FORTY YEARS A GIANT

FORTY YEARS
A GIANT
THE LIFE OF
HORACE STONEHAM

STEVE TREDER

University of Nebraska Press • LINCOLN

Library of Congress Cataloging-in-Publication Data
Names: Treder, Steve, author.
Title: Forty years a Giant: the life of Horace Stoneham / Steve Treder.
Other titles: 40 years a Giant
Description: Lincoln: University of Nebraska Press, 2021. | Includes
bibliographical references and index.
Identifiers: LCCN 2020041748
ISBN 9781496224194 (Hardback)
ISBN 9781496227232 (ePub)
ISBN 9781496227249 (mobi)
ISBN 9781496227256 (PDF)
Subjects: LCSH: Stoneham, Horace, 1903–1990. | Sports team owners—
United States—Biography. | New York Giants (Baseball team)—History. |
San Francisco Giants (Baseball team)—History. | National League
of Professional Baseball Clubs—History. | Major League Baseball
(Organization)—History. | Baseball—New York (State)—New York—
History. | Baseball—California—San Francisco—History. | Baseball—
United States—History.
Classification: LCC GV939.S7457 T74 2021 | DDC 796.357/64092 [B]—dc23
LC record available at https://lccn.loc.gov/2020041748

Set in Questa by Laura Buis.

Contents

Introduction • vii

Prologue • xv

1. Horrie, I Bought You a Ball Club • 1

2. Roaring into the Twenties • 20

3. Hard Truths • 37

4. Brooklyn Is Still in the League • 69

5. War, Peace, and Nice Guys • 92

6. We Knew Segregation Was Wrong • 116

7. Horace Stoneham Has Finally Got a Winner • 143

8. We Have No Chance to Survive Here • 178

9. Open Your Golden Gate • 204

10. It's Bye-Bye Baby • 228

11. No Cigar • 268

12. Certainly the Move Will Hurt Us • 305

13. Resilience • 333

14. I Never Thought I Would Trade Willie • 368

15. You Can't Get Discouraged • 397

Epilogue • 423

Acknowledgments • 429

Notes • 431

Bibliography • 459

Index • 465

Introduction

In professional baseball, as in every other sport, the players and field managers (or head coaches)—the athletes and their direct supervisors—are the star attractions and fan favorites. No ordinary fan roots for or against a given franchise based on its upper management structure, let alone its owner; indeed, it's likely that few fans of any team are interested in the chief executive at the top of that club's corporate organization chart.

This is entirely sensible and a phenomenon hardly unique to sports. The vast majority of entertainment choices, and consumer purchase decisions generally, are made on the basis of the consumable product itself and not with regard to who might be—in a commanding high-backed chair in some lavishly paneled office—ultimately accountable for creating it. In baseball the players and the games they play are the product, with the owner only a producer, at the distant end of a long chain of contractual and hierarchical connections.

As fans focus on the game on the field, so do baseball writers and broadcasters in their standard coverage. This has always been true. Thus, the cultural literacy enveloping the sport has always presented ample room for the names, faces, and stirring exploits of celebrity players and star skippers—part of the management regime, of course, but colorfully visible and accessible, right there in the dugout and right there with the media. The players and field managers are the show, after all.

So, once we leave the clubhouse and head upstairs to the front office, fan and media attention quickly diminishes. To be sure, there have been a few famous general managers in history—say, Ed Barrow, Branch Rickey, and George Weiss—and the modern era has celebrated Billy Beane and perhaps some others like Pat Gillick, John Schuerholz, and Theo Epstein. But they're the exceptions; most GMs, today and in the past, are dull and forgettable. The same is true of owners: history has highlighted a Bill Veeck here and a George Steinbrenner there, but for the most part fans and writers have been content to grant the occupant of the owner's suite little more than a perfunctory glance.

However, to the extent that one endeavors not just to be entertained by professional baseball but to understand it, a better reckoning is required. The easy choice of relegating owners to deep background may be normal, but that doesn't make it a good idea. Failing to examine the teams' ownership structures, and the business realities and implications attending to those structures, is to ignore an irreducibly huge factor in determining how this sport we love is presented to us. While the owner himself (and today as in the past, it's nearly always a man) may remain obscure, the owner's impact pervades everything, for good or ill.

With this in mind, we turn our attention to Horace Stoneham, who presided as owner of the National League's Giants from 1936 to 1976. That's an extremely long time to preside over a baseball team; indeed, it's one of the very longest ownership runs in the history of the business. Moreover, that four-decade period through the heart of the twentieth century was percolating with remarkable events and changes, both in professional baseball and in the nation at large: among the issues Stoneham grappled with were the racial integration of the sport and the relocation of his franchise across the breadth of the continent. It is the case that many of the decisions made by Horace Stoneham would have profound effects, both within professional baseball and within the larger communities it inhabited.

And on top of that, Stoneham didn't operate his organization in the manner that had become the norm by the time he came along in the 1930s: that is, hiring a general manager to take responsibility for the "baseball operations" (including determining the player roster, executing trades and other player transactions, negotiating player contracts, and supervising the farm system), with the owner focusing only on the financial side of the business. When Stoneham's GM, Bill Terry, resigned in 1942, he was never replaced; instead, from that point forward, it was Stoneham who served as his own GM. The roster was managed by Stoneham himself. Every trade, every waiver claim, every demotion, and every promotion was his personal decision; every Giants team from the mid-1940s until the mid-1970s was built, or torn apart and rebuilt, by Horace Stoneham himself.

Thus, Stoneham was an extraordinarily important figure in the history of professional baseball, both as a business operator and as a competitor for championships. Yet his story has never been told in any detail or depth. Certainly, a large part of the explanation for Stoneham's historical obscurity is baseball's institutional direction of the spotlight to the game on the field and away from the front office. But in Stoneham's case that "baked-in" bias was amplified by his own personality: Stoneham was shy and introverted and avoided public appearances and statements as much as he could. He was rarely quoted in the newspapers or on the airwaves, and even then he rarely offered more than inoffensive clichés. As owner of one of the most grand ball clubs in all of sports, Stoneham couldn't escape prominence, but he bore it reluctantly and went out of his way to reveal as little about himself as he was allowed. He was more than happy, eager, to let the media and the fans devote all their attention to his players and his field manager and to personally remain as invisible as possible.

That was his choice to make, but like all choices, it had consequences, both intended and not. Stoneham succeeded at becoming far less famous than many of his contemporary owners and GMs. He attracted only the tiniest fraction of the press action generated by such scene-stealers as Branch Rickey or Bill Veeck or Larry MacPhail or Charlie Finley. And notably, Stoneham never approached the public profile attained by Walter O'Malley—his fellow owner, with whom Stoneham enacted an unofficial partnership when deciding to leave New York for California. Yet the Stoneham-versus-O'Malley contrast illustrates an unintended effect of Stoneham's publicity shyness: while the ever-loquacious

O'Malley was (rightly or wrongly) cast as a crass villain by the New York media and as a visionary genius in Los Angeles, Stoneham's side of the relocation story effectively remained untold. Instead, what little public image of Stoneham did emerge was that of neither villain nor genius but, rather, as a well-meaning bumbler, as O'Malley's gullible follower. This wasn't at all accurate, but since Stoneham attempted no public correction, it was the only image of him that persisted.

Another consequence of Stoneham's reticence was the thin written record he left for historical researchers. Relative to the importance of his position and his high level of activity in the sport, remarkably little was written about him in the newspapers of his day: those who don't offer juicy quotes don't get many column inches. Moreover, Stoneham felt absolutely no sense of attention to building an official record of his deliberations and actions as the chief executive of the Giants and left essentially zero files, letters, and other documents to posterity. This, again, stands in vivid contrast to O'Malley, who spent his long career painstakingly filing memoranda and carefully wording voluminous letters; to his estate and to the research community, O'Malley left tall stacks of boxes of elegantly organized and impeccably preserved documentation. A cynic might observe that in so doing, O'Malley was artfully presenting the version of events he wished to present, but that doesn't negate the fact that he was providing contemporaneous information, and lots of it, while Stoneham was providing nothing at all. And it seems, those who leave behind little for researchers to study don't get much research attention.

So, Horace Stoneham has succeeded (until now, one hopes) at remaining largely unknown to the huge majority of baseball fans. But his very lack of interest in seeking attention, in crafting his legacy—frustrating though that might be to a researcher such as yours truly—also provides a guiding light to perceiving what sort of fellow he actually was. Because, if it's obvious that Stoneham simply didn't give a rip about his public image and reputation, then the question must be: what *did* he care about? What occupied his interest? What did he dream of and worry about?

The answer, as discovered by this researcher in scrutiny of the written accounts that do exist and in conversation with Stoneham family members who knew him, is surpassingly simple and obvious: what he cared about was *the Giants*. The team, their performance on the field, the regard among their fans, and, yes of course, their delivery of financial return on investment: that was what Horace Stoneham cared about and attended to. And to a remarkable degree, that was all that he cared about and attended to.

Horace Stoneham, as it turns out, was not a person with a diverse range of interests. He was, in the best sense of the term, a simple man. (In this regard Horace stands in dramatic contrast to his father, Charles Stoneham, who was the very definition of a complicated and conflicted man.) Horace Stoneham wasn't just a baseball fan; he was something far deeper than that: he was a baseball devotee who intensely viewed thousands of games in his lifetime and grew to comprehend—and marvel in—the factors resulting in games won or games lost, to a depth achieved by few others in his time or any other. He *loved* baseball and therefore loved his Giants, and there was never anything more important to Stoneham than how his Giants were doing.

That was it, pretty much. He held no other interests. Stoneham pursued no additional business operations and, indeed, no hobbies. He didn't take vacations. The modern idea of "decompressing" from "the stress" of operating the Giants by escaping to a remote beach or a mountain cabin would have struck him as ridiculous. Being away from the Giants would be the only thing that could "stress him out," and so he never did that. He loved his family, but some of the choices he made suggest that he loved his family business even more.

By all means Horace Stoneham made sure that he enjoyed himself while attending to his Giants. His indulgence in alcohol was legendary—this one aspect of his behavior was well known—even amid a macho sports culture in which holding one's liquor was a central test of manliness. While shy in public, Stoneham could be gregarious among friends and took endless delight in drinking and talking with them—talking baseball, of course, because that's what Stoneham loved to talk about, and virtually all of his friends were within the realm of baseball.

Therefore, the best way to tell the story of Horace Stoneham is to tell it as he lived it: wrapped up in baseball and the Giants. Win or lose, good or bad, Stoneham's life was all about his Giants. To genuinely present Stoneham's life is to present the fortunes of the Giants, win or lose, good or bad, through his long relationship with the franchise. The threads are inextricable.

But to tell that story honestly—to inhabit, as best we can, the world inhabited by Stoneham and his Giants—we'll also endeavor to place these events within their proper mid-twentieth century social, economic, and political context. We'll consider what Stoneham and his contemporaries would likely be reading about when they scanned the newspaper headlines or caught the evening news on TV and the ways in which those things changed over the decades. We'll confront the notion that as much as he might have loved to, Stoneham could never truly just lose himself within the tidy realm of baseball, for both he and the tidy realm of baseball were inevitably pushed and pulled by forces wide and great and continually required to adapt.

So, this narrative is less a standard biography of Horace Stoneham than it is the history of the New York and San Francisco Giants while Horace Stoneham was intimately engaged with that major league baseball franchise. This was a more-than-half-century span in which several of the greatest figures within the history of the sport came and went through the organization, but the one constant presence was Stoneham's. Though the shy introvert expended no effort at conjuring a public image or a self-conscious personal legacy, the ball club itself was, of course, always his legacy. Not only was it his life's work; it was the life's work presented to him by his father, as his inheritance.

The relationship between father and son was not simple, and the behavioral example provided by Charles to Horace—as different in personality as a father and son could be—was, to say the least, perplexing. But whatever else Horace might have felt about his father, the inherited legacy of the Giants was something he cherished. It would become Horace's deep ambition to sustain that legacy and pass it along to his own son, in due time—yet that would never come to pass, finally coloring the family legacy with a hue of profound sadness.

It was, indeed, a complicated situation. The Giants achieved many things under Horace Stoneham. The organization was a leader in the process of racially and culturally integrating professional baseball in the United States—yet the organization struggled with racial and cultural clashes within its own clubhouse. The franchise pioneered in introducing major league baseball to the West Coast and in developing the robust San Francisco Bay Area market for the sport—yet its abandonment of the New York market was a blow to that city, one among many factors that would lead to an economic and social crisis in New York in the 1960s and '70s. The Giants ball clubs built by Stoneham routinely displayed a gallery of the sport's most brilliant stars—yet they were unable to muster the sufficient supporting cast and roster depth to achieve sustained championship success.

The Giants of Horace Stoneham were good, but greatness eluded them. Stoneham himself wasn't a great man, but he was a good man, and his life's work has all the stuff of a great story.

Prologue

SUNDAY, SEPTEMBER 21, 1975

Horace Stoneham rose at his customary hour, about 9:00 a.m. He was a man of regular habits and routines.

He shaved and showered, then dressed in the clothes cleaned, pressed, and impeccably prepared for him. Stoneham was fastidious in his grooming and appearance, and his custom-tailored apparel was always stylish and tasteful. For today it would be a creamy yellow Egyptian cotton dress shirt, crisply ironed and starched yet supple and smooth. He wore it unbuttoned at the top, no tie today. Then perfectly creased charcoal worsted gabardines, butter-soft dark-brown English loafers, and a sporty herringbone tweed blazer. Then a rose-colored pocket square. Just so.

Back in his New York days, he'd regularly worn a hat, but out here in San Francisco, with the wind and everything, he usually just went without, as he decided to do today.

He was seventy-two years old. He was in good health for a man of his age and, well, for a man with his fierce lifelong devotion to cocktails. He was of average height, pudgy but not portly. His distinctly round face was often punctuated with eyeglasses, and the round-shaped frames he favored could sometimes give him an owlish look. His hair, once curly and blond, was now thin and gray around a bald scalp. Always, it was neatly trimmed. His resting gaze was genial, his countenance calmly confident.

Horace Stoneham ate the hearty breakfast prepared for him by his Chinese American houseman. Often Stoneham's breakfast was hotcakes with butter and syrup, or just as often it was eggs, with bacon or ham. He was never a heavy eater and certainly never one to fuss over fancy cuisine, but Horace Stoneham enjoyed his meals. The breakfast was excellent. With it he had coffee: sugar, no cream.

After breakfast Stoneham sat back and savored a second cup. He enjoyed the commanding morning view of the bay and the city from his Telegraph Hill windows. He read the newspaper and lit a cigarette. After a bit, with a glance at his wristwatch, he patted a napkin to his lips, stood, and bid goodbye pleasantries. He took the several staircases down to the street-level garage. There he found his tarragon-gold Cadillac Fleetwood Eldorado convertible, gleaming and ready to go. The key was in the ignition. The garage door was conveniently opened.

Often Valleda (pronounced "VAL-uh-duh"), his wife of more than fifty years, would accompany Stoneham on this daily errand. But that was usually when the grandkids were coming too, in the summertime. With the girls back in school now, Valleda had quietly let him know that he could go by himself today. He was more than fine with that, as she had known he would be, in that rhythm of unadorned understanding purchased exclusively by the hard experience of multiple decades of companionship.

He donned sunglasses, but Stoneham kept the convertible top closed. It wasn't foggy but still overcast at this point in the morning. It was September, though, often the nicest month of the year here, and a warm sunny afternoon dependably awaited.

Despite a calm demeanor, Stoneham was an impatient, lead-footed driver, roaring and screeching from each signal to the next. Happily, today was a Sunday morning, and the traffic was light. After a few steep and twisting blocks of city streets came the ramp up to the Embarcadero Freeway, and Horace Stoneham's morning pull into the Candlestick Park lot was not even twenty minutes away.

The parking attendant, who normally just waved him in with a nod, made a point today of flagging Stoneham's Cadillac to a stop, walking over and reaching in to the rolled-down driver's side window, and shaking this driver's hand. "Thank you, Mr. Stoneham," he said.

After Stoneham parked his car, he walked through the EMPLOY-
EES ONLY doorway, and the guard there stood up from his stool
and also gave him a handshake. This was not standard protocol.

This was not a normal day.

So many faces so familiar to Stoneham made a point to give
him a greeting this morning. Ushers. Cops. Concessionaires.
Janitors. Some offered big clunky handshakes, some just shy
nods and smiles. Stoneham did his best to acknowledge every
last one. He knew many of their names. It wasn't easy to keep
his composure. He was a sentimental man, and he was deeply
touched. They knew it.

Stoneham made his way up familiar staircases and through
familiar hallways, cheerfully responding to still more expres-
sions of gratitude and well wishes. At last he entered the owner's suite. He stood there alone for a long while, in the cool quiet.
He savored it. Horace Stoneham had been a public figure all his
life, and he took some enjoyment in that. But by a strong nature,
he was introverted. Being alone was always good.

Presently, Horace Stoneham opened the sliding glass door
and stepped outside. He stood awhile, contemplating the vista
presented, then took his familiar comfortable chair on the broad
concrete balcony overlooking the ball field. The cool morning
breeze said its customary hello but gently for now. Already the
marine layer was breaking up, and it was pleasant here, no over-
coat needed. It was going to be a really nice day.

Today's was the last home game of the season, an event that
in years past was sure to generate a great big crowd. They'd give
away new cars and trips to Hawaii. Fan Appreciation Day. The
crowd today wasn't going to be big. It would be small. Stoneham
wasn't surprised or even disappointed anymore. He'd long since
come to terms with the situation.

But he watched. Closely.

With his rare depth of experience and knowledge, Stoneham
watched batting practice—

both teams, the complete routine, as well as the full infield
fungo drills. He watched the grounds crew rake and water the
infield dirt. He then watched the entire game—every inning,

every pitch. Between each inning he watched the infielders perform the casual ritual of tossed grounders and the climactic peg from catcher to second base, then the ball once more snapped around the diamond.

The game Horace Stoneham watched that day was a beauty. John Montefusco, a colorful character and one of Stoneham's dearest favorites, went the distance with a brisk five-hitter, winning it 2–1. A really nice ball game.

Horace Stoneham had presided over thousands of Giants games. He had no idea exactly how many games, in San Francisco and in New York and everywhere else. Everywhere. In Florida and Arizona, in the Caribbean and even in Japan. And on those old springtime barnstorming tours they used to take, halfway across the country riding the train, in small towns and rickety little ballparks. For so many, many years, so many, many games.

This would be the last. The team, his family business, was hopelessly insolvent. Stoneham had no choice but to put the franchise up for sale. He hoped the buyer would be local and keep the team in San Francisco, but no matter what, he had to sell. He didn't want to, but he had to.

The ballpark people knew it. They understood.

The crew was still with him. That's what provided Horace Stoneham with the profound measure of strength, he believed, to be able to make it through this hardest of all days. And, yes, with a smile. Why not?

FORTY YEARS A GIANT

1

Horrie, I Bought You a Ball Club

The summer of 1876—the centennial of the United States of America—was the first summer for the National League of Professional Baseball Clubs. In that season's original configuration, the league fielded eight franchises, representing Boston, Chicago, Cincinnati, Hartford, Louisville, Philadelphia, St. Louis—and New York.

The New York entry was the Mutual Base Ball Club. The Mutuals were among the blossoming sport's longest-established clubs, in continuous operation since 1857, well before open professionalism had taken hold. They'd been based in Hoboken, New Jersey, through 1867 and in Brooklyn beginning in 1868. In 1871 they became a charter member of the National Association of Professional Base Ball Players, the first professional league, and the Mutuals competed there through the five seasons that league sustained before it dissolved in 1875.

In the National League the Mutuals were not a success. In August 1876, mired in sixth place with a record of 19–26, the cash-poor Mutuals refused to travel anymore, forcing their road game opponents to cancel those scheduled games for the rest of the season. Though they did fulfill their commitment to take part in eleven more home games (of which they would lose nine), at season's end the Mutuals were expelled by the fledgling league.

There would be no succeeding New York franchise in the National League, not just in 1877 but for the next half-decade. Perhaps it would make for a grand storyteller's point that the

National League badly suffered for failing to include the nation's largest city within its struggling young ranks, but such a statement wouldn't have much truth behind it. To be sure, the National League enterprise suffered mightily through the late 1870s and early 1880s. But its struggles were so basic and plentiful as to suggest that the concept of full-time professional baseball generally and the manifestation of the National League specifically were still so fly-by-night that a nicety like market size optimization was as yet an aspirational problem.

But year by year the toddling league gained surer footing. In 1879, the National League's fourth year of operation, it was able to expand back to its original eight-team size. And with the opening of the 1881 season, the six-year-old National League surpassed the life span of the National Association. If such things were modest benchmarks of progress and prosperity, they were benchmarks still.

A storyteller could be tempted to present the 1883 remarriage of the National League and New York City as a pageant of ceremony, summoning great notice and interest far and wide, but that would also be a fib. If New York baseball sort of stumbled its way back into the National League's good graces in the early 1880s, it's also the case that for most of the time New York was absent, the National League's good graces didn't count for all that much.

In any case, the instrumental characters in getting New York back into the NL were James J. "Jim" Mutrie, a Massachusetts-born minor league player and manager, and John B. Day, an up-and-coming tobacconist from Connecticut making his entrepreneurial fortune in the big city. It was in September 1880 that the twenty-nine-year-old Mutrie, well known within the baseball realm but newly arrived in New York, and the forty-two-year-old Day, well connected in New York circles, joined forces to found the New York Metropolitans. In late 1880 and through the 1881 and 1882 seasons, the Metropolitans operated as a loosely configured independent club, not quite an outlaw but not embraced by any league either—not an unusual make-it-up-as-we-go-along approach in professional baseball's still-not-ready-for-prime-time realm.

In 1882 another major league was launched, the American Association, the first direct rival to the National League. The growing popularity of the New York Metropolitans was such that at the conclusion of the 1882 season, Mutrie and Day accepted offers from both the National League and the American Association. So, in 1883 the Metropolitans would step out as a professional baseball syndicate, fielding two major league franchises. Interestingly enough, the American Association entry was the flagship, bearing the "Metropolitans" brand, stocked with the best talent, and managed by Mutrie himself. The National League would have to settle for the B side, a team generally known as the Gothams, skippered by a journeyman named John Clapp. Both newborn ball clubs would play their home games in a semi-developed complex at 110th Street between Fifth and Sixth Avenues that had sometimes been a venue for polo matches and, though it now was emerging as a home for baseball and football, was commonly known as the Polo Grounds. Even when, several years later, the ever-expanding city grid forced the operation to relocate and build a new stadium farther north in Manhattan, all the way up in Harlem at 155th Street and Eighth Avenue—beneath a promontory known as Coogan's Bluff—the quaint Polo Grounds moniker moved with it.

It had been way back in 1792 that the first formal stock exchange was established in New York, an endeavor known as the Buttonwood Agreement. Securities and commodities were avidly traded in reasonably coherent markets in New York and New Jersey (as well as in Philadelphia and Boston, and so on) through the decades to come. In the closing decades of the nineteenth century, the 1870s, '80s, and '90s, propelled by the long-distance communication capability of the telegraph, American stock, bond, and "commercial paper" markets boomed as never before. With rapid growth came ever-mounting concentration of financial power and influence in the densely packed blocks surrounding the headquarters of the New York Stock Exchange, located at Ten and Twelve Broad Street, near the corner of Wall Street, at the southern tip of Manhattan.

Situated just across the Hudson River from Lower Manhattan is Jersey City, New Jersey. Then as now, the ever-growing skyline of Wall Street and the Financial District loomed in direct view of the denizens of Jersey City, tantalizing, taunting, and inescapable. In the wide-open business and financial markets of that Gilded Age, every ambitious, enterprising up-and-comer in New Jersey understood that no matter how successful he might become within the context of the home neighborhood, ultimately the only place for the sharpest and the toughest to be was across the river. New York was where you had to go to prove yourself, to make your mark and make it big. One particular such ambitious, enterprising up-and-comer was Charles Abraham Stoneham, born in Jersey City on July 5, 1876.

Charles Stoneham's father was Bartholomew F. Stoneham, a New Jersey–born bookkeeper of Irish and Welsh descent. His mother, Mary E. Holwell Stoneham, was an Irish immigrant. Charles was one of four sons born to this aspiring Catholic family, making their way into the emerging industrial middle class on the teeming streets of urban New Jersey. This particular son would quickly prove to be something else again.

The profoundly American boyhood of Charles Stoneham (his middle name of Abraham was given in honor of President Lincoln) is vividly imaginable. Amid dusty, raucous, and fragrant Jersey City backstreets and weedy lots, he would be introduced to baseball by his chums and neighbors, watching and playing with bigger kids and even grownups. It's likely that young Charley could scarcely remember a world without baseball games.

By the mid-1880s Charley was a diehard bug for the New York National League team that would forever be known as the Giants—so named in early 1885, the legend goes, by Jim Mutrie, entering the clubhouse following a particularly stirring victory and declaring: "My big fellows! My giants!"[1] After guiding his Metropolitans to the American Association pennant in '84, Mutrie decided the following season to refocus his priorities on the erstwhile Gothams. The 1885 Mutrie-managed Giants, now his "A" team, were stocked with stars in outfielder Jim O'Rourke, first baseman Roger Connor, catcher William "Buck" Ewing, and a pair of ace pitchers in Mickey Welch and Tim Keefe.[2] They fashioned a scintillating 85–27 record that year, finishing in second just behind Adrian "Cap" Anson's juggernaut Chicago White Stockings, and promptly became the top entertainment in New York baseball.

Yet there was great ballplaying afoot in New Jersey too. A particular local hero captivating the admiration of Charley Stoneham was a quiet, steady Irish Catholic teenager from Trenton named "Silent Mike" Tiernan. In 1885 the eighteen-year-old Tiernan starred for the Trenton minor league team, and in 1886 he moved up to Jersey City and was the toast of the town. It seemed just the next natural step when, in 1887, Day and Mutrie recruited Tiernan to join the Giants. He would blossom into an all-around star right fielder and would remain a Giant for all of his distinguished thirteen-year major league career. It they hadn't before, the New York Giants had now for certain hooked Charley Stoneham as a lifelong devotee.

Of course, baseball wasn't the only activity Charley pursued. He loved sports and games of all types, and he loved to gamble on the games, and he loved to gamble in general. And even as an adolescent, the sharp-eyed, energetic, and upwardly mobile Charley took ever-keener interest in the biggest, most sophisticated, and most lucrative from of real-life gambling: the markets.

Charley Stoneham had a family connection pointing that way. Among the hundreds of exchange offices jostling for space in Lower Manhattan was a brokerage house called Haight and Freese—Mr. Freese was Stoneham's uncle. In 1892, at the age of sixteen, Stoneham finished whatever school he'd had and took a job at Haight and Freese as a "board boy," updating transactions. The ever-hustling Stoneham soon was promoted to salesman.[3] Still living with his parents in Jersey City, he commuted across the river every morning into the swarming pits of cutthroat competition in a wildly unregulated securities racket, in which amorality and illegality were never hard to find. Stoneham was very good at it. He steadily worked his way up the trading ranks.

In his early twenties the rising financial sharpie married and started a family. Indeed, while it's impossible to know for certain, it appears very likely that Charles Stoneham married more than once and led at least one bigamous family life in secret. The one certain union—publicly presented—occurred in 1900, when Stoneham wed twenty-year-old Hannah Monahan. Together they would promptly have three children, first a son whose name is unrecorded, then a daughter named Mary Alice, and then, on April 27, 1903, son Horace Charles Stoneham, his first name in honor of one of Charles's brothers.

But murky records suggest that Charles might have already been married, since 1897, to an Alice Rafter and possibly never divorced, and whether through this relationship or still another, upon his death decades later there would be claims, valid or not, advanced by others claiming his paternity.

Whatever else Charley Stoneham was doing, he was getting rich. It was in 1903, the same year little Horace was born, that twenty-seven-year-old Charles became a partner at O. F. Jonasson & Company, a brokerage house specializing in mining stocks. There were fortunes to be made (and lost) in the dubiously honest trade of mining stocks, and Charley was seeing to it that the fortune being made was his own.

In 1902 the United States won the Philippine-American War, a three-and-a-half-year insurgency of Philippine Islands nationalists, and now that sprawling former Spanish colony was firmly under American authority. In February 1903, as part of the Cuban-American Treaty of Relations formally resolving the terms of the 1898 Spanish-American War, the government of Cuba leased the southern portion of Guantanamo Bay, including the Guantanamo Bay Naval Base, to the United States "in perpetuity." For the first time, a globally muscular United States held essentially colonial dominion over the Caribbean Sea and Central America and a prominent position in Southeast Asia and the western Pacific Ocean. In March 1903 the United States Senate ratified the Hay-Herrán Treaty, granting the United States the right to complete the Panama Canal across the Isthmus, a project begun by the

French in 1881 but abandoned in the early 1890s. It would be a monumental feat of technical capability and steadfast will, and when completed in 1914, it forged a dramatic link in the developing chain of rapid, high-volume round-the-world transportation and communications.

In January 1903 the first wireless transatlantic radio message was successfully transmitted. Radio technology would be rapidly applied to nautical communications, to law enforcement, and, broadly and deeply throughout the modern world's militaries. (Broadcast radio as an entertainment medium remained a generation away.) In June 1903 Henry Ford founded the Ford Motor Company in Detroit, Michigan. Before then the automobile had largely been a curiosity for hobbyists but would soon be mass-produced, reliable, and commonly affordable and adapted to military as well as civilian uses. The machine's overwhelming popularity would force the wholesale redesign and reconstruction of not just roads, streets, and highways but cityscapes themselves, a pervasively transformative impact on everyday life that would prove even greater over the coming decades of the twentieth century than the advent of the railroad had been over the course of the nineteenth. In December 1903 Wilbur and Orville Wright, self-taught small-town midwesterners, demonstrated the first successful flight of an internal combustion engine–powered heavier-than-air craft. This novel technology would also soon find itself widely applied to military purposes.

On Thursday afternoon, October 1, 1903, at Huntington Grounds in Boston, Massachusetts, Cy Young of the Boston Americans delivered his first pitch to Pittsburgh Pirates leadoff hitter Ginger Beaumont, and the first modern World Series was underway. After several decades of often fractious development, the business of professional baseball in 1903 had "declared peace" and formally assumed the major and minor league organizational structure (within a framework called the National Association) it has essentially held to this day. The enterprise had matured, and its newfound stability would deliver sustainable and significant profitability to savvy investors in the decades to come.

The whiff of scandal would always lurk around Charles Stoneham. On Saturday, May 6, 1905, Mrs. Olivia Gray, a thirty-something woman, perhaps or perhaps not a widow, perhaps or perhaps not wealthy, residing in high style at the Hotel Imperial at Broadway and Thirty-Third Street, committed suicide with a revolver shot to the temple. She died leaving multiple letters addressed to Charles Stoneham, pleading: "Charles, Sweetheart, how can you treat me this way? What have I done? I am half crazy at your treatment of me. . . . And your promises not kept with me! . . . God forgive me. . . . I love you better than my life."

It was front-page news across New York, and Stoneham (inaccurately named in the papers as "Charles H. Stoneham") was suddenly a notoriously public figure. Hotel staff identified him as the man who'd recently registered with her at the Imperial as "Mr. J. W. Gray," the "husband" of the late Olivia. Not only that—another of the letters found with Olivia Gray's body was addressed to a landlady named Mrs. Minnie G. Sanford, at 62 West Sixty-Sixth Street. Mrs. Sanford told the *New York Times* that in the fall of 1904, Olivia Gray had lodged in her building under the name of "Mrs. Stoneham" and that her frequent companion was known to all as "Charley."

For his part Stoneham not only categorically denied having known or met her but dropped a bombshell of his own. His business partner at Jonasson, J. J. Bamberger, issued this statement to the press: "My partner is a married man. He lives in Clark Street, Jersey City, with his wife and two little children. An older child, a boy of four, was drowned in the Morris Canal on April 25, and was buried a week ago to-day. My partner was very much cast down over his loss. He has been with me every night for the past two weeks." For her part Mrs. Hannah Stoneham, the grieving young mother, was quoted in the *New York Times*: "Mr. Stoneham felt so badly about the drowning of his little boy that he did not leave Jersey City at all for the rest of the week, and only went to his office on Monday. Someone in the office told my husband three or four days ago that some other man in the building had been using his name in telephoning."[4]

Whatever the tawdry truth, in this tragic moment, with both

his wife and his business partner supporting (some version of) his story, Stoneham avoided any criminal or civil charges.

This time.

The New York Giants ball club Charley Stoneham had come to love was a grand success in the 1880s. With Mike Tiernan on board, they won back-to-back National League pennants in 1888 and '89 and topped it off with back-to-back triumphs in that era's version of the World Series against the American Association champion.

But in the decade to follow, things went less well. By the end of the 1891 season Mutrie was fired, and Day was forced to sell his controlling interest. In 1895 the franchise was acquired by thirty-five-year-old Andrew Freedman, a Tammany Hall–connected real estate developer who would prove to be among the least popular moguls in baseball history, openly detested by players and fellow owners alike. The Giants floundered while managers were frantically hired and fired: in the seven and a half seasons from Opening Day 1895 through mid-1902, no fewer than thirteen skippers came and went.

But Freedman's fourteenth skipper, arriving on Saturday, July 19, 1902, would alter the destiny of the New York Giants. He was five feet, seven inches tall, twenty-nine years old, and a personality of exceptional force.

John McGraw's appointment with the Giants was an extraordinary circumstance, one of the key battles in the "war" for talent that was raging between the National League and the upstart American League challenger in 1901–2. McGraw had made his name in the mid-1890s as a standout third baseman for the National League champion Baltimore Orioles. But though he wasn't yet thirty, he suffered from knee trouble, and in 1902 his career stood at a crossroads. He was now player-manager for a new Baltimore Orioles franchise, this one struggling in the upstart American League. He was also bitterly feuding with AL president Byron Bancroft "Ban" Johnson.

By July 1902 McGraw was under league suspension, and the debt-plagued Orioles' ownership group was fed up with Johnson. A stunning midseason conspiracy was hatched to sabotage the Baltimore franchise. Orioles team president John Mahan purchased the shares owned by players McGraw, Joe Kelley, and Wilbert Robinson to gain a controlling interest and then immediately sold that interest to a partnership between New York Giants' owner Freedman and Cincinnati Reds owner John T. Brush. Freedman and Brush commenced to plunder the Baltimore roster: Kelley was named playing manager of the Reds, and along with him to Cincinnati went power-hitting outfielder James "Cy" Seymour. The haul Freedman extracted for the Giants was even greater: not just McGraw as playing manager but also ace pitcher Joe McGinnity, standout first baseman Dan McGann, and budding young catcher Roger Bresnahan.

The newly invigorated Giants didn't transform into champions overnight. The team was in last place, at 23–50, when McGraw and company arrived, and though their performance under McGraw for the balance of the season wasn't that bad (25–38), it was still bad, and they finished last. But the turnaround that began in 1903 was indeed stunning: the Giants leaped all the way to second place that year, and in 1904 they dazzled the baseball world by running away with the National League pennant with a record of 106–47—the most regular season wins yet achieved by a major league team.[5] McGraw was catapulted to A-list New York superstar celebrity status, hailed as a genius, and was on his way to an epic thirty-year tenure with the Giants.

It's unclear whether it was Freedman or Brush who'd been the primary orchestrator of the bold piracy that brought McGraw to New York. What is known is that following the 1902 season, amid the tectonic plate–shifting machinations going on throughout organized baseball, John T. Brush—from Upstate New York, fifty-seven years old, gaunt and sallow, a onetime clothing store entrepreneur who'd been pretty much full-time in the baseball business since the early 1880s—sold his stake in the Cincinnati Reds and purchased from Freedman the controlling share of the New York Giants. Despite chronic ill health, Brush would sustain ownership of the Giants until his death in late 1912. Brush and McGraw were mutual admirers who worked smoothly together, and together they forged a tenure of extraordinary on-field achievement and financial prosperity.

When McGraw arrived in 1902, the Giants roster was sparse, but it did include one exceptional diamond in the rough: right-handed pitcher Christy Mathewson, not yet twenty-two years old but already the ace of the meager New York staff and clearly a tremendous prospect. Perhaps under any manager, Mathewson would have swiftly blossomed into an all-time great. But perhaps not, as even the most tremendous prospects sometimes fail to fulfill their promise. What we know is that it was under the handling of John McGraw that Mathewson did, in fact, more than fulfill his.

Indeed, McGraw and Mathewson developed a remarkably close bond. They were the oddest of couples: one was a short, foul-mouthed, hard-drinking, pugnacious Catholic, the other a tall, handsome, temperate, well-spoken Presbyterian. Yet they found not just common ground but genuine respect and enjoyment in one another's company. They became so close that they lived side by side in a grand apartment building on Manhattan's west side.[6]

To achieve a dynastic run in major league baseball requires sufficient talent, of course, but among the other important conditions is that the team's manager and its reigning superstar are consistently on the same page, mutually respectful, believing in each other. With McGraw and Mathewson the Giants absolutely had that, and as the team reeled off five pennants in the ten seasons from 1904 through 1913, the fiery, tightly wound McGraw and the cool, even-tempered Mathewson had each other's back and provided twin poles of positive leadership in the clubhouse.

It's impossible to overstate how broadly and deeply celebrated John McGraw and Christy Mathewson were. The New York Giants were quickly established as the flagship brand in the now solidly thriving enterprise of major league baseball, and McGraw and Mathewson were the faces of that brand, the toast of the dynamic metropolis, brilliant luminaries.

Moreover, it's important to comprehend just what a genius manager John McGraw truly was. Descriptions of him never fail to mention his hot temper and general bellicosity, and that much is accurate. But those aspects of McGraw's character mustn't obscure how superbly intelligent he was and how loyal and generous he could choose to be. Remember that at this stage of professional baseball history, the position of "manager" encompassed the responsibilities charged to at least two full-time jobs today: field manager and general manager. McGraw didn't just set the lineups and call for the bunts; he also crafted the roster; executed trades and drafts; scouted, signed, and farmed prospects; and negotiated all player contracts. McGraw was a wizard at all of this for thirty years.

He was great at everything, but McGraw's mastery was perhaps most clearly revealed in his unsurpassed understanding of the subtle tactical advantages to be gained through artfully applied pitching staff rotation and deployment, left-right batter platooning, and in-game substitutions of pinch hitters and defensive replacements. He was years, if not decades, ahead of his contemporaries in these regards, to a degree not again demonstrated by any skipper until Casey Stengel (who would be mentored by McGraw) in the 1950s.

Modern New York City had been formed in 1898, with the consolidation of Manhattan, Brooklyn, the Bronx, Queens, and Staten Island into a five-borough unit. New York was by far the largest city in the United States—the 1900 census counted more than 3.4 million New Yorkers, more than twice the size of its second-largest rival, Chicago—and a burgeoning economic juggernaut. The pace of growth was sensational, and New York added nearly 40 percent more in population between the census counts of 1900 and 1910. It was also rapidly being built into its signature modern physicality. This period heralded the openings of the New York City Subway, Penn Station, and the Grand Central Terminal; of the Williamsburg Bridge, Columbus Circle, and the Plaza Hotel; of the New York Public Library Central Building; and of the Metropolitan Life Insurance Tower (at the time the tallest building in the world).

Meanwhile, though periodic panics and crashes persisted, the volume of business flowing through American securities markets, and especially New York securities markets, grew ever larger. This was a time of extraordinary confidence in the long-term return the markets would deliver and thus a time of extraordinary risk undertaken (wittingly or not) by many investors. There were no structural safeguards protecting investors and precious little legal regulation of any kind governing the various business operations breeding like rabbits around Wall Street. This was the financial equivalent of the Wild, Wild West: the financial products and services developing and competing within this maelstrom were often wildly creative, of questionable credibility, and of dubious legality even under the loose standards of the day.

This was Charley Stoneham's world. He'd grown up within it, and he readily prospered within it. He understood pitches, he understood negotiations, he understood deals, he understood cons, and he understood hustles. He was a quick-shooting gambler who seemed to always figure out a way to beat the house.

On January 16, 1908, the *New York Times* reported a banner headline on page 2, "BROKER STONEHAM ACCUSED BY FARMER." Stoneham, by now the thirty-one-year-old president of O. F. Jonasson, was arrested on civil charges (and shortly thereafter released). He was accused by an investor, a Vermont farmer with eleven children, of misappropriating $1,300 out of his account with Stoneham's firm.[7] Denials ensued and motions to dismiss. This case would never proceed to trial. Another day, another dollar.

Soon Stoneham's name would be closely associated in the papers with that of George Graham Rice—one of the most notorious financial swindlers of the era, who would serve five separate terms in prison—regarding the issue of essentially worthless, and possibly fraudulent, mining stocks.[8]

Yet Stoneham avoided legal consequences. He was well connected enough within the Tammany Hall Democratic machine— particular Stoneham Tammany friends were Thomas "Big Tom" Foley and Al Smith[9]—to ensure that the appropriate arrangements were available, as necessary, to keep Stoneham not just out of jail but generally out of court.

He was getting richer, that's for certain. In the 1905 Olivia Gray scandal, Stoneham had presented himself as a humble Jersey City commuter, a modest family man living quietly across the Hudson from the wicked excesses of Manhattan itself. But it wasn't long before he forsook that image. Now typically referred to as "C.A.," Stoneham relocated himself as well as Hannah and their two surviving young children full-time into the swirl of nouveau riche New York City.

Little Horace learned to walk and talk in a realm of pampered luxury. He would describe his childhood as a virtually endless tour of Manhattan's finest hotels. The earliest photographs of the young boy Horace Stoneham feature him dolled up like a prince, seated in elegant carriages or astride fancy ponies, in the most chic neighborhoods of the gleaming city.[10]

C. A. Stoneham continued to gain prominence, not just among his fellow operators within the shady edges of the securities business but among the city's community of rich-guy "sports." Stoneham went to the tracks and played the horses. He went to the invitation-only parlors and played high-stakes cards. He held a season ticket box at the Polo Grounds, and there is every reason to believe that Stoneham enjoyed betting on the games.

Arnold Rothstein, the glitzy-yet-shadowy New Yorker, was instrumental in developing organized crime into a big business, run like a corporation, and Stoneham came to know him well.[11] Rothstein was a ubiquitous manager of relationships, racketeer to racketeer and racketeer to politician.[12] Stoneham was a charter member of the Partridge Club, Rothstein's "permanent, floating" crap game that moved around New York hotel rooms (and would be immortalized in Frank Loesser's *Guys and Dolls*), and a regular at The Brook, Rothstein's palatial casino outside Saratoga, where both were big men about town and owned racehorses.[13]

The Federal League opened play in 1913, operating defiantly as an "outlaw," not respecting the regulations regarding player contracts and the reserve clause that girded the National Association. In 1914 the Federal League declared itself a major league, the third major league, pitting itself in ruthless to-the-death competition with the National and American.

As the business of baseball again found itself in a state of virtual war, in the summer of 1914 the continent of Europe lurched into the real thing. Though the United States wouldn't be drawn into the Great War as a combatant until 1917, the bitter, fruitless, and shockingly bloody war dragging on in Europe dampened the American mood, as a large proportion of Americans were recent European immigrants, with family members and friends caught up in the slaughter.

Such was the bleak landscape upon which baseball's war of attrition was staged. It endured for two years before concluding with a negotiated Federal League surrender after the 1915 season.[14] "Organized Baseball" won the war, but the cost was significant: major league baseball attendance plunged by nearly a quarter in 1914–15, and many minor leagues failed.

For the Giants the blow was particularly severe, as Polo Grounds turnstile rotations slowed by 40 percent. The 1914 Giants, three-time defending National League champions, were overtaken by the "Miracle Braves" of Boston and finished second. And in 1915 McGraw's ball club humiliatingly tumbled all the way to last place. McGraw reacted swiftly, swinging several major trades to rebuild. The revamped 1916 Giants came in fourth (though pulling off an all-time record twenty-six-game winning streak along the way), and in 1917 the payoff came in full, as the Giants ran away with the pennant, their sixth in McGraw's tenure.

The Federal League's demise and a rejuvenated Giants' ball club led to improved Polo Grounds attendance in 1916 and 1917. But ticket sales didn't regain the heights the franchise had previously enjoyed. As the United States fully entered the European war, big-league attendance, which had rebounded by 33 percent from 1915 to 1916, fell back 20 percent over the course of 1917.

As the nation shifted to a modern industrial "total war" posture, professional baseball was hit hard by the combined effects of players joining (or drafted into) the military,[15] of inhibited leisure time and money, and of—worse yet—a debilitating worldwide influenza pandemic. As the 1918 season limped along, multiple minor leagues began to fold. The National and American Leagues saw attendance crater to just over three thousand per game, a level significantly below where it had wallowed during the Federal League crisis. By Labor Day of 1918 major league owners decided to cancel the remaining regular season schedule and just go ahead and stage the World Series and be done with it. (This World Series would not include the Giants, who, despite a blazing 18–1 start, wound up in second when the season was cut short, behind the Chicago Cubs.)

When John Brush died in 1912, the controlling share of Giants' ownership had gone to his son-in-law, Harry Hempstead. Though his stewardship of the Giants was sound, Hempstead lacked his father-in-law's passion for the sport, considering it just another investment. Confronted first with the Federal League and now the war, Hempstead concluded he'd had enough. At some point during the 1918 season, he let it be known that the New York Giants were for sale.

The boyhood of Horace Stoneham was ever so grandly different from that of his father. There was no hustling through Jersey City alleyways for Horace, no working his way up from the bottom rung of a brutally competitive exchange racket. Horace's days were soft and easy, spent in lavish salons, fawned over by servants and maids.

An interesting question to ponder is just how much time high-flying C. A. Stoneham spent with his surviving son. This wasn't quite the era of "involved dads" anyway, and the lifestyle ardently pursued by C.A. wouldn't appear to block out many "quality time" father-son one-on-ones. Yet the relationship the two would exhibit as adults indicated warmth and closeness. In whatever way it was fashioned, the two formed a bond, and Horace revered his father.

More than sixty years after the fact, a septuagenarian Horace Stoneham would readily remember his first Giants' game: the first half of a doubleheader on the Fourth of July 1912. The Giants' battery was Christy Mathewson and John "Chief" Meyers.[16] Horace was nine years old, and the person taking him to the Polo Grounds that day was undoubtedly C.A., whom Horace would always affectionately call "Pop." Both Stonehams, father and son, truly loved baseball, never tired of it, and this shared devotion anchored their relationship.

Young Horace would be boarded away to the finest schools. He began at the age of eleven at Trinity-Pawling, in Pawling, New York, and then moved to the newly opening Princeton Math School in Princeton, New Jersey. As a teenager, he attended Loyola, an elite Jesuit boys' high school at 980 Park Avenue in Manhattan, where he played on the baseball team, modestly describing himself as a "mediocre second baseman." In photos of the adolescent Horace, beneath slightly curly blond hair neatly parted and groomed, he offers a sly and mischievous grin.

His father kept getting richer. In 1913 C.A. founded his own brokerage firm, Charles A. Stoneham & Company. It was, in the vernacular of the day, a "bucket shop," a securities trading establishment that took orders to buy and sell stock but never directly executed the orders, instead waiting for market fluctuation to skim a profit off the change in price. This activity wouldn't be explicitly illegal until the 1930s, but it was considered unscrupulous, taking advantage of unsophisticated small investors.[17] Stoneham became a multimillionaire at a time when the purchasing power of the United States dollar was roughly twenty times what it is today.

C.A.'s investment portfolio diversified. In 1915 he was a founding investor in the Oriental Park Racetrack, in Havana, Cuba, and he also purchased hotel and casino properties in Havana. Stoneham acquired ownership stakes in silver and copper mining operations in Nevada and California.

He threw parties on a scale that stripped the town of Saratoga of its entire stock of champagne, and at evening's end Stoneham tipped each waiter $100 and the wine steward $500.[18] Stoneham would think nothing of wagering a thousand dollars per turn of the roulette wheel at Rothstein's casino or of dropping $70,000 in an evening's gambling.[19]

Exactly when Charles Stoneham first met John McGraw is not recorded. It seems likely to have occurred before 1918, given their New York City prominence, their shared association with

Tammany Hall, and especially their shared enthusiasms for baseball, gambling, horses, liquor, and Havana. What's known is that their paths did cross in 1918.

Probably the very first person whom Harry Hempstead would have notified about his decision to seek a buyer of the Giants was McGraw. This would be not only because of McGraw's towering status as the essential employee of the enterprise but also because Hempstead surely understood that McGraw, now in his midforties and contemplating the next stage of his career, had keen interest in forming an investment group and promoting himself to the rank of ownership partner. In any case, 1918 scuttlebutt in McGraw's circles had him reaching out for backing to luminaries such as oil magnate Harry Sinclair, who'd been a significant investor in the Federal League, and Broadway superstar George M. Cohan famously a diehard Giants fan.

However valid those may have been, a serious possibility involved George Loft, a candy-making magnate connected to McGraw through their interests in horse racing. McGraw arranged a meeting between Loft and Hempstead at the Waldorf Hotel in December 1918, but the discussions foundered over Loft's insistence on purchasing the shares of all Giants' investors, not just the controlling portion owned by Hempstead.[20]

Where Stoneham might have been through all this isn't known. What's clear is that the connection that eventually fused him to McGraw went straight through Tammany Hall: one Francis Xavier McQuade, an intriguingly well-capitalized New York magistrate,[21] a Catholic, and an ardent Giants fan. Judge McQuade knew C. A. Stoneham, and he also knew John McGraw, and he was eager that they should all get to know one another better.

The deal was engineered as 1918 gave way to 1919. The announcement came on January 14 of the new year: Stoneham had purchased a controlling interest in the club and would serve as president; McGraw and McQuade each acquired smaller interests and would serve as officers, with McGraw as a vice president as well as manager and McQuade as treasurer. The price paid by the trio for the Brush stock was estimated at $1.1 million.[22] Formally, the privately held corporation of which Stoneham now held a 58 percent share was called the National Exhibition Company, which included the New York National League Baseball Club and the Polo Grounds stadium facility, on land leased from the Coogan family.

Multiple accounts present differing versions, but it seems essentially factual that among C. A. Stoneham's very first actions upon acquiring the grandest brand and most valuable property in professional sports was to seek out his fifteen-year-old son and coolly announce, "Horrie, I bought you a ball club."[23]

2

Roaring into the Twenties

The Great War's battle line that came to be known as the western front—several hundred meandering miles, from the North Sea to the Swiss Alps, of entrenched, barbed wire, rat-infested, machine-gunned, artillery-bombarded, poison-gassed hellscape across which the German army faced west, and the French and British armies faced east—remained locked in ghastly stalemate from 1914 through 1917. No previous warfare in history so monstrously produced casualties. Three battles alone (Verdun, the Somme, and Passchendaele) delivered about 2.3 million dead and wounded while providing zero resolution to the conflict. In 1918, at last, with the entry of the United States on the Allied side, the balance tipped. Economically and politically exhausted, the German Empire negotiated a surrender, and on November 11, 1918, the appalling devastation finally reached its end.

During the conflict, and especially in the period immediately following, the Great War was frequently described as the "War to End All Wars." This decidedly optimistic reckoning was based on logical observations: no conflagration on such an epic scale had ever occurred before because the world's nations had never been so extensively interconnected and military technology had never been so deadly effective. This cataclysmic event had plainly demonstrated the futility—the negative return on investment of lives for territory—that modern war would now and forever present. Thus, the lone positive consequence of the horrific War to End All Wars seemed to be that nothing like it would ever take place again.

In the United States the postwar environment was fraught with fundamental change. Forty-six of the forty-eight states approved ratification of Amendment 18 of the United States Constitution, which declared the production, transport, or sale of "intoxicating liquors" to be illegal. On January 16, 1920, alcohol prohibition became the law of the land. On the heels of the nation's eighteenth constitutional amendment came its nineteenth, on August 18, 1920, granting women in every state the right to vote.

Amid this environment of dizzying transformation, major league baseball grappled with another crisis. The World Series of 1919, the first World Series held following the Great War and the first while C. A. Stoneham was counted among the fraternity of baseball owners, was the infamous Black Sox series. Perceived by some at the time as fishy, it was soon exposed to have indeed been crooked, its outcome preordained by gamblers promising large bribes to key Chicago White Sox stars to lose to the Cincinnati Reds on purpose. Suspicions of gambler-bought players and gambler-fixed games here and there were nothing new in baseball, but the sport had never before faced a scandal on this scale.

The closest precedent to the Black Sox series had been the World Series of 1914, in which the heavily favored dynastic Philadelphia Athletics were stunningly swept in four straight games by the upstart Boston Braves. No investigation was undertaken and no specific accusations made, but the circumstances around that series—not just the underdog's (and thus the long odds') improbable win but the fact that A's owner-manager Connie Mack, not a man easily angered, was so disgusted that he immediately blew up his roster, casting away his core stars and willingly sending his ball club from the penthouse to the cellar—raised more than a few eyebrows.[1]

And there was the fact that shortly before the 1914 series began, none other than George M. Cohan had placed a series of large bets against the Athletics. The bookmaker taking Cohan's wagers was Joseph J. "Sport" Sullivan, a Boston-based gambler with a record of multiple arrests.[2]

This was the same Sport Sullivan who would be named by 1919 White Sox first baseman Arnold "Chick" Gandil as having approached him with the proposal of throwing that year's series. And though it was never proved, it was widely suspected at the time, and deemed accurate by the school of Black Sox Scandal research, that Arnold Rothstein was at the very least aware of the 1919 scheme, was probably involved to some degree, and was possibly the major financier.[3]

The Black Sox scandal was front-page news across the country in 1920, and it was terrible publicity for professional baseball. A number of major league owners had long been dissatisfied with the ineffectual governance of the sport since 1903 under the National Commission, a three-man panel consisting of the president of the American League, the president of the National League, and the chairman, who had always been Garry Herrmann, who also happened to be a minority owner and president of the Cincinnati Reds (coincidentally, the very team to whom the Black Sox had thrown the 1919 series). Seeing the need to at least appear to do something to prevent a reoccurrence of this fiasco, the owners agreed to bring in an independent outsider with no conflicts of interest to take over as chairman of the National Commission.

The outsider they chose was Kenesaw Mountain Landis, a high-profile federal judge. He agreed to take the job but only under two conditions: the three-man National Commission was to be dissolved, and Judge Landis alone would exercise absolute authority without appeal; and he could not be fired for the entirety of his seven-year contract (at a whopping $50,000 per year, nearly seven times what he was making as a judge). The owners, all too aware of their meager bargaining position, acquiesced. On November 12, 1920, Landis became the first commissioner of baseball. In the photo recording the event, Judge Landis is seated in the center, signing his contract, with all the baseball owners standing behind him. Over Landis's left shoulder, in the second row, stands C. A. Stoneham.

Landis would, of course, take dramatic action to "clean up" baseball's image regarding the influence of gambling: even though the eight White Sox players implicated in the scandal were all acquitted of fraud charges (in a criminal proceeding of highly dubious validity), Landis immediately and permanently banned them from professional baseball anyway, and he banned several other major and minor league players also merely suspected of fixing games. Given this, it's worth considering whether Commissioner Landis, with absolute power over everything, would have permitted Stoneham—not only a close associate of the notorious Rothstein but a high-stakes gambler himself, heavily invested in horse racing and casinos—to purchase a major league franchise.

But we'll never know. Stoneham had bought in a year and half before the Black Sox scandal erupted and twenty-two months before Landis became commissioner. C. A. Stoneham got into baseball, one might say, just under the wire.

While it isn't clear when C. A. Stoneham and John J. McGraw first met, it's certain that once partnered with the Giants, they got along very well. Stoneham's love for baseball in general and the Giants in particular were genuine, as was his deep respect for McGraw's wisdom and capability. The division of labor was clear and simple: McGraw would run the baseball operation as well as serving as the public face of the franchise, meeting with the press; Stoneham was happy to stay out of the limelight as much as he could and to provide McGraw with whatever financial resources he deemed necessary.

The matter of financing was dramatically illustrated during Stoneham's first season as owner, when on August 1, 1919, he approved a McGraw trade of two journeymen and two prospects, along with a prodigious $55,000 in cash, to the Boston Braves in exchange for young standout pitcher Art Nehf. The ace southpaw would go 9–2 with a 1.50 earned run average down the stretch for the Giants, and though that wouldn't be enough to deliver a pennant (the Giants finished second again in 1919), the bold and confident deal was a signal that Stoneham was an owner committed to victory. For McGraw it was a welcome return to the manner of trusting alliance he'd enjoyed with John Brush.[4]

Moreover, Stoneham's commitment wasn't just to putting the best possible team on the field; it would also be to providing the best possible ballpark experience for the fans. When announcing their purchase in January 1919, Stoneham, McGraw, and McQuade issued a joint statement: "The new owners realize that the New York Baseball Club is something more than a private business enterprise, and we take possession with a keen sense of responsibility to the public of this city and of the entire country. . . . In the playing department, it belongs primarily to its patrons."[5]

Such flowery pronouncement has since become customary fodder from corporate public relations departments, but at the time it was not typical, and Stoneham's subsequent actions indicated that for him at least, it was sincere. C. A. Stoneham was a complicated figure; shady and ruthless in his securities enterprises, pathologically deceitful in his personal affairs, and a high-living playboy, yet he had come from humble origins and never forgot the passionate perspective of the common fan. Eddie Brannick, a Giants front office secretary through nearly the entire Stoneham (both father and son) tenure, put it this way: "Mr. Stoneham was a fan—he held a season box for years—before he bought the club . . . and he always considered policy from the point of view of the fan. He got the feel of the business after two or three years as an official, and thereafter he was a sincere pleader at league meetings for the cause of the fans. I recall a time when he quashed what he believed to be an unpopular scheme by saying, 'Gentlemen, we must always remember one principle first of all. This game doesn't belong to us. It belongs to the fans. We are their servants.' He gathered support to vote down the motion."[6]

And like McGraw—perhaps it was from McGraw that he came to understand it—Stoneham perceived the New York Giants as more than a transactional business; for him they were also a community, an institution—something important—with a past that deserved respect and dignity. The story is told that one day C.A. walked through the pass gate at the Polo Grounds and nodded a greeting to the old man at the turnstile. "Who is that old fellow?" Stoneham asked an aide. "I've seen him here every day."

"That's Jim Mutrie," was the reply. "He used to manage the Giants. In fact he gave them their name."

"What? You don't mean it. And now he's a gate-tender!"

Jim Mutrie never tended another gate after that. Stoneham saw to it that the old manager was provided with a pension that afforded a fitting retirement.

McGraw had long made it a policy to provide some money or a job for old ballplayers down on their luck. At the Polo Grounds in the 1910s and '20s, some of the biggest names of the 1880s and '90s were tending gates, serving as night watchmen, or sweeping the grandstand, performing humble honest jobs and sustaining an identity with baseball.[7] (Decades later Horace Stoneham would sustain the legacy as a paternalistic employer with "scouting" jobs and pensions for those in the Giants "family.")

The 1919 season was C. A. Stoneham's first at the Giants' helm. The war-cratered attendance totals of 1918 had spooked major league owners, and to mitigate risk, the 1919 schedule lopped off 2 games between each team, so that the standard 154-game regular season was shortened to 140. But that fear soon proved to be unwarranted, as fans in both leagues were readily clicking the turnstiles. And no team enjoyed that renaissance more than Stoneham's New York Giants, whose 1919 attendance nearly tripled that of 1918 on an absolute basis (from 256,618 to 708,857) and more than doubled it on a per-game basis (from 4,582 to 10,273). Giants' attendance at the Polo Grounds in 1919 was the highest in all of major league baseball, and their per-game rate was indeed the second best in franchise history, surpassed only by that of 1908. Though the team fell short of a pennant, with everything considered it was a highly successful first year for the Stoneham-McGraw partnership, and all signs pointed to greater achievements soon to come.

But that winter a loud and colorful threat would arrive, suddenly and literally, upon the Giants' doorstep.

That Baltimore Orioles franchise that the Giants (and Reds) had plundered back in 1902 was reorganized in 1903 and relocated to New York, as the American League desperately grabbed a presence in the nation's largest city. The meager ballpark in which they played, situated on a ridge in Manhattan's Washington Heights neighborhood, was informally known as Hilltop Park, and the ball club was nicknamed the Highlanders.

They had a few contending seasons early on but weren't consistently good, generally finishing in the American League's second division and a couple of times in the cellar. Rarely did their attendance approach that of the Giants; it was plain to everyone that the Highlanders, along with Brooklyn's never-competitive Superbas, were a second-tier baseball attraction in New York, while the Giants were the glamorous headliner.

By 1913 the Highlanders gave up on rickety Hilltop Park and just moved in as a tenant in the Giants' newly remodeled steel-and-concrete Polo Grounds, paying rent to the top dog in an arrangement that could hardly have been more symbolic. Now couch surfing with the Giants in the bottomlands between Coogan's Bluff and the Harlem River, the Highlanders name no longer fit, and soon the team came to be called the Yankees.

It wasn't particularly big news in 1915 when the Yankees franchise was sold, for $480,000, to the partnership of Jacob Ruppert and one Tillinghast L'Hommedieu "Cap" Huston. But the German American Ruppert was heir to an enormous brewery fortune and could afford to spend lavishly to improve the club. By 1919 the Yankees were no longer a mediocrity, matching the Giants' second-place National League finish with one of their own in the American and setting a franchise record for attendance with 619,164. But though the 1919 Yankees' roster was solid and well rounded, it lacked a core superstar.

The most dynamic superstar in baseball in 1919 was the Boston Red Sox's twenty-four-year-old prodigy, George "Babe" Ruth. He was an ace pitcher but so devastatingly powerful with the bat that over the course of 1918 and '19 he'd been moved from the mound and become an outfielder. In 1918, despite appearing in just ninety-five games (twenty of them as a pitcher), Ruth had tied for the major league lead with eleven home runs; bear in mind that under the extremely pitcher-friendly conditions then prevailing, the rest of the Red Sox roster hit just four homers, all year long, and their pitching staff allowed a grand total of nine.

In 1919, playing every day for the first time, Ruth was sensational, blasting twenty-nine home runs to set a major league record (the second most in either league that season was twelve). Babe Ruth was the sport's greatest attraction, a box office smash wherever he played, not just for his amazing feats on the field but also for his brash and freewheeling personality. One would imagine that such a player would be the very definition of "untouchable" by any team seeking to acquire him.

But these were peculiar circumstances. For one thing, Boston owner Harry Frazee was a theatrical producer, not a beer baron or a Wall Street hotshot, and he was chronically strapped for cash. Right now he was in particular need of the means to pay off the loan he'd used to buy the team in 1916, a loan that came due in November 1919. For another thing, Frazee was feuding with imperious American League president Ban Johnson, and he understood that Johnson—who usually got what he wanted— was seeking a way to force Frazee out. And for a third, the brash and freewheeling personality of young Babe Ruth, while rollicking fun for sportswriters and fans, was a headache for management: Ruth was frequently drunk and/or bellicose, often tardy and sometimes absent, and entirely heedless of team rules and norms.

So when, that winter, Jacob Ruppert presented Frazee with the proposal to take Ruth off his hands in exchange for $25,000 in cash, plus three promissory notes worth $25,000 each, and on top of that a $300,000 loan secured by the mortgage on Boston's Fenway Park, Frazee reasoned that it was, well, an offer he couldn't refuse. On January 5, 1920, Babe Ruth became a member of the New York Yankees.

So it was that the New York Giants faced the prospect of the most spectacular player baseball had yet known playing not just for a rival team within their city but playing his home games in their very ballpark. The Giants' long-held status as the titan of New York baseball was about to be tested, and in 1920 the test did not go well: Ruth obliterated his own home run record, clouting an unbelievable total of fifty-four, and while the Giants and Yankees again both came in second place in their leagues, it was the Yankees now outdrawing the Giants at the Polo Grounds. Riding the high-revving postwar economy, the Giants established a

National League record attendance of 929,689, but that imposing figure was dwarfed by the Yankees, with a staggering 1,289,422, more than twice what they'd ever drawn before.

No one felt the humiliation more bitterly than John McGraw. He was being upstaged as the king of New York baseball and on his own home turf to boot. The more McGraw derided Ruth as a goon, a circus freak, exhibiting a crudely unrefined slugging style that was obviously, inherently inferior to McGraw's complex, cerebral brand of "inside" baseball, the louder Yankee fans cheered Ruth's next tape measure shot. So long as the Yankees had been no threat to the Giants' hegemony, McGraw had been happy to allow them to play at the Polo Grounds, and Stoneham, of course, was happy to receive the lease revenue. But once the Ruth-centered Yankees became the top attraction, the wisdom of hosting them was quickly diminished.[8]

While the Giants' selfish motivation to send the Yankees packing was obvious, an additional factor, at least suspected by Ruppert, was that McGraw and Stoneham were being encouraged by Ban Johnson to evict the Yankees. McGraw wasn't the only party feeling threatened by the Yankees' rapid emergence as an American League powerhouse, as the ironfisted Johnson was now feuding with Ruppert. It was Ruppert's belief that Johnson was hoping to force a crisis regarding the Yankees' ballpark status as a means of revoking their charter as a member of the league, a provision of which required having a venue in which to play home games.

In any case, barely a month into the 1920 season, on May 14 Stoneham suddenly announced that beginning in 1921, the Yankees would no longer be welcome as tenants at the Polo Grounds. In Ruppert's own account, as he recalled nearly twenty years later, this provoked an exchange of threats between Johnson and himself:

"The constitution of the American League says that if you have no park to play in, your franchise may be confiscated," Johnson informed us.

I owned a plot of ground on Madison Avenue, from 102nd to 103rd streets. It measured 600 feet by 200, far too small for a ball park. "Mr. Johnson, if you force me to it, the Yankees will play in a park seating exactly 1500 persons," I informed Ban. I was serious about building on that ground on Madison Avenue. "If you press us to the wall we will play Yankee games where every hit will be a home run. Your league will become the laughing stock of the country."

Johnson must have called off McGraw, because we got a new lease for two years.[9]

However serious either Johnson or Ruppert may have been, it was indeed the case that a week after his May 14 announcement that the Yankees would be out of the Polo Grounds next year, Stoneham reversed his decision and said that the teams would enter negotiations for a long-term lease. In fact, however, Ruppert and Huston had for a few years been pondering their options for building their own facility—a serious and permanent home, not the stopgap farce on Madison Avenue—and this kerfuffle simply meant that they would stop thinking about it and start doing it. In October 1920 the Yankees signed a two-year lease of the Polo Grounds, providing them with the time to get busy building Yankee Stadium.[10]

The Giants' second-place finish in 1920 had been their third in a row, which was frustrating enough for John McGraw. Being very good was never good enough for him. But worse yet, the club nosing them out for the 1920 pennant had been Brooklyn, of all teams, coming out of nowhere. Brooklyn manager Wilbert Robinson (the team was now known as the "Robins" in his honor) had been a Baltimore teammate of McGraw in the 1890s, and they'd once been close, but that just made it harder for the hypercompetitive McGraw to lose to him.

Between the obnoxious Ruth and his Yankees and the upstart Robins, McGraw deeply understood that he was being challenged as never before, not just to win a championship but to win the battle of New York. With Stoneham's full commitment of financial support behind him, McGraw steeled himself for victory in the most competitive environment he'd yet faced. He would succeed—and to an extraordinary degree.

The terrific Giants' ball clubs McGraw would present in the early 1920s were the crowning achievement of his marvelous career. Unlike the string of winners he'd had early in his New York tenure, built around the phenomenal Christy Mathewson, this time McGraw had no dominant superstar at his disposal. He certainly had no Babe Ruth. Instead, these teams were exceptional for their depth and balance and for their deft mixture of young standouts McGraw had signed and developed himself (infielders Frankie Frisch and Travis Jackson, outfielder Ross Youngs, first baseman George Kelly, and pitchers Wilfred "Rosy" Ryan and Virgil Barnes) with key veterans he acquired through shrewd trades and purchases (shortstop Dave Bancroft, outfielders Emil "Irish" Meusel and Charles "Casey" Stengel, catcher Frank Snyder, and pitchers Hugh McQuillan and Jack Bentley).

To be sure, McGraw's capacity to acquire talent was enabled by Stoneham's hefty bankroll. Starting with the Art Nehf deal in 1919, McGraw was able to spend more than half a million dollars in player purchases through 1924.

Though the Giants were the favorite of most prognosticators to win the 1921 National League pennant,[11] they spent most of that season in second place, trailing Pittsburgh. When the Pirates came to the Polo Grounds in late August to begin a five-game series, their lead was seven and a half games, the largest margin all year, and for the Giants it was do-or-die. The Giants did, sweeping all five games, launching a blistering 24–9 stretch run that delivered the seventh pennant of McGraw's tenure. And the 1921 flag would be the first of four straight for the Giants, the first achievement of that feat in major league history.

Yet even that wasn't the pinnacle. Babe Ruth's Yankees began their run of American League dominance in 1921, setting up the Giants and Yankees to face off in an all–Polo Grounds World Series, not just that year but again in 1922. McGraw's team now had the chance to knock the big loudmouth down a peg, and they did it. In 1921 the Giants won it in dramatic fashion, coming back from two games to none, and then from three games to two, winning the series going away by taking the final three in that year's best-five-out-of-nine format. And in 1922 they delivered an emphatic four wins–to–naught whitewashing of the Yanks. And perhaps even very best of all, Giants' pitchers shut down the mighty Ruth himself, limiting him in those two series to seven hits in thirty-three at bats (a .212 batting average), with just one double and one home run (a solo shot in a Giants win) and eleven strikeouts. McGraw never tired of explaining that he'd personally signaled, from the dugout, every pitch to Ruth.[12]

The New York rivals would square off yet again in 1923, with brand-new Yankee Stadium now the venue for the American League home games. This time around Ruth was able to exact some revenge, delivering three homers as well as a double and a triple, leading the Yankees to a four games–to–two championship. In the 1924 Series the Giants finally faced a different opponent, the Washington Senators. Capping off an epic see-saw struggle, in a twelve-inning seventh game in which thirty-six-year-old Walter Johnson heroically provided four shutout innings in relief, the Senators prevailed on a walk-off bad-hop groundball double.

Back-to-back-to-back-to-back World Series appearances placed Stoneham and McGraw's New York Giants squarely again at the center of the baseball realm. And Stoneham was quick to realize that with the Polo Grounds in his possession, he had more than baseball to offer his patrons. The 1920s economy was, well, roaring along, and other sports were rapidly growing in popularity and could be engaged to sell lots of tickets. In a way his predecessors hadn't imagined, C. A. Stoneham developed the Polo Grounds into a year-round sports palace (including a major expansion of the facility in 1923, increasing the seating capacity from thirty-four thousand to fifty-five thousand).

Through the 1920s Stoneham operated the crown jewel of sporting venues. In September 1923 the Polo Grounds hosted the wildly intense two-round heavyweight championship boxing match between Jack Dempsey, the "Manassa Mauler," and Luis Firpo, the "Wild Bull of the Pampas"; that event sold eighty-five thousand tickets, a large portion of them standing room only, while another twenty thousand or so were left outside the gates. Other big-name boxers who fought at the Polo Grounds in 1923 were Eugène Criqui, Johnny Dundee, Francisco "Pancho Villa" Guilledo, Johnny Kilbane, Benny Leonard, Jack McAuliffe, Lew

Tendler, Jimmy Wilde, and Jess Willard. Football coach Knute Rockne's immortal "Four Horsemen" of Notre Dame were so christened at the Polo Grounds in 1924, in a game against Army. The Army-Navy football game was held at the Polo Grounds six times between 1919 and 1927. Harold "Red" Grange, the most celebrated college football player of the era, gave professional football a boost with the New York football Giants, when he attracted a crowd of seventy thousand to the Polo Grounds for a game against the Chicago Bears in 1925.[13]

C. A. Stoneham had surely made a fortune on Wall Street, but he fully recognized the shadiness of his business enterprises there and knew all too well the stress involved in skirting the edges of legality and propriety. He wanted something better for his son.

The great love C.A. and Horace shared was that of baseball—and the Giants. What better career for Horace to pursue than operating the New York Giants and the Polo Grounds? These were endeavors refreshingly free of the dark bucket shop shadows, and indeed, the sports business was a means not to just make money but to be part of the civic fabric, delivering a wholesome public good. It was C.A.'s intention that this was the business Horace should learn and in due time take over its management, and when C.A. would someday pass away, Horace would inherit the Giants and the Polo Grounds. He could hardly imagine a greater legacy than that the New York Giants, the team of Jim Mutrie and Mike Tiernan, of John McGraw and Christy Mathewson, would forever be the Stoneham family business.

But in 1921 Horace was just eighteen years old and certainly not ready yet. That spring he had graduated (just barely, perhaps) from the Loyola School. For now he should go to college and be formally educated. This had been a privilege denied to C.A., a missing piece of his own experience and achievement that he was too often reminded of when dealing with business colleagues and other professionals who were college men—despite his great wealth and stature, C.A. recognized the glint of condescension in their eyes, the inescapable sense that there was a social class above him that he could never attain. C.A. was genuinely proud of his hard climb from Jersey City to Wall Street to the executive offices of the Polo Grounds, but he was self-aware enough to know that he had a rough edge that could never be polished. In the classic tradition of the American Dream, Stoneham wanted his son to climb higher still. And so he enrolled Horace as an undergraduate at Fordham University, the prestigious Jesuit institution, the third-oldest university in the city of New York.

Many years later Horace would toss off the line that he lasted at Fordham "for about four days." While this is almost certainly an exaggeration for the sake of a good story, it is true that Horace dropped out. He was hardly the first nor last teenager to disappoint his parents by dropping out of college. It's easy to imagine the arguments between exasperated father and willful son, the strict ultimatums and the defiant shrugs. Such has been the dynamic in many a family.

But this dynamic revealed particular truths about this family. C.A. and Horace were different people, with distinctly different personalities. C.A. had always been self-directed, obsessively driven to achieve success. Horace was more prone to take it easy, to enjoy the moment, and C.A. was no doubt kicking himself that the childhood of pampered luxury he'd provided for his son had allowed this trait to develop all too fully. There was a positive aspect of this—C.A. was often harsh and ruthless, while Horace would almost never be that way—but that was probably not something C.A. was finding very valuable at the moment. Still, while son Horace was a genuinely nice person, gentle and sensitive in ways that didn't come naturally to his father, C.A. remained perplexed that his nice-guy son didn't perceive a college education to be a priority, no matter how thoroughly and sensibly he explained it.

There was, however, at least one characteristic that father and son shared: both loved to drink. Though alcohol was by now illegal in the United States, it was plainly true that it was still readily available. For C.A. drinking had always been an integral part of the evening party, blowing off steam with the boys while dealing cards or shooting dice. To C.A.'s way of thinking, having a few belts was the just reward for a day's work done. And now C.A.

had to contend with his shiftless son, neither going to school nor working for a living, with nothing but time on his hands, time that was happily devoted to going out with fellow spoiled brat pals and indulging in bootleg booze.

This uneasy father-son stalemate lasted for a year or two. Finally, C.A. was fed up. If Horace wasn't going to educate himself through book learning, then it would have to be the school of hard knocks. He needed to experience some painful lessons, to grow up, to develop a work ethic. And C.A. came upon an idea.

C.A. understood that the one thing Horace loved even more than lazing around was the Giants. And so he played that card. C.A. issued an ultimatum: if Horace did not do exactly what his father now told him to do, he would never take over the Giants. C.A. made it clear that he would have no difficulty finding someone else to do that job. With this, at last, C.A. succeeded in focusing his son's attention. Horace readily agreed to now do what he was told.

Among C.A.'s properties was a copper mine, operated by the Calaveras Copper Consolidated Company, in the rugged Sierra Nevada foothills of California.[14] A copper mine in the rugged Sierra Nevada foothills of California was, in every sense, just about as far away from the cushy salons and speakeasies of Manhattan as could be. C.A. needed his listless boy to become a serious man, and if a year in a copper mine couldn't make that happen, then maybe nothing could.

Though obviously named for local copper mining, the town of Copperopolis is located in the region of California known as the Gold Country, in Calaveras County. It's about eighty miles southeast of Sutter's Fort, where gold was first discovered in the territory, in rocky, semiarid ridge land where extensive gold mining had occurred during the gold rush of the mid-1800s. Copper was and is less lucrative than gold, and certainly less glamorous, but a mineral in persistent demand for industrial applications.

The town is in the low foothills, at about one thousand feet of elevation, with California's broad Central Valley to its west and the towering Sierra Nevada mountain range to its east. In 1865, in a shack on a Copperopolis promontory called Jack Ass Hill,

Sam Clemens, using the pen name Mark Twain, was said to have written his short story "The Celebrated Jumping Frog of Calaveras County." By the 1920s the town had a population of roughly two thousand people. While not especially remote, it was entirely rustic, a tough, hard place. It would not suffer fools gladly.

And so it was that at some point in 1922 or 1923, the nineteen- or twenty-year-old Horace Stoneham, a big-city rich kid who'd never worked a day in his life, went to Grand Central Station and boarded the 20th Century Limited to Chicago and from there on to Sacramento, California. It took him several days to traverse the continent, and the very journey itself had to be an education. Between New York and Chicago he observed the hardwood forests of the Appalachians, then the rolling hills of the coal and oil country of Pennsylvania and Ohio. Then he came within sight of Lake Erie and then Lake Michigan. Heading west from Chicago, the two thousand–mile journey to California took him across the broad flat cornfields and prairies of Iowa and Nebraska before crossing the Continental Divide in Wyoming via the South Pass. As he headed farther west, the vistas he encountered were ever more alien to anything he'd known. In particular he spent many hours crossing the vast deserts of Utah and Nevada, with enormous skies and magnificent reaches of vividly open space, as different from jam-packed Manhattan as could be. Stoneham would come to love this environment, in time relocating the Giants' spring training headquarters to the Sonoran Desert of Arizona and living there until the end of his days. This was his introduction to that extraordinary landscape.

Once he finally reached California, from Sacramento to Copperopolis there was no railroad. Someone from the mine was sent to meet young Horace Stoneham at the station and drove him up into the craggy hills by automobile, a trip that took several hours, via dusty, rutted mule wagon roads.

One can only imagine what the miners must have made of the big boss's son, this city slicker, dandy kid who didn't know a shovel from a shitter. Exactly what work Horace was assigned to do at the mine is unrecorded. It seems highly unlikely that he would have been expected to do much toiling within the pits or tending to the smelters. Probably he was taught to handle administrative chores, the business operations.

C. A. Stoneham's decision to send Horace out to Copperopolis can properly be understood as a last resort, a desperation move. It was reform school. But all evidence suggests that it succeeded perfectly. Horace did indeed learn humility and learned to respect authority, to show up every day on time, and to respect hard work and the people who perform it. Corny though it may be, it appears essentially true that Horace Stoneham arrived in Copperopolis a boy and there became a man.

That was likely true in more ways than one, of course, at least in the version of the story that Horace would love to tell. "I don't know what Pop expected," Horace would recall. "But when it came to handling liquor, those boys in that camp really completed my education. They were the greatest collection of two-fisted drinkers you could find anywhere." Even a hardworking Horace, it would seem, was Horace wherever he went.

It was during this time in California that Horace Stoneham first visited San Francisco, 120 miles to the west. In the 1950s—under very different circumstances—he would explain to the Bay Area press: "I've always liked San Francisco, since I was a kid. I worked in Calaveras County, and it was always a treat to be able to get up to San Francisco."[15] He would, of course, come to love the city, which presented many of the charms and pleasures of Manhattan, though on a cozier scale and in a far more picturesque setting.

In any case, the reports on Horace's deportment and progress that Sam Levy, the Copperopolis mine foreman, sent back east to Mr. Stoneham were positive. In March 1924 C.A. contacted Horace and directed him to pack his bag and head to Sarasota, Florida, for spring training. He was going to start working for the Giants.

3

Hard Truths

Figuring out how to get his son to straighten up and fly right wasn't the worst of C. A. Stoneham's problems in 1923 and 1924. His less-than-honest Wall Street wheeling and dealing caught up with him again, and this time around he wouldn't be able to have everything "fixed" as easily as before. Even as his team prepared for their World Series showdown with the Yankees in 1923, Stoneham was facing federal criminal charges in connection with the transfer of his customer accounts, two years earlier, to firms that had quickly fallen into bankruptcy. On August 31, 1923, a grand jury indicted Stoneham for perjury. This was bad, but worse soon followed. On January 11, 1924, Stoneham was charged with conspiracy to defraud.

Stoneham had built his great fortune by expertly navigating the dark channels of sketchy securities and the Tammany political machine. Now his prominence in those places, once an asset, increasingly presented itself as a liability. Stoneham found himself pitted against Tom Foley's bitter foe, newspaper publisher William Randolph Hearst, whose papers railed against the bucket shop racketeers who swindled customers. Stoneham's efforts to divest himself of his brokerage operations—which had made possible his purchase of the Giants—rendered him squarely in the line of fire of the Hearst press crusade. Compounding the issue was that one of Hearst's primary Tammany Hall villains, Judge McQuade, had of course been the crucial actor in securing Stoneham's placement within the Giants' executive offices.[1]

Though Stoneham would eventually succeed in evading conviction—on February 27, 1925, he was acquitted of the fraud charge, and the perjury indictment would be finally dismissed in 1927 (though Stoneham was forced to settle multiple civil suits)—the drawn-out, expensive proceedings were a major distraction from his capacity to focus on operating the Giants and a hindrance to his ability to spend as freely as before.

Moreover, it wasn't just that Stoneham was no longer able to invest outside wealth into the ball club. Whether by necessity or just bad habit, Stoneham was actively extracting profits from the ball club for his personal purposes. He reliably paid himself an annual salary of $45,000 (about $670,000 in 2020 dollars) as team president. Between 1920 and 1930 the Giants yielded $2 million in profits, which funded $1.5 million in dividends, leaving just a quarter of retained earnings to be reinvested into the company. Beyond even that, the team advanced Stoneham $280,035 in "loans," which were entirely unsecured and, shall we say, not promptly or thoroughly documented.[2]

The dodgy loan activity would eventually provoke a bitter public and legal falling-out between Stoneham and club treasurer McQuade. All of this trouble and acrimony stood in stark contrast to the operation of the Giants' formidable rival, the Yankees. Jacob Ruppert's sound stewardship of that franchise was dedicated to ensuring long-term success for the team and the business, as opposed to lining the principal owner's pocket. In the decade of the 1920s the Yankees recorded profits of over $3.5 million and paid zero dividends to investors: the entire profit was available for reinvestment in club operations, paving the way for an already dominant team to gain yet more strength. Ruppert didn't rely on his ball club's earnings for personal income and thus was able to focus on winning in both the present and the future. Stoneham, increasingly less wealthy than Ruppert and ever-more financially dependent upon his team, lived lavishly on its earnings. Meanwhile, across the river Ruppert and Ed Barrow—the genius Ruppert employed to run the baseball operation, in the role that would come to be known as general manager—were constructing the foundation of the greatest dynasty in baseball history.[3]

In November 1920 the National Exhibition Company's share-holders had elected seventeen-year-old Horace Stoneham a direc-tor.[4] It was, of course, a formality; he was still in high school and took no authority or responsibility. But it was a clear indication of his father's intentions regarding Horace's future. When Horace arrived in Florida for spring training in 1924, now almost twenty-one years old and fresh from his Copperopolis boot camp, he was ready to begin pulling his weight.

C.A. saw to it that his son would indeed perform real work and be held accountable. He was given no empty title. Horace worked every day, all day, and was apparently eager to do so. He was expected to learn everything about the operation of the ball club from the bottom up—by doing it. He started in the ticket office; half a century later he recollected: "We had a lady, Miss Wilson, who ran it all then. None of this computer business."[5]

In that year of 1924, upon the team's return to New York from spring training, Horace sprung a surprise. He eloped to Atlantic City, marrying Valleda Pyke on April 14. Like Horace, she was a few weeks shy of her twenty-first birthday. Petite and high-spirited, she'd worked as a dancer on Vaudeville stages. She and Horace had been sweethearts before his exile to Copperopolis and had corresponded in his absence and decided to tie the knot upon their first reunion.[6]

It was, perhaps, a measure of Horace's newfound sense of adult responsibility that he got married on the ball club's off day, between their arrival in New York and their Opening Day game of April 15. Newlywed Horace reported for work the next day. And it was also, perhaps, an indication that Horace—while cer-tainly not identical to his father in this regard—might develop his own issues regarding commitment to marriage.

Perhaps especially because he was the big boss's son, Horace's willingness to perform humble toil, to listen and learn, earned him the respect of many in the organization. In later years a capacity to treat every employee with dignity and respect would become a hallmark of his executive style. And also perhaps espe-cially because he was the big boss's son, Horace's natural shy-ness served him well in his earliest years with the club: he was never overbearing, never arrogant, but instead cheerful and self-effacing and genuinely happy to be doing what he was doing. Horace had an innate quality that his father had not: he was simply likable.

None other than John McGraw took a particular liking to him. "I remember that Mr. McGraw called me up to his room [in Sarasota] and showed me a letter he had just written to my father about a young prospect named Hack Wilson, who'd been on a Class B team in Portsmouth, Virginia. He wore a red undershirt under his uniform. Mr. McGraw had written, 'If hustle counts, he's sure to make it.' Everybody called him 'Mr. McGraw'—everybody but my father, of course. Mr. McGraw, he called my father 'Charley' or 'C.A.'"[7]

Horace didn't let his natural inclination to shyness prevent him from engaging with the Giants players themselves, at least the ones closer to his age. "I came to know the ballplayers then, of course. I used to see them in the mornings. I got to be friends with some of them, like Ross Youngs, the great outfielder who died so young. Ross Youngs, from Shiner, Texas. When he first came along—before I knew him—he was signed by the Giants at a time when the team was on the road. Ross was in town and the Giants were away, and he went right over and got into a pickup game over by the docks on 79th Street, next to the railroad yards there. It's where they have the marina now. He had that intense desire to play ball."[8]

Piece by piece Horace learned the various aspects of running the Polo Grounds, and eventually C.A. put him in charge of operations. In the 1920s the facility was open for events about two hundred days throughout the year. In addition to the boxing matches and football games, the Polo Grounds regularly hosted soccer matches as well as tennis. It held midget automobile races and ice skating and even outdoor opera. As Stoneham liked to say, they had every sport at the Polo Grounds except polo, though he tried to arrange it.

The hardworking young executive started a family with Valleda. In 1925 they had a daughter, named Valleda Mary, and two years later a son, Charles Horace Stoneham.

While C. A. Stoneham was preoccupied with mounting his legal defenses, John McGraw's team on the field encountered frustration. In 1925 the four-time defending National League champions bolted out to a great start and were in first place by six and a half games in June but played .500 ball the rest of the way and wound up in a distant second. And the 1926 Giants remained sluggish all year, finishing at 74–77, in fifth place, with a losing record and in the second division for the first time since 1915 and just the second time in McGraw's quarter-century at the helm.

It was, perhaps, just one of those years. The array of talent still seemed there for this team to rebound to contention, with a careful adjustment or two. But McGraw was in no mood for careful adjustments.

The Giants' best player was fast, versatile, switch-hitting second baseman–third baseman Frankie Frisch. He wasn't a superstar but excellent all around and was the team leader. McGraw, in one of the few significant blunders of his career, fouled up this important relationship. The intensely competitive Frisch had quickly become a favorite of McGraw, who saw in him a kindred soul, and Frisch was appointed team captain early in his playing career. There were no problems between the two while the Giants won pennants in the early 1920s, despite the roughness of McGraw, who was especially hard on the Giants' captains. But as the Giants' performance deteriorated, McGraw became more irritable, and after difficult losses the manager singled out his captain for verbal abuse in the clubhouse. The harsh words were meant not so much for Frisch as for others to hear, which the captain understood. Frisch bridled at the tongue-lashing but bore it for the sake of the team.

But as the losses and the insults mounted, Frisch's capacity to bear them wore down. By mid-1926 he was barking back at McGraw. At last, after a particularly tough loss in St. Louis and yet another sour and cruel postgame trashing from McGraw, Frisch packed his bag, left the team, and returned home to New York. Entreaties would be made and apologies accepted, and Frisch would return to finish the season, but his relationship with McGraw was poisoned forever.[9] McGraw had needlessly painted himself into a corner and was essentially forced to put his team captain on the trading block. Fortunately—or perhaps, as it would turn out, merely interestingly—McGraw was able to find a trading partner making an extremely attractive offer.

Rogers Hornsby, "the Rajah," was the greatest player in the National League in the 1920s, a second baseman who hit with destructive force. Moreover, he was a keenly intelligent student of the game who'd been promoted to player-manager of the St. Louis Cardinals at the age of twenty-nine. In 1926 Hornsby had guided the Cards to the pennant and a World Series championship over none other than Babe Ruth and the Yankees.

However, there were two sides to the Hornsby coin. He was entirely unlikable: blunt, mean, and self-absorbed. St. Louis owner Sam Breadon groaned that listening to Hornsby speak to him was like having the contents of a rock crusher emptied over his head.[10] The proximate cause of Breadon's desire to deal Hornsby following the 1926 season was a contract dispute, but the larger truth is that Breadon was just sick of dealing with Hornsby and wanted him gone, World Series title be damned.

So it was that on December 20, 1926, in what is to this day among the very biggest bombshell deals in major league history, McGraw's Giants traded Frisch along with journeyman pitcher Jimmy Ring to the Cardinals for Hornsby.[11] It's no slight toward Frisch to acknowledge that, terrific as he was, the combination of Frisch and Jimmy Ring didn't compare to the on-the-field value delivered by the Rajah. That Breadon was okay with that (and significantly, so was his brilliant right-hand man, Branch Rickey) is strong suggestion as to just how severe an off-the-field headache Hornsby could also deliver.[12]

Furthermore, a key question loomed: how well would Hornsby, having enjoyed the status in St. Louis of being his own manager, deal with having to defer to a skipper again, especially one as harsh and demanding as the Little Napoleon? The not-quite-fifty-four-year-old McGraw himself anticipated that question. He addressed it in coy language when meeting with Hornsby following the trade: "You just go your own way around here, watch yourself carefully, and keep your mouth shut. You never can tell what might happen. I'm not going to go on managing this team forever, you know."[13] However McGraw meant Hornsby to interpret that, what's known is that on the not-infrequent occasions in 1927 in which McGraw's nagging health problems kept him away from the ballpark, he designated Hornsby to serve as his substitute manager.[14]

Hornsby's performance for the Giants was utterly brilliant. He played every inning of every game, batting .361 with twenty-five home runs, leading the league in runs scored, walks, on-base percentage, OPS, and OPS+.[15] However, though the 1927 Giants contended strongly, in an agonizingly close race they finished third, two games behind Paul Waner's pennant-winning Pittsburgh Pirates and a half-game behind the second-place Cardinals and Frankie Frisch.

And there was that other side of the Hornsby coin. McGraw got along with him well enough, but C. A. Stoneham assuredly didn't. Hornsby's rude and cantankerous personality made him something of an antihero among a certain segment of the Giants' fan base, who, like many fans then and now, enjoyed the spectacle of someone telling the big boss to go to hell. The big boss himself, however, didn't enjoy it at all. So it was that on January 11, 1928, Rogers Hornsby, after just one season in New York, was traded to the Boston Braves.

The deal wasn't close to a fair exchange of talent: all the Giants received in return for the best player in the league was Frank "Shanty" Hogan, a high-potential but not-yet-established young catcher, and journeyman outfielder Jimmy Welsh. It was a plain and willful giveaway of Hornsby and his trainload of baggage. Yet even that wasn't the most significant aspect of the transaction: Stoneham had executed the deal entirely on his own, without so much as a consultation with McGraw, who was away in Havana that January, merrily enjoying his winter holiday.[16]

Never before had Stoneham acted so impulsively, and non-collaboratively, on such a momentous decision, directly overriding the partners' established division of labor. McGraw was furious and had every right to be. For the first time in their nearly decade-long partnership, Stoneham and McGraw found themselves facing one another as antagonists.

Indeed, the original three-man managing partnership of Stoneham, Vice President McGraw, and treasurer Francis McQuade was fully and bitterly imploding in 1928. Stoneham at this point was in the midst of forcing McQuade out of the organization altogether, in a battle prompted by McQuade's understandable outrage at having discovered Stoneham's secret, unsecured "loans" from the treasury.[17]

In neither of these intraorganizational disputes had Stoneham's choice of actions been defensible. And in McQuade's absence the dark mood would get no lighter. Since 1920 Jim Tierney had quietly served as club secretary; with McQuade out, Tierney newly asserted himself and quickly was accused by McGraw of some foul deed or another. Stoneham publicly sided with Tierney, and McGraw felt yet more isolated and aggrieved.[18]

The grand days of pennants and glory, though a mere half-decade past, increasingly seemed more distant than that, more irretrievably gone. With each passing year in the late 1920s, it was ever more blindingly inescapable that Babe Ruth and his Yankees now just flat-out *owned* New York. The Bronx Bombers racked up three straight pennants in 1926, '27, and '28 in utterly dominant fashion, giving them six league flags and three World Series titles in eight years. The Babe continued to clout his sensational home runs, notably the staggering sixty of 1927, and Yankee Stadium rudely outdrew the Polo Grounds year in and year out, whether the Yankees won the pennant or not. The fussy, fusty old Giants were now just another ball club, yesterday's news. In 1928 they came in second again—behind Frisch's Cardinals—and in the following seasons the Giants were no longer a serious contender, strolling in for a gentleman's third place in 1929 and '30 and an easy-does-it distant second to a runaway St. Louis gasoline tanker in 1931.

If frustrations, regrets, jealousies, grudges, fears, and tense alcoholic exhaustion weren't a dysfunctional enough potpourri to sour the air in the Polo Grounds executive offices, there was more. Following the stock market collapse that began in October 1929, C. A. Stoneham felt genuine financial alarm too. By 1932 he was facing the sickening hard reality of financial ruin. Stoneham's elaborately complicated fortune, mostly invested one way or another in stocks and other securities, had steadily and irretrievably disappeared. His real estate ventures, the hotels and casinos, were heavily leveraged luxury properties that were among the first dominoes to fall as the economy relentlessly failed. Stoneham lost many millions of dollars in the crash— wiped out, as the writer Roger Kahn would put it, of "everything but the Giants. That was his jewel, the one possession above all others, he would not part with, whatever the cost."[19]

While Stoneham was helplessly watching his lifetime's accumulation of wealth evaporate, John McGraw—now barely on speaking terms with C.A. yet still his essential, irreplaceable partner in that jewel of a possession—was suffering the steady loss of his very health. Though just in his late fifties, McGraw increasingly looked and acted like a much older man. His maladies were numerous, chronic, and progressive, his decades of hard living and bad habits exacting a pitiless toll.

This was the office within which junior executive Horace Stoneham, twenty-eight years old in 1931, was pursuing his apprenticeship, watching, listening, and learning. It's obvious that the day-to-day environment he was experiencing at the heart of the Giants' operation was quite different than that of the halcyon early 1920s, much less harmonious and satisfying than C.A. had envisioned for his son. Undoubtedly, much of it was hard for Horace, unpleasant for everyone, disappointing and disillusioning.

Yet it's also worth considering that in some ways this lugubrious state of affairs would provide a more bracing apprenticeship for the young heir than a run of good times could have done. There's an old saying in business: any fool can manage when things are going well; it's in the tough times that ability is tested. Horace was presented with the opportunity to learn, all right, and the lessons presented were the hardest ones.

Among the unadorned realities laid bare for Horace to study was the tireless, endless demand of the business. C.A. and McGraw could wallow away in distraction and weariness and gloom, but the business didn't care. It took no time-outs. Not only was the baseball operation continuing to require more attention than McGraw could deliver; the Polo Grounds itself was busily active as a year-round entertainment venue. There was always more work to be done, whether the organization's top leaders were up for it or not.

And thus it may well be that this lesson was among the most profound that Horace could embrace, and it may well be that he comprehended it deeply. The work continued to get done by and large, even as the attentiveness and passion of C.A. and McGraw faded. The work continued to get done because the organization by and large manifested its own institutional intelligence and energy—in modern parlance, its own positive "culture"—as competent employees properly placed in responsible roles continued to assert their own attentiveness and passion and did their jobs.

Over his long tenure as the Giants' chief executive, Horace Stoneham would exhibit his share of foibles and failings. But he would also demonstrate enduring strengths as a manager. Chief among them would be his keen sense of loyalty and support to everyone in his employment (a trait he would sometimes exhibit to a fault) and his genuine respect for the dignity and importance of the work, all of the work to be done, every day, no matter what.

As the 1930s began, though the Giants were no longer closely contending, they were a good ball club, featuring several extraordinary performers. This closing-phase John McGraw team was still a John McGraw team, after all. These Giants flashed a pair of pitching aces: friendly, easygoing right-hander "Fat Freddie" Fitzsimmons and gaunt, laconic southpaw Carl Hubbell. Right fielder "Master Melvin" Ott, though still barely out of his teens, was already well established as one of the game's top stars, an on-base machine with exceptional home run power.

But the Giants' biggest star was veteran first baseman Bill Terry. "Memphis Bill" was famous as a slick fielder and a powerful and consistent high-average hitter (notably batting .401 in 1930) and also as an intelligent team leader, but even on top of that, he was known for having a strong and independent personality. The story of then-amateur Bill Terry's remarkable negotiation with John McGraw back in 1922 was well known.

It was April 1, 1922, and McGraw's Giants were in Memphis, Tennessee, barnstorming their way back north from spring training. On a tip from Norman "Kid" Elberfeld, the manager of the Little Rock Travelers in the Southern Association and a trusted old friend, McGraw had arranged to meet with a hot local prospect, some kid named Terry, who was lighting it up as both a hitter and a pitcher for the semipro Standard Oil company team in Memphis. Elberfeld told McGraw that he'd tried to recruit Terry himself but had been rebuffed by the young man, who explained that he was already making more money working for the oil company and enjoying far greater job security than any minor league offer could match. He'd listen only to a big-league offer.

This was rich, coming from an early-twenties amateur whose only experience in pro ball amounted to scattered bush-league appearances as a teenager in 1915–17. He'd "listen" to an offer from the defending world champion New York Giants, represented by none other than John J. McGraw himself, in person? Well, even John McGraw had a sense of humor, and besides, Elberfeld's counsel was worth taking seriously, and what the hell, the team was in Memphis today anyway. So, the word was passed along, and Bill Terry made his way downtown that early spring day to the Peabody Hotel, the finest in the city, to pay a call on Mr. John J. McGraw.

The young man who walked into McGraw's suite that morning was much bigger than McGraw. He was tall and muscular, well dressed, and entirely self-assured. Though he was only twenty-three years of age, his demeanor was mature and confident. When they shook, McGraw noticed that Terry's hands were unusually large, even for a six-footer. The young man's grip was firm but not threatening, and he looked at John McGraw without glancing away. McGraw asked him to sit down, and Terry took off his hat—he always wore a hat—and politely took a seat.

Young Bill Terry was a family man, a devoted husband and father. He'd not only married his childhood sweetheart; he'd converted from his Baptist faith and joined the Episcopal Church because she was Episcopalian. He behaved in a disciplined and orderly manner and took his decisions seriously. Terry was committed to his family's best interest as the top priority, outweighing any personal ambition to be a ballplayer.

John McGraw, the greatest figure in the business of professional baseball, at the very peak of his success, asked the young man if he wanted the opportunity to play for the World Series champion New York Giants, a team that at that point featured five future Hall of Famers occupying the first six spots in its batting order.[20]

Without hesitation Terry calmly asked McGraw how much he would be paid. This startled McGraw. He answered by asking Terry how much he wanted. Terry named a figure that was at least equal to his Standard Oil paycheck, maybe a little higher. McGraw said that was too much. Terry politely declined the offer and got up to leave.

John McGraw had seen quite a few things in his day, but he'd never seen anything like this. The great manager was astounded. This apparently sensible young stranger—a courteous, dignified, well-groomed aspirant, in whom McGraw couldn't help but find himself reminded of a young Christy Mathewson—was being offered the chance of a lifetime, and he was asking about a salary.

McGraw sputtered: "Don't you realize what I'm offering? A chance to play baseball in the Polo Grounds, for the New York Giants?" Terry did. He wasn't confused. But for the sake of his young family, he wouldn't take a cut in pay, and that was all there was to it. He thanked Mr. McGraw for his time and consideration and said goodbye.[21]

Bill Terry walked away from the Peabody Hotel that morning, leaving the un-stunnable McGraw fully stunned. John J. McGraw of the New York Giants wasn't used to being blithely dismissed by anyone, let alone by bush-league nobodies. Yet there was something to admire in this busher's fearlessness. Whether McGraw spent the next several weeks waiting to hear from Terry again or whether he spent that time seeking reports from scouts on Terry's performance with the Memphis ball club—probably both—it was about a month after their initial meeting that Terry received a message from the Giants.

Terry was invited to join the major league club on a road trip in Philadelphia, and from there he accompanied them to Manhattan and the Polo Grounds. After several days of working Terry out on big-league fields with big-league players, McGraw was satisfied. He met Terry's original demand, presenting him a three-year contract at $800 per month, an amazing deal for a prospect so utterly unproven.[22]

Secure under the terms of the big-league contract he'd so brazenly secured, Terry then accepted McGraw's assignment to the Toledo Mud Hens of the top-rung American Association to further his development. At McGraw's insistence Terry would pitch no more and instead would play strictly first base and focus on his hitting. Memphis Bill did so and barely seemed to break a sweat, handling American Association competition with ease over the balance of the 1922 season and the full year of 1923. In September 1923 he would be called up to the Giants to begin his stellar big-league career.

From such a dramatic start, one might have expected the relationship between Terry and McGraw to become difficult. But mostly it didn't. Contract negotiations between the two were always spirited, and indeed, Terry held out multiple times, but it wasn't acrimonious. It was business. Terry's manner was invariably dignified, confident, and direct. McGraw, in his way, respected that, and as between Matheson and McGraw long before, the gentleman Bill Terry developed and sustained a productive relationship, if a distant one, with the ruffian John McGraw. It wasn't a warm friendship, as McGraw had enjoyed with Matty and with Ross Youngs, but it was a stable business understanding.

The cool professionalism that Terry seemed to project even onto the likes of McGraw perhaps explains how their relationship didn't fall apart as McGraw's had with Frankie Frisch. In that case McGraw had openly chosen Frisch as his special protégé and presumed successor. This overamplified the pressure in a situation in which the last thing either personality needed was amplification. It brought out the worst in both and led to their bitter parting.

After Frisch was gone (and then, in turn, Hornsby), it was Bill Terry who calmly and naturally rose to the status of Giants' field leader. Never did McGraw promote it or call attention to it. Both parties just allowed it to come to be; indeed, into the 1930s the two rarely even conversed. They just acted. It was handled, perhaps, with modern Terry-style understatement instead of old-time McGraw-style bluster. Perhaps some manner of torch was already being passed.

The national and worldwide economic disaster that would come to be known as the Great Depression had begun with the United States stock market collapse in the autumn of 1929. The years to follow were bad ones, but none was as terribly bad as the year of 1932; indeed, across the entire twentieth century there would never be a worse year in the United States than 1932. In his epic social and political history, *The Glory and the Dream*, William Manchester presented a particularly vivid account of the widespread misery enveloping the nation and the nation's largest city:

> U.S. Steel, the key to heavy industry, was operating at 19.1 per cent of capacity. The American Locomotive Company didn't need much steel. During the 1920s it had sold an average of 600 locomotives a year; in 1932 it sold one. Nor was the automotive industry the big steel customer it had been. Month by month its fine names were vanishing: the Stutz Motor Company, the Auburn, the Cord, the Edward Peerless, the Pierce Arrow, the Duesenberg, the Franklin, the Durant, the Locomobile. One rash man decided to challenge Ford with another low-priced car. He called it the Rockne, lost 21 million dollars, and killed himself. . . .
>
> New York drew countless job seekers from surrounding states, though the city had a million jobless men of its own. A few strangers joined Manhattan's seven thousand nickel shoeshine "boys" or found furtive roles in the bootleg coal racket—10 per cent of the city's coal was being sneaked in by unemployed Pennsylvania miners—but most outsiders wound up on one of New York's 82 breadlines. If a man had a dime he could sleep in a flophouse reeking of sweat and Lysol. If he was broke he salvaged some newspapers and headed for Central Park, or the steps of a subway entrance, or the municipal incinerator. The incinerator's warmth drew hundreds of men on winter nights, even though they had to sleep on great dunes of garbage.[23]

Such was the ghastly scene within which the New York National League Baseball Club began its fiftieth season of continuous operation, which also represented the thirtieth consecutive Opening Day for John McGraw managing the Giants. That April 12 opener, against the Philadelphia Phillies at the Polo Grounds, should have been a gala event; a telegram from President Hoover was delivered to the Giants' dugout, congratulating John McGraw. But the ceremony was minimal, and the game itself was long and dispiriting, as the Phils crushed the Giants 13–5.

Things improved little as the season progressed. It was an unusually cold and wet spring in the Northeast, and the Giants' schedule was riddled with delays, postponements, and miserable gray afternoons. They lost five of their first six and were languishing in the second division, sometimes in last place, for all of April and all of May. McGraw, suffering from painful sinusitis that blurred his vision, was even more grouchy than usual, and for the first time in his long career, he seemed to have lost control of the team.[24]

It was a dismal Giants season playing out within a dismal economic realm. In 1930 and '31, despite the advancing Depression, attendance at the Polo Grounds, though no longer at record levels, had remained strong. But in the early months of economically desperate 1932, Giants' attendance was plunging. As May gave way to June, the New York Giants were in last place in the National League. John McGraw, in ever poorer health, lacked the energy to face the ever mounting set of challenges. At long last he decided that he was done.

McGraw sought a private meeting with C. A. Stoneham and, with whatever spirit he had left, told him so. Stoneham accepted McGraw's decision (which likely didn't come as a surprise), and the longtime partners discussed what to do. They came to a decision.

On June 2, a darkly clouded Thursday, the Giants suited up for a Polo Grounds doubleheader, but the games wouldn't be played, due to the threatening weather. After the postponement was announced, McGraw called Terry into his office. McGraw had a quirky rule of requiring a visitor to stand, facing his desk, his back to the open office door. Terry was told to assume this posture and did so. Over McGraw's desk were his only concessions to sentimentality: framed photos of his stricken favorites, Mathewson and Youngs.[25] "He called me in," Terry recalled, "and asked me, 'How would you like to be manager of this club?' I said, 'I'll take it.' 'Well,' he said, 'wait just a minute.' He said, 'you got to go upstairs and talk to Mr. Stoneham.'"

Terry showered and changed, and then he and McGraw went upstairs to Stoneham's office. There they were joined by club secretary Jim Tierney. Terry, in his characteristic cool-but-firm manner, said that he would accept the job only if it meant that he was to be the complete boss, with no interference from the front office. Stoneham promptly assured him of that. Then Terry, without missing a beat, requested that the team trainer, "Doc" Knowles, be fired immediately. Stoneham said that was fine.

Everyone in that room understood why Terry wanted Knowles gone: he'd been McGraw's curfew enforcer and general clubhouse spy. For Stoneham to immediately grant Terry's wish, with McGraw sitting right there, was utter humiliation for the once-great manager. After thirty years of running the Giants, he suddenly had zero juice. McGraw's later public announcement contained a promise that he would remain with the team "as general adviser and counselor in business as well as baseball matters," but McGraw understood the truth, that his influence wasn't just diminished when he sat meekly in Stoneham's office that afternoon; it was forever gone. No matter how the front office or the press might choose to present it, the great McGraw was now a figurehead.[26]

The next morning the communication to the rest of the players took the form of a one-page typewritten sheet of paper, signed by McGraw, tacked to the clubhouse wall:

> For two years, due to ill health, I have been contemplating the necessity of turning over the management of the Giants to someone else. My doctor advises me, because of a sinus condition, that it would be inadvisable to attempt any road trips with the club this season, so I suggested to Mr. Stoneham that another manager be appointed,

inasmuch as it is impossible for me to handle the team unless I accompany it.

It was my desire that a man be appointed who is thoroughly familiar with my methods, who had learned his baseball under me. We, therefore, agreed on Bill Terry, who, I think, has every qualification to make a successful manager. While my illness may be temporary, I want it thoroughly understood that Terry will have complete charge and control of them team and also will have to assume entire responsibility in the future.[27]

With that, after thirty-one years, McGraw was gone, retired overnight with his wife, Blanche, to their suburban home in Pelham Manor, north of New York City. Indeed, before the news reached the public, McGraw had already returned home to inform Blanche. In later years Mrs. McGraw recalled that her husband had seemed pleased that evening. He behaved, she said, like a man who had had a great burden eased from his back.[28] The unburdened John McGraw would have twenty months to live.

The news of John McGraw's retirement sent a shockwave through not just New York but the greater baseball world. This wasn't just the end of an era, it was the end of an epoch. McGraw would now spend occasional time at the Polo Grounds, watching the games from the office window overlooking center field, but there was nothing there for him to do. He never appeared in the clubhouse, the dugout, or the grandstand. Once, when the team was on the road, McGraw entered the office he'd commanded for three decades and quietly removed his portraits of Mathewson and Youngs from the wall. Most of his time was spent at the racetrack.[29]

McGraw, for all his late-career failings, left enormous shoes for Terry to fill. Memphis Bill, in his confident manner, just strapped it on and went to work. He continued the policy of a curfew on the road (even without Doc Knowles to administer it), but he moved it back to midnight, and if a player could present a good case for an occasional waiver, Terry would cheerfully grant it. And even though Prohibition was still the law of the land, Terry discreetly let it be known that what *New York Post* writer Westbrook Pegler called "the inhalation of small beers" would be permitted, and maybe, if he was in a good mood, the new boss might even buy.

Terry now occupied McGraw's office, but unlike the old man, he didn't lurk inside it like a crab defending its lair. Terry kept the office door open and eliminated McGraw's old-fashioned standing-at-attention rule for players visiting the office. Moreover, Terry suggested that the players didn't need to use the pay telephone in the clubhouse because they could just use the phone on his desk for free.

In Pegler's description, within a matter of days "the carpet on the floor of McGraw's own office had begun to show the wear-and-tear of baseball spikes, and the mystery of the old man's office had been completely dispelled." Terry had maintained structure but purposefully updated it, and the Giants' players were, at long last, treated like adults and professionals.[30]

Not only was Terry a personality of different temperament than McGraw; he was also just of a different generation. Bill Terry was a distinctly modern American type, twentieth century made, at ease with the present and optimistic about the future, an earnestly ambitious go-getter, a "bright young man." However tough a taskmaster he might prove to be, the thirty-three-year-old Terry was incomparably easier for every modern ballplayer to get along with, and to listen to, than the cranky old-school McGraw.

Terry made one significant roster move in 1932, promoting rookie Joe "Jo-Jo" Moore from Jersey City of the International League (where McGraw had farmed him out) and installing him as the regular left fielder. The Giants didn't suddenly improve with Terry at the helm; they'd been 17–23 under McGraw and went 55–59 the rest of the way. Their sixth-place finish was the Giants' worst since the last-place debacle of 1915. Polo Grounds attendance plummeted to its lowest since the wartime season of 1918. Still, in a show of confidence, in September, C.A. signed Terry to a two-year contract extension.

So, into that autumn of 1932 went the suddenly struggling New York Giants, navigating their first off-season since 1901 without the legendary McGraw in command. The trade talks, winter meetings, contract negotiations, and all the rest would be the responsibility of young Memphis Bill, facing the challenge of his lifetime.

The modern organizational apparatus that would become familiar in subsequent decades as the "front office" of major league baseball teams hadn't yet formed in the early 1930s. There were two franchises in this period endeavoring to build out sophisticated operational structures: in the National League the Cardinals, in which Sam Breadon employed "business manager" Branch Rickey, and in the American the Yankees, in which Jacob Ruppert employed "team secretary" Ed Barrow, both in roles that would soon be called "general manager." But they were the exceptions.

Most baseball teams were still run like small businesses, in some variation of a broadly applied American organizational model that dated to the mid-1800s: the man (and it was virtually always a man) in charge typically was granted the title of president, and under him would be a general superintendent who supervised the labor force and was accountable for day-to-day administration. Major league baseball teams were similarly directed well into the twentieth century. Nearly all were administered by the president—typically the controlling member of the ownership group—and the manager, who guided the players (the labor force) on and off the field. The distribution of authority between manager and president depended mainly on the level of control the president wished to retain for himself, but usually it was the manager who was responsible not only for tactical game supervision (lineups and bunt and steal calls, for example) but also for determining the roster (trades, releases, minor league call-ups, and the like).

Teams also employed a business manager—in the parlance of the day, a "secretary"—reporting to the president, responsible for "back office" administrative functions such as financial accounting, ticket sales, travel accommodations, and ballpark operations, including uniforms and equipment. The secretary had no responsibility for the acquisition or disposition of players, just the supporting platforms. The president and the manager were responsible for the product on the field.[31]

The New York Giants firmly remained old-school. C. A. Stoneham had granted McGraw complete authority over the baseball operation (until undercutting it with the Hornsby-for-Hogan trade), and the team's back-office operations were the responsibility of secretary Jim Tierney. (Reporting to Tierney was all-around office factotum Eddie Brannick, who'd started with the team as an "office boy" at the age of thirteen, back in 1905, under John T. Brush, and it was Brannick under whom Horace was learning the operational ropes.)

McGraw's performance in managing the Giants' baseball side had been brilliant, of course, all the way back to the start. But in old-time fashion he'd done everything almost entirely on his own, employing very little in the way of staff. He would keep one or two trusted old ballplayer friends in-house as coaches (and spies) and sincerely rely upon them for advice and counsel. Also, he listened to his favorite scouts and his broad network of associates throughout the game, such as Kid Elberfeld. But it was McGraw's show, with the old man making every strategic decision as well as overseeing nearly every tactical detail himself—right up until he could just no longer do it. That was the breadth of responsibility he handed to Bill Terry in 1932. And Terry was also still playing first base and batting in the middle of the order.

Moreover, McGraw hadn't been open to the wisdom of the new minor league "farm" concept. Indeed, McGraw publicly derided the very idea of a farm system. At one point, when the esteemed National League umpire Bill Klem raved about the quality of baseball he'd seen being taught at Branch Rickey's spring tryout camps, McGraw scoffed, "It will never work."[32] McGraw discouraged Stoneham from even considering the investment in a chain of minor league teams (though, as we've seen, Stoneham after the mid-1920s wasn't investing much in the franchise anyway).[33] In this regard the generally brilliant McGraw was showing a blind spot. Increasingly in the late 1920s and early '30s, the issue of the farm system—and all the complicated ways in which it impacted the economic and existential basis of the minor leagues—was the subject of intense debate among owners and between the owners and Commissioner Landis.

Stoneham and McGraw largely ignored this debate, while Rickey and Ruppert forged it. By 1932, quite against the wishes of Landis, the owners had agreed to update the system of rules governing rosters, drafts, and the ability of major league teams to control the contracts of players under option to the minors, and with that the modern farm system was formally permitted and sanctioned.[34]

Rickey's Cardinals had led the way. In 1930 and '31 the Cards' system was by far the largest in existence, as only five other franchises—the Chicago Cubs, Cleveland Indians, Detroit Tigers, Pittsburgh Pirates, and St. Louis Browns—had any minor league affiliates at all. But in 1932 the liberalization of the rules opened the barn door wide. Despite the Depression's harrowing depth, teams began full-scale investments in farm systems, in land rush mode.[35] The Cardinals were still the leader, but others were seriously buying in as well, most notably Ruppert and Barrow's Yankees, who hired the impressive young George Weiss to build their system.

Of the sixteen big-league franchises in 1932, only the moribund Philadelphia Phillies would remain without a farm team. Stoneham's Giants, bowing to the competitive pressure, inaugurated their own farm system that year, but it was rudimentary, including just the Bridgeport (Connecticut) Bears of the Class-A Eastern League and a Class-B Piedmont League entry that played in both Winston-Salem and High Point, North Carolina. The Giants had ceded a head start to others in the development of what would prove to be the sport's indispensable method of establishing and sustaining on-field competitiveness.

Such was the circumstance Bill Terry found himself in the 1932–33 off-season. But he was never one to be intimidated. On October 10, 1932, barely two weeks after the conclusion of play, Terry confidently engaged with the ever-energetic Rickey to complete a six-player Giants-Cardinals trade. The key element surrendered by Terry was crafty southpaw Bill Walker, who'd led the National League in earned-run average in both 1929 and 1931, and the significant piece coming from St. Louis to New York was a good-all-around young catcher, Gus Mancuso.

In December, at the annual winter meetings, Terry collaborated with the Pirates and Phillies in a three-way blockbuster. Center fielder Fred Lindstrom, generally one of the Giants' best players since arriving in the majors as a teenager in the mid-1920s, was sent to Pittsburgh, and in exchange Terry received journeyman center fielder George "Kiddo" Davis from Philadelphia. While this one made little sense on a pure talent-for-talent bases, the backstory was that the still-young Lindstrom had believed he'd been ahead of Terry in line to replace McGraw as manager. Though the relationship between Lindstrom and Terry remained friendly, Lindstrom (however sensibly) felt betrayed by McGraw and Stoneham, and though he didn't demand a trade, both he and Terry felt it best that he be moved along.[36]

That same week Terry acquired, from the Buffalo Bisons of the International League, John "Blondy" Ryan, a light-hitting but slick-fielding young shortstop. And in late December, Terry sold catcher Shanty Hogan—now rendered surplus with the acquisition of Mancuso—to the Boston Braves for $25,000 cash. Within the space of ninety autumn and winter days, Terry had retooled three starting positions; on top of the Jo-Jo Moore promotion back in June, it amounted to half of the non-pitcher lineup. Memphis Bill was decisively stepping out of McGraw's towering shadow.

It was a season for changes everywhere, it seemed. On November 8, 1932, Franklin D. Roosevelt was first elected president of the United States. It was a landslide, as Roosevelt trounced incumbent Republican Herbert Hoover with 57 percent of the popular vote, winning 472 of 531 Electoral College votes. Riding the wave of a major U.S. political realignment unleashed by the Depression, Roosevelt was just the second Democrat to be elected president in forty years. The 1932 election was a major historical demarcation, signaling the end of the Republican-dominated Progressive Era and ushering in FDR's New Deal Coalition that would hold until the 1970s.

The landslide gave the Democrats not just the White House but huge majorities in both houses of Congress. A rush of New Deal legislation would soon be enacted to alter the dynamics sustaining the economic depression. (Helping to brighten the mood would be another piece of legislation, the repeal of alcohol prohibition, which sailed through Congress, was ratified by the states, and was signed by the president on December 5, 1933.)

The Great Depression wasn't just an American phenomenon, of course. It was global, and on that scale 1933 was the year in which recovery generally began to take hold. It would be years before many economic metrics would regain their 1929 levels, and there would be setbacks along the way, but from 1933 forward, in the United States and abroad, it finally was becoming evident that the dreadful economic bottom had been found and that better financial times were ahead at last.

But the overwhelming economic crisis had provoked dramatic political reordering in many places, nowhere more dramatically than in Germany. Adolf Hitler's Nazi party achieved a plurality of seats in the country's parliament in 1932, setting up a circumstance in which he was appointed chancellor in January 1933.

John McGraw's legacy was daunting, but on the other hand, the Giants hadn't won a pennant since 1924, hadn't strongly contended since 1928, and in 1932 they'd tumbled to sixth place. No prognosticator expected Bill Terry's partially remodeled version to immediately reclaim franchise glory in 1933.

Yet that's just what Terry's partially remodeled version did. The 1933 Giants spent the season's early weeks jockeying for first place, then took it over in June and won the National League pennant going away. In the World Series, Terry's club faced the Washington Senators, the team that had bested them in 1924, and this time it was the Giants breezing to victory in five brisk games. It was seemingly easy and altogether astonishing.

An earlier generation of Giants fans had marveled when John McGraw took over a cellar-dwelling team and transformed it into a pennant winner in a bit more than two years. Now here was Terry pulling off a comparable feat. C. A. Stoneham was so thrilled that he signed his player-manager to a five-year contract at $40,000 per year, a massive deal that was, pointedly, equal to the highest annual salary paid to John McGraw.[37]

To be sure, the stunning 1933 success was keyed by the nucleus of stars Terry had inherited from McGraw. Carl Hubbell, at the age of thirty, broke out as one of the game's elite pitchers, capturing the Most Valuable Player award.[38] Freddie Fitzsimmons was excellent as usual, and in 1933 the Giants produced a third ace, as twenty-two-year-old Hal Schumacher blossomed into stardom. Right fielder Mel Ott remained a dynamic offensive weapon, and the team still had Terry himself at first base, past his prime at thirty-four but still among the league's better hitters. But few championships are won by star players alone; the supporting cast must hit its marks too. And in this regard the '33 Giants were a Bill Terry production, as all of the changes he made after taking the helm in mid-1932 worked out well. Catcher Mancuso, left fielder Moore, center fielder Davis, and shortstop Ryan all settled in as sold regulars (and Mancuso and Moore would shortly emerge as stars).

Perhaps Terry's most impressive work came during the 1933 season. In April, Memphis Bill himself was hit by a pitch and broke his wrist and was sidelined for more than a month. His backup, Sam Leslie, filled in wonderfully. When Terry returned to the lineup, Memphis Bill promptly traded Leslie to the Brooklyn Dodgers for heavy-hitting veteran outfielder Frank "Lefty" O'Doul, who was terrific as a spot starter in left and right field as well as pinch-hitting.

John McGraw spent the 1933 baseball season as an occasional spectator. His only "work" for the year was to serve as manager of the National League team in the first-ever major league All-Star Game, in Chicago. McGraw's public appearances became less frequent. Just before the World Series, he took part in a photo shoot with a dozen Giants, all wearing stylish fedoras in an advertisement for a hat company.[39] The day after the Series, upon the team's return to New York following their clinching victory in Washington DC, McGraw hosted a reception for them at the gleaming ultramodern New Yorker Hotel, a party that was as robust and went as deep into the night as any he had ever given.[40]

But he was suffering from uremic poisoning, and his energy was ebbing. That winter, for the first time in memory, McGraw and his wife, Blanche, didn't vacation in Havana but, instead, stayed home in Pelham. He was content now to sit quietly before the fireplace, reading or listening to the radio. He still received frequent invitations to dinner and to parties and shows in New York, but he now routinely declined.[41]

On February 4, 1934, he did accept an invitation. McGraw attended the annual dinner of the New York Baseball Writers Association, and following that, he dropped by a New York Giants "victory dinner" celebration. He only stayed for an hour.[42] It would be his final evening out.

Two weeks later, running a high fever, McGraw was hospitalized in New Rochelle. He endured abdominal hemorrhaging, and it was clear that his end was near. His wife and C. A. Stoneham were at his bedside when John McGraw passed away at 11:50 a.m. on February 25, 1934, at the age of sixty. The funeral service would be held at St. Patrick's Cathedral in New York, before his remains were interred in a vault at Cathedral Cemetery in Baltimore.

Reporters asked Bill Terry for a statement, and he said: "Well, here I am alive and in his position. I once threw my pitching glove away in disgust because of McGraw. He insisted I play first base. He even went out and bought me a first baseman's mitt. He trained me, gave me my big chance. All that I know of plays, percentages, and the psychology of handling teams I owe to him. He was the greatest manager of all time."

The press tracked down sixty-nine-year-old Wilbert Robinson—who himself had just months to live—sitting on his porch at Dover Hall, his winter home on the Georgia coast. "This is one of the saddest messages that has ever come to me," Robbie said. "I can't say enough in his praise and words can't express how I feel about his death."[43]

The New York Times rarely devoted front-page space to sports stories, but this event was exceptional. The February 26, 1934, headline was large: "JOHN J. MCGRAW IS DEAD AT 60. CALLED BASEBALL'S GREATEST FIGURE."

On July 10, 1934, the second-ever major league All-Star Game was hosted by the Giants at the Polo Grounds, attended by 48,368. As manager of the preceding year's National League pennant winner, Bill Terry was honored as manager of the National League All-Star team (this was the start of that tradition). Terry selected his own Carl Hubbell as starting pitcher. The American League lineup was as fearsome as any ever assembled, with every position except pitcher manned by a future Hall of Famer. In the top of the first inning Hubbell found himself in immediate trouble, as Charlie Gehringer singled and Henry "Heinie" Manush walked. It was two on with nobody out and Babe Ruth stepping up to the plate. But Hubbell struck out the Sultan of Swat. Next up was Lou Gehrig. Hubbell struck him out too, and then he struck out Jimmie Foxx. In the second inning Hubbell fanned Al Simmons of the A's and Joe Cronin of the Senators for five straight punch-outs of Hall of Fame–bound hitters. He would finish his three-inning scoreless stint with six strikeouts and eternal glory in All-Star Game lore.

In January 1934 Bill Terry had been in New York to attend the annual business meetings of the American and National Leagues. At the Hotel Roosevelt a gaggle of sportswriters converged upon him, and the Giants' manager held court on his team's chances for 1934, which were widely viewed as excellent. He named Pittsburgh, Chicago, St. Louis, and Boston as potential threats to dethrone the champion Giants.

> "What about Brooklyn, Bill?" asked Roscoe McGowen, who covered the Dodgers for the *New York Times*.
>
> "Brooklyn?" asked Terry, gently teasing McGowen. "I haven't heard anything from them lately. Are they still in the league?"
>
> The writers laughed. The writers reported the remark. But in print the next day the question didn't have the playful tone in which it had been spoken.[44]

Everyone, certainly including the Dodgers themselves, knew as plain truth that Brooklyn wasn't going to contend in 1934. They hadn't contended for ten years. So nobody thought Terry should pretend that the Dodgers were a threat, but nobody likes a bully. Terry's quip, however inoffensively intended, was perceived (or at least played up in the press) as an unprovoked, rude taunt. The story stayed alive all season long, and it blew up in Terry's face on the season's final weekend when the Giants, tied for first place with the "Gashouse Gang" St. Louis Cardinals, lost back-to-back games to the lowly sixth-place Dodgers—all too vividly still in the league—while the Cards waltzed past them for the pennant. The papers rode the Terry-humiliating "is Brooklyn still in the league" yarn for everything it was worth. It wasn't a substantive issue, of course; it was a media-manufactured pseudo-controversy. But neither was it a good look for Terry or the Giants. It was a lesson for Terry, and though he would always exhibit a quick, dry sense of humor, never again would Memphis Bill allow himself to be quite so sarcastic with the press.

The frustrating finish of 1934 was followed by another disappointment in 1935, when after roaring out to a 47–19 record by the Fourth of July, the Giants' pitching staff threw a rod over the second half, and they wound up in third. But the late-season letdowns weren't due to any missteps on Terry's part. Indeed, he continued to demonstrate a knack for knowing when to say "hello" and when to say "goodbye" to players at various positions and for making successful trades. In 1934 Terry opted to reinstall veteran Travis Jackson—who'd been relegated to secondary status in 1932–33 because of knee trouble—as his first-string shortstop, and the power-hitting Jackson bounced back with a fine year. Then Terry packaged Blondy Ryan, whom he'd acquired to start ahead of Jackson at shortstop in 1933, along with incumbent third baseman Johnny Vergez and a couple of others (plus some cash), to the Phillies in exchange for star shortstop Dick Bartell. This allowed Terry to shift Jackson to the less-demanding position of third base in 1935, improving the infield at two positions.

As the team played well, attendance at the Polo Grounds continued to improve. During the dismal season of 1932, the Giants had drawn fewer than 500,000, by far their lowest since the wartime year of 1918. But in 1933 attendance rebounded to better than 600,000, and amid the still depressed but recovering economy, it continued to grow in 1934 and '35. Indeed, in 1935, for the first time since 1925, the New York Giants sold more tickets than the New York Yankees, 749,000 to 658,000. The Bronx Bombers were going through a lean period, if only by their own exceptional standard. Between 1929 and 1935 the Yanks won the pennant just once, as Babe Ruth finally declined from his epic peak, and Joe DiMaggio hadn't yet arrived. The Giants, now fully emerging as Bill Terry's team, were ascending.

The organization gradually expanded its toddling farm system. By 1935 the Giants were affiliated with four minor league teams, and the big-league roster featured two standouts who'd successfully climbed their minor league ladder: twenty-four-year-old center fielder Hank Leiber, blossoming as a power-hitting star in '35, and twenty-three-year-old catcher Harry Danning, now the understudy to Gus Mancuso but destined for stardom of his own.

Terry's responsibilities were growing so broad (at the age of thirty-six he was still playing first base every day and still performing so well that he placed sixth in the league's Most Valuable Player Award balloting) that on May 14, 1935, C. A. Stoneham approved the hiring of a full-time junior assistant (in the parlance of the day, a "secretary") for him in the front office. Twenty-two-year-old Bronx-born John "Jack" Schwarz would become a fixture in the Giants organization for nearly fifty years.

His hiring into the organization was a lucky accident. Growing up, young Schwarz had no interest in baseball. But when Terry instructed an office assistant to place a call to the local YMCA to see if anyone might be interested in a temporary job, Jack Schwarz happened to be standing near the person who took the call. The assertive young man overheard the request, volunteered for the opportunity, and got the job. Schwarz was a voracious reader and a quick study. He asked questions, observed, and examined everything he could to learn baseball. After a few months, when the temporary gig expired, Schwarz began packing his belongings. Terry came into the office and asked what he was doing, and the young man explained that he'd accepted a position with an oil company and was going to Venezuela. "You're not going anywhere," Terry corrected him.[45]

That C.A. was willing and able to finance these expenses was an illustration of his renewed investment in the franchise. The stock market crash had vaporized his fortune, but he steadfastly held onto the Giants. In the 1930s he was no longer the high-rolling big spender he'd been for so long, but not only was C.A.'s great wealth a thing of the past, so were his chronic legal battles. He was now living far less lavishly, and he was also far less distracted and agitated. Gone was Francis McQuade, and gone even was John McGraw, and gone with them was all of that argument and tension. C. A. Stoneham was able at last to focus all of his daily attention on his beloved Giants, no longer as a source of ready cash to be exploited but as a business—*the* business—to be responsibly managed and sustained. Indeed, C.A. was now dependent upon the healthy financial performance of the franchise as never before.

The Giants weren't just the business; they were the *family* business, the one and only, at last. His son, Horace, was now at his side, working closely with him every day. In these years their relationship became the closest it would ever be. With all the battles he'd fought and all the things he'd won and lost, C. A. Stoneham was, perhaps, satisfied at last. His ambition to have the great New York Giants stand as his legacy to his son and to the family name was not just a dream but a daily reality.

Horace's responsibilities continued to deepen. He was no longer just handling event management at the Polo Grounds; he was involved now in everything, including financial and legal administrative details, contract negotiations, organizing and managing the staff, and even sitting in on the baseball strategy discussions with Bill Terry. C.A. was proud of his son and trusted his capability and judgment, and Horace, for his part, unquestionably felt the deepest respect for his father's strength and intelligence.

It was a happy time. It wouldn't last long.

Just like John McGraw, in his late fifties C. A. Stoneham developed serious health problems. He was diagnosed with what was then called Bright's disease and would now be understood as nephritis, an inflammation of the kidneys, a condition no doubt exacerbated by many years of immoderate drinking and eating.

We don't know if C.A. was feeling ill over the course of late 1935. It's likely that he was, and if so, that was requiring Horace to take on still more executive responsibility. In any case, we do know that thirty-two-year-old Horace was in fact taking on more. For the first time, in September 1935, Horace traveled with the team on a long road trip, a three-week western swing through Cincinnati, Pittsburgh, St. Louis, and Chicago (and a fateful one, concluding with four straight losses at Wrigley Field that knocked the Giants out of the race). In December, for the first time, Horace represented Giants' ownership at the National League winter meetings, and on December 9, 1935, for the first time, Horace delivered the public announcement of a Giants' trade (a four-for-one blockbuster with the Cardinals that netted a fine young second baseman, Burgess Whitehead).[46]

Whatever symptoms C.A. may have been suffering before then, in mid-December his condition gravely worsened. Stoneham realized this was a crisis, but he wanted to avoid it being discovered by the press. He called upon the man he felt would be the most reliable and discreet in this situation, and it was not his son. It was Bill Terry.

At C.A.'s urgent request, Terry traveled from Memphis to New York, and there he found a dying man. Stoneham asked Terry to take him to the resort spa of Hot Springs, Arkansas, far from prying newspaper eyes. Stoneham wished to also be accompanied by Alfred, his Black servant, and asked Terry to handle the logistics of that, a careful maneuver given that they would be staying at a segregated hotel. Almost as an afterthought, Stoneham requested that Terry arrange for his doctor to meet them in Hot Springs.

"When do you want to go?" Terry asked.

"As fast as we can get the tickets," Stoneham said.[47]

Terry made the necessary calls, then he, Stoneham, and Alfred quietly boarded a southbound train. When they arrived at the hotel in Hot Springs, a week before Christmas, they were shown to a large suite with a separate room for Alfred, so that he wouldn't be seen in the halls. Stoneham's doctor was already there. Terry would remember seeing the suffering man drained of enormous amounts of fluid, nearly filling two two-gallon buckets. Then Stoneham asked for a drink, and while they were sending out for one, he said again, "I've got to have a drink."[48]

It was at this juncture that Terry called Horace Stoneham in

New York and gave him the terrible news that if he wanted to see his father alive, he'd better get down to Arkansas quickly. Whether he was surprised by this dreadful message is unknown, but Horace immediately came. Terry said his goodbyes and went home to Memphis, and it was Horace who with his father at the end.

Charles A. Stoneham, fifty-nine years of age, died on January 6, 1936. He'd successfully completed his life's final task of keeping his ordeal private, and the press was told of his illness only after his death. Horace Stoneham had his father's body embalmed in Little Rock and then placed on a train bound for Newark, New Jersey. In St. Louis, Terry joined the train. As had been the case when McGraw died, Terry was the only Giants player in the funeral party. In Jersey City, Charles Stoneham's birthplace, a requiem mass was held in All Saints' Church, where he had served as an altar boy. He was buried in nearby Holy Name Cemetery.[49]

As close as C.A. and Horace may have grown, it's notable that the Stoneham family dynamic was such that it was Bill Terry, not Horace, to whom C.A. first turned for help in his desperate time. And nowhere in the accounts of his final days is any mention of C.A.'s wife and Horace's mother, Hannah Stoneham. Indeed, C.A.'s murky, reckless, and complicated personal life would yield a contentious settlement of his will.

Charles Stoneham left his ownership stake in the Giants to his son, Horace, and to his daughter, Mary Alice, the mother of future team executive and National League president Charles Stoneham "Chub" Feeney. But C.A. almost certainly had other children from what apparently was a second, secret marriage, to a Margaret Leonard Stoneham. Claiming herself to be the mother of these children, Margaret went to court in April 1936 to sue for the ejection of club treasurer Leo Bondy and of Horace A. Stoneham, C.A.'s brother, as trustees of a fund in the children's name. They were, she insisted, holding back the money. The *New York Times*, in its January obituary, had mentioned neither Margaret nor her children and had unaccountably identified his widow as "Kate."[50]

What was already a sad and stressful episode for Horace could only have been made more wrenching by these scandalous revelations. What Horace might have previously known or suspected regarding his father's sordid personal life isn't recorded, but he had no choice but to confront it now. Nevertheless, Horace and his sister were awarded full inheritance of their father's controlling interest in the New York Giants. The psychological legacy left to Horace Stoneham by his extraordinarily powerful and duplicitous father was far less straightforward.

The sporting press, at least, was quite willing to ignore the mess of a personal life C. A. Stoneham had led and focus on the handing down of the Giants franchise, about which the late owner's intentions had never been in doubt. So cheerfully opined the *Brooklyn Daily Eagle*:

> The executive reins of the New York Giants will pass into the hands of Horace Stoneham, son of the late President Charles A. Stoneham, though the exact terms of Mr. Stoneham's will are not yet known. It was always the wish of the elder Stoneham that the baseball properties should remain in the family.
>
> There are two men who will probably figure a great deal in the club's policies after the new directorate is organized. Leo Bondy, the treasurer, is expected to exercise a strong influence on the club affairs, while it is probable, too, that Bill Terry will also become a dominant figure in the club's future. . . .
>
> Should Horace Stoneham succeed his father as president of the club, the choice will be a popular one.[51]

4

Brooklyn Is Still in the League

The year in which Horace Stoneham took control of the New York Giants included several worldwide developments with resounding effects. In 1936 Italy conquered and annexed Ethiopia, a signature achievement for Fascist dictator Benito Mussolini. Meanwhile, right-wing militarists took full control of the Japanese government. It was the year when Nazi Germany, in blatant violation of the Treaty of Versailles, occupied the Rhineland. Historians would later assess this as the last opportunity for the Allies to confront the German military with overwhelmingly favorable odds.

In the summer of 1936 the Games of the XI Olympiad were held in Berlin, Germany. Presented in grand ultramodern venues, it was the first televised sporting event in history. Much to Adolf Hitler's disappointment, African American Jesse Owens would capture four gold medals in sprint and long jump events. That year seventeen-year-old Jackie Robinson was a junior at John Muir High School in Pasadena, California, and he won the junior boys singles championship in the annual Pacific Coast Negro Tennis Tournament and was named to the Pomona Baseball Tournament all-star team, which also included seventeen-year-old Ted Williams and sixteen-year-old Bob Lemon.

Meanwhile, Stoneham assumed the responsibility to which he'd been apprenticed for more than a decade. The president's desk within the Polo Grounds office was now his. He was not yet thirty-three years old. Horace Stoneham would see to it that upon the wall behind that desk, literally towering above it, there would always hang a large formal portrait of Charles A. Stoneham.

Jim Tierney, who'd been C.A.'s secretary since 1920, chose to retire. Horace then made his first executive decision, promoting Eddie Brannick to replace Tierney, and "the announcement was unanimously cheered in the press."[1] Thereafter, like his father before him, Horace Stoneham would strive to keep a low public profile and would usually (though not always) succeed. As had become C.A.'s custom in his later years, Horace would usually watch the games from the center field clubhouse office windows. Rarely, in the early years of his ownership, would Horace issue statements to the press. Instead, Leo Bondy or Brannick spoke for the club.[2]

Certainly, the baseball operation was entirely Bill Terry's domain, and though he was polite about it, Memphis Bill wasn't about to be seeking advice or approval from young Stoneham. In addition to the December trade acquiring second baseman Burgess Whitehead, Terry executed two key purchases that off-season, buying journeyman right-handed pitcher Dick Coffman from the St. Louis Browns and reacquiring first baseman Sam Leslie from the Brooklyn Dodgers.

Horace Stoneham's first Opening Day as owner was on April 14, 1936, at the Polo Grounds, hosting the Dodgers, packed to the rafters with 54,992 fans. The Giants won handily, 8–5, pounding out seventeen hits, including home runs by Mel Ott and Dick Bartell.

The National League celebrated its sixtieth anniversary in 1936, and young Stoneham led the festivities at the Polo Grounds on August 13. The *New York Herald Tribune* reported: "Merry memories of the past will come tumbling back to many an old resident of New York as a colorful parade of gay mustachioed ballplayers, riding in barouches and landaus with their wicker bat baskets hanging from the drivers' seats, wind their way through upper Manhattan from the site of the old ball park to the new. Horace Stoneham, the young owner of the Giants, has been scouring the metropolitan area for weeks for varied forms of ancient equipage, and this afternoon there will be a colorful pageant of baseball as it was enacted in 1876."[3]

But not everything was fun for the 1936 Giants. After a fast start they slumped in midseason, dropping below .500 and falling to fifth place in mid-July. In a rare unguarded moment a fretful Stoneham allowed himself to be quoted: "I guess the best thing that could happen would be if the team were torn to pieces and rebuilt from the ground up."[4] But in the second game of a July 15 doubleheader against the Pirates at Forbes Field, the Giants broke up a shutout with a six-run fifth inning and waltzed to a 14–4 laugher. That launched a stupendous five-week run in which they took thirty-five out of forty and vaulted into first place by late August.

At this point Stoneham's confidence was revived, as reported in this newspaper piece from September: "Young Stoneham, who looks more like a hustling young college football halfback than a club president, insists the only mystifying element in the rush of the Giants is that they didn't start their drive two months early and clinch the flag by now. . . . 'This team is probably the greatest bunch of hustlers baseball ever saw,' he said. 'Why, even when we hit fifth place on July 16 and I rushed out to Pittsburgh to have a talk with Bill Terry, we couldn't understand what was holding us back. Not once has the team loafed in the face of defeat or victory. And man for man, it is a greater and better team than the World Series winner of '33.'"[5] They would never look back, breezing to the 1936 National League pennant by a margin of five games ahead of the defending champion Chicago Cubs. No teardown and rebuild needed to be undertaken.

The central superstars Mel Ott and Carl Hubbell were never better: Ott hit a lusty .328, leading the league with 33 homers while driving in 135 and drawing 111 walks, and Hubbell was voted Most Valuable Player for his second time with a scintillating 26–6 record and a major league–best 2.31 earned run average. Key members of the supporting cast included Terry's off-season acquisitions: the slick-fielding Whitehead at second base and Coffman in the bullpen, effectively deployed by Terry in newfangled fashion as a relief specialist. And in this season thirty-seven-year-old player-manager Terry voluntarily sat himself out of the regular lineup for the first time, turning over the first-string first base job to Sam Leslie, who performed capably, though not as a star.

The World Series was a ballyhooed matchup against the resurgent New York Yankees—with sensational rookie Joe DiMaggio now starring alongside Lou Gehrig—in the first all–New York Fall Classic since 1923. But after Hubbell laid down a complete game, eight-strikeout 6–1 victory in the Series opener, the Bronx Bombers proceeded to obliterate the Giants the rest of the way, outscoring them 42–17 and allowing the Giants to scratch out just one additional win. Bill Terry's assessment was typically honest and blunt: "That's the toughest club I ever faced. They have everything. They're just a great team."[6]

It was a sobering finish, but on balance Horace Stoneham's inaugural season was a grand success. The pennant-winning Giants led the National League in attendance with 837,952, their biggest draw since 1930. While stuck again with second-banana New York status behind the mighty Yankees (who drew nearly a million in 1936), the young owner's franchise was at the top of its own league both competitively and financially. Pop would be proud.

And remarkably, events would proceed almost exactly the same in 1937. The Giants' roster was mostly unchanged, with three modifications: Terry retired as a player and installed twenty-seven-year-old journeyman Johnny McCarthy as the new first baseman, with Leslie as the backup; Terry purchased twenty-five-year-old southpaw Cliff Melton from Baltimore of the International League, and the rookie went 20–9; and in June, Terry spent $35,000 of Stoneham's money to acquire veteran outfielder Wally Berger from the Boston Bees—the four-time All Star slugger was no longer up to everyday play, but Terry spotted him to excellent effect as a part-timer.

The boldest move Terry made in 1937 was a midseason position shift. Fed up with weak hitting from journeyman third baseman Lou Chiozza, in August, Terry made the stunning decision to shift twenty-eight-year-old right fielder Mel Ott to third, a position at which he had a grand total of sixteen games of prior professional experience. The amazing Master Melvin confidently met the challenge, and while his defense at the hot corner wasn't great—in the assessment of biographer Fred Stein, Ott was "not a polished third baseman, but he played a sound, dependable game"[7]—the shift allowed Terry to play Jimmy Ripple, a better hitter than Chiozza, in right field. The gamble paid off, as the second-place Giants caught fire, roaring in at a 37–14 clip and again nosing out the Cubs for their second straight pennant. And again, the Giants were the most popular attraction in the National League, drawing 926,887, their highest total since the glorious championship season of 1922.

Yet while the Giants 1937 stretch run heroics were underway, Stoneham and the team faced some off-field drama. A rumor hit the newspapers that Alva Bradley, the owner of the Cleveland Indians, was engaged in discussions with Terry about that team's managerial job. Bradley denied it, but the rumor persisted. On September 7 Stoneham put it to rest by signing Terry to a new five-year contract, explaining: "We felt it was much better to take this action now and end all the rumors rather than wait until the end of the season. Bill will continue as manager, and he will also be responsible for directing our farm system, making deals, and signing players."[8]

With Terry and the franchise recommitted, the familiar pattern of events ensued. Not only did the Giants win the pennant again with a late-season rush, in October they again squared off against the cross-river Yankees, who'd waltzed through yet another American League runaway. The World Series result was also a near-replica of the previous year's, as again the Yanks won easily, dispatching the Giants in five games while outscoring them 28–12.

If the outcome of the 1937 all–Big Apple Series was anticlimactic, it provided the backdrop for a blockbuster transaction executed by the third Big Apple franchise. Just as the Series was getting underway, Brooklyn Dodgers manager Burleigh Grimes announced a trade of four players to the St. Louis Cardinals in exchange for one: shortstop Leo Durocher. The deal attracted attention because of its voluble and magnetic centerpiece, whom Baseball Hall of Fame historian Lee Allen would describe as "possessed of more brass than a Burmese junk shop."[9] Durocher was thirty-two years old and entering the closing phase of his playing career, but one year later he would be named manager of the Dodgers, and his intelligent, high-energy leadership would become an essential factor in the dynamic transformation of that long-struggling franchise.

Durocher traveled to New York that October to meet with his new employers, and Stoneham, in a spirit of good fellowship, took the opportunity to invite Leo to be his guest in the owners' box to watch the World Series. This was the first time they met. That night Stoneham and Durocher stayed up until dawn drinking and talking baseball, then had breakfast and headed straight back to the ballpark for that day's game. "That was my introduction to the guy," Durocher would later tell *Sports Illustrated*.[10]

Through his years of apprenticeship in the Giants front office, Stoneham had kept a low profile, as he avidly sought his father's approval. The limited public image he had projected, however accurately, was meant to signal "solid citizen." Young Horace, heir to the throne, was married and the father of two. The shiftless misbegotten youth of the pre-Copperopolis days was secreted away. He didn't closely resemble his father physically, and Horace was described at the time as "affable," which no one was known to call his old man.[11] Horace was not only affable but steady and reliable, and the future of the business was seen to be in capable hands.

That perky assessment rested on a foundation of truth. Horace was, in fact, a pleasant fellow and a disciplined worker, and he was indeed the married father of two growing children. But he was also a young man who'd never really forsaken his eager delight in hard-drinking bonhomie. Horace had simply managed to learn, as his father had learned long before, to sufficiently compartmentalize the partying and to sensibly (enough) keep a clear eye on the bottom line. Reality was complicated.

And complicated as well were the behavioral lessons Horace's father had daily presented on issues such as parental devotion and spousal fidelity. What we know is that beginning in the late 1930s, married father Horace Stoneham—not succeeding at keeping his profile all that low—began to develop a reputation as something of a "man about town" in the New York sporting community.

It was in this period that Stoneham developed a close relationship with Bernard "Toots" Shor, a robustly colorful New York figure, a former traveling shirt and underwear salesman and bar bouncer who through sheer force of effort and ebullient personality made himself into a famous Manhattan saloonkeeper and restaurateur. New York was the capital city of American sports, and Toots Shor's place at 51 West Fifty-First Street billed itself as "the country's unofficial sports headquarters." Shor himself was straight from central casting, as the tough Jew with the heart of gold, both abrasive and sentimental, resentful and affectionate. The crowd his saloon attracted was routinely studded with celebrities, the regulars including actors such as Pat O'Brien and Jackie Gleason, novelists such as James Michener, and nearly every New York sportswriter. However, in Shor's assessment the most important among the famous guests were the star athletes, definitely including Leo Durocher and, of course, Joe DiMaggio. But Toots himself was a Giants fan, and few among his regulars were more honored than Horace Stoneham.[12]

Toots Shor's place was described as a "clubby kind of barn . . . with all the chic warmth of [a] boarding school gymnasium."[13] The food there was, as Shor put it, "nuttin' fancy"—standard American guy-food basics like shrimp cocktail, steak, and baked potato—but the raucous establishment, centered around an oversized circular bar, quickly became famous for its high-profile clientele and the back-slapping, fast-talking manner in which Shor hosted. He was a fearless wisecracker, intimidated by no one, and ran the place strictly on his terms. Shor tirelessly cultivated his celebrity following by giving them jocular admiration, loyal friendship, and a certain kind of heartily boozy, old-fashioned male privacy—among his firm house rules were that his famous guests were never to be pestered by autograph seekers or otherwise nosy nobodies and that wives were not really welcome. It was boys' night out, every night.

Certainly, Shor was motivated to cultivate the owner of the New York Giants as one of his prize house celebrities. And there is no reason to doubt that the sporty, macho, cocktail-rich atmosphere Toots Shor's place provided could hardly have been more inviting for Stoneham. Yet their relationship was more than transactional; they were genuinely close friends, near-exact contemporaries in age, sharing authentic relish for sports and stars and joyful New York brotherhood. Stoneham provided financial assistance to Shor in getting his restaurant established. In 1951, when Stoneham's daughter gave birth to his first grandchild, the godparents were none other than Toots Shor and his wife, Marion. In 1958, when Stoneham relocated his ball club across the continent, Toots and Marion made the three thousand–mile journey to attend the inaugural Opening Day in San Francisco.

Yet as genuine as the Stoneham-Shor friendship was, it could be that a lifestyle of regularly carousing at Toot's place was less than healthy for Stoneham's marriage. At some point Horace and Valleda separated; whether it was in the late 1930s or sometime in the '40s isn't known, but it was an established fact by the 1950s. They would never divorce—perhaps a function of Stoneham's Catholicism (though he was obviously less than devout), or perhaps it was "for the sake of the children," or perhaps it was that Stoneham feared that in a divorce proceeding he could lose control of his beloved Giants—but in any case Stoneham and his wife lived mostly apart for many years. They would maintain a luxurious family apartment overlooking the Hudson at 54 Riverside Drive; indeed, that's where Valleda and the children continued to live. Horace, for his part, often lived at the Polo Grounds, literally; on the top floor of the old green-painted blockhouse that contained the locker rooms and the Giants' stadium offices, towering over the furthest reaches of center field, was a small apartment adjacent to Stoneham's private office, and he spent many of his nights there. Writer Roger Kahn quipped, "As far as I can learn, no teetotaler ever crossed that threshold."[14]

Later, in San Francisco, Horace and Valleda would reunite. It wasn't so much his drinking that was the problem for Valleda as it was his roving eye. Like his father, Horace Stoneham, at least for a time, had difficulty with monogamy.[15]

As of 1937, the Stoneham family had owned the New York Giants franchise for nineteen seasons, seventeen with C.A. at the helm and two under Horace. It had been a remarkable run of success: those nineteen seasons had featured three World Series titles, seven National League pennants, six second-place finishes, and four times in third. Just twice in nineteen years had the team failed to make the first division. They'd been just as successful financially, as 1937 marked the fifth straight year the Giants had topped the league in attendance, adding up to eleven such seasons of the nineteen. Moreover, their high-capacity stadium, the Polo Grounds, served as a profitable year-round rental venue for a variety of sports and other attractions. Young Horace Stoneham could be forgiven if the vista he perceived into the future shimmered with perpetual promise.

Meanwhile, the same period had delivered little but frustration for the Brooklyn Dodgers (who were going with that nickname again, after having been known for many years as the "Robins" under John McGraw's friend Wilbert Robinson). They'd last won a pennant in 1920. Brooklyn wasn't bad exactly, but the team was stuck in a rut of dull mediocrity: in the seventeen seasons from 1921 through 1937, they never came in last but were in the second division thirteen times, including no fewer than ten times in sixth place. In 1937, plodding along to their familiar sixth-place oblivion, the Dodgers drew slightly more than half as many fans to Ebbets Field as the Giants did at the Polo Grounds. Indeed, the intense Giants-Dodgers rivalry that would become so vivid in later decades was inert in 1937. The Dodgers were "Dem Bums," the butt of jokes, not to be taken seriously. A rivalry is fueled by competition, and the Dodgers were providing none.

All of that was about to change. The Brooklyn Trust Company, the bank that held controlling ownership of the Dodgers, was fed up with the team's chronically poor performance, especially on the balance sheet. Seeking an experienced baseball executive to turn the organization around, Dodgers ownership asked Ford Frick, the president of the National League, for suggestions. Frick recommended forty-eight-year-old Leland Stanford "Larry" MacPhail, an explosive redhead who in three years in charge of the operation in Cincinnati had lifted the Reds from the cellar to the middle of the pack while demonstrating a rare genius for promotion. It should be noted that MacPhail had also rapidly worn out his welcome in Cincinnati with his mercurial, hard-drinking behavior and was available because he was now working as a lawyer for his father's investment business. But the Dodgers were in no position to be choosy.

As Lee Allen would put it, "Everything that MacPhail did was accompanied by the blare of trumpets."[16] He was loud, brash, hyperactive, and brilliant. He well understood a business fundamental that largely escaped many of that era's baseball executives, namely that it was necessary to spend money in order to make money. In Cincinnati he had painted the ballpark, introduced night baseball to the major leagues, made intelligent use of radio broadcasting, and established an extensive farm system. Attendance more than doubled.

MacPhail arrived in Brooklyn on January 19, 1938. He greeted the press contingency expansively, announced that there was going to be some action, and left the writers with the electric feeling that things would begin to hum. Within a span of a few months, first Durocher and then MacPhail had arrived in Brooklyn. It was evident that whatever would happen, it wasn't going be the dull mediocrity-as-usual for the Dodgers.

For the Giants, back-to-back defending National League champions, 1938 started off sensationally. They bolted out of the gate, winning eighteen of their first twenty-one, and remained in first place into mid-July. But they couldn't sustain it: Bill Terry's team slumped after the '38 All-Star break and never made a challenge in September. They finished third, five games behind the pennant-winning Chicago Cubs. The key development contributing to the Giants' second-half disappointment was a pitching elbow injury suffered by longtime ace Carl Hubbell, who underwent season-ending surgery in August. Terry kept Mel Ott at third base until late in the year, with the team reeling, he was returned to right field, where he would spend the rest of his career.

It was a disappointing season for the Giants yet hardly a disaster. Ticket sales declined to 799,000, but that was still good enough for second highest in the league. No team could be expected to win the pennant every year (well, apparently except for the Yankees, who ran away with the American League flag for the third straight time in 1938). There wasn't necessarily reason for Stoneham or Terry to be overly concerned.

Yet across town in Brooklyn, as MacPhail had promised, things were happening. The Dodgers sent a cool $45,000 cash to the ever-desperate Philadelphia Phillies in exchange for slugging star first baseman Dolph Camilli. Though the Dodgers' on-field improvement was modest—they went from sixty-two wins to sixty-nine but dropped from sixth place to seventh—the overall operation was decidedly not Dodger-normal. The difference in Ebbets Field itself was astonishing. For years the stadium had been allowed to deteriorate, but now every seat was freshly painted one shade of blue or another, with the exits a flaming orange. The Dodger players were no longer wearing uniforms trimmed in long-familiar kelly green but were instead natty in the clean, bold royal blue-and-white scheme that's been their signature ever since. Gone were swearing ushers who fought with patrons for foul balls, and in their place were neat collegians who located seats with courtesy. For the press there was free lunch and a bar. In the first base coach's box was none other than Babe Ruth.

In the middle of May, MacPhail grandly announced not just that he was installing lights at Ebbets Field, but that the first night game would take place on June 15. That the construction could be accomplished so quickly seemed fantastic, but with MacPhail the fantastic seemed to be expected.[17] (The first night game in Brooklyn was indeed held on June 15, 1938, and it featured Cincinnati Reds southpaw Johnny Vander Meer shutting out the Dodgers with his second consecutive no-hitter.)

Though the 1938 Dodgers were never a factor in the pennant race, the excitement of a more fan-friendly product and a leading-edge presentation greatly stimulated fan interest. Ebbets Field attendance boomed by more than a third. And it wasn't just the size of the crowds in Brooklyn that was exciting; it was a newfound MacPhail-infused spirit of fun and mischief. The mood at the ballpark was festive. MacPhail installed a stadium organ, and organist Gladys Gooding played "Three Blind Mice" when the umpires entered the field. A super-fan named Hilda Chester merrily rang a cowbell and became known as the "Queen of the Bleachers." Once she had a messenger deliver a note to manager Leo Durocher in the dugout: "Casey looks tired. Better get somebody warmed up." In section 17, behind first base, a fan by the name of Shorty Laurice organized an extremely amateur little musical band he called the "Sym-phoney" that joyfully played drums, cymbals, and a loud trombone.[18]

The third-place Giants lost more than 125,000 ticket buyers between 1937 and 1938. The seventh-place Dem Bums Dodgers gained more than 180,000. Something was going on.

New York City baseball fans of 1938 were a diverse lot, split at least three ways from the get-go by the three-franchise status the metropolis had enjoyed for decades and fractured as well along all of the perennial fault lines of geography, ethnicity, and tribalism. But varied as their perspectives and rooting interests would be, all New York baseball fans had one thing in common: nobody's games could be heard on the radio. New York City, by agreement between the Giants, the Yankees, and the Dodgers, was in 1938 the last of the country's "dry" baseball radio markets.

Way back in the medium's infancy—when radio was just as often still called "wireless," an eternity of almost twenty years ago in this ever-modernizing twentieth century—the very first baseball games ever broadcast were Giants games. They were Yankees games, too, because they were World Series games between the clubs, one each from 1921 and 1922. Radio/wireless was just a curiosity then and not much of a business.

That would quickly change. However, the rapid development of the radio broadcasting business over the 1920s and into the '30s didn't occur identically in every region and every market of the country. Differing business conditions applied across a diverse economic landscape. Depending on one's perspective, introducing broadcast radio into a given situation wasn't necessarily a good idea.

In the baseball business the crucial question was: would routinely broadcasting a team's home games in its home market help or hinder live attendance? It was a debate unable to find resolution even as the 1930s advanced and radio became an ever bigger business. Two opposing camps formed: the pro-radio contingent, led by Chicago Cubs general manager Bill Veeck Sr.; and the anti-radio side, led by St. Louis Cardinals owner Sam Breadon and joined by general manager Ed Barrow of the Yankees as well as C. A. Stoneham's Giants.

Breadon argued that broadcasting games on the radio could undermine the business of newspaper sports sections and imperil the free publicity that newspapers had provided baseball for so many decades. Veeck responded that the decision to broadcast, or not, was an inherent right of each team that couldn't be infringed by other owners. He asserted that radio advertises the product, it brings women and other new fans to the ballpark, and it had helped build the Cubs into a successful franchise. Both Boston teams joined with Veeck, as did the Chicago White Sox. A consensus was uneasily established that for the time being, each club could independently choose to broadcast or not, but the arguing didn't cease.

It was no accident that the center of gravity of the pro-radio side was Chicago and that its opponents were situated in New York. Chicago, way out on the major league frontier, sat as the economic hub of a vast multistate market, in which radio broadcasting served to develop the fan base far and wide, whose members might then be inclined to take in a Cubs or a White Sox game when it was time to visit the city. None of the New York teams were in such a circumstance, placed as they were within the most densely packed metropolis in the country, surrounded by other large cities with four competing teams. The New York clubs were largely required to fill their ballparks with just the locals, arriving at the games on foot or in local commuter streetcars and subways. Radio plainly provided a service to the Chicago teams that didn't translate to New York. Interestingly, Breadon's Cardinals catered to a far-flung fan base like the Cubs and White Sox, but his worry was that St. Louis and a large section of its hinterlands were too easily within reach of overwhelmingly powerful Chicago-based radio signals for the smaller-town Cardinals to successfully compete.

In 1934 the Cardinals persuaded the St. Louis Browns to commit to a no-broadcasting policy from Sportsman's Park, the stadium they shared. In New York the Giants under C. A. Stoneham, the Yankees under Jacob Ruppert, and the Dodgers under Steve McKeever mutually agreed to a five-year ban on radio broadcasting, including not just live games but also re-creations. Nevertheless, sponsors were bidding ever-increasing fees for broadcasts. In the mid-1930s the hardcore anti-radio contingent was increasingly representing a minority of interests and would never be able to muster the votes to impose league-wide restrictions. The economics of radio were becoming ever more irresistible.

It was in 1934 that Larry MacPhail had introduced Walter "Red" Barber as the radio broadcaster for his Cincinnati Reds, and MacPhail quickly assessed the arrangement to be an unqualified success. Upon his arrival in Brooklyn, MacPhail was prohibited from bringing Barber along by the existing New York no-broadcasting pact. But at the end of the 1938 season the five-year ban expired, and there was no way the Dodgers were going to take part in any extension. In December 1938 big-time advertisers General Mills, Socony-Vacuum, and Procter & Gamble signed agreements with Brooklyn to sponsor broadcasts of both home and away games. The Dodgers were going all in with radio.

This meant that "the Ol' Redhead" was coming to the New York baseball radio market for 1939. Red Barber was from the Deep South and peppered his broadcasts with colorful colloquialisms such as "black-eyed peas" and "the catbird seat." Nevertheless, the Flatbush fan base quickly adopted him as their own "verce of Brooklyn." His delivery included more than just homespun accents; Barber's vocabulary was in fact highly literary, and he developed a sophisticated style that worked perfectly within the drawn-out pace and rhythm of baseball. Moreover, he was a serious student of the game and helped his audience learn its nuances. Barber became the first superstar baseball broadcaster, and his deep popularity would be as impactful as that of the team's stars on the field in generating and sustaining loyalty from the fans.[19]

Horace Stoneham and Ed Barrow knew it was time to fold. In January 1939 both the Giants and Yankees signed with the same big three Dodgers sponsors for the rights to their games, though they took the leap more cautiously, limiting it to home games and excluding Sundays. The Giants and Yankees shared broadcasters: in the first few years, calling both teams' games on the radio were Mel Allen, Joe Bolton, Connie Desmond, Garnett Marks, and Arch McDonald. In just a year's time MacPhail's impact with night baseball and radio was revolutionizing the presentation of baseball in New York. Things were happening, indeed.

Especially when considering how grim and desperate the early 1930s had been for New York City, by the end of the decade there was a growing sense of achievement in the mood of the metropolis and a confident display of cutting-edge modernity. More than ever before, there was no other place in the world that had ever been like New York. It was an era in which New York City reveled in the beauty of the brand-new things it had made. On April 30, 1939, the New York World's Fair opened a two-season run at Flushing Meadows in Queens. It was the first of such expositions to be explicitly focused on the future, with the slogan "Dawn of a New Day" and featuring exhibit after exhibit demonstrating the wonders of emerging technologies, including air conditioning, television, and a prototype computer called "the electric calculator." The Empire State Building itself, having opened way back in 1931, was almost old hat by now. A 1939 guidebook touted the "towering shaft of the RCA building" in the dazzling new Rockefeller Center: "If that doesn't make you catch your breath, you might as well go home." At Radio City Music Hall glamorous dancers high-kicked above semicircles framing a huge stage lit up in any desired sequence of vivid colors by a "color orchestrator" behind a switchboard.[20] A tourist book from 1937 marveled at "the loveliness of naked steel and cable" as "the splendid example of the sheer beauty of form following function" in the brand-new George Washington Bridge.

Amid this giddy atmosphere the New York Giants suddenly found themselves struggling to keep up. As 1938 became 1939, Bill Terry endeavored, in his customarily decisive fashion, to reenergize his roster, executing two big trades. The first, rather remarkably, was with the pennant-winning Chicago Cubs—it's rare for directly competing contenders to engage in significant player transactions—and it was also unusual as a three-for-three "challenge trade" that swapped outfielder Hank Leiber, shortstop Dick Bartell, and catcher Gus Mancuso for outfielder Frank Demaree, shortstop Billy Jurges, and catcher Hank O'Dea.[21] The second deal—in whose negotiation Stoneham was prominently involved—was with the American League's Washington Senators, and it was more of a purchase than a trade: the Giants expended two marginal players along with $20,000 cash and received first baseman Henry "Zeke" Bonura, a heavy hitter and dreadful fielder. The *Indianapolis Star* reported it on December 12, 1938: "President Horace Stoneham of the Giants and Clark Griffith of the Senators discussed the deal at several sittings the past week. They met this afternoon at the New York Giants–Green Bay Packers professional football game and settled the details. Then 'Griff' phoned manager Buck Harris of the Nats to get his final 'okay.' In acquiring Bonura, the Giants hope their first base problem, which has been a source of considerable worry ever since Bill Terry gave up active playing, has been finally settled."[22]

Bonura became an immediate favorite among the New York writers as a made-to-order source of good copy, with his valiant struggles with the glove, his booming bat, and his uninhibited exuberance. His first meeting with Stoneham was the talk of spring training. The team was in New Orleans, Bonura's hometown, and upon being introduced to his new boss, Zeke responded with a blithe: "Say, Horace, for a club owner you're a fine-looking young fellow. You ought to be playing ball yourself. By the way, how about coming out to my house for one of my mother's famous Italian dishes?"[23]

Another change Terry instituted for 1939 was to name thirty-year-old Mel Ott as team captain. While unquestionably the team's best player, Master Melvin was a shy personality, hardly the type to display animated leadership. Though his teammates teased Ott, telling him he was required to learn the rule book line by line, he took it seriously. As Terry described it, "Mel took over as captain as solemnly as though he were taking over control of the U.S. Army."[24]

Demaree, Jurges, and the colorful Bonura would all perform well in 1939, but Captain Ott had to sit out nearly thirty games with the first significant injury of his career, a nagging "charley horse" in his leg. Moreover, with Carl Hubbell no longer able to carry a heavy workload, the pitching was problematic. Overall the 1939 Giants could muster only a bland 77–74 record, falling to fifth place. It was by far their worst showing since 1932, and attendance slid again, to 702,000, third in the league. And what team enjoyed the highest attendance in the National League in 1939? Why, the Brooklyn Dodgers, at 955,000, leading in ticket sales for the very first time in their fifty seasons as a franchise. MacPhail installed Durocher as playing manager, and the Dodgers that year also passed the Giants in the standings, surging to third place at 84–69. It was altogether a circumstance that had been unimaginable just a couple of years earlier.

It was obvious that major changes needed to be undertaken by the Giants. Stoneham and Terry pondered their next moves. Their conclusive decision was that strategically, the best course of action was to double down on investment in and expansion of the organization's farm system. When Terry took over in 1932, the Giants had a grand total of twenty-seven players in their organization. By 1939 the Giants owned the contracts of well over one hundred, including eighty-two minor leaguers assigned either to the three farm clubs now directly owned by the Giants or to the four teams with which they had a working agreement. With the farm system grown so large, Terry finally convinced Stoneham that its supervision was a full-time job. In December 1939 Jack Cook, until then the secretary of the Jersey City farm team, was placed in this new position.[25]

As with radio, Stoneham had resisted the innovation of night baseball. In 1935 he'd pondered: "Suppose Hubbell or Terry or

Bartell was fooled by the lights and hit by the ball. In one night my team would be ruined for the season." Now, however, prodded by the competition from MacPhail's Dodgers, on November 14, 1939, Stoneham announced that the Giants were investing $135,000 to install lights at the Polo Grounds.[26] As with radio, modernity implacably had its way.

In the spring of 1940 Terry decided that one year of Bonura at first base had been enough, selling him back to Washington for the familiar figure of $20,000. In his place Terry went with twenty-three-year-old rookie Norman "Babe" Young, a powerful left-handed hitter whose pull-hitting stroke looked to be a great fit for the short porch in the Polo Grounds. As the *Brooklyn Daily Eagle* reported: "After a brief look at Young at the tail-end of last season and another quick glance during spring training, manager Bill Terry announced that he had found the first baseman he had been looking for ever since he hung up his spikes several years ago. . . . The Giants had been flirting with the idea of unloading Bonura to the Senators for the past two months but it wasn't until after Young's fine showing yesterday that Terry, Leo Bondy, and Horace Stoneham had a hasty conference and decided to go through with the transaction."[27]

Terry shifted thirty-year-old incumbent second baseman Burgess Whitehead to third for 1940, giving the second base opportunity to rookies Mickey Witek and Al Glossop. Young would do well, but neither Witek nor Glossop proved to be the answer, and Terry couldn't avoid another disappointing season. After a good first half, the Giants fell apart and finished at 72–80, in sixth place. Although Polo Grounds attendance improved a bit, to 748,000, that was still far less than MacPhail and Durocher attracted in Brooklyn (976,000, again leading the league), while the Dodgers improved again, to eighty-eight wins and second place.

It was now a sustained cycle of poor results for the Giants, something Bill Terry had never before encountered. During spring training of 1941, Memphis Bill proposed an ambitious three-club deal in which the Giants would reacquire power-hitting outfielder Hank Leiber from the Cubs and also receive catcher Ernest "Babe" Phelps from the Dodgers while sending star catcher Harry Danning to Chicago. The trade negotiations were nearly complete when Terry suddenly announced the deal was off. This was confusing, given that it was Terry who'd conceived it. Brooklyn's MacPhail was furious, and he sent a statement to the press blasting Terry. What seems to have happened was that at the last minute Terry was overruled by Stoneham, at the request of Leo Bondy, who deemed the contracts the Giants would be taking on to be too expensive. It was the first instance of Stoneham asserting such power over Terry, and the manager was frustrated, not only because he couldn't get the players he wanted but because he'd been made to look foolish.[28]

Nothing was going right. In 1941 the Giants turned in yet another listless performance, at 74–79, fifth place. And this time the National League pennant winner whose dust they ate was Brooklyn, for which MacPhail and Durocher had succeeded in building a one hundred–win powerhouse. Dolph Camilli led the league in home runs and RBIs and was named Most Valuable Player, and he was now flanked in the lineup by big-hitting Joe "Ducky" Medwick (purchased from the Cardinals for a staggering $125,000) as well as sensational twenty-two-year-old sophomore center fielder Pete Reiser. On the mound the Dodgers boasted a pair of aces in Kirby Higbe (bought from the Phillies for $100,000) and late-blooming veteran Whitlow Wyatt. MacPhail was rewarded for his free-spending ways not just with a championship but with booming ticket sales at 1,214,990, a franchise record and the highest attendance in the major leagues for 1941. The Brooklyn Dodgers had outdrawn not just the Giants but the mighty Yankees as well.

Not only were the Dodgers now beating the Giants like a drum—twelve wins in twenty-two games in 1939, sixteen in 1940, and fourteen in 1941; worse yet, a distressing pattern emerged at Polo Grounds turnstiles: the ballpark was popular only when the Dodgers played there. The crowds with Brooklyn as the visitor were comprising 30 to 40 percent of Giants' attendance in just eleven of the seventy-seven games played at the Polo Grounds.[29] Stoneham was six years into his ownership tenure, and on his brief watch the franchise suddenly faced its most bleak predicament in the forty years since John McGraw and John T. Brush had come to the rescue. It was time for the young owner to make some hard decisions.

Bill Terry became fed up late in the 1941 season, while the team fell apart, from eight games over .500 in July to six under by the end of August. In early September, on their final western road trip, a grumpy Terry told the writers he would be making a "sensational" announcement soon. But he later said he'd reconsidered, and no announcement was forthcoming. It would become evident that Terry had planned to announce his resignation in Pittsburgh; he'd called Stoneham from the road and told him so. The owner immediately flew to Pittsburgh and talked Terry into remaining. Stoneham told the writers that there would be a general housecleaning of the roster for 1942, noting that only Carl Hubbell, Mel Ott, Babe Young, and twenty-four-year-old sophomore center fielder Johnny Rucker were sure of their jobs and that Terry would remain as manager "for as long as he wants."[30]

The issue, of course, was that Terry didn't want. Even with Jack Schwarz working as his assistant, he was exhausted by the status quo and needed a change. Terry could no longer handle the two jobs of field manager and general manager, and "he knew which of the two positions was no longer responding to his touch or maintaining his interest."[31] He and Stoneham agreed to take some time for careful consideration before reconvening to seek a consensus.

The meeting of the minds took place on the first of December 1941, at the annual minor league meetings in Jacksonville, Florida. Stoneham, at the urging of Leo Bondy, had decided that Terry was out, but being Stoneham, he wasn't eager to fire him, especially with a year remaining on his contract. So the owner allowed Terry to speak first, hoping that Terry would resign voluntarily. As it turned out, Terry was prepared to do so if it came to that, but he had a different proposal for Stoneham: Terry said he wanted to stay with the organization but serving full-time as general manager, with particular focus on overseeing the scouting and farm system operations while giving up the responsibility as field manager.

Whether Stoneham had previously been considering such an arrangement isn't clear, but he was delighted with the idea. That resolved, the discussion then turned to the question of who to hire as the new manager. Among those considered were Charles "Gabby" Hartnett, who'd just retired as a player, and Dick Bartell and Billy Jurges, both veteran infielders still playing regularly. It's not recorded who suggested it should be thirty-two-year-old Mel Ott instead, but that choice seems more likely to have come from Stoneham than from Terry. In any case it was Ott upon whom they decided.

Coincidentally, on that very day Ott himself arrived in Jacksonville. Though in the past he'd attended such baseball conventions as a social break in the long off-season, this time Ott was there with a purpose. He was worried that with lagging Polo Grounds attendance, Stoneham and Terry might be preparing to cut his salary, and his insecurity was heightened by the fact that Terry had given a September look-see in right field to Herbert "Babe" Barna, a minor league slugger. Ott went to Jacksonville prepared to put up an argument.

But once there, he hesitated about barging in on Stoneham and Terry. Working up his nerve, Ott ate lunch by himself down the street from the hotel where Stoneham and Terry were meeting. Meanwhile, they'd come to their big decision and were ready to announce the great news to Ott. Stoneham placed a telephone call to Ott's home in Louisiana, and he and Terry were surprised when Ott's wife, Mildred, told them that Mel was in Jacksonville.[32]

And so, rather comically, Stoneham and Terry sent someone out to find Ott and deliver the message to join them at the hotel. When Ott entered the Giants' suite, Stoneham heartily greeted him with "Hi ya, manager! I have a new job for you, at more money!" Dumbfounded, Ott looked from Terry to Stoneham and said, "You aren't kidding, are you?" Terry assured him that no one was kidding and said, "Go on, son, take it." Ott thought a minute, then said soberly, "I guess a fellow couldn't refuse a chance like this, could he?" The men shook hands all around, and Ott said, "I've got to call Mickey [his nickname for Mildred]."

With that done, Ott sat in a daze, shaking his head in disbelief at how this day had turned out.

Ott had long been Stoneham's favorite player, and the owner was eager to spread the good news. He called Toots Shor at his restaurant. "Hello, kid, I've got swell news for you," declared a jubilant Stoneham. "Ottie is my new manager. Yeah, Ott. I need a drink. Wait a minute, here's Mel." Ott told Shor: "I can't believe it. That's right. I'm the man." They talked excitedly, with Shor offering hearty congratulations, and finally they hung up. Back at the restaurant someone asked Shor, "What's going to be done with Terry?" Toots answered, "Jeez, I forgot to ask." He hesitated a moment, then shouted: "Who cares, anyway? Ottie's the new manager now!"[33]

With the crucial communication to Toots Shor taken care of, it was time for Stoneham to assemble the members of the press covering the Jacksonville meetings and make the formal announcement. There was a great deal of surprise expressed by the writers, even more than when Terry had named Ott team captain in 1939. Some were skeptical as to how much authority the hard-driving Terry would cede to the mild-mannered Ott; though Stoneham and Terry both said Ott would be his own man, that he wouldn't take orders from Terry, the writers weren't so sure. Bob Considine of the *New York Journal-American* wrote that he didn't remember Ott ever having taken a stand on anything regarding the running of the team. Dan Daniel of the *New York World-Telegram* came right out and said the promise that Ott would run things by himself was "difficult to believe."[34] No one had seen this coming, certainly including Ott himself.

Thus, in his first truly strategic decision as owner of the Giants, Stoneham had made a most peculiar choice. It didn't appear to have been based on any sort of careful analysis, nor was it consistent with the conventional baseball wisdom regarding what kind of man is best suited to perform as a leader of men. Indeed, based on Stoneham's giddy manner in offering the job to Ott (and in immediately telling his best pal Toots about it), the compelling motivation for Stoneham might have been little more than avoiding the grim task of negotiating an austere contract with his favorite player in lean times and, instead, being able to delight Ott with a grand promotion, worthy of celebration. If so, it was a brilliant maneuver in the service of conflict aversion, but it did not bode well as an indicator of hardheaded business management.

In any case both Terry and Ott were given two-year contracts. Terry took a cut in annual salary from $42,500 to $30,000 to help persuade Stoneham to create his newly focused role. Ott, instead of the pay cut he'd been fearing, got a raise to $25,000.[35]

How well it all might turn out was the question raised by stunned New York sportswriters. But within just a few days that sort of question would be overwhelmed by worries of a vastly more serious nature. On November 26, 1941, a Japanese navy task force comprised of six aircraft carriers had departed Hito-kappu Bay on Kasatka Island, northeast of Hokkaido, heading for a rendezvous northwest of the Hawaiian Islands, transporting a fleet of 408 fighter planes. The United States was about to be swept into the greatest armed conflict in human history.

5

War, Peace, and Nice Guys

Exactly when World War II started is a matter of interpretation. It is generally considered to have been September 1, 1939, when Germany invaded Poland, provoking France and the United Kingdom to declare war. But it was in 1937 that the Empire of Japan fully invaded China, and it had been in 1931 that the Japanese army occupied Manchuria. But there could be no question in December 1941, with the Japanese attacks on American and British targets in Hawaii, Malaya, Guam, Wake Island, and the Philippines, that this ever-widening conflict was truly global, with its multiple theaters all inextricably interconnected. It was at this point that the World War II nomenclature came into prominence, and the combat of a generation earlier, which had been known at the time as the Great War or the World War, came to be understood as World War I.

The major theater of battle in World War I had been the western front, stretching hundreds of miles and yielding, over a four-year period, about 3.2 million military deaths and several hundred thousand more civilians. In World War II the eastern front between the Nazis and the Soviets would be the largest military confrontation in history, spanning more than two thousand miles from the Gulf of Finland to the Black Sea, involving hundreds of thousands of tanks, artillery pieces, and aircraft and tens of millions of military personnel. The eastern front was epic not just in size but in ruthless atrocity-rich cruelty. Casualties would total roughly fifteen million military dead and—in stark difference to the earlier war—an approximately equal number of civilians killed.

World War II would be the circumstance in which Nazi Germany undertook the deadliest genocide in history, murdering about six million Jews, Romani, and mental patients. In the largest camp within the carefully organized system of extermination, at Oświęcim, Poland (called Auschwitz in German), over 1.1 million people were slaughtered in a period of less than four years. World War II would be the circumstance in which the United States detonated atomic bombs over the Japanese cities of Hiroshima and Nagasaki, vaporizing perhaps 100,000 people instantaneously, with a comparable number succumbing to injuries within the next few months. It was the world's first and (so far) only combat deployment of nuclear weapons.

Though combat in World War II took place almost entirely outside of the United States, the war's impact on the lives of nearly all Americans was immense and lasting. First, of course, were those who entered military service itself. In addition to recruiting volunteers, the United States employed a military draft that was prodigious in scale.[1] At its peak in 1945, the U.S. military had more than eleven million members in service, a total about one-sixth the size of the nation's entire workforce.

At the same time, the war effort created enormous demand for industrial and agricultural production, and therefore, the United States quickly developed a severe manpower shortage. The unprecedented need for labor motivated millions of retirees, women, and teenagers to go to work. Labor shortages were especially difficult in agriculture, even though most draft-age farmers were given an exemption, and few were conscripted. Many farmworkers joined the military or moved to cities for better-paying factory jobs, yet agricultural produce was in greater demand than ever before. Civilians were encouraged to grow "victory gardens" in backyards, schools, and empty lots. The United States and Mexico collaborated to develop the Bracero Program, a labor agreement in which some 300,000 braceros ("strong arms" in Spanish) were imported to work in agriculture and railroads.[2] In addition, more than 400,000 Italian and German prisoners of war were used as farm laborers, loggers, and cannery workers.[3]

Both the American Federation of Labor (AFL) and the Congress of Industrial Organizations (CIO) dramatically grew in membership. These major unions committed to a wartime no-strike pledge, and in return the federal government offered arbitration to determine wages and other terms of collectively bargained contracts. Applying the leverage afforded by lucrative defense contracts, the government pressured employers to recognize unions and avoid the labor confrontations that had characterized the 1930s. Struggling to attract and retain talent in the extraordinarily competitive labor market, many employers introduced new "fringe benefits" (such as paid vacation, retirement pension, and medical insurance), which increased real incomes even when wages were frozen.[4]

An elaborate rationing system was constructed to guard against hoarding and shortages and to prevent inflation. Price controls were imposed on most products, and wages were also controlled. Personal income was higher than it had ever been, and consumer goods were rarely available for purchase, so Americans saved money at an all-time high rate, in private savings accounts and insurance policies but mostly in War Bonds, which were championed in rallies featuring movie stars and radio personalities. The success of this campaign enabled over 40 percent of the United States gross domestic product to be devoted to military spending, with only moderate inflation.

Along with heavy borrowing, high taxes were required to pay for the war effort. Top marginal income tax rates rose above 90 percent for the duration of the war, and the income level subject to the highest rate was lowered from $5 million to $200,000 annually. Congress also enlarged the tax base by lowering the minimum income to pay taxes and by reducing personal exemptions and deductions.[5]

The "war footing" economy demanded migration on a massive scale. Hundreds of military training bases were established or enlarged, and millions of wives followed their enlisted husbands to take up residence in base towns or moved away to live with extended family. The immense growth in military hardware production attracted workers into industrial centers, including many thousands of African Americans who departed the rural South. In these suddenly overcrowded cities, adequate housing was ever more difficult to find, with virtually no nonmilitary construction being undertaken.

These disruptions stirred racial tension, erupting most notably in a three-day riot in Detroit in June 1943 that resulted in thirty-four deaths and more than four hundred injuries, as well as "Zoot Suit" riots in Los Angeles that same month. Wildcat strikes occurred in Detroit, in Baltimore, and in Evansville, Indiana, where white migrants from the still-segregated South refused to work alongside Blacks. The African American community in the United States organized a "Double V" campaign, highlighting the dual need not only for victory over the Axis abroad but also to overcome systemic discrimination in employment, housing, and education at home. (The United States military services themselves remained racially segregated throughout the entire war.)[6]

Despite the looming labor shortages, on February 19, 1942, President Roosevelt signed Executive Order 9066, which set up designated military areas "from which any or all persons may be excluded." This authorized the forcible internment of more than 100,000 Americans of Japanese descent who were living in California, Hawaii, Washington, Oregon, and Arizona. Zero Americans of German or Italian descent were interned.

Professional baseball executives remembered how disruptive World War I had been to the business, with seasons shortened and many minor leagues forced to fold. Major league owners fretfully wondered what might be in store this time, and they persuaded an initially reluctant Commissioner Kenesaw Mountain Landis to seek direction from the president himself on how to best proceed. On January 14, 1942, a bit more than a month following America's entry into the war, Landis sent a short handwritten letter to Franklin Roosevelt. Landis got straight to the point, writing: "The time is approaching when, in ordinary conditions, our teams would be heading for spring training camps. However, inasmuch as these are not ordinary times, I venture to ask what you have in mind as to whether professional base-ball should continue to operate."

FDR responded the very next day with a thoughtful and encour-aging message. In what would become known as the "Green Light Letter," Roosevelt began by stipulating that he was provid-ing his personal opinion, not a legal order, and that the author-ity to decide what to do would be with the commissioner and the owners. But, wrote the president, "I honestly feel that it would be best for the country to keep baseball going." Roosevelt observed that baseball could helpfully serve as a source of entertainment and comfort for stressed American workers, whose sustained productivity would be a requirement of military victory. As the president elaborated: "Baseball provides a recreation which does not last over two hours or two hours and a half, and which can be got for very little cost. And, incidentally, I hope that night games can be extended because it gives an opportunity to the day shift to see a game occasionally." He laid out the cost-benefit math, comparing the combined scale of major and minor league base-ball against that of the nation at large: "If 300 teams use 5,000 or 6,000 players, these players are a definite recreational asset to at least 20,000,000 of their fellow citizens—and that in my judgment is totally worthwhile."

Nonetheless, while President Roosevelt was clear that he wanted baseball to be played, he would not exempt its players from military service. And though he understood the risk teams faced if popular star players were drafted, the president remained confident that fans would understand. "Even if the actual qual-ity of the teams is lowered by greater use of older players," he wrote, "this will not dampen the popularity of the sport."

And so, green-lighted to swing away, professional baseball endeavored to serve the needs of a nation prosecuting total war. As with every other industry—indeed, more acutely than most, given that professional ball players were exclusively able-bodied young men—the first problem was that of attrition of the play-ers themselves, through voluntary induction as well as the draft. There would be a total of 71 players with prior major league expe-rience missing the 1942 season due to military service, 219 in

1943, 342 in 1944, and 384 in 1945. Every team was hit hard: the St. Louis Browns lost the fewest, with "only" 19, while the Philadelphia Athletics contributed the most, at 36.[7]

And as impactful as wartime military service was in the majors, it was devastating for the minors. In 1941 there were forty-one minor leagues operating within the framework of "organized baseball," but in 1942, the first season under wartime conditions, that total was trimmed to thirty-one. Then the lesser leagues began to fold in rapid succession; in 1943 and '44 just ten minor leagues were able to operate and twelve in 1945.

Quality of play was, of course, severely undermined by the accelerating shortage of qualified players. Then there was the quality of the actual, physical baseball itself. Rubber was a commodity restricted from nonmilitary use, and baseballs were traditionally constructed around a cork-and-rubber core. With rubber unavailable, ball manufacturers were forced to experiment with alternatives. The first version used balata, an organic rubber substitute, which rendered the balls resoundingly "dead," and the term *balata ball* would become a derisive nickname for a nonresilient baseball. A newly developed form of synthetic rubber was then adopted, and while it performed better than balata, power-hitting and run-scoring rates were greatly depressed at every level of professional baseball throughout the war.

Another issue was travel restriction. Beginning in 1943, all major league teams were ordered to undertake spring training north of the Mason-Dixon Line. The regular season schedule was revamped to incorporate longer series and less-frequent travel, so that the teams visited each other three times rather than the customary four. The 1945 All-Star Game was cancelled because by that midsummer the nation's railroad grid was overburdened with the traffic of military demobilization.

Though the president had expressed a wish for more night games, Atlantic coastal teams, including the Giants, were inhibited in staging them because of after-dark citywide "blackouts" intended to frustrate potential German night bombing. In an attempt to attract fans with daytime jobs, several contests were scheduled to begin near twilight. On successive evenings in August

1942, games at the Polo Grounds were terminated by "dim-out," abruptly halted amid dramatic action in the ninth and tenth innings. After that Stoneham announced there would be no more games by twilight.[8]

The New York Giants' December 1, 1941, announcement that Mel Ott would take over as playing manager had been a bombshell. Bill Terry, now fully dedicated to the GM role, wasted no time before detonating another one. On December 11 Terry executed the biggest deal he'd ever made: the Giants sent pitcher Bill Lohrman, catcher Ken O'Dea, first baseman Johnny McCarthy, and $50,000 of Horace Stoneham's cash to Branch Rickey's St. Louis Cardinals and received in return first baseman Johnny Mize. It was back-to-back stunners from Stoneham's Giants, and as one newspaper reported, "If a bolt of lightning had struck the National League it couldn't have shocked the circuit any more than the rebirth of the New York Giants."[9]

Johnny Mize, "the Big Cat," a hulking, soft-spoken Georgian with a sweet, powerful swing, was a prize acquisition indeed. Still just twenty-nine years old, Mize wasn't a well-rounded player, average at best with the glove and on the base paths. But his bat was stupendous: he'd led the National League in batting average once, in home runs twice, in RBI once, and in slugging average three times; indeed, since the mid-1930s, the only National Leaguer who might have been a better hitter than Johnny Mize was Mel Ott himself.[10] This extravagant purchase was a lusty expression of rediscovered competitive fury on the part of Stoneham's Giants, who'd been surpassed by the Dodgers more or less flat-footed. Well, now, the Giants had radio too, and now the Giants had night games too, and damn right, they now had a high-priced imported superstar in their lineup too. The Giants were no longer flat-footed: they were fighting back.

"I know what kind of baseball New Yorkers want and I promise to give it to them," Ott said not long after the Mize trade.[11] Presumably, he meant winning baseball, but he could also have been referring to his own specialty of home run production. It was simply true that in pairing Ott and Mize in their lineup, the Giants were doubling down on their commitment to power hitting. To whatever extent this represented a shrewd strategic decision, within a few years Giants' rosters would be critiqued for valuing home run power to a fault.

And it was the case that notwithstanding Mize's remarkable talent as a hitter, it was his limited value outside of the batter's box that likely motivated Rickey to accept the Giants' offer. The Cardinals certainly didn't need to be peddling Mize, as they were a perennial contender who'd finished a close second behind the Dodgers in 1941. Yet Rickey made this calculation in keeping with his proactive "better to trade a man a year too soon than a year too late" maxim, cashing in the Big Cat ticket while his value was high, especially considering that the St. Louis fan base, despite the team's sustained success on the field, had never delivered attendance revenues comparable to the New York and Chicago teams.

For the Giants, while it could be dismissed as "a good problem to have," fitting Mize into the lineup created a complication. Though the Giants in 1941 had their weaknesses, first base wasn't among them: twenty-six-year-old first baseman Babe Young's 25 home runs were fourth most in the league, and his 104 runs batted in second best. But the lumbering Mize could play nowhere except first. Therefore, if Young's powerful bat were to remain in the lineup, he'd need to learn to play the outfield, where he'd never spent a professional inning. Alternatively, Terry might put Young on the trading block and leverage his value to address other team needs, such as pitching.

But Young wasn't traded, and Ott's choices in determining how to deploy him can charitably be described as "odd." Through the entire first half, Ott limited Young to a strict pinch-hitting and backup first baseman role, playing him almost not at all. But then in mid-July Ott suddenly inserted Young into the regular lineup as the Giants' *center fielder*—a strange way to introduce him to the outfield. When finally given the chance to play, Young delivered strong offense, but he was, unsurprisingly, out of his depth in center field, particularly the vast expanse of the home field Polo Grounds.[12] A sportswriter didn't mince words regarding Young's misadventures in the outfield, asserting that he "was unable to make the grade there because of a weak throwing arm and his inability to untrack himself quickly enough on fly balls."[13]

As inscrutable as Manager Ott's wisdom may have been in this regard, the Giants were clearly better with Mize on board. In 1942 Ott and Mize formed the best back-to-back slugging duo in the major leagues. With Master Melvin batting himself third and the Big Cat cleanup, Ott led the league in runs scored, home runs, and walks, while Mize led in RBIS and slugging.[14] Together they were sensational, everything the Giants could have hoped for. As a team, the Giants improved from 74 wins to 85 and were back in the first division, in third place. Alas, it was a distant third, trailing far behind Rickey's dynamic 106-game-winning who–needs–Johnny Mize Cardinals as well as MacPhail's brassy Dodgers, who tied the all-time major league record for second-place wins with 104 while selling over a quarter-million more tickets than the Giants. Stoneham's team had achieved progress, but there was still a long way to go.

And none of this was easy for Ott, balancing the player-manager double duty. He was the first in the majors since Ty Cobb and Tris Speaker in the 1920s to handle the concurrent duties from an outfield position. This was before the rules limited a manager's number of visits to the pitcher's mound, and often Ott would call time more than once in an inning and trot in from right field on his aging legs. Once he reported "being startled" in right field while concentrating on game strategy and looking up to see a hard-hit ball coming his way. On another occasion Ott was at bat with the bases loaded in the tenth inning when he inadvertently gave the signal for the suicide squeeze play by tapping the plate with his bat. Seconds later the runner at third was charging as the pitch was delivered. Though surprised, Ott was able to get his bat on the ball at the last split-second, and the Giants scored the game-winning run.[15]

All told, the results of 1942 were positive. Subsequent seasons might have allowed the team to add critical pieces to supplement the robust Ott-Mize offensive axis and, well, to figure out what to do with Babe Young. However, World War II butted in. In '42 the Giants had been hit lightly by the military draft, losing just a few utility players, but in the ensuing off-season Uncle Sam took command. First came the news that Johnny Mize himself was gone, off to the navy. Soon off to military service as well were Babe Young, catcher Harry Danning, outfielder Willard Marshall, and pitchers Hal Schumacher, Bob Carpenter, and Dave Koslo.

"Total war" reality had now fully engulfed the New York Giants and all of major league baseball. Normality had to be set aside, to wait for a happier day. The general assumption among Americans, soundly reasoned or not, was that the Allies would win the war, but no one knew how long it would take, perhaps five years, maybe ten. As it turned out, after the United States actively entered the war in December 1941, it took a bit over three and a half intensely eventful years. "Soldiering" through on the home front, the major league baseball seasons of 1943, '44, and '45 succeeded in fulfilling President Roosevelt's wish for a familiar entertainment—attendance was down from prewar levels but not dramatically—but draft-riddled rosters meant that the standings and pennant races weren't taken seriously by many fans. Unfamiliar players came and went, and moreover, a significant portion of every team's most faithful fans were also overseas; altogether, the atmosphere at the games took on a sense of confusion.[16]

The Giants tumbled to last place in the helter-skelter National League standings of 1943—and Stoneham nonetheless re-signed Ott to a three-year player-manager contract at a modest raise—then came in fifth in both 1944 and '45. The archrival Brooklyn Dodgers, after winning one hundred–plus games in both 1941 and '42, dropped to third place in 1943, down to seventh in 1944, and back to third in 1945. For both franchises events occurring on the field weren't nearly as significant as those in the front office.

On September 23, 1942—in the closing week of the regular season, with the second-place Dodgers still closely battling the Cardinals for the pennant—Brooklyn president Larry MacPhail suddenly announced his resignation. He considered that his job in Brooklyn was done: the franchise had led the National League in attendance for four straight years, and he'd paid off much of the club's debt while winning one pennant and coming very close to another. MacPhail was fifty-two years old, but his nation was at war, and he believed it was his duty to help. He called a meeting of the Brooklyn directors, tore up the contract that would have paid him $75,000 a year, and announced that he was joining the army as a lieutenant colonel.[17] This stunning turn of events created a high-profile opening at the Brooklyn helm, and it would almost instantly be filled by the most high profile of candidates.

Sixty-year-old Branch Rickey, working in close partnership with St. Louis Cardinals owner Sam Breadon for more than twenty years, was the celebrated architect of that remarkably innovative and extremely competitive organization. But by 1942 their relationship was wearing thin. Rickey was upset over Breadon's refusal to back him in a dispute with Commissioner Landis over farm system rights and over Breadon's payment of a large bonus to himself while cutting Rickey's budget for salaries. Rickey was considering leaving baseball altogether, for a top executive post with a large insurance company.

Back in 1937, Brooklyn Dodgers board member James Mulvey had first approached Rickey, but at that point he wasn't interested in leaving his comfortable life in St. Louis. But now he was, and the wooing was quick. The *New York Times* first reported on October 4, 1942, that the Dodgers and Rickey were talking, and it was on October 29 that Rickey was introduced as the team's new general manager at a lunch at the Brooklyn Club. At that lunch Rickey was introduced to a thirty-nine-year-old lawyer, also newly hired to work for the Dodgers, named Walter O'Malley.[18]

Rickey could hardly be more different from MacPhail in personality. In Lee Allen's words: "In many ways [Rickey] was the antithesis of MacPhail: devious and subtle rather than direct and obvious, serene rather than mercurial, pensive rather than impulsive. The borough to which he came was loud, wet and Democratic—Rickey was quiet, dry and Republican."[19]

Just a month after Rickey's startling arrival in Brooklyn, it was the Giants' turn to make big news: on November 30, 1942, Bill Terry announced his resignation as general manager. He explained that the decision was entirely his own and was a consequence of the wartime-imposed decimation of the Giants' farm system. His statement read: "Some months ago I suggested to Mr. Stoneham that I did not believe the curtailed activities of the Giants in the minor leagues warranted my remaining. I did not feel I would be able under any conditions to earn my salary. So I suggested that if it met with the club's approval, my contract for next year be terminated."[20]

Terry had always kept his hand in various investment enterprises outside of baseball. Over the next few years there were rumors in the press that Terry was being considered for an executive job with this or that ball club, but none would materialize. Instead, Terry focused his energy on a lucrative cotton manufacturing business headquartered in Memphis. Just over twenty years after his memorable first negotiation with John McGraw, Memphis Bill Terry would never again work in professional baseball.[21]

Stoneham's response to his ball club's sudden vacancy in the front office was distinctly different from that of the Brooklyn ownership group. Not only did Stoneham not seek to recruit a big-name executive to take Terry's place; there's no indication that he considered looking outside of the organization at all. Nor was any protégé (such as Jack Schwarz) promoted from within; Terry was simply not replaced in the role of general manager. Instead, Horace Stoneham himself just quietly assumed the responsibility, and for the next thirty-plus years as owner of the Giants, he acted as his own GM. From the point of Terry's resignation onward, there would never be any ambiguity about who was in charge: this was now, in every way, Horace Stoneham's ball club.

One aspect of Stoneham's behavior, indeed of his essential personality, that cannot be overstated is how much he genuinely loved baseball—not the business of it so much as the sport itself. Like his father before him, in his capacity as Giants' owner, Horace Stoneham would sometimes host distinguished guests—politicians or other celebrities—in the owner's box in the Polo Grounds grandstand. But like his father, that wasn't his preferred vantage point. His favorite perspective was far away from the crowd, through the window from the center field offices above the clubhouse. He would often be accompanied there by a member or two of his staff, but usually he was alone.

In either case he watched every home game—every game—and not out of a sense of duty but because it was what he truly wanted and loved to do. The games, all of them, completely absorbed his attention, fascinating him. He scrutinized them with unflagging intensity, bordering on obsession. The Giants were vastly more than a business to Stoneham. They were the most important thing in the world to him, his heart and soul.

Horace Stoneham's devotion to the ball club was total. He never took vacations. Quite unlike his father, he didn't partake in gambling or horse racing. He had no hobbies; he dabbled at golf but was far more involved in it as a social endeavor than a competitive one. He would occasionally watch a movie (and in later years sometimes watch television—he enjoyed westerns) but not regularly. He wasn't one for listening to music, nor did he read books. He took no particular interest in much of anything except baseball and his Giants, and talking about baseball and his Giants, eagerly and inexhaustibly, with his beloved pals, over round after round of cocktails—indeed, to the extent that he could be overbearing; in later years longtime Giants broadcaster Lon Simmons described Stoneham's road-trip party routine: "He would have everyone into his room, and then wouldn't let you leave. You tried to make sure not to be the last one there because you might have to spend the night."[22]

Bill Terry's contention that the diminution of the minor leagues during wartime eliminated the need for the job of general manager was, shall we say, not how Branch Rickey looked at it. As Rickey reasoned, the very fact that other teams were reducing their scouting and development operations presented a competitive opening to be exploited. While most organizations were hoping merely to survive the war, Rickey's Dodgers, a jump ahead as usual, began to sign every free agent they could locate. He directed his staff to mail letters to eighteen thousand high school coaches, asking for player recommendations, and the best of these were then tried out in camps all over the country. Rickey knew, of course, that most of these boys would soon end up in the military, but he focused on what many other teams did not:

at war's end they would be returning, and with that the Dodger farm system would instantly be the strongest in the business.[23]

The Brooklyn farm system had included fourteen teams in 1941, but the impact of the war shrunk it to just four clubs by 1943. But under Rickey's direction they began to expand the chain even as the war continued. In 1944 they fielded seven minor league teams (including two at the very highest classification, with Montreal in the International League and St. Paul in the American Association), and in 1945 they stocked eight.

Stoneham did not sit idly by. In 1943 forty-year-old Carl Hubbell's great pitching career finally reached its end. Stoneham insightfully perceived in the laconic southpaw not just an abiding devotion to the game of baseball but an analytical insight for it and a keen eye for judging talent. So, at the end of the '43 season, Stoneham proposed that Hubbell stay with the Giants and created for him the position of general manager for Farm System and Scouting Development, reporting directly to Stoneham.

Hubbell began in 1944 with a staff of eight scouts (Hank DeBerry, Mel Logan, George Mack, Gordon Maguire, Bill Pierre, Marty Purtell, Frank Rickey, and Johnny Vergez) and went to work reconstructing the Giants' system. Rickey had gotten a head start in Brooklyn, but Stoneham and Hubbell ensured that the Giants would keep pace. They'd squeaked through 1943 with just three farm teams but grew the list to five in 1944 and to eight in 1945—equaling the size of the Dodger system and including, just like the Dodgers, two affiliates at the highest level (then still called "AA," or "double-A"): the Jersey City Giants of the International League and the San Francisco Seals of the Pacific Coast League (PCL). Both the Dodgers and Giants were committing to long-term investments that would yield extraordinary returns in the postwar period.

Hubbell abundantly justified Stoneham's faith in his ability to comprehend and master the subtle art of not just recognizing raw talent, but most crucially of applying effective techniques to develop it, while always remembering that every prospect was unique. In an interview in the 1950s, Hubbell described his nuanced approach:

First of all, few kids can execute plays exactly as their instructors did; and, when the instructors demand such performance, there is likely to be frustration on both sides. I never saw two hitters or two pitchers who were just alike in my life. Therefore, the teacher has to size up the boy's physical equipment and acquired mannerisms first of all and try to go with them, if no gross error is involved. Second, it is very important for any teacher to realize that the youngster coming to a professional baseball camp is probably mentally tight or physically tight, and sometimes both, and that progress has to wait until the boy loses that raw edge of the nerves.

Sometimes, I go so far as to say no teacher is the best prescription for a particular boy. That happens when we have a boy who may be a slow learner but has good physical qualities, who will only be confused in his greenness if he is asked to think of too many things at one time. Each boy is a distinct individual in that connection. A few can absorb a good deal of instruction so readily as if they were snapping a picture; a few have to put things together slowly and methodically as if it were a case of laying one brick on top of the other. There are all sorts of variations in between, and I know of no system which is going to turn them all out like autos on an assembly line.[24]

Stoneham forged another partnership in 1944 that didn't appear to be momentous but would become so. As an element in his ongoing program to optimize the revenue generated by the Polo Grounds, in June he struck a deal with Alejandro "Alex" Pompez, the owner of the New York Cubans of the Negro National League: Stoneham leased the Polo Grounds to Pompez as the Cubans' home field. The relationship between Stoneham and Pompez would flourish in the coming years, creating unique opportunities for both.[25]

Meanwhile, in Brooklyn, Branch Rickey was taking steps to consolidate his authority. On November 1, 1944, Rickey called a press conference to announce that he and two partners—Walter O'Malley and Andrew Schmitz—had purchased 24 percent of the Dodgers' stock. O'Malley was an attorney who'd been hired to represent the club's legal interests after MacPhail departed, and Schmitz was a prominent Brooklyn businessman. In August 1945 Rickey, O'Malley, Schmitz, and a fourth partner named John Smith purchased the stock held by the heirs of Charles Ebbets, giving Rickey, "the Mahatma," controlling interest.

The very next day Japan surrendered, and World War II was over. Rickey understood, as few others did, how dramatically different the future would be. "Great changes are coming," he told an interviewer that day. "In the postwar world of baseball there is going to be a revision of the map. Such cities as Los Angeles, Miami, San Francisco, Dallas, Montreal, and Houston are going to demand that their growth be recognized by organized baseball. Eventually one or more of these cities will demand major league status, and it will not be denied them."[26]

He wasn't yet ready to announce it in August 1945, but for more than a year Rickey had been undertaking a secret project to identify a Black player or players worthy of being signed by his organization, with the intent of nothing less than defying the six-decades-old practice of racial segregation in professional baseball in the United States.

While Rickey's particular endeavor was being pursued secretly, the issue it was confronting was increasingly the subject of public debate in the mid-1940s, especially in New York City. The world war's irresistible force in disrupting long-established social and economic norms reverberated everywhere, and baseball, loftily touting itself as "the national pastime," was inescapably visible in this modern light. There was a growing sense of conviction within much of the African American community, in the "Double V" spirit, that once the war ended, a resumption of prewar Jim Crow standards and expectations would be intolerable.

Several New York political candidates had featured the issue in their 1945 campaigns. Communist city councilman Ben Davis, a former college football star running for reelection, distributed a flyer featuring two Blacks—one a dead soldier, the other a baseball player—with a caption reading, "Good enough to die for his country, but not good enough for organized baseball." A state delegation investigating violations of the Quinn-Ives Act, a 1945 law prohibiting racial discrimination, called upon the three New

York major league owners in October and demanded that they sign a pledge not to discriminate in hiring. They refused, and the normally reticent Stoneham even spoke out in complaint, denouncing the delegation as coercive. New York mayor Fiorello LaGuardia, never one for reticence, joined the clamor. On his Sunday radio program LaGuardia touted the work of the Mayor's Committee on Baseball, which was preparing to issue a report criticizing the three baseball teams and calling for immediate action. The mayor predicted that, as a result of the committee's work, "baseball would shortly begin signing Negro players."[27]

It was amid this mood, on October 23, 1945, that Rickey revealed his secret, introducing twenty-six-year-old Jackie Robinson to the New York press and announcing his signing of a minor league contract with the Dodgers organization. While it wasn't the huge national story that Robinson's eventual debut in the majors would be eighteen months later, his initial signing was a very big deal and stimulated significant discussion. Not all the reactions were positive, but many were, though probably the most common observation expressed was skepticism regarding Robinson's realistic likelihood of achieving success as a big-league player, given that while he'd been well known as a collegiate football and track star, his baseball experience was limited.

The public reaction from the community of major league baseball owners and executives could best be described as "guarded." Commissioner Albert "Happy" Chandler, National League president Ford Frick, and American League president Will Harridge were all conveniently "unavailable for comment." Philadelphia Athletics owner Connie Mack tersely stated: "I'm not familiar with the move and don't know Robinson. I wouldn't care to comment." Eddie Collins, general manager of the Boston Red Sox, and Alva Bradley, owner of the Cleveland Indians, both denied the existence of a color line. Collins noted that the Red Sox had given Robinson a tryout and asserted, though it was patently untrue, that Black players "always have a chance to prove themselves in the minors." Bradley pursued the same convoluted logic, arguing that "Colored players have never been discriminated against in the major leagues. They have simply never been able to get into the minor leagues to get the proper training for major league competition." Most other executives remained silent on the issue.

For his part Horace Stoneham offered a qualified endorsement of the Robinson signing. "It is a fine way to start the program," he stated. "But we have hundreds of returning servicemen and only if they fail to make the grade will we have room for new players."[28] Indeed, by the end of 1946 approximately three-quarters of the eleven million Americans who'd been in the military would be demobilized. Therefore, however sincere Stoneham's enthusiasm for Rickey's "fine way to start the program" of racial integration in baseball, he was clearly correct in acknowledging that the glut of players returning to baseball from military service was going to be intense.

To help accommodate the returning hordes, for the 1946 season the size of major-league rosters was expanded: the standard forty-man total roster was enlarged to forty-eight, and the mid-season active roster, normally set at twenty-five, was stretched to thirty, with final "cut-down day" moved back from mid-May to June 15. Accordingly, every team in 1946 would undertake an extraordinary rate of player turnover. The intense competition for playing time and roster spots was abnormally stressful, given that the great majority of players would end up without a job. Moreover, even for those who would make the harrowing cut, the oversupply of labor gave all the salary negotiation leverage to ownership.

This created an atmosphere in which many players were suddenly open, as never before, to an offer to pursue their athletic careers in new and exotic locales. Jorge Pasquel, president of the Mexican League, was eager to launch that venture into "major-league" status and saw the U.S. ballplayer surplus as his opportunity. Through the winter and early spring months of 1946, Pasquel and his representatives openly courted countless major and minor league players. The U.S. players were contractually forbidden by the reserve clause to accept any offers, but as an "outlaw"—unaffiliated with stateside "Organized Baseball"—Pasquel's Mexican League paid no heed. He was apparently willing to spend whatever he wished, and that became the driving force.

Pasquel wanted everyone he could get and reportedly made "blank contract" offers to the likes of Joe DiMaggio, Bob Feller, Stan Musial, and Ted Williams. Alas, he could persuade no superstar to jump his way. But he would find success with several lesser-paid big leaguers, including five from Stoneham's New York Giants: outfielder Danny Gardella, infielders George Hausmann and Nap Reyes, and pitchers Sal Maglie and Adrian Zabala. Alarmed, in late March, Commissioner Chandler announced that any stray player who failed to report to his U.S. team within ten days would be banned from Organized Baseball for five years. Nonetheless, all of the Giants' defectors stayed south, willing to accept the U.S. ban in exchange for fat new Pasquel-funded paychecks. And it didn't stop there. Despite full awareness of Chandler's edict, in late April 1946 Giants star relief pitcher Ace Adams said, "Adios."[29]

Over the course of the 1946 season, reports filtered back that perhaps everything wasn't quite so sunny down in Old Mexico. There were shabby playing conditions and dodgy accommodations as well as the big question of Pasquel's capacity to fulfill his lavish contract obligations, given that growth in Mexican League attendance wasn't keeping up with increased expenses. In 1947 and '48 Pasquel's ambitious Mexican League scheme would fall apart. The banned U.S. players straggled away from Mexico to become outlaw-league nomads, and several of them (most notably Gardella) filed suit against Major League Baseball in objection to the ban on constitutional grounds. In 1949, fearing this legal challenge to the reserve clause, MLB would settle with every banned player and permit their return.

Like everyone else, the Giants came into the 1946 season with pent-up hope, but they also had legitimate reasons for optimism. In 1942, the last season with a "real" roster, the Giants had finished in third place, propelled by the slugging duo of Johnny Mize and Mel Ott. Both were now four years older, but neither yet seemed to be "too" old. Mize would be thirty-three, an age at which many stars (such as Ott) had remained productive. While this year's Ott would be thirty-seven, he'd performed as a regular and a star throughout the war, slowing down in right field and giving himself more days off but remaining among the game's most productive power hitters.

And Stoneham spent lavishly to acquire a third star to join them in the heart of the Giants' order. On January 5, 1946, Stoneham parted with a whopping $175,000 in straight cash—among the very largest such transactions in baseball history—to purchase catcher Walker Cooper from the St. Louis Cardinals. Cooper was thirty-one years old; he'd served most of the 1945 season in the navy but was the Cards' first-string catcher for their pennant-winning seasons of 1942, '43, and '44, an All-Star each time, a right-handed hitter of excellent quality, with extra-base power and a career batting average of .298. For reasons undisclosed, Cooper was unhappy with the Cardinals. He confirmed that he'd asked to be traded and said that he considered going with the Giants "the best break I ever had."[30]

Asked to comment on his big spending, Stoneham reasoned: "I figure that when you buy baseball players you should either pay a lot for a good one who will make your club, or buy the $10,000 to $15,000 players who might develop but don't set you back too much if they don't. It's the $35,000 players who break your back."[31]

Stoneham's confidence was further expressed in full-on investment in the farm system. With no more player shortages to worry about, Hubbell was given the green light to hire scouts, sign prospects, and stock the largest system the Giants organization had ever put together: seventeen minor league teams. Beginning in 1947, Hubbell would employ not just Jack Schwarz but also Clarence "Bubber" Jonnard as full-time lieutenants overseeing the operation.

But 1946 would prove to be a Giants season in which just about everything would go wrong. On Opening Day, in his first at bat of the year, Mel Ott whacked a two-run homer. But the next day Ott tweaked a knee diving for a fly ball and had to sit out for a few days. When back in the lineup, he struggled at the plate and then sat himself back down for a couple of weeks. He tried some more intermittent starts but utterly failed to find his stroke and eventually just benched himself. Master Melvin would play in just thirty-one games in 1946, while recording a pitiful batting average of .074, or five for sixty-eight. The Opening Day homer was the last he would ever hit.

Walker Cooper spent his first year with the Giants unable to shake off a nagging elbow injury. He took part in just eighty-seven games and compiled a batting average of .268, far below his standard. Johnny Mize appeared to be the one big name delivering as expected. In early August he was hitting .339 and leading the league in home runs but was hit by a pitch and broke a finger. He missed more than a month, then in his first game back, Mize broke his toe in a collision at first base and was out for the season.

Ott was still unable to figure out a productive way to make use of Babe Young. He gave Young another shot at the center field job, but not on a sustained basis, before again relegating him to strict pinch hitter status. Young finally got a chance to play regularly at first base when Mize was out, and he hit well then, but still it was another mostly lost season for the now thirty-year-old Young. (In the early 1947 season Young would be deployed by Ott only as a pinch hitter until he was traded in June for a journeyman relief pitcher.)

The 1946 Giants had an 11–10 record on May 11, good for a single day in third place, but they lost the next six in a row and would never again sniff .500. They achieved zero winning months. They finished in last place, with a record of 61–93. As if that weren't humiliating enough, there were the Dodgers across town, enjoying another splendid year. They finished in a first-place tie with St. Louis, before dropping a best-of-three playoff to the Cardinals. Branch Rickey's disappointment at winding up in second was assuredly lightened by the fact that they set a National League attendance record, drawing nearly 1.8 million to cozy Ebbets Field.

The Dodgers, indeed, were in a position to crack wise at the Giants' expense—and Leo Durocher was never one to miss a chance. It was July 5, 1946, and the Dodgers were warming up to play the Giants at the Polo Grounds. Brooklyn broadcaster Red Barber was needling Durocher about the five home runs the Giants had hit over the course of the previous day's double-header. Several sportswriters were within earshot, and multiple slightly differing versions of the conversation would appear in the various papers.

Barber's teasing got Durocher going, no doubt as intended. The Brooklyn manager looked across the diamond at the muscular, ponderous Giants hitters and their amiable manager, Mel Ott, whose career total of 511 home runs wasn't just the National League record; it was the record by a margin of more than 150. "Home runs?" snorted "Leo the Lip," as if anyone could think that the mere act of hitting a ball over a fence was supposed to be impressive.

"But Ott's a nice guy," offered Barber.

"A nice guy!" Durocher erupted. "I've been in baseball a long time. Do you know a nicer guy in the world than Mel Ott? He's a nice guy. In last place! Where am I? In first place. I'm in first place. The nice guys are over there in last place, not in this dugout."[32]

Or something like that, anyway. In fact the Giants had spent the past month or so bouncing between last place and seventh, and the Durocher quotation as originally published in the *New York Journal-American* was "The nice guys are all over there, in seventh place."[33] But shortly afterward the headline in *The Sporting News* recapping the story was "'Nice Guys' Wind Up in Last Place, Scoffs Lippy," and Leo the Lip's most vivid catchphrase was launched forever.[34]

But the Giants really did wind up the 1946 season in last place, and Mel Ott was, without question, a genuinely nice guy. So, indeed, was Ott's boss, the "affable" Horace Stoneham. But with this 1946 humiliation at hand, the sporting press began to target the Giants' owner with criticism of a sort he'd never before received and definitely not of a sort that his "not affable" father had known. The emerging thesis was that Horace Stoneham was just too nice a guy for the rough-and-tumble baseball business.

A *Collier's* magazine article that appeared in the winter of 1946–47 lampooned the Giants' owner. As a trade negotiator, it contended, Stoneham was overmatched by more shrewd operators such as Sam Breadon of the Cardinals and Branch Rickey of the

Dodgers, and the article mocked Stoneham's penchant for reacquiring veterans who'd played for his team years earlier. These players were called members of Stoneham's "Two-Timers Club," performing as older, slower versions of their former selves. Such players were presented as evidence of Stoneham's endearing personality traits of loyalty and sentimentality: he considered the baseball team he'd inherited to be part of his family, and he seemed to want everyone who donned its uniform to gather with him forever around his ever-welcoming fireplace.[35]

Thus was born a certain public image of Horace Stoneham, a caricature, as a well-meaning softie, warmly welcoming all within his clubby circle while being routinely outsmarted by competitors who were more cynical and less forgiving. It was an image Stoneham would never shed, resting as it did on some obvious level of truth, though like many caricatures, it failed to capture the complicated layers of reality.

In fact, Stoneham was seriously concerned by his team's bad 1946 showing, and the papers openly speculated about whether nice-guy Mel Ott's job was in jeopardy. Ott remained tremendously popular with the fans, but the team hadn't been in the first division since 1942. Debate was conducted regarding the extent to which the team's lackluster performance during the war could be written off, but 1946 hadn't been a war year. It was widely understood that Stoneham was asking himself the same questions. A rumor made the rounds that the Giants' owner had contacted San Francisco Seals manager Lefty O'Doul to inquire whether he'd be interested in replacing Ott, but according to this story, O'Doul didn't want to leave his West Coast hometown.

The sports columnists speculated about Stoneham's deliberations. Certainly, the club needed improvement, but the crushing injuries to Mize and Cooper weren't likely to happen again, and there was a lot of young talent ripening on Hubbell's prodigious farms. Moreover, the New York Giants' business had performed quite well financially in 1946, and Stoneham was feeling no pressure from his shareholders to replace Ott. Indeed, there were four more years to go on Ott's contract, so firing him would be a wasteful fiscal move. And of course, Mel Ott was among Stoneham's dearest friends and one of the very finest men—yes, nicest guys—he could ever hope to know. Stoneham didn't want to replace Ott and decided that at this point he didn't need to either. Ott would be back to manage the Giants in 1947.[36]

There were, in fact, positive portents. The postwar attendance boom had delivered a franchise record 1,219,873 fans to the Polo Grounds despite the last-place performance. And the team, despite all its setbacks, had led the National League in home runs with 121. Thirteen of those long balls, along with a .282 batting average, had been contributed by twenty-five-year-old Willard Marshall, stepping forward as the team's primary center fielder. Another impressive young hitter on hand, flashing a hot bat as a September call-up after blasting 26 homers for Jersey City, was twenty-two-year-old Bobby Thomson.

The 1946 Giants' pitching struggled overall, but two young left-handers, Dave Koslo and Monte Kennedy, had emerged as effective starters. Another highly promising pitching prospect was twenty-six-year-old right-hander Larry Jansen, purchased at the close of the '46 season from the Giants' San Francisco affiliate, in which he'd been the sensation of the Pacific Coast League with a 30–6 record and a glittering 1.57 ERA.

6

We Knew Segregation Was Wrong

The 1946 New York Giants' league-leading total of 121 team home runs wasn't a remarkable figure by historical standards. The Giants' franchise record for home runs in a season was 143, set in 1930, and they'd exceeded the 121 mark four additional times. The National League record for team homers was 171, set by the Chicago Cubs of 1930, powered by Hack Wilson's league record 56 big flies. The major league record was 182 by the 1936 Yankees, with Lou Gehrig contributing a career-high 49. While the Giants entered 1947 with home run power as their key strength, there was no reason to perceive the team as an all-time great lineup of sluggers, particularly with Ott's bat no longer productive. No one anticipated what was about to happen.

But in the season's home opener against the Dodgers on April 18, the Giants clubbed six home runs in a 10–4 romp. By the end of May the 1947 Giants had accumulated 41 homers in 35 games, a record-threatening pace. And then they got hot. In the month of June the Giants blasted 44, bringing their total to 85 through 61 games, and it was clear that something special was underway. At the season's precise midpoint, the 77th game of the scheduled 154, the Giants had launched 118 home runs, very nearly their season-long league-leading total of 1946.

On August 2, in the second game of a doubleheader in Pittsburgh, Bobby Thomson's 21st of the year was the team's 144th, surpassing the franchise record. The National League mark of 171 went down on August 24, and on the first of September, Giants third baseman Jack "Lucky" Lohrke hit their 183rd of the year, a new major league record with a month still left to play.

The final tally of 221 buried the Yankees' old record by more than 20 percent. It was a previously unimaginable feat, a silly number. The barrage was led by Mize, who hammered a career-high 51. The Big Cat scored 137 runs and drove in 138, both also career highs and major league–leading totals. Willard Marshall blossomed into stardom with 36 home runs. Walker Cooper, whose previous most was 13, muscled up for 35 big flies. Thomson, in his first full year, belted 29 while taking over as the center fielder, with Marshall now full-time in right.

It was well understood that the Polo Grounds' long, narrow horseshoe configuration, yielding comically short porches of 279 feet down the left field line and 257 to right, provided an extremely friendly home run environment, even with the cavernously deep center field.[1] So there's no question that the 1947 Giants' home run total was enhanced by playing half their games in the Polo Grounds: that year the ballpark yielded home runs (for the Giants and their opponents combined) at a rate 46 percent above the league-average yard, a mark typical of how the Polo Grounds played throughout the late 1940s and early 1950s. But to conclude that their achievement was a park effect illusion would be a miscalculation. The 1947 Giants hit 131 home runs at home, far and away the most in the league, but they also hit 90 on the road, also far and away the most in the league and also a new league record. Their power production was completely genuine.

The fans simply loved it, and the Giants in 1947 set a new franchise attendance record by a mile, drawing 1.6 million. Eddie Brannick, as he merrily toted up gate receipts, affectionately nicknamed the long-balling crew "the Windowbreakers," and the colorful moniker stuck. After the season Stoneham was so delighted that he presented every member of the team with a 14 karat gold ring, with the inscription "New York Giants 1947 HR Record" encircling a red baseball diamond, with "221" at its center.

But as much fun as it all was, the 1947 Giants weren't an especially good ball club overall. They were briefly in first place in June but then fell back and never challenged again, finishing at

81–73, in fourth. While the team was terrific at generating runs (830, the most in the major leagues), they weren't adept at preventing them (allowing 761, second most in the majors). They led the major leagues in errors, while converting balls in play into outs at a below-average rate. Rookie Larry Jansen was marvelous, going 21–5 with a 3.16 ERA, but beyond him the pitching was a headache, compiling a ballpark-adjusted earned run average that was fourteenth worst among the sixteen big-league staffs. And while shattering the record for home runs might be celebrated as the year's big event in some seasons, in the National League of 1947, it was fully overshadowed by the doings of—who else?—the Dodgers.

The journey taken by Jackie Robinson, from his signing with the Brooklyn organization in October 1945 to his major league debut in April 1947, was laden with challenges. In his 1946 spring training, as a minor leaguer in Florida, his team struggled to secure not just lodging for Robinson but local ballparks that would permit him to play. Clay Hopper, the manager of the Montreal Royals farm club, to which Robinson was assigned, didn't want him and had to be forced by Branch Rickey to accept his presence. Throughout the International League season Robinson was subjected to vicious taunts and threats. Nonetheless, he led the league in batting average, on-base percentage, and runs scored and was second in stolen bases.

During spring training in 1947, Fred "Dixie" Walker, the Dodgers' star right fielder, drew up a petition demanding that the Dodgers keep Robinson off the big-league roster and asked his teammates to sign it. Manager Leo Durocher immediately called a team meeting. He was furious. Durocher declared that Robinson was playing, whether they liked it or not. "I don't care if the guy is yellow or black," he roared, no doubt punctuating with choice expletives. "I'm the manager of this team, and I say he plays." Then, for his clincher, Durocher appealed to everyone's common denominator. "I say he can make us rich. And if any of you can't use the money, I'll see that you're traded."[2]

Alongside his real flaws and abundant bad behavior, all evidence demonstrates that Durocher was full-on supportive not only of Robinson specifically but of the concept of racial integration in baseball generally. It's easy to find fault with Durocher but not in this regard. His performance in this episode was among the great deeds in the history of baseball managing.

Still, Durocher, being Durocher, also engaged in reckless behavior with gamblers and organized crime figures, and just prior to Opening Day of 1947, Commissioner Albert "Happy" Chandler suspended the Dodgers' manager for a period of one year, for "conduct detrimental to baseball." So it was that Jackie Robinson's fraught and fateful rookie major league season would not take place with Leo Durocher as his skipper. Instead, that role would be filled by sixty-two-year-old Burt Shotton, a faithful employee of Rickey. Calm, dignified, and old-fashioned—he and Connie Mack were the last big-league managers to wear a suit and tie in the dugout instead of a uniform—Shotton was as different from Durocher as could be. Perhaps, in his way, he served as a more helpful figure to Robinson through his 1947 trials than a scene-stealing Durocher would have. Or perhaps not. In any case Shotton was steady as a rock.[3]

What we know is what Robinson knew—better than anyone—that he was being relentlessly tested, on two equally crucial scales. The first was his measure as a man: could he withstand the suffocating scrutiny and pressure, hold the moral high ground, and behave impeccably through punishing emotional ordeals? And simultaneously, his measure as a baseball player: was his presence on the roster and in the lineup legitimately justified by hard, objective, won-and-lost results? Was he actually helping the Dodgers win, as Durocher claimed he would?

The degree to which Robinson would succeed at passing both tests is staggering. Fiction could hardly have invented a more worthy heroic protagonist, off the field and on. Over that 1947 season, while enduring the brunt of bitter resistance, Robinson's performance on the field of play was amazing. It wasn't just that he was extremely good, a remarkable enough fact given that Robinson was twenty-eight years old and his entire experience playing professional baseball before 1947 consisted of one year at AAA on top of a partial single season in the Negro National

League. It was, instead, the *way* in which Robinson was really, really good that was the most striking.

Certainly, he was a superb physical specimen, with gifts of strength, speed, and agility. But his success as a baseball player wasn't just an expression of his natural "tools." The performance profile of a merely "toolsy" prospect is all too familiar to fans of every team: the strapping young fellow impresses everyone on the practice field, but his real-game performance, while including some dazzling high points, is agonizingly unreliable. His physical talent is great, but his mastery of the finer skills involved in winning baseball games is not so much in evidence. Our typical toolsy prospect hits for power but not for average, draws few walks while striking out too much, commits base-running blunders, and plays erratic defense. Pundits anticipating Robinson's performance, with all sensible empirical experience on their side, readily predicted such results from the toolsy-but-raw Jackie Robinson.

He could not possibly have proven them more wrong. From the beginning Robinson performed as a superbly nuanced *baseball player*, displaying ease with the sport's finest points of skill as though he'd been in the majors for years. He had formidable natural power at the plate but didn't focus on pulling the ball for home runs, instead adroitly spraying it to all fields, like a cagey veteran. He was a terrific bunter. His strike zone discipline was extraordinary; from the get-go he knew exactly when to swing or take. He ran the bases with controlled ferocity; he knew when to go but also when not to go, and indeed, his feints were as much a feature of his justly celebrated base running as his dashes. He adapted to multiple defensive positions, rapidly grasping the footwork and relay positioning fundamentals. His performance was steady and consistent, not prone to slumps.

Much more than just a great athlete, Robinson was a particularly great practitioner of the sport—indeed, the art—of baseball. His exceptional intelligence was manifest. This was perhaps the most devastatingly effective argument on his behalf. He laid waste to the notion that Negroes, regardless of athletic prowess, just weren't capable of excelling at "inside baseball." This guy was an instant master of it.

Robinson was voted National League Rookie of the Year in 1947 (a brand-new award), a judgment plainly warranted with or without the Jim Crow–defiant backstory. He was that good, and everyone could see it. The Dodgers won the pennant. They set yet another National League record for attendance with 1.8 million. Robinson couldn't possibly have more fully justified Rickey's high-risk decision to bring him in, and Rickey's record of success in Brooklyn was dramatically mounting.

Leo Durocher, his suspension served, returned to the Brooklyn dugout as manager for 1948. His roster was reshaped by a couple of significant off-season transactions. First, Rickey granted Dixie Walker's wish to be traded, sending him off to Pittsburgh in a remarkably sharp deal that netted the Dodgers infielder Billy Cox and pitcher Elwin "Preacher" Roe. And in early 1948 Rickey sold second baseman Eddie Stanky to the Braves, clearing room for Robinson to shift from first base.

Horace Stoneham, meanwhile, stood pat with his Window-breakers roster. Ott would introduce two modifications in 1948: twenty-one-year-old rookie Carroll "Whitey" Lockman, a heralded all-around prospect who would have made the club in 1947 if not sidelined by a broken ankle, was installed as the regular left fielder; and strong-hitting veteran Sid Gordon was shifted from left field to third base. But mostly the Giants were status quo.

Though their rate of blasting home runs cooled off from the historic 1947 pace, the Giants remained the most powerful club in the league. And in the season's early weeks, Giants pitching was much improved over 1947, and so into June the Giants were jockeying for first place.

This year, for once, it was in Brooklyn that things were discombobulated. As May turned to June, the defending champion Dodgers were languishing in seventh place. Everyone was stunned. Both the local and national press were playing the how-the-mighty-have-fallen angle, and there was rampant criticism of Rickey's choice to deal away Walker and Stanky. During an eight-game losing streak, Ebbets Field fans booed Durocher, a sound heard never before. Attendance was down, and Rickey knew he would be hearing about that from his ownership group, including the particularly vocal and hard-nosed Walter O'Malley.[4]

Worse yet, Jackie Robinson was struggling. Robinson had reported to spring training about 30 pounds over his ideal playing weight of 185 to 190 pounds. Durocher was shocked and angry when he saw Robinson's condition. "You look like an old woman," the manager bellowed. "Look at all that fat!" The reinstalled skipper drove Robinson extremely hard to shape up, drilling him for hours under the broiling Dominican sun in the spring of 1948. "Robinson will shag flies until his tongue hangs out," Durocher vowed. "He was thin for Shotton, but he's fat for me."[5]

Over the first half of 1948, as he played himself into shape, Jackie Robinson was a disappointment. Though he was able to keep his batting average around .300, he wasn't running the bases with anything close to his former verve: he didn't steal a single base until late June. And even with Stanky out of the way at second base, Robinson's range in the field was so limited that through the end of June, Durocher had still deployed him more frequently at first base than at second.

That Robinson was overweight was hardly the fault of his manager. But as the team continued to drag, mired in sixth place as the Fourth of July approached, Rickey began to think Durocher himself was off his game as well. Their relationship went back to the early 1930s, with the Cardinals, and Rickey had long regarded the strong-willed and ambitious young Leo with an almost paternal concern. In Rickey's estimation something seemed to be missing in Durocher's attitude since his return from the suspension. Rickey couldn't put his finger on it, but Leo seemed to have lost some of the intensity that had always been his trademark. Rickey found himself wondering if Durocher's recent marriage (to Laraine Day) had rendered the fiery Durocher a bit too domesticated. "The management of a baseball club is a jealous mistress," Rickey would say. "In earthly terms, he can have no other God."

In seasons past Durocher and Rickey would vehemently argue about player personnel decisions before reaching consensus. Now Rickey was sensing less vigor from Durocher. When the

Dodgers stumbled into a six-game losing streak in late June 1948, Rickey decided that Durocher had to go. But Rickey, tough-minded though he was, was also a gentle personality and could rarely rouse himself to fire an employee, especially someone as dear to him as his prodigal son, Durocher. He struggled to decide upon the best way to handle the situation.[6]

Simultaneously, the Giants' fortunes were souring. A slump knocked them from first place in mid-June to fifth by the Fourth of July. Stoneham, not for the first time but more seriously than ever before, considered whether it was time to replace his beloved Ott.

Rickey, trying to avoid the hard conversation, sent traveling secretary Harold Parrott to the Ebbets Field clubhouse on July Fourth as his emissary to Durocher. Parrott told him that Rickey wanted him to resign, and Durocher flatly refused. "The old man will have to fire me himself, face-to-face, and he hasn't got the guts," roared Leo the Lip.[7] Having stalemated Rickey, the media-savvy Durocher then leaked word of the situation to columnist Bill Corum of the *New York Journal-American*, and for the next week speculation swirled in the press that Rickey and Durocher were at odds. Therefore, Horace Stoneham, like everyone else who could read a newspaper—including Mel Ott—had to be aware that Durocher's term as Dodger manager might soon be at its end.

A version frequently offered as to what happened next is that Stoneham somehow decided that the manager he wanted to replace Ott was none other than former Brooklyn manager Burt Shotton, now sixty-three years old and quietly back in semiretirement in Florida. So, Stoneham contacted Rickey, this story goes, and asked for permission to contact Shotton, who remained under contract with the Dodgers as a "scout." Rickey then supposedly told Stoneham that Shotton wasn't available but that, say, how about this, he could have Durocher instead, and Stoneham, surprised and delighted, then moved to hire Durocher. This version of the story has persisted, probably because it perfectly supports the easy narratives of Rickey as a brilliant manipulator of events and Stoneham as a dumb-lucky bumbler. It's also not true.

No evidence indicates that Stoneham ever had the slightest interest in bringing "Kindly Old Burt Shotton" (as Dodger players called Shotton behind his back) out of retirement to manage the Giants.[8] Moreover, it's not plausible that Stoneham was unaware of Durocher's precarious status with the Dodgers, as Durocher himself had seen to it that the story was known to the public. Instead, the truth is very likely the far simpler sequence of events that Stoneham would present in his press conference on July 16, 1948, in which he announced that the New York Giants had replaced Mel Ott as manager with Leo Durocher. The reporters asked, when had Stoneham decided to make the change? He answered, at about one o'clock the day before. Was the change a surprise to Ott? Stoneham answered, whether or not truthfully: "I had already discussed this with Ottie. He was the one who suggested getting Durocher if it were possible."

What about getting the okay to talk to Durocher? Stoneham responded, "I called [National League president] Ford Frick and obtained his approval. I then contacted Rickey and told him we would like to have Leo manage the Giants. I was agreeably surprised when Rickey gave me permission to negotiate with Leo. I met with Leo about 10:30 last night at his apartment, and we came to terms pretty quickly."[9]

Whatever the background sequence of events had been, the announcement that Lippy Leo Durocher was suddenly manager of the Giants was a shock of seismic proportion. For fans of both teams, it was unbelievable. It was front-page banner headline news in the *New York Daily News*:

LIP REPLACES OTT!

BURT BACK WITH FLOCK!!!

It wasn't clear from whose point of view the transaction was most stunning. To Brooklyn fans, the concept of their brassy, pugnacious hero Durocher skippering the archrival Giants had never been imagined, and for Giants' fans, to have hired this most reviled of filthy villains was equally beyond the pale. Yet here it was.[10]

Among the many surprises was that Horace Stoneham had not only recruited his team's fiercest enemy but that he'd actually fired Master Melvin, whom everybody loved, no one more than Stoneham himself. He admitted to being brought to tears by the decision, and Stoneham's twenty-three-year-old daughter—whom her father adored—was so fondly attached to Mel Ott that she refused to speak to her father for a month.[11]

Stoneham used the opportunity of the press conference introducing Durocher to announce that the Giants were forever retiring Ott's uniform number 4 in tribute.[12] Al Laney of the *New York Herald Tribune* reported on the reactions of the Giants players at the Hotel Schenley in Pittsburgh: "It was as though a wake were being held in the lobby. Men sat around or wandered around, saying nothing. Ott was through. The players had an air of bereavement, as though a well-loved member of the family had died suddenly and unexpectedly. Most appeared stunned."[13]

As for Ott himself, it wasn't as though he was tossed into the street. He remained under contract with the Giants through 1950, and Stoneham was assigning him to work with Hubbell in the farm system. Still, though Ott was gracious as always in public, privately he took it hard. Once the decision was official, Ott walked manfully to the phone to call his wife. He did his best to suppress his disappointment, but when his beloved Mickey, at the other end of the phone, began to cry, he cried too. Mel Ott was never any good at faking anything.[14]

That manner of authentic vulnerability—his sheer niceness—was, of course, the reason everyone who knew Ott liked him so much. He related easily with everyone in the organization. A few days after Ott was replaced, he went to the Polo Grounds to clean out his office. He saw Giants clubhouse man Eddie Logan, who recalled: "Mel had such a great sense of humor, even under such circumstances. The first thing he said when I came in to offer sympathy was that he was glad to get out of there because I was the worst clubhouse man he had ever seen. I told him, 'Yeah, but I haven't been fired,' and then he laughed and took out the bottles of Scotch and Bourbon that were always in the manager's office, and we sat down and polished them off."[15]

As the dust settled following the explosive announcement of Durocher's jump to the Giants, the true meaning of it began to become clear. By sacking the beloved Ott in favor of his utter antithesis, Stoneham had acted in a way thoroughly at odds with his established image as a too-nice owner afraid to upset his happy family and make the bold move. It was a plain admission by Stoneham that the status quo was not acceptable, that all prior assumptions were now in question, and, whatever it might turn out to be, that a new Giants chapter was about to be written.

It may have been true, as Stoneham said in his press conference, that he was acting upon Mel Ott's suggestion when seeking to hire Durocher. Most likely, however, was that Ott was only suggesting an idea to Stoneham that he'd already arrived at himself.

Stoneham and Durocher had known each other since the 1937 World Series, when Stoneham had welcomed Durocher to New York by drinking the night away with him. No doubt their paths had crossed many times since then, at Toots Shor's place for sure and quite likely at other of the sorts of watering holes that both were known to frequent. Durocher's record as Dodgers manager was superb, and Stoneham recognized his exceptional talent, even packaged as it was with a high-maintenance ego. Stoneham knew what he was getting. Gone would be the days of amiable, no-drama Mel Ott in the dugout, and coming, instead, would be perpetual rhubarbs and controversies. This wasn't going to be easy. But Stoneham accepted the inevitable headaches as the price to pay for a meaningfully more competitive ball club.

Horace Stoneham was forty-five years old. He'd been at the helm of the Giants' franchise—the gift grandly provided by his father—for a dozen years, and his record of accomplishment was not impressive. He knew it. He was dissatisfied. He was ready to do whatever he had to do to achieve the kind of results that would have made Pop proud. That would mean listening to Durocher's input and taking action on his suggestions, however hard they might be to hear.

As with so much Durocher lore, different sources provide different versions of the ensuing tale. But whether it occurred soon upon his arrival with the Giants or as a post-1948 review of their situation—or, perhaps, at both of those times and others as well—it's certain that Durocher's advice to Stoneham was that the roster needed a fundamental overhaul. The smart-aleck phrase all versions have Durocher using is "Back up the truck."

Which players should stay? Who should go? Was a major overhaul necessary? Durocher's pithy assessment to his new boss, to back up the truck, meant the Giants needed to liquidate the roster of its current inventory and completely rebuild. It was tough advice for Stoneham, who loved every single one of his ballplayers and held a particular affinity for his Windowbreakers. "Powder River" was Stoneham's favorite turn of phrase for a batting order presenting sequential power bats, the style of baseball he most loved. The Giants were the most prolific home run-hitting team in all of baseball history. But Durocher told Stoneham that this approach wasn't working. They spent many days and nights arguing the questions, nights of much disagreement and much alcohol. "To say that Stoneham can drink," Durocher would quip, "is to say that Sinatra can sing."[16]

Yet as blustery and dismissive as Durocher's assessment may have been, in fact he didn't introduce any significant changes to the Giants' lineup upon his arrival in mid-1948. Instead, he just rode out the season sticking with the deployments Ott had chosen. The only change Durocher made was to move twenty-six-year-old right-hander Sheldon Jones from the bullpen to the regular starting rotation, and there Jones flourished. But mostly Durocher stood pat—interestingly, displaying patience and careful assessment, qualities he was perhaps developing as a maturing manager—and the Giants under Durocher in 1948 weren't much different than the Giants under Ott in 1948, going 41–38 for Durocher after 37–38 for Ott. He inherited the team in fourth place, and they finished in fifth.

Nor would any backing up of the truck take place in the 1948–49 off-season, a period of months in which the Giants would execute exactly zero major transactions. Durocher and Stoneham, whether as part of a strategic design or, more likely, because they just couldn't yet agree or decide upon what to do, were in practice playing a long game. They would be making changes of a most fundamental sort but not just yet.

June 1949 brought a joyous event to Horace Stoneham's family. Valleda Mary Stoneham, born February 2, 1925, was the elder child of Horace and Valleda. Though named for her mother, in public she was normally known as "Mary," and within the family, for reasons lost to history, she was "Wootchie."

As the daughter of Horace and the granddaughter of C. A. Stoneham, from her youngest days Wootchie was a regular subject for newspaper photographers and columnists. A grainy news photo survives from the mid-1930s of Wootchie at the Polo Grounds with her mother and her little brother, Charles (named for his grandfather but always known as "Pete"), happily munching on hot dogs. In another from the same period Wootchie and Pete are isolated in close-up, leaning over what's likely the Giants' dugout, she comfortingly draping her arm around Pete's neck and clutching his elbow.

In both shots Wootchie stands out as a strikingly attractive girl, with a broad, vivid smile and a posture of supreme confidence. She graduated from high school at the Convent of the Sacred Heart on East Ninety-First Street, on the Upper East Side, and then attended Finch College, an exclusive women's liberal arts school in the same neighborhood. Later, as a twenty-year-old, she was the cover model for *Cue* magazine, a New York City arts-and-entertainment weekly, mugging with a pack of Chesterfield cigarettes. She had inherited none of her father's shyness and all of her mother's spunky vivacity. Wootchie Stoneham was a "catch," sought after, or at least wished for, by many a young Giants fan.

The suitor who would win her hand was a most impressive young man. Charles B. "Chuck" Rupert had grown up in a working-class family in Springdale, Pennsylvania, near Pittsburgh. Bright, energetic, and enterprising, through hard work he made his way to the University of Pittsburgh and earned a bachelors' degree in industrial engineering. Immediately upon graduation, Chuck Rupert was awarded by his congressman with an appointment to the United States Army Military Academy in

West Point, New York, the first ever from the town of Springdale to receive such an honor.

At some time during his West Point studies, Rupert had a day off and took the trip down the Hudson to visit New York City. He seems to have gone to a Giants game and some way or another found himself introduced to Wootchie Stoneham.

By the time Rupert graduated from West Point in 1945 and was commissioned as a second lieutenant, World War II was nearly over. But he found himself deployed into active service nonetheless. Trained as a pilot, Lieutenant Rupert flew numerous Douglas C-54 Skymaster missions into Germany as part of the Berlin Airlift in 1948–49.

Chuck Rupert was twenty-eight years old when he and Wootchie Stoneham were married, on Saturday, June 4, 1949, at St. Ignatius Loyola Catholic Church in New York City, at 980 Park Avenue.[17] The building had been dedicated in 1898, and it was, and still is, a glorious space. The Reverend Henry C. Avery, SJ, presided. The reception was held in the Jade and Basildon Rooms of the Waldorf-Astoria Hotel, the forty-seven-story Art Deco landmark completed in 1931.

It was a magnificent New York event. Many baseball luminaries were in attendance, certainly including, of course, Wootchie's dear Mel Ott. Horace and Valleda, at least for the day, were reunited in joyous celebration. In a photo they flank the beautiful white lace–gowned bride: Valleda looks radiant in a pastel dress, hat, and veil, with elbow-length white gloves and corsage, while Horace beams as well, dapper in a striped-pants three-piece suit with a glimmering watch chain across his vest, a silver-white handkerchief tucked just so in his pocket, and a white carnation boutonniere.

Among the groomsmen was Wootchie's brother, Pete, not quite twenty-two years old. The young man resembled his father and his grandfather but was more handsome than either, with a stronger jawline, thick dark hair, and piercing brown eyes. Another groomsman was tall, congenial twenty-seven-year-old Charles "Chub" Feeney, Wootchie and Pete's cousin and Horace's nephew.

Feeney had been taken under Horace's wing as a child, serving as the Giants' batboy at the Polo Grounds in the 1930s. Unlike his uncle, Feeney was a keen student and graduated from Dartmouth and then Fordham Law. He served as a U.S. naval officer in World War II, and upon his discharge in 1946, he went to work for Stoneham in the Giants' front office as vice president. As with Uncle Horace before him, Feeney was no empty-titled figurehead but was assigned real work and performed it seriously and well. By the time of Wootchie's wedding, he'd assumed broad responsibility in business administration.

Yet Chub Feeney, devoted though he was to his uncle, understood that he wasn't in the line of succession to be trained as Horace's understudy, to be groomed to one day take over as president, the heir to the controlling share of ownership of the National Exhibition Company. That was for Pete.

Horace Stoneham's son was attending Dartmouth. Pete would undergo no banishment to Copperopolis. How rigorous his dedication to university training or moderate his indulgence in campus partying is unknown. What's known is that Horace Stoneham would soon decide that Pete was ready to begin apprenticeship in the management of his father and his grandfather's New York Giants.

Jackie Robinson's ringing success with the Brooklyn Dodgers in 1947 quickly motivated thirty-three-year-old Bill Veeck Jr., the flamboyant owner of the Cleveland Indians and son of the previous Chicago Cubs owner, to integrate his own club. Young Veeck deserves great credit for this. But it's also true that Veeck hadn't gone first, and it's also true that the baseball magnate who had gone first was actively recruiting Veeck to go second.

Branch Rickey deeply wanted a second club to integrate. Such a development would reduce the intense pressure on Robinson and the Dodgers while also giving the greater enterprise a big vote of confidence. Looking around at his ownership brethren to find a likely candidate, Rickey quickly determined that Veeck was his man. Rickey understood that Veeck took much pleasure in ruffling the feathers of the conservative baseball establishment. The young owner found most fellow owners and general managers stuffy and inflexible and undoubtedly received fellow iconoclast Rickey's entreaties as a breath of fresh air. Red Barber describes the interaction between the two:

> Rickey, I'm certain, simply purred on the phone as he told Veeck how Robinson and the Dodgers had overflow crowds on the field at Pittsburgh, turned away thousands of fans at Cincinnati and Chicago, filled the park at St. Louis despite a transit strike, jammed the Polo Grounds, and that tickets for Ebbets Field were worth their weight in gold. Rickey would pause, puff his cigar, and then tell Veeck the fans were coming to games in Boston as they hadn't in years, and records were being set in Philadelphia. Yes, Robinson was a tremendous attraction. Yes, indeed.
>
> Veeck was never an "afraid man." Once he got an idea he thought had merit, he tried it. The more he talked with Rickey, and the more Robinson played and drew people with ready money in their eager hands, the more Veeck's eyes brightened. After all, it was his money he had in the Cleveland club, his finances weren't deep, and he was willing to shoot for the moon. He needed to.[18]

On July 5, 1947, Veeck signed twenty-three-year-old Larry Doby, who was generally considered the best young player in the Negro Leagues. Doby was leading the Negro National League in home runs and batting average, and Veeck decided to dispense with any minor league development and put him directly on the major league roster.[19] Nevertheless, Cleveland manager Lou Boudreau wouldn't rush the rookie and cautiously deployed Doby over the balance of the 1947 season, training him vigorously but giving him just twenty-nine game appearances, mostly as a pinch hitter.

Also in July 1947, Bill DeWitt, the general manager of the last-place St. Louis Browns, persuaded owner Richard Muckerman to step forward. DeWitt purchased two players from the Kansas City Monarchs: Willard Brown, a thirty-two-year-old star outfielder; and Hank Thompson, a twenty-one-year-old infield prospect. Like Veeck, DeWitt bypassed the minor leagues with his acquisitions and put them straight into the majors, but unlike the Indians, at DeWitt's request, St. Louis manager Herold "Muddy"

Ruel inserted both Thompson and Brown into the everyday start-ing lineup.

If Doby's experience in the American League in 1947 could be described as anticlimactic, languishing on the Cleveland bench, in St. Louis things turned out less well than that. A local newspa-per described Browns players as "none too happy over the addi-tion of two Negro players." Indeed, Alabama-born outfielder Paul Lehner delivered an ultimatum to the club, threatening to quit the team if Brown and Thompson were kept on. "The gloom that pervaded the dressing room and bench of the Browns was thick enough to make one gasp for air," one writer reported, "and tem-pers were taut." When Brown and Thompson joined the club, their teammates greeted them with glum silence.

Like Robinson and Doby, Brown and Thompson endured rac-ist taunts and brushback pitches, but with little organizational support.[20] Perhaps unsurprisingly, neither player performed impressively. As they failed to lift the Browns from the cellar, neither did they boost the Browns' meager home attendance. On the road Black fans poured out to see them, but in St. Louis, where Jackie Robinson had packed Sportsman's Park, the pres-ence of the two Black players had no effect on attendance. The Browns were quick to assess the experiment as a failure, and on August 23, barely a month after their signing, St. Louis released Brown and Thompson, and the first Black teammates in the major leagues became the first Blacks to be cut from a major league roster.

Still, the very next day, August 24, 1947, Brooklyn's Branch Rickey purchased the contract of twenty-seven-year-old pitcher Dan Bankhead from the Memphis Red Sox of the Negro Amer-ican League and brought him straight to the majors, rendering Bankhead and Jackie Robinson the second set of major league Black teammates. While Bankhead would make just four relief appearances with the Dodgers down the stretch in 1947, it was the case that within four months of Robinson's debut on the big-league field, four additional African American players had arrived. While none met with anything remotely comparable to Robinson's success, by the end of the 1947 season the "program" of racial integration in baseball, as Stoneham had termed it in 1945, was, however hesitantly, underway.

In 1947 twenty-five-year-old catcher Roy Campanella completed his second season in the Brooklyn minor league system, impressing observers as a can't-miss prospect for AAA Montreal. Twenty-one-year-old pitcher Don Newcombe, also in his second year in the Dodger chain, starred in the Class B New England League. Newcombe, the sole Black player on the Nashua roster, roomed with a white player on the road, another first in organized baseball.[21]

Bill DeWitt's Browns organization signed another Black player in 1947, twenty-three-year-old Chuck Harmon, a former basketball star at the University of Toledo, and he played in the Class C Canadian-American League. Also in that league was a third Black Dodgers prospect, eighteen-year-old Sammy Gee, "the Wonder Boy of the Detroit scholastic athletic circles."[22]

In 1948 Rickey promoted Campanella to the majors, and he took over as the Dodgers' starting catcher. Larry Doby, rewarding the Indians' patient handling, blossomed over the course of the 1948 season into an all-around star center fielder. In July, Veeck hired the legendary veteran Negro League superstar Leroy "Satchel" Paige onto his pitching staff, and he along with Doby would help Cleveland win the pennant and the World Series. The Indians' opponent in that series was impressed: Boston Braves' owner Lou Perini announced that there would be a "delegation of Negro players" in his 1949 training camp. Several other teams dispatched scouts to the Latin American winter leagues.[23]

Horace Stoneham's Giants had stood by, but they would no longer. The organization never issued a formal policy comment, but in the winter of 1948–49 they acquired and signed three Negro Leaguers: from the Kansas City Monarchs, twenty-three-year-old infielder Hank Thompson (the very same ballplayer who'd had the stint with the Browns in '47) and thirty-year-old pitcher John Ford "Speedball" Smith; and from the Newark Eagles, thirty-year-old outfielder Monte Irvin. The trio would be assigned to AAA for the start of the 1949 season.

"Of course we knew segregation was wrong," Chub Feeney would recall. "My uncle knew it and I knew it, but pure idealists we were not. Competing in New York, against the Yankees and the Dodgers, the resource we needed most was talent. In 1949, the Negro leagues were the most logical place in the world to look for ballplayers."[24] The integration of professional baseball was a complicated intersection, with dire implications for the Negro Leagues themselves. If stripped of their most attractive talent, the financial viability of the operation, never stable, faced a looming crisis.

It was in this suddenly new era in professional baseball's development that Alex Pompez, owner of the New York Cubans, and Horace Stoneham, his landlord at the Polo Grounds, took a fresh gaze at one another and began to cultivate a special relationship. Pompez recognized that he was being forced to design a new business model, and so he forged an agreement with Stoneham's Giants. Starting in 1949, Pompez's Cubans would operate informally as a farm team for the Giants—the first time a Negro League team served in such a capacity. The arrangement gave the Giants the first option to purchase New York Cuban players whom they deemed worthy. In return, the Cubans would play their home games exclusively at the Polo Grounds at a discounted rental rate, and Carl Hubbell would gain Pompez's guidance on which Negro Leaguers the Giants should sign.

The first transactions between the Giants and Cubans took place in the middle of the 1949 season: in June, Pompez sold the Cubans' player-manager and veteran star third baseman Ray Dandridge, along with their starting catcher, Rafael "Ray" Noble, and starting pitcher Dave Barnhill to the Giants for a total of $21,000. Thus, Pompez was able to stay afloat, but the long-term viability of the Cubans was further undermined.[25]

Another development that would have long-term implications was the hiring in 1949 of Russ Hodges as the team's primary radio and television broadcast voice. Born in Tennessee in 1910, Hodges was raised in Kentucky. He attended the University of Kentucky on a football scholarship but was injured and, instead, watched the games from the press box, working as a spotter and occasionally filling in as public address announcer. Hodges paid his way through law school at the University of Cincinnati in the 1930s by working at radio stations, and though he would pass the bar exam, he pursued his career as a sports broadcaster. Before joining the Giants, Hodges had called college and professional football games and major league baseball, including both Chicago teams, the Washington Senators, the Cincinnati Reds, and the New York Yankees.[26]

Hodges was never as literary in his voicings as a Red Barber, but he brought warm intelligence and an earthy, muscular spirit to his game calling. Though the Giants had been broadcasting their games since 1939, they'd never developed a particular "voice" of their team, but now they would, and Hodges soon become a great favorite of Giants fans. He would be a key figure in the team's commercial success for the next two decades.

With the roster and lineup configuration he'd inherited in July 1948 still essentially intact, Leo Durocher had the Giants playing well in the opening months of 1949. But in mid-June they hit a slump and tumbled to fifth place, and it was at this point that Stoneham acceded to Durocher's plea and began maneuvering that truck into place by the loading dock.

Catcher Walker Cooper was a mischievous, practical joking sort, a trait that didn't endear him to the hyperintense Durocher. Following his monster 35-homer, 122-RBI career year of 1947, Cooper had missed much of the 1948 season with injuries, and thus far in 1949 the thirty-four-year-old Cooper was hitting poorly. Stoneham agreed it was time to cut him loose. On June 13, 1949, Cooper was traded to Cincinnati for thirty-seven-year-old backup catcher Ray Mueller; the deal was essentially a salary dump, as Mueller was of marginal value. Twenty-six-year-old sophomore Wes Westrum, a superior defender with a questionable bat, was recalled from AAA (triple-A), and Durocher went with Westrum as his primary catcher from that point forward.

When Cooper departed for Cincinnati, he told Bill Roeder of the *New York World-Telegram*: "I've always felt that Durocher would ruin any good ball club. There's a lot of feeling on the Giants about the way Durocher handles men and pops off." The writers promptly relayed Cooper's parting shot to Durocher, and he responded in kind. "Have you got a nice, big bath towel?" Durocher sneered. "Well, send it to him. I'm tired of being a nice guy."[27]

Two of the Giants' newly signed ex–Negro Leaguers, Monte Irvin and Hank Thompson, were tearing it up in their minor league auditions, and on July 7, 1949, both were promoted to the majors. In typical Stoneham style the Giants did it quietly, unaccompanied by any Rickeyesque flourish, but twenty-seven months after Jackie Robinson's debut with Brooklyn, the New York Giants became the second National League ball club to racially integrate. From the modern perspective it's easy to conclude that the full-scale integration of baseball was inevitable. However, in 1949—with only two, the Dodgers and Indians, of the sixteen major league rosters integrated—this outcome was not so obvious. The Giants' commitment to integration in 1949, while by no means as courageous as that of the Dodgers in 1947, was still a momentous act. The Giants were in, and thereby "the program" was given a crucial push toward the unstoppable momentum it would eventually achieve.

Worthy of real credit as well was Durocher, rising to this occasion with the Giants as positively as he had with the Dodgers in the spring of 1947. Irvin would express gratitude for Durocher's gracious handling of the situation. "He couldn't have been nicer," Irvin recalled. "He welcomed us warmly, and introduced us around. Then he talked to us privately. 'Fellows,' he said, 'it's no different from what you've been doing everywhere else. Just go out and play your game and you'll be all right.'"[28]

Second base had been a revolving door for Durocher's Giants in 1949. Durocher gave Thompson the opportunity to win the job, and he promptly did so. Thompson's defense at second was rocky, but at the plate he was very good, delivering a solid batting average with power and excellent strike zone judgment. However, for the thirty-year-old Irvin, Durocher had no such decisive plan. As a youngster in the Negro Leagues, Irvin had been capable of handling shortstop, but at this point he was a corner outfield–corner infield player, and the Giants didn't have immediate room for opportunity at those positions. So, there just wasn't much for Irvin to do. Durocher gave him a handful of spot starts, but largely he was a pinch hitter. In the backup role Irvin was unable to get his stroke going.

First baseman Johnny Mize, thirty-six years old, was hitting reasonably well into midsummer of 1949, but then, bothered by a sore shoulder, the Big Cat slumped. On August 22, 1949, Stoneham backed up the truck once again, clearing National League waivers on Mize and selling him to the Yankees for $40,000 cash.[29] Durocher didn't take Mize's departure as an opportunity to give Irvin an extended look at first base. Instead, down the stretch most of the first base playing time went to Joe Lafata, a journeyman who'd been hitting well as Mize's understudy. But Lafata flopped in his big chance.

Despite the midseason retooling, the Giants finished fifth again in 1949. The pennant went to the Dodgers, under Kindly Old Burt Shotton, emphatically bouncing back from their disappointing 1948. Jackie Robinson was in fighting trim this time around, and he delivered a sensational MVP-winning performance while now joining him as Dodger stars were Roy Campanella and Don Newcombe.

Giants' attendance in 1948 had been down a bit from their 1947 Windowbreakers peak, though it was enough to lead the National League. But in '49 that bit of good news vanished, as ticket sales at the Polo Grounds declined to fourth in the league and 25 percent behind what the resurgent Dodgers were drawing at Ebbets Field. A season and a half past the Giants' shocking recruitment of Leo Durocher, the fundamental rebuilding he recommended was underway, but its progress was incremental, and the competitive imperative was growing more urgent.

Stoneham again boldly acted. On December 14, 1949, the Giants traded third baseman Sid Gordon, right fielder Willard Marshall, shortstop John "Buddy" Kerr, and a pitching prospect to the Boston Braves, in exchange for shortstop Alvin Dark and second baseman Eddie Stanky. The negotiation between Stoneham and Braves general manager John Quinn had been long and intense, as Quinn hesitated for weeks before agreeing to surrender Dark, the key player in the swap. But when Stoneham pledged Gordon, Quinn committed to give up Dark.[30] In Gordon and Marshall, Stoneham was surrendering two outstanding hitters, each still in his prime. Kerr had been the Giants' regular shortstop since 1943, but though his defense was well regarded, his hitting had receded to the point of unacceptability. (There was also, as reported by the Associated Press, the issue that "Buddy and Leo had not always seen eye to eye, to put it mildly.")[31]

In this ambitious trade Stoneham and Durocher expended significant middle-of-the-order power—the Windowbreakers were surely broken up now—in order to gain a huge upgrade at the keystone. The move was the central piece in Durocher's effort to remake the Giants in the image he liked to project, of heady "small ball" tactics rather than brute power.

Alvin Dark would turn twenty-eight in early 1950 (though like more than a few ballplayers, he was lying about his age, passing himself off as a year younger than that). He'd played just two full major league seasons, his progress delayed by a college career (where he was a star in football as well as baseball), then a hitch in the U.S. Marine Corps. But he'd been terrific for the Braves (who'd lavished him with a $50,000 signing bonus), winning the major league Rookie of the Year award in 1948 and following it up with a solid season in '49. And in Eddie Stanky, Durocher was reunited with one of his Brooklyn favorites. Undersized and utterly lacking in athletic grace, Stanky was nonetheless a fine player, a bat control artist adept at slapping singles and especially at working bases on balls. As Branch Rickey famously overstated it, "He can't run, he can't hit, and he can't throw, all he can do is beat you."[32] Moreover, Stanky's personality was a lot like Durocher's: he was "The Brat," loud, brash, and fearless, the very definition of "scrappy." Yet The Brat was thirty-four now, and as the Giants took the risk that he had useful mileage left, his age was an indicator that this Giants rebuild wasn't a long-term strategy but an expectation to improve and win now.

An additional aspect of the big trade was a deed Stoneham undertook in its wake that vividly displayed his sentimentality and personal generosity in relationships with players. The big hitting Sid Gordon had been a holdout in the spring of 1949, but he finally came to terms for $2,500 less than he'd demanded. Stoneham was always uncomfortable with salary disputes, and in December 1949 he mailed Gordon a check for $2,500—a remarkable parting gift for a player no longer employed by the Giants.[33]

Stoneham was unusually busy in December 1949. As Polo Grounds landlord to not just one but two National Football League teams, the New York Giants and the New York Bulldogs, Stoneham was centrally engaged in the negotiation to merge the NFL with it upstart professional rival, the All-America Football Conference. Stoneham's interest in the issue was financial: several years of competition between the two football leagues—neither robust on its own—was bleeding them both dry, and Stoneham was sensibly concerned that failing franchises, or worse yet a failing NFL, would eliminate this source of stadium rental revenue. It was Stoneham who called on NFL commissioner Bert Bell to meet with the AAFC's representative—J. Arthur Friedland, the general counsel and secretary of the AAFC's New York Yankees franchise, which played in Yankee Stadium—and he effectively brokered the deal, signed on December 9, 1949, five days before Stoneham closed his blockbuster trade with the Braves. Stoneham was credited as "the one man responsible" for the merger that brought the Baltimore Colts, Cleveland Browns, and San Francisco 49ers into the expanded and more stable NFL. In his genial and collaborative way he accomplished what apparently no one else could, bringing the parties together and facilitating the discussion until they agreed to terms.[34]

The Giants' big trade with the Braves presented Durocher with several decisions in assembling the 1950 lineup. Hank Thompson, who'd taken over at second base in 1949, would be shifted to third, a move that neatly replaced Gordon while allowing Thompson to play a less demanding defensive position. To replace Marshall in right field, an obvious option was Monte Irvin, but Durocher would instead make a regular of twenty-three-year-old Don Mueller. This was a curious choice, as Mueller had neither power nor speed, had no capacity to draw walks, and offered modest defensive aptitude. He did only one thing well: Mueller was nearly impossible to strike out, and by reliably slapping and poking the ball into play, he could deliver a high batting average.

Independent of the trade was the situation at first base, with Mize gone. Again, Monte Irvin was quite available, but again, Durocher opted against him. Instead, two power-hitting rookies, first Jack Harshman and then Harold "Tookie" Gilbert, would be given the starting opportunity, with no success.[35] Meanwhile, the thirty-one-year-old Irvin's 1950 season would be an odyssey. Sent back to AAA to start the year, Irvin made an immediate mockery of that decision: in eighteen International League games, he hit .510 with ten homers, and Stoneham hustled him back to the majors. Durocher played Irvin for a while in right and left field, until finally giving him a shot at first base at the end of July. In that role the veteran caught fire, hitting .341 with ten homers over his final sixty-one games, and the first base question was resolved.

It was a sweeping revision of the starting lineup. Only Bobby Thomson in center field (entering his fourth full big-league season) and Lockman in left (entering his third) were returning established Giants. Wes Westrum behind the plate, Irvin at first base, Thompson at third, and Mueller in right field became major league regulars for the first time. Then there were Dark and Stanky, the veteran imports anchoring the middle of the infield. Both performed wonderfully for the Giants in 1950, rendering the risky trade a great success. Dark added to his breadth of skill with newfound power at the plate, while Stanky delivered the best year of his career, hitting an even .300 and leading the major leagues with 144 walks and an extraordinary .460 on-base percentage—the highest OBP achieved by any National Leaguer between 1935 and 1975.

The big changes didn't yield immediate success. The 1950 Giants started badly, losing twenty of their first thirty. At the All-Star break they were in sixth place, ten and a half games behind the league's surprise, the "Whiz Kid" Philadelphia Phillies. But over the second half the Giants were red-hot: their 52–28 record was the best in the National League, raising them to an 86–68 third-place finish.

The key to the turnaround was dramatically improved pitching. The Giants had made no major deals to acquire a pitcher since Durocher's arrival, nor had any hot prospects been promoted from the minors, and so behind ace Larry Jansen, the primary Giants starters remained southpaws Dave Koslo and Monte Kennedy and righties Sheldon Jones and Clint Hartung.[36] But in 1950 two key newcomers arrived. Right-hander Sal "the Barber" Maglie was thirty-three years old, yet his major league history consisted of thirteen appearances with the Giants in 1945. Maglie had jumped to the Mexican League and was then banned from Organized Baseball. In 1950, the ban rescinded, Maglie returned to the Giants and made Durocher's Opening Day staff as a mop-up reliever, and in July Durocher gave him a chance to start. He won and kept on winning, finishing with a stunning record of 18–4.

Right-hander Jim Hearn, aged twenty-nine, was wasting away at the end of the Cardinals' bullpen bench in July 1950, when Stoneham claimed him on waivers. Giants coaches Frank Shellenback and Freddie Fitzsimmons worked with Hearn and had him drop his arm angle from overhand to three-quarters, transforming his straight fastball into a sinker.[37] Just like Maglie, Hearn pitched himself into the Giants' starting rotation, and just like Maglie, his performance was brilliant: for the Giants in 1950, Hearn compiled an 11–3 record with a sparkling 1.94 ERA.[38]

And there was something else that happened in 1950.

The Boston Braves had a scout by the name of Bill Maughn, who lived near Birmingham, Alabama. In 1949 he saw a teenager playing for the Birmingham Black Barons of the Negro American League who stunned him as the best youngster he'd ever seen play ball. Maughn strongly urged the Braves to acquire and sign the kid, but sluggish negotiations ensued over many months concerning the purchase price, complicated by young Willie Mays's enrollment as a high school student and therefore, by modern major league rules, not eligible for signing.

The effort fell apart, and the Braves instructed Maughn to forget about Mays. Then on June 17, 1950, Maughn bumped into New York Giants scout Eddie Montague at a high school all-star game in Alabama. Montague said he was on his way to Birmingham to evaluate the Black Barons' first baseman, Alonzo Perry. "Listen," Maughn told him, "you forget about Perry. Willie Mays is the one you want."[39] On this tip Montague invited fellow Giants scout Bill Harris to join him. They undertook a thorough look at this supposed hotshot player, not just in game action but in batting and fielding practice and in the locker room, up close.

Jack Schwarz later recalled that he was reading the newspaper at his home in Massapequa, New York, when the telephone rang. It was Harris on the line, from his hotel in Birmingham. "He told me he had seen enough of Perry to know he was not the man we wanted," Schwarz said. "But he thought the Black Barons had one player worth having, a nineteen-year-old kid named Mays—Willie Mays. Harris reported that Mays could hit to either field, that he could run, that he had a real good arm. As I listened, it added up to a routine description of a player who happens to strike a scout favorably. Nothing more, nothing less. Then Montague got on the phone. Now it was different. Montague fairly exploded. 'You've got to get this boy!' he shouted. 'He'll be in the big leagues in two years. Don't ask any questions. Just go get him.' That was the convincer. From then on, we went after Willie."[40]

On June 20, 1950, the Giants acquired his rights from the Black Barons and signed nineteen-year-old Willie Howard Mays Jr. Carl Hubbell assigned the kid to Trenton in the Class B Inter-State League. Mays proceeded to tear up the league, hitting .353 with slashing power and astonishing speed, accompanied by breathtaking range, arm, and aptitude in center field. He would be in the big leagues far more quickly than two years.

In the autumn of 1950 came huge news from Brooklyn: Branch Rickey had been forced out of ownership by Walter O'Malley, and Rickey was leaving to become the general manager of the Pittsburgh Pirates. In his eight-year tenure Rickey's Dodgers had not only pioneered the racial integration of the sport; they'd also won two pennants and finished in the first division seven times. Moreover, Rickey had built a top-to-bottom organization of such soundness that the franchise would remain a power in the National League for years to come.[41] To replace Rickey as GM, O'Malley promoted thirty-six-year-old Emil "Buzzie" Bavasi, who'd been running the Montreal Royals. O'Malley also fired Rickey's faithful servant Burt Shotton as field manager and hired in his place the voluble veteran Chuck Dressen.

1. Charles Abraham Stoneham, Horace's father, born in 1876 to a middle-class family in Jersey City, New Jersey, was a New York Giants "bug" from early on.

2. At the age of sixteen Charley Stoneham finished whatever schooling he'd had and went to work at a stock brokerage firm on Wall Street.

3. Horace Charles Stoneham, the son of a nouveau riche Wall Street hotshot, learned to walk and talk in a realm of pampered luxury.

4. Charley Stoneham— now usually called "C.A."— perfected shady and exploitative securities-trading techniques to become a millionaire before he was forty years old.

5. Horace Stoneham would describe his childhood as a virtually endless tour of Manhattan's finest hotels.

6. C. A. Stoneham owned racehorses, hotels and casinos, and silver and copper mines. He could breezily lose $70,000 in an evening's gambling.

7. Among C. A. Stoneham's properties was the Oriental Park Racetrack in Havana, Cuba.

8. Boarded away to the finest schools, Horace Stoneham loved sports but was an inattentive student.

9. When C. A. Stoneham purchased the New York Giants—the most valuable franchise in sports—he presented them as a gift for his teenaged son, Horace.

10. C. A. Stoneham and John McGraw shared passions for horses, gambling, liquor, and baseball. They mostly got along well as they operated the Giants.

11. Horace Stoneham began working for the Giants at the age of twenty-one, and his father required him to work seriously at it, learning every aspect of stadium and business operations.

12. Horace Stoneham inherited ownership of
the New York Giants at age thirty-two. Here
he hosts President Franklin D. Roosevelt in
the owner's box at the Polo Grounds.

13. (*opposite top*) During World War II, Horace Stoneham hosts New York mayor Fiorello LaGuardia (not one to fuss over his appearance) and General of the Army Dwight D. Eisenhower.

14. (*opposite bottom*) Horace Stoneham's children: son Charles, nicknamed "Pete," and daughter Mary, nicknamed "Wootchie."

15. (*above*) Horace Stoneham and his wife, Valleda, flank Wootchie on her wedding day in 1949.

16. Horace Stoneham adored his daughter, and her wedding celebration was a grand New York event, with the reception at the Waldorf Astoria Hotel.

17. Horace Stoneham's close friend Toots Shor joins Wootchie and her husband, Chuck Rupert, at the Polo Grounds.

18. It was Horace Stoneham's fondest
wish that his son, Pete, would
methodically learn the entire business,
as he had done under his own father,
and someday inherit the franchise.

19. But Pete Stoneham struggled with alcohol, and a deadly drunk driving car wreck in 1958 ruined his reputation and his career.

20. After relocating the Giants to San
Francisco, with his team ascending
competitively and financially, Horace
Stoneham's future appeared bright.

21. (*opposite top*) Horace Stoneham's nephew Charles "Chub" Feeney served him loyally and well as his second-in-command from 1946 through 1969.

22. (*opposite bottom*) Frank "Lefty" O'Doul and Horace Stoneham were pioneers in developing the relationship between baseball in the United States and baseball in Japan.

23. (*above*) Horace Stoneham's grandchildren called him "Pops," and he loved visiting with them. Here he is with granddaughter Jaime Rupert.

24. Horace and Valleda Stoneham with granddaughters Kim and Jaime Rupert and son-in-law Chuck Rupert in the late 1960s.

25. (*opposite top*) Horace Stoneham's Giants toured Japan multiple times, and he was a greatly honored guest. His final tour was in the spring of 1970.

26. (*opposite bottom*) Horace Stoneham strove to treat his employees like family, and his own family was close to the team. Manager Clyde King and Stoneham both autographed this photo for granddaughter Kim.

27. (*opposite top*) By the early 1970s Horace
Stoneham's beloved Giants were in financial
distress, and the owner was feeling increasingly
beleaguered.

28. (*opposite bottom*) For his entire forty-year
tenure as owner of the Giants, Horace Stoneham
kept a huge portrait of his father, C. A. Stoneham,
on the wall above his desk.

29. (*above*) Horace Stoneham loved the desert,
and he and Valleda made their winter home in
Scottsdale, Arizona, and retired there.

30. His son, Pete, was a profound disappointment to Horace Stoneham, and their relationship would be described as "silent if not distant."

31. After selling the team, Horace Stoneham remained close to his Giants "family." In spring training 1979 he and Valleda visit with coaches Salty Parker and Hank Sauer, farm director Carl Hubbell, and (likely but not certainly identified) new owner Bob Lurie.

7

Horace Stoneham Has Finally Got a Winner

Stoneham and Durocher were feeling confident about their team's capability entering the 1951 season, and they weren't alone. In a preseason poll of sportswriters conducted by *The Sporting News*, the Giants were the consensus favorite to win the National League pennant.[1] Their great second-half performance in 1950 had gained wide notice.

So it was that the Giants opened the season with the lineup unchanged. They proceeded to face-plant right out of the gate, losing twelve of their first fourteen. But Durocher didn't panic, and they pulled themselves together and began to play well. By May 20 the Giants' record was 16–18, putting the team in sixth place but just three and a half games behind the first-place Dodgers. Things appeared to be heading in the right direction. Yet it was at this point that Durocher shook things up.

For reasons never articulated, Durocher suddenly had first baseman Monte Irvin and left fielder Whitey Lockman swap positions. This was a puzzling move, given that Lockman had never played an inning of professional baseball anywhere except the outfield, and there was no apparent advantage to be gained by the switch. It was just once of Leo's hunches, though it may have been driven by the polite-but-persistent Irvin's ongoing suggestion to his manager that he was most comfortable in the outfield.[2] The ever-resourceful Durocher no doubt also perceived in the earnest Lockman an uncommon capability to learn and adapt: Lockman started out literally not knowing which foot to use on the bag, but his daily improvement at first base would be rapid and remarkable.[3] For the rest of his career Lockman would be considered one of the best-fielding first basemen in the game.

Next came something more substantial. On May 24, 1951, Stoneham made the decision to promote just-turned twenty-year-old center fielder Willie Mays to the major league roster. Playing for AAA Minneapolis, in thirty-five games Mays had produced a batting average of no less than .477, punctuated with lots of power. Earlier that spring the calm counsel of Carl Hubbell had persuaded the owner to give this very young prospect some more developmental experience. But .477 will prompt reconsideration.

Still, Mays wasn't eager to come along. Minneapolis manager Tommy Heath called Mays into his hotel room to give him the great news.

"Congratulations!" he said.

"What for?" Mays said.

"You're going up to the big league."

"Who said so?"

"Durocher," Heath said. "That's who."

"Not me," Mays said. "Call Durocher up and tell him I'm not coming."

When Heath realized Mays was serious, he phoned Durocher and explained the young fellow's reluctance. Durocher told Heath to put Mays on.

"What do you mean, you're not coming up?" Durocher said.

"I mean it. I can't play that kind of ball."

"What can't you do?"

"I can't hit that kind of pitching."

"What are you hitting for Minneapolis now?" (As if Durocher didn't know.)

"Four seventy-seven."

Durocher said quietly, "Do you think you could hit half that for me?"[4]

Mays was thus persuaded to step into what he knew would be an oppressively intense environment. It wasn't the same circumstance by any means as that which Jackie Robinson had faced in 1947. But as good as Robinson was—and Doby, Campanella, and Newcombe too—everyone, certainly including Mays himself, understood that there hadn't yet been a young Black player arriving in the major leagues with an aura as prodigious as this one. Mays wasn't oblivious; he knew how great a player he was, and he could sense the perturbation around him in Minneapolis and in Trenton and Birmingham before that. His exceptional talent meant relentless scrutiny and expectation, as it always would. Barely a year out of Fairfield Industrial High School, Mays properly anticipated that he was about to be stepping into the hardest time of his young life. Consider the headline and lead in the *Brooklyn Daily Eagle* when Mays was called up:

NEW GIANT WHIZ IN CENTER TONIGHT

> The New York Giants today brought up a 20-year-old Negro outfielder with less than a year of experience in organized baseball and asked him to win the National League pennant for them—beginning tonight.[5]

Though Mays's tenure in Minneapolis had been brief, his astounding performance had made him an instant local superstar, and Millers' fans were devastated to see him quickly depart. Stoneham felt compelled to take out quarter-page advertisements in the Minneapolis newspapers that read in part: "We appreciate Mays' worth to the Millers, but in all fairness, Mays himself must be a factor in these considerations. Merit must be recognized. On the records of his performance since the American Association season started, Mays is entitled to his promotion, and the chance to prove that he can play major league baseball. It would be most unfair to deprive him of the opportunity he earned with his play."[6]

Mays caught a United Airlines flight to New York. He'd been to the city before and had even played in the Polo Grounds, when he was with the Black Barons. But this was quite a different situation. His first appointment was to meet with Mr. Horace Stoneham in the Giants' Midtown Manhattan office suite at 100 West Forty-Second Street.[7]

Mays was visibly nervous, and Stoneham wondered if he would be tough enough to handle the challenge facing him. But the fidgety kid showed the owner something in their verbal back-and-forth.

"Willie, they're going to try to find out about you fast up here," Stoneham told him. "They're going to try you out with pitches at your cap."

Mays shrugged. "That's okay, Mr. Stoneham. When I played in the Negro League, they threw at me too, only it didn't count."

"What do you mean?"

"They couldn't hit me."

"They throw harder up here," Stoneham warned.

"They can throw as hard as they want," Mays said. "I won't be there."[8]

After signing his major league contract (at an annual salary of $5,000), Mays boarded a train to Philadelphia, where the Giants were playing that night. There he met his new roommate, the gracious Monte Irvin, who would eagerly and well serve as Mays's mentor—a relationship best described as his "big brother"—for the next few years.

Irvin phoned Durocher to let him know that the kid was there. Durocher invited Irvin and Mays up to his hotel suite and happily greeted the new arrival. "Glad to see you here, son," Durocher said. "Glad you're hitting .477." He told Mays how he had wanted him to be with the club since spring training, but Stoneham wouldn't let him. "He said you needed more seasoning, but I could see you were a natural and only needed to play." Durocher told Mays not to worry about anything.[9]

In the visitors' dressing room at Shibe Park, next to Irvin's locker, was one prepared for Mays. Durocher came over with more smiles and welcomes. Mays noticed that the manager's manner with him was gentle and fatherly, a tone he didn't use with other ballplayers. "Son, you're batting third and playing center field," Durocher told him.[10] Mays suited up, donning number 24 for the first time, and took the field for pregame warmups.

When Mays stepped into the cage for his big-league batting practice, the ballplayers in Shibe Park—both Giants and Phillies, all of them—stopped whatever they'd been doing, and a hush fell over the field. As Russ Hodges recalled it, "Willie began to comb the ball," rocketing line drives all around the greensward, and jaws dropped.[11]

Stoneham had driven to the game with other team executives, and after Mays was done hitting, Durocher walked past Stoneham's box. The owner yelled, "Hey, Leo, how do you like him?"

"I'll marry him," Durocher shouted back.[12]

But despite his showing in batting practice, Mays was nervous and played badly in his debut. He took a called third strike in his first big-league at bat and went 0 for 5. In the field he misjudged a fly that went for a triple, and on another play he collided with the right fielder. He could hardly have performed any worse. Yet the Giants won, and John Drebinger's lead in the *New York Times* read, "Inspired by the presence of their flashy rookie star, Willie Mays, the Giants rallied for five runs in the eighth inning."[13]

Mays went hitless for the entire three-game series in Philadelphia, but the Giants swept it. They returned to New York for their flashy rookie's debut before the home fans, 23,101 of them, against the Boston Braves, on Monday evening, May 28. Durocher still had him batting third. In the bottom of the first, with two outs and the bases empty, Mays stepped into the box to face Warren Spahn, the Braves' superstar left-hander.

Spahn delivered, and Mays took a backdoor curve for strike one. Then Mays got a fastball and swung and missed badly. No balls, two strikes. He was 0 for 12 and looking overmatched. But the rookie guessed that the 0–2 pitch would be a curve, and he guessed right. He swung and connected, with a piercing crack.

For a moment there was silence in the grandstand, then a collective gasp. The ball didn't tower or loft. It shot straight up and out in an instant, rocketing clean over the double-decked left field Polo Grounds roof, still rising on one astounding line as it disappeared into the twilight. The stands erupted as Mays jogged purposefully around the bases, head down, unsmiling, all business. Spahn stood with his hands on his hips, looked down, and kicked the dirt behind the rubber. When Mays reached the dugout, he finally allowed himself a grin and slapped hands with Durocher, who beamed.

On the radio Russ Hodges proclaimed, "If it's the only home run he ever hits, they'll still remember him."

Spahn's postgame assessment was, "For the first sixty feet, it was a helluva pitch."

And Durocher's: "I never saw a fucking ball leave a fucking park so fucking fast in my fucking life."[14]

Yet following this most imposing first major league hit, Mays continued to slump. He went hitless in his next thirteen at bats, running his bad start to one for twenty-six. Mays told Durocher he didn't think he would ever hit in the big leagues, that he was doing the team no good and ought to be taken out of the lineup. But Durocher calmly and soothingly told the young man to relax, that he would start hitting, that he was still his center fielder, the best center fielder he'd ever seen, and that if Willie didn't make another hit all season, he would still be his boy.[15]

Mays promptly busted out. Before the end of June his batting average was over .320. He cooled off from that pace, finishing at .274 with twenty home runs, and was voted National League Rookie of the Year in a landslide. He instantly became, of course, a tremendous favorite of the fans, not just for how well he played but also for the *way* he played, with vibrant spirit and vivid joy—what Lee Allen termed "a rare éclat"—reliably losing his cap during mad dashes on the bases, ranging far and wide in center field to convert impossible plays into routine outs, and endearing himself to everyone with his authentic good nature. Durocher, who regularly chewed out others, understood Mays perfectly, encouraged him fully, and never criticized him.[16]

Stoneham also understood his obligation to take special care of the young man, far distant from his family and friends, all alone in Jim Crow reality. Stoneham employed Frank Forbes, an African American New York boxing official and former athlete, to serve as Mays's guide and guard. Forbes located a boarding-house in Harlem that provided clean sheets and hearty meals. He steered Mays to an agency to handle the endorsement offers and to approve the press interviews. And Forbes personally saw to it that Mays was steered clear of the wrong sort of company, certainly including female companionship.

Forbes would recall: "When I met him, I immediately knew that Willie was the most open, decent, down-to-earth guy I'd ever seen—completely unspoiled, completely natural. But I was worried to death about the kind of people he might get mixed up with. He'd have to live in Harlem, and believe me, that can be a bad place, full of people just waiting to part an innocent youngster from his money. Somebody had to see to it that Willie wasn't exploited, sift the chalk from the flour, figure out who was in a racket and who was representing a decent organization."[17]

Another development in 1951 was the formalization of the Giants' relationship with Alex Pompez. They were already affiliated, but as the New York Cubans dissolved, Stoneham put Pompez directly on the payroll as a senior scout and advisor. With this move Horace Stoneham's Giants became the first major league team to employ a Black man in the front office. Jack Schwarz explained: "Alex Pompez was a very good friend of the Giants . . . and I suggested to Mr. Stoneham that we engage [him] as a scout. And we got into the Caribbean area in a big way because Pompez was making friends with or renewing his acquaintances with all his connections down there. And he had hundreds of them, ex-ballplayers who played for him in the Negro leagues that were living down there, and that he'd been very kind to and they remembered him. He had a great many connections."[18]

Prominently among Pompez's many connections were Pedro Vasquez (who'd been hired by the Giants as their first Spanish-speaking scout in 1946), Puerto Rican Pedro Zorrilla, and Horacio "Rabbit" Martínez, a Dominican who'd been the star shortstop for the New York Cubans in the 1930s and '40s. The dividends would soon accrue for the Giants in their capability of identifying and recruiting amateur prospects, not just in the Caribbean but also within African American communities in the States, where Pompez was also a knowledgeable and trusted figure with, indeed, a great many connections. The Giants would quickly become the leading major league organization in signing and developing players of color, a pipeline that would yield a gusher of talent.

Over many years, as the number of Latino and African American players within the Giants organization grew, Pompez's role became deeper than just scouting prospects. As a Spanish-speaking Black Cuban, he served as advocate and advisor to all Blacks and Latinos in the organization. He helped with contracts and U.S. employment law and the business of professional baseball. He instructed them in the English language and advised them regarding cultural assimilation. Many of these young athletes came from backgrounds of extreme poverty and had no experience handling money. Pompez assisted them with cashing checks, opening bank accounts, and transferring funds, particularly across borders. And not always with success, he advised them not to spend frivolously.[19] Pompez was a remarkable figure whose impact was profound.

When Mays took over in center field in May 1951, Durocher had to decide how to reconfigure his lineup. He fiddled with it for a while, juggling Bobby Thomson, Monte Irvin, and Don Mueller between left and right. Finally, in mid-July Stoneham optioned slumping third baseman Hank Thompson back to AAA, and Durocher shifted Bobby Thomson from the outfield to third. Thomson, agile for his size (six foot two, 180 pounds), had played mostly third base as a minor leaguer and for the Giants as a September call-up in 1946. He would start every game at third for the rest of the 1951 season. The lineup shuffling was now finished: from July 20 forward, it was set with Westrum catching, Lockman at first base, Stanky at second, Dark at shortstop, Thomson at third, Irvin in left field, Mays in center, and Mueller in right.

The twentieth of July was, coincidentally, the day upon which Durocher set up an elaborate sign-stealing system at the Polo Grounds. A telescope was mounted at a window in the manager's office in the center field clubhouse, affording a view of home plate and the catcher's signals. Durocher directed the ballpark electrician to install a button next to the telescope that was wired to a buzzer in the Giants' bullpen in deep right-center field, within the batter's line of sight. Coach Herman Franks, a longtime catcher and expert sign stealer, used the telescope to study the opponent's signs. Once he was confident he'd cracked the code, he would press the button to sound the buzzer in such a manner as to indicate "fastball" or "curve," and someone in the bullpen (usually backup catcher Sal Yvars) would quickly relay that signal to the Giants' batter by standing up or sitting down.

In 2006 writer Joshua Prager published a book-length exposé of the scheme, presenting the thesis that this sign-stealing gambit largely explains the Giants' red-hot second half in 1951, and Bobby Thomson's home run off Ralph Branca in particular. The weight of evidence fails to support that thesis. The key to their turnaround wouldn't be improved hitting; it would be improved pitching. Moreover, while it's true that the particular telescope-and-buzzer arrangement was unique to the Giants and that ballpark, it's also the case that there was nothing in the rules of baseball prohibiting sign stealing, and the Giants were far from the only team in that era endeavoring to deploy remotely placed sign stealers. Indeed, it's a fair assumption that in every major league game, historically and to this day, someone is attempting to steal the opponent's signs and relay them to the batter. So long as catchers have given signs to pitchers, signs have been stolen; it's normal, not exceptional.

July was the Giants' third strong month in a row, and at month's end they were 56–44, comfortably in second place. Yet for all their progress they were still far behind the first-place Dodgers, who were a blistering 21–7 in July. The Dodgers, indeed, looked unbeatable, playing better with every month. At the trade deadline in June, they'd improved their already star-laden lineup, as rookie GM Buzzie Bavasi swung an eight-player blockbuster with the Chicago Cubs that brought power-hitting All-Star outfielder Andy Pafko to Brooklyn. *The Sporting News* called it "the big steal of 1951" and said it meant the pennant for the Dodgers.[20]

The Giants started the month of August losing seven of ten. At the close of play on Saturday, August 11, the Giants were at 59–51, thirteen games behind the 70–36 Dodgers and barely ahead of the third-place, 58–52 defending champion Philadelphia Phillies.

As the Dodgers surged, Brooklyn manager Chuck Dressen was irrepressible. One afternoon in early August he was asked to provide the writers with his assessments of various National League teams.

"What about the Giants?" someone asked. It was a question reminiscent of the one that Roscoe McGowen had addressed to Bill Terry back in 1934: "What about the Dodgers, Bill?"

But Dressen's response wasn't "Are the Giants still in the league?"

"The Giants," Dressen proclaimed, "is dead."[21]

Such was the situation on Sunday, August 12, 1951, when the Giants played a doubleheader at the Polo Grounds. The visiting Phillies were poised to overtake the Giants for second place. But the Giants swept them, 3–2 and 2–1. At the conclusion of that victorious day, in the established custom of the Polo Grounds with a Giant win, a blue flag was hoisted above the center field clubhouse, while the stadium loudspeakers played a recording of the Giant Victory March:

> We're calling all fans
> All you Giant ball fans
> Come watch the home team
> Going places 'round those bases
>
> Cheer for your favorites
> Out at Coogan's Bluff
> Come watch those Polo Grounders
> Do their stuff.[22]

The Phillies would not overtake the Giants. That doubleheader sweep would be the start of sixteen straight wins for Stoneham's team, and the pennant chase of the century was underway. The hot streak of the 1951 New York Giants achieved—winning thirty-seven of their final forty-four regular season games, to tie the Dodgers and force a playoff—was a run as incandescent as any major league team has ever achieved.

It was a magical spell, a day-upon-day, week-upon-week fury of astonishing performance. Player after player stepped forward to deliver as never before. Right at the outset, when the charge was just gathering force, it was the rookie center fielder.

On Wednesday afternoon, August 15, the Giants faced the Dodgers at the Polo Grounds before 21,007 fans. The Giants had won the first game of the series, giving them four in a row and perhaps stirring thoughts of a comeback, though the Dodgers still had an eleven and a half–game lead. Brooklyn was batting in the eighth with one out, the score tied 1–1. Ralph Branca was on first, speedy Billy Cox was on third, and Carl Furillo, a powerful right-handed hitter was at the plate. Center fielder Willie Mays shaded him to left-center. Furillo stung a high line drive into right-center, and Mays took off for it. A run appeared certain to score, as the ball would either fall safely for a double or, less likely, Mays would catch it and the quick-footed Cox would easily tag up and score. As Mays closed in on the ball, Cox stood poised at third in a sprinter's ready stance.

Running at full speed, Mays one-hand speared the drive on the fly, a terrific catch. Cox bolted for the plate. Mays was still barreling toward right field, in no position to throw, but he somehow instantly planted his right foot and pivoted counterclockwise. For an instant his back was to the plate as he spun, in a whirling pirouette of perfect and powerful rhythm, with his cap (of course) flying off, and Mays blindly fired the ball homeward as his body corkscrewed to the ground in a heap.

The ball, as described by one writer, "took off as though it had a will of its own," cutting through the air like a bullet taking dead aim at cut-off man, Whitey Lockman. As catcher Wes Westrum screamed, "LET GO," Lockman ducked, he later said, "more out of self-preservation than anything else." Westrum hadn't even removed his mask because the last thing he expected was a play at the plate. He later estimated that when the throw reached him, it was traveling eighty-five miles per hour and said that if the umpire had called it, it would have been a strike.

Russ Hodges had the call on the radio: "Willie Mays . . . is reaching up with one hand, he's got it, he spins 180 degrees. Cox breaks for home. Wait a minute! Wait a minute! The ball comes into Westrum on the fly. Cox slides. And Westrum cuts him down at the plate! Cox is out! Billy Cox is out!"[23]

Eddie Brannick, who'd been watching games for half a century, called the play "the greatest I've ever seen." Mays himself called it his best throw. Chuck Dressen said Mays would have to do it again before he'd believe it, and Furillo said flatly that the play was impossible, and that was that.[24]

The impossible was something the Giants were somehow ready to deliver, no sweat. Take the game of September 1, in which Don Mueller, the slappy singles hitter, hammered home runs in the first and third innings. In the fifth inning the Giants turned a triple play. In the seventh, just before Mueller came to bat again, the Giants' bench received news that Mueller had become a father, so he went out and whacked another homer and then two more the next day. The Dodgers—about whom the only question had been how soon they would clinch—were crushed by scores of 8–1 and 11–2.

There was Bobby Thomson, the converted outfielder playing third base. In another September game against the Dodgers, this one at Ebbets Field, Thomson made a play at third that one New York newspaperman thought was the best he'd ever seen. The Giants were leading 2–1 in the bottom of the eighth, with one out. Jackie Robinson was on third and Andy Pafko at bat. Robinson took his customary long lead—one step too many, it would prove to be, and maybe this one step was the pennant— and Pafko pulled a shot down the third base line, headed for the left field corner.

Thomson—playing close to the bag, as one had to with Robinson, lest he get a running lead to steal home—stretched full-out and backhanded the wicked liner on its first short hop. Robinson desperately dove back to the bag, but Thomson smoothly swept his gloved hand back to tag him out before straightening up and firing to first to nail Pafko for a dazzling, inning-ending, game-saving double play.[25]

The astounding stretch drive was a team effort, for sure, but the key wasn't run production—which actually declined during the streak—but stupendous run *prevention* by their pitching and defense. In those forty-four games the Giants allowed just 2.8 runs per game, lowest in the league by a vast margin.[26]

So it was that the Giants and Dodgers squared off for the historic best-of-three playoff. The league had conducted a coin toss to determine the home field assignments in the event of a regular season tie, and Stoneham had lost the flip to Jack Collins, the Dodgers' business manager. Brooklyn had then chosen to host the first game at Ebbets Field, allowing the Giants to have the next game—or two—at home. That decision rankled Branca. "It was stupid. Someone remembered that in 1946 we had opened the playoffs on the road and we lost, and so they decided that in 1951 we'd open at home. But there was one exception. In 1946 the road trip for us was to St. Louis. We were exhausted by the time we got there after a 26-hour train ride. In 1951, it was Manhattan. Wouldn't you rather have your last two games, if you had to play two, at home?"[27]

On Monday, October 1, before a crowd of 30,707 at Ebbets Field, the heavy-hitting Dodgers were stifled by Jim Hearn, who tossed a complete game five-hitter and won 3–1, supported by home runs from Thomson and Irvin. Brooklyn's decision to go all in on the first game had backfired. The Giants now happily considered their prospects in the ultra-friendly Polo Grounds, where they'd been 24–3 since mid-August.

Yet baseball games have a way of defying expectations. On Tuesday, October 2, with their backs to the wall, the Dodgers rallied, not just surviving but emphatically trouncing the Giants 10–0. Brooklyn pounded four home runs off three Giant pitchers, while Dodgers rookie Clem Labine, making just his sixth major league start, breezed to a complete game six-hitter, and the vaunted Giants defense committed five errors.

The morning of Wednesday, October 3, 1951, dawned gray in New York City and never brightened. Rain threatened all day. The sky was so relentlessly thick and dull that in mid-game, in midafternoon, the Polo Grounds lights were turned on, but in the hazy, shadowless atmosphere, they had no discernible effect. The day's unpleasant hue seemed a visible manifestation of tight, uneasy stomachs rumbling within every participant in that day's undertaking, on the field and in the grandstand.

It was a stern matchup of hard-as-nails aces, twenty-game winner Don Newcombe for the Dodgers against twenty-three-game winner Sal Maglie of the Giants. The game was grim and austere. Tied 1–1 in the Dodger eighth, events then turned quickly: four singles, an intentional walk, and a wild pitch fueled a three-run rally, and Brooklyn suddenly commanded a 4–1 lead. The Giants went out quietly in the bottom of the eighth, as did the Dodgers in the top of the ninth.

So the Giants now faced the end against Newcombe, working on a four-hitter. But Alvin Dark led off with a single to right. The Dodgers then chose to have first baseman Gil Hodges hold the runner on the bag—not unreasonable, given the quick-footed Dark, but questionable with a three-run lead. Don Mueller then slapped a ground ball through the right side for a single that, perhaps, the slick-fielding Hodges might have flagged down if playing back.

With runners at first and third, Irvin was up. He was a pearl of a hitter, the Giants' best. But Irvin, "trying to pull one of Newcombe's sliders into the left field stands," fouled out to Hodges.[28]

One away. Up stepped Whitey Lockman.

In the biggest at bat of his life, Lockman connected with Newcombe's one hundredth pitch and lined it sharply into left center for a double. Dark scored easily, but Mueller slid awkwardly into third and sprained his ankle. While he was being carted off to the clubhouse on a stretcher (Clint Hartung would pinch-run), Dressen decided it was time to relieve Newcombe. He had two right-handers warming up, Clem Labine and Ralph Branca, but the report from his bullpen was that Labine (who'd pitched nine innings the previous day) was bouncing his curve. Therefore, Dressen opted for the hard-throwing Branca to come in and face power-hitting Bobby Thomson with one out in the bottom of the ninth, runners at second and third, and the score Dodgers 4, Giants 2.

The subsequent home run—"The Shot Heard 'Round the World"—became as celebrated as it did not just because of its exquisite drama as a baseball play but also because of the amazing radio call delivered by Russ Hodges, shouting, "The Giants win the pennant!" four times at the top of his lungs.[29] The event became such an iconic touchpoint, both in baseball culture and in the broader American imagination, that nearly half a century later author Don DeLillo used it as the opening scene in his best-selling and highly acclaimed novel *Underworld.* The 848-page epic opens with a masterful dramatization of that afternoon and its climactic at bat, finally focusing on the ecstatic exclamations of Russ Hodges:

> Then he raises a pure shout, wordless, a holler from the old days—it is fiddlin' time, it is mountain music on wcky at five-thirty in the morning. The thing comes jumping out of him, a jubilation, it might be *heyyy-ho* or it might be *oh-boyyy* shouted backwards or it might be something else entirely—hard to tell when they don't use words. And Thomson's teammates gathering at home plate and Thomson circling the bases in gamesome leaps, buckjumping—he is forever Bobby now, a romping boy lost to time, and his breath comes so fast he doesn't know if he can handle all the air that's pouring in. He sees men in a helter-skelter line waiting at the plate to pummel him— his teammates, no better fellows in the world, and there's a look in their faces, they are stunned by a happiness that has collapsed on them, bright-eyed under their caps. . . .
>
> Russ has got his face back into the mike. He shouts, "I don't believe it." He shouts, "I don't believe it." He shouts, "I do *not* believe it."[30]

What broadcaster Hodges said next, once ready to report on more than his own level of astonishment, was this: "Bobby Thomson—hit a line drive—into the lower deck—of the left-field stands—and this blame place is goin' crazy! The Giants! Horace Stoneham has finally got a winner! The Giants won it— by a score of five to four—and they're pickin' Bobby Thomson up—and carryin' him off the field!"

It's meaningful that at this most ecstatic of moments, the broadcaster would choose to invoke the name of the Giants' owner. One doubts that if the Dodgers had dramatically won the game, Red Barber would have similarly shone a verbal spotlight on Walter O'Malley. It's suggestive of the depth to which Stoneham was ingrained in the Giants enterprise, how emblematic of its fortunes he was, how deeply understood it was by everyone close to the team that Horace Stoneham had striven for so long to get beyond the towering shadow of his father, how much he wanted and needed this pennant at last.

Yet the finally victorious owner, captive to his quirky behaviors as always, had not even seen Thomson's home run. Following Sal Maglie's removal from the game for a pinch hitter in the bottom of the eighth, Stoneham had left his normal viewing perch at his office window in center field and gone downstairs to the Giants' clubhouse to commiserate with his valiant pitcher. Down by three runs entering the ninth, Stoneham couldn't bear to watch what he expected to be the sad end of this inexplicable down-and-up-and-apparently-down season. Giants infielder Bill Rigney, who'd struck out as a pinch hitter in the eighth inning and then retired to the clubhouse, described it: "Horace had already come into the clubhouse and said he had decided that we weren't going to win. He was a pessimist. He was not an optimist. That was just his nature. I don't mean that as a putdown of the owner of the Giants. But he said another thing, too, that he'd have a drink with the entire group of players when they came off the field, because this had been the darnedest season he'd ever been a part of."[31]

So, the Giants went on to their first World Series appearance since 1937. They once again squared off against the Yankees, who were making their ninth World Series appearance since that year. The Giants could be forgiven for experiencing this all–New York Fall Classic as a bit of an anticlimax, following their exhausting pennant chase and playoff. For the Yankees it was just another day at the office.

The 1951 New York Yankees, though capturing their third pennant in a row and their fourth in five years, were a team in transition. This was thirty-six-year-old Joe DiMaggio's final season and nineteen-year-old Mickey Mantle's first. Their best player was power-hitting catcher Yogi Berra, the league's MVP, and their key strength was a starting pitching rotation that featured a trio of aces in Allie Reynolds, Eddie Lopat, and Vic Raschi.

Though the 1951 World Series wasn't particularly memorable, it had a great start. In the opening game, at Yankee Stadium—on Thursday, October 4, the very afternoon following the stunning playoff victory—in the top of the very first inning, Monte Irvin stole home, as the Giants instantly and dramatically took the lead. They won that opener 5–1.

The next day the Yankees evened it up behind Lopat. Back across the river in the Polo Grounds, the Giants took the third game, and a World Series cherry on top of the Miracle of Coogan's Bluff was within reach. But it was not to be. The following day's game was rained out, and the interruption perhaps broke the Giants' breathless momentum. Or perhaps it was just that Casey Stengel's New York Yankees—midway through their unmatched run of five straight World Series championships— were a tremendous ball club. In any case, following the first inning of Game Four, the Giants would never have another lead. The Yankees calmly and methodically won three in a row, and the magical season came to a quiet end.

The Giants' success in 1951 included another major contribution from second baseman Eddie Stanky. But at the age of thirty-five, he finally began to decline, hitting .229 in the second half. Rookie second baseman Davey Williams, called up in July, frequently spelled him in late innings. The Cardinals were interested in acquiring Stanky for the purpose of naming him their manager, so in December 1951 Stoneham traded him to St. Louis in exchange for veteran left-handed starting pitcher Max Lanier and utility outfielder Chuck Diering. Stoneham explained: "Eddie won a place in our esteem, and I was reluctant to let him go to the Cardinals. But Stanky told me he wanted to go to St. Louis and I couldn't stand in his way. But Lanier and Diering should strengthen us."[32] The twenty-four-year-old Williams, a steady gloveman with a so-so bat, would be the Giants' new regular second baseman in 1952.

The Giants' chances of repeating as NL champions were given a boost by the arrival of an odd duck named Hoyt Wilhelm: a twenty-nine-year-old rookie (though he was passing himself off as twenty-eight), a right-handed pitcher who threw the knuckleball almost exclusively and whose record at the AAA level had been mediocre. Wilhelm's meandering and unlikely path to the big leagues included three years in the Class D North Carolina State League and three years in the United States Army (in whose service he was awarded the Purple Heart for combat injuries sustained in the Battle of the Bulge). But in spring training of 1952 Durocher was impressed with the tough, taciturn North Carolinian's work and placed him on the Opening Day roster.

Wilhelm had been deployed mostly as a starter in the minors, but Leo envisioned him strictly as a reliever. "The knuckler can fool 'em for four or five innings, even if Wilhelm doesn't have the hard stuff to go nine."[33] Before long Wilhelm was Durocher's ace reliever, and the more heavily he was worked over the course of the 1952 season, the better he performed. He finished the year with remarkable statistics: 71 major-league-leading appearances, all in relief, and 159 innings pitched, 15 wins against just 3 losses, and a National League–leading ERA of 2.43.[34] Wilhelm was fourth in National League MVP voting in 1952 and second in balloting for Rookie of the Year—behind only a fellow sensational reliever, African American Joe Black of the Dodgers.

Two significant absences would strike the Giants in 1952. First, Monte Irvin suffered a compound fracture of his ankle when his spikes caught in a spring training game, and he was out of action for several months. To replace him in left field, Stoneham immediately traded pitcher Sheldon Jones and $50,000 cash to the Boston Braves for Bob Elliott. The highly respected Elliott—his non-ironic nickname was "Mr. Team"—was a longtime power-hitting star and a former MVP. But he was thirty-five and hit poorly for the Giants. Irvin rejoined the team in the second half, and while his bat remained potent, he was hobbled and would never again be the smooth all-around performer he was before the injury.

Nevertheless, in the season's early weeks the Giants were hot, and on May 28 they were in first place. But that was the end of the season for center fielder Willie Mays, who was ordered for induction into the United States Army. Mays played his last game of the year at Ebbets Field, and on the occasion of his final time at bat, the spirited Brooklyn fans, gracious to few of the Giants, rose to their feet and applauded him warmly.[35] With Mays gone, the Giants immediately lost eight of their next ten, dropping to second. They would never fall to third, but neither would they see first place again in 1952. This time the Giants finished in second, by four and a half games.

At the season's close Durocher—who'd given no indication of being dissatisfied—made a strange announcement: he said he would quit baseball after 1953 and try a career in the movies. Stoneham rarely angered, but he did now. He told Durocher that he had one month to decide if it was going to be the movies or the Giants. If the manager was indeed planning to quit after 1953, then Stoneham wouldn't wait and would just fire him now. "I thought at first it was a press agent's stunt," said Stoneham. "But Leo told me he had three offers he should examine."

Pressured now, Durocher called a press conference and announced that he would manage the Giants in 1953 and be available for the 1954 season. When asked about his future beyond that, he replied: "Not movies necessarily. But that television is something else. There's big money there."[36]

It was reasonable for Durocher to plan his next career move, whatever it might be, but his manner of flatly announcing his intention to the press while still under contract with the Giants and having not discussed it directly with Stoneham had been graceless. For all of his capacity to charm and cajole, Durocher could also be rude and mean; he wasn't called "Leo the Lip" for nothing. Over his long career in baseball Durocher demonstrated great capacity to make friends, but his ability to sustain positive important long-term relationships was far less in evidence. This kerfuffle with Stoneham was the first instance of difficulty between the two. They would get past it, and indeed, Durocher would eventually be re-signed by Stoneham to manage the Giants through the 1955 season. But more trouble would come.

By 1952 it was obvious that the business of professional base-ball, in both the major and minor leagues, was facing a new and broad-based economic challenge. The great boom in atten-dance that had erupted following World War II, that had gushed fresh revenue into the game and funded ambitious growth in farm systems and minor leagues generally, was plainly over. Major league attendance had peaked at nearly 21 million in 1948 and declined every year since, down to 14.6 million in 1952. The decline was even more pronounced in the minors and was now causing league after league to go out of business. The size of the minors had peaked in 1949 and 1950, with fifty-nine leagues in operation each year, but that total had contracted to fifty in 1951 and to forty-three in 1952.

Just what might be causing these distressing trends was the subject of widespread inquiry and debate. There were multiple potential culprits. One issue was that other sports and leisure enterprises in the vibrant postwar economy had expanded to compete for the entertainment dollars baseball had been rak-ing in: professional football was a growing enterprise, as was automobile racing, and so, too, were recreational sports such as boating, bowling, and golf. Beyond sports, general entertain-ment and leisure options were growing everywhere, including drive-in movies, amusement parks, and automobile sightsee-ing vacations—made more accessible than ever before by rap-idly developing networks of modern highways.

Another factor was the widespread adoption of modern air conditioning. Especially in places that were likely to get hot in the summertime—in other words, just about everywhere that professional baseball was presented—it was increasingly harder to persuade someone to pay money to sit in the sun for a couple of hours, especially for a minor league game.

All of these issues were impactful to one degree or another. But the primary explanation for baseball's attendance bust, nearly everyone agreed, was television. In 1948 only one American in ten had even seen a television set. By 1953 one-half of Ameri-can households would own one. Just as with radio in the 1930s, there was now quite divided opinion within the ranks of baseball executives on the question of whether televising was ultimately good or bad for the business. Bob Carpenter, owner of the Philadelphia Phillies, thought television would be "the greatest boost the game ever had." Chicago Cubs owner Phil Wrigley supported televising games as a promotional boost, but based on baseball's slow acceptance of radio broadcasts, he thought it would take years to get other owners to agree with that position.

The Sporting News, the "baseball bible," saw in television both potential and peril. In May 1947 that paper editorialized that "television does not constitute a problem for baseball yet, but it inevitably will." Owners would need to capitalize on the promotional value of the broadcast media by "formulating plans to incorporate their radio and television rights to get the most out of them, not merely in money, but in advertising value. After all, baseball, too, has a product to sell to the public." Yet just a few weeks later, *The Sporting News* cautioned that television was different than radio: "Listening to a game, a man may develop the desire to see it. But seeing it from his easy chair, at no cost and free from parking problems, he might decide that only a darn fool would make the trip to the ball park."[37]

When the ballpark business was roaring in the late 1940s, the TV naysayers weren't much heeded. But by the early '50s, with all the needles leaning toward the red, the chorus of accusation was sounding. Consider these headlines from the period:

"Does TV Empty the Ballparks?" *Business Week*, 1951

"Baseball Is in Trouble: High Costs, TV Are Blamed," *U.S. News & World Report*, 1952

"TV Can Kill Baseball," *Newsweek*, 1953

"Can Baseball Survive TV?" *Business Week*, 1953[38]

However well-informed or sensibly balanced such analyses may have been, there could be no question that television legitimately presented a threat of some magnitude to the viability of professional baseball's traditional business structure. It did so in two ways. The first was local fans simply choosing to watch the hometown team's games on TV instead of at the ballpark. While a challenge, this was within the realm of baseball management's control, insofar as it could be determined what number of games to be televised would optimally stimulate fan interest without depressing attendance.

But the second issue was beyond baseball's remotest control, and that was the existential question of how each potential customer might choose to invest precious leisure time following baseball at all within the television entertainment era now noisily dawning. In *Baseball Magazine* John Drebinger suggested: "Television itself, apart from its baseball offerings, could very easily have made a deep inroad in the game. The novelty of the thing, the fact that it offers many other attractions—the Milton Berles, Jimmy Durantes, and the like—could also have contributed much to keeping folks at home evenings, when otherwise they would be going out to the ballpark."[39]

In baseball's executive suites far more questions were known than answers. But by 1952 and '53 it was becoming the majority view to acknowledge an imperative: whatever form it might take, change was now unavoidable in the baseball business. The world wasn't standing still. Baseball owners would need to adapt, in one way or another, or be left behind.

For Stoneham's Giants attendance at the Polo Grounds had indeed been skiing downhill since the grand peak in the Windowbreakers season of 1947, from 1.6 million to 985,000 in 1952, their lowest attendance since the war year of 1944. In 1948 Stoneham had funded a farm system for Carl Hubbell that included twenty-one affiliates. By 1952 economic necessity had reduced that total to fourteen, yet Stoneham well understood that allowing competitors to gain significant advantage in talent development was simply not an option. Even as he contracted the system's minor league chain, Stoneham made no reduction to Hubbell's staff of scouts, which continued to number more than twenty in the early 1950s.

It's worth acknowledging that even though the vast farm systems that mushroomed in the late 1940s were economically affordable so long as gate receipts were record shattering, their size itself rendered it difficult to apply focused attention on talent assessment and skill development. Jack Schwarz recalled a Florida minor league spring training camp in the postwar period that gathered more than five hundred players. "Such a horde was wasteful in money and time," Schwarz admitted. "No organization could possibly screen all those boys adequately in the limited time, and they were there only to pad farm systems which were overextended anyway. Along with other clubs, we found we could squeeze a lot of water out of our holdings. Mere size was not an indication of strength."[40]

The issue of televising the games was a competitive arena too, of course. Stoneham himself was in the skeptical-of-TV school; in 1948 he'd been quoted with the opinion that television was hurting the Giants' attendance, particularly for night games, and also hurting the attendance at the organization's minor league affiliates, and he favored a ban on night telecasts.[41] But Stoneham was, as always, a realist, and he did what he had to do. Both the Dodgers and Yankees were ardent TV advocates, eagerly televising all seventy-seven of their home games each season in the late 1940s and into the 1950s, and so Stoneham, competing for the attention of those viewers, felt compelled to have all of the Giants home games broadcast on the tube as well.[42] (A few years later, in a different competitive environment in San Francisco, Stoneham would play this card very differently.)

Yet the televising of games was a two-sided coin. The exclusive right to broadcast the action was a commodity sold by the teams. So, whatever revenue might be sacrificed in terms of ticket sales was, at least partly and perhaps significantly, available to be replaced by broadcast rights revenue. Especially for teams in big media market locations—and none was nearly as big, by a long shot, than New York—as the size of the TV viewing audience would grow, the value of the advertising time purchased on the broadcasts would grow, and thus the value of the broadcasting rights themselves was certain to grow. This point was rarely acknowledged in the "TV is killing baseball" pearl clutching of the early 1950s, but it was true: television could potentially prove to be the furthest thing from a problem for major league baseball (while in the minors, it genuinely was a serious problem) but, instead, a great benefactor. That wasn't yet the case in the early 1950s, but things were rapidly changing. Figuring out how to leverage this changing landscape and convert TV from a threat into an asset was a central challenge presented to Stoneham and his fellow owners.

While television per se wasn't the driving factor, it was the "we have to change" spirit that animated the decision of the Boston Braves to relocate their franchise to Milwaukee for the 1953 season. This was the first relocation of a major league team since 1903, fully half a century. No other team in baseball had seen its attendance vaporize quite like the Braves: as National League pennant winners in 1948, they'd drawn a franchise-record 1.45 million. But the descent since had been frightening, all the way down to a pitiful 282,000 in 1952. It was a plain economic emergency, and the desperate remedy of relocation, a radical notion for decades, was suddenly acceptable. Their fellow National League owners voting to approve the momentous action—including Stoneham—would surely keep a careful eye on the Braves to see how they might make a go of it in Milwaukee. Perhaps at this point Stoneham conceived the possibility of his Giants one day taking such a dramatic step.

It was a period in which forward-thinking baseball operators recognized that the time was at hand for, in the business parlance of later decades, "thinking outside of the box," considering unprecedented options to promote their sport and brand and cultivate new potential markets. Stoneham had known Frank "Lefty" O'Doul since 1928, when the pitcher-turned-outfielder first joined the Giants. Their paths had crossed again in 1933–34, after Bill Terry reacquired the heavy-hitting veteran, and still again in 1945–46, when the San Francisco native O'Doul was the hugely popular and successful manager of the San Francisco Seals of the Pacific Coast League, and the Giants briefly incorporated the Seals as a farm system affiliate. O'Doul had delivered pitcher Larry Jansen to the Giants from the Seals, and O'Doul had been rumored to be on Stoneham's short list when he was considering the replacement for Mel Ott as the Giants' manager.

In addition to his exploits as a star player and manager, for more than twenty years O'Doul had been a tireless and passionate leader in fostering friendship and collaboration between American professional baseball and that of Japan. In the post–World War II period of reconstruction of war-ruined, American military–occupied Japan, O'Doul was the single most instrumental figure in the campaign—fully supported by General Douglas MacArthur, effectively the viceroy of Japan—to leverage baseball as a means of regenerating harmony and trust between the recently combatant populations.

It was in this capacity that O'Doul contacted Stoneham in early 1953 and arranged an exhibition game to be held in the town of Santa Maria, California, between the Yomiuri Giants of Tokyo and the New York Giants. The connection between these two geographically distant baseball clubs was already strong: not only had the nickname of "Giants" been bestowed upon the Yomiuri team by O'Doul himself in the 1930s; they further purposefully emulated Stoneham's team right down to the black-and-orange color scheme.

During this visit Stoneham met Tsuneo "Cappy" Harada, a native of Santa Maria. The Japanese American Harada's bilingual skill had allowed him to be spared internment and drafted into wartime U.S. military intelligence service in numerous Pacific combat theaters against the Japanese.[43] Harada had been a star high school baseball player who desired a career in the game, and following the war he became O'Doul's counterpart on the Japanese side, coordinating tours of American players and teams. It was because of Harada that the Yomiuri Giants were holding their 1953 spring training camp in Santa Maria. Stoneham and Harada hit it off. Stoneham accepted Harada's offer to host the New York Giants on a trip to Japan in the autumn of 1953, the first of several that Stoneham's team would undertake in years to come. Harada would eventually be hired by the Giants organization as a scout, a relationship that would one day produce a most extraordinary collaboration.[44]

In the early 1950s Horace Stoneham's son, Pete, was formally beginning his career in the Giants organization. Stoneham well remembered the rigorous, no-shortcuts approach his father had demanded of him back in the 1920s, given hard humble work and expected to complete it and to learn from it. While Horace lacked the capacity to be as stern as C.A., Pete was given a similar course to navigate. In the late 1940s, during school summer vacations, Pete was dispatched to minor league outposts to toil as a forty dollar–per–week "handyman."[45] In 1950, at the age of twenty-two, he was placed in his first full-time job as traveling secretary for the Class B Trenton Giants of the Inter-State League (the very same ball club with which Willie Mays began).[46]

It would be a long climb from such a rung in the low minors to a position of significant responsibility in the major league front office. That was the point. By the time he would someday stand at his father's side at the top of the organization, he would be ready for it, having learned the totality of the business, the nature of the many jobs to be done, and the people who performed them. About this outcome no doubt was felt, or at least expressed, inside the organization or within the sporting press: "If, by chance, you should see Stoneham's good-looking son, Pete, around town some evening, you will see, except for Pete's snappy black eyes, a dead ringer for 'Old Pop,' the way he looked in those days when flappers were flapping around and about. Someday Pete will be the president of the Giants. Or a fellow can hope and believe that he will. For these Stonehams, stubborn and sentimental, form one of the . . . real baseball dynasties left in the game."[47]

But for Pete the ascent would not come easily. He didn't possess the same personality as his father, who at a similar age had disarmed potentially resentful rank-and-file organizational employees with his quiet humility and cheerful disposition. Nor was Pete in the same mold as his cousin Chub Feeney, who impressed everyone with calm competence in handling the details of financial and business administration. Pete was not so patient or easygoing or self-confident. Earning the genuine respect of those around him for his capability, and not just for his name, would prove to be a challenge.

One characteristic Pete did share with his father was a distinct inclination to drink. Generally (though not always), Horace was able to contain his ardent tippling and responsibly fulfill his professional obligations. Pete would have a much harder time with that, with dire consequences.

Upon the departure of Willie Mays to military service in late May 1952, Durocher took a while to decide who should handle center field. The alignment he finally settled upon put Bobby Thomson back in center, with Hank Thompson—hitting well again after his poor showing in 1951—back as the third baseman. There they would remain through 1953 as well.

Two rookies would play key roles in 1953. Ruben Gomez was a hard-throwing Black Puerto Rican right-hander who'd purchased his own release from the New York Yankees organization and then was signed by the Giants on the recommendation of Alex Pompez.[48] Gomez made the major league staff as a long shot and delivered an excellent year as a starter, even attracting some down-ballot MVP votes. Twenty-four-year-old Daryl Spencer, a versatile infielder promoted from Minneapolis, was big and strong as well as agile. He impressed Durocher so much that despite a bat that delivered a feeble batting average (with fine power), Spencer was deployed extensively at shortstop, second base, and third.

Overall the team's performance in 1953 was poor; they started slowly and were never close to contention, finishing fifth, at 70–84. There were two big stories in the National League of 1953, and neither involved the Giants. The first was the archrival Brooklyn Dodgers, who repeated as pennant winners, capturing their fourth flag in seven years. This time they did it in spectacular runaway fashion, with a franchise record 105 wins. Brooklyn's brutally punishing offense plated 955 runs, by far the most by any National League team since the wild scoring year of 1930. Naturally, they once again handily outdrew the Giants, this time by more than 40 percent, as the Polo Grounds' attendance continued to slide.

Yet this dominant Dodger team didn't lead the league in attendance; indeed, Brooklyn's second-best gate trailed the league's top draw by more than 50 percent. That best-attended team in 1953, setting a National League record with 1,826,397 turnstile clicks, was none other than the Milwaukee Braves. Their desperate gamble on relocation halfway across the continent delivered immediate and dazzling success. Led by veteran ace pitcher Warren Spahn and sophomore third baseman Eddie Mathews, the Braves soared from seventh place to second and were poised to be a formidable contender for the rest of the decade.

Notice was widely paid. Shortly following the 1953 season, American League owners forced St. Louis Browns owner Bill Veeck to sell to an investor group in Baltimore, and for the 1954 season the American League would present its own first franchise relocation in more than fifty years. Racial integration wasn't the only "program" now getting underway.

At multiple points during his army service, Willie Mays applied for discharge on the grounds of family financial hardship. Every time he was denied, even when, on April 15, 1953, his mother died while giving birth to her eleventh child. Mays was distraught, but though he was given leave to attend her funeral in Fairfield, Alabama, to his deep frustration he wasn't discharged. It wasn't until the winter of 1953–54 that he and the Giants were informed that he would be discharged in time for spring training.[49]

Secure in the knowledge that Mays would be back in center field in 1954, Stoneham then made a key decision as to how he would fit into the lineup. Bobby Thomson wouldn't be shifted to third base this time. Instead, on February 1, 1954, Stoneham traded Thomson to those surging Milwaukee Braves, along with a backup catcher, in exchange for pitchers Johnny Antonelli and Don Liddle, a backup catcher, a minor league infielder, and $50,000 in cash. It was a remarkable haul, and it would turn out to be one of the most beneficial trades in the history of the Giants' franchise.

Stoneham explained: "Thomson always played fine ball for us and always will be remembered as the hero of the Giants' 1951 pennant victory. But the Giants had to strengthen their pitching staff and we had to include Thomson in the deal to do it."[50] The key for the Giants was Antonelli. Not quite twenty-four years old, the left-hander had been a prized prospect, a $75,000 "bonus

baby" signed by the Braves out of high school in 1948.[51] His progress was slow, and delayed by two years in the army, but in 1953
he was deployed for the first time as a regular starter, and his
performance was impressive. He was a special young pitcher;
indeed, Thomson-for-Antonelli straight up would have been a
reasonable deal. But Stoneham was able to negotiate quite a bit
more from Braves general manager John Quinn, including the
twenty-nine-year-old southpaw Liddle, a solid spot starter–long
reliever. The nationally syndicated *New York Herald Tribune*
columnist Red Smith wrote of the departing Thomson: "He is
a good man to have on your side and a bad one to have against
you, and the Giants know it. Still they had no choice save to let
him go. As well as it is possible to judge in midwinter, it was a
good deal for New York."[52]

So, the Giants went into 1954 with Mays in place of Thomson in center field but otherwise the same starting lineup as in
1952 and '53: Westrum catching, Lockman at first base, Williams
at second, Dark at shortstop, Thompson at third, Irvin in left,
and Mueller in right. The only other significant change was that
Daryl Spencer, a semi-regular infielder in 1953, was now himself away in the army. The team's renovation was focused on the
mound. Veteran left-handers Dave Koslo, Monte Kennedy, and
Max Lanier were all discarded and replaced by Antonelli, Liddle, and John "Windy" McCall, acquired by Stoneham from the
San Francisco Seals.

The 1954 Giants did not start well. Through the games of
Wednesday, May 5—the eve of Willie Mays's twenty-third
birthday—they were 9–10, in fifth place. Their 1951 Rookie of
the Year center fielder had hit three home runs in these earliest
weeks but done little else at the plate. In his exciting but choppy
and brief 174-game major league career so far, Mays had compiled a cumulative batting average of .263 and hit twenty-seven
home runs. He was a peerless defensive center fielder, but with
the bat, though he was powerful, he was inconsistent, a danger-
ous hitter but hardly a great one.

It was in May 1954 that Willie Mays suddenly and emphatically turned that corner. In sixty-five games from his birthday

until the All-Star break, Mays hit twenty-eight home runs. His batting average in that span was .356, his slugging percentage .805, and the Giants went 48–17. Mays wound up as the 1954 National League batting champion, breaking Mel Ott's franchise record for extra-base hits. He was the first National Leaguer since Rogers Hornsby to lead the league in average while hitting over forty homers.[53] He led the league in slugging and was voted Most Valuable Player.

His pattern of production at the plate dramatically shifted in midseason, from one form of domination to another. Through July, Mays was a big-swinging home run hitter: at the All-Star break he had thirty-one homers. On July 28, when he hit his thirty-sixth—a 447-foot bomb into the upper left-center field stands at the Polo Grounds—the game was the Giants' ninety-fifth, and the papers made much of the fact that in 1927, the year Babe Ruth hit his record sixty, he didn't achieve his thirty-sixth until August 10, in the Yankees' 110th game.

Yet from that date forward, Mays hit just five home runs, and two of those were inside-the-park jobs. But though Mays surely encountered a home run drought—Ruth's record was safe for now—he continued to deliver amazing offensive production. In that stretch Mays hit .379, filling the box scores with doubles and triples, shots whistled between the outfielders or pounded over the center fielder's head.[54] The cause of Mays's change in batting results wasn't certain, but likely it was a combination of the league's pitchers deciding, through bitter experience, to refuse to give him anything to pull and instead feed him nothing but away, away, away, and Mays's lightning-quick maturation as a hitter, instantly adapting and squaring up line drives to the big part of the outfield.

The superstar on the field of play became a nationally famous celebrity off it. He was nicknamed "the Say Hey Kid" for his habit of greeting everyone with a chirpy "Say Hey," as he was (so the legend goes, anyway) terrible at remembering names. He played stickball in the Harlem streets with the neighborhood kids; this was well known because six national magazines ran stories on it. One neighborhood sixteen-year-old let the truth out. "Willie's a con man," the boy said. "He tells us we'll get our turn to hit, but we never do." Stickball wasn't the half of it. Mays would come around to shoot baskets or have a hardball catch if gloves were available or a rubber ball catch if not. "Somebody's got to teach these kids right," Mays said. Then he would round up the neighborhood for ice cream sodas, until Mrs. Ann Goosby, who ran his boardinghouse, stuck her head out the window and yelled Willie home for supper. It was quite a summer.[55]

Songwriters Jane Douglas and Dick Kleiner wrote one in his honor, "Say Hey (The Willie Mays Song)," and its recording by the rhythm-and-blues group the Treniers was an instant hit. The record was routinely blared through the public address speakers at the Polo Grounds, and fans joyfully sang along.[56]

> Say hey! Say who? Say Willie
> Say hey! Swingin' at the plate
> Say hey! Say who? Say Willie
> That Giants kid is great.

Propelled by Mays, at the 1954 All-Star break the Giants were in first place by five and a half games. In the second half the Dodgers mounted a couple of charges but could never catch the Giants, who clinched the pennant with a week to spare by blissfully trouncing Brooklyn 7–1 at Ebbets Field. Stoneham had endured thirteen years of frustration before finally capturing the flag in 1951. This time around it had taken just two.

As in 1951, this 1954 team could hit plenty, but it was in the realm of run prevention—fielding and pitching—that the 1954 Giants were truly outstanding. They led the National League in both defensive efficiency (converting 72.2 percent of balls in the field of play into outs, against a league average of 70.7 percent) and in estimated runs saved (with fifty, against a league average of eight).[57] Decades later Stoneham would recall the 1954 team this way: "It's funny, but the thing I remember about that club is all the double plays they got that year that ended up with a base runner caught out of position—being put out by a throw behind him, or something like that. A great heads-up team."[58]

Excellent fielding is a pitcher's best friend, of course, and with such support the Giants' pitching staff achieved glittering statistics in 1954. Their aggregate earned run average of 3.09 led the National League and was the best ERA from a Giants staff between 1933 and 1967. Adjusting for ballpark and league context, the Giants' ERA+ of 132 was among the best in league history.[59] Leading the way on the 1954 Giants staff was Antonelli, bounding into stardom at 21–7 with a major league–leading 2.30 ERA; if there had been a Cy Young Award in 1954, Antonelli surely would have won it. Ruben Gomez and thirty-seven-year-old Sal Maglie both delivered strong years, and the bullpen was superb as well, with ace fireman Hoyt Wilhelm now joined by thirty-six-year-old Marv Grissom, a scrap heap reclamation who blossomed under Durocher as a relief specialist.

The other breakthrough for the Giants in 1954 came from a bench player, twenty-seven-year-old Jim "Dusty" Rhodes, a one-dimensional, left-handed-batting slugger. His honest self-appraisal was "I ain't much of a fielder and I got a lousy arm, but I sure do love to whack at that ball."[60] In the first half of 1954 Durocher deployed him exclusively as a pinch hitter, and Rhodes hit so extraordinarily well in that role that he gained increasingly frequent starts ahead of Monte Irvin in left field and finished the year at .341, with fifteen homers and a remarkable fifty RBI in 164 at bats. (He would never have another year like this one, but then, neither would just about anyone else.)

In the World Series, for once the American League wasn't represented by the Yankees. Instead, the Giants faced an exceptional Cleveland Indians team that had set a league record with 111 wins. The Indians had a formidable offense, featuring batting champion Bobby Avila and a power-hitting core of Larry Doby, Al Rosen, and Vic Wertz. But like the Giants, their key strengths were fielding and, especially, pitching. Flashing a trio of elite aces in Bob Lemon, Early Wynn, and Mike Garcia, the staff ERA of 2.78 was the best in the American League since the "dead ball" season of 1918. Cleveland was heavily favored by pundits and oddsmakers.

The opener was on Wednesday, September 29, before a throng of 52,751 at the Polo Grounds. The game was a beauty, a tense pitchers' duel between Lemon and Maglie. Into the top of the eighth it went, tied 2–2, when the Barber began to tire. He walked Larry Doby to lead off the inning, then surrendered a single to Al Rosen, advancing Doby to second with no outs. Next up was Wertz, a left-handed-batting slugger, and Durocher made a move that is commonplace today but was aggressive for 1954: he brought in a left-handed reliever, Don Liddle, to face just this key lefty hitter. Liddle hung a curve above the belt, and Wertz got every ounce of it.

Watching from a seat in the center field bleachers was Arnold Hano, a thirty-two-year-old sometime novelist and former fiction editor, now seeking his fortune as a freelance magazine writer. His peerless recounting of the subsequent play in his book *A Day in the Bleachers* became an eternal gem of sports literature:

> And this was not a terribly high drive. It was a long low fly or a high liner, whichever you wish. This ball was hit not nearly so high as the triple Wertz struck earlier in the day, so I may have assumed that it would soon start to break and dip and come down to Mays, not too far from his normal position.
>
> Then I looked at Willie, and alarm raced through me, peril flaring against my heart. To my utter astonishment, the young Giant center fielder—the inimitable Mays, most skilled of outfielders, unique for his ability to scent the length and direction of any drive and then turn and move to the final destination of the ball—Mays was turned full around, head down, running as hard as he could, straight toward the runway between the two bleacher sections.
>
> I knew then that I had underestimated—*badly* underestimated— the length of Wertz's blow.[61]

In any other ballpark on the planet except the Polo Grounds, Wertz's blast would have been not just a game-breaking three-run homer but an epic tape measure bomb, a titanic shot to be forever recounted in World Series lore. And even within the weirdly configured Polo Grounds, with any other center fielder on the planet except Willie Mays, it would have safely landed for a two-run triple, still with no outs. In either case it would have been a devastating eighth-inning blow for the Indians against the Giants, quite possibly a mortal blow, the turning point of the game.

With Mays's astonishing catch-and-throw—a play so iconic it would become known simply as "The Catch"—it was a turning point, indeed, but in the very opposite direction, a sudden and bewildering reversal of momentum. Cleveland, instead of busting the tight game wide open, would fail to score in the eighth. Into extra innings the game would go instead, still deadlocked at 2–2, when in the bottom of the tenth, with one out and two runners on, pinch hitter Dusty Rhodes (who else?) lofted a soft fly ball down the right field line—not much more than a pop fly, really, as Indians second baseman Bobby Avila gave chase going out while right fielder Dave Pope came in and toward the corner—and it landed *just* over the wall, *just* fair, the chintziest possible Polo Grounds–only home run (Stoneham's characterization of it was "real Chinese") to win the game. What bitter irony it had to be for the Indians, after what had become of Wertz's colossal clout.

Rhodes and the Giants now could do no wrong. The next day Durocher summoned him as a pinch hitter again, this time in the fifth inning, and Dusty swiftly delivered a game-tying RBI single off Early Wynn. Rhodes remained in the game, and his next time up, in the seventh, he hit another home run, this one not a cheapie but an upper-deck monster ("went nine miles," according to Stoneham), and the rout was on. The teams traveled to Cleveland, and the Giants proceeded to knock out the great Indians' starters, Garcia and Lemon, early in each game, breezing to no-sweat 6–2 and 7–4 wins. The Giants had not just beaten the 111-win Cleveland juggernaut to win the World Series; they'd swept it in four straight, a feat every bit as impressive as those once achieved by the mighty John McGraw. Horace Stoneham, no question about it, had finally got a winner.

In the victorious locker room following the closeout win, Stoneham made a grand tour, congratulating every last player. He repeated: "That's the way to do it. Get it over with quick!" As

Stoneham moved along the benches, shaking hands and slapping backs, Dusty Rhodes, drinking a bottle of beer, tapped the owner on the shoulder. "Hey, Mr. Stoneham," asked the World Series hero, "Where's the champagne?" Stoneham grinned and replied, "It'll be on the plane!"[62]

That Giants' party plane returning from Cleveland was just the warmup, delivering its passengers to a truly special celebration. Hosted by Stoneham at the Waldorf, it was of a style and scale equal to any ever presented by C. A. Stoneham or John J. McGraw.[63] As Stoneham sliced an enormous cake, topped by a Giants' cap sculpted in frosting, Leo the Lip, wiping tears while hugging Willie Mays, testified: "I've never won the big one until now. I wondered whether there was something in me that prevented it."[64]

The Giants were graced with a remarkable honor, as the City of New York threw them a ticker tape parade down Broadway through the Canyon of Heroes, an honor never before bestowed upon any baseball team, not even the Yankees. It was a tremendous height for Horace Stoneham's Giants to have seized. It would be the apex.

8

We Have No Chance to Survive Here

ollowing their dust-up in the 1952–53 off-season, Leo Durocher
and Horace Stoneham had patched things up. But the relationship was never the same again, and in the spring of 1954
it heated up once more. The Giants were training, as usual, in
Arizona. Durocher that spring found it more frequently convenient than usual to make his way over to nearby Palm Springs or
LA and party it up in immoderate form with whichever Hollywood celebrities were available. This activity was gleefully highlighted in the gossipy rags but wasn't happily received by those
who thought it unbecoming. Included in the latter category was
Alvin Dark, the Giants' star shortstop and team captain, and a
conservative Southern Baptist.

Dark complained to Stoneham, who then found himself in the
awkward position of having to take a side in a quarrel between
his star player and his manager. Stoneham chose to side with
Dark and had it out with Durocher. In the subsequent interrog-
atories Stoneham (perhaps, at that specific moment, a cocktail
or so past prudent) told Durocher he was fired. The next morning came without this threat being acted upon, but word of the
confrontation got back to Dark. He went to Stoneham and suggested that it would be best left to him and the rest of the team's
veterans to make sure that Leo the Lip didn't get out of hand.[1]

So, it was cooled down, for now. However, nobody was around
Durocher to keep him in line during the celebratory off-season
following the 1954 championship. Back on his Hollywood turf,
hanging out and showing off with his cool-cat show business

friends, Durocher repeatedly griped about Stoneham behind his back, ridiculing him as a tiresome drunk. The showbiz pals, who only knew of Stoneham what Durocher told them, happily ran with the gag.

Among the many banquets at which Durocher was feted as the guest of honor that autumn and winter, one was a particularly raucous stag party at the Friars Club on East Fifty-Fifth Street in New York. On the dais were A-list celebrities including Jack Benny, Groucho Marx, and George Jessel. A special feature was Danny Kaye's imitation of a drunk Horace Stoneham. Kaye had Stoneham's signature old-school patter just right—"pally," "by golly"—and Kaye's exaggerated drunken diction was brutal.

"The greatest thing," Durocher chortled later, "was when Danny opened his fly and pulled out his pecker and put it on a saucer. He's doing Horace. I mean, the sloppy talk and the stupid speeches and the rest. He's doin' Horace with his pecker hanging out. I never laughed so hard in my life."[2]

Hilarious though it may have been, there was an inescapable element of self-destructiveness in Durocher's carrying on. He had to realize that Stoneham, sooner or later, was going to get word of all this, and he had to have some realistic expectation of how Stoneham might react. Indeed, Stoneham heard about it. Everyone in baseball heard about it; the scene became the hottest baseball business gossip of that winter.[3]

Stoneham was not about to fire his star manager following a World Series sweep, especially with a year remaining on his hefty contract. But Stoneham was understandably hurt, humiliated, and furious with Durocher. Leo's days as manager of the Giants were now numbered, probably no matter how well the team might perform in 1955.

From Stoneham's perspective what Durocher had done was not only insult his employer; he'd blatantly violated a fundamental trust. Bill Veeck knew Stoneham very well, and Veeck's father—who was president of the Chicago Cubs from 1919 to 1933—had known Stoneham's father very well. Bill Veeck's perception of the dynamic seems astute: "Basically, he is little different from his father. . . . The Stonehams, father and son, lived in the Broadway gambler's world of impulsive, compulsive, and colorful characters, a world held together by a rigid code. Your word was good. You paid your debts. You didn't presume to judge the kind of life your friends and acquaintances lived, just so long as they observed the code, too. . . . With Horace, the Irish-Catholic clannishness and the Broadway gambler's sense of loyalty come together to produce a man to whom friendship and loyalty are so much a way of life that disloyalty becomes an act of treason."[4]

Repeating as champion is an extremely difficult thing to do in baseball (well, unless you are the Yankees), but with the Durocher-Stoneham relationship in tatters, it was going to be that much harder for the Giants in 1955.

Stoneham stood pat with his roster that off-season, and the cast from 1954 returned. With that the Giants in 1955 lost five of their first six games and were unable to get above .500 until mid-May. The Dodgers, meanwhile, blasted out white-hot at 22–2, led wire to wire, and the pennant race was essentially over as soon as it had begun. The Giants would not repeat. They finished a mediocre 80–74, in third place, miles behind the runaway Dodgers.

There was a sense of listlessness and tedium to the season. Several Giant veterans showed their age: Monte Irvin, at thirty-six, hit poorly and was cast away to the minors; Wes Westrum, at thirty-two, receded into second-string status; thirty-three-year-old Alvin Dark was nagged with injuries for the first time in his career; and Sal Maglie, thirty-eight years old, pitched less than his best, and Stoneham let him go on waivers to the Cleveland Indians.

Second baseman Davey Williams, though just twenty-seven, was overcome with chronic back trouble and forced to retire before the season's end.[5] Third baseman Hank Thompson, at twenty-nine, began an early decline as years of excessive drinking took their toll.

Willie Mays was sensational again, not only leading the major leagues with fifty-one home runs but now adding the skill of base stealing to his dazzling all-around game, swiping twenty-four in twenty-eight attempts. But nevertheless, this Giants' team wasn't good enough to contend.

Durocher, apparently understanding at last that he'd blown it with Stoneham, casually phoned it in all year while still talking big with the Hollywood crowd. Durocher would frequently arrive at the Polo Grounds just a few minutes before game time.

"You can't believe what I put up with," Durocher would tell Spencer Tracy. "The boss is a full-time drunk."

"I used to be a drunk myself," Tracy replied. "That was in the old heimerdeimer days."

"Not like Horace," Durocher said. "We got to make some moves. He says, 'We'll be okay, pally.' I'm sick of this."[6]

To the press Durocher spun it that he'd be willing to stay with the Giants if Stoneham would make him the general manager. To anyone who knew the situation, that was laughable, but it was a way for Durocher to attempt to save face as the inevitable occurred. At season's end, when Leo Durocher's contract with the New York Giants expired, he was pointedly not invited to return. A distinct era was flatly finished.

The New York Giants' humdrum third-place performance on the field in 1955 could properly be understood as the least of Horace Stoneham's worries. In the pennant-winning season of 1954, Polo Grounds attendance had rebounded to 1.1 million, second highest in the league, but in '55 it dropped all the way to sixth best, at 824,000.

By the mid-1950s several long-developing economic and demographic dynamics were well underway in the United States. More people than ever before were choosing the automobile as their primary means of transportation. Doing so allowed them to move away from congested city centers and out into suburban developments, which were, consequently, rapidly developing. The widespread construction of modern roads and freeways supported this trend, accelerating the cycle.

It was, of course, the more affluent households that were most able to move out to the leafy suburbs in the station wagon, which also meant, disproportionally, the white households. Racism abided, often in the form of exclusionary real estate covenants, a widespread practice that continued unofficially after being declared unconstitutional in 1948. As the suburbs boomed, the inner cities grew poorer and Blacker. This was "white flight."

This phenomenon wasn't simply one of older downtowns surrendering residents to younger suburbs. It played out as well along the axis of the broader geography, as the nation's population shifted away from older, densely packed cities (mostly in the East and Upper Midwest) and into more modern, sprawling metropolitan areas that had been purposefully built out to prioritize cars. The country was migrating west and south, and this movement helped propel the economic dynamism of such younger, fast-growing places as Greater Los Angeles, the San Francisco Bay Area, Seattle, Minneapolis–St. Paul, Kansas City, Dallas–Fort Worth, Houston, and Atlanta while simultaneously draining the economic vitality of the downtown districts of older cities like New York, Boston, Philadelphia, Washington, Cleveland, and Detroit.

This was a broad change, impacting all industries and businesses in various ways, positively and negatively. But for the business of baseball teams such as the New York Giants, staging their games deeply inside congested inner cities, in deteriorating old-fashioned facilities, with inadequate and insecure parking, in increasingly downscale minority-majority neighborhoods, all the news was bad. Their long-established customer base was moving away, as the convenience and attractiveness of their product was steadily degrading. The trends were all downward, and it was obvious that significant changes were inevitable. Commissioner of baseball Ford Frick assessed it plainly in October 1954: "Baseball is trying to operate as it did in 1900—and it can't be done. Population and business have gone West. Baseball must follow."[7]

The 1955 season was the third in a row in which a major league team relocated, as the Philadelphia Athletics moved to Kansas City. And for the third time in a row, the relocating team was rewarded with an enormous increase in attendance. The Boston Braves had drawn fewer than 300,000 in their final year, and then the Milwaukee Braves had averaged just under 2 million per year in their first three seasons. The St. Louis Browns had also posted attendance under 300,000 in 1953 and then averaged about 950,000 in their first two years as the Baltimore Orioles. And the A's went from drawing 304,666 in Philadelphia in 1954 to nearly 1.4 million in Kansas City in '55. And unlike the Braves, who had simultaneously shown great improvement on the field, both the Orioles and Athletics enjoyed their attendance booms while remaining dismal tail-enders in the standings. In light of this, by mid-1955 speculation was widespread regarding the possible relocations of other clubs, certainly including the Giants.

In August 1955 Walter O'Malley announced that in 1956 the Dodgers would play seven of their home games in Jersey City. To Dodgers fans the news was ominous. They were aware that the seating capacity of Ebbets Field was small and that parking facilities were outmoded and inadequate, and they could see that although the Dodgers were headed for their third pennant in four years, attendance was dropping steadily. But why Jersey City? What did it mean? O'Malley explained that since 1948 he'd been seeking a new home park and that Ebbets Field would definitely not be used after 1957. He added that a new facility could be built with private capital and that he had secured six million dollars for that purpose but that he needed help from the city in securing a desirable site. The move to Jersey City, even for seven games, was seen as a demonstration of the team's readiness to vacate Brooklyn altogether. Several days after O'Malley's announcement, Stoneham sent a telegram to New York mayor Robert F. Wagner asking that the possibility of a new stadium for the Giants be considered if similar action were to be undertaken on behalf of Brooklyn.[8]

Shortly after that, none other than Memphis Bill Terry, alarmed by the swirling rumors he was hearing that Stoneham was considering the relocation of the New York Giants and/or the sale of the franchise, bluntly inserted himself into the disquiet picture. Terry was alarmed at the idea of the Giants moving, and he told sportswriter Dan Daniel of the *New York World-Telegram* that he was going to try to buy his old club. He said he could likely raise sufficient cash and that he'd already consulted with several potential partners in the effort. "I mean every word of it," Terry said. "If Horace Stoneham wants to sell the Giants, let him put a price on them." Terry added that the Polo Grounds, badly in need of refurbishment, would present no problem since the park would no longer be used. "We would move into Yankee Stadium," said Terry. "I am pretty sure I could field a team that would give the Yankees a run for the patronage."

However, the relationship between Terry and Stoneham was a bit fraught. Through they'd parted on friendly terms when Terry resigned as general manager in 1942, Stoneham understood that Terry had essentially considered him as merely the boss's son—a lightweight—and there was never warmth between them.

Stoneham now took Terry's uninvited pronouncements as a public challenge, and he wasn't pleased. Stoneham's response to Terry was icy, as a headline in the *World-Telegram* suggested:

GIANTS ARE NOT

FOR SALE EVER

TO BILL TERRY

Stoneham was quoted: "The New York Giants are not for sale. If they are for sale, the negotiating will be done with one of several New York City individuals or groups who from time to time have expressed an interest in the New York Giants."[9] Stoneham's wording was ambiguous, on the one hand indignantly denying any intention to sell the team and on the other saying he might negotiate with those who had "expressed an interest." What was clear is that with whomever Stoneham might have discussed the idea—if anyone—it hadn't been Bill Terry. After Stoneham's statement Terry admitted that no formal offer had been made, but he repeated his initial comment to the press. "Yeah, I'd like to have the Giants," he said in the *Times*.

Nothing would ever come of Terry's sudden interest in purchasing the Giants, and indeed, there's no evidence that Stoneham ever seriously considered selling the team to anyone. But finding a new and modern ballpark that optimized automobile access and parking—whether in New York or elsewhere—was certainly a very serious priority for Stoneham, just as it was for O'Malley.

Following the 1955 season, Stoneham didn't need the urging of Leo Durocher or anyone else to "back up the truck." His terrific team that had won two pennants in the first half of the 1950s was now aging out and falling apart, and it was time for a rebuilding. Stoneham understood that. However, he wouldn't execute a large volume of trades to revamp the roster; instead, he would rely on the increasingly robust production from his remarkable farm system to provide in-house regeneration.

Indeed, it was from the farm system that he harvested his new manager to replace Durocher. Bill Rigney, the Giants' infielder from 1946 through 1953, had been appointed by Stoneham as manager of the AAA Minneapolis Millers in 1954, and in '55 he'd guided them to the American Association pennant. He turned thirty-eight years old in January 1956 and represented a departure from Leo the Lip in a number of ways, not just that he was much younger but more that he was far less egotistical and attention seeking. Rigney was sharp-witted and energetic but fundamentally decent and pleasant to work with. Everybody liked "Rig."

The new manager's lineups in 1956 would make liberal use of younger talent, including infielder Daryl Spencer, who returned from military service, along with rookie first baseman Bill White and rookie infielders Foster Castleman and Eddie Bressoud. Stoneham did swing one big midseason trade, sending Alvin Dark and Whitey Lockman in a package to the St. Louis Cardinals, with the key talents in return being veteran star second baseman Albert "Red" Schoendienst and promising rookie outfielder Jackie Brandt.

So, the 1956 Giants were younger, by and large. But they weren't good. The pitching overall was decent, but the Giants' run production in 1956 was atrocious, last in the league by a wide margin. Willie Mays remained spectacular—in 1956 he became the second player in major league history to achieve thirty-plus home runs along with thirty-plus stolen bases, a feat he would repeat in 1957—but the '56 Giants offense featured little else.

The team trudged in at 67–87, in sixth place, twenty-six games behind the pennant-winning (yet again) Brooklyn Dodgers. Attendance at the Polo Grounds spiraled down to 629,000, dead last in the National League. The soaring heights of the world championship had been theirs just two years earlier, but it now seemed like two decades.

What else could go wrong? Well, the New York Giants of the National Football League could decide to stop renting the Polo Grounds from Stoneham to play their games and move to Yankee Stadium instead. That could go wrong in 1956. That source of income was now gone. The sinking ship essence was now palpable.

Walter O'Malley had been pursuing options of new stadium construction with various New York stakeholders more assertively than had Stoneham, who had never appeared to take that avenue very seriously. In May 1956 Stoneham for the first time publicly acknowledged that, instead, relocating his franchise was a real possibility, as he was considering moving the franchise to Minneapolis–St. Paul.[10] Indeed, Chub Feeney was dispatched to the Twin Cities multiple times to discuss the idea with local government authorities and business leaders and to assess progress in the construction, which had begun in 1955, of Metropolitan Stadium in suburban Bloomington. This was a publicly financed and owned facility being built to modern standards and priorities—in other words, sited in the comfortably white suburbs, away from the dingy and "dark" (wink wink) old downtown, easily accessible by car, and surrounded by vast acres of parking lot—and intended precisely for the purpose of attracting a major league tenant. The project had been inspired in 1953 by the colossal success of the Milwaukee Braves at County Stadium—which was itself a public property purpose-built to attract a big-league team.

New York city fathers could see what was going on, and there was lots of talk, at least, about the feasibility of accommodating either or both of the Giants and Dodgers with a new stadium or stadiums to keep them from leaving. The improbably named president of the Manhattan borough, Hulan Jack, announced a spectacular plan for a new ballpark that would seat 110,000 spectators. Jack asserted that negotiations were underway to explore the construction of such a park to be built upon stilts, suspended above a railroad yard along the Hudson River in Midtown Manhattan. In addition to the baseball park, there was to be a thirty-story office building and a garage for twenty thousand cars.[11] Needless to say, that one never got past the conceptual phase. New York City was, alas, an exceptionally complicated entity, and it was proving highly difficult to get all of the necessary interests and forces in alignment, particularly when the city was no longer doing well economically and there were endless competing and overlapping priorities to be addressed.

But neither the Giants nor the Dodgers could afford to wait forever. Time was not on the city's side. On October 30, 1956, the Dodgers, announced that Ebbets Field had been sold to Marvin Kratter, a Brooklyn real estate operator, and that the property would be redeveloped as a housing complex for middle-income families. The Dodgers signed a lease allowing them to stay on through 1959. "The lease insures us of a home until the new stadium can be built," said assistant GM Arthur "Red" Patterson.

But would such a stadium ever be built? Patterson's words seemed to indicate that O'Malley had been assured Brooklyn would have its new park. Earlier that summer the New York state legislature had passed a bill creating a Brooklyn Sports Center Authority, a group authorized to investigate the situation. But investigate was all it did; there was much talk but no meaningful action. "We're at a standstill right now," said Charles J. Mylod, head of the new commission. "We don't have the funds to go ahead. We know what we want to do and are anxious to get going on the job, but the budget for the Authority has not been okayed."[12]

Meanwhile, the inexorable economic pressure intensified, especially on the Giants. Among the elements in the fast-changing dynamic was, of course, the perplexing issue of television, an impact getting larger every year. On the one hand, revenue from broadcast rights was growing steadily—the Giants yielded $490,000 in television money in 1954, and that figure expanded to $646,000 in 1955 and $731,000 in 1956—but on the other, for the Giants that growth was being more than offset by the decline in ticket and concessions revenue. In these years there was always one, often two, and sometimes three free TV games broadcast in New York every day during the baseball season, a volume of programming unique to the New York market. It was widely considered that TV was the primary driver of depressed attendance, and in New York it was the Giants suffering the most. This was the reality facing Stoneham.[13]

We don't know at exactly what point in the autumn and winter of 1956–57 that Stoneham firmly resolved a decision to move. But he did. He was leaning toward Minneapolis, but he was moving somewhere. Stoneham simply had no realistic alternatives in New York, and the examples of the Braves, Orioles, and Athletics alluringly sang that relocation to a virgin market offered not just economic survival but a jackpot. It was therefore pointless to put it off any longer. Indeed, Stoneham may well have felt a sense of competitive urgency: if he didn't soon grab the best destination available, some other team would.

So, sometime during that fateful off-season, Stoneham came to know that the 1957 season was going to be the Giants' last in New York. Especially and profoundly for fifty-four-year-old Horace Charles Stoneham, ever-devoted son of Charles Abraham Stoneham—as pure and thorough a creature of New York as there ever was—that must have been a hard reckoning indeed.

The roster changes Stoneham undertook in 1956–57 seemed calculated to goose dwindling Polo Grounds ticket sales more than improving the team. He signed thirty-nine-year-old veteran slugger Hank Sauer, who'd been released by St. Louis, anticipating that the onetime MVP might have enough left to whack some home runs and give the fans something fun to watch. He reacquired Whitey Lockman, whose performance in recent years was in decline but who had long been popular with Giants fans. Most interestingly—in a transaction not quite as shocking as the hiring of Leo Durocher back in 1948 but still jaw-dropping—Stoneham sent $30,000 and a second-line player to O'Malley's Dodgers in exchange for none other than Jackie Robinson, the most fiercely intense enemy. Robinson would be thirty-eight in 1957 and was plainly nearing the end of his playing days, but he could surely serve as a box office attraction. However, Robinson himself put the kibosh on that, deciding to retire rather than change uniforms, and the deal was quickly voided.

In June 1957 Stoneham accepted a trade offer from the Milwaukee Braves for Red Schoendienst, still performing very well at thirty-four. The humdrum package the Giants received included old hero Bobby Thomson, now thirty-three and heading downhill but a sentimental valentine to the Polo Grounds fans. In any case the 1957 Giants again slogged their way to another sixth-place finish and again were last in the National League in attendance.

It was all, of course, an entirely secondary consideration. In March 1957, at an owners' meeting in Clearwater, Florida, O'Malley had pulled Stoneham aside and asked what he was planning to do. Stoneham answered that he was probably going to relocate to Minneapolis. It was at this point that O'Malley proposed to Stoneham the idea of them moving together, to California. He reasoned that the long-standing Dodger-Giant rivalry had always been good for both of their businesses and that dynamic could be sustained on the West Coast. Following this meeting, O'Malley and Stoneham jointly commissioned a survey to be conducted by a market research firm to assess the receptiveness of California fans to the Dodgers and Giants. Meanwhile, O'Malley asked Los Angeles mayor Norris Paulson if he might be able to coordinate with San Francisco mayor George Christopher, and Paulson said he was already doing so. For his part Stoneham was already in contact with Christopher's office.[14]

Having the Giants accompany the Dodgers to California made sense from O'Malley's perspective in two ways. The first, just as he told Stoneham, was that keeping the traditional rivalry alive— indeed, reimagining it in two new natural rival cities—could only serve to stimulate fan interest. The second was logistical but nonetheless important: there were meaningful travel efficiencies to be gained by having two teams out on the West Coast instead of one. It would be better for everyone in the league.[15]

For Stoneham, Minneapolis–St. Paul had been his primary relocation candidate, of course, and the only destination to which he'd yet dedicated serious resources and investigation. But neither is it plausible that O'Malley's suggestion of San Francisco was the first time that idea had ever crossed Stoneham's mind. For one thing, the city of San Francisco itself was hardly a passive bystander. San Francisco had sought a major league team for years. Way back in 1932, John McGraw himself visited the city and toured Seals Stadium, telling San Francisco Seals owner Charley Graham, "You'll have major league baseball here someday, Charley." In the early 1950s San Francisco supervisor Francis McCarty and Downtown Association secretary Tom Gray were leading an active campaign to attract a major league franchise. Mayor George Christopher appointed McCarty head of the major league committee. In 1954 a $5 million bond issue was placed before the San Francisco voters for the purpose of building a stadium "if a major league franchise can be obtained." It passed overwhelmingly.

Many clubs were invited in for talks prior to the Giants' interest. The Washington Senators, Cleveland Indians, Cincinnati Reds, Philadelphia Athletics, St. Louis Browns, and even the Boston Red Sox, who owned the San Francisco Pacific Coast League franchise for its final two seasons, were asked to "please investigate." Both the National and American League offices were visited by San Francisco representatives, happy to discuss expansion if no team wanted to relocate.[16] The notion that Stoneham could have been unaware of all this, or indeed not keenly interested in it, is preposterous. There's every reason to believe that Stoneham had at least thought about the possibility of San Francisco, just as he would have sensibly thought about other potential destinations such as Dallas and Houston. The concept of relocation had been vibrantly alive throughout major league baseball for years before 1957, in the front of the minds of all teams, including the Giants.

The quickness with which Stoneham embraced the notion of "partnering" with O'Malley in this way and how swiftly the decision process was resolved in 1957 also suggest that the idea wasn't brand new. It just made so much practical sense, from the Giants' perspective every bit as much as from the Dodgers'. Moreover, there was the rather important fact that the San Francisco

Bay Area was a bigger market, more affluent and faster growing than Minneapolis–St. Paul. Finally, it probably wasn't trivial that downtown San Francisco presented a sense of beauty, charm, and style that few others—sorry, Minneapolis—could match. For Manhattanite Stoneham, that unquestionably meant something.

In any case Stoneham, being Stoneham, played it coy with the press. Following his spring training consultations with O'Malley, Stoneham revealed that he had offers to transfer the Giants to Minneapolis, San Francisco, and a city of the Southwest, either Houston or Dallas. "If the Dodgers should move to Los Angeles," Stoneham said, "our rivalry with them would suffer considerably, even though we should still be in the same league. In that case, we would have to decide whether it would be better for us to move too, or try to continue in New York at Yankee Stadium, if we were invited to play there, or in some other place in the city."[17]

But things were moving along now. O'Malley visited Los Angeles in early May 1957 to meet with Poulson and Christopher. Following that meeting, O'Malley called Stoneham in New York and told him that all signs were positive. Stoneham reminded O'Malley that he had a ballpark already constructed and available in Minneapolis, and he was uncertain about the stadium deal San Francisco could offer. O'Malley then decided that it was time for Stoneham and Christopher to meet directly.

So, Christopher flew to New York, and on May 10 they met at the Hotel Lexington in Manhattan, hosted by O'Malley. Among the topics discussed were stadium lease terms, and Christopher admitted that he had no experience with such contracts. At this O'Malley took a pen and a Hotel Lexington envelope and, yes, scribbled some numbers on the back of the envelope. Christopher and Stoneham studied the figures, and both found them workable. Christopher left the meeting and announced to the press that a preliminary agreement had been reached. Commissioner Ford Frick then requested that the parties refrain from public discussion on the issue unless and until a formal deal was struck.[18]

On May 28, 1957, National League owners held a special meeting and voted, unanimously, to grant permission to the Brooklyn Dodgers and New York Giants franchises to relocate to Los Angeles and San Francisco, respectively, if they should so choose. League president Warren Giles explained: "Previously they were unable to make any definite commitments despite a number of meetings with the mayors of the two California cities involved. They are now free to make a decision one way or another."

In July, Stoneham called a press conference and announced: "I am going to recommend to my board of directors that we leave the Polo Grounds after this season. I can show them that we face an anticipated decrease in revenue for every year we stay here. We have no chance to survive here."[19]

On August 19, 1957, the board of the National Exhibition Company voted eight to one in favor of relocating their National League franchise from New York, New York, to San Francisco, California. The New York Giants, the team of Jim Mutrie and John McGraw, of Christy Mathewson, Bill Terry, and Mel Ott, and of Charles A. Stoneham, would exist no longer.[20]

In the decades to follow, popular lore never tired of playing the angle that O'Malley had somehow hoodwinked Stoneham into something he hadn't thought through. It plays to the easy narrative caricatures of both O'Malley as master player / Brooklyn villain and of Stoneham as useful idiot / lucky bumbler. Over the years O'Malley, ever alert toward his reputation in the press, carefully made no comment disavowing that interpretation, while Stoneham probably paid no attention. In any case the plain truth is that no one hoodwinked anyone in this grand episode in baseball history. Stoneham understood exactly what he was doing, and he was every bit as fully invested in it as O'Malley.

Independently of O'Malley, Stoneham had already committed to the decision to move. The only part to which Stoneham wasn't yet committed was his destination. Yes, it was probably going to be Minneapolis, but it's always prudent to consider all of one's options before deciding.[21] Besides, having the Minneapolis deal pretty much in his pocket—his to take or leave— afforded Stoneham bargaining leverage with San Francisco. When O'Malley proposed the possibility of San Francisco to Stoneham, it isn't difficult to imagine Stoneham's grinning reply to be something along the lines of "Why, Walter, I thought you'd never ask." There was a notable absence of hesitation on Stoneham's part. As author Harvey Frommer put it: "Stoneham was not pushed. He jumped."[22]

Among the things that made the story so colorful, and such fertile material for myth, was the sheer difference between the rival owners as personalities. "O'Malley came across as a political wheeler-dealer, a smoker of big, long cigars, a duplicitous man who had greased the way for the exile of Branch Rickey to Pittsburgh. A roly-poly type, his thick eyebrows and accentuated speech pattern suggested the kind of person who would foreclose mortgage payments on a widow and four children. Stoneham was quieter, gentler. He looked like an out-of-uniform Santa Claus."[23]

In this story the abiding myths, as all myths do, serve to make sense out of confusion by forging a simplified narrative in place of a complex and nuanced truth. In author Robert Garratt's words, "Myth, as the scholars tell us, often wanders into the fabulous and the marvelous, but it conveys nonetheless a truth of its own, revealing and explaining type and character."[24] O'Malley and Stoneham did in fact each exhibit distinctive and defining predilections, which laid the foundation for creative extensions among various commentators, and the story tended to get better with every successive retelling.

The persistence and exuberance of the O'Malley trickster myth was served by the interactions of sportswriters with the two owners. O'Malley cultivated the writers, worked the relationships, and was outgoing and loquacious, while Stoneham, while polite, was reclusive and taciturn. This assisted the invention in the press of O'Malley as a manipulator who convinced Stoneham to move. But that characterization was never supported by facts, regardless of how convenient such a narrative might be.[25]

Perhaps a reason that chroniclers were prone to inaccurately describe Stoneham was that it was difficult to accurately understand him. Horace Stoneham was broadly depicted as trusting, bibulous, and generous to a fault, all of which had basis in truth, but those who knew him well understood that he was also stubborn, smart, damn hardworking, and despite his essential shyness, a great and true friend to many, far and wide.[26] In a *Sports Illustrated* feature on Stoneham in 1958, Robert Shaplen considered him to be "one of the most complicated men in the game."[27] In the same magazine a year earlier, Robert Creamer wrote of Stoneham: "No one has ever said he lacks courage, and no one has ever called him stupid. . . . Horace Stoneham doesn't talk as much as Walter O'Malley, and he has no compulsion for forcing events, like O'Malley, but when the situation demands drastic action, Stoneham throws the dice with the best of them."[28]

Bill Veeck was never one to miss a chance to point out, if perhaps in a wry way, the shortcomings of famous baseball executives, many of whom he considered fools. But he never expressed anything other than admiration for Stoneham's quiet sense of gamesmanship and diplomacy. Veeck even compared Stoneham with Branch Rickey in this regard, considering that pair as "the two men I least cared to match myself against" in trade negotiations. He assessed that both excelled at disguising their purposes by lurking one step ahead of their proposed bargaining positions. Sure, Stoneham "could get plastered twice a day" (never a concept foreign to Veeck himself), but "you always seem to find that everybody sets out to take advantage of Horace and, by dint of great effort, manages to trick him into doing what he has already decided to do."[29]

The fundamental marvel about Horace Stoneham is how such a sensitive person, for whom the New York Giants were essentially flesh and blood and for whom the Polo Grounds was not only a shrine in which he watched every game from the same clubhouse perch as his father but also had often been literally his very home, could then coolly chuck it all and move away. The explanation was not that he was a fool but, instead, that he was the furthest thing from it.

When announcing the decision, Stoneham was presented with a question about what the team's departure would mean to the ranks of innocent kid Giants' fans. His reply was sly: "I feel bad about the kids, but I haven't seen many of their fathers at the ballpark lately." There's no reason to doubt that Stoneham did truly feel badly about the kids, but he had a hard business decision to make, and he'd made it.[30]

Stoneham was called to testify before the United States House of Representatives on July 17, 1957, in an antitrust hearing chaired by Congressman Emanuel Celler of Brooklyn. The Giant owner's language revealed clean decisiveness. While he hadn't yet made his formal announcement of the move, Stoneham all but laid out precisely what he was going to do. In contrast to Walter O'Malley's prior testimony, which was evasive and equivocal, Stoneham was straightforward, especially on two essential points. First, when asked, "Am I correct in understanding that if a suitable proposition is made, you would move the Giants to San Francisco next year?" Stoneham replied unambiguously, "I would recommend it to our board, yes, sir."

The second question revealed Stoneham's resolve. The same member asked, "Would you recommend this move to San Francisco even if the Dodgers remained in Brooklyn?" Stoneham directly answered, "I think I would, yes, sir." Then the congressman probed, "In other words, your decision would not be predicated on any decision that the Dodgers would make," and Stoneham responded, "No, sir."[31]

It was, then, all done except for the formalities. And so the 1957 season played out to its end. Many Giants fans expressed anger, but the more typical response was shocked numbness. And of course, whatever Giants fans were feeling, few were purchasing tickets at the Polo Grounds.

The last Giants game at the old stadium was on Sunday, September 29, against the Pittsburgh Pirates. Stoneham did his best to see to it that an appropriate sense of ceremony was observed, inviting a long list of former players, including George Burns, Larry Doyle, Carl Hubbell, Rube Marquard, Rosy Ryan, and Hal Schumacher, as along with recent favorites Sid Gordon and Sal Maglie. Manager Bill Rigney presented a bouquet of long-stemmed red roses to the widow of John McGraw.

The august event attracted a "crowd" of 11,608. Horace Stoneham himself did not attend. "I couldn't go to the game," he would explain. "I just didn't want to see it come to an end."[32]

Rigney put as many familiar veterans in the starting lineup as he could, including Thomson, Lockman, Westrum, Mueller, and Rhodes as well as Mays. The Giants lost 9–1. When Rhodes grounded out to shortstop to end the game, the small crowd stormed the place. Swarming fans filled the playing field, not with the joy of a celebration but with something more like the intensity of an attack. The ballplayers sprinted in headlong retreat toward the center field clubhouse. More than one writer would describe the scene as some form of mass psychosis, essentially a riot. The mob dug up home plate and fought for possession of it and also uprooted the bases, the pitching rubber, and great swatches of turf. They yanked down the bullpen canopies along the outfield walls, ripped out the dugout telephones, and stripped off various signs, including the plaque memorializing Eddie Grant, the Giants player who'd been killed in the Great War. At last the crowd, clutching their spoils, massed around the clubhouse. "Stay, team, stay!" they chanted. Others countered, "We want Stoneham!" Then it was "We want to stone him!" And "We want Stoneham—with a rope around his neck!"

On television station WPIX, Channel 11, Russ Hodges, who'd ecstatically called Bobby Thomson's heroic home run just six years earlier, narrated the disquiet scene as the camera panned across the melee on the field and the now-empty grandstands. Finally, he offered: "This, ladies and gentlemen, is the Polo Grounds, historic in baseball memory, where the New York Giants played for some 70 years, to so many friends and so many fans—with Mathewson and Terry, Mel Ott, Willie Mays, Leo Durocher and many others. Yes, ladies and gentlemen, that is the Polo Grounds. The tumult and the shouting may die. The captains and the kings may depart. . . . Lest we forget! Lest we forget!"[33]

Horace Stoneham had another reason to favor San Francisco over Minneapolis, and it involved the potential development of cutting-edge technology: pay television. The concept wasn't new and had been proposed and experimented in a number of ways over the years, under such names as Phonevision, Subscriber-Vision, Telemeter, and Telemovies, but had never successfully caught on. But one version being promoted in the 1950s appeared to have real promise for baseball, called Subscription Television, or STV, whose parent company was called Skiatron. STV was different in that it was hard-wired via cable, enabling it to avoid the problems facing pay television services relying upon Federal Communications Commission–licensed broadcast stations to distribute the signal. Skiatron was attracting attention with its announced project to wire the San Francisco and Los Angeles markets, a development of distinct significance for the Giants and Dodgers as they considered the move to the West Coast.[34]

Stoneham had long been dissatisfied with the impact of broadcast television on his baseball business in New York. He longed for a situation in which he could exercise more power over the delivery and consumption of his team's games on television, in which he could limit the TV coverage at his discretion so as to minimize the risk to attendance, and he sought a means to do all of this in a manner more directly lucrative than the broadcast rights status quo.

Thus, it was that another important figure in persuading Stoneham to decide on San Francisco as his destination was Matthew "Matty" Fox, the owner of Skiatron. A visionary technologist and a flashy salesman, Fox had been in O'Malley's ear since early 1957. Once O'Malley was sold on the idea, Fox trained his formidable energies on the Giants' owner.[35]

Fox's concept delighted Stoneham. It worked in two ways. Partnering with O'Malley, the Giants and Dodgers could package the programming of their own games to pay-per-view subscribers not just in California—where Los Angeles was the largest television market in the country and San Francisco the seventh biggest—but potentially elsewhere as well.

And the most intriguing other place was the New York market itself. Skiatron presented the possibility of marketing Giants and Dodgers games directly back to their New York fan base, hitting the vast New York market from the outside. Night games from the West Coast would make for a wonderful late, late show for stay-awake New Yorkers. Day games from California would hit New York in late afternoon and into the dinner hour, a popular viewing time. Indeed, pay TV could be worth the most in New York when the team was no longer there.[36]

There was no Matty Fox pitching any such idea in Minneapolis. Stoneham was all in, especially when Fox sweetened the deal. He offered Stoneham an escrow payment of $1 million to be paid in October 1957 and a second $1 million to be delivered on January 1, 1958. Stoneham was so enthusiastic that he purchased one thousand shares of Skiatron stock, which appreciated in value amid the speculation of San Francisco and Los Angeles business.[37]

Alas, the reality would prove far more complicated than the theory. Skiatron encountered delay after delay in getting STV operational. Political roadblocks arose, as the FCC was undecided on how to deal with subscription television, and intense lobbying against the concept was applied by established Hollywood interests. Moreover, in both San Francisco and Los Angeles practical complications emerged regarding the extensive cable installations required, which led to insufficient capital investment. In September 1958 the Giants announced that home games would appear on STV in 1959, but that proved not just premature but altogether false.[38]

Matty Fox's dream to wire San Francisco and Los Angeles and make Skiatron the first company to offer pay-per-view sports in the United States ended unhappily. Within a few years the whole thing collapsed. Cable television would have to wait another decade and a half before becoming a reality, but its promise had been a crucial influence on Stoneham's and O'Malley's decision to bring major league baseball to California.[39]

There was yet another factor tipping Stoneham's decision in favor of San Francisco over Minneapolis, and that was California's proximity to the state of Arizona. Stoneham first visited the Great West and its vast desert landscapes in 1923, on his journey to Copperopolis. Likely, he toured the area again at some point or points in the 1930s, when the Giants passed through Arizona during their meandering preseason barnstorming trips that were common in that period.

We know that in 1947 Stoneham partnered with Cleveland Indians owner Bill Veeck to transfer the spring training base of operations for both teams from Florida to Arizona. Veeck established his camp in Tucson and Stoneham 120 miles to the northwest, in Phoenix. With this the Cactus League was founded, as additional big-league teams would join the Giants and Indians in Arizona in the years to follow. One sometimes hears that the explanation for Stoneham and Veeck choosing Arizona for spring training, instead of Florida, was the absence of Jim Crow segregation policies in the western state, but that wouldn't have been relevant in the spring of 1947, when neither team had yet signed any players of color, and indeed, Jackie Robinson hadn't yet appeared in a major league game.

The actual reasons were more prosaic. Veeck loved the Southwest and owned ranches in the region, including one near Tucson. Stoneham had grown to love the desert as well and was looking into real estate investments there of his own. Arizona in the 1940s was a significantly cheaper place to do business than Florida; indeed, investing in Arizona real estate in that period was a case of "buying in on the ground floor" of an as-yet undeveloped market that many envisioned booming in the decades to come as a vacation and retirement destination, much as Florida had already done. Stoneham knew Del Webb, a Phoenix resident who'd become one of the owning partners of the New York Yankees in 1945 and was making a fortune in the construction business in Phoenix, Tucson, and Las Vegas.

And there was the practical consideration of reliable weather: when conducting training and staging exhibition contests in the Sonoran Desert in the springtime, one would practically never have to worry about a rainout, a frequent annoyance in tropical Florida.

Stoneham greatly preferred spring training in Arizona. Except for the spring of 1951, when the Giants and Yankees swapped Phoenix for St. Petersburg to give Webb the opportunity to show off his world champion Yankees in his hometown, the Giants would never again train outside of Arizona. Stoneham purchased a rambling Southwest ranch–style house in Scottsdale, just outside of Phoenix, which became his winter residence and eventually, in retirement, his year-round home. San Francisco was, conveniently, a whole lot closer to sunny Scottsdale than was Minneapolis.

Once the Giants transferred to San Francisco, Stoneham undertook the investment and development of an ambitious and forward-looking Arizona real estate venture. He endeavored to leverage baseball with a vacation resort. He chose the location of Casa Grande because that small town was roughly halfway between Phoenix, fifty miles to the north, and Tucson, seventy miles to the south. Therefore, Stoneham reasoned, Casa Grande was right in the center of the state's spring training action, accessible to both of the region's biggest towns.

Stoneham purchased a big patch of empty desert near Casa Grande, and in the late 1950s construction began. The complex was envisioned to incorporate a state-of-the-art baseball training facility, with multiple diamonds and bullpens and central observation towers for coaches and scouts to oversee it all, plus barracks to efficiently house his young players, far from the worldly temptations of Phoenix or Tucson taverns. Adjacent to that would be the Francisco Grande, a nine-story high-rise resort hotel with its roof shaped like a baseball cap, plus a big swimming pool in the shape of a baseball bat (with the hot tub serving as its baseball), and a plush restaurant and the Hall of Fame Cocktail Lounge (off-limits to players) and, adjacent to that, an eighteen-hole championship golf course.

The idea was that Stoneham would attract visitors to Casa Grande not only during spring training but throughout the long Arizona vacation season from October through April. No longer did he have the revenue stream from staging events in the Polo Grounds, but instead, he could supplement his earnings from the baseball business as the operator of a unique Arizona resort. And as the resort grew in popularity and the town of Casa Grande prospered, Stoneham would be able to develop and sell home lots on the expanses of land he owned adjacent to the resort property.

It was a bold vision, foreseeing the development of spring training—historically a ragtag affair—into the profitable vacation attraction it has become in recent decades. However, Stoneham's Casa Grande project would prove to be too far ahead of its time.

Stoneham spent the autumn and winter of 1957–58 busily engaged in the many logistical chores necessitated by the relocation. He paid an indemnity to the Pacific Coast League for the territorial rights to San Francisco and the termination of the San Francisco Seals franchise. He deeded his AAA team in Minneapolis to the Boston Red Sox, to compensate them for the Seals, who'd been their affiliate. He founded a new Giants AAA farm club in Phoenix, playing in the PCL.

Stoneham wanted to sell his lease on the Polo Grounds structure, but there were no buyers forthcoming. For all the same reasons that venue had become unattractive to baseball fans, it was no longer an in-demand site for sports of any sort—at least not until the Mets would be launched in 1962. By then Stoneham had agreed to relinquish control of the aging facility to the city of New York, but the Mets' need for the use of the Polo Grounds suddenly revived its market value. It became a complicated and contentious episode and wouldn't be settled until 1968.

And there was the practical exercise of moving the business of the Giants, setting up a box office and initiating ticket sales in San Francisco, and so on. Stoneham, loyal and paternalistic employer that he was, promised a job for every single employee in his organization. Anyone willing to make the move across the continent would keep his or her position. Virtually everyone took Stoneham up on his offer, including the front office staff of vice president Chub Feeney, treasurer Edgar Feeley, secretary Eddie Brannick, farm director Carl Hubbell and his chief lieutenants Jack Schwarz and Frank Shellenback, public relations director Garry Schumacher, and senior scout Tom Sheehan as well as clubhouse and equipment manager Eddie Logan, trainer Doc Bowman, and groundskeeper Matty Schwab. In San Francisco, Stoneham hired Jerry Donovan in the newly created position of business manager; Donovan, a former Pacific Coast League player, had been working in the front office of the San Francisco Seals, and he provided the Giants with a link to the Bay Area baseball and business communities.

Stoneham went house hunting in San Francisco. He and Valleda had reconciled, and she was moving to California with him. They settled on a multistory place on the steep slope of Telegraph Hill, with a delightful view of San Francisco Bay. All through this frantic period the San Francisco press was busy capturing and presenting their images of Horace Stoneham to San Francisco Bay Area readers. Stoneham was described as a debonair sophisticate who would appreciate San Francisco's high culture, while, in fact, Stoneham's favorite entertainment, other than baseball games, was watching westerns on television.

It was true, however, that Stoneham readily took enjoyment in San Francisco's great downtown restaurants. His favorite hangout came to be Bardelli's, on O'Farrell Street between Powell and Mason. Bardelli's offered a confident midcentury San Francisco setting, with vaulted ceilings and extravagant art deco stained glass and tuxedoed waiters serving the house specialty: calves' brains with brown butter and capers. The operator of Bardelli's was named Stu Adams, and he delivered a high-energy hosting style comparable to that of Toots Shor.

San Francisco newspaper columnists—not just sportswriters like Curley Grieve and Prescott Sullivan but also, significantly, the *Chronicle*'s top "society" columnist, Herb Caen—made Stoneham's social outings a frequent topic. By the end of 1957, when Stoneham had lived in San Francisco for just three months, he'd already been mentioned in Caen's column five times. Consider Caen's further offering on January 21, 1958: "Giants boss Horace Stoneham, dining at the Owl 'n Turtle, hosted six pals. When the check arrived Horace displayed an autographed baseball and grinned to owner Bill Varni, 'Have we got a deal?' Varni was quick to respond. 'Well, if the autograph is Bill Rigney, you pay half the check. If it is Willie Mays, dinner is on the house.' It was. Now do you think Willie Mays is overpaid?"[40]

Among the many employees in the Giants organization undertaking the relocation to San Francisco was Pete Stoneham, who'd been granted the title of vice president in 1957. Pete was spending his winter in Scottsdale, Arizona. But there, on Tuesday night, February 4, 1958, Pete Stoneham recklessly drove his car into a ghastly wreck that would be reported in newspapers nationwide:

[On February 7] a coroner's jury ruled . . . an automobile operated in "a negligent manner" by Charles Horace (Pete) Stoneham, son of the San Francisco Giants' owner Horace Stoneham, caused the death last Tuesday night of a British Columbia tourist. Mr. Stoneham, 30 years old, was involved in a head-on collision with Mr. and Mrs. William Leach of Victoria, B.C. Mrs. Leach, 55, was killed. Her husband and Mr. Stoneham are still undergoing hospital treatment for minor injuries.

Sgt. Paul Mullenix testified that Mr. Stoneham "definitely was under the influence of alcohol and unfit to drive" at the time of the accident. Deputy Sheriff Earl Alexander said Mr. Stoneham's car was on the wrong side of the road.[41]

A preliminary hearing on a charge of felony manslaughter was soon held. If convicted, Horace Stoneham's only son, and heir apparent to the beloved family business, could face a prison term of one to five years.

9

Open Your Golden Gate

The town of San Francisco, originally called Yerba Buena, was founded by Spanish colonizers in 1776. It remained a sleepy outpost until the United States forcibly seized control of California. With the discovery of gold in California in the late 1840s, San Francisco became an American boomtown and continued to grow. By the turn of the twentieth century San Francisco was by far the largest city in the western United States, with a population of nearly 350,000, much larger than Los Angeles (100,000) or Seattle (80,000).

The entire San Francisco Bay Area suffered damage in the devastating earthquake of 1906, nowhere more terribly than San Francisco itself, which largely burned down. But on a long-term economic basis, the disaster's impact on the city and the region was negligible. Growth continued unabated, though as the twentieth century progressed, the more explosive growth in California was increasingly taking place in the Greater Los Angeles region.

Baseball had come to the Bay Area no later than 1849, for that's when Alexander Cartwright, who'd founded the Knickerbocker Base Ball Club in New York in 1842, arrived in San Francisco to seek his fortune in the gold rush. He didn't stay long, soon moving along to Hawaii, but whether or not it was through Cartwright's personal introduction, in the 1850s and 1860s baseball was commonly present in San Francisco and its surrounding towns. By 1879 the sport had gone fully professional, with the founding of the California League, fielding three representatives from San Francisco (the Athletics, the Californias, and the Mutuals) and the

Oakland Pioneers. By 1891 the California League's four entries now included just one San Francisco team, known either as the Friscos or the Metropolitans, along with the Oakland Colonels, the San Jose Dukes, and the Sacramento Senators.

In 1903 the Pacific Coast League was founded and has remained in operation in one form or another to this day. Its founding members included the San Francisco Seals and the Oakland Oaks as well as entries from Los Angeles, Portland, Sacramento, and Seattle. The Seals and Oaks would be PCL mainstays until the existential changes of the mid-1950s. San Jose would most always field a team in the lower-classification California League (or California State League).

The Pacific Coast League wasn't a major league, of course, though in the late 1940s it would attempt to be reclassified as such. But it was always placed at the highest of minor league classifications, and in its heyday in the 1920s, '30s, and '40s, the PCL was the most glamorous of the minor leagues. The Bay Area became well known as a producer of top-tier baseball talent, flowing to the majors through the Pacific Coast League channel, including stars such as Harry Hooper, Harry Heilmann, Tony Lazzeri, Joe Cronin, Lefty Gomez, Ernie Lombardi, Dolph Camilli, and most famously, the DiMaggio brothers.

In the 1930s the San Francisco Bay Area completed two ambitious high-profile transportation infrastructure projects, with the San Francisco–Oakland Bay Bridge rising to busily connect those key cities and the Golden Gate Bridge connecting San Francisco to Marin County, producing one of the region's most beautifully iconic symbols.

The Bay Area was already a hot-running economic engine, and then the impact of World War II accelerated the motor. As a major seaport, the region became a center of military force training, organization, and transport. It was also a center of shipbuilding and other military engineering and manufacturing. Moreover, the Bay Area locus of elite science and engineering schools— including the University of California, Berkeley; Stanford University; and Santa Clara University—rendered it a national center of technological research and development activity, and the intensified investment in these endeavors both during the war and in the Cold War period that followed laid the structural groundwork for the extraordinary techno-industrial phenomenon that would become known worldwide as "Silicon Valley."

In the 1950 census the nine counties comprising the greater San Francisco Bay Area had a population of 2.7 million. By 1960 that would swell by more than a third, to nearly 3.7 million. The region into which Horace Stoneham was relocating his franchise in the late 1950s was an exceptionally dynamic, affluent, and burgeoning place. If it didn't closely resemble the New York of the 1950s, it did recall, in many ways, the younger and more confident New York of the early decades of the twentieth century, the place of Horace Stoneham's boyhood.

Yet for all the Bay Area had to offer, the key attribute that Stoneham sought was not yet in place: a new ballpark of modern design, in a location easily accessible by car, and with ample and secure parking. That facility was coming soon—indeed, ground was being broken in 1958—the project financed entirely by the City and County of San Francisco. The agreement between the Giants and the city called for construction of a stadium with seating capacity between forty and forty-five thousand, with parking for ten to twelve thousand cars; that all concessions revenue would go to the Giants; and that the cost to the Giants would be 5 percent of the gross annual receipts, or $125,000 per year, whichever was greater.[1]

In the meantime the San Francisco Giants would play their games in what had long been regarded as one of the finest parks in the Pacific Coast League, "the Queen of Concrete," crisply white-painted Seals Stadium. Located in San Francisco's Mission district, it had opened to much fanfare on April 7, 1931. Ty Cobb threw out the first ball. A state-of-the-art facility for its time, it was designed for night games, with six light-tower banks. At its opening Seals Stadium's seating capacity was 16,000, and it was expanded in 1946 to seat 18,500. The stadium had no roof over the single-deck grandstand because of San Francisco's absence of rainfall during the summertime and San Franciscans' fog-weary preference to sit in the sun if at all possible.

Seals Stadium underwent a $75,000 upgrade in preparation for the Giants. The seats were repainted dark green, and the seating capacity was increased to nearly twenty-three thousand with the addition of bleachers in left field. A new row of ten lights was added to each of the light towers, with the total wattage boosted from 300,000 to 540,000. A new auxiliary press box was added, and a new photographer's stand was built as well as a new press room in the clubhouse.

One thousand curb parking spaces were added to the streets adjacent to the stadium, along with seven hundred spaces in areas underneath the nearby Central Freeway skyway and three hundred off-street spaces elsewhere (offsetting the loss of some three hundred spaces eliminated by the addition of the left field bleachers). Shortly before Opening Day, two thousand more parking spaces were added on land made available to the city by the Hamm's Brewery, across Bryant Street, behind home plate.[2]

Meanwhile, in the spring of 1958 Horace Stoneham cleaned up his son's mess. Pete Stoneham would never go to prison on the felony manslaughter charge. His father had sufficient financial capacity to engage the necessary legal representation as well as sufficient pull within local governmental jurisdictions to have the tragic matter quietly "fixed" for his son. The civil settlement was in the hundreds of thousands of dollars.[3] After the early public reports, the incident was never again mentioned in the newspapers, as American news media then adhered to a different code of editorial discretion than it would adopt in later decades.

But even though the Giants' owner was able to avoid a broadly public scandal for his son, to a great extent the damage was already and forever done. It remained a dreadful scandal throughout the ranks of the Giants organization and permeated into the business of professional baseball generally. Everyone heard about it. Everyone talked about it. Pete Stoneham had killed someone while driving drunk. *Killed* someone, driving drunk. It was a case of *felony manslaughter* that had needed to be hushed up by Pop. It was a very big deal, a catastrophic turn of events, impossible to dismiss or to undo.

If the heavy-drinking and less-than-popular Pete Stoneham had struggled to gain professional respect and to earn major responsibility within the organization before the deadly crash, his case now became hopeless. His sketchy reputation was now toxic, the stench of irresponsible recklessness clinging to him like a shadow.

Perhaps if Pete had been able to take this rock-bottom moment in his life and use it as a turning point, to quit drinking and deeply and sincerely mend his ways, he might have regained trust in those around him and, as much as one ever can, put the terrible incident behind him and rebuild his career. But he did not.

Robert Shaplen's feature article on Horace Stoneham ran in the May 5, 1958, issue of *Sports Illustrated* and was therefore written when Pete's Scottsdale wreck was still heavily fresh in the atmosphere, when indeed the negotiations that would settle the case were likely still going on inside important Arizona offices. The magazine piece was as penetrating an examination into the psyche of Horace Stoneham as anyone ever attempted, but Shaplen—again, in a manner that was the journalistic norm in those days and is no longer—treaded lightly around the subject of Pete and the relationship between father and son and the elephant in the room, the issue of alcoholism: "The most significant thing about Horace Stoneham as an individual is his truly massive loneliness. . . . It is no secret that Stoneham . . . an extremely shy man, has frequently found solace in drinking. He does it publicly as well as privately and is the first to admit it. [His relationship with Pete is] silent if not distant [perhaps because Pete] shares many of his father's psychological problems."[4]

Pete Stoneham's defining challenge, before he could hope to salvage his reputation with the key decision makers surrounding his father, was to rebuild his relationship with his father, whom more than anyone else he had so profoundly let down. But he did not. "Silent if not distant" would forever be their status.

It was perhaps perfectly emblematic of the Stoneham family dynamic—of the shared "psychological problems" of father and son—that Pete's problem was dealt with by not talking about it. Horace was frosty toward his only son, in whom he was bitterly disappointed, but he didn't fire Pete or demand that Pete seek help to stop or limit his drinking or take steps to stop or limit his own drinking. Pete remained on the payroll and kept the title of vice president. Stoneham, in public, pretended as though nothing had changed.

But everyone in the organization knew that everything had changed. While Pete's title had been perceived as somewhat phony before, it was now accepted as entirely phony. He would never gain respect as a member of his father's brain trust, never have his opinion sought by Chub Feeney or Carl Hubbell or Jack Schwarz or Eddie Brannick. Pete stayed on the payroll, but the cheery puff pieces about how he would someday replace his father as team president would never again be written. He was vice president in charge of nothing, and everyone knew it.

Pete continued to drink, more than ever as the years would pass. No one around him came to expect otherwise, nor did he himself. Drinking was what Pete Stoneham did, and increasingly, it was all he did.

Horace Stoneham, in his way, steeled himself and got back to work running his ball club. The team Horace Stoneham brought to San Francisco had been a sixth-place dud in both of their final seasons in New York. But he well understood that the important issue wasn't that; it was the action going on in his farm system. The years of work that Carl Hubbell and Alex Pompez and the rest of the organization's scouting and development operation had invested was about to pay off like never before. Stoneham had an exceptional talent pool bubbling up like an underground river, eager to splash.

The Giants' roster moves in the 1957–58 off-season were strictly about clearing space for the kids. Discarded were first baseman Gail Harris and infielders Foster Castleman and Ozzie Virgil, young players who'd gotten some chances in New York, because there were better youngsters coming on fast. Discarded as well were veterans Wes Westrum, Don Mueller, and Bobby Thomson. The 1958 Opening Day starting lineup included four rookies: first baseman Orlando Cepeda, third baseman Jim Davenport, right fielder Willie Kirkland, and catcher Bob Schmidt. Two additional rookie outfielders, Felipe Alou and Leon Wagner, would be called up in June and see significant playing time. The roster counted six other players who were twenty-five or younger, and two additional youngsters who'd arrived in 1956—first baseman Bill White and outfielder Jackie Brandt—would return from military service during the '58 season.

Despite an unusually rainy winter in San Francisco, the Giants sold more than $1 million in season tickets.[5] The ball club won the Cactus League, with the many youngsters shining, especially Cepeda. Watching the team in Phoenix, Stoneham said, "If Orlando Cepeda doesn't make this ball club, I'll give the franchise away."[6]

Following spring training, the team itself at last came to the Bay Area, arriving at the San Francisco airport late in the evening of April 13, 1958. Mayor Christopher and a crowd of four hundred fans were there to greet them. The next day the city feted the Giants with a ticker tape parade down Montgomery Street. Police estimated the spectators watching from street side and from windows above to be in the hundreds of thousands. The players were seated two per car in sparkling new convertibles. The team's two most well-known stars, Willie Mays and Hank Sauer, rode together. Mayor Christopher rode in his own car, as did Horace Stoneham (though the signs on the owner's car were mismarked as "Stoneman").

Shirley Temple Black, the former child movie star who now lived near San Francisco, rode as the parade queen. She then signed autographs at a luncheon in the team's honor at the Sheraton-Palace Hotel, where about one hundred patrons paid five dollars per plate. In the accompanying ceremony Mrs. John McGraw received a standing ovation, and Bill Rigney was presented with the key to the city.[7]

The day after that, a sellout, standing room–only crowd of 23,449 at Seals Stadium beheld the first official major league baseball game ever played west of the state of Missouri. The day was sunny, warm, and this being San Francisco, breezy. The opposing team was—who else?—the one from Los Angeles.

During the player introductions the biggest ovation was for Mays, but the iconic Dodger stars Pee Wee Reese, Duke Snider, and Gil Hodges provoked cheers that nearly matched his. Hall of Famer Ty Cobb, who lived down the peninsula in ritzy Atherton, was in attendance, and he asserted that seventy-five thousand would have eagerly showed up if there had been enough seating. He also said the Giants' arrival had rekindled his long-dormant interest in watching games.

It was the most heavily covered regular season game in major league history, with 110 credentialed journalists on hand. Dick Young of the *New York Daily News* wrote: "The general consensus of visiting newsmen is that the new Giant fans have big-league maturity. They are not the wild, fanatically partisan fans of the Milwaukee breed. They seem hep about baseball: Cheer when a play rates it, and not over a routine catch of a foul pop. And they are fair."[8]

The game itself could hardly have gone better for the home team. Daryl Spencer and Orlando Cepeda connected for home runs, and the Giants won in an 8–0 rout, with Ruben Gomez tossing the shutout. As the season unfolded, the very young team continued to play excellent ball. At the end of May their robustly powerful offense, the best in the league, had propelled them to a virtual tie for first place with the defending champion Milwaukee Braves.

Alas, the Giants fell into a slump in June—a "June swoon" seasonal pattern would come to frustrate fast-starting Giants teams in the years to come—then in July they again threatened the Braves with another charge, before fading in August and September. The 1958 Giants finished at 80–74, in third place—precisely their record of 1955, but this time it felt entirely different. This was a season of positive energy and great hope.

The 1958 San Francisco Giants drew 1,272,625. That figure was fourth highest in the league, and the Giants achieved it in a teensy, minor league–caliber facility with inadequate parking and half of any normal stadium's capacity. Given that and everything else, Stoneham was thrilled. He hadn't quite experienced the Braves' astounding 1953 bounce, but this was still great.

Back in New York, only in the postwar boom years of 1947 and 1948 had the Giants ever drawn better. The big-risk roll of the dice was paying off well and fast and promising more to come.

One factor that had helped maximize the Giants' attendance in the Bay Area, Stoneham believed, was that none of the games were televised—they were on the radio but not on the tube. Stoneham was waiting for the Skiatron pay-per-view system to become operational, but until that was to happen (which, of course, it never would), Stoneham was resolute that he would not inhibit the demand for tickets by broadcasting the action on TV. He sacrificed broadcast rights revenue, secure in the calculation that he optimized overall revenue by not "competing against himself" for ticket sales, not falling into what he perceived as the trap of TV in which he'd found himself in New York.

When still in Boston, the Braves, competing for attention with the cross-town Red Sox, had televised their games, but once in Milwaukee, they televised none, and Stoneham interpreted their attendance boom as partially explained by that decision. The same dynamic was repeated by the Athletics when they moved from Philadelphia to Kansas City in 1955. Both Stoneham and Walter O'Malley found these examples instructional (and, of course, O'Malley was betting on the pay-per-view model along with Stoneham). In 1958 the Braves, Athletics, Giants, and Dodgers were the only major league teams not televising.[9]

The resurgent 1958 Giants team was led by the incomparable Mays, of course, that grizzled twenty-seven-year-old. He achieved career highs in hits and batting average and led the league in runs scored, stolen bases, OPS, and OPS+. He won a Gold Glove award and was second in Most Valuable Player balloting. Yet Bay Area fans had already heard about Mays and knew he would be great. They loved him, but in that inaugural San Francisco season, it was often noted that the player local fans seemed to shower with the most enthusiastic favor was the rookie Cepeda, their own discovery. "The Baby Bull" played with a Mays-like ebullient spirit and hit with a ferocious free-swinging abandon. Cepeda was unanimously voted the National League Rookie of the Year.

The club was so suddenly overstuffed with impressive young

talent that it was a challenge for Rigney to squeeze everyone in. In left field Sauer was shouldered aside by Leon "Daddy Wags" Wagner, a colorful character and an adventurous fielder who hit a ton. In right field the rookie Kirkland had a good year but had to fight off a challenge to his starting job from multitalented fellow rookie Felipe Alou. When the "veterans" Bill White and Jackie Brandt rejoined the roster in the second half, both found the regular jobs they'd seized in 1956 were taken, and both now had to grind it out as utility men.

Despite playing home games in the cool and breezy pitcher-friendly San Francisco environment, the 1958 Giants led the league in extra-base hits and runs scored. It was on the run prevention side that the team had its issues. Staff ace Johnny Antonelli, now all of twenty-eight, was still very good, and Stu Miller, a journeyman blossoming at the age of thirty, led the league in ERA as a starter-reliever. But after them it was often a struggle. Stoneham's own public assessment, though extravagant, correctly diagnosed the problem: "If we had any kind of pitching, we would have won the pennant in 1958 by a dozen games."[10] The owner-GM therefore devoted his off-season energy to finding a way to meaningfully improve his sparse pitching staff, to shore it up to a contender-worthy level. He would find not just one way but two.

Horace Stoneham was always sentimental and paternalistic in his relationships with the players in his organization, seeing them as people first and not merely employees or assets. It's not too strong a word to say that Stoneham loved his players, in his way, considering them a huge and ever-expanding extended family. But Stoneham never held any player in higher regard than Mel Ott.

Because of their closeness in age, the Stoneham-Ott relationship wasn't father-son; it was big brother–little brother. Stoneham was in his early twenties and Ott a shy seventeen-year-old when they met in 1926. They grew up together within the New York Giants world of John McGraw and C. A. Stoneham. Everyone loved Ott; there was just an endearing, guileless sweetness about him. Horace Stoneham's anguish at disappointing Ott by firing him as manager in 1948 was completely genuine.

In 1951–52 Ott managed the Oakland Oaks in the Pacific Coast League. When he wasn't retained for '53, Ott returned to his hometown of Metairie, Louisiana (a suburb of New Orleans), and was out of baseball for a couple of years. But he missed the game. In 1955 Ott accepted an offer to join the Mutual Network's "Game of the Day" broadcasting team, re-creating games on the radio. The following year he was hired by the Detroit Tigers, and through 1958 he partnered there with play-by-play man Van Patrick on radio and television.

In the fall of 1958 Ott was spending the off-season at home with his wife, Mildred ("Mickey"). The couple was in the process of building a vacation cottage in Bay St. Louis, Mississippi, on the Gulf Coast about sixty-five miles to the east of Metairie. On Friday, November 14, 1958, they drove over to inspect the progress of construction. Before heading home, they stopped for dinner at a roadside café.[11] After their meal Ott drove the family car, a 1956 Ford Custom station wagon with wood-paneled sides, back onto the highway after dark, in dense fog. There he collided head on with another car, whose driver, fifty-year-old Leslie S. Curry, was killed at the scene. Mel and Mildred Ott were both critically injured. A coroner's jury immediately returned a verdict of accidental death for Curry.[12]

Ott's injuries were horrifyingly massive. He was taken to Memorial Hospital in Gulfport, Mississippi, where he underwent preliminary surgery. He developed complications. On November 20 he was transferred to Touro Infirmary in New Orleans, where the following day he died on the operating table. He was forty-nine years old.[13]

Ott's two daughters and his brother were with him at the hospital in New Orleans when he passed away. Mildred was still hospitalized in Gulfport and was not immediately told of his death because of her condition.[14] She would eventually recover.

Stoneham was devastated. He was in Ciudad Trujillo in the Dominican Republic, watching winter league games and scouting prospects. The agonizing weeklong vigil while Ott was helplessly suffering ruined the time for him.

The evening before Mel Ott died, many of his New York friends and fans gathered at Toots Shor's restaurant. The normally jovial atmosphere was somber, everyone speaking in hushed tones about Ott's tremendous career and the kind of man he was. Upon the news of Ott's death the next day, Shor called Stoneham, and the old friends shared their loss. Stoneham, weeping, lamented to Shor, "Toots, the worst has happened." Stoneham broke short his Caribbean trip to attend the funeral in Louisiana, after which he told reporters: "I'm so shocked. Mel was not only a great Giant player but also a very dear personal friend."[15]

With a heavy heart, once again Stoneham returned his focus to the Giants, heading to the baseball winter meetings in December with pitching on his shopping list. On December 3 Stoneham traded Ruben Gomez and a backup catcher to the Philadelphia Phillies for right-handed starting pitcher Jack Sanford. Not yet thirty years old, the hard-throwing Sanford had been a late bloomer with an inconsistent track record, but his upside was far higher than that of Gomez, and this was an astute acquisition.

Toward the end of spring training, Stoneham landed an even bigger arm. Thirty-three-year-old African American right-hander "Toothpick Sam" Jones (so nicknamed for the toothpick that might as well have been surgically implanted between his lips) threw even harder than Sanford. Indeed, Sam Jones was one of the very hardest throwers of the 1950s, and combining the heater with a nasty sweeping curve, the long, lean six-foot-four-inch, 192-pound Jones was a devastating strikeout pitcher. For a long time he'd racked up prodigious numbers of bases on balls as well, but year by year he'd gotten better and better. With St. Louis in 1958 Jones stepped into stardom: he was fourth in the league in starts, sixth in complete games, fifth in innings, and second in earned run average, and his 225 strikeouts were the most by a National League pitcher since 1936.[16]

Horace Stoneham acquired the remarkable Toothpick Sam Jones from the Cardinals on March 25, 1959, along with minor league pitcher Don Choate, at the price of young first baseman Bill White and utility player Ray Jablonski. Choate and Jablonski were throw-ins; the essence of the deal was White-for-Jones, an exchange of a potential star hitter for a veteran star pitcher. This was another astute move, from several perspectives. First, it was a confident stroke by Stoneham, signaling to his team, to his fans, and to the rest of the league that the Giants, laden with rookies in 1958, weren't content to be merely a high-potential young team but were serious about winning right now. Second, it was a purposeful act in drawing from his team's surplus in one area to address a legitimate shortage elsewhere. And third, simply in terms of talent exchange, the Giants got fair value for value; they didn't steal Jones, but neither did they give White away. It was a very good piece of business.[17]

At spring training in 1959, sitting in his favorite isolated spot twenty-two rows up in the left field bleachers at Phoenix Municipal Stadium, Stoneham was happy to allow himself to be quoted, saying: "This is a very good baseball team. Maybe the best Giant team I have seen."[18]

In early 1958 construction began on the new baseball stadium in San Francisco, whose very promise had been the key to attracting the Giants to come this way. The new facility's story began in 1953, when the news about the booming success of the Braves in Milwaukee was fresh in the air. It was sweet news indeed to other cities interested in attracting a major league team of their own. San Francisco Republican mayor Elmer Robinson, backed by the city's business community, asked the board of supervisors to approve a $5 million bond proposition to construct a new baseball stadium. Among the supervisors voting for approval was fellow Republican George Christopher, soon to succeed Robinson as mayor.

In July 1953 Charles Harney, a local construction contractor, purchased sixty-five acres of empty land from the City of San Francisco at a place called Candlestick Point, for the price of $2,100 per acre. The reason that land was empty was that Candlestick Point was the very least attractive real estate in all of the city and county of San Francisco. It was a windswept, muddy, and marshy no-man's-land between a towering hill to the west and the bay itself to the east—and not the picturesque part of the bay. The sights to be seen from here were the grim, gray cranes and towers of the Hunters Point Naval Shipyard and the big green empty expanse of the bay. This was the very broadest part of the San Francisco Bay, with the East Bay shore, more than ten miles dimly distant, offering only the hazy vista of mundane working-class burgs San Leandro, San Lorenzo, and Hayward.

And because it was at the very broadest part of the bay, Candlestick Point was maximally exposed to what that seriously big bay would regularly dish up—namely, almost ocean-like weather conditions of wind and of fog—even, this being San Francisco, right through the heart of summer. (The peculiar charm of notoriously grumpy San Francisco weather is that the sunniest and warmest months are usually September and October. February can sometimes be beautiful as well.)

In 1954 a group of enthusiasts spearheaded by the sports editor of the *San Francisco Examiner*, Curley Grieve, mounted a campaign in support of the stadium bond proposition, and it was easily passed by the voters in November. With that the imperative became the choice of a site, around which discussion and speculation would consume 1955 and 1956, without resolution. In early 1957 Mayor Christopher was ready to appoint a site search committee.

Coincidentally, the discussions between Christopher and Stoneham were moving briskly. It was in their May 1957 meeting in New York when the subject of the cost of a stadium presented itself: when Christopher proudly played his $5 million stadium bond card, Stoneham, confidently holding his Minneapolis ace, patiently explained to him that a modern stadium suitable for a major league baseball team—the kind that would be attractive to someone like, say, himself—would cost a whole lot more than that. Realistically, it would be something more like $10 or $11 million.

So, Christopher hastened back to San Francisco to raise that kind of money, and things turned in a particularly interesting direction. Since the idea of suddenly doubling the original stadium bond amount would likely not be approved by the voting public, Christopher decided to create a nonprofit corporation called Stadium, Incorporated, as a legal arm of the city. Operating through this dummy corporation, the Christopher administration could bypass the voters to raise the cash. None other than construction contractor Charles Harney—the very same who'd purchased vacant Candlestick Point real estate from the city back in 1953—and two of his employees found themselves selected as the first board of directors of Stadium, Inc.[19]

In an appalling backdoor deal, in the summer of 1957 Christopher and Harney struck a bargain via the Stadium, Inc., device: the city would locate the stadium at a city-owned Bayview site that just happened to abut Harney's Candlestick Point parcel; the city would buy Harney's parcel to complete the site at the Harney-specified price of $65,853 an acre (bear in mind that he'd paid $2,100 an acre for it in 1953); and Harney's construction company would be the no-bid contractor for 100 percent of the project. This most remarkable arrangement was rubber stamp approved by Christopher's board of "supervisors." The mayor's spin was that this was a great deal for the city because it was just so gosh darn efficient; Harney was in fact a contractor with a reputation for getting things done in a timely manner, known in the construction trade as "Hurry-Up Harney."[20]

All of this was coming together in the summer of 1957. Following Stoneham's own board approval of the move in August, he traveled to San Francisco to formally celebrate the deal. Local lore has never tired of spinning the yarn that Christopher and Harney nervously ushered Stoneham around the Baypoint-Candlestick site at midday, when it was sunny and nice, careful to hustle him back downtown before midafternoon, when the wind would faithfully begin to howl. In Stoneham's casual look-see, so goes the story, he focused exclusively on the expansive room for a huge parking lot, and he never asked (nor did anyone stupidly volunteer) about the weather. Then it was, all right, boys, let's move along to lunch.

The problem with this bit of folklore is that it insinuates dereliction on Stoneham's part. It presumes that Stoneham was the client of the stadium project, that he had the power to issue a ruling on the merits of the Bayview-Candlestick location, when, of course, he never had anything of the sort. Stoneham wasn't the project's client; he was its tenant. He had no input on the location, which in any case had been resolved long before this photo op pseudo-event. Stoneham's visit to the site was a courtesy, not a matter of decisive concern for any of its parties.

Indeed, there was a perspective expressed at the time that Stoneham was maneuvering the situation beautifully. In Los Angeles, O'Malley had determined to construct his stadium with private financing instead of allowing the city to build it for him, and that project was going to take years longer to complete than San Francisco's. John Drebinger of the *New York Times* wrote: "O'Malley played it smart and got stung; he forced Los Angeles to let him build a stadium and so far, he has nothing. Stoneham played it dumb and got a stadium; he let San Francisco build him a beautiful park for only $125,000 a year rent and total concession revenue."[21]

In any case the deal that contractor Harney had secured with the city stunk to high heaven. It wasn't long before Christopher was forced to acknowledge the obvious conflict of interest with Harney's role as director of Stadium, Inc.[22] Many in the city were outraged, and a grand jury was convened, overseen by Henry North of the District Attorney's office, and its report, issued on December 1, 1958, exposed that at the time of Harney's sale of his Candlestick site to the city for $65,000 per acre, adjacent pieces of tideland were sold by the city for about one-sixteenth of that. Further, the report charged that all of the bond issues negotiated by Stadium, Inc., were illegal evasions of the city charter.[23]

But though the corruption exposed by the grand jury's report was egregious, the temper of most of the local press, at least, was to ignore it, if not smear it. The chorus led by Curley Grieve of the *San Francisco Examiner* first tried to bury the story and then belittled it as grandstanding on the part of North. Editorials in the *Examiner* and the *Chronicle* dismissed the report and blamed North for exceeding his authority. Christopher labeled the grand jury report a private vendetta against his office and a vote against progress. Mayor Christopher bluntly insulted North, labeling him a drunkard and insinuating that he was the corrupt actor. North responded with a libel suit, and the ugly argument raged for months.[24]

And all this was apart from the construction work itself.

From the outset Harney and stadium architect John Bolles bickered, each casting the other as the source of the project's delays. In the winter of 1958–59 Harney declared that if any further changes to the plans were issued, he would cease construction altogether. Yet the contractor's budget had failed to account for an extensive array of basic elements, including landscaping, lighting, and fire and safety items. Bolles argued that such fundamental features were logically implied as part of broader categories, but Harney insisted that every detail needed to be specifically itemized. Ingress and egress to the parking lot hadn't been adequately addressed in the plan. A radiant heating system underneath the lower grandstand was insufficiently funded and botched in design and construction.

Amazingly, Harney initially put in the soil and sod of the playing field itself without an underground sprinkler system. When this was discovered by groundskeeper Matty Schwab, Harney's familiar response was that there was no line item in his budget calling for an irrigation system. When ordered by the city to dig up the field and install the system, Harney's crew performed the work shoddily, resulting in sprinkler heads standing four inches high above the outfield grass.[25]

That shoddy sprinkler system was then torn out and replaced, and recriminations flew. The schedule was delayed again and the budget blown some more. Meanwhile, Harney had audaciously campaigned for the facility to be named "Harney Stadium," and when the Parks and Recreation Committee, heeding a poll of the taxpaying public, decided on "Candlestick Park," Harney took it as an insult.

And here was the meeting that took place in Mayor Christopher's office in August 1959, when it appeared that the Giants might very well win the pennant, and the question was whether the new ballpark might be able to be opened for the World Series. Only half of the seats were in place, and at issue were a hundred details: no place to steam the hot dogs, no handrails for the box seats, two ramps unfinished, the seats not yet numbered, no backstop, no womens' restrooms. The mayor emphatically stated the problem: "The biggest disgrace we could possibly suffer is not being ready. Those boys are playing their hearts out for us."

Contractor Harney replied, "There's nothing involved here that somebody spending some money can't help."

"I want that stadium ready!" expounded Christopher. "By God I want that stadium ready, if some of you want to keep doing business with this office."

"Now listen here," shouted Harney, "if you want to threaten me—"

"I mean Bolles," said the quick-thinking mayor.

Stoneham was aghast. "The handrails," he said, "are a safety measure. We can't open without them. The seating and the tickets are the most important things. Will the seats be numbered?"

This touched off a ruckus on who would pay for numbering the seats. "Horace," asked Harney, "when do you need the seating plan?"

Groaned Stoneham, "We needed it a couple of months ago."[26]

This was Candlestick Park. It hadn't even opened yet.

At Seals Stadium in 1959, Sam Jones and Jack Sanford could hardly have fit any more neatly into the Giants' starting rotation. The pair of right-handers joined the team's incumbent left-handed starters—ace Johnny Antonelli and steadily developing young Mike McCormick—to provide a balanced set of rotation anchors. Stu Miller, who'd been the top swingman in 1958, would make some spot starts but was now primarily deployed by Rigney as the bullpen ace, joined there by another former starter, Al Worthington. The staff was significantly improved.

For 1959 Rigney decided that Jackie Brandt would be his primary left fielder, and Leon Wagner was mostly deployed as a pinch hitter. The other adjustment Rigney made was in the middle infield: incumbent second baseman Danny O'Connell was demoted to the bench, and shortstop Daryl Spencer was shifted to second, thus opening up the starting shortstop job for twenty-four-year-old André Rodgers.

The first Bahamian to appear in the major leagues, Rodgers was a grade-A physical specimen, six foot three on a broad frame that would fill out to two hundred pounds. He was a graceful and agile athlete with a superb throwing arm and power at the plate. The road he'd traveled was unlikely and circuitous.[27] It had included an introduction to the game of baseball at the age of eighteen, stupendous minor league batting stats, a pundit's prediction of 1957 Rookie of the Year status,[28] nervousness, struggle, and still more stupendous minor league batting stats. Stoneham and Rigney believed Rodgers was ready at last in 1959, his ceiling sky-high.

But in 1959 the young shortstop experienced a nightmarish defensive struggle. He committed two errors on Opening Day and eight in the season's first eight games. Rigney sat him down for few days, and when Rodgers returned to the lineup, he did fine for a while, with bat and glove. But in June he came down with another case of the yips, making five errors in a four-game span. Rigney's patience was starting to wear.

The situation came to a head at the end of the month. On June 30, against the Dodgers in Los Angeles, the Giants were leading 2–0 with two outs in the eighth inning—and Sam Jones was working on a no-hitter. Jim Gilliam hit a slow chopper to shortstop, and Rodgers scooped it up, then lost the handle and failed to throw as Gilliam was safe at first. Official scorer Charlie Park of the *Los Angeles Mirror-News* immediately signaled "hit," and the press box exploded in derisive disagreement. Jones completed his shutout with a one-hitter, and on the radio Russ Hodges roared: "If ever a man deserved a no-hit game, Sam Jones did tonight. The ball was a routine grounder."[29] Instead of celebrating Jones's great performance, the postgame attention was focused on the scorer's blunder—and that of Rodgers.

In the Giants' next game Rodgers booted another grounder, and this one was charged as an error, his twenty-second in sixty-three games. Rigney was now done with it. Rodgers was benched and then sent back to the minors, and twenty-seven-year-old Eddie Bressoud, a solid player but with nothing close to Rodgers's promise, was now the first-string shortstop.

Through it all the Giants were in the thick of a three-way battle for first place in 1959, contending with the Milwaukee Braves and the Los Angeles Dodgers. Those teams presented a fascinating contrast. The Braves were the two-time defending National League champions, with an all-time great talent core led by right fielder Hank Aaron, third baseman Eddie Mathews, and ageless ace Warren Spahn. Yet the Braves lacked depth and had a gaping hole at second base.[30]

The 1959 Dodgers were utterly different. Several years removed from their magnificent "Boys of Summer" peak in Brooklyn, the Dodgers were in a rebuilding phase and had zero superstars. Their lineup instead was a patchwork of fading but still productive veterans, a few solid pros, and some aspiring youngsters. The Dodgers' strength was a young pitching staff, led by twenty-two-year-old ace Don Drysdale, with journeyman Roger Craig and rookie Larry Sherry both taking unexpected star turns.

The Giants spent most of July narrowly in first place. But on July 29 a fourth straight loss knocked them into second, and Stoneham decided it was time to send for help from Phoenix. The call went to first baseman Willie McCovey, who'd been signed in 1955 out of Mobile, Alabama, as a tall and skinny seventeen-year-old. From the get-go he was a tremendous hitter, but McCovey's progress was slowed by a knee injury he suffered in 1957; knee trouble would forever be his kryptonite. With Phoenix in 1959 he was healthy, and that combined with the hitter-friendly desert conditions created a perfect storm: in ninety-five games through late July, his production could best be described as frightening, as he was hitting .372, with twenty-six doubles, eleven triples, and twenty-nine home runs.

On Thursday, July 30, 1959, McCovey made his major league debut at Seals Stadium. The weekday afternoon game against the last-place Philadelphia Phillies drew a little over ten thousand, and it would become an event embedded in the heart of Giants lore. The Phillies' starting pitcher was future Hall of Famer Robin Roberts, at thirty-two years old no longer the superstar he'd once been but still a serious presence. Rigney went all in, starting his rookie at first base, batting him third in the order, behind Mays and ahead of Cepeda.

In the bottom of the first inning, in his first major league at bat, McCovey singled to right field. He led off the bottom of the fourth with a titanic triple to center field. In the next inning he again pulled a single to right—not just an ordinary single but a line drive rocket off the wall that rebounded to right fielder Wally Post too quickly for McCovey to reach second. In the bottom of the seventh, still against Roberts, he blasted another triple, this one to left-center field. When asked what pitches he threw to McCovey, Roberts said: "Everything. He hit everything."[31] The Giants won, 7–2, and it was safe to assume that the rookie would be in the lineup again the next day.

In his first week in the major leagues, McCovey hit .467 with two doubles, two triples, and three homers. As he tore it up off big-name pitcher after big-name pitcher—Roberts, Harvey Haddix, Elroy Face, Spahn, Bob Buhl, and Lew Burdette—the stunned appraisals continued. Said Buhl: "You ask me what I threw to him? Whatever the hell it was, it was the wrong pitch."[32]

Giants fans were agog, of course, and so was the national press. On one particular morning McCovey was awakened at home by a reporter-photographer from the *San Francisco News-Call Bulletin* to be interviewed and photographed at breakfast. Once at the ballpark, in the clubhouse he was surrounded by four New York baseball writers and a dozen local feature writers who examined every flaw—even the chip on his front tooth (later capped) and the two corns on his third toes. At batting practice he was photographed by cameramen from *Life, Time, Sports Illustrated, Look, Saturday Evening Post*, the Associated Press, the United Press International, and the local papers. After batting practice he posed and spoke for a local TV program, then taped a weekend bit for NBC's *Monitor*. In the game he hit two home runs into the right field bleachers as the Giants regained first place.[33]

In fifty-four games for the Giants in 1959, McCovey's batting average was .354, with thirteen home runs and thirty-eight runs batted in. As Orlando Cepeda had been in 1958, McCovey was unanimously voted the National League Rookie of the Year.

Ah, but Cepeda. There was the rub. Along the lines of the arrival of Johnny Mize back in 1942, the arrival of McCovey in 1959 created a logjam for the Giants at first base. What to do?

McCovey, known even in those days as "Stretch," was central casting's ideal of a first baseman: he was six foot four, left-handed all the way, and a slow runner. In five minor league seasons he'd never played anywhere except first base. Cepeda was six foot two, right-handed, and fast for a big man; he'd been a third baseman as well as an outfielder in the minor leagues. So, it wasn't a perplexing decision to conclude that Cepeda should be moved to make room for McCovey.

Left field, the least demanding defensive position other than first base, would be a logical place to put Cepeda, but the Giants were already overstocked in the outfield. However, at third base they weren't quite as strong; Jim Davenport was an excellent fielder (he would win a Gold Glove in 1962), but his hitting was mediocre. Cepeda had played a lot of third base in the minors, and he was still only twenty-one years old, a superb athlete whose complete skill profile was yet to be fully shaped. Giving Cepeda an opportunity to become a major league third baseman would make a lot of sense: even if Cepeda's fielding was poor, Davenport was on hand as a late-inning defensive replacement, and if Cepeda could manage to develop into anything approaching an average fielder at third, the Giants would have an asset of exceptionally rare value on their hands.

Placing a power hitter with limited defensive skill at third base was hardly an unusual move. Examples from the 1940s and '50s were Bob Elliott, Frank Thomas, and Harmon Killebrew, and others to follow would include Dick Allen, Tony Perez, Pedro Guerrero, Bobby Bonilla, Albert Pujols, and Miguel Cabrera. Under Stoneham's own authority the Giants had moved Mel Ott to third in 1937, Sid Gordon in 1948, and Bobby Thomson in 1951. None of these moves yielded a slick-fielding third baseman, but that was never expected. In every case the choice was made to get another big bat into the lineup, the calculation being that runs gained at the plate would outnumber those conceded in the field. In every one of these cases the move turned out to be a positive one for the ball club and a career-enhancing skill gained by the player. Cepeda had defensive aptitude equal to most of these players and had played more minor league third base than many of them. With proper coaching and patient encouragement, a serious, sustained effort by Cepeda at third base may very well have paid off handsomely for the Giants.

Instead, what happened was this: when McCovey came up, Rigney shifted Cepeda to third base for four games. He handled a total of eight chances at third, made three errors, and the Giants abandoned that idea forever. Cepeda moved to left field for the remainder of 1959, but the situation would remain unresolved for years to come.

The Giants held on to first place into late September 1959, though never by much. The final San Francisco home stand of the season brought the Braves and then the Dodgers into Seals Stadium, with the Giants two games in front of both with ten to play. In their two-game series the Braves and Giants split, and now the mathematical logic was simple: if the Giants could simply play .500 ball for the remaining eight games, the other teams would have to win six out of eight to tie, seven out of eight to win.[34]

Yet winning baseball games is harder than calculating statistics. The Friday night game against the Dodgers was rained out—just the second rainout in two seasons in San Francisco, another benefit of playing in California—necessitating a Saturday doubleheader. In the first game the Giants played sloppy, three-error defense and lost 4–1. In the nightcap Don Drysdale started for the Dodgers, and he was wild. To open the first inning, he walked Bressoud, McCovey, and Mays. But an overanxious Cepeda, biting at balls that hit the plate, struck out swinging. So then did Willie Kirkland and Daryl Spencer. Had Cepeda waited for his walk, Drysdale would likely have been lifted. But Drysdale righted himself, struck out eight in seven innings, and the Dodgers won 5–3. The Giants and Dodgers were suddenly tied for first.

Hoping to turn it around, on Sunday, Rigney handed the ball to Toothpick Sam Jones.[35] Exhausted by a grueling workload—this was his second start and third appearance in five days—Jones didn't last through the fourth, and it was never a contest as the Dodgers went on to win 8–2.[36]

Though the Giants were still right in it—while now in third place, they were just one game behind the first-place Dodgers, with five to play—emotionally they were reeling. The team flew to Chicago for a two-game series with the Cubs. There the Giants lost both games on walk-off home runs, and they were two games behind with three to play. They'd be eliminated on the season's final Sunday.

It ended sadly. But with perspective Stoneham and the Giants had to conclude that 1959 had been a remarkable, exciting season. In *Sports Illustrated* Roy Terrell summed it up: "All the Giants lack is experience and the steadiness it brings; they still make mistakes; they get rattled; sometimes they seem to lack confidence in their own skills. But to make up for this, the Giants have a blend of bubbling enthusiasm which keeps them battling to win. These three teams, so different in ability, so widely separated in style, have combined to make 1959 one of the most memorable years in National League history. It's a shame that two of them had to lose."[37]

It surely had been a successful year financially. In their little bandbox of a temporary home, the Giants drew 1,422,130 in 1959. Stoneham was so delighted with the support that during the final home stand, he inaugurated a "Fan Appreciation Day" event that would become an annual tradition. Lucky fans would be awarded prizes if their seat number was drawn. The prizes in 1959 included a fifteen-cubic-foot freezer, a hi-fi set, a black-and-white television, a color television, and the grand prize, a brand-new Cadillac.[38]

Beginning in 1960, they would need that little bandbox no more, as the big, modern, car-friendly stadium Stoneham had long sought would now at last be his. In just a few years' time, Stoneham had sidestepped what had seemed to be intractable, existentially threatening problems, and now, placed within a dynamic, affluent, fast-growing region in what would soon be the nation's largest state, with an exceptionally talented, still very young team ready to take that brand-new field, it's difficult to imagine how the future could have appeared much brighter.

10

It's Bye-Bye Baby

The first task Horace Stoneham assigned to himself following his team's sooner-than-wanted finish to the 1959 season was to rehire manager Bill Rigney. In the immediate aftermath of the frustrating final week, the local papers speculated that Rigney might be replaced. *San Francisco Examiner* columnist Prescott Sullivan suggested Lefty O'Doul as the obvious choice.[1]

But Stoneham never seems to have seriously considered anything other than bringing Rigney back. On October 23 Stoneham held a press conference announcing that Rigney had signed a new one-year $40,000 contract. *San Francisco Examiner* columnist Charles Einstein diagnosed that the explanation for Stoneham's not making the announcement immediately at the season's end was his hope that waiting a few weeks would let emotions cool and protect Rigney (and by extension, himself too) from criticism: "Mr. S. has one fault, if fault it is, that is shared by most of us. He is a human being."[2]

Another topic of discussion in these months was a proposed third major league, calling itself the Continental League. In July 1959 the prospective league had announced its initial five franchise locations as New York (having lost the Giants and Dodgers), Minneapolis–St. Paul (having missed out on the Giants), Houston, Toronto, and Denver. In the months to follow, other sites were debated, and one speculation that came to Stoneham's attention was that a Continental League team might join the Giants as a cotenant in the new San Francisco ballpark. Stoneham weighed in with a strongly worded (for him, anyway) assertion that sharing Candlestick Park would be a bad idea, and unfair to the Giants, in a "white paper" (read: press release) published in the *Examiner*:

> It has been the experience of all baseball people that two clubs operating in one ballpark have been uniformly unsuccessful. This experience convinces us that each team should maintain its own identity. I am sure that everyone is aware that the Giants in moving to San Francisco have had to assume heavy financial obligations that involve territorial equities as well as the obligations imposed by their occupancy of the new Candlestick Park. I am surprised by the suggested interest of the Continental League in the San Francisco area. It was my understanding that the proposed new league was interested primarily in bringing major league baseball to new territory.[3]

Though the Continental League would never get beyond the conceptual stage, it was a serious effort put forth by serious people, and it gained the serious attention of all current major league owners, not just Stoneham. The threat it presented became the primary motivator behind the decision of both the American and National Leagues to undertake expansion within the next few years.

But mostly Stoneham's focus that off-season was on balancing his roster, which in 1959 presented surplus strengths alongside key shortcomings. He entered the trading season with a sense of purpose, acknowledging: "Our strength is in the outfield. We'd like to help ourselves everywhere else."[4]

On November 30 came the first of two big moves. Jackie Brandt was shipped to Baltimore, along with two marginal players, for two-time All-Star left-handed starting pitcher Billy O'Dell and a journeyman reliever. Brandt, the odd man out when McCovey came up, was an obvious trading piece, and O'Dell was a substantial return, not yet twenty-seven years old and already very good. This was a sweet trade for Stoneham.

In mid-December, Daryl Spencer and Leon Wagner went to the St. Louis Cardinals in exchange for second baseman Don Blasingame, another All-Star. Given the Giants' outfield depth, the poor-fielding Wagner was never going be much more than a pinch hitter for the Giants. Spencer had been a solid all-around performer, but the left-handed-batting Blasingame—a little guy, five foot ten, 160 pounds—though he had no power, hit for a higher batting average than Spencer, was better at drawing walks, was much quicker on the bases, had better range in the field, and moreover, he was three years younger. He represented a plain upgrade at second base.

Yet again, Stoneham had negotiated an ambitious and soundly reasoned transaction. He'd never been a frantic wheeler-dealer along the lines of a Larry McPhail or Frank Lane, but since the mid-1950s Stoneham had engaged in more frequent trading, and he was exhibiting confidence and something of a flair for it. The Giants entered 1960 with a more diversely talented roster than the one that had come so close in 1959.

Though Stoneham served as his own general manager in this regard, his management style was collaborative. The major final decisions were always his, but he usually came to them cautiously, after thorough consultation and debate within his circle of advisors. Stoneham was often quick to credit Chub Feeney for successful transactions. Feeney, however, would have none of it, admitting: "You kidding? Horace instigates the deals. I merely carry out his orders."[5] Stoneham was candidly self-aware of his strengths and weaknesses in the difficult but necessary endeavor of player transactions. "Well," he said, "you always hate to see your players leave. Maybe I'm too much of a sentimentalist. You can make mistakes trading, of course, but if you never make a mistake, you're not really trying."[6]

The opening of Candlestick Park in 1960 could have been an episode of grand delight and celebration, the realization at last of the shared dream of the San Francisco Bay Area and of Horace Stoneham's Giants for a gleaming showplace at the cutting edge of modern design and efficient functionality. But this place was, well, not that.

Instead, it was an instant laughingstock. The immediate and incessant complaint was about the wind. Of course, everyone knew there was plenty of wind in San Francisco, but it wasn't supposed to present a problem at Candlestick Park. "The Bay View Hill," said the stadium planners, "will cut off the wind. It is a natural windbreak. The wind will go around the side of the hill, rush beyond center field and out to the bay." The very first batting practice proved them wrong. Perfectly struck balls had to fight hard to reach the fences. The wind didn't go around the hill; it came over it, full force, and swooped down into the stadium, roaring and twisting.[7] Stray hot dog wrappers and old newspapers blew across the field, making crazy dives and dips in the swirling gale. In other parks this might cause a delay while the annoyance was removed, but everyone soon learned that here that was pointless, and the umpires and players just did their best to ignore them.

And the wind was just the start of it. The fifty-six-acre macadam parking lot was slowly sinking into the bay, reported Sam Francisco director of public works Reuben Owens, who told the board of supervisors that $5,000 or more per year would be needed for continual paving. Fans griped that the ticket windows were too high, and players complained about the exposed dugout, at ground level.

In the first fourteen games at Candlestick Park, the alarming total of five people suffered fatal heart attacks, and half a dozen more were overcome. San Francisco coroner Henry Turkel blamed the steep incline of the ramp, about twenty-seven degrees, leading from the parking lot to the front gates. Giants public relations director Garry Schumacher retorted: "This is really something, to blame a small hill in San Francisco for those five tragedies. If that were the case there wouldn't be a soul alive around the City of Seven Hills." But then he added: "For my part, though, they could have forgotten the radiant heating that doesn't work and put in some elevators. I go into the main gate of the stadium and I see my office just overhead, but I have to walk 200 yards of ramps to get there."

Fans had been advised not to fear the San Francisco evening cold: the box seats would be radiant heated, and the warming glow would make baseball a cozy game for the highest-paying spectators. But the warmth didn't get through, as the hot-water pipes were too far from the concrete, and the concrete was too thick. After firing the boilers again and again, the whole thing was abandoned—though it wouldn't be forgotten.[8]

Even the stadium structure itself—overbearingly massive, dead gray, and oddly asymmetrical—received negative reviews. Roger Angell wrote in the *New Yorker*, "Candlestick Park . . . with its raw concrete ramps and walkways and its high, curving grandstand barrier . . . looks from the outside like an outbuilding of Alcatraz."[9] Herb Caen observed that the ballpark "sometimes gives the uncomfortable impression that a giant had taken the Embarcadero Freeway and bent it into a horseshoe."[10]

Still, one of the design features built into Candlestick Park is something that is taken for granted today but was innovative then: a level of partially enclosed "suites" incorporated into the overhanging upper deck of the grandstand. One hesitates to describe them by the modern phrase of "luxury boxes" because in the 1960s they were spartan in terms of creature comforts, but their inclusion in the architecture was an important way in which Candlestick was the first of the new standard of sports facilities. Two of these adjoining suites, just to the first base side behind home plate, near the broadcast booths and the press box, were occupied by Horace Stoneham and his front office staff. It was from this concrete balcony that Stoneham intently watched. As had long been his custom and would remain so to the end, Stoneham virtually never missed a game and rarely missed an inning.

The huge anticipation for the new stadium had stimulated a great advance sale of season tickets, and Giants' attendance at Candlestick Park was nearly 1.8 million, second most in the league. But it might have been noted that their attendance grew by one-quarter while their seating capacity had nearly doubled. It would become a fair question to wonder how many fans would consider themselves satisfied customers in 1960, given the singularly uncomfortable ballpark experience and, as it turned out, given the performance of the team on the field.

The Giants entered 1960 as an extremely serious contender. It might not be accurate to say that Stoneham and Rigney flat out expected this team to win the pennant, but the quality of this roster demanded very high expectations. Good was no longer good enough. And in the early weeks, while the stink bomb reviews of Candlestick Park grabbed most of the attention, the Giants played superbly. On Opening Day, in the first game ever played in the new stadium, the Giants beat the Cardinals 3–1 behind a Sam Jones three-hitter. They took five out of seven in the opening home stand and stayed hot. By May 15 they were 19–8, in first place by a game and a half. But then things started to go sideways.

Third baseman Jim Davenport was enjoying a fine early season when on May 19 he vomited blood in a Milwaukee hotel room and was diagnosed with a gastric ulcer. He would be out of the lineup for a month.[11] The question then arose of who should fill in at third for Davenport, and Rigney and Stoneham disagreed on the answer. Here's Rigney's recollection:

> I called Horace and told him [about Davenport]. And he said, "Who's going to play third base?" And I said, "Joe Amalfitano." So he said, "What's the matter with André Rodgers?" And I said, "Well, nothing, Horace. But right now I think Joe's a little better player for us." He said, "I want to tell you something. André Rodgers is going to be around here a devil of a time longer than Joe Amalfitano, and maybe longer than the manager." And I said, "Well, I've got to do what I think is right." And we hung up.
>
> Now, Joe Amalfitano played third base that night and he got two hits and we won three to two, and he drove in two runs. So the next day the phone rang again. "Who's playing third base tonight?" I said, "Well, I'm going to play Joe Amalfitano."[12]

This was a peculiar quarrel for Stoneham to pick with his manager. It wasn't a strategic decision as to who should play third base for a month; it was tactical, within the realm understood (in those days) to be every manager's discretion. And moreover, when this question was presented to the Giants, the team had won twice as many games as they'd lost: it wasn't as though there was reason to invest much worry over this. But Stoneham did, and Rigney, literally put on notice, felt his strings tightened.

The Giants didn't sustain the 19–8 pace, of course, but they didn't slump exactly, playing .500 ball from mid-May to mid-June. They were still hot in the race, in second now but right on the heels of the Pittsburgh Pirates. Yet the mood expressed by Rigney didn't exude confidence. After a 2–1 victory Rigney fretted, "We can't seem to get even a good pop."[13] He criticized his pitchers: "I gotta get a guy who can get me three outs in the ninth inning. I can't keep coming back with my starters and expect to keep the pitching staff from falling apart." He complained: "Whatever wins we get have been scratchers. I have to sit on the edge of my seat in the dugout every inning." Sweating under the heat of glowing preseason predictions, Rigney shook up the lineup.[14]

Such was the sense of unease when the Pirates, in first place by one game, arrived in Candlestick Park for a three-game series beginning June 14. In the opener, before 35,465 on a Tuesday night, errors by Bressoud and Blasingame led to four unearned runs in the first two innings, and the Giants lost 6–3. The next day 19,180 fans watched the Pirates pound six Giants' pitchers for nineteen hits, including six doubles and two triples, in a 14–6 laugher. For the Thursday afternoon finale the crowd was down to 17,237 when Jack Sanford took a 2–0 lead into the top of the fifth, but before an out was recorded, the Pirates had scored six runs. The final would be 10–7 Pirates, and their first-place margin was now four games.

The next day Bill Rigney was fired. In Rigney's assessment: "Horace had been told by everyone that if the Russians didn't attack, we should win the pennant by 20 games. Well, Milwaukee, the Dodgers and Pittsburgh were still pretty good. But even though we were only two and a half games behind, Horace got it into his head that we should have been ahead by eight or 10 games."[15] Yet Rigney would harbor no bitterness. "My relationship with Horace Stoneham was like I'm sure a lot of relationships with Horace, never good, yet never strained. We had a lot of arguments, a lot of battles. And I found one thing out the first half year I was up there, I couldn't stay up and drink with him. But he enjoyed talking about his team, and he wanted people to sit around and talk baseball, that was the whole thing."[16]

Stoneham's explanation was simple, if puzzling. "This is no reflection upon Rigney as a manager. I still think he is a good one. But I believe the club got away from Rig. We were losing a lot of ground on this home stay, and although we were as young, or younger than the other clubs, they outhustled us. I've been thinking about a change for some time."[17] Just how much time might that have been, after re-signing the manager the previous autumn, was left unspecified. But while the firing itself was odd, the truly bewildering aspect was Stoneham's choice to replace Rigney: Tom "Clancy" Sheehan. He was sixty-six years old and had never been a manager before at any level. He'd been a journeyman pitcher from 1913 through 1934, mostly in the minors. He'd worked in Stoneham's organization for a long time, officially as a scout, but he was firmly within Stoneham's inner circle.

Sheehan told the press that Rigney was fired because he was too nervous, too high-strung. Dick Young of the *New York Daily News* wrote that Sheehan had been responsible for the firings of both Leo Durocher and Rigney, that he played Richelieu to Stoneham's Louis XIV. Asked about this, Sheehan so much as said he hadn't come across those names in the *Baseball Guide*.[18]

Among the questions hanging in the air was that of Sheehan's longer-term status. Stoneham's plan was not evident. Though Sheehan wasn't announced as an interim manager, Stoneham nonetheless explained that he had several others in mind for the job and couldn't reveal their names because they were under contract to other clubs. So, the guessing game began in the papers as to who Stoneham might be considering. The only clarity Stoneham offered was, "Durocher is not on my list."

Shortly after taking over, Sheehan called a clubhouse meeting and told the players, "I'm the nicest guy in the world when we're winning." This failed to instill its intended motivation. The club began to sag almost immediately, fell out of contention, and finished fifth.[19] Indeed, if one presumes Stoneham's thinking was that Sheehan would serve as a calming presence in place of the tightly wound Rigney, instead he was the substitute teacher the classroom freely ignores. The players knew they had a lame-duck manager, and they ran wild on Clancy. They broke curfew and played cards all night. Willie McCovey was overweight. Shee-han called time to go out to the mound to pull Jack Sanford, but instead of waiting for the reliever to arrive, Sanford just walked to the dugout, leaving Sheehan standing there. Sheehan fined Sanford $200. Eddie Bressoud failed to chase a pop fly, allow-ing it to land safely. Willie Mays loafed after hitting a fly ball that would be misjudged, denying himself extra bases.[20]

Stu Miller described the atmosphere:

You remember Tom Sheehan [imitates a big, burly, mumbling guy]? A big, old ex-pitcher. He was not only Stoneham's right-hand man, he was the head scout and his best drinking buddy [laughs]. He sat up there beside Stoneham in their box and, I'm sure, proceeded to tell Stoneham, "Well, Rigney's doing everything wrong, we should be doing this," and on and on. So Stoneham fired Rigney and said to Sheehan, "You get down there and run that club" [laughs]. For cry-ing out loud, he didn't even have a uniform for four days until they made one for him. I think Omar the Tentmaker had to make it. But Sheehan got that ball club and we laughed all the way down to the lowest point in the standings we could find.[21]

It wasn't just undisciplined carousing that explained the Giants' second-half collapse. There was also the fact that Sheehan refused to play Willie McCovey. Rigney had deployed the 1959 Rookie of the Year as his everyday first baseman. When Rigney was fired, McCovey's batting average in 170 at bats was just .244—a disap-pointing fall from his heady .350 hitting the previous summer—but in every other regard the twenty-two-year-old McCovey was delivering an outstanding sophomore season, among the league leaders in home runs, RBIs, and bases on balls.

But Sheehan benched him, moving Cepeda in from left field to play first base, with Felipe Alou taking over in left. McCovey played strictly as a backup the rest of the way, and Stoneham even optioned him back to AAA for a few weeks.

Though the 1960 season was frustrating for the Giants in nearly every regard, there was one bright ray amid the gloom. In 1958, on the recommendation of scouts Frank "Chick" Geno-vese, Horacio Martínez, and of course, Alex Pompez, the Giants had signed a Dominican right-hander named Juan Marichal to a $500 bonus. He proceeded to torch the minor leagues, and on July 19, 1960, the twenty-two-year-old made his major league debut at Candlestick Park. He was stunningly brilliant, tossing a one-hit shutout over the Phillies, striking out twelve. Marichal's singular windup featured a dramatic sky-high leg kick, and the flamboyant delivery produced a baffling array of fastballs, curves, and sliders; impeccable control; and a pitching guile and poise far beyond his experience.[22] For the third straight season the Giants had introduced a future Hall of Famer into their lineup.

The inscrutable Stoneham's intentions regarding his manager became clear in October. The wire services carried a brief notice to the effect that the Milwaukee Braves had traded thirty-eight-year-old utility infielder Alvin Dark to the San Francisco Giants in exchange for the disappointing young shortstop André Rodgers. Speculation immediately sprouted that this wasn't just a swap of infielders. It wasn't long before a Braves official confirmed the hunch: the Giants had acquired Dark for the purpose of naming him manager.

Horace Stoneham was in Japan, but a press conference was held in San Francisco, with Chub Feeney introducing Dark as the new skipper. "Dark will operate on a two-year contract," Feeney said. "He and Eddie Stanky were the only two candidates ever considered."

The appointment received general approval. The only concern expressed about Dark was his lack of managerial experience, but he'd long been a team captain and field leader, and no one had ever questioned his competitive intensity. John McHale, the Braves' GM, summed up the prevalent feeling when he said: "We couldn't very well stand in Alvin's way when he had a chance to manage. The Giants got a terrific guy and I think it's wonderful that he can start managing in the major leagues. We just didn't have that to offer him."[23]

Dark was a peculiar character. Writing in 1954, during Dark's peak as the Giants' all-around star shortstop, Arnold Hano had pondered his unique combination of traits:

The Giant captain . . . fails to paint a picture of athletic grace, and this is surprising because he was a football, track, and baseball star at Louisiana State University, and such all-around skill usually makes for a rhythmic performer. Dark seems to have another talent that makes him a star. It is an intangible quality, and though the spectator views it much as you can see smoke coming from the mouth of a smoldering volcano, the real fire is down underneath, unseen. . . .

I am still fascinated by the mystery of Alvin Dark. It may be that there is something in his name that has impelled him. Dark. Sometimes he is called Blackie Dark. He uses a black bat, the only ball player I've ever seen using one regularly. He is a man of dark and glowering looks. There is nothing light colored about him, nothing bright or joyous. His is a dark spirit, a raging spirit, the kind that takes losing bitterly and broodingly, and thus, the kind that must win.[24]

And there was Jim Bouton's memorable recollection of an interaction with Dark he had experienced as a boy: "I was a big New York Giants fan when I lived in New Jersey as a kid. . . . I remember once leaning over the dugout trying to tell Alvin Dark how great he was and how much I was for him and, well, maybe get his autograph too, when he looked over at me and said, 'Take a hike, son. Take a hike.' Take a hike, son. Has a ring to it, doesn't it? Anyway, it's become a deflating putdown line around the Bouton family. Take a hike, son."[25]

Dark wasn't an easy one to figure out. His manifest contradictions were noted: he could be uninhibited, then cautious; he was deeply religious yet prone to profanity; he could exhibit calmness, then emotionality and a vicious temper.[26]

In Dark's autobiography he reflected on becoming manager of the Giants:

I admit I was surprised that Horace Stoneham wanted me to manage. It had been five years since I had played for him, and I had never managed anywhere. . . . Mr. Stoneham put himself on the spot with the move. I heard Chub Feeney was against it. . . . The most notable thing about Stoneham, besides his abiding love for home-run hitters and the time he took making decisions, was that he was very loyal. In turn, he appreciated loyalty. Rigney . . . was smart, and he was loyal; Stoneham liked that. I had played for him six years and was also . . . loyal. I suppose it counted for something. . . .

Chub Feeney had dinner with me and told me I might have some trouble because there were so many Negroes on the team. I told him that he was wrong—that he didn't know how I feel about Negroes. . . . I told him . . . that my feelings were to treat every man individually and that's the way I'd run my ball club.[27]

This was Stoneham's fifth managerial hire: Ott, Durocher, Rigney, Sheehan, and Dark. Only Durocher had previous major league managing experience, and neither Ott, Sheehan, nor Dark had managed at all. Ott, Rigney, and Sheehan were all organizational insiders, and Dark, as he himself perceived, was still seen by Stoneham as an insider, or perhaps more accurately, as a loyalist.

The outlier in every regard had been Durocher. To the extent that this small sample revealed a pattern, it was that Stoneham plainly preferred his managers to be *his* guys, loyal to him and perhaps, as rookie managers, indebted to him. The dynamic was as different as could be from that surrounding the Durocher hire, and Stoneham knew how that had ended. Stoneham perhaps never uttered truer words than when he had stated, in June 1960, "Durocher is not on my list."

But Alvin Dark was on Stoneham's list—indeed, at the very top of it. Stoneham well remembered Dark's intense presence as the Giants' team captain and anticipated that he would provide more forceful leadership than Bill Rigney. Stoneham was so confident about Dark that he not only hired him on the spot; he traded for the right to hire him on the spot, without even a stint at the minor league level. Dark himself sensed that Chub Feeney wasn't nearly as confident about it. It was the issue of Dark's capacity to handle the racially and culturally integrated complexity of the Giants' roster that worried Feeney. Interestingly, in Dark's recollection of Feeney's addressing the subject with him over dinner, the focus was entirely on African Americans, with no mention of the Latino players (generally called "Latin" at the time).

239

When Dark took over, he made several antagonizing moves. He believed the team's three factions—whites, Blacks, and Latinos—should spend more time together, so in spring training he changed the locker assignments in order to facilitate more intermingling. But the players didn't appreciate the microman-agement, and eventually Dark gave in and let the players choose their own lockers. Another idea of Dark's was even less popu-lar. He posted a sign in the spring training clubhouse that read: SPEAK ENGLISH, YOU'RE IN AMERICA. He called a meeting of the Latino players and said that the other Giants were complain-ing that they didn't understand what the Latino players were say-ing. There were almost a dozen Latinos in the camp, and many of them, pointedly including Orlando Cepeda, viewed the edict as an insult. The Alou brothers—who now numbered three— thought it odd to speak among themselves in a foreign language. The rule was unenforceable, and Dark dropped that one as well.[28]

Years later Cepeda remained bitter:

> The guy who really messed the Giants up was Alvin Dark. When he got the team he separated the blacks and the whites, he separated the whole team. . . . I remember when he first came to the Giants, he don't want any Latins to speak Spanish in the clubhouse. And I told him it was a disgrace to see two Latin guys, two Puerto Rican guys, me and José Pagán speaking English. First, we can't commu-nicate in English as well as we can in Spanish, and second, it was a disgrace to our people and to our language to have to speak another language. . . . Dark couldn't put it together. He's not a manager. The only thing to be a good manager is to know your ballplayer and respect the ballplayer, so that he can respect you. . . . He didn't know how to deal with people. He always thought about himself. . . . He was very cruel to me.[29]

Next on Stoneham's list was to address the other problems that had dogged the team in 1960. Candlestick Park itself was an issue. Stoneham was powerless to do anything about the many discom-forts the stadium presented to the fans, but he could do some-thing about the way in which it played as a ballpark. With the wind and cool temperatures, it was going to be a pitchers' park regardless, but its spacious outfield dimensions had made it an even more difficult environment for home run hitting. In 1960 the Giants hit eighty-four home runs on the road, the league-leading figure, but just forty-six at home, least in the league; a San Francisco disc jockey said he was dedicating the next tune to the Giants: "Don't Get Around Much Anymore."[30]

Among the Giants' key strengths was power hitting, and of course, everyone knew how much Horace Stoneham loved home runs. Robert H. Kingsley was a St. Louis–based engineer who'd established a thriving consulting practice in the 1950s, ministering to baseball teams on the issue of optimizing the rate of home runs produced in their ballparks. Much as a golf course groundskeeper can adjust golf scores by pin and tee placement, Kingsley was able, by keeping complete records of all home runs hit in every major league park—the distance and the direction of the hit—to calculate a fair placement of outfield fences.[31]

Upon the opening of Candlestick Park, Kingsley had confidently predicted it would be a terrible park for home runs. Climatological factors such as wind, temperature, and air density, together with the spacious configuration of the park, would make it the most difficult major league stadium for home runs in at least the last twenty-five years, claimed Kingsley.[32] Engineer Kingsley was proved correct, and he succeeded in winning a new client. Stoneham engaged him to make recommendations about installing a chain link outfield fence closer to the plate. Kingsley advised bringing in the Candlestick fences as much as thirty-two feet in left-center field and by ten feet at the corners.[33] So would the field be reconfigured for 1961.

Stoneham executed two big trades to reconfigure the roster. At the winter meetings in December, he sent right fielder Willie Kirkland and longtime ace pitcher Johnny Antonelli to the Cleveland Indians in exchange for outfielder-infielder Harvey Kuenn. Trading either or both Kirkland and Antonelli wasn't a surprise, given that the high-potential Kirkland hadn't developed as anticipated, and Antonelli had suffered a down year in 1960. However, expending both of them for Kuenn was a curious choice. He was a high-average hitter and an eight-time All-Star, but at the age of thirty he showed signs of slowing down. Moreover, it wasn't clear what position he would play for the Giants and whether his presence would limit the opportunity for fellow right-handed batter Felipe Alou, who appeared ready to step into a regular outfield job.

The other deal was swung two weeks after Opening Day in 1961. Second baseman Don Blasingame, who'd been a major disappointment in 1960, hitting just .235, was traded to the Cincinnati Reds, along with catcher Bob Schmidt, and the Giants received power-hitting three-time All-Star catcher Ed Bailey.[34] Like Kuenn, the thirty-year-old Bailey was past his peak but provided a clear upgrade behind the plate. The curious part of this one was that dispensing of Blasingame in this way meant that second base was now left to obscure rookie Chuck Hiller, a twenty-six-year-old who'd never before played as high as AAA, along with utility infielder Joey Amalfitano.

Dark would spend the entirety of the 1961 season shuffling his lineup. Kuenn, a onetime shortstop, rotated from third base to left and right field. Alou played most of the time in right but also quite a bit in left. Willie McCovey, in irregular stints, wound up in about half the games at first base, while Orlando Cepeda, starting every day, rotated from right field to left to first. Hiller took over as the regular second baseman until he was sent back to the minors in early July, when the job went to Amalfitano. At shortstop Eddie Bressoud gradually gave way to José Pagán, in his first full big-league season.

Catch all that? It was dizzying, and a method was difficult to comprehend. But through it all the Giants generally played good baseball. They occupied first place for nearly all of May and remained close until July, before finishing third, eight games behind pennant-winning Cincinnati.

Kingsley's prescription to liven up the action at Candlestick Park succeeded perfectly. In 1960 the Giants and their opponents had combined for 80 home runs in the windswept ballpark. In 1961 that total leaped to 174, with 97 of them by the home team. The biggest individual beneficiaries were the right-handed sluggers Mays and Cepeda, whose pull field was into the wind. With now-reachable power alleys, Mays hit 40 home runs in 1961 (21 at home), his highest output since 1955, and Cepeda exploded for a league-leading 46 (24 at home) and topped the majors with 142 runs batted in. As a team, the Giants led the league in runs, scoring 48 percent of them at home.

It wasn't a great year, but it was a good one, a rebound from the flop of 1960. Attendance dropped from the new ballpark boom of 1960 but was still strong, at 1.4 million, second highest in the league. It was in 1961 that Stoneham came to the conclusion that the Skiatron cable TV arrangement wasn't coming together, so he reluctantly assented to lease out his broadcast television rights. But it was a very limited showing: Oakland-based KTVU, broadcasting on Channel 2, was granted exclusive authority to televise the eleven games in which the Giants played the Dodgers in Los Angeles and only those games.

The 1961 season saw the Giants host the All-Star Game on July 11.[35] It was the introduction to Candlestick Park for all of the American Leaguers and most of the national media. The facility made quite an impression. In the early innings it was windless and broiling hot, causing ninety-five fans to be treated for heat prostration and five for suspected heart conditions. But then the weather capriciously turned, bringing swirly, slamming winds in the late innings, creating havoc for fielders. The National Leaguers, who knew Candlestick best, committed the most errors (four behind Giants ace reliever Stu Miller in the ninth and tenth innings), but it was the Americans who yelped loudest about it.

Observed Baltimore's Hoyt Wilhelm, "Chewing tobacco and sand isn't a tasty combination." Paul Richards, the AL manager, said: "The wind—you have to feel it to believe it. Conditions were as near impossible as anything I've ever seen." Arthur Daley of the *New York Times* tore into his typewriter with the same high-blown force as the wind and concluded, "Whatever it is, this isn't a major league ball park."[36] The incident usually associated with this game (which the National League won 5–4) is reliably described as "Stu Miller was blown off the pitcher's mound," though that didn't happen; in reality a gust hit Miller in his stretch position, briefly staggering him. But the legend, as legends will, became the story.

Below its loftiest mountaintop elevations, the San Francisco Bay Area very rarely sees snow. Therefore, it was an unusual event indeed when in mid-January 1962 the entire region, including downtown San Francisco, received a heavy dusting—it was, in fact, the first time in thirty-eight years that it had snowed in San Francisco. The frigid weather served as a fitting backdrop for a civil trial underway that month in a San Francisco courtroom.

The plaintiff was Melvin Belli, a flamboyant and publicity-savvy attorney who was suing codefendants, the City and County of San Francisco and the San Francisco Giants, for the sum of $1,597, which was the cost of a six-seat box at Candlestick Park he'd purchased for the 1960 season. Belli's complaint was that he'd been promised that the radiant heating system built into the brand-new stadium would ward off the evening chill.

The story of Candlestick's built-in heat went back several years. Before the stadium plan was approved, San Francisco supervisor Clarissa McMahon, a rare realist regarding Candlestick Point weather, had demanded heating and a roof. She got a partial overhang on the upper deck and a $50,000 radiant heating installation. However, in only–in–Candlestick Park fashion, instead of being embedded within the grandstand's several-inches-thick steel-reinforced concrete floor, the radiant heating steam pipes were set about an inch below it.

The Giants, as tenants, contended the city was responsible for the heat. They attested that the boilers were fired for days in advance, to no avail. On the first night game of the 1960 season, local sportswriters were crawling under the stands and knocking on the engineer's door to ask why the floor was stone cold. After the buck was passed back and forth between the Giants and the City Recreation Department, Stoneham announced that the heating system was a failure.[37]

Belli argued that the system's failure amounted to a breach of warranty. He introduced into evidence a copy of the 1960 *Giants*

Yearbook, which included an article asserting that the floor underneath all the box seats would be warmed to a toasty eighty-five degrees. The barrister called the president of the Giants to the stand, and asked Stoneham about the yearbook statement.

"We didn't write it," said Stoneham. "We exercise no control over what the contributors write."

"If they wrote stories and said the Giants were a bunch of bum players, that certainly wouldn't go in the yearbook, would it?" asked Belli.

"No," said Stoneham, "but they have written such stories in their papers."

"Let's hope they don't have to write them this year," tossed in Judge Andrew J. Eyman from the bench.

Stoneham said the Giants never promised anything more than a seat and a major league ball game. "Then why," demanded Belli, "did you keep turning on the heat all the time if you knew it wouldn't work?"

"To protect ourselves from criticism," said Stoneham. "They were screaming."

"This was to take the heat off, then," said Belli.[38]

Belli called a succession of further witnesses who testified how miserably cold it could get in the Candlestick Park grandstand. One said he had to leave a game with the score tied, and another, who regularly swam in San Francisco Bay, found the ballpark unbearable. Belli claimed he tried giving his tickets away, only to have them returned. The attorney pulled out all the rhetorical stops, referring to "the bitterest winds this side of the Himalayas" and offering, "Even with long underwear and an Alaskan parka, the same one I wore to Siberia last year, I couldn't keep warm in Box J, Section 4."

Belli had sent a man from his office, Gordon McGlendon, to Candlestick Park to buy the tickets on March 3, 1960. McGlendon's orders were to buy a box for the season, one of the heated ones. The order was repeated to ticket manager, Peter Hoffmann, and Hoffmann reportedly answered, "Yes, the box is one of the heated ones."

Defense attorney Morris M. Doyle didn't call on Hoffmann to attempt to repudiate McGlendon's testimony. Instead, Doyle told the jury: "The question was merely, 'Was there radiant heat?' It was not whether the heating system worked."

Belli then rocked the court by saying: "That's like having a man come into City Hall asking, 'Where are the elevators?' and getting an answer, 'They're right over there,' without bothering to tell him they're not working. So he steps into the elevator shaft and falls down to the basement."[39]

The jury voted in Belli's favor. With a final flourish he announced to the press that he would donate the $1,597 to the city for the planting of trees but not at Candlestick Park "because they would freeze out there." Belli concluded, "This decision is a mandate to the Giants to keep the fires burning."

On October 10, 1961, immediately following the conclusion of the World Series, in the Julep Room of the Netherland-Hilton Hotel in Cincinnati, the National League held its first-ever expansion player draft, to establish the player rosters of the newborn Houston Colt .45s and New York Mets. The Giants surrendered thirty-six-year-old Sam Jones (who, after great seasons in 1959 and '60, had severely declined in 1961) and journeyman infielders Eddie Bressoud and Joey Amalfitano to Houston, while to the Mets all they gave up were backup catcher Hobie Landrith and a grade-B minor league pitcher.

While these hardly amounted to deep losses, Stoneham's choice to allow both Amalfitano and Bressoud to be drafted, just six months after trading away Don Blasingame, meant that second base now belonged exclusively to twenty-seven-year-old Chuck Hiller. While he played with lots of hustle and grit, Hiller was an athlete of modest capability, with neither power nor speed nor particular defensive aptitude—his nickname, rather cruelly, was "Iron Hands"—and with the Giants in 1961 he'd hit .238 and found himself demoted to AAA in midseason. But Hiller was now Stoneham and Dark's guy, as no competitor for the second base job would be introduced.

The only significant deal the Giants swung that off-season was to shore up the pitching staff. Stoneham leveraged his organizational depth, sending a package of young talent to the Chicago White Sox for two well-known veterans: thirty-five-year-old southpaw Billy Pierce and thirty-two-year-old right-hander Don Larsen. Both seemed to have enough left to help a team ready to win now.

The only other change for 1962 was in Alvin Dark's deployment of Orlando Cepeda and Willie McCovey. There would be no more of the herky-jerky indecisiveness of 1961, and the decision was this: "McCovey will play left field for us this year, and maybe a little first base. Cepeda is my regular first baseman. There will be no more running Orlando on and off first base every day."[40]

Back in 1959 the Giants' election to not persist with Cepeda at third base could be understood. Their young star admitted to no confidence in his ability there—he described himself as a "butcher"—and so it might have been wise to not press that position with him. But when he continued to whine about having to play the outfield in 1960 and '61, Stoneham and his managers should have told him to knock it off. There was no reason why Cepeda couldn't have become an adequate, if not a good, defensive corner outfielder; he had more than enough athletic ability. But he refused to work at it, bitching all the while.

"I could understand his reluctance," Bill Rigney would recall. "But Cepeda was the better athlete, so I thought he could make the move to another position more easily. But he would come up to me and say, 'Bill, I'm the first baseman not the left fielder.' What could you do? He was the most popular San Francisco Giant. It was very hard not to like Orlando Cepeda. But this became an unresolvable situation."[41]

It wasn't unresolvable. The Giants just didn't steel themselves to sensibly resolve it. The boisterous, prodigiously talented, and deeply popular Cepeda intimidated Rigney, Stoneham, and the Giants organization, and they indulged him. "I just wasn't ready mentally," Cepeda said years later. "I know I could've played left field if I'd put my mind to it, but I was only 21 years old and very sensitive. Friends and other players kept telling me I should demand to play first. It was all pride with me. And ignorance."[42]

Cepeda and Dark hadn't gotten along well in 1961, and the manager's decision in the spring of '62 to give in to Cepeda's wishes was an attempt to ease the tension. But even if this would resolve that problem, it actively created another: they were now going to introduce the spectacle of Stretch McCovey in the outfield.

Through this entire episode Stoneham and the Giants were disregarding the best interests of not only of the team itself but of McCovey, their other prodigious young slugger. McCovey was quiet, and Giants management never seemed to be concerned about how Cepeda's noisy complaints must have felt to him. When Dark moved McCovey to the outfield, he went without a murmur of protest and gave his best effort, although to no one's surprise he was a horrible defensive outfielder. McCovey's utter lack of grace and aptitude in the outfield prompted the description of him there as "a huge flamingo flopping around."[43]

The Stoneham organization's mishandling of the young Willie McCovey could scarcely have been more complete. Overly fearful of undermining Cepeda's confidence, they were quite the opposite with McCovey. When Dark moved McCovey to the outfield in 1962, he didn't offset that indignity by providing the chance to finally play full-time. Instead, McCovey that season would be a pure second-stringer, rarely starting, and allowed a grand total of twelve plate appearances against left-handed pitching. Bill James observed, "McCovey is probably the only truly great player in history to have been platooned for several years at the start of his career."[44] It was McCovey, not Cepeda, whose career was genuinely stalled and who might have rightly complained about it.

In the decades to come, McCovey—especially after his late-career return to the Giants—would become the single most beloved baseball player in the San Francisco Bay Area, more than Cepeda, more even than Mays, more even than Mays's godson Barry Bonds. McCovey would come to be genuinely adored by the team's fan base, admired not just for his marvelous play but for his gentle humility, his warm humor, and his steely determination against the painful ravages of steadily degenerating knees.

But McCovey was not so beloved by the fan base in the early 1960s. When he proved unable to sustain the other-worldly rate of hitting he flashed in 1959, McCovey was widely derided in the local press and perceived by many of the fans as a flop, a bust, a clumsy bum. Through the 1960–62 period McCovey endured frequent boos and insults at Candlestick Park. He became the team's designated fall guy, the magnet for blame, the whipping boy. Through it all the young man maintained gentlemanly composure.[45]

Upon arriving in San Francisco, the local radio station to which Stoneham had sold broadcast rights was KSFO.[46] The station engaged songwriters Allyn Ferguson and Hugh Heller to compose a song for the Giants, "It's Bye-Bye Baby." The lyric was inspired by broadcaster Russ Hodges's signature home run call, "Tell it bye-bye baby!" (which he'd been too flummoxed to utter when Bobby Thomson hit that particular homer). The song was recorded, a marching tempo with a drums-brass-and-piccolo band accompanying a men's chorus, and the lusty result was introduced as the theme song of the Giants on the radio. It was a perfect fit, honoring the hugely popular Hodges and celebrating the fact that this truly was a home run–hitting ball club, just the way Horace Stoneham loved it. The song was an immediate hit and remains prominently deployed in the Giants' local television broadcasts to this day.

During spring training of 1962 the team enjoyed a particularly nice moment, recalled by Billy O'Dell:

> When we went out to spring training out in Casa Grande, Horace Stoneham really went out of his way for us. He had the wives and the kids and everybody there, took care of everybody, and just saw to it that everybody was real comfortable, beyond what normally would be done. So we decided . . . to do something for him, so everybody threw in a few dollars and we bought him a watch. Just an ordinary watch, maybe a hundred bucks or something like that. And we asked him to come to the clubhouse and we gave it to him. And he broke down and cried. Couldn't say anything at all, and finally just had to turn around and leave. Later he said he'd been in baseball for so many years and he'd never thought about anybody giving him anything. That's just the kind of guy he was.[47]

Opening Day of the 1962 season was at Candlestick Park, on Tuesday afternoon, April 10, when a crowd of 39,177 braved the breezes to watch the Giants face the Milwaukee Braves and perennial ace Warren Spahn. In the bottom of the first, Willie Mays dug in for his first at bat of the year. On KSFO the voice of Russ Hodges: "And center fielder Willie Mays steps up to the plate now, and fans today are seeing something they've never seen. Willie is wearing a batter's helmet this year. In previous years he always wore the cap with the plastic inner lining, but at the request of manager Alvin Dark, he went for the full helmet. He wears it right over his baseball cap.... Spahn throws to the Giants' center fielder. There's a swing and a long drive, to deep left-center field, and you can tell it—bye-bye-baby!... What a way to start off a season! One pitch! One home run!"[48]

The Giants would chase Spahn in the fourth inning and breeze to a 6–0 win behind a ten-strikeout three-hitter from Juan Marichal. The starting eight behind Marichal that day—Ed Bailey catching, Cepeda at first base, Chuck Hiller at second, José Pagán at shortstop, Jim Davenport at third, Harvey Kuenn in left field, Mays in center, and Felipe Alou in right—would essentially be intact all season long. Dark would tinker with the batting order, but the zig-zagging of lineup combinations he exhibited in 1961 was absent this year. The only alteration would be at catcher, where sophomore Tom Haller would step ahead of the veteran Bailey for most of the second half because Haller was hitting better.

Similarly, with the pitching staff, roles were set and generally held. Marichal, Billy O'Dell, and Jack Sanford were locked into the starting rotation. In the bullpen the big three were Stu Miller, Don Larsen, and hard-throwing sophomore Bob Bolin. Billy Pierce was usually the fourth starter and would occasionally make a bullpen appearance. Twenty-three-year-old Mike McCormick would have been a regular starter, but he came down with a sore arm in 1962 and in the custom of the time was expected to "pitch through it"; he was given intermittent starts and long-relief appearances, nearly all ineffectively.

The Giants in 1962 started extremely well. They swept the opening series with the Braves, then took two out of three from the defending champions Reds. In their first meeting with the Dodgers, the Giants mauled them 19–8.[49] The Giants finished April with fifteen wins against five losses, in first place, and they'd scored nearly seven runs per game. They rolled on through May, and by the end of that month their record was a sizzling 35–15. Yet their first-place lead was only a half-game because the Dodgers were on fire too.

It was at this point in the 1962 season that the Dodgers and Giants made their first visits to New York since 1957, in back-to-back series against the brand-new Mets in the Polo Grounds.[50] Roger Angell of the *New Yorker* took the opportunity to watch these seven games, which, these being the 1962 Mets, were all won by the visiting teams, by a combined score of 56–26. Angell was deeply impressed by the talent displayed by both California teams and vividly described them:

> Both the Dodgers and the Giants, who are currently running away from the rest of the league, are stocked with large numbers of stimulating, astonishingly good ballplayers. . . .
>
> Frank Howard, the six-foot-seven Dodger monster, striding the outfield like a farmer stepping through a plowed field; Ron Fairly, a chunky, redheaded first baseman, exultantly carrying his hot bat up to the plate and flattening everything thrown at him; Maury Wills, a skinny, lizard-quick base-runner. . . . Willie Davis, the Dodger center fielder, is the first player I have ever been tempted to compare with Willie Mays. Speed, sureness, a fine arm, power, a picture swing—he lacks nothing, and he shares with Mays the knack of shifting directly from lazy, loose-wristed relaxation into top gear with an instantaneous explosion of energy.
>
> . . . Orlando Cepeda, the Giants' slugger, stands with his hands and the bat twisted back almost behind his right shoulder blade, and his vast riffles look wild and looping. Only remarkable strength can control such a swing. . . . Harvey Kuenn, by contrast, has the level, controlled, intelligent swing of the self-made hitter. He is all concentration, right down to the clamped wad of chewing tobacco in his left cheek; he runs with heavy, pounding determination, his big head jouncing with every step.

Mays, it is a pleasure to say, is just the same—the best ballplayer anywhere. He hit a homer each day at the Polo Grounds, made a simple, hilarious error on a ground single to center, and caught flies in front of his belt like a grocer catching a box of breakfast food pulled from a high shelf. All in all, I most enjoy watching him run the bases. He runs low to the ground, his shoulders swinging to his huge strides, his spikes digging up great chunks of infield dirt, the cap flies off at second, he cuts the base like a racing car, looking back over his shoulder at the ball, and lopes grandly into third, and everyone who has watched him finds himself laughing with excitement and shared delight.[51]

But with June came the swoon to the 1962 Giants, and it was a doozy: twelve losses in sixteen games, dropping them to second. But they rebounded. A four-game Giant-Dodger showdown at Candlestick Park in early July had the rivals fighting over first place. The teams split, resolving nothing, but the four games drew nearly 150,000, a throng unprecedented in San Francisco baseball.

In the final game of that series, the winning pitcher for the Dodgers was twenty-six-year-old Sandy Koufax. A bonus baby back in 1955, he was slow to blossom, struggling to harness control of his lightning bolts. He began to figure it out, though, and by 1962 Koufax had fully arrived. The win over the Giants put his record at 13–4, and he was leading the league in earned run average by a mile and in strikeouts by a mile and a half, with a staggering 202 in 168 innings. At this pace he would shatter the twentieth-century record for strikeouts. But Koufax would make just two more starts before a circulatory condition in the index finger of his pitching hand sidelined him for two months. It would be the most impactful injury of the season.

The Giants and Dodgers remained close in July, but then Los Angeles began to pull away. The Dodgers came to Candlestick in August with a lead of five and a half. Maury Wills was running wild: 60 steals in 116 games. Alvin Dark ordered the Candlestick grounds crew to be extra-generous in watering down the infield, especially around first base. The Dodgers loudly complained, and the umpires ordered two wheelbarrows of sand dumped along the base path. Still the footing remained precarious; moreover, the infield grass had been mowed so high that Los Angeles writer Bob Hunter suggested that Giants groundskeeper Matty Schwab should be considered for MVP.[52]

As it turned out, Wills would reach base just once in the series and not attempt to steal. In the second game Don Drysdale—sporting a record of 21–4—took a 3–2 lead into the Giants' half of the sixth inning. The six-foot-five-inch right-hander's sweeping sidearm delivery rendered him exceptionally tough on right-handed hitters and naturally more vulnerable to lefties. Willie McCovey was one lefty who just owned him: his career batting average against Drysdale at that point was a neat .500 (15 for 30), with three doubles, a triple, and six home runs. "Earlier in the season [Drysdale] had said, 'I wish that McCovey would play in some other league.'"[53]

With two outs in the sixth, the Giants had runners on first and second, and Dark sent McCovey up as a pinch hitter for Billy Pierce. Hodges had the radio call: "It's three and it's two with two down and the Dodgers lead three to two, and Alou is at second and O'Dell is at first. McCovey waiting on the three-two pitch from Don Drysdale, who has struck out seven Giants so far, and got his sights set on number eight. . . . Drysdale is ready. He winds, throws. McCovey hits a long drive and TELL IT BYE BYE BABY! . . . That's one of the big thrills in the history of Candlestick Park, to see Willie McCovey put the Giants ahead five to three!"[54]

Hodges marveled: "Drysdale threw it, and it was just gone. I don't think anybody really knows where or when it landed."[55] The Giants won the game and swept the series. In the tense weeks to come, the Giants would squeeze the margin to as little as a half-game. But into mid-September they still couldn't catch the Dodgers.

On September 12 the Giants embarked on a road trip to Cincinnati and Pittsburgh, and disaster struck. In the first game at Crosley Field, Willie Mays, overwhelmed with physical and mental exhaustion, fainted in the dugout. He was hospitalized and missed all or part of four games, and with him out, the team stopped hitting and lost six straight. The Dodgers' lead went back up to four, and the Giants were starting to run out of time.

By September 22 the Dodgers' record was 100–55 and the Giants' 96–59, still a four-game lead, now with just seven left to play. The situation resembled that of 1959, only this time it was the Dodgers holding the advantage: if Los Angeles could win four games in the final week, it would be impossible for the Giants to catch them. The '62 Giants then promptly won three in a row, while the Dodgers were losing two out of three, and it was down to a two-game lead with four to play. On September 26 the Giants lost, but instead of closing in for the kill, the Dodgers lost too, and the Giants were two games behind with the final three games of the season to be played.

On that closing weekend the Giants hosted the Houston Colt .45s at Candlestick Park, while the Dodgers faced the St. Louis Cardinals in Los Angeles. On Friday night, September 28, the Giants game was rained out, the first home rainout of the year. (It would be an unusually rainy Bay Area autumn. More on that later.) A Dodger victory would clinch a tie, but the Dodger Stadium crowd of over fifty-one thousand watched their game go, excruciatingly, into extra innings, before the Dodgers lost yet again, 3–2. It was their eighth defeat in eleven games, and the lead was down to a game and a half.

Saturday afternoon's doubleheader at Candlestick drew 26,268. The Giants romped in the opener, 11–5, but lost the second, 4–2. All attention turned to the south, where that evening the Dodgers could wrap it up. But in front of 49,012 agonized fans, the Dodgers failed again, 2–0. The margin was now a single game entering the last day of the regular season.

The pitching match-up in San Francisco was hard-throwing right-hander Dick "Turk" Farrell for the Colts against Billy O'Dell. The Dodgers were playing a day game as well, though it started a bit later than the Giants'. It was scoreless at Candlestick with one out in the bottom of the fourth when Ed Bailey stepped in against Farrell. Bill King, the Giants' third broadcaster behind Hodges and Lon Simmons, was at the KSFO mike: "Whitey Lockman, Wes Westrum, pacing up and down in the third and first base coaching lines, respectively. Crowd sitting in anticipation, waiting for some fireworks. . . . The pitch, there's a swing and a long drive, that might BE the fireworks, it's deep into right field. It is—FOUL, by inches. . . . Full count, with one out to big Ed. Farrell into the motion, here it is. There's a swing, another drive, way back into right field, that one is going, it IS GONE, for a HOME RUN!"[56]

So the Giants had a 1–0 lead. The 41,327 fans in Candlestick Park, as well as listeners on the radio, waited for updates from Dodger Stadium, where Curt Simmons and Johnny Podres were scoreless in the early innings.

At Candlestick, in the sixth, the Colt .45s put together three singles off O'Dell to tie the score 1–1. While it remained nothing-nothing in LA, the Giants came to bat in the bottom of the eighth. Willie Mays led it off. Hodges had the call:

> As Farrell is warming up for the bottom of the eighth inning, Lloyd Fox, the very fine organist here at Candlestick Park, who uses so much showmanship, is suggesting, faintly, you know, putting in the subtle hint, as he's playing "Bye Bye Baby."
>
> As Willie Mays, Willie McCovey, and Ed Bailey will face Dick Farrell, in the bottom of the eighth inning, with the score tied here at one and one, and tied at the end of five innings at Dodger Stadium nothing to nothing, the Cards against the Dodgers. The entire one hundred sixty-two games, wrapped right up here today on the West coast, at Dodger Stadium and here at Candlestick Park.
>
> Here's Farrell winding, he throws to Mays. Willie swings, slaps it foul, deep to right field.
>
> Oh-one pitch, MAYS—HITS ONE A LONG WAY—TELL IT BYE, BYE, BABY!
>
> Mays—put one in orbit! That's as long a home run as he's ever hit in his career, hit far back up into the left field seats, and the Giants lead two to one. Mays's forty-seventh home run.[57]

Stu Miller retired Houston one-two-three in the top of the ninth, and the Giants had won the game. But if the Dodgers won theirs, it wouldn't matter. Most of the throng at Candlestick Park remained in their seats, listening to pocket radios and the periodic updates from Los Angeles relayed over the public address system. It was an odd mood, happy but nervous.

It remained a scoreless tie in Los Angeles, through six innings and then through seven. But with the Cardinals batting in the top of the eighth, over the Western Union telegraph ticker in the Candlestick Park press box came the most welcome message in San Francisco's sports history: "HR, OLIVER, STL, 8th, NONE ON." The Cardinals' catcher Gene Oliver had taken Podres deep, and that game was scoreless no longer.

Yet it was far from over. The Dodgers had six outs. A hush hung above Candlestick. Across the Bay Area cars pulled to curbs, occupants straining to hear the voice of Russ Hodges on the radio relaying the action from the south.[58] Curt Simmons set down the Dodgers in the eighth, but St. Louis didn't score in the ninth, and so the Cardinals took their 1–0 lead into the final half-inning.

Simmons, the veteran left-hander, was working on a five-hitter. Leading off was rookie Ken McMullen, pinch-hitting for Podres. Hodges relayed the messages as they came in. McMullen, the ticker said, flew out to right field. One away. Next up was none other than Maury Wills, who, unnervingly, had 204 hits, had stolen a record-setting 100 bases, and had scored 128 runs. But Hodges was able to report that Wills, batting right-handed against the southpaw Simmons, smacked a line drive that carried straight to right fielder Charlie James, who was, of course, playing shallow. Two down.

Russ Hodges, we'll recall, had started in the sports broadcasting business in the 1930s, when it was common to "call a game" from the studio, reporting each play as its result was received via telegraph line. He well knew this drill. The technique in this circumstance wasn't to merely state the results of each play as it came across the wire; it was to paint a mental picture for the listener, making it seem as though the broadcaster was actually watching the game. This required an active imagination on the part of the broadcaster and a forgiving suspension of disbelief on the part of the listener.

This was Hodges's artful on-air monologue as he waited, with two outs in the bottom of the ninth, to learn the result of Jim Gilliam's at bat against Curt Simmons: "Simmons checks with the resin bag, and fiddles around. He knows the importance of this pitch. So does Gilliam. So do the some 50,000 fans at Dodger Stadium—HE POPS UP TO JAVIER, WE HAVE A PLAYOFF!"[59]

Just as they had in the 1951 playoff, the Dodgers won the home field coin toss. Quite unlike 1951, this time they elected to open on the road and finish at home. So, the Dodgers flew that night to San Francisco for the first game, on Monday afternoon, October 1. Despite zero advance ticket sales, a crowd of 32,652 assembled at Candlestick Park.

The reeling Dodgers, whose killing slump over the past two weeks—ten losses in thirteen games—had opened the door for the Giants, desperately turned to Sandy Koufax. Their sensational star had been rushed back into action for the regular season's final ten days, but though his finger injury was healed, the two-month hibernation put him now essentially in spring training form. He'd made three appearances in late September and was plainly far from his best, but manager Walt Alston had little choice but to give him a try, as the Los Angeles staff was in a state of exhaustion.

It didn't go well for the gallant young ace. After Giants starter Billy Pierce set down the Dodgers in the top of the first, Koufax took the mound. He retired Harvey Kuenn and Chuck Hiller on fly balls, but Felipe Alou raked a line drive double to left field. Up came Mays. Koufax attempted a high fastball, and Willie blasted his forty-eighth home run of the season far over the fence in right-center, and just like that the Giants had a 2–0 advantage.

In the bottom of the second, Jim Davenport greeted Koufax with another homer, and Ed Bailey followed with a loud single. Alston sighed and walked out to the mound to pull his great young southpaw, facing the reality that his overtired bullpen was going to have to handle a big workload today. Against Dodger relievers the Giants would pile on—Mays and Cepeda hit back-to-back homers in the sixth, and José Pagán delivered a three-run double in the eighth—but the insurance runs were superfluous, as the deeply slumping Dodger offense, already shut out in their previous two games, was easily blanked by Pierce, who barely broke a sweat with a three-hitter, 8–0. If ever a team looked help-lessly whipped, it was these Dodgers.

The teams repaired to Los Angeles for the second playoff game. The Dodger fan base seemed as dispirited as their ball club, as despite a day of notice, only 25,321—less than half of capacity—showed up for this do-or-die last stand. Their lack of faith seemed validated when the Giants chased a worn-out Don Drysdale in the top of the sixth, and Jack Sanford took a 5–0 shutout into the bottom of the inning.

Then, at long last, the ice-cold Dodger bats thawed, and sud-denly it was the Giants looking rattled. As Roger Angell vividly portrayed it:

> In the first playoff game, on Monday at Candlestick Park in San Francisco, the Dodger team displayed the muscle, the frightfulness, and the total immobility of a woolly mammoth frozen in a glacier; the Giants, finding the beast inert, fell upon it with savage cries and chopped off steaks and rump roasts at will, winning 8–0. The feast continued here for a time yesterday, and after five and a half innings the Giants led, 5–0. At this point, the Dodgers scored their first run in thirty-six innings, and the Giants, aghast at this tiny evidence of life, stood transfixed, their stone axes dropping from their paws, while the monster heaved itself to its feet, scattering chunks of ice, and set about trampling its tormentors.[60]

The awakening Dodgers stunned the Giants with a seven-run sixth-inning rally, the combined effect of four hits, two walks, a bases-loaded hit batsman, and an error. Dark relieved Sanford with Miller, then relieved him with O'Dell, then relieved *him* with Larsen, before the nightmare was done.

In the eighth three Giants' singles, a Dodger error, and a sac-rifice fly tied the score at 7–7. But in the bottom of the ninth Bob Bolin issued a lead-off walk to Maury Wills—the worst possible idea. Three more pitching changes, two walks, a sacrifice bunt, and a sacrifice fly later, Wills scored the game-winning run. The appallingly sloppy contest had consumed four hours and eighteen minutes, setting a record for the slowest nine-inning game in major league history.[61]

Most improbably, the Dodgers had new life, and this time around they had the decisive third game taking place in their home park. Dodger fans were suddenly feeling a whole lot better about the situation, as this time 45,693 made their way to Chavez Ravine on Wednesday afternoon, October 3. They were presented with another episode of clumsy, messy baseball, as both teams were now burned to a crisp.

Podres started for the Dodgers and Marichal for the Giants. The top of the third inning played like a scene from *The Bad News Bears*, when the Dodgers reacted to three Giant singles by committing three errors and making a throw to the wrong base. Yet all the Giants could muster were two runs, missing—crucially perhaps—the opportunity to break it open.

And the Dodgers had some fight left. They scratched a run off Marichal in the fourth inning, and in the sixth Tommy Davis connected for a two-run homer, and they suddenly gained the lead, 3–2. In the seventh Wills single-handedly manufactured an insurance run by singling, stealing second base and then third, and scoring as the throw to third was wild.

So, the Dodgers took their 4–2 lead into the ninth inning, and though the echoes of 1951 were inescapable, the odds were surely against the Giants mounting another last-ditch comeback. But the bone-weary Dodger bullpen obliged them. Reliever Ed Roebuck was working his fourth inning of the game and eighth of the three-game playoff. Matty Alou—the slight, quick younger brother—led off as a pinch hitter and promptly grounded a single into right field. Kuenn grounded into a force out, but McCovey, pinch-hitting for Hiller, drew a walk. Felipe Alou then came up as the potential go-ahead run, and Roebuck, reeling now, walked him too, loading the bases.

This brought Mays to the plate. He wasn't inclined to wait for another walk. Instead, Willie hacked at a neck-high pitch and lined it viciously straight back at Roebuck, who deflected it with his glove to the grass for an infield single. The score was now 4–3, still one out, the bases still loaded.

At this point Alston made a move that would be roundly crit-icized: he called in right-hander Stan Williams to face Cepeda. Williams was a very hard thrower, and usually a Dodger starter, but he'd endured a poor year in 1962. To be fair to Alston, all of his relievers were exhausted, and it isn't obvious what better options he had.

Williams retired Cepeda, but it was on a fly ball to right field deep enough to allow the tying run to score. There were now two outs, and Alston made another decision that would draw heat, ordering Williams to intentionally walk left-handed-batting Ed Bailey, reloading the bases and bringing up right-handed-batting Jim Davenport. Williams was not a pitcher noted for his control, and the Chavez Ravine fans looked on in dread as he proceeded to unintentionally walk Davenport, forcing in the go-ahead run—the run carrying the weight of the pennant.

Alston now replaced Williams with left-hander Ron Perra-noski, who induced Pagán to hit a grounder to second base, but rookie Larry Burright booted it, and it was 6–4 San Francisco. The third out was then recorded, but the Giants had plated four runs while achieving just one single to the outfield, with the Dodgers contributing four walks and an error.

Dark called upon Pierce to close out the bottom of the ninth, and he briskly did so, one-two-three. The San Francisco Giants had won the pennant. "At the Curran Theatre on San Francis-co's Geary Street, where the musical *Oliver* was playing a mat-inee, a great cheer rose up from spectators pressing transistor radios to their ears."[62]

The victory celebration in the Giants' clubhouse was exultant indeed, but the party had just started. The team gathered itself and boarded a bus to Los Angeles International Airport and from there a chartered jet to San Francisco International. But as they flew home, an immense and ever-growing crowd was gathering at sFO, overwhelming local security, spilling out onto the tarmac. As the Giants' plane swung toward San Francisco, the pilot came on the intercom and warned, "We may have to land in Oakland."

The plane headed for Oakland, then turned around and con-tinued to circle; a sportswriter aboard commented that he hoped they'd remembered to fill the fuel tanks before takeoff. The DC-7 then began an approach to land in San Francisco but aborted it, and some thirty-eight minutes after the first announcement, the pilot took the microphone again: "We can't go in. Two big jets are stalled down there. We'll have to land at the west runway."

At last the plane was able to land at SFO, and it taxied to the United Airlines maintenance base, far from the terminal, behind locked gates. The crowd, now grown to 75,000 or 100,000, surrounded the area, but actually only thirty-seven workers on duty—hangar police, maintenance men, a switchboard attendant, and the driver of the team's bus—greeted the victors, applauding politely.

The team boarded a bus to head for the terminal building, where their own families were waiting. But they never made it. The immense crowd had overwhelmed the police. The bus was swarmed, and two of its windows were broken. Things began to look ugly. Chub Feeney ordered the bus driver to back up and retreat from the airport entirely. The bus escaped the milling crowd, and Feeney directed it to a nearby hotel. "In all my born years," Feeney said, "I've never seen anything like this. It certainly wasn't like this when we won in 1951." The Giants disembarked the bus at the hotel, and one taxicab after another picked them up and finally took them home.[63]

Bay Area newspapers frantically tried to keep up with it all. The circulation manager of the *San Francisco Chronicle* approached the news editor and said, "What's the headline?"

"It's 'WE WIN!'—white on black," the news editor said.

"How big?"

"Same size as 'FIDEL DEAD!'"[64]

Roger Angell arrived in downtown San Francisco at eleven that night, and the scene he encountered was still wild:

The gutters were awash with torn-up newspapers and office calendars, and Market Street, Geary Street, and Kearney Street were solid with automobiles crawling bumper to bumper, horns blasting. The faces inside all had the shiny-eyed, stunned, exhausted expression of a bride at her wedding reception. The police, who had planted red flares at intersections to guide the processions, were treating it all like cops in a college town after a big football victory—a little bored, a little amused, a little irritated. . . . The total identification of this attractive city with a baseball team is a sado-masochistic tangle. The gala this week has offended a good many proud old-time locals, who think the city should be less naïve. "Good God!" one of these said to me. "People will think we're like *Milwaukee*, or something!"[65]

So, twice in the space of a dozen years—and bracketing the width of the continent—Horace Stoneham's Giants had forged a dramatic late-season comeback to catch the Dodgers in a tie and prevailed two out of three to win the playoff. That much was repeated. But the nature of the dramatic come-from-behind triumphs were different. In 1951 it wasn't so much that the Dodgers blew it as it was the Giants flat out surpassed them with inspired play. In 1962, well, the Dodgers just blew it: while the Giants' stretch performance was okay, the Dodgers' was terrible, and the Giants were looking increasingly frazzled themselves.

Thus, while the Giants had roared into the 1951 World Series matchup against the Yankees *en fuego*, in '62, again facing (of course) the Bronx Bombers, one could reasonably expect that these well-rested Yanks would likely make quick work of the worn-out San Franciscans.

It wasn't to be. In contrast to the dreadful quality of play in the 1962 National League playoff, the World Series was a crisp, professionally executed, low-scoring affair, and by no means did the Yankees have an easy time with the Giants. Indeed, it was about as evenly matched a series as there ever was, not only going the full seven games but with neither team able to win two games in a row and with the overall tally of runs at Giants twenty-one, Yankees twenty.

But though the 1962 Series was a hard-fought seesaw affair, the individual games themselves were less so. In six of the seven, the team that scored first won, with zero lead changes. Thus, the contests, though well played and mostly close, weren't dramatic or especially memorable—until Game Seven, which, especially in its final half-inning, was indeed dramatic and memorable, if achingly so for Giants fans.

The New York Yankees in 1962 were riding the crest of a dynastic wave that was the greatest even in their own storied history, the greatest ever known in major league baseball. Their 1962 American League pennant was their third straight, and their thirteenth in sixteen seasons, and they'd gone on to win the World Series in nine of those twelve preceding appearances. Their 1962 edition hadn't run away with the flag, but one of the interesting characteristics of the Yankee teams through this period is that they rarely did; they just ground it out, avoiding any significant slumps, methodically compiling just enough victories to get the task accomplished. In '62 they took over first place for good in mid-July, and their final winning margin of five games was very nearly their biggest all season. It was cold, hard efficiency.

The team they brought into the 1962 World Series was more impressive for its depth and balance than for any individual superstars. Their greatest player, center fielder Mickey Mantle, was voted the American League's Most Valuable Player that year, but at the age of thirty he was beginning to break down and appeared in just 121 games. Right fielder Roger Maris had been the AL's MVP in both 1960 and '61, and of course had set the new major league record with sixty-one home runs in 1961. But in '62 Maris was frequently booed by his home fans in Yankee Stadium because he was unable to repeat the previous year's stunning long ball production, delivering "only" thirty-three homers. Giants pitching bottled up both of them in the World Series, as the "M and M Boys" combined to go seven for forty-eight (.146); Mantle drove in zero runs.

But Mantle and Maris, in top form or not, were just the beginning of what the Yankees brought to bear. The lineup of catcher Elston Howard, first baseman Bill Skowron, second baseman Bobby Richardson, shortstop Tony Kubek, third baseman Clete Boyer, and Rookie-of-the-Year left fielder Tom Tresh didn't just lack a weakness; it featured nothing but strengths. The team's pitching staff in 1962 didn't match that kind of depth, but their pair of aces up front were world class: Hall of Famer Whitey Ford, still sharp as ever at age thirty-three, and twenty-six-year-old Ralph Terry, who led the league in innings and wins. Manager Ralph Houk would ride those two big horses hard in the World Series, starting each three times and having them handle three-quarters of the innings.

The Series opener was in San Francisco on Thursday, October 4; for the Giants it was their tenth game in ten days and thirty-sixth in thirty-eight. Candlestick Park was filled to standing room only, with 43,852 ditching work or school. The Yankees were unimpressed, getting right to work with two runs in the top of the first and cruising to a 6–2 win behind Ford.

At this point the Giants would have been forgiven for thinking that maybe they'd gone about as far as they could. Angell was in the Candlestick Park grandstand for Game Two:

> The apparently inevitable outcome of yesterday's game seemed to afflict the home team and its fans deeply this afternoon. A man seated just in front of me was suffering from a severe case of the uh-ohs. "Uh-oh," he would murmur to his companion, "here comes Yogi Berra." . . . "Uh-oh, Mantle comes up this inning." Meanwhile, the Giants were clustering under pop flies like firemen bracing to catch a baby dropped from a burning building (they muffed one baby, right behind the mound), and wasting their substance in overexuberant base-running. In the seventh and eighth innings, they combined a home run by Willie McCovey, three singles, a walk, two successful sacrifices, and a Yankee error for the grand total of one run, which may be another Series record.[66]

Yet Jack Sanford was brilliant, shutting out the Yankees on three hits, and the win-loss ping-ponging was underway. After a merciful travel day on Saturday, the third game was in Yankee Stadium, and before a massive sellout of over seventy-one thousand, the Yankees won 3–2. But on Monday it was the Giants' turn, and their 7–3 win was notable in that the big hit was a grand slam by, of all people, Chuck Hiller; it was the very first grand slam by a National Leaguer in World Series history. With the Series now tied at two, the fifth game was postponed because of rain—there would be more of that to come—and when it was played on Wednesday, October 10, the Yankees won 5–3 behind Terry. The teams flew back to the West Coast with the Giants facing elimination.

Among the benefits of playing baseball in California is the region's near-total absence of summertime rainfall. In their five seasons since arriving from New York, the Giants had suffered just six home rainouts. However, in 1962, a big storm arrived in mid-October, just in time for the scheduled conclusion of the World Series. Game Six was supposed to take place on Thursday, October 11, but it was postponed to Friday and then to Saturday and then beyond, as steady, heavy rain drenched the Bay Area. On Sunday the sky finally cleared, but the Candlestick Park outfield was too wet for play. The teams were bussed to Modesto, a San Joaquin Valley farming town one hundred miles to the east, where it hadn't rained as much, to work out on the Modesto Junior College ball field. Meanwhile, Stoneham hired three helicopters to hover over the Candlestick outfield to try to dry it out.

On Monday, October 15, though things were still soggy, Commissioner Ford Frick deemed the field playable, so a sellout crowd of 43,948 filed into Candlestick. The long layoff allowed both managers to reshuffle their starting pitchers as desired. Houk went with Ford, owner of a record ten World Series wins against just four losses. Dark couldn't select Marichal because in Game Four he'd broken a finger while attempting to bunt. So instead, it was Billy Pierce. The Giants roughed up Ford, knocking him out in the fifth inning, while Pierce tossed a three-hit gem, and it was on to Game Seven.

It was another sellout, and these fans witnessed Ralph Terry and Jack Sanford present one of the most grindingly tense Game Sevens of all time. Terry was masterful, rendering the power-laden Giants—whose offense in 1962 scored the most runs of any major league team between 1953 and 1982—whisper-quiet. Sanford wasn't so sharp, but he bulldogged his way out of jams. He made just one critical mistake: in the fifth inning, with runners at first and third and no outs, Sanford walked Terry. He then induced Tony Kubek to ground into a double play, but the run scored from third, and it was 1–0 Yankees.

Terry was perfect through five and two-thirds innings until Sanford himself, allowed by Dark to bat with two outs in the sixth, sliced a single to right-center. He was stranded. In the bottom of the seventh Mays drilled a liner deep into the left field corner, but Tom Tresh made a spectacular, sprinting, backhanded snow cone catch. Next up McCovey—getting his fourth start of the Series—blasted a searing drive over Mantle's head in center field and legged it out for a triple. But Terry struck out Cepeda to end the inning. In the top of the eighth Billy O'Dell, in relief of Sanford, wriggled out of a bases-loaded, no-outs jam. It remained 1–0 into the bottom of the ninth inning.

Matty Alou led if off, pinch-hitting for O'Dell. The Yankees may not have been surprised when he laid down a drag bunt, but he executed it perfectly, pushing it past Terry, and was aboard with a single. His brother Felipe attempted to sacrifice but was unable to get his bunt down, and Terry then struck him out. Next up was Hiller, who laid down a marvelous bunt along the third base line that wouldn't have been just a sacrifice but another single, except that it rolled just foul. Then Terry struck him out as well.

That left it up to Mays. Later a reporter asked: "You were just trying to hit the ball, weren't you, Willie? Just trying for a base hit?" Mays shot him a look and said, "You crazy, man? I was trying for a home run!"

Terry's first pitch was a fastball, slightly outside. Mays hit it right on the nose but without home run loft. The ball sped on a line to the right field corner, touching down deep for a base hit. Matty Alou, a fast runner, was off at the crack of the bat, flying around second and into third full steam, eager to score the World Series–tying run. But third base coach Whitey Lockman put up the stop sign and held him at third. Later, in a calm, controlled voice, Harvey Kuenn said: "On any normal day, that ball goes through to the fence. And Alou scores."[67]

But this, alas, wasn't any normal day. This was the day after six days of rain, and the outfield grass was thick, high, and soaking wet, and Mays's bullet was slowed down so much that Roger Maris was able to cut it off before it bounded to the fence. Marvelous fielder that he was, Maris not only cut it off but kept his balance on the slick wet turf while smartly pivoting and threw a strike to cutoff man Bobby Richardson, who wheeled and threw a strike to catcher Elston Howard.

Lockman made the right call. As Ed Bailey put it: "And wouldn't THAT have been a helluva way to end the season, Willie McCovey coming up and the tying run thrown out by fifteen feet? Crazy, man!"[68]

So, McCovey was up, with the tying run on third, the World Series–winning run on second, first base open, and two outs and Orlando Cepeda on deck. Consider that the left-handed-batting McCovey had hit the daylights out of the ball for a triple in his previous at bat against the right-hander Terry. Consider that McCovey had homered off Terry in Game Two. Consider as well that the right-handed-batting Cepeda had struck out twice and popped up against Terry in this game, was three for nineteen in the Series, and was benched by Dark against Terry in the second and fifth games. Everyone in the world understood that the obvious move here was to walk McCovey intentionally and allow Terry to face Cepeda, instead, in this do-or-die situation. McCovey was the worst possible opponent for Terry to deal with.

So, Ralph Houk called time and went out to the mound to confer with his pitcher, catcher, and infielders. Everyone in the world understood that the discussion was about how to pitch to Cepeda with the bases loaded, after McCovey was given his free pass. But, no. Houk somehow allowed Terry to persuade him that the right move was for him to face McCovey. With a decision that would be recalled for eternity as one of the all-time howling managerial blunders if it hadn't turned out as it did, Houk returned to the dugout, and McCovey eagerly dug in against Ralph Terry.

Willie Mac yanked Terry's first pitch deep to right but clearly foul, hooking into the grandstand. On Terry's second offering McCovey nailed a smoking, sinking line drive. Second baseman Richardson—playing in extreme pull position way around toward first base, at the edge of the outfield grass—was in precisely the right place. He caught the liner easily, reaching just a bit down and to his left. The 1962 World Series was over.

11

No Cigar

The 1962 San Francisco Giants were a great achievement of baseball team building. The bountifully talented roster—that came within exactly one differently placed line drive of beating the dynastic New York Yankees in the World Series—was the result of many years of sound work and patient investment on the part of Horace Stoneham and the organization he had created. The core pieces of the team—not only the key stars Willie Mays, Orlando Cepeda, Juan Marichal, and Felipe Alou but much of the productive supporting cast, including Willie McCovey, Jim Davenport, José Pagán, Chuck Hiller, Tom Haller, and Bob Bolin—were homegrown products of the Giants' extraordinary farm system, which had gained much of its competitive advantage by committing to scouting and pipeline development efforts in the Caribbean and in African American communities in the United States before most other teams had even begun to do so. As Bill James put it, the Giants farm system in these years "was producing ballplayers like McDonald's produces hamburgers. . . . It may have been the most productive farm system in the history of baseball."[1]

But Stoneham had complemented his internal sources with ambitious and well-reasoned trades. Stu Miller, Jack Sanford, Billy O'Dell, Harvey Kuenn, Ed Bailey, Billy Pierce, and Don Larsen were all trade acquisitions imported by Stoneham in an era in which it was no longer feasible to simply purchase major talent, as it had been in previous decades, and it was not yet feasible to sign major talent on the free agent market, as the reserve clause was still in place. In the 1950s and 1960s, for a team to bring in talent from outside the organization, it was necessary to give up talent in return, a circumstance not for the faint of heart and one in which a poor bargainer would lose ground. Stoneham and his staff deserve real credit for assembling this 1962 Giants roster. One could certainly question a couple of their choices— namely, in failing to perceive just what they had on their hands in McCovey and in going all in with Hiller at second base—but on balance the organizational performance had been excellent.

Now having achieved a National League championship, the challenge was to sustain the success, not merely to avoid "falling apart," as pennant winners sometimes do, but to win another flag or two, continually refreshing the roster as necessary and remain at the top of the game. Such a thing is far easier said than done, of course, but the Giants in the early 1960s appeared to be in a good position to pull it off. Their best players were still young, with years of peak performance likely to come, and the pipeline from the minors showed no signs of shutting off. Rookie pitcher Gaylord Perry played only a bit part on the major league roster in 1962 but offered extraordinary promise. Additional prospects glimmering in the Giants' minor league chain included twenty- year-old third baseman Jim Ray Hart, nineteen-year-old short- stop Charles "Cap" Peterson, twenty-year-old right fielder Jesús Alou (yet another brother), and eighteen-year-old center fielder José Cardenal.

In the off-season following the 1962 pennant, Stoneham didn't stand pat, executing two trades. The first was with Houston in November, surrendering a pair of youngsters—outfielder Manny Mota and pitcher Dick LeMay—to return infielder Joey Amalf- itano to the Giants. Neither Mota nor LeMay projected as a star, and reacquiring Amalfitano, a competent major league second baseman, signaled recognition that Hiller could use some help.

The second deal, in December, packaged Stu Miller, Mike McCormick, and young catcher John Orsino to the Baltimore Orioles, in exchange for pitchers Billy Hoeft and Jack Fisher and backup catcher Jimmie Coker. This one was a head-scratcher. Miller and Hoeft were both veteran relievers (the former a righty and the latter a lefty), McCormick and Fisher were both impressive young pitchers who'd struggled in 1962 (the former a lefty and the latter a righty), and Orsino and Coker were both right-handed-hitting catchers, so it all balanced out in that way. But comparing the quality of talents, it didn't balance at all. Miller had delivered an off-year in '62, but Hoeft's was worse, and moreover, Hoeft had a history of arm trouble, and Miller didn't. McCormick and Fisher had both endured bad seasons as twenty-three-year-olds in '62, but McCormick's record of success before then dwarfed Fisher's. Orsino was two years younger than Coker and had outhit him in both the minors and majors. Stoneham's logic was mysterious.

Manager Alvin Dark made one significant lineup change for 1963. In '62 McCovey, deployed irregularly in the utility role, had hit tremendously well and not just against Don Drysdale: McCovey's slugging percentage in 1962, had he played enough to qualify, would have placed him fourth in the league, and his home run rate, projected to six hundred plate appearances, would have yielded forty-six, placing him second. It dawned on the manager that even though McCovey presented a serious defensive liability in left field, a bat like his would surely outweigh it. So, for '63 it was now McCovey as the first-string left fielder, with the veteran Kuenn—who was still a good player but no star—now in the utility role.

In 1963 the Giants started well and spent most of the early season in first. But in June, once again, they swooned, losing seven in a row. They made subsequent charges, then fell back and weren't close down the stretch. They finished third, eleven games behind the pennant-winning Dodgers.

The Giants in 1963 were a team of extremes, with tremendous strengths alongside glaring weaknesses. The extraordinary hitting trio of Mays, Cepeda, and McCovey wasn't just the best in baseball in 1963; it was one of the very greatest ever seen.[2] Felipe Alou was excellent as well. For the second straight year the remarkable catcher tandem of Ed Bailey and Tom Haller combined for thirty-five home runs. And twenty-five-year-old Juan Marichal blossomed into superstardom, tying Sandy Koufax for the major league lead in wins, with twenty-five. (On July 2, 1963,

Marichal hooked up with forty-two-year-old Warren Spahn for one of the greatest games in history, a double shutout into the bottom of the sixteenth inning, both aces stubbornly going the distance, ended at long last by a Willie Mays home run.)

But there were the weaknesses. At second base Chuck Hiller had held his own with the bat in 1962, slapping out a .276 average, but his twenty-nine errors led the major leagues at the position. In 1963 he got off to a 9-for-71 (.127) start and wound up at .223; moreover, his fielding percentage, as in '62, was the worst among major league regular second basemen. Joey Amalfitano, imported for the very purpose of stopgapping Hiller, was no help; he hit .175 and was shipped out to AAA. Neither José Pagán nor Jim Davenport hit well either, so the infield's offensive contribution was meager.

Indeed, in early July, Davenport's batting average was in the .230s, so Stoneham reached into his minor league bag of tricks for some third base help. Twenty-one-year-old Jim Ray Hart, leaving a trail of battered minor league pitchers in his wake, was summoned from AAA, and Dark immediately installed him as the new starting third baseman. However, Hart encountered the worst of luck: in his second major league game he was hit by a Bob Gibson fastball, broke his shoulder blade, and missed a month. Upon his return, in his fifth game back, Hart was again struck by an errant St. Louis pitch, this one from Curt Simmons, fracturing his skull and finishing his season.

The trade with Baltimore turned out disastrously. Failing to bolster a Giants staff that had issues with depth, Hoeft was sore armed and of little use, and Fisher was ineffective as a spot starter–long reliever. (Meanwhile, for the Orioles, Miller bounced back with a great year, and Orsino blossomed with a nineteen-homer season.)

The Giants did make a bit of history in September 1963. One of their late-season call-ups was Jesús Alou. On September 15, in the closing innings at Forbes Field in Pittsburgh, the Giants featured an outfield of Matty Alou in left, Felipe in center, and Jesús in right, the first and only time in major league history that a trio of brothers played in a single lineup. It was to Horace

Stoneham's organizational credit that the brothers achieving this feat were Black and Latino.

On top of the disappointment of dropping to third place in 1963, the team faced an awkward issue with manager Alvin Dark. Often preachy with his players regarding his Baptist religion and openly judgmental about the morality of others, over the course of the '63 season it became all too evident that Dark was conducting an extramarital affair with a flight attendant, whose name was Jackie Rockwood. Many Giants players were bitter over their manager's rank hypocrisy. Word about it reached Stoneham, and he was furious. Dark described the situation in his autobiography:

> Mr. Stoneham called me into his office and said he knew what was going on and I would have to stop seeing Jackie. He said it didn't look good. "You can't handle your ball players if you can't handle yourself. You've got rules *you* are breaking."
>
> He was right, of course. I was not much of an example. I'd had a rule, a $250 fine for any player who brought anyone to his room on the road. I had the house detective get a girl out of one player's room in Pittsburgh when we were driving for the pennant in '62. I had him tell the girl she was going to jail, and that I was going to fine the player. I had the managers of the hotels alert their detectives to watch certain guys. It was effective when I wasn't guilty myself. Your actions drown out your words every time.
>
> The players knew. They always knew. Maybe if I'd been Leo Durocher they'd have applauded, but as a professing Christian I was more likely to get raspberries. That's one of the problems of presenting a self-righteous profile. . . .
>
> Mr. Stoneham . . . always resented the fact that I wouldn't join his drinking parties—his "sit-sees" he called them. "Come sit-see with me." I hated that because I don't drink and I don't enjoy watching what drinking does to people. I loved Mr. Stoneham, but I wanted nothing to do with that part of his life.
>
> It probably didn't bother him until he found out about Jackie, and then it got in his craw. (Who is this Holy Joe who won't drink or smoke or curse, but now he's got a girlfriend?) From then on, our relationship cooled.[3]

Stoneham's team remained exceptionally strong at its core. Its problems were with specific portions of the supporting cast, so Stoneham made an effort to address the issues. His key move was a big trade with the Milwaukee Braves, executed on December 3, 1963. The Giants' main surplus was (as usual) in the outfield, and the Giants were blessed with two power-hitting catchers. So, Stoneham sent right fielder Felipe Alou and catcher Ed Bailey to the Braves, along with Hoeft, and received pitchers Bob Shaw and Bob Hendley and veteran catcher Del Crandall. Shaw was thirty years old, a crafty right-hander—particularly crafty in a way that we'll explore—who'd pitched very effectively for the Braves in both 1962 and '63, flexibly working as either a starter or reliever. Hendley was a twenty-four-year-old southpaw starter who hadn't achieved consistent success but appeared capable of it. The thirty-three-year-old Crandall had long been a star but at this point would fit as the backup to Tom Haller, who looked more than ready for regular play.

Felipe Alou had been an outstanding all-around performer for the Giants but was no longer a young player—he would be twenty-nine in 1964—and his kid brother Jesús seemed ready to take over in right field. Jesús, who would be twenty-two in '64, had made All-Star teams right up the minor league chain, hitting for a consistently high average with moderate power, and he had the kind of size—six foot two and 190 pounds—that often brings home run production with maturity.

In the infield the announced solution was in-house. A healthy Jim Ray Hart, recovered from his 1963 beaning injuries, would take over as the regular third baseman, allowing Jim Davenport to shift to second base and bumping Chuck Hiller to the bench. Davenport had always been a superb defensive third baseman, but his hitting was up and down. His bat would be adequate for a second baseman, however, and in any case he was a better hitter than Hiller and certainly more sure-handed.

But for no apparent reason, Dark would fail to carry out the plan. Davenport started just three games at second to open the 1964 season, and then Hiller was back in there, and from then on they alternated, with Davenport generally deployed as the utility infielder. Neither he nor Hiller nor shortstop José Pagán hit at all well in 1964, rendering the Giants' middle infield an offensive wasteland. Therefore, in June, Stoneham called up twenty-two-year-old Hal Lanier, who took over as the everyday second baseman, with Hiller at last truly demoted to a backup role.

The baseball seasons of 1963 and 1964 played against a backdrop of increasing racial turmoil and cultural change in the United States. In early 1963 George Wallace was inaugurated as governor of Alabama, and in his address he proclaimed, "Segregation now, segregation tomorrow, and segregation forever." In May of that year, thousands of African Americans, including many children, were arrested for protesting segregation in Birmingham, Alabama, the hometown of Willie Mays. Public safety commissioner Eugene "Bull" Connor authorized the weaponization of fire hoses and police dogs against the demonstrators. On August 28, 1963, during the March on Washington for Jobs and Freedom—the single largest political protest in United States history—Dr. Martin Luther King Jr. delivered his epic "I Have a Dream" speech from the steps of the Lincoln Memorial to an audience of at least 250,000. Two weeks later, in Birmingham, the Sixteenth Street Baptist Church was bombed by white supremacists, killing four children and injuring twenty-two others. In the spring of 1964 the landmark Civil Rights Act of 1964 was moving toward approval in Congress and would be signed into law by President Lyndon B. Johnson in July.

In early 1964 Jackie Robinson published a book titled *Baseball Has Done It*. In later years Robinson would speak with bitterness about baseball's slow progress in racially integrating beyond the playing field. But this book was largely a celebration of the sport's role within the larger civil rights dynamic. Much of *Baseball Has Done It* was in the form of lengthy interviews with prominent players and managers, discussing the subject of race relations within baseball. None other than San Francisco Giants manager Alvin Dark—against whom Robinson had fiercely competed amid the Dodger-Giant rivalry in New York in the 1950s—found himself quoted extensively:

Since I was born in the South I know that everyone thinks that Southerners dislike Negroes or even being with them. This isn't true at all.
The majority of the people in the South, especially the Christian people that I have associated with, have really and truly liked the colored
people. . . . The way I feel, the colored boys who are baseball players
are the ones I know best . . . all these boys were, as far as I was concerned, wonderful boys and I never had any kind of trouble with any
of them. In fact, I felt that because I was from the South—and we
from the South actually take care of the colored people, I think, better than they're taken care of in the North—I felt when I was playing
with them it was a responsibility for me. . . . As far as my thoughts on
integration are concerned, I'd rather stay away from it as much as
possible. I think it's being handled a little wrong in that . . . too many
people are trying to solve the Southerners' problems in the North.

  . . . The way I run a ball club is just like the way I played. As long
as a man does his job, I don't care who he is. I don't pick on anyone
in particular. If a fellow loafs, if a fellow misses a sign, if a fellow
doesn't produce, it makes no difference to me what color he is. . . .
There has never been any trouble between colored boys and other
players on this club during my connection with it. Colored boys have
never given me any trouble as manager.[4]

As condescending a tone as this was, neither Dark's viewpoint
nor his vocabulary were unusual among a large segment of the
white population. However, to acknowledge the pervasiveness
of this mind-set is not to dismiss how offensive it had to be to
the players of color under Dark's direction. And 1964 was a new
time, in which much of the nation was no longer accepting racial
business as usual. Dark's quotations in Robinson's book were
widely noted and criticized.

With Dark's racial comments freshly prominent, on May 21,
1964, the Giants manager called Willie Mays into his office. Dark
informed Mays that he was appointing him team captain. Neither
Dark nor Mays needed to point out that there had never before
been a Black major league team captain. Both knew it. Mays pondered, then accepted, though telling Dark that he didn't have to
do it. Dark insisted.

Mays understood that the timing, on the heels of the controversy over Dark's comments, would be seen as intended to give the manager cover. Naming a captain in the middle of a season was strange, and the Giants hadn't even had a team captain since 1956, when, interestingly enough, it had been Alvin Dark. But Mays had nothing to apologize for. He believed he deserved to be captain. He was no aloof superstar but was, in fact, the club's dedicated elder statesman, helping to position fellow defenders on the field. Off the field Mays gave away to teammates the sweaters, shirts, and neckties that endorsement companies sent him, and—as Willie McCovey admitted—Mays reliably "laughed at our jokes even when they weren't funny."[5] Mays accepted the appointment.

In early 1964, among the Giants' frustrations was the lack of progress achieved by twenty-five-year-old Gaylord Perry. The organization had invested a $60,000 signing bonus in him, and he'd easily climbed the minor league ladder. Big and strong at six four, 205 pounds, with a superior fastball and fine control, major league success and even stardom seemed within his reach. But in both 1962 and '63 with the Giants, Perry struggled, failing to establish himself, and in both years he was ignominiously sent back down to AAA. In 1964 he opened the season as Dark's mop-up reliever and last-resort spot starter. Through May 30 he'd appeared just eight times, and his earned run average was 4.76.

On May 31, 1964, in the second game of a doubleheader against the Mets at Shea Stadium, the Giants found themselves ensnared in extra innings. In the thirteenth, rookie Ron Herbel, the Giants' fourth pitcher of the contest, was spent. Dark handed the ball to Perry, his last man in the bullpen, and everyone understood that this was going to be Perry's game, win or lose.

The spitball, or any manner of defacing or applying a foreign substance to the ball, had been banned in major league baseball since 1920. Nevertheless, in the decades since, everyone understood that more than a few pitchers, perhaps many pitchers, surreptitiously threw some version of it, as the rule was difficult to enforce. In the 1950s and '60s future Hall of Famers Whitey

Ford and Don Drysdale were among the most prominent suspects. But probably no pitcher in that era was more commonly assumed to deploy the moist pitch than longtime Milwaukee Braves star Lew Burdette.

We'll recall that in the previous winter, the Giants had acquired veteran pitcher Bob Shaw from the same Milwaukee Braves. It was the case that the erstwhile journeyman Shaw had turned his career around with the Braves. Rumor had it that among the new tricks he'd learned was a wicked spitter, taught to him by Mr. Burdette.

The craft of pitching is one in which grizzled veterans hand down hard-won wisdoms and secrets to aspiring youngsters. Some wily old hurler—it may or may not have been Hall of Famer Burleigh Grimes—had many years ago passed the forbidden art along to Burdette.[6] In 1964, with the Giants, it became Bob Shaw's turn to forge another link in that eternal chain. Perry came to spring training all too aware that his window of opportunity might be closing and worked with pitching coach Larry Jansen on a new slider, to augment his fastball, curve, and changeup. And in secret, under the tutelage of Shaw, he also learned to throw the spitball. Perry used it in a few spring training games.[7]

In the bottom of the thirteenth inning at Shea Stadium in May 31, Perry decided he had nothing to lose, perhaps even fearing that his very career was at stake. He'd toyed with the spitball in meaningless situations, but on this day he and catcher Tom Haller decided it was time to try it out for real, with the game on the line. And this game went on and on, as Perry heroically delivered ten sudden-death shutout innings. He earned the victory, at last achieved by the Giants in the twenty-third, and he finally earned the confidence of his manager.[8]

With that stunning performance, Perry dramatically turned around his season and his career. He would pitch brilliantly as a long reliever through June and July, and when Dark inserted him into the starting rotation for the season's final two months, he was superb in that role as well. Perry was the best Giants pitcher in 1964 outside of superstar ace Juan Marichal.

On July 21, 1964—two months to the day after Alvin Dark had appointed Willie Mays as the first Black team captain in major league history—the manager of the Giants sat down in his Candlestick Park office for an interview with Stan Isaacs, a columnist from *Newsday* magazine. It's a fair question to consider whether Alvin Dark should have known better than to be interviewed by Stan Isaacs. As a major league baseball manager in the 1960s—indeed, as a public figure—one could argue that Dark had a responsibility to gain some knowledge of the current media landscape and in any case to be careful about what he said on the record. But Dark was heedless and obviously had no idea what type of writer Isaacs was.

Isaacs was a prominent member of an unofficial but extremely self-aware "club" of young New York–based sportswriters dubbed the "Chipmunks." The nickname had been given to them, deprecatingly, by old-school sportswriter Jimmy Cannon, who was annoyed by their busy chattering, but the Chipmunks bore it proudly. They saw themselves as outsiders, reinventing the work and perhaps even the role of sportswriting. Unlike the previous generations of beat writers, the Chipmunks weren't interested in sustaining carefully arranged heroic images of famous jocks and teams. Instead, they intended to cover sports like a news beat, asking hard questions and treating the subject objectively, if not skeptically. While there was never an official roster of Chipmunks, those who considered themselves members of the fraternity along with Isaacs included Steve Jacobson and George Vecsey at *Newsday*, Larry Merchant at the *New York Daily News*, Phil Pepe and Paul Zimmerman at the *New York World-Telegram and Sun*, and Leonard Shecter, Maury Allen, and Vic Ziegel at the *New York Post*.[9]

Isaacs's interview with Dark—in which the manager, well, spoke freely—would appear in *Newsday* in two installments, the first on July 23. The article's gist was that the Giants were squandering great talent with dumb mistakes. Dark concurred with that assessment and explained to Isaacs that he had identified the cause. "We have trouble because we have so many Negroes and Spanish-speaking players on this team," Dark was quoted.

"They are just not able to perform up to the white ball player when it comes to mental alertness. You can't make most Negro and Spanish players have the pride in their team that you can get from white players. And they just aren't as sharp mentally."

Some Black players, such as Willie Mays and Jackie Robinson, were exceptions, Dark allowed, but he elaborated: "You would have to be here day in and day out to see what happens. They are not the kind of thing a manager can correct—missed signs and such—but they are inabilities to cope with game situations when they come up. And one of the biggest things is that you can't make them subordinate themselves to the best interests of the team. You don't find the pride in them that you get in the white player."

Dark went on. "You don't know how hard we've tried to make a team player, a hustling ballplayer, out of Orlando [Cepeda]. But nothing has worked for so long. He doesn't sacrifice himself. I'd have to say he's giving out only 40 percent."

When Isaacs suggested that basketball's Boston Celtics had been quite successful with Black players, Dark shrugged it off, saying: "I only know what I've seen on this team and other base-ball teams. If I'm wrong, then I have been getting an awful number of the slow ones."[10]

It took a week or so, in that pre-internet age, for Dark's quotations to become widely circulated. Once that happened, it was a bombshell. Dark was nationally skewered, especially on the heels of his utterances from the Jackie Robinson book. In reaction to the furor, Dark protested that he'd been misquoted, but as writer Charles Einstein put it, "Too many people knew Dark too well" for that to be credible.[11] Dark initially threatened to sue, but he withdrew that notion when he was told that his private life would be made public in any trial.[12]

The Giants' players of color, especially Cepeda, were enraged, vowing open rebellion. The team was on the road in Pittsburgh, and Willie Mays, in his newfound role of team captain, called a meeting of all the Black and Latino players in his room at the Carlton House. Mays was not well, in the depths of a bad cold, so bad that he kept a decongestant inhaler in his hand and periodically took it to his nose for a weary whiff. He stood and confronted the loudly griping crew filing into the hotel room.

"Shut up!" he told them. "Just shut up."

"You don't tell me to shut up," Cepeda said. "I'm not going to play another game for that son of a bitch."

"Oh yes you are," Mays told him. "And let me tell you why."

Mays informed them that Horace Stoneham was so upset that he was planning to fly to Cincinnati, where the club was headed in a couple of days, and fire Dark. Mays further told them that in his own opinion as well as those of Chub Feeney and of coach Herman Franks, firing Dark right now would be a disaster because it would turn him into a martyr for the racist cause. Mays said that he, Feeney, and Franks were working to persuade Stoneham to hold off. "I tell you for a fact, he is not going to be back next year," Mays said. "Don't let the rednecks make a hero out of him."

Mays also had a practical reason. Were the team to fire Dark now—or if the players should quit on him—their pennant chances would likely disappear. They were two games out of first place, and Dark gave them the best chance to win. "I don't say it'll happen, but it's money if we do, and we ought to take our best shot. We changed managers in the middle of 1960 and look where that left us."

Mays noted that Dark, no matter what he said or how he felt, didn't discriminate when he filled out the lineup. Though both Cepeda and Marichal had complained about incidents to the contrary, Mays's point was that Dark, in hard fact, regularly played more Black and Latino players than any other manager in baseball. Mays went back a long way with Dark, and he told the players that he knew the man better than anyone else there. "I know when he helped me and I know why," he said. "The why is that he's the same as me and everybody else in this room: he likes money. That preacher talk that goes with it he can shove up his ass. I'm telling you he helped me. And he's helped everybody here. I'm not playing Tom to him when I say that. He helps us because he wants to win, and he wants the money that goes with winning. Ain't nothing wrong with that."

Thus, Mays used the same argument that Leo Durocher had used in 1947 when Dodger players had objected to Jackie Robinson. Money trumped all else. In this case Cepeda mildly objected, but Mays reiterated that Dark was color-blind when necessary. "Suppose him and a lady friend went to a picture show together in Birmingham, where I'm from, and one of them passes out. And somebody shouts, 'Is there a doctor in the house?' And it turns out the only doctor is colored. You think Dark's gonna turn him away?"

Willie McCovey, standing beside the window, said, "Be a while for him to get there, that doctor, seeing as he'd have to make his way down from the balcony."

That broke the tension. Mays had quelled the uprising. Cepeda later said that he wished Mays had spoken out publicly against Dark, but it was Mays's way to work from within. The team would carry on.[13]

The Giants' next stop on their road trip was New York. There the Giants manager was summoned to meet with Commissioner Frick, who instructed Dark to hold a press conference to better explain himself and stabilize the situation. That didn't go well either, as among the things Dark said was "I thought I proved my feelings when I named Willie Mays captain. If I thought Negroes were inferior, would I have done that?" To Mays that sounded like an admission that Dark's sudden concern with naming a team captain was indeed just an attempt to shield himself from criticism, and Mays felt humiliated.

On Wednesday night, August 5, Mays suited up for the Giants game at Shea Stadium, but his cold had only worsened. His throat was raw and his voice all but gone. Dark handed Mays the lineup card to take out to the umpires. Logically, Mays ought not to play, as he was plainly ill. However, if he didn't start tonight, Mays reasoned, in the light of what Dark had said the day before, the baseball world might take it as a refusal to play, and Mays would find himself making a bad situation worse for everyone.

Silently, Mays took the lineup card. He looked. His name was not on it. "I actually felt sorry for the man," he said later. "So I did the only thing I could do." What he did was take a pencil, write his name back in the lineup, and go out and hit two home runs to beat the Mets.

With this, Stoneham was persuaded to call off his plan to fire Dark. The owner would let his manager stay for the time being, allowing the immediate heat to cool off. The grace period ended on the final day of the season, when Stoneham announced that Herman Franks was the new manager. That day upon which sore-throated Mays took the lineup card from Dark and wrote his own name on it was two full months before the end of the season. In those two months Willie Mays never spoke to his manager again.[14]

So, the team did carry on, but they were plainly dispirited, and everybody understood that Dark was a dead man walking. They'd been in the thick of contention when the *Newsday* bomb-shell hit, but in the month of August they fell out of it. They finished in fourth place, and though their final margin was just three games behind the pennant-winning St. Louis Cardinals, that was an illusion created by the infamous season-ending collapse of the front-running Philadelphia Phillies, and the Giants were never in a realistic position to reclaim first place.

Jim Ray Hart was indeed healthy in 1964, and he was outstanding. His defense at third base was iffy, but his bat was tremendous, as he hit .286 with thirty-one home runs at the age of twenty-two. Hal Lanier's installation at second base turned out well and appeared to have solved that problem for a long time to come. He was a terrific defensive infielder, and at the plate, though he lacked power and drew precious few walks, he hit for a .274 average, and his minor league statistics suggested that Lanier should be able to deliver that kind of hitting going forward.

The third rookie in the starting lineup, right fielder Jesús Alou, performed less well. He also hit .274, which his minor league track record indicated to be at the low end of his capability. Alou also exhibited poor strike zone discipline and failed to provide anything close to the kind of extra-base power that's expected of a corner outfielder. But Alou was just twenty-two years old himself and could be expected to develop further.

The Giants were struck with a major disappointment in Willie McCovey. After all the ups and downs in his early career, in

1963 he'd appeared to have finally achieved enduring stardom, leading the league with forty-four home runs. But then, at the prime age of twenty-six in 1964, he slumped terribly, finishing at .220 with just eighteen homers, and was mostly benched for the last month and a half. For most of the year there was no explanation provided for his struggles—McCovey was profoundly disinclined to complain or excuse—until at last he admitted to be suffering from a chronically painful condition in the soles of his feet, which prevented him from properly planting and driving for power. Alvin Dark—of course—didn't believe him.[15]

In the years since their first tour of Japan in 1953, Horace Stoneham's Giants had sustained their fellowship and exchange with Japanese baseball. Not coincidentally, the organization's relationship with Cappy Harada had grown closer. Harada, who maintained homes in both California and Japan, was on Stoneham's payroll as a scout, but he also was employed by the Nankai Hawks of the Japanese Pacific League, setting up a conflict of interest at the core of an eventual international incident.[16]

In 1963 Harada came up with a bold idea.[17] He proposed a joint venture in which the Hawks would provide the Giants with a handful of young low minor league players for the 1964 season. The Giants would deploy the Japanese prospects within their farm system, generating a nice bit of publicity, selling some extra tickets, and providing a challenging and enriching developmental experience for the young players. The arrangement was approved all around.

Early in spring training of 1964 the Hawks sent the Giants three players. Two were eighteen-year-olds: third baseman Tatsuhiko Tanaka and catcher Hiroshi Takahashi. The third was a left-handed pitcher, not quite twenty years old, named Masanori "Mashi" Murakami. The visas granted to each of the trio under U.S. immigration law required them to either hold roster spots in the Giants minor league organization at the end of spring training or return to Japan. All was unprecedented in the history of both American and Japanese baseball. Stoneham's announcement simply noted that "it would help Japanese-American relations, and it was also good publicity for the Giants." Jack Schwarz was more elaborate: "It is a great benefit to Japanese baseball because they'll get a year of development in our farm system. And if one of them should be a Willie Mays or a Mickey Mantle we'll certainly put him right on our roster." That last notion would prove problematic.[18]

Tanaka, Takahashi, and Murakami arrived in the Sonoran Desert of Arizona. By now the grand complex in Casa Grande was fully constructed and brightly operational, and in every conceivable respect it was a very long way from Fukuoka, the hometown of the Nankai Hawks. The three Japanese youngsters were to compete for 1964 roster spots with over two hundred ballplayers striving to play within the Giants' seven-club minor league system. None of the three spoke English, and the only thing familiar to them was the baseball.

Nonetheless, when the Giants broke camp, each of the Japanese prospects got a roster spot. For Tanaka and Takahashi it was the lowest rung on the Giants' ladder, to the Rookie classification Pioneer League. But Murakami was sent to the Fresno Giants of the full-season Class-A California League.

Like many California cities, Fresno had a large Japanese American community full of baseball fans, and Murakami was taken in by a Japanese American family to live for the season. The Fresno manager was Bill Werle, himself a former pitcher, who'd played for Lefty O'Doul's San Francisco Seals and had twice toured Japan as a player. He'd even learned a bit of the Japanese language. Prior to Murakami's joining the team, Werle called a meeting and told his players to treat Murakami with respect and warned them to never use the term *Jap*.[19]

The 1964 Fresno Giants club would prove to be excellent, running away with the pennant, and their best pitcher by far was none other than Masanori Murakami. The southpaw was deployed by Werle as a relief ace, and he was astonishingly good: in 49 games and 106 innings, he allowed just 64 hits while striking out a jaw-dropping 159 against just 34 walks, posting a won-lost record of 11–7 and a 1.78 ERA. Those kinds of statistics are normally the signature of a high-velocity fastball pitcher. But

Murakami wasn't that. He wasn't small, but at six feet even and 180 pounds, Murakami wasn't big either, certainly not by the standards of American pitchers. But though his fastball was below ninety miles per hour, he threw a wicked screwball as well as a curve, changed speeds and painted corners with everything, and delivered it all with a sidearm motion that baffled California League hitters. As impressive as his numbers was the fact that he was achieving them as a fully realized *pitcher*, not just some raw heat–throwing kid.

Stoneham and the rest of the Giants brass were bowled over, ecstatic with the rare pearl that had been dropped into their laps. At the conclusion of the minor league season, the Giants bade sayonara to Tanaka and Takahashi and shipped them back to Japan. But not Murakami. On the first of September, as soon as the major league roster limit expanded to allow late-season call-ups, the San Francisco Giants promoted Murakami to the major league club. Chub Feeney's announcement made it clear that this was no publicity stunt, no field trip for Murakami. The Giants were embroiled in a pennant race, and down the stretch they wanted the best bullpen they could muster. The rookie was there to pitch.

Murakami was instructed to join the Giants on a road trip in New York. Still speaking no functional English, he flew cross-country unaccompanied and somehow succeeded in finding his way to the Roosevelt Hotel in Manhattan. The next day at the ballpark Murakami signed a major league contract of which, of course, he couldn't read a word.

That very evening, Tuesday, September 1, 1964, against the Mets at Shea Stadium, the first Japanese player in major league history made his debut, relieving in the eighth inning. He struck out the first batter he faced, on his way to a scoreless inning. It was the first of eight consecutive shutout relief outings delivered by Murakami in the coming weeks, as the rookie sliced through National League hitters just as effortlessly as he had all summer in the California League.

Murakami's success was widely noted across the United States and a huge story in Japan. The Giants were delighted and eager

to have him back for the full season in 1965. However, the Nankai Hawks would have something to say about that.

While no one could have predicted just how badly things would
go during the managerial tenure of Alvin Dark, Stoneham's decision to hire him in the first place was ill considered. All too obviously, Stoneham had failed to consider the implications of a
manager with Dark's social perspective in a clubhouse with the
racial and cultural composition of this one. It revealed Stoneham's fundamental contradiction: he was progressive enough to
hire Alex Pompez and lead the way in the diverse integration of
the sport but oblivious enough to fail to comprehend that Alvin
Dark as manager would now be a terrible fit.

In any case the decision to replace him with Herman Franks
indicated that Stoneham seemed to have learned that lesson.
Significantly, the promotion of Franks truly pleased Orlando
Cepeda. Franks had managerial experience in Puerto Rico's winter league, so he'd already dealt with a diverse, multicultural
locker room. The hire suggested a new awareness on Stoneham's part that the handling of the team's clubhouse dynamics was important and that the manager must devote careful
attention to the balance of talent and psyche of those on its big-
league roster.[20]

Cepeda would put it simply: "Herman was a good man. He
understood the Latin ballplayer."[21] Like Alvin Dark before him,
Herman Franks would be making his major league managerial
debut with the Giants, but that's where the similarities ended.
In every other respect Franks was Dark's opposite. Unlike Dark,
Franks hadn't been a star player but, instead, a scrub, a backup
catcher who played far more in the minors than the majors.
Unlike Dark, Franks came to the job with many years of coaching experience as well as minor league and winter ball managing experience. Unlike Dark, Franks spoke some Spanish and
got along well with Latinos and African Americans. Unlike Dark,
Franks was one of the boys, who cussed a blue streak, chewed
tobacco, smoked cigars, and was quite comfortable knocking
back a few belts with Stoneham.

Franks was blunt and brusque, and he would demonstrate no aptitude for schmoozing with the media. Unlike Dark, Franks wasn't one for clubhouse meetings and lectures. He imposed few rules. He was decidedly a "players' manager." A guidebook from 1967 would interestingly observe: "He can be ingratiating with writers one day and lock the clubhouse door on them the next, which he did a couple of times last season. The one area in which he can be counted on for consistency is with his players, to whom he extends unwavering loyalty. Herman will never allow himself to be trapped into saying anything about one of his players that might be construed as a knock. He is careful about assessing their talents publicly, and evidently enjoys a solid relationship with them."[22]

Franks certainly understood that his most precious asset was Willie Mays, and quite like Leo Durocher—under whom Franks had played and coached—he would go out of his way to support and encourage his superstar center fielder. It was Stoneham's wish that Mays should take on more responsibility, to be not just team captain but something like an assistant manager. Franks embraced the idea, and Mays was happily elevated to this new standing. "I'm going to put more responsibility on his shoulders," Franks said. "I can get only so close to a club. The coaches can get a little closer. But a player like Mays can get real close. I expect to have him in my office a lot and talk to him about the club. I won't hesitate to ask him if he thinks I should play this or that man. He's very smart. I'm not too proud to ask for suggestions."[23]

Beyond replacing his manager, Stoneham didn't make any big moves following the 1964 season. He did execute three trades, all of them involving catchers, to inscrutable purpose. The first deal, in November, sent twenty-one-year-old outfielder José Cardenal to the Los Angeles Angels for twenty-two-year-old catcher-outfielder Jack Hiatt. This was an exchange of top AAA prospects, both of whom appeared ready for the majors, but Cardenal was clearly the superior talent. The apparent reason Stoneham was willing to accept this lowball offer was that young Cardenal had developed a reputation as a difficult personality. A newspaper comment on the trade put it this way: "José Domec Cardenal is one of the most gifted youngsters in baseball, but he never has unwrapped all of his gifts, never has applied himself fully to the job at hand."[24]

If it seemed premature to give up on a prospect with Cardenal's upside over disciplinary issues—many young people need a few more years than that to attain emotional maturity—it was also odd for the Giants to exchange him for a young catcher because the organization was already overloaded with that commodity. At the AAA level in 1964, the Giants had no fewer than three impressive catchers: Randy Hundley, Bob Barton, and Dick Dietz. Exactly why the Giants needed Hiatt was a puzzle.

Then, in February 1965, veteran southpaw Billy O'Dell—who'd lost his spot in the starting rotation in '64 but was effective in relief—was traded to the Braves for a veteran catcher, old friend Ed Bailey. With Bailey back in the fold, Stoneham then dumped off Del Crandall to Pittsburgh for a couple of marginalities. On the heels of acquiring one catcher the team didn't need, Stoneham expended left-handed pitching—in which the team was anything but deep—for another catcher the team didn't need. All this activity suggested a solution in search of a problem.

Early in the 1965 season Stoneham finally decided it was time to cut Chuck Hiller loose and sold him to the New York Mets. Hiller recalled how graciously Stoneham handled the notification: "I'll say one thing about Horace Stoneham, I don't think there was a nicer owner to the players than he was. I knew I was going to go. I wasn't playing and I wasn't doing anything, you can't blame that on them. But after Herman told me in his office the phone rang and it was Mr. Stoneham. And he personally thanked me on the phone, and how sorry he felt that he had to get rid of me, and thanked me for what I did for his team. And I'll never forget the nice feeling it gave me. What the hell, I was just a humpty-dumpty player, he didn't have to do that for me. And I appreciated it. And I do to this day."[25]

On April 24, 1965—two weeks after the start of the major league baseball season in the United States—civil war broke out in the

Dominican Republic. The small nation was quickly consumed by violence, and the U.S. Marines were deployed to the island to help suppress the rebellion. Few Americans paid much attention, but Dominicans in the United States, including the Alou brothers and Juan Marichal, were deeply worried for their families and friends back home. For Marichal it was especially agonizing, as his mother and siblings lived on a rural farm without a telephone, so he had no way of knowing what their situation might be.

The news dispatches coming from the Dominican Republic became increasingly distressing. The marines weren't able to restore order. The capital city of Santo Domingo was consumed in a chaotic urban guerrilla war, each outrage more ghastly and provocative than the last. Observed *Time* magazine, "Santo Domingo was a city without power, without water, without food, without any semblance of sanity."[26]

The Alou brothers and Marichal finally received word that their loved ones were unharmed, for the time being. But the war raged on through the summer, and the stress of it weighed heavily on twenty-seven-year-old Juan Marichal, who spent the 1965 season plagued with anxiety, which manifested as chronic sinus trouble and sneezing fits.

After Mashi Murakami's great September in 1964, the Giants wouldn't hear of the phenomenal youngster returning to Japan. They directed him back to Arizona to play for the Giants' fall Instructional League team, where he continued to dominate opponents. That winter, before allowing Murakami to return to Japan, the Giants were quick to offer the young pitcher a major league contract for the 1965 season. Seeing no reason not to sign it—or probably more accurately, not understanding what he was signing—Murakami complied.

It was upon his return to Japan that things got complicated. While everyone at home was thrilled with what a success Murakami had been in the United States, when the Hawks learned that the Giants had signed him for 1965 and expected him to return, they were furious.

Certainly, Cappy Harada could have done a much better job of ensuring clear understanding of the terms of the project. It was now obvious that the Hawks and Giants held highly divergent perceptions. The Hawks believed they'd been loaning Muraka-mi's services and his contract remained their property and that whenever they chose to recall him to play in Japan, they could. And they were quite ready to do just that: the Murakami stat sheet was vivid in any language.

Thus began a protracted cross-Pacific argument over the exceptional young pitcher. It went on for months and eventually involved both Major League Baseball commissioner Ford Frick as well as his Japanese counterpart, Yushi Uchimura, and various lawyers in both countries. But perhaps possession is nine-tenths of the law, and the fact is that Japan now possessed Murakami. There's no question he was feeling immense pressure to stay in his homeland. Murakami sent a letter to Stone-ham: "I feel that my place is with my family, since I am an only son. I didn't know how much Japan meant to me, but now I have a girl in Osaka and I feel I will be homesick if I leave."

However sincere Murakami's plea was perceived by the Giants, at last they backed down. With Frick's consent Stoneham cabled Japanese commissioner Uchimura: "In spite of bad faith and unwarranted action of the Nankai Hawks and because we do not desire to interfere with the career of a player, if Murakami reports for this season, we will agree to give him the right to choose where he will play in 1966. If he elects to return to Japan, then he will be placed on the voluntarily retired list of the Giants." While the Hawks weren't happy with this, they were confident enough in what Murakami's choice would be that they agreed to Stoneham's offer. The issue was resolved at last.[27]

But the stalemate had dragged on all through the spring, while Murakami's legal limbo status had prevented him from working out with either team. He reported to the Giants on May 4, 1965, three weeks into the regular season, without the benefit of spring training. He was rusty and got knocked around in his early outings. But he eventually found his groove and pitched very effectively over the balance of the season. His basic 1965 statistics—in forty-five games and seventy-four innings, a won-lost record of 4–1, with eight saves and an ERA of 3.75—were decent numbers, but the details were remarkable, as he ranked among the very best in the major leagues in hits per inning, in walks-plus-hits per inning, in strikeout-to-walk ratio, and in strikeouts per inning. He was a very special young pitcher.

As expected, at the close of the 1965 season Murakami chose to return to Japan and the Nankai Hawks. Superstardom there was roundly expected but didn't materialize; though he pitched until 1982, overall his was a good career but not extraordinary. After retiring as a player, Murakami became a baseball broadcaster in Japan. He also renewed his relationship with the Giants, was honored at Candlestick Park, and worked for the organization as a scout.

Masanori Murakami's legacy loomed large for a very long time. The eagerness of the Giants to claim Murakami as their own and have him pursue his career in the United States, instead of Japan, greatly alarmed Japanese baseball owners. The Murakami episode confirmed their worst fears of losing their best players to the Americans, decimating the quality and popularity of the Japanese leagues. So, for the next thirty years there was absolutely no more "loaning" of Japanese prospects to major league baseball organizations. Until Hideo Nomo was acquired by the Los Angeles Dodgers in 1995, every Japanese player spent his entire career in Japan.

For the Giants' archrival Los Angeles Dodgers, 1963 had been a glorious year. Sandy Koufax rebounded from his finger injury to burst into megastardom, capturing both the Cy Young and Most Valuable Player awards, and the Dodgers handily won the National League pennant and then stunned the Yankees in the World Series with a four-game sweep. But in 1964 they fell all the way to sixth place, and general manager Buzzie Bavasi then retooled the roster in multiple ways. A big trade brought in Claude Osteen, one of the better young starting pitchers in the game, and young players were given opportunities for starting jobs at three positions: sophomores Wes Parker at first base and John

Kennedy at third base and rookie Jim Lefebvre at second. The lineup was further revamped early in the season when star left fielder Tommy Davis went down for the season with a broken ankle and was replaced by a minor league journeyman, Lou Johnson. The new-look Dodgers in 1965 would struggle to score runs, but they would be exceptionally adept at preventing them, and on balance they were a superb competitor, setting up a pennant race of rare quality.

For Orlando Cepeda the 1965 season could have been a great relief, liberated from his poisonous relationship with Alvin Dark. Instead, a new problem arose. Cepeda had been bothered by a troublesome right knee in 1964, missing twenty games, and by spring training of 1965 the condition had worsened to the point that he was barely able to run. The Giants hoped that Cepeda could "play through it," pinch-hitting and playing sparingly while the knee came around, but it was soon clear that wasn't happening. On May 4 he was placed on the disabled list, with the plan that a period of extended rest would do the trick.

With Cepeda unavailable, for the first time since 1961 the first base job was open for Willie McCovey. A custom ripple sole had been developed for McCovey's shoes that successfully relieved the foot pain that had plagued him in 1964, and McCovey retook the job with a vengeance, delivering a great year as the full-time first baseman in 1965.[28]

In each of the seven seasons the Giants had been in San Francisco, the team had started well, and following that, the pattern had been the problematic June swoon. But in 1965 the Giants started poorly. In late May, in fourth place well behind the pace of the first-place Dodgers, Stoneham took action and swung two trades.

José Pagán served the Giants well as their shortstop during the pennant-winning season of 1962. But since then he'd declined with both the bat and glove, yet he remained the team's regular shortstop because they simply didn't come up with anyone better. On May 22, 1965, he was thirty years old, hitting .205 and exhibiting ever-less range in the field, and Stoneham traded him to the Pittsburgh Pirates straight up for shortstop Dick "Ducky"

Schofield. The thirty-year-old switch-hitting Schofield was pretty much the definition of "journeyman," but he was still a sound defender at shortstop, and at the plate he'd been consistently able to get on base reasonably well, certainly better than Pagán. This appeared to be a no-brainer upgrade for the Giants, to tide them over at shortstop until a longer-term solution could be found.

A week later Stoneham executed the second deal, this one focused on shoring up left field. That position had opened up with McCovey's return to first base, and Franks had opted for a platoon of Matty Alou and Harvey Kuenn, but neither was hitting. So, the Giants traded Kuenn, along with southpaw Bob Hendley (who'd done pretty well in 1964 but couldn't get anyone out so far in '65) and catcher Ed Bailey (who was three for twenty-eight at the age of thirty-four), to the Chicago Cubs in exchange for outfielder Len Gabrielson and catcher Dick Bertell. Gabrielson, just twenty-five years old, was a big, strong left-handed batter who hadn't yet broken through as a consistent hitter but seemed on the verge. Bertell, meanwhile, was a humdrum journeyman, just as superfluous on the Giants' overstocked catching depth chart as Bailey had been.

The reconfigured Giants avoided a June swoon, but they never found a hot streak. They entered July in third place, four games behind the Dodgers. They were doing as well as they were primarily because of the terrific play of thirty-four-year-old Willie Mays, enjoying one of his best years with the bat, hitting .332 and leading the majors with twenty-two home runs.

But the month of July was miserable for him. Beset with accumulated nagging injuries to his groin, his hip, and his hand, Mays limped noticeably and started only twenty of the team's twenty-five games, with a couple of the appearances in left and right field instead of center, which he'd never done before. At the plate he suffered the worst month of his career, batting .231 with two homers and seven runs batted in. The Giants spent another month marking time, bouncing between third and fourth place. The injury-wracked midsummer slump tormenting Mays was ominous, suggesting that his decline was at last arriving and raising the serious question as to whether the 1965 Giants, already without a healthy Cepeda, were even capable of mounting a strong stretch drive and contending for the pennant.

Problems abounded. The Giants' yawning need for a left-handed starting pitcher—a vacant spot since Hendley was dealt away—was such that Stoneham signed forty-four-year-old Warren Spahn as a free agent. Once peerless but now reeling, Spahn was available after having been released even by the rock-bottom New York Mets. But Stoneham, with no better options, took the gamble that the longtime ace might have something left.[29] Dick Schofield, instead of resolving the shortstop issue, was hitting barely over .200. (In mid-August the Giants would call up twenty-year-old Rigoberto "Tito" Fuentes, who'd been mostly a second baseman in the minors, and give him a shot at shortstop, but he wouldn't hit either.) Hal Lanier, the slick-fielding young second baseman who'd held his own with the bat in 1964, was hitting poorly, as was normally strong-hitting catcher Tom Haller. Gaylord Perry, who'd turned the corner in 1964, was making a U-turn in '65, and Jack Sanford, aged thirty-six, had contributed little and would soon be sold to the Los Angeles Angels.

This was the third season since the Giants' pennant of 1962. Stoneham might have figured he could give himself a mulligan for 1963; repeating, especially in a league as competitive as the NL in this period, was really hard to do. And 1964, well, all the controversy with Alvin Dark was a huge distraction. But here they were, more than halfway through 1965, and the excuses were getting stale. With Mays, the magnificent superstar upon whom the team had so long depended, suddenly struggling, it wasn't a promising picture.

But then, most improbably, thirty-four-year-old Willie Mays, as Arnold Hano put it, "took a beaten ball club, hoisted it on his shoulders, and with his bat and glove carried the team to the top."[30] On Sunday, August 1, Mays had five hits in a doubleheader for his best day in more than a month. The next day Mays hit his twenty-fifth home run. The Giants then suddenly went on an eight-game winning streak, driven by the torrid hitting of Mays, who went sixteen for thirty-four (.471), with six home runs. Overnight he'd somehow overcome his assortment of aches and hit as well as he'd ever hit in his life. With the winning streak, the Giants reclaimed second place and closed to within just one game of the first-place Dodgers.

On Wednesday, August 11, the San Francisco Bay Area experienced a very rare midsummer rain, and the Giants had their only home rainout of the 1965 season. But down south in Los Angeles the weather was fine; indeed, it was a particularly warm evening in which the Dodgers defeated the Mets 1–0. Dodger Stadium, located in Chavez Ravine, was thirteen miles due north of the Watts district of Los Angeles.

Watts was a broad, flat, African American slum of concentrated poverty and blight, the product of decades of real estate covenants that tightly restricted where Blacks could buy or rent housing in Los Angeles and of structurally unequal opportunities for education and employment. African Americans in Los Angeles had numbered 60,000 in the 1940 census, and they were 350,000 in 1965, nearly 15 percent of the city's population. A profound sense of bitterness and frustration pervaded the community, as so many had left behind the deprivations of Jim Crow only to have landed in a place where racial segregation was forbidden by law yet social and economic mobility was stifled nonetheless and political representation was absent.

The Los Angeles Police Department, under the forceful leadership since 1950 of Chief William H. Parker, was organized in a paramilitary form that prioritized a mobile and mechanized "war on crime" approach instead of neighborhood or community policing. The police department was perceived as openly adversarial by the city's African American and Mexican American communities, a posture exacerbated by years of recruitment of white officers from the South. The baton routinely carried by LAPD officers was known within the department as a "n— knocker."

At about seven in the evening on Wednesday, August 11, a white California Highway Patrol officer pulled over a Black driver for speeding on South Avalon Boulevard in Watts. The traffic stop attracted a small crowd, and the symbolic image of white law enforcement oppressing Black citizenry became a flash point.[31]

A cascade of terrible escalations was set into motion. The confrontation devolved into a small fight and that into a big fight. The big fight then devolved into a small riot. More law enforcement resources were dispatched, which attracted ever-larger crowds, and the violence spiraled horribly out of control.

Rioting would rage for six full days, metastasizing over a forty-six-square-mile area. It was one of the most massive breakdowns of civil order in United States history. Over thirty thousand people engaged in rioting, looting, and arson. Nearly a thousand buildings were damaged or destroyed, and four thousand National Guard troops were mobilized. Both Chief Parker and California governor Edmund G. "Pat" Brown described the rioters not just as lawbreakers but as insurgents. Over thirty-four hundred arrests were made, more than a thousand people were injured, and thirty-four died, twenty-three from gunshots fired by law enforcement.

The Watts riots horrified and shocked the Los Angeles region, where the widespread belief among many, if not most, in the white community was that Southern California was a special place, a wholesome bastion of prosperity and progress. Televised images of the mayhem and destruction were broadcast nationwide, and it was a sickening tableau, a gut punch to the confidence of a country already grappling with a crisis of racial tension and civil rights inequality.

Among the unnerved were the Los Angeles Dodgers, who played a home stand right through that awful week, just a few miles north of the anarchy. Dodgers outfielder Willie Crawford, who lived near Watts, was arrested by the LAPD because he was eighteen years old and Black. Everyone at Dodger Stadium could see the smoke billowing in the distance, where fed-up African Americans chanted, "Burn, baby, burn!" The Dodgers announced that fans who feared coming to the ballpark could exchange tickets for a September game. The stadium scoreboard helpfully listed highway exits closed by the rioting.[32]

No Dodger was put more on edge than African American catcher John Roseboro, who lived with his wife and children in Compton, adjacent to Watts. Roseboro was thirty-two years old, and he'd been around. He'd attended a historically Black university, had played in the minor leagues in the early years of integration, and had served in the military. Yet nothing he'd seen prepared him for this. The rage and the violence that built up and exploded here was unlike anything he'd comprehended. The riots laid bare to him the scale of institutional racism and its consequences, and he was sickened.

When that troubled Dodger home stand came to its end, the team's first destination was San Francisco, for a four-game show-down, beginning on Thursday, August 19. One thing at which Horace Stoneham and Walter O'Malley had abundantly succeeded when transplanting to California was sustaining the archrival status between the ball clubs. It wasn't just something hyped up by the teams or the media either; it was genuinely felt by the players themselves. "When you stepped off the plane in Los Angeles, you could *hear* the electricity," recalled Willie McCovey. "Even the skycaps at the airports were all wrapped up in the rivalry. It carried over to the hotel and finally the ballpark. The tension was always there." Observed Don Drysdale, "Those of us who have been around a while always play this series just a little harder, and it's contagious among the young players who aren't as familiar with the background."[33]

As in New York, the intensity of Giants-Dodgers games in California often boiled over in "chin music" back and forth and in on-field brawls. The 1965 season was no exception, with con-frontations and snarling language. As they began the series in San Francisco, the pennant race tension was thick, and the bad blood between the California rivals was at peak level.

In the second game of the series, a nasty verbal exchange occurred between John Roseboro and Juan Marichal—both already frazzled with nervous exhaustion. Though nothing more came of it at the time, neither Roseboro nor Marichal consid-ered it "over."

This series finale, on Sunday, August 22, 1965, was an epic matchup between each team's Hall of Fame–bound ace: Sandy Koufax, with a record of 21–4 and an earned run average of 2.10, against Marichal, 19–9 and 1.73. Arnold Hano memorably described the scene: "It was a windy, slightly chilly August afternoon, the sun shining brilliantly out of a hard blue sky . . . and if there has been a more bitter baseball game played in my lifetime I do not recall it. . . . There was an almost frightening quality to the contest."[34]

In the second inning Marichal flattened Maury Wills with a high fastball. The at bat ended uneventfully, but Roseboro wanted vengeance.[35]

When the Dodgers took the field on defense, the Giants' first batter was Willie Mays, who could be seen as San Francisco's equivalent of Wills, the veteran team captain and emotional leader. Roseboro thought the situation called for the Dodgers to send a message.

Crouching behind the plate, Roseboro flicked his index finger, the sign for Koufax to put the batter in the dirt. Koufax well understood pitching hard inside. He wound up and sailed a fastball well over Mays's head to the backstop. Koufax later said to reporters: "It was a lousy pitch. I meant it to come much closer." But he'd fulfilled his duty, even if it was a token gesture.[36] Mays had expected a gesture just about like that and considered it message received and acknowledged. He subsequently flied to center and considered—well, hoped, anyway—that the skirmish was concluded.

It wasn't. In the next inning Marichal threw a pitch that may or may not have been too far inside, and Ron Fairly may or may not have overreacted in jackknifing out of the way. What's undisputed is that the crowd and both dugouts yelled in reaction and that home plate umpire Henry "Shag" Crawford called time.

Everyone heard Crawford bellow a loud-and-clear warning to both dugouts: on the next goddam pitch from anyone that was goddam remotely inside, that goddam pitcher would be goddam ejected from the goddam game. Crawford had seen more than goddam enough.

Roseboro got the message; after all, he was its primary recipient. He couldn't direct Koufax to protect his hitters any further. To give Sandy that signal now would be to place him in an impossible bind, given the umpire's plain notice. What happened next, fatefully, was that Roseboro decided he would handle it himself.

Leading off for the Giants in the bottom of the third, conveniently enough, was Marichal. The Giants' ace gingerly stepped into the batter's box, not sure what to expect. Everyone on the field, in both dugouts, and all through the jammed grandstand of more than forty-three thousand fans was stiff with tension. Koufax threw a first-pitch curve, amiably breaking over the plate for a called strike. Marichal breathed a sigh of relief. Koufax had sent another message, and it was one of peace.

Roseboro called for the fastball, down and in. Koufax delivered it, and Marichal had a notion to swing but held up as the pitch was a bit off the plate. A ball, and the count was now 1–1.

Roseboro had artfully boxed the pitch into the dirt and moved to retrieve it as it rolled behind the right-handed batter's box. The catcher picked up the ball, and without hesitation or notice, without taking the slightest step to clear his throwing lane, Roseboro fired a smoking-hard return throw to Koufax. The ball flashed just past Marichal's face; it may or may not have nicked his right ear.

Roseboro later said his throw passed two inches past Marichal's nose, but he readily acknowledged his intent—to scare the shit out of Marichal. Mission accomplished. Wills would say, "When a hard-thrown ball goes past you that closely, it makes a noise like a bullet." Mays, watching from the bench, couldn't believe it. He'd never seen a duster thrown by a catcher, and he now knew that something bad was about to happen.[37]

It did. Things now moved extremely fast. Marichal turned to Roseboro and accusingly screamed at him. Roseboro now had Marichal just where he'd wanted him, ready for a serious ass kicking. Roseboro had twenty pounds on Marichal, he was far stronger, and he was older, wiser, and just plain tougher. He very well knew how to fight, having been trained in both boxing and karate, and as one writer put it, "When Johnny Roseboro comes at you, you should be entitled to call a priest." Roseboro dropped his catcher's mitt and stepped aggressively toward Marichal, yelling in his face, "Fuck you and your mother," and then took a wild right-handed swing. Marichal then raised his bat above his head and brought it straight down, like an ax, upon Roseboro. The blow didn't strike squarely, glancing off the side of Roseboro's skull. It opened a two-inch gash above his left eye.[38]

The instantly resulting melee was epic in scale and intensity. This was nothing like the usual baseball brawl, with some ineffectual swinging and tagging and a lot of yelling and milling about. This was a genuine fight, with angry young men fully intent on delivering pain and injury. It was a terrible scene. In the immediate wake of Watts, what was rapidly unfolding on the field at Candlestick Park all too well resembled that sickening chaos. The umpires were completely overwhelmed, helpless to restore control.

Though Marichal's action shocked so many who knew him for his gentle personality, his teammates observed that he was unusually on edge. Matty Alou said: "Juan wanted to fight all day. He had the devil inside him that day." While Roseboro had started this fight—or, at least, this manifestation of the ongoing fight—Marichal's bludgeoning of him completely violated the sport's unwritten rules and transformed the dynamic. The *New York Times* reported: "In the melee that followed within a few seconds, peacemaking seemed desperately urgent. . . . Everybody seemed horrified by the nature of the attack and by the sight of blood streaming down Roseboro's face." Adding to the mayhem was the fear that Roseboro had lost his eye. "I thought the bat had knocked Roseboro's eye out," said Dodger manager Walter Alston. "There was nothing but blood where his left eye should have been."[39]

Willie Mays was afraid that if this wasn't stopped quickly, many in the grandstand would leap the railings and there would be a genuine riot. Mays determined that the crucial priority was to get Roseboro away from Marichal, off the field, and to provide him first aid. Mays, an extraordinarily strong man himself, grabbed Roseboro, gently but firmly, and held him closely in an embrace, a posture of comfort and consolation.

Mays took Roseboro's face in his hands and said in a voice that scarcely hid tears: "Oh, John, I'm so sorry. You're hurt." He began to lead Roseboro away. But when Dodger trainer Bill Buhler arrived with a towel and wiped the blood from Roseboro's face, somehow the sight of the blood, or perhaps just the fact that he could see again with both eyes, triggered a new attack response from Roseboro. Again, he struggled to get at his tormentor, but again Mays interceded, placing his muscular body between the antagonists. Once more he cupped Roseboro's face and spoke soothingly. "You're hurt, John," Mays said as he led the injured man away.[40]

Though Roseboro was still enraged enough to flip the bird to the Candlestick fans, he now submitted to Mays. Roseboro walked, with Mays's arm tight around his shoulder, toward the Los Angeles bench. A photograph shows Mays, hatless, pulling Roseboro along while surrounded by nine Dodgers. Blood from Roseboro's face has splattered his chest protector. He is looking in apparent disbelief at his right hand, also covered with blood. Flecks of blood are scattered on Mays's uniform as well.

Mays led Roseboro to the visitors' dugout and sat on the bench next to him. Mays used some towels to help stanch the bleeding and then cradled Roseboro's head while Buhler examined the injury. Roseboro had a two-inch wound on the left side of his head near the top of his scalp. This was allowing blood to pour into his eye, but the eye itself was fine.

With both Marichal and Roseboro in their respective dugouts, the brawl finally wound itself down, like a spent windstorm. Roseboro wanted to stay in the game, but his trainer and his manager ordered him to the clubhouse. To get there, he had to walk to the right field corner. He was showered with jeers from the stands, so he bent over and patted his rear end.[41]

At long last order was restored. Though there'd been more than ample brawling of the sort that normally results in multiple ejections, the umpiring crew sensibly concluded that sorting it all out was well beyond their capability. Only Marichal was ejected. Crawford told Koufax: "Whatever you do, don't throw at anyone. We don't want a riot here."

Koufax quickly recorded two outs but was still rattled; he then issued back-to-back walks. That brought up Mays.[42] Koufax uneasily toed the rubber and took his stretch position. Among the superstar southpaw's best pitches to right-handers was his alarmingly hard fastball just off the inside corner. Hitters would obviously lean back and were then helpless with his next pitch, the big curve, started away and then back-doored across the plate. But in this situation Koufax was robbed of his "jammer," and Mays could confidently crowd the dish. Koufax threw him a high hard fastball. Mays crushed it high into the left center field bleachers for his thirty-eighth homer of the season. "I don't take much pride," Mays later said, "in the advantage I had over him."[43]

Just minutes after the horrific fight, it was suddenly a 4–2 Giants lead. The rest of the game was sullen and anticlimactic.[44] In relief of Marichal, Ron Herbel blanked the Dodgers nearly the whole way, and Murakami saved it in the ninth, with the final score Giants four, Dodgers three. The utterly draining four-game series had ended in a split.

Johnny Roseboro went to the hospital and received fourteen stitches in his scalp but missed just two games. Juan Marichal was suspended by the National League for eight games—effectively, two starts—and was fined $1,750, the largest fine ever assessed in baseball to that point, amounting to about 3 percent of his $60,000 annual gross salary, and league president Warren Giles pointedly specified that the fine must be paid by Marichal alone, not covered by the team.

Roseboro remained bitterly angry for years. Marichal was deeply saddened and sorry. The incident was truly out of character for the young man, who'd simply lost his mind for a terrible moment, and that awful truth tormented him. Roseboro, with time, would come to accept his own fault in provoking the fight. He would nobly forgive Marichal, and their sincere and public rapprochement was a profoundly positive conclusion to the dark episode. They became close. When Roseboro died in Los Angeles in 2002, Marichal gratefully accepted the invitation from the Roseboro family and eulogized his unlikely friend.

Following that infamous game, the Giants traveled back east for an extended road trip. Mays kept on hitting, pounding three home runs on the eastern swing to finish the month with seventeen, a new National League record. In early September the

Giants swept a two-game series in Los Angeles, giving them four straight wins, and for the first time all season they were in first place. They kept on winning. On September 13, on the road in the Houston Astrodome, Mays launched his forty-seventh home run of the season and the five hundredth of his career—becoming the fifth player in major league history to achieve that milestone—as the Giants won their eleventh straight, and their first place lead was two and a half games.

But the next night the Astros had a 5–3 lead with two outs in the ninth, and the winning streak seemed done. Houston's best reliever, Claude Raymond, a smallish right-hander from Quebec with a lively fastball and superb control, was on the mound with a runner on first, facing Willie Mays as the tying run. Raymond didn't want to walk him, as that would bring up the left-handed-batting McCovey as the go-ahead run. So, Raymond challenged Mays with his best fastballs.

In an epic confrontation Raymond fired heater after heater, and again and again, Mays fouled them off. Perhaps Raymond thought about an off-speed pitch, but that might now seem, well, unmanly. "I kept waiting for a breaking ball," Mays said later. "A curve, a slider—something other than a fastball. But that's all he threw. Nothing but fastballs." They were two heavyweights throwing their best haymakers. On the bench a rapt Herman Franks muttered, "It's like challenging God."

On the tenth pitch of the at bat, with the Astrodome fans on their feet and shouting, Raymond threw another fastball on the inside part of the plate. As Raymond recalled, "Willie bailed out but opened up on the ball at the same time, the way only he could." Mays connected squarely and hit a high line drive to left field. The fans gasped as the ball sailed over the fence, and the Giants' dugout exploded in astonishment and celebration.[45]

The Giants went on to win it in ten innings. It was twelve wins in a row, and they now led the league by three and a half games. They beat the Astros twice more to make it a fourteen-game winning streak—the team's longest since, that's right, 1951—and their lead was four and a half. With sixteen games left to play, the newspapers started to present the Giants' "magic number," which was now twelve: any combination of Giant wins plus losses by their closest pursuer adding up to at least twelve meant the Giants would clinch.

But no magic was forthcoming this time. The rest of the way the Giants' pitching staff burned out, and they played .500 ball. Meanwhile, the Dodgers put together an astonishing hot streak: they won fifteen of their final sixteen games, eight of them shut-outs, allowing a total of seventeen runs. They flashed past the Giants and won the pennant by a margin of two games.

Willie Mays had followed up his seventeen-homer August with an eleven-homer September. His major league–leading final tally of fifty-two home runs was not only a career high; it was the third most in National League history. Mays led the major leagues in on-base percentage, slugging, OPS, and OPS+; his OPS+ mark of 185 was the highest yet achieved in twentieth-century Giants franchise history, higher than any by Mel Ott or Johnny Mize.[46] He was voted Most Valuable Player, eleven years after he'd first won the award in 1954. But the vote was close because Sandy Koufax presented a compelling case too: he went 26–8, led the league with a 2.04 ERA, shattered the modern major league record for strikeouts with 382, and in the regular season's gruel-ing final month, he had six complete games, four shutouts, and an earned run average of 1.51.

12

Certainly the Move Will Hurt Us

The so-near-but-so-far finish of 1965 was excruciating. In fairness it wasn't so much a case of the Giants blowing the lead down the stretch as it was the Dodgers just playing near-perfect baseball and blowing past. In that respect it resembled the dynamic of 1951, with the teams reversing roles. Sometimes the cap must be tipped.

Horace Stoneham was determined to bolster his team's bullpen, a particular priority given that Mashi Murakami wouldn't be back. At the winter meetings in December 1965 the Giants swung two deals acquiring good veteran arms. Matty Alou was sent to the Pittsburgh Pirates for southpaw Joe Gibbon, while catcher Randy Hundley and right-handed pitcher Bill Hands—top AAA prospects—went to the Chicago Cubs for top-shelf reliever Lindy McDaniel and a utility outfielder.

The middle Alou brother had been a puzzle for the Giants. Much slighter in build than either of his siblings, Matty wasn't destined to hit for power, but otherwise, he was a useful ballplayer: fast on the bases, with the defensive capability to handle center field, and at the plate a short-swinging contact hitter (and a superb bunter) apparently ready made to produce a high batting average. But after good years in a utility role in 1961 and '62, Alou steadily failed to produce in 1963, '64, and '65, performing especially badly as a pinch hitter (twelve for ninety-four, a .128 batting average). Pinch-hitting is a challenging assignment, but someone has to do it, and Matty Alou hadn't delivered in the role they needed him to fill.[1] Gibbon was a good return, a solid southpaw who could spot start as well as relieve.

Hundley and Hands both had promise.[2] But the Giants were plenty deep in young catchers, and their starting rotation, while glaringly free of a southpaw, was chock full of right-handers in Marichal, Shaw, Perry, Bolin, and Herbel. Parlaying this pair into Lindy McDaniel made perfect sense. Joining him with Gibbon and young right-hander Frank Linzy, a sinker baller who'd performed splendidly for the Giants as a rookie in 1965, the Giants' bullpen looked to be a strength for 1966.

But Stoneham was unable to find a trade partner to help with his problem at shortstop, where neither the import Dick Schofield nor the rookie Tito Fuentes were adequate in 1965. Schofield would be discarded in early '66, and Herman Franks would go mostly with Fuentes, but the position remained in a state of flux.

The biggest question the Giants faced heading into 1966 was the condition of Orlando Cepeda's right knee. Following his lost '65 season, he'd undergone surgery, and by spring training of 1966 Cepeda was markedly improved, though still in the process of rehabilitation. He could run—in 1965 he really couldn't— though he wasn't running nearly as well as he had a few years earlier. And he could hit; while the knee wasn't affording the capacity to run fast, it was now again providing Cepeda the stability to push off in the batter's box and rotate his hips for power.

This was great news. It was, of course, also a problem, the Giants' familiar dilemma of what to do with Cepeda and McCovey. Stretch McCovey had reclaimed the first base job in 1965 with a terrific thirty-nine-homer performance. Franks wasn't about to make McCovey go back to left field and humiliate himself, particularly with the fragile condition of his feet. So, Franks decided that if Cepeda was going to play for the Giants in 1966, like it or not, he was going to have to play left field.

Cepeda was now twenty-eight years old and grown-up. He was far more understanding about the situation than he'd been back in 1959, '60, and '61. He didn't like it but humbly followed his manager's direction and did his best to play left field in 1966. In earlier years Cepeda had plenty of athletic capacity to play well

in the outfield, but he didn't have the willingness to try. Now trying wasn't the issue: he just could no longer run well enough to
cover ground out there. For the first few weeks of 1966, Franks
gave Cepeda eight starts in left and also five at first base against
left-handers and five pinch-hit appearances. He hit quite well.
But this wasn't a sustainable arrangement, as Cepeda's outfield
defense was problematic, and platooning him at first base with
McCovey would be a waste of both great hitters.

Thus, Stoneham's Giants found themselves painted into a corner. All along, trading either Cepeda or McCovey had been an
option, but now it was the imperative: this team urgently had
to make the trade that Stoneham had been avoiding for years.
Everyone in baseball knew it, and this put the Giants in the worst
of bargaining positions.

Given that both of the Giants' other top hitters (Willie Mays
and Jim Ray Hart) were right-handed batters, McCovey's lefty
power bat was essential. Therefore, it was Cepeda who had to
go, and so it was that in the evening of May 8, 1966, the Giants
accepted a standing offer from the St. Louis Cardinals of left-
handed pitcher Ray Sadecki straight up for Orlando Cepeda.

The trade was received with complete horror in the San Francisco Bay Area. Cepeda had been a local superstar since his smash-
ing debut in 1958, not just because of his great play but also his
vivid spirit and his direct and ongoing connection to the region's
Latino and Black communities. He was beloved. The Bay Area was
aghast to see him go. But if he had to go (and there was begrudg-
ing acknowledgment that, yes, under the circumstances, he did
have to go), the Giants' fan base expected that only a marquee
star in exchange would be fair. But Ray (blanking) Sadecki? *Who?*

Sadecki had in fact once been among the game's top pitching prospects, a fireballing teenager who'd signed to a big bonus
out of high school and was in the St. Louis starting rotation at
the age of nineteen. But the anticipated success never materialized. At the time of his trade to the Giants, the stories on Sadecki
all stressed that he'd been a twenty-game winner in the Cardi-
nal's pennant-winning season of 1964, but a cursory glance at
his stat line revealed that the achievement was more a function

of extraordinary run support than pitching excellence. And in 1965 he'd been unambiguously bad: 6–15 with a horrendous 5.21 earned run average. In 1966 he was still only twenty-five years old but not throwing that hard anymore, and in his best years he'd been a league-average starter; Sadecki's career record was a plodding 67–64, with a 4.16 ERA. Orlando Cepeda was a Rookie of the Year, a six-time All-Star, and a career .308 hitter with 226 home runs. The equation of him with Ray Sadecki was laughable.

But it was a stark demonstration of the Giants' poor bargaining posture. Since the trade was occurring in May rather than in the fall-winter trading season, Cepeda couldn't be traded to any American League team without clearing National League waivers, and that wasn't going to happen. So, right away that reduced the scope of possible trading partners from nineteen to nine. Moreover, Cepeda could—alas—only play first base, which meant the only teams interested would be those with a need at that position. That eliminated most of them, and though the Dodgers could certainly have used Cepeda, they weren't about to help the Giants out of their bind.[3] Realistically, then, the only teams with whom the Giants could seriously negotiate were the Houston Astros and the St. Louis Cardinals. Given that the obvious need the Giants were seeking to fill was a left-handed starting pitcher, the possibilities were more limited still. The only southpaw starter the Astros had was twenty-nine-year-old journeyman Mike Cuellar, a reclamation project who would break out as a surprise star over the course of 1966, but that hadn't happened yet.

That meant it would have to be the Cardinals. They were a logical fit, as they had a gaping hole at first base, having traded away longtime star first baseman Bill White (the former Giant) over the winter, while they had no fewer than four lefty starters on their staff. In addition to Sadecki, the Cardinals had veteran Curt Simmons, rookie Larry Jaster, and journeyman Al Jackson. For whatever it was worth, Sadecki was doing well early in 1966, with a 2.22 ERA in five appearances. None of the options the Cards could present were very compelling, but this was a deal Stoneham had to make.

The decision wasn't hasty or impulsive. The St. Louis offer had been on the table for a while, and it was roundly debated by Stoneham and his circle of advisors. His own inclination was against it, as was Tom Sheehan's. But both Chub Feeney and Herman Franks advised him to take it, to get the Cepeda-McCovey predicament behind them at last. Stoneham reluctantly decided that he had to settle for Sadecki.[4]

With Cepeda absent, left field was again open. The first candidate was twenty-four-year-old Jesús Alou, the incumbent right fielder, bumped out of that spot by twenty-two-year-old rookie Ollie "Downtown" Brown, a powerful right-handed hitter with a tremendous throwing arm and clear star potential. Jesús Alou was coming along slowly. His rookie year performance in 1964 had been underwhelming, and while in '65 he was better, his strike zone discipline remained egregiously poor, and overall his offensive production still wasn't good for a corner outfielder. The other left field candidate was twenty-six-year-old lefty-swinging Len Gabrielson, who'd hit well as a semi-regular in 1965.

The Giants started very well in 1966, reviving their familiar pattern. When Cepeda was traded, they were flying along at 18–7, easily in first place, in the midst of a twelve-game winning streak. The Giants would remain in first for the rest of May and for most of the summer. However, the race they were leading was extremely close, as at the Giants' heels were not only the defending champion Dodgers but also the Pittsburgh Pirates. The Pirates hadn't won the pennant since 1960, nor had they closely contended. But in '66 they were a legitimate threat, featuring the major leagues' best double-play combination in shortstop Gene Alley and second baseman Bill Mazeroski and a heavy-hitting offense led by right fielder Roberto Clemente, left fielder Willie Stargell, and first baseman Donn Clendenon. The Dodgers, featuring the same lineup and the same smothering pitching and defense approach they'd won with in 1965, spent most of the year in a close third.

When the Giants traveled to Los Angeles for a three-game series in early September 1966, the California rivals were in a virtual tie for second place, two games behind Pittsburgh. In the first game, on Labor Day afternoon, the Dodgers won, and Willie Mays pulled a thigh muscle and had to leave the game. It appeared that he would be out of action for at least a few games, but the thirty-five-year-old Mays wouldn't hear of it. The next evening he told Franks he would play, though he accepted the manager's compromise measure that he play right field instead of center. Mays, limping badly, contributed a two-run homer, and the Giants won.

Wednesday night, September 7, would be the final game of the year between the archrivals. It went into extra innings tied 2–2, and in the top of the twelfth, Mays came up to bat with two outs and the bases empty. Dodger reliever Joe Moeller worked him carefully. On a pitch in the dirt, catcher Johnny Roseboro blocked the ball so it popped straight up in the air. Without missing a beat, Mays stuck out his bat, caught the ball on the very tip, balanced it for a moment, then casually flipped it back to Roseboro, delighting even the Dodger Stadium crowd.[5]

Behind in the count, the Dodgers decided to just make it an intentional walk, and Mays limped to first base. A raw rookie named Frank Johnson, in his first major league game, then came to bat. He swung at the first pitch and looped it into short right field for a single. Right fielder Lou Johnson fielded the ball and whipped it to Jim Lefebvre, the Dodger second baseman.

Willie Mays may or may not have been limping as he made his way around second and over to third base; no one was paying attention. But everyone noticed that Mays was not limping at all as he suddenly cut around third and lit out for home, flying like the Willie of old. A startled Lefebvre threw to John Roseboro, who set up to block the plate. Just before Mays got there, Roseboro received the ball, but not quite solidly, and as Mays slammed into him, it popped loose. In the swirl of dirt Willie Mays rose from his slide, one hand on a sprawled Roseboro, while the other pointed to the ball resting on the ground. "Out," roared umpire Tony Venzon, then, "No, goddam, safe!" as he followed Willie's pointing finger.

The Giants were ahead, 3–2, yet the rabid Los Angeles crowd delivered peals of applause for the astonishing Mays as he, yes, limped out to right field to take his position for the last of the twelfth.[6] Frank Linzy retired the Dodgers, and the Giants were alone in second place.

But they couldn't convert the dramatic win into momentum. The Giants came home for a fatefully unsuccessful two-week home stand that concluded with three losses in four games to the Pirates, while the Dodgers were winning ten out of thirteen in Los Angeles, including a four-game sweep of the Astros *in four consecutive shutouts*. As the season entered its final week and a half, it was the Dodgers in first place.

Nearly knocked out, the Giants took to the road and fought back. They swept a series in Atlanta that left them with a chance to catch the Dodgers on the concluding weekend. But though the Giants swept the Pirates in Pittsburgh, knocking them into third, on the last day of the season Walt Alston handed to ball to Sandy Koufax on two days' rest, and the Left Arm of God came through with a ten-strikeout complete game victory, his twenty-seventh complete game of the season and his twenty-seventh win—the final win of his career. For the second year in a row, the Dodgers had won the pennant over the Giants by an eyelash.

The 1966 season was the first since the Giants' arrival in San Francisco in which Stoneham was persuaded to televise more games than the team's road trips to Los Angeles. In addition to those nine, another eight away games were selected, most of them on weekends, for a total of seventeen. Not included among the seventeen was the game in Atlanta on Tuesday night, September 27.

The Hunters Point district of San Francisco was essentially that city's version of Watts. Adjacent to the Bayview district that housed Candlestick Park, Hunters Point included a large United States Navy shipyard and other industrial dock works. Its residential neighborhoods were grim, poor, and in the 1960s, almost entirely African American. On the evening of September 26, 1966, a Black teenager who'd been pulled over for speeding fled from his vehicle, and a white police officer fired two shots. The cop later said they were meant as warning shots, yet they struck the young man and killed him.

Within minutes the Hunters Point district was a riot zone. Mobs looted stores, lit fires, and overturned cars. A curfew imposed by Mayor Jack Shelley was ignored, and 349 people were arrested. As the violence continued the following morning, the mayor concluded that force alone could not keep the rioters off the street. Maybe a baseball game would.[7]

Early that morning Shelley's office called Horace Stoneham and asked if it would be possible for that evening's game to be televised back to the Bay Area from Atlanta. Stoneham agreed to do it if he could, but given that no telecast had been scheduled, a lot would need to be done in a very short time. The Giants' broadcast station, KTVU, contacted a station in Atlanta to help with the technicalities, and the unions representing the television crew members granted their approval. Giants broadcasters Russ Hodges and Lon Simmons agreed to do the telecast for free.

The San Francisco afternoon newspapers published the announcement of the hastily arranged telecast on the front pages. Hodges called Willie Mays in his room at the Marriott Hotel in Atlanta to ask for his help in publicizing the telecast. Mays asked, "How much time have we got?" Hodges replied: "None. Seven hours till game time. They can spot-announce it back home, but I told the mayor it'd be five times as valuable coming from you."[8]

Hodges sat Mays down and they tape-recorded a message that would be telephoned to every Bay Area radio station. The script made no reference to the riots, raised no alarms, and implied no threats. All it carried was the moral authority of its messenger. "This is Willie Mays," the announcement began. "Channel 2 is carrying a special program, a game against the Atlanta Braves at five o'clock. I, for one, wish and hope each and every one will be tuned in, wishing us well. I'll be out in center field trying to do my best."

The short spot aired on station after station, repeated almost three hundred times. An hour before the game, shooting broke out in Hunters Point, and a large fire was set. But shortly after the broadcast started, the unrest diminished, and by the time the game ended, the rioting had come to a virtual halt. Both Mayor Shelley and the chief of police, Tom Cahill, said the broadcast played a major role in restoring peace, and the ratings supported that view: citywide the telecast ranked number one, with 33 percent of the market, and in the riot areas the game captured a 42 percent share.[9]

In that game the Giants were trailing 3–1 in the sixth inning when Mays launched a three-run homer to turn it around. They won 6–3.

"If you're going to San Francisco, be sure to wear some flowers in your hair." So proclaimed the lyrics of the song written by John Phillips of the pop-folk group the Mamas and the Papas and sung by Scott McKenzie. Released as a single on May 13, 1967, it was a smash hit, heralding across the ubiquitous AM radio airwaves the 1967 social phenomenon known as the "Summer of Love." It was a startling, amazing, disorganized—journey? destination? both?—occurring in some form in many places but centered as nowhere else in the Haight-Ashbury neighborhood of San Francisco.

Haight-Ashbury, adjacent to Golden Gate Park, the University of San Francisco, and the Castro, was a pleasant, (previously) sedate, older middle-class district featuring many Victorian houses. It was suddenly overrun during the summer of 1967 with as many as 100,000 groovy visitors.[10] The hippie culture celebrating the Summer of Love vowed rejection of established social conformity and shallow materialist values and preached communal sharing and peaceful coexistence. While the commitment to such lofty ideals was often genuine, there was more than a little white privilege and oblivious self-indulgence being exhibited as well. There was no Summer of Love going on over in Hunters Point.

Along with rock and roll music and "uninhibited" sex, an overt pleasure central to the Summer of Love experience was consumption of psychedelic drugs. In addition to the cannabis that had long been favored by beatniks—the 1950s precursors of hippies and a prominent presence in ever-bohemian San Francisco—many hippies were advocates of the synthetic hallucinogen LSD. While ingesting "acid" would usually stimulate a euphoric and revealingly introspective state of mind, it also presented the danger of a negative experience, an anxiety-filled "bad trip." The bummer side of the Summer of Love in Haight-Ashbury was a detritus of drug-fueled illness, vagrancy, and squalor. Utopia was a work in progress.

It was in the year of 1967 that Horace Stoneham's son-in-law joined the San Francisco Giants' front office. Chuck Rupert, since marrying Stoneham's daughter Wootchie in 1949, had led a successful air force career. After serving as a pilot flying large transport aircraft, he then became an aeronautical engineer, migrating with his young family to various bases around the country on missile and nuclear assignments. His security clearance became so rarified that the State Department forbade him from leaving the United States. When he retired in 1966 after twenty years of service, it was at the rank of lieutenant colonel. Rupert was in his midforties and not ready to sit on a porch. He had zero baseball experience, but he'd always been a fan and, more important, in his long military career was familiar with establishing and managing project plans and budgets, overseeing staffs, and solving problems.

It was a hard but obvious truth that Stoneham's son-in-law was, in fact, about as different as could be from his son, Pete, still emptily on the payroll as a vice president. Stoneham had always been impressed with Rupert and was happy to bring him into the family business. Stoneham placed Rupert in the newly created position of controller, learning the revenue and expense details of the baseball business from treasurer Edgar Feeley, one of Stoneham's old guard who'd been counting the beans for two decades.

Working for his father-in-law presented Rupert with the opportunity to settle in the Bay Area. He and Wootchie had four children: three daughters (Sonja, Kim, and Jaime) and a son (Peter); the oldest was now in high school and the youngest a preschooler. Rupert and Wootchie bought a midsized ranch-style house in the plush peninsula enclave of Atherton, a half-hour commute from Candlestick Park. For the first time the family had a permanent address, and the kids were now provided the opportunity to get to know their grandparents more closely than ever before. Valleda and Horace adored them; the grandchildren called Stoneham "Pops" and enjoyed regular attendance at games at Candlestick as well annual spring training Arizona vacations.

Looking forward to a second career in a fun and exciting new profession, Chuck Rupert had no way of knowing that he was joining the Stoneham family business at just the point when it would begin to collapse.

In the four seasons following their 1962 pennant, the Giants had drawn over 1.5 million fans at Candlestick Park every year and won eighty-eight, ninety, ninety-five, and ninety-three games, respectively. But a repeat championship teased and eluded them, a frustration rendered especially bitter by the fact that it had been the archrival Dodgers winning the pennant in three of those four years. Horace Stoneham's Giants were very, very good but, so frustratingly, not quite good enough.

No other team in baseball presented a core of talent equal to that of the San Francisco Giants. The 1966 edition was particularly striking in this regard. As measured by wins above replacement (WAR), Willie Mays that year was the best center fielder (and indeed the best position player) among all twenty teams in the major leagues, Juan Marichal was the second-best pitcher, Willie McCovey was the second-best first baseman, Jim Ray Hart was the third-best third baseman, Tom Haller was the third-best catcher, and Gaylord Perry—who at age twenty-seven broke into stardom for good in 1966—was the ninth-best pitcher. No other roster was nearly as star laden.

Yet they couldn't win the pennant because the supporting cast severely let them down. The Giants' middle infield remained truly problematic. Hal Lanier, deployed mostly at second base but sometimes at shortstop in 1966, was fine with the glove, but for the second year in a row his hitting was woeful. Tito Fuentes, mostly at shortstop but sometimes at second, hit better than Lanier but not well. In the outfield Jesús Alou regressed, delivering a middling batting average but utterly no power and practically never drawing a base on balls. The Giants sent Alou back to AAA for a couple of weeks in mid-June to try to get him untracked, but to no avail. He played poorly on defense as well, completing the dismal picture: no position player in baseball compiled a worse WAR score in 1966 than Alou's minus 1.8.

His struggle provided an opportunity for Len Gabrielson to grab the left field job, but Gabrielson flopped as well in 1966. So, twenty-three-year-old Cap Peterson now had a chance to seize the day, but he didn't hit either. Literally, no position on any team in major league baseball in 1966 was less productive than left field for the Giants—it wasn't just a hole; it was a crater. Nor was right field much better, as the rookie Ollie Brown had a disappointingly rough time with the bat. The corner outfield positions are counted upon by teams to provide offense, but the Giants in 1966 got none of it.

The Giants' pitching staff in 1966 was outstanding, one of the very best in the game. Marichal and Perry were both brilliant, and Bob Bolin was good as the third starter. Lindy McDaniel and Frank Linzy were strong in the bullpen, and Joe Gibbon was solid as a long reliever and spot starter. The staff had just one problem, but it was a doozy: Ray Sadecki, burdened with the pressure of being the one for whom Cepeda was traded, performed terribly. The only player in the major leagues with a worse WAR figure than Jesús Alou in 1966 was Sadecki, whose valuation in twenty-six games and 105 innings with the Giants was minus 2.2.

Since Ray Sadecki so profoundly failed to fulfill the Giants' need for a dependable left-handed starting pitcher, in the ensuing off-season Stoneham went back to the trade market to address it. He found an attractive option available: on December 13, 1966, the Giants reacquired southpaw Mike McCormick, taking him off the hands of the Washington Senators in exchange for Cap Peterson and second-line pitcher Bob Priddy.

McCormick had endured a career crisis after the Giants traded him to Baltimore. Sore armed, the former bonus baby hit bottom in 1964, landing in the minor leagues for the first time. Picked up from there by the lowly Washington Senators, McCormick reinvented himself: his old fastball was gone, so he learned to rely on changing speeds and artfully spotting a new pitch, a screwball. McCormick noted, "I re-established credibility in myself, and got my feet back on the ground to where people recognized that, 'He's not the same type pitcher that he used to be, but he can pitch.'" McCormick put up solid stats with the second-division Senators in 1965–66.[11] He was still just twenty-eight, and the price the Giants expended for him was eminently sensible.

Still, Stoneham executed no transactions to shore up the middle infield. In the outfield he dealt away not only Cap Peterson but also Len Gabrielson and shopped Jesús Alou but found no takers.[12] So, the corner outfield spots in 1967 remained even more exclusively the province of Alou and Ollie Brown.

The Giants started the 1967 season on a literal bad trip, opening on the road and dropping seven of their first eight games. It was a long climb out of that ditch. They reached .500 in mid-May and got to within semiserious contention at a couple of points in June and July. But that was it. In August the St. Louis Cardinals—led by National League Most Valuable Player Orlando Cepeda, thank you very much—blew the race apart and won it in a runaway. The Giants were hot down the final stretch, going 21–7, but all that did was raise them to their familiar second place, and they were never close to the top.

In midsummer of 1965 Willie Mays had encountered the first injury-nagged slump of his career. He won the MVP anyway because he hit ridiculously well the rest of that year. In 1966 he was able to avoid any bad stretches, but he didn't find the sustained red-hot streaks he'd enjoyed in '65. His thirty-seven home runs in '66 were a great total, third most in the league but Mays's fewest in a season since 1960. His 1966 batting average was .288, a very good mark but the lowest of any full season in his career. He sat out ten games in '66, the most he'd ever missed. He was still a superstar, but evidence of inevitable decline was seeping into the edges of his performance.

In 1967, at age thirty-six, the decline began in earnest. In the season's first week Mays pulled a hamstring and was slow to recover. He finally began to hit well but was no longer performing among the game's elite, and for the first time since his return from the army, he wasn't elected as a National League All-Star starter. Mays was peppered with questions about his downgrade. Did he feel slighted? Was he angry? "Look, time marches on," he said. "I'm honestly not disappointed at losing the chance to be a starter. Let's face it. I'm not a kid anymore and there are so many fine young outfielders coming up, and some are already here, that I feel good just finishing as high in the voting as I did."

The 1967 All-Star Game represented the passing of an era, as both Mays and Mickey Mantle entered as pinch hitters—and both struck out. Mays stayed in the game, but he didn't look right and went 0 for 4 in the National League's fifteen-inning victory. "He looked tired and weak and sick," noted Ernie Banks, "and he told me that was just how he felt."[13]

He was ill. Back at Candlestick Park following the All-Star break, Mays was feverish and asked Franks for the night off. But when his substitute (utility man Ty Cline) pulled a muscle, Mays volunteered to play. His legs were heavy, and his bat was slow; after he misplayed a line drive into a triple and struck out twice, Mays took himself out of the game and went home.[14] (Catcher Tom Haller had to play in the outfield.)

The next day Mays was admitted to St. Mary's Hospital in San Francisco, where Stoneham insisted he be placed under the care of his own personal physician. A battery of tests yielded no diagnosis beyond flu virus and exhaustion, and Mays spent five days in the hospital sleeping and recuperating. Upon his return, over the balance of the season, the longtime superstar would start just fifty-four of the Giants' sixty-eight games as his batting average dwindled to a pedestrian .263, with twenty-two home runs.

Not just Giants fans but the national press viewed the situation with sadness. Columnist Furman Bisher in the *Atlanta Constitution* summed up the sense of a wonderful magic spell having been broken: "Willie Mays wasn't supposed to grow old. He was supposed to go on forever, his cap flying off as he broke the sound barrier on foot, face bright and two eyes twinkling like stars. Willie Mays was born for eternal youth. Age is acting in direct violation of that code."[15]

Mays wasn't the only Giants superstar encountering unaccustomed struggle in 1967. Through the end of June, twenty-nine-year-old Juan Marichal was enjoying perhaps his best season. But he had several rough outings in July, and in early August, while running in the outfield between starts, he tore a hamstring and was essentially finished for the season.[16] Willie McCovey, also twenty-nine, encountered issues with sore knees in '67, and while he hit with his standard fury, his playing time was diminished.

But Jim Ray Hart and Gaylord Perry both delivered great years in 1967. And left-handed starting pitching, the dire weakness of 1966, emerged in this season as a grand strength. Mike McCormick had a career year, leading the league with twenty-two wins and being awarded the National League Cy Young Award. Ray Sadecki, banished to the back of the bullpen after his disastrous 1966 performance, pitched his way into the rotation in the summer and was superb in '67, the very best of his career.

Yet the Giants' major shortcomings remained unresolved. Ollie Brown hit wonderfully in the early season, but he then pulled a groin muscle and struggled the rest of the way. Jesús Alou again played as a regular, and while he hit for a good average, in every other regard he remained a deficient player, and it was now all too obvious he would never develop as anticipated. Shortstop and second base were festering problems all season long; as one guidebook put it, "The middle of the Giants infield has been like an ulcer to manager Herman Franks."[17] The manager finally resolved that Hal Lanier would play short and Tito Fuentes second, but stability didn't deliver positive results. Lanier's 1967 OPS+ of 42 was the very worst of any regular in the major leagues—a distinction he'd also achieved in both 1965 and '66. Fuentes flopped dreadfully in 1967: in late June he was hitting .146, and he finished at .209.

The 1967 season was the Giants' tenth in San Francisco, and it was the first in which the team was never in first place at any point. Nor did they mount any serious challenge for it. It was a season with little drama, about as uncompelling as a second-place finish can be. The fan base was bored with it, as Candlestick Park attendance dropped by 25 percent from that of 1966, to the Giants' lowest since moving west. In the month of September, with no pennant race at stake, in fifteen dates at Candlestick the Giants attracted crowds of fewer than 10,000 seven times and fewer than 5,000 five times. On Monday afternoon, September 25, 1967, against the last-place Mets, the sparse gathering of 2,818 was the smallest the Giants had ever drawn in San Francisco.

The championship joy of 1962 was receding ever further into the rearview mirror, and the sense of optimism that this extraordinarily talented ball club would win again was rapidly draining. With Mays in decline, and with the injury issues encountered by Marichal and McCovey, the notion now loomed that the window of opportunity for this team was closing. The failure to seal the deal in either of the close chances in 1965 and '66 began to nag like a toothache.

The city of Oakland occupies the eastern shore of the San Francisco Bay, directly across the water from San Francisco. The fact that the prominent estuary is known as the "San Francisco Bay" and the region is known as the "San Francisco Bay Area" may provide a hint regarding the status that Oakland has always held. From the very beginning of Spanish settlement in the 1700s, through the incorporation of the State of California within the United States in the 1850s, and ever since, Oakland has been the "other place," the supporting player, the sidekick to the area's glitzy, overbearing, egotistical star.

The name *Oakland* implies a leafy, pastoral hamlet, and through much of the nineteenth century that's what Oakland was, nestled between the blue bay to the west and the grassy, oak-dappled hills to the east. But by the twentieth century Oakland was rapidly growing: between 1890 and 1910 the population tripled to 150,000, and it would be double that again by 1940. In the middle of the twentieth century, Oakland was anything but pastoral; it was a dense, tough, working-class city. It became a huge seagoing port (larger than San Francisco in that regard), glutted with warehouses, train yards, and trucking depots. San Francisco had developed as the picturesque tourist attraction, with the cute cable cars and fancy restaurants; Oakland was the district of loading docks and lunch pails. To use a New York analogy, if San Francisco is Manhattan, then Oakland is Newark, New Jersey.

Whether many Oakland residents cared much about their city's second-banana status is debatable, but the city's politicians and business leaders sure didn't appreciate it. Following the 1955 baseball season, the half-century-old Oakland Oaks franchise in the Pacific Coast League had relocated to Vancouver, Canada, and coupled with the Giants' arrival in San Francisco in 1958, Oakland's movers and shakers were feeling left out in the cold. They sought to attract a major league sports team of their own to help improve the city's dull image.[18]

To that end, a civic effort was undertaken to explore the construction of a new multipurpose stadium that could host either baseball or football, and by 1960 a joint city-county project was officially underway to allocate public financing and spearhead the development of the facility. It would open in 1966 as the Oakland–Alameda County Coliseum, built alongside a companion venue, the indoor Oakland–Alameda County Arena (suitable for basketball, hockey, and large-scale entertainments), in very modern fashion, amid a huge parking lot alongside the city's major freeway.[19] (The promise of the Coliseum's construction was a key factor in the decision of the American Football League in 1960 to grant one of its charter franchises to the Oakland Raiders, and the National Basketball Association's San Francisco Warriors would rename themselves the Golden State Warriors and call the Oakland Arena home from 1971 to 2019.)[20]

With the new stadium in the works, the Oakland city fathers began actively courting major league baseball owners with the idea of relocating a team to Oakland or placing an expansion franchise there. The City of Oakland itself still wasn't nearly large enough to support an MLB team; its population of 360,000 was about half that of San Francisco and significantly smaller than Kansas City, the smallest major league city. But like San Francisco, in 1960 Oakland was at the geographic center of a multicity metropolis of 3.7 million, which was still growing at a frantic pace. Even half of that market, which a second Bay Area team would presumably have to work with, made it bigger than not only the Kansas City metropolitan area but also the markets of Cincinnati, Pittsburgh, St. Louis, or Cleveland. The Oakland boosters had a strong product to pitch.

Horace Stoneham wasn't at all pleased with this idea. He'd moved to the Bay Area with the understanding that the territory would be his alone. However, given that the two major leagues operated almost entirely independently in those days, as a National League owner he only had a vote on where National League franchises would be placed. If the American League opted to put a team in Oakland, there was nothing Stoneham could do about it.

The Philadelphia Athletics had pioneered westward three years ahead of the Giants and Dodgers, arriving in 1955 in Kansas City, Missouri. The A's enjoyed booming attendance in their first few years in Kansas City, but as the team on the field remained a tailender, enthusiasm and fan support waned. When owner Arnold Johnson died in 1960, his estate sold the franchise to Charles O. Finley, an insurance millionaire from Chicago.

Finley was a singular character, one of the very most colorful owners in baseball history. He was brilliant, energetic, and innovative. He was also a tireless proponent of the tackiest, corniest, and most peculiar marketing schemes, and above all, Finley demonstrated the remarkable capacity to make a bitter and lasting enemy of nearly everyone who ever met him.

He genuinely loved and understood baseball and would prove to have an extraordinarily great eye for talent and team construction. But Finley had no particular affinity for Kansas City, which he accurately recognized as the smallest of big-league markets. Though at the time of his purchase Finley had explicitly pledged to never move the franchise away from Kansas City, that was a blatant lie—something Finley was quite prone to do— as he almost immediately began looking to find a more lucrative home. Kansas City fans soon grew wise to it, which further undermined attendance and soured his relationship with the city government, business leaders, and local news media.

His fellow American League owners were aghast at the notion of relocating the Athletics less than a decade after they'd arrived in Kansas City and properly feared legal action if they allowed the team to move. Among other concerns the Athletics held a lease on the use of Kansas City Municipal Stadium that ran through 1967. American League president Joe Cronin explained to Finley that he would get zero votes from the other owners if he formally proposed a relocation. Undeterred, Finley actively courted Dallas–Fort Worth, as well as Atlanta, Oakland, and Seattle, all the while demanding that Kansas City build him a brand-new stadium at taxpayer expense.

In early 1964 Finley went so far as to sign an agreement with the city of Louisville, Kentucky, promising to move his team there. The AL not only voted down that plan, but Cronin and the other franchises now seriously threatened to expel Finley from the league. With this, Finley finally backed down. But by mid-1967, with his Kansas City lease nearing expiration, Finley and the league worked out an agreement allowing him to relocate to Oakland in 1968, while the league promised Kansas City an expansion team beginning in 1969. One of the factors working in favor of the move was the league's desire to place a second team on the West Coast, mitigating the travel costs currently borne by teams flying to California for a single series with the Angels.[21]

United States senator Stuart Symington of Missouri, exasperated by his involvement in the negotiations with Finley, declared on the Senate floor: "The loss of the A's is more than recompensed by the pleasure of getting rid of Mr. Finley. He is one of the most disreputable characters ever to enter the American sports scene. Oakland is the luckiest city since Hiroshima."[22]

Horace Stoneham wasn't feeling very lucky himself, as his Giants, on the heels of their most troubling season since the move from New York, now had to contend with a business competitor in their territory. His nephew Chub Feeney issued a cheery, innocuous public welcome to the Athletics, saying he hoped it would work out for everyone, but Stoneham couldn't bring himself to be anything but bluntly worried: "Certainly the move will hurt us. It is simply a question of how much and if both of us can survive. I don't think the area at the present time will take care of us both as much as [the Athletics] think it will."[23]

So, the San Francisco Giants entered 1968. In *The Glory and the Dream* William Manchester would ponder the national mood of 1968, a troubled year within a troubled decade that just wasn't turning out the way it was supposed to:

> The hundred-and-twenty-one-year-old Pennsylvania Railroad and the hundred-and-fourteen-year-old New York Central merged, and service was twice as bad. . . . In Washington, the Willard Hotel, where at least seven Presidents, beginning with Franklin Pierce, had been guests at one time or another, went bankrupt. . . .
>
> The postal system was a disgrace. Everybody had his horror story about the mails. Waitresses brought you somebody else's order. Cab drivers couldn't find your destination. Your evening paper wasn't delivered. The druggist filled the wrong prescription. The new washer-dryer was a lemon. Deliverymen double-parked and wouldn't move. . . .
>
> Airliners were late taking off; because they didn't reach your destination on time you had to wait, stacked over it, and when you did land you discovered that your baggage had gone on to another airport. This was so common that frequent travelers bought luggage expressly designed to fit under their seats. Bus and train timetables were fictive. Nearly everyone was dunned at one time or another for bills that were already paid. Nothing, it seemed, functioned any more. . . .
>
> The fault was difficult to pin down, but it was everywhere. People didn't seem to care whether things worked any more. The discipline that knits a society together was weakening and at some points giving away altogether. John Kenneth Galbraith attributed it to prosperity. Richard Nixon blamed it on permissiveness.[24]

On January 30, 1968, the Viet Cong and the North Vietnamese army began their ambitiously coordinated campaign known as the Tet Offensive. Militarily, it would produce little more than heavy casualties on all sides, but it would be a strategic political success for the North, demonstrating that this war was never going to be won by the South. In the spring of 1968 a graphic photograph of a Viet Cong officer being executed by a pistol shot to the head was published in newspapers and magazines around the world and would win the 1969 Pulitzer Prize. The image would become an iconic symbol of the anti–Vietnam War movement in the United States that rapidly gathered strength in 1968. On March 31 fifty-nine-year-old President Lyndon B. Johnson, defeated in spirit by the nightmare of Vietnam, announced that he would not stand for reelection. The exhausted incumbent president had lost control of his own party.

Four days later Dr. Martin Luther King Jr. was assassinated in Memphis, Tennessee. That evening, in Indianapolis, U.S. senator and Democratic presidential candidate Robert F. Kennedy spoke to a largely African American crowd at a rally and for the first time talked publicly of the horror of his own brother's murder just a few years earlier. He extemporaneously concluded with the words: "What we need in the United States is not division; what we need in the United States is not hatred; what we need in the United States is not violence or lawlessness, but love and wisdom, and compassion toward one another, and a feeling of justice towards those who still suffer within our country, whether they be white or whether they be black." Indianapolis remained calm that night, while rioting consumed some 168 other U.S. cities.

King's funeral service was scheduled for Tuesday, April 9, which coincided with major league baseball's scheduled Opening Day games, raising the question of whether they would be postponed in a gesture of respect for the civil rights leader's memory. Baseball commissioner William "Spike" Eckert declined to issue a blanket ruling, instead declaring that it would be the decision of each home team to play or postpone. All the home teams opted to postpone except the Houston Astros and the Los Angeles Dodgers, but they both relented when met with threats of boycotts by the visitors (the Pittsburgh Pirates and Philadelphia Phillies, respectively).

On June 5, 1968, Robert Kennedy himself was shot in the head at the Ambassador Hotel in Los Angeles. He died in the hospital the next day. Again, the question arose of the appropriate response from major league baseball, and again Eckert deferred it to the teams. Instead of calling off games, Eckert announced that two days later—Saturday, June 8—no scheduled games would start before Kennedy's burial, set for that day. But the funeral began later than scheduled, and baseball teams took the field to play in Baltimore, Cincinnati, Boston, and Detroit.

The Major League Baseball Players Association sent a telegram to Eckert asking him to declare an official day of mourning for RFK. Eckert again declined to act, leaving the chaos of each club deciding independently. Many players were furious. Some teams voted not to play, including the New York Mets, who were scheduled to face the Giants in San Francisco.

Stoneham, however, declared that the Giants wanted to play. The Mets' refusal, he complained, would cost him $80,000 in lost revenue. While the nation was mourning the horrible assassination, Stoneham filed a grievance with Warren Giles, the National League president. Giles promptly ruled that if the Mets did not play, it would be considered a forfeit, and moreover, the Mets' front office would be fined and their players would be docked a day's pay.

Chub Feeney stepped forward at this point and persuaded both Stoneham and Giles into de-escalating and allowing the game to be postponed. "It would give baseball a black eye," he told reporters. "It doesn't look good." That ship, though, had already sailed. It was a rare demonstration of pique on Stoneham's part and entirely poor judgment.[25]

The dismal summer proceeded. On August 20–21, 1968, 750,000 Soviet-led Warsaw Pact troops with sixty-five hundred tanks and eight hundred planes invaded Czechoslovakia—the largest European military operation since World War II—and crushed the "Prague Spring" of liberalization. From August 26 through 29 the 1968 Democratic National Convention was held in Chicago. Inside, a bitterly fractured and dissatisfied party membership would struggle to nominate Vice President Hubert H. Humphrey for president. Outside, a clash between antiwar protesters and the police resulted in appalling violence that would be described as a "police riot."

In the 1920s rates of hitting and scoring in major league baseball had dramatically risen, following the ban of the spitball and the introduction of a new, clean baseball whenever the current one became soiled or nicked. The offensive heyday peaked in the 1930s and gradually declined from the mid-1930s until the early 1960s (with a temporary extra dip in offensive production occurring in World War II with the inferior-quality ball). The causes for the decline were many, including the introduction and growing frequency of night games, the ever more liberal and sophisticated deployment of relief pitchers, improved quality of fielding, and generally larger, more pitcher-friendly new ballparks being phased in during the 1950s and '60s.

But in 1963 major league baseball owners unwittingly turned a gradual reduction in hitting and scoring into a rapid and immediate dive when they revised the rules to increase the size of the strike zone. The motivation for the change wasn't to reduce scoring; it was an attempt to speed up the pace of games, which were getting ever longer with the increasing rate of mound visits and pitching changes. Enlarge the strike zone, the reasoning went, and batters will more readily swing, put the ball in play, and resolve the at bat.

That line of reasoning proved to be, shall we say, misguided. Batters were indeed forced to swing, but the result was more weak contact, more foul balls, and particularly more swings and misses. The rate of strikeouts had already significantly increased since the 1940s, but now it soared, while batting averages plunged. The rate of runs scored in 1963 was the lowest since 1919, with the exception of one balata ball wartime season. It would go still lower from there in subsequent seasons, as on top of everything else, in the 1960s teams seized on a new method of helping their pitchers: building up the height of the pitcher's mound so that the pitch would have a sharper downward trajectory. And then came 1968.

Hitting and scoring plummeted to such forlorn depths in 1968 that nearly everyone was struck with a sense of dismay, heightened by the fact that this baseball season was playing out within a nation that seemed to be unraveling. In the *New Yorker* Roger Angell considered the situation:

327

The 1968 season has been named the Year of the Pitcher, which is only a kinder way of saying the Year of the Infield Pop-Up. The final records only confirm what so many fans, homeward bound after still another shutout, had already discovered for themselves; almost no one, it seemed, could hit the damn ball any more. . . . Adding up zeros is not the most riveting of spectator sports and by mid-July of this year it was plain to even the most inattentive or optimistic of fans that something had gone wrong with their game. Why were the pitchers so good? Where were the .320 hitters? What had happened to the high-scoring slugfest, the late rally, the bases-clearing double? The answers to these questions are difficult and speculative, but some attempt must be made at them. . . . All the technical and strategic innovations of recent years have helped the defenses of baseball; none have favored the batter. Bigger ballparks with bigger outfields, the infielders' enormous crab-claw gloves, more night games, the mastery of the relatively new slider pitch, the persistence of the relatively illegal spitter, and the instantaneous managerial finger-wag to the bullpen at the first sign of an enemy rally have all tipped the balance of this delicately balanced game.[26]

With the events (or from the hitting perspective, nonevents) of 1968, even baseball owners whose obtuseness had led to the sport's unprecedented form recognized that they were at a point of crisis. Following the 1968 season, the rules committee voted to restore the strike zone to its pre-1963 dimensions and also established a rule limiting the height of the pitcher's mound to ten inches.

Stoneham engaged in just one trade in the 1967–68 off-season, and it was notable: catcher Tom Haller, along with a secondary minor league pitcher, was traded to Walter O'Malley's Los Angeles Dodgers for second baseman Ron Hunt and utility infielder Nate "Pee Wee" Oliver. This action violated the unwritten rule, scrupulously followed for decades by the archrival teams, to not deal with each other.[27] Haller wasn't a major star, but he was consistently among the most durable and productive catchers of the 1960s; in 1967 he'd made his second straight National League

All-Star team. But he would be thirty-one in 1968, and in Jack Hiatt, Dick Dietz, and Bob Barton, the Giants had ample depth in younger candidates for the job.

Ron Hunt was, in every significant regard, the second coming of Eddie Stanky—a player who'd never impressed anyone with athletic prowess, but with almost painfully determined will, he gritted and hustled his way into being a productive major league second baseman. Unlike Stanky, Hunt didn't specialize in drawing bases on balls, though he was pretty good at it; instead, Hunt eagerly endured literal pain by crowding the plate and, on any pitch a few inches inside, just turning his body and letting the ball drill him in the side or the back for the free pass to first base. He had his limitations, but nonetheless, Hunt presented a substantial offensive upgrade over Tito Fuentes at second base.

To open the 1968 season, Franks gave most of the catching starts to Hiatt. Jim Ray Hart had spent the second half of 1967 playing left field, and that's where he was to begin '68, so thirty-four-year-old Jim Davenport, for the first time since 1963, opened the year as the regular third baseman. In right field, in a puzzling choice, Franks went with Jesús Alou as the first-stringer and Ollie Brown as backup.

The Giants in 1968 started reasonably well, and a hot streak in May put them in first place for the week before Memorial Day. June, however, brought its swoon, and by the latter part of that month the Giants had fallen to six and a half games behind the St. Louis Cardinals, who'd caught fire and were threatening another runaway. Right field for the Giants had been a black hole, as neither Alou nor Brown was hitting at all, even by 1968 standards. Stoneham now shipped Downtown Brown back to AAA and gave the call for twenty-two-year-old Bobby Bonds. Signed out of high school in Riverside, California, by scout Rex Carr, young Bonds was nothing less than the organization's most impressive power and speed athlete since Willie Mays himself. He'd dazzled at every minor league rung, and all he was doing at AAA Phoenix so far in '68 was hitting .370, with thirty-one extra-base hits, including eight homers, and twelve steals in fifteen attempts.

Bobby Bonds made his major league debut on Tuesday evening, June 25, 1968, at Candlestick Park against the Dodgers, playing right field. In his third trip to the plate, Bonds belted a grand slam as his first big-league hit. The drive was the prototype for so many he would deliver in the years to come: a high liner to left-center field that seemed hit hard enough to pierce the outfield barrier if it didn't clear it. The athletic capacity of Bonds was the sort that comes along only rarely—six foot one, 180 pounds, of lean muscularity and blinding speed. He performed every task on a baseball field with excellence and élan but for one flaw: his fiercely confident, almost balletic swing could get loopy, and he was quite prone to the strikeout, the only factor that would prevent him from sustaining a high batting average.

Because of his spectacular ability, Bobby Bonds was, of course, widely characterized as "the next Willie Mays," with all the scrutiny and pressure that would bring. (To help out with that, the Giants issued him uniform number 25.) For his part Mays readily did his best to take young Bobby Bonds under his wing and help him succeed. Mays also took a warm liking to Bobby's son, a precocious and energetic kid named Barry, almost four years old, to whom Mays would become godfather.

The 1968 Giants, as in '67, played their best ball in the second half. However, once again all that strong finish brought them was a distant, never-threatening second-place finish behind the runaway Cardinals. Willie McCovey, sustaining satisfactory knee health, had his best year yet, leading the league in home runs, RBIs, slugging percentage, OPS, and OPS+. Juan Marichal, also healthy, was tremendous, as was Gaylord Perry. Thirty-seven-year-old Willie Mays enjoyed a resurgent season, maintaining a schedule providing periodic rest and avoiding the exhaustion and illness that had overwhelmed him in 1967. Ron Hunt gave the Giants exactly what they were looking for: adequate second base defense and an on-base percentage sixth best in the league, helped considerably by twenty-five hit-by-pitches, the most in the major leagues since 1911. Ray Sadecki sustained the good performance he'd found in 1967, working in the starting rotation all season and setting career highs in complete games, innings, and strikeouts. Mike McCormick slumped off, but Bob Bolin delivered a terrific year and largely replaced McCormick in the second-half rotation.

For all this core excellence, in their recurrent pattern the 1968 Giants brought to bear entirely too much counterbalancing weakness. Jim Davenport proved to be not up to the rigors of the everyday job at third base, so for most of the second half, Hart was moved back to third, where his defense was now plain bad. Hart hit well in '68 but not his best, as a chronically sore right shoulder caused him to miss twenty-six games. Dick Dietz hit so well that Franks ended up giving him most of the playing time at catcher, even though Dietz's defensive performance was ghastly.[28]

In earlier seasons the team's persistence in providing Jesús Alou and Hal Lanier with regular playing time, while not to be commended, could be understood: both were very young players with strong minor league records that could justify patience through developmental struggles. But by 1968 it was no longer defensible: this was the fifth big-league season for both, and by now it was obvious that neither was going to develop into an acceptable first-stringer. Alou was again dreadful in 1968, presenting below replacement-level performance both at the plate and in the outfield, yet he soaked up 436 plate appearances. Lanier's hitting continued, amazingly, to get worse, and his 1968 OPS+ was for the fourth consecutive year the worst of any major league regular, yet Lanier remained unchallenged as the Giants' full-time shortstop.

Putting together a competitive major league roster is a genuinely difficult endeavor, and every general manager makes mistakes. Horace Stoneham, as the architect of this ball club, deserves full credit for the scouting and farm system operations that delivered the remarkable talent core. But Stoneham must also be held accountable for the failings of so much of the supporting cast, especially given the pattern of ongoing lineup holes left unfilled year after year in this period. Stoneham seemed to develop blind spots, either not recognizing serious problems or perhaps being complacent that his ever productive farm system would soon provide handy solutions.

By 1968 the Giants' persistent failure to fulfill their promise and win another pennant was more than just a sporting disappointment. With the presence of the Athletics in Oakland, the financial competition was now real and pressing. Bay Area baseball fans could now choose to spend their ticket money on a young, exciting, and improving A's ball club that was introducing new stars such as Reggie Jackson, Sal Bando, and Jim "Catfish" Hunter. In their first season in Oakland, Charlie Finley's Athletics drew 837,466, which was more than they'd drawn in Kansas City since 1959. The Giants in 1968, the bloom off their rose, drew a near-exact total of 837,220, not only by far their least since arriving in San Francisco but about a third less than their attendance of 1967 and a bit over half of what they'd drawn in 1966. This amounted to more than a million dollars in suddenly vanished ticket and concessions revenue.

The Giants played seventy-five home dates at Candlestick Park in 1968, and at only nine of them did they attract a crowd of 20,000 or more. In forty-five of their dates the gathering was below 10,000, and eighteen times it was below 5,000. On Monday afternoon, September 16, the Giants beat the Cincinnati Reds 8–4 at Candlestick in front of just 2,361, another new record for the least-attended major league game in San Francisco history.

13

Resilience

One party who'd become exhausted with the Giants' second-place treadmill to nowhere was manager Herman Franks, who tendered his resignation at the close of the 1968 season. It wasn't a surprise, as Franks hadn't sought a long tenure. In one of several ways in which he defied the stereotype of the spittin'-and-swearin' baseball lifer, Franks was independently wealthy. Many years before, with his meager baseball savings, Franks had begun investing in real estate in and around his hometown of Salt Lake City, Utah—there goes another stereotype—and through shrewd and attentive management and trading of his properties, by the mid-1960s he didn't need to work in baseball for the money, not even for the substantial salary of a major league manager. (Among his other side gigs was serving as a financial consultant and money manager, and among his clients, in a breathtaking conflict of interest, was Willie Mays.) So Herman Franks, burned out by four straight years of close-but-not-close-enough, voluntarily retired from baseball at the age of fifty-four in order to focus on his business pursuits.[1]

It's a fair question to wonder if Franks might have been less ready to retire if the Giants had finished in first instead of second in 1968 and, for that matter, in '67, '66, or '65. But they didn't. And over the 1968 season, looking around the massive wind-blown edifice of Candlestick Park and seeing acres of empty seats wasn't encouraging, particularly to someone as keenly tuned to the hard realities of balance sheets as Herman Franks.

Stoneham wasn't happy about Franks's decision to retire, but they parted as friends. With ample time to consider his options to replace Franks, Stoneham chose once again to promote from within: he gave the job to Clyde King, who'd been manager of the AAA Phoenix Giants in 1968. Very different from Franks in personality, King's manner was studious and soft-spoken. He was forty-four years old and had known a journeyman's major league career as a pitcher from 1944 to 1953. He'd then become a minor league manager for several organizations, a roving minor league pitching instructor, and then the major league pitching coach for the Pittsburgh Pirates in 1965–67.

There was obvious wisdom in promoting the AAA manager, as he was familiar with the key young players working their way up to the majors. But the move had its downside. King himself would be a rookie manager in the major leagues, and he would misstep in attempting to establish his authority over the big-league veterans in his charge. Moreover, with just the lone minor league season under his belt within the Giants organization, King was naive about the particular history and culture of the clubhouse he was entering.

Crucially, King failed to establish a good relationship with Willie Mays. He didn't know Mays and didn't appreciate how other managers had handled him. Even as a veteran, Mays was a vulnerable personality, still needing encouragement and support and remaining hypersensitive to slights. He was, in short, a bit of a diva. He'd been doubly protected by Franks, his financial advisor, who allowed Mays to determine his own playing schedule and serve as an unofficial assistant manager. Mays, the longest-tenured player in the big leagues, believed he'd earned special privileges and that both he and the club were better for it. King didn't understand any of this, and troubles were inevitable.[2]

It took no longer than King's introductory press conference to get off on the wrong foot with Mays. King was concerned that he might be accused of favoring the young players he knew from Phoenix over the team's established regulars. So, as his opening statement, he announced an even-handed policy: all Giant players, regardless of seniority, would be required to practice equally and would be treated as equals in all ways. No doubt this was well intended, but as Charles Einstein memorably put it, "Where Mays was concerned it was like Rudolf Bing taking over the Metropolitan Opera and telling Maria Callas she had to sing scales."[3]

The National League expanded again following the 1968 season, adding the Montreal Expos and San Diego Padres. Whatever else this accomplished, it provided Stoneham and the Giants with a one-time windfall of $2 million cash—a million from each of the new franchises as their purchase fee. Coincidentally, in 1968 the long-negotiated settlement of a lawsuit going all the way back to the Giants' relinquishment of the Polo Grounds was finalized at last, and it delivered another $1 million to Stoneham. While such income couldn't be counted upon going forward, it was eagerly accepted by the suddenly cash-poor Giants.[4]

In the expansion draft the price in players the Giants surrendered for their $2 million was negligible. They lost right fielder Ollie Brown to the Padres as the very first pick in the draft; he remained a high-potential player, but though he'd shown flashes, overall Brown hadn't hit well in multiple opportunities with the Giants. The only other major leaguers they lost were outfielders Jesús Alou and Ty Cline, both to Montreal, and they were both more than replaceable. The Giants also surrendered three second-tier minor leaguers, none of whom would enjoy a substantial major league career. Following that, Stoneham executed no significant deals. The departures of Brown, Alou, and Cline created vacancies in the Giants' outfield, and heaven knows they had room for improvement in the infield, but Stoneham's plan was to address all the team's needs—to the extent they would be addressed—from within.

In spring training rookie manager King came up with another fresh idea. He announced that Mays was going to hit leadoff, so his speed could be optimized at the top of the order. If King had privately approached Mays with the notion, it's possible that Mays might have bought in, or at least he could claim some ownership of it, and the switch would have been easier for him. But

King didn't do that. He thought he should treat Mays like every other player, and Mays balked.

"Why do you want me to bat leadoff?" he asked. "I'm no kid, you know."

"I know that, but you're not hitting home runs like you used to," King said.[5]

This was not a managerial approach destined to win the loyalty of Willie Mays. Publicly, Mays offered no more than mild misgivings, but plainly, he wasn't persuaded with the wisdom of the concept and was displeased with the way it was thrust upon him. King, for his part, would stick with the plan for a grand total of nine games (in which Mays hit .317 with two home runs and two stolen bases) before abandoning it without explanation and moving Mays back to his customary third slot in the order. Bobby Bonds, who'd batted third when Mays led off, was moved back to leadoff (where he'd mostly hit in 1968), and Bonds would be the Giants' primary leadoff batter for the balance of 1969.

The King-Mays relationship did not improve. In the early weeks of the 1969 season, Willie McCovey was hitting up a storm. But Bonds, now in the leadoff position, and Mays, now hitting third, were the only other productive bats; none of the candidates King batted behind McCovey in the fifth spot in the order—Jim Ray Hart, Dick Dietz, and Jack Hiatt—were hitting well, so McCovey was drawing a bucketful of intentional walks. He took eight in the month of April alone and five more in May, while his previous full-season high had been twenty.

So, Mays, batting ahead of McCovey, fashioned a creative solution. Multiple times he got what appeared to be a two-base hit but would put on the brakes and settle for a long single. His reasoning was that to be on second base with first base open was to take the bat out of McCovey's hands: the opponent would walk McCovey intentionally. With Mays on first, instead, there was pressure to throw strikes to McCovey, and moreover, with the first baseman playing on the bag to hold Mays, the right side was opened up for the dead-pull-hitting McCovey. "I told King time and again why I was doing it," Mays later said. "I just don't know if it ever got through."[6]

The tension between the team's rookie manager and its aging superstar finally boiled over before a game in Houston on June 24. Mays thought he was getting the night off, but a teammate told him that his name was on the lineup card, posted in the dugout. Mays retreated to the clubhouse to take off his sweats and put on his uniform. When it was time to present the lineup to the umpires, King didn't see Mays. Instead of finding out where he was, King assumed Mays didn't want to play and erased his name from the card. Mays returned to the dugout, saw his name removed, and erupted with an anger that few had ever seen in him.

He thought King was trying to show him up—first putting him in the lineup, then taking him out. He barked at King, waved his arms, and appeared ready to charge the manager before McCovey, Gaylord Perry, and pitching coach Larry Jansen held him back. Mays continued to shake his finger at King before at last settling down.

In the second inning left fielder Jim Ray Hart aggravated his troublesome shoulder. King asked Mays if he wanted to play. "You're the manager," Mays said. He played the rest of the game.

Afterward King told Mays that he would be fined. Mays would have none of it. "If I'm fined," Mays told him, "I quit." Stoneham was not about to let that happen. No fine was levied, and Chub Feeney persuaded Mays to apologize to King. In the *San Francisco Examiner* columnist Prescott Sullivan noted that the tantrum was the first for Mays "in some eighteen years as a professional player [and] he had us wondering if he'd ever get around to it. . . . It's only human to foul up now and then, and Willie, who had baseball's longest good conduct record going for him, finally did it."[7] At that point the thirty-eight-year-old center fielder was having another excellent year, appearing in fifty-six of the team's sixty-six games, and was hitting .315 with nine home runs. From then on he struggled, nicked up and sitting out more than one-third of the time and hitting .252, with four homers.

The frustrating season for Mays was just one of many setbacks the Giants encountered in 1969. Jim Ray Hart had been bothered by the problematic right shoulder in 1968, and in '69 it overwhelmed him: he was limited to ninety-five games and hit just three home runs. Hart's absence from the lineup thrust twenty-three-year-old Ken Henderson into Jesús Alou's left fielder–by–default role, and while the switch-hitting Henderson demonstrated all-around breadth of capability, he hit just .225, and left field remained a weakness.

Hart played almost no third base in 1969, and Jim Davenport, now thirty-five, was again asked to handle more than he was able. In the second half, most of the third base playing time went to twenty-five-year-old Tito Fuentes, recalled from the minor leagues and reinvented as a switch hitter. Batting from the left side, Fuentes had no power at all, but he could slap out a decent batting average. He was a stopgap, and third base for the Giants remained a problem. At shortstop Hal Lanier was, yet again, the full-season uncontested regular. He showed no improvement. On the mound starting pitchers Ray Sadecki and Bob Bolin, both excellent in 1968, struggled in '69, rendering the back end of the Giants' rotation another problem.

Yet the 1969 Giants were a strong contender in the newly created National League West Division. They started out hot, finishing April in first place, and spent the year engaged in an intensely close battle for the division flag. Twenty-three-year-old Bobby Bonds, in his first full season, hit thirty-two home runs while stealing forty-five bases in forty-nine attempts, making him just the fourth major leaguer to achieve the "30–30" combination. Bonds also established a new major league record for batters' strikeouts, with 187, and to King's credit, the manager didn't panic over that, just playing Bonds every day, recognizing that even with all the whiffs, on balance he was a terrific performer. Gaylord Perry delivered his best year yet but remained the Giants' second-best pitcher, as Juan Marichal was again brilliant, an All-Star for the eighth straight season, a twenty-game winner for the sixth time in seven years, leading the National League in shutouts and leading the major leagues in ERA and ERA+.

Best of all in 1969 was Willie McCovey, with his greatest year. He hit a career-high .320 and led the National League with 45 home runs and 126 runs batted in, both also personal bests. He led the major leagues in on-base percentage, slugging, OPS, and OPS+. McCovey's OPS+ in 1969 was 209, far above what Mays had achieved in 1965, thus setting a new franchise record.[8] McCovey in 1969 shattered the major league record for intentional walks, with forty-five, breaking the mark of thirty-three set by Ted Williams in 1957.[9] McCovey was voted the National League Most Valuable Player.

The 1969 National League West race was amazingly tight, a five-way free-for-all. Consider the standings at the close of play on Wednesday, September 10: the Giants (78–64) were in first place, with the Cincinnati Reds (76–63) and Atlanta Braves (78–65) in a virtual tie for second, a half-game behind, and the Houston Astros (75–65) and Los Angeles Dodgers (75–65) tied for fourth, two games behind. Over the final three weeks it narrowed down to a two-team fight between the Giants and the Braves, who were led as usual by perennial superstar right fielder Hank Aaron as well as knuckleballing ace pitcher Phil Niekro.

On Monday, September 22, when the Giants took the short flight from San Francisco to San Diego to play the Padres, they'd just swept the Dodgers at Candlestick, and the current standing had the Giants in first and Atlanta in second by a half-game. The first-year Padres were a 48–105 cupcake, desperately struggling to attract fan interest. Their attendance in 1969 would be 512,970, the lowest in the major leagues since 1958. The Monday night game against the Giants drew 4,779, a pitiful showing within vast San Diego Municipal Stadium, an ultramodern baseball and football facility with a seating capacity of well over 60,000.

Willie Mays wasn't in the starting lineup, as he'd played the complete ten innings of the Giants' Sunday win over the Dodgers. Mays had hit 23 home runs in 1968, which brought his career total to 587, second most in major league history behind only Babe Ruth's legendary 714. When Mays had hit his five hundredth in 1965, he joined an elite club whose only prior members were Ruth, Jimmie Foxx, Ted Williams, and Mel Ott. With his six hundredth, Mays would be alone at that pinnacle with the Sultan of Swat, and it was an event widely anticipated by the national sports media.

With his strong start in 1969, it had appeared he'd reach the lofty mark in midsummer. But then came his long power drought; Mays hit number 596 on June 21 but didn't achieve his 597th until August 15. When he delivered number 598 a couple of days later, it did now seem imminent, but then number 599 wouldn't come until September 15.

The Adirondack Bat Company had sent Frank Torre, the retired major league first baseman (and Joe's older brother), to present Mays with some gifts when he hit the milestone homer. Waiting for the moment, Torre followed Mays for six weeks.[10] Now Torre accompanied the Giants down to San Diego, but it looked like another night for waiting, as Mays sat in the dugout.

In the top of seventh the score was tied 2–2, and Ron Hunt led off with a single. Next up was raw rookie George Foster, with just one major league plate appearance under his belt. King called upon Mays to pinch-hit. Rookie right-hander Mike Corkins threw him a first-pitch fastball, and Ron Fimrite reported it in the *San Francisco Chronicle*: "In the privacy of San Diego's Municipal Stadium, the great center fielder—staggered by injuries, haunted by the specter of old age and the taunts of critics who have been burying him for the better part of four years— lofted a 391-foot home run to the empty left field seats. . . . As Mays rounded the bases, the tiny crowd rose to its feet and gave him the reception that rightfully should have been his from a far greater multitude."[11]

The entire Giants dugout swarmed onto the field and gleefully greeted Mays at home plate. "It was my most satisfying home run," he said after the game, "because of all those guys waiting for me when I crossed home. There was nobody left on the bench. That really got to me." Mays acknowledged that he had been trying too hard and the pressure had affected him. He waved off the possibility of reaching Ruth's record. He was just glad the team won the game.

The only man happier than Mays was Frank Torre, who estimated that he'd seen forty games, traveled twelve thousand miles, and spent $4,200 waiting for the historic swing. Not expecting Mays to pinch-hit, Torre almost missed it entirely, but he scurried onto the field to present Mays with his awards: a trophy made up of three bats on a plaque with the number 600 tying the bat-handles together at the top, a $12,500 Italian sports car, and a share of Adirondack stock for each foot the ball had traveled; at $9 a share, it was a $3,519 clout. Said Mays, "I'm just glad Torre can go back to his family."[12]

Mays's two-run homer gave the Giants the lead, and they won 4–2. But the Braves won too, in Houston, and the Giants' first place margin remained just a half-game. That would be the high point of the season. The Giants dropped the next two games to the lowly Padres, while the Braves completed a sweep of the Astros to move into first, and they never looked back. Atlanta wouldn't lose again until the final day of the regular season, after they'd clinched. The Giants had a good September, at 16–11, but the Braves were a blistering 20–6, with five of the wins recorded by Niekro.

The Giants' run of four consecutive second-place finishes from 1965 through 1968 was unprecedented in major league history, and now their bitter fate was to add a fifth. Being in the thick of the 1969 division race through September had been good for attendance at Candlestick Park, but it was still just 873,603, ninth best in the twelve-team National League. And in the season's two final games, Wednesday and Thursday afternoon dates against the Padres after the Giants were eliminated, drew 2,184 and 1,995. Horace Stoneham would stand pat no more. This was a harsh new economic reality, and many changes were on the way.

Chub Feeney had loyally and effectively served as Horace Stoneham's vice president since his graduation from college in the 1940s. It isn't easy to describe exactly what Feeney's job was. He's usually named as the Giants' "general manager," but in the specific major league baseball usage of that term, it isn't accurate—Stoneham himself handled *that* role—but Feeney might be understood as the organization's general manager in the general industry sense of the title, in a business sense. Feeney was the top executive in charge of the operation, first advisor to the president, and accountable for all administration. He was liked and respected, inside and outside the Giants organization, for his integrity and competence and his pleasant good humor. He wasn't a bold thinker or an innovator; Feeney just got everything that needed to get done *done*, without drama or difficulty. That's a truly valuable executive asset. Feeney's contribution to the success of the Giants in the 1950s and '60s was immense. Horace Stoneham deeply understood this, and Feeney knew he did, and their relationship was always close and mutually respectful.

It was, of course, more than a professional relationship; it was familial and loving. But the bond between them was uncle to nephew, not father to son. Feeney understood that too. He understood that when Pete Stoneham was brought into the organization in the early 1950s, Pete was being groomed as the successor. As the years passed and Pete proved ever more incapable of assuming a position of serious responsibility, perhaps Feeney might have begun to think that he would become Uncle Horace's successor. If so, once Stoneham's son-in-law, Chuck Rupert, was hired into the family business in 1967, that idea would have gone out the window. Chub Feeney was nothing if not a realist. He knew where he stood.

Yet Feeney never issued a syllable of complaint or a hint of dissatisfaction. This was in keeping with his sense of decorum and loyalty but also, no doubt, because he never actually felt unhappy. Chub Feeney loved the Giants, loved his uncle, and loved his job. But Feeney was good at math, and the Giants' financial numbers in the late 1960s weren't captivating. And when a very special opportunity arose for Feeney in late 1968, an opportunity that would require him to leave the Giants organization, Feeney pursued it, and his uncle fully supported him in that pursuit.

The fourth commissioner of baseball following the iconic original, Judge Kenesaw Mountain Landis, was retired United States Air Force lieutenant General William D. "Spike" Eckert. Commissioner Eckert's office had a peculiar history. Baseball owners had never been happy with Landis because the judge believed that he did, and should, wield supreme authority. In the aftermath of the Black Sox scandal, ownership recognized that they had no choice but to accept Landis, and once they had him, they had to stick with him. So they did until his death in 1944. When Landis passed away, the owners were eager to replace him with a commissioner more ready to act in their service.

The man they chose was United States senator Albert B. "Happy" Chandler of Kentucky. He was hired to be a political fixer, as professional baseball understood the seriousness of potential legal challenges to their antitrust exemption. But Chandler's appeal quickly wore thin. He totally botched baseball's first big television contract: in 1949 Chandler sold World Series TV rights to shaving razor company Gillette for six years at $1 million annually. Gillette then turned around and resold the rights to NBC, for $4 million a year. St. Louis Cardinals owner Fred Saigh took to calling Chandler "the blue-grass jackass." Saigh, together with Yankees co-owners Dan Topping and Del Webb, engineered Chandler's ouster in 1950.[13]

Taking his place was Ford C. Frick, a onetime sportswriter who'd been president of the National League since 1934. Frick understood exactly what the owners wanted in a commissioner— which was not much at all—and he provided it to their great satisfaction. Frick busied himself with enforcing routine rules, taking care of administrative details, and giving little offense. Frick retired in 1965 after two terms, saving his only notes of criticism for the end. In his farewell address Frick strongly recommended that the owners put some teeth back into the office of commissioner, and he frankly admitted problems in the business, admonishing his employers: "So long as the owners and operators refuse to look beyond the day and the hour; so long as clubs and individuals persist in gaining personal headlines through public criticism of their associates; so long as baseball people are unwilling to abide by the rules they themselves make; so long as expediency is permitted to replace sound judgment, there can be no satisfactory solution."[14]

In the annals of wise parting words, if this ranked somewhere up there with President Eisenhower's 1961 warning about the looming military-industrial complex, it would be paid about the same heed.[15] Indeed, the complacency of most ownerships in this period brings to mind a quote from Charlie Finley, who found his fellow owners every bit as exasperating as they regarded him. Finley offered this acidly sarcastic advice on the best way to curry favor within the community of owners: "Do not go into any league meeting looking alert and awake; slump down like you've been out all night and keep your eyes half closed, and when it is your turn to vote you ask to pass. Then you wait and see how the others vote, and you vote the same way. Suggest no innovations. Make no efforts at change. That way you will be very popular with your fellow owners."[16]

To replace Frick, the owners hired Spike Eckert. He had an impressive record as a logistics and supply expert in the military. This was no small deal, but it didn't translate into competence within the unique economic and social space occupied by major league baseball. Eckert's low-profile ineffectuality came to symbolize baseball's increasingly "out of it" image in the late 1960s. At a time when the charismatic Pete Rozelle was leading the National Football League to new heights of popularity and top ratings on TV, Eckert had zero sense of marketing. Nor did he have any clue about labor relations, this at a time when Major League Baseball Players Association executive director Marvin Miller was bringing that issue to the fore. Eckert didn't even know baseball; he required his assistant Lee MacPhail (Larry's son) to sit in on his phone calls, and explain to him what was going on. After three years of this, Walter O'Malley had seen enough. At the December 1968 winter meetings he orchestrated Eckert's "retirement," and like the good soldier he was, Eckert went quietly.[17]

O'Malley was the most influential of all baseball owners—at least, that is, within the National League. His favored candidate to be the next commissioner was none other than Chub Feeney. This was a many-layered situation, and on one layer the arrangement was an act of mutual tribute between the old rivals-partners O'Malley and Stoneham. In Feeney, Stoneham gave O'Malley a quietly effective, NL-friendly commissioner, and in return O'Malley gave the financially strapped Stoneham a gracious exit ramp for his most appreciated nephew.

For his part Stoneham was proud, even honored, that his nephew and protégé might attain such a high office and no doubt felt that his own Pop would have been proud, indeed, to see the family legacy extended so prominently. Stoneham was committed to what was best for his nephew, and this would be the best for everyone—because on another inescapable layer, cutting an executive salary from the Giants' payroll would seriously help. Reality was being responsibly faced all around.

In December 1968 the owners convened a special meeting at the O'Hare Airport Hilton Hotel in Chicago to elect their new commissioner. It didn't go as O'Malley had hoped. The National League was firmly lined up behind Feeney, but American League owners instead solidly backed Mike Burke, the New York Yankees' president.

Feeney and Burke were entirely different personalities, and those differences were reflective of the two leagues. Though Feeney was still a relatively young man of forty-seven, as Stoneham's nephew he'd long moved comfortably within baseball's old-boy circles. Burke, fifty-two, had been in baseball only since 1964, when CBS, for whom he was a vice president, purchased the Yankees. Burke wore his hair in a fashionably longish cut and presented a long and colorful résumé: the OSS, the CIA, Ringling Brothers, and CBS. The National League owners disdainfully called him "the circus guy."

The meeting began at 4:15 p.m. and went through round after round of deadlocked votes. A commissioner needed 75 percent approval from both leagues, and it seemed hopeless. The arguments went on and on and on. At 4:55 a.m., after nineteen ballots, they gave up.[18]

They would try again in February 1969, this time in Bal Harbour, Florida. Immediately, however, the Feeney-Burke stalemate reappeared, and it was obvious that neither of them was going to be able to be elected. O'Malley then proposed the name of Bowie Kuhn, the National League's assistant legal counsel, and it was Kuhn whom the owners chose, on a one-year contract. Chub Feeney's bid to become commissioner of baseball fell short, and he stayed with the Giants.

However, Feeney's esteem among National League owners was such that less than a year later, when league president Warren Giles announced his retirement at the 1969 winter meetings, Feeney was promptly elected as his replacement. Stoneham's nephew was elected by unanimous acclaim and given a four-year contract at $75,000 per year.

Chub Feeney said farewell to the Giants after all.[19] A most significant page was turned. There would be more.

Candlestick Park had laid an egg in its initial public reception in 1960, and nothing had happened since to improve its sad reputation. The weather was still dreadful. Access to the parking lot was still a choke point, and the lot itself, asphalt struggling to coat dirt-and-gravel fill over tidal salt marsh, still never really drained or settled. The stadium entry ramps were still as steep and the amenities still as Soviet-bloc joyless.

When the Giants had featured the incomparable Willie Mays at his peak, presenting epic pennant race marathons and climactic showdowns against peak Sandy Koufax and the extraordinary mid-1960s Dodgers—and, of course, when there was no other major league baseball locally available—the Giants had regularly drawn a million and a half per year, as fans just bundled up and lived with the grim Candlestick setting, focusing on the extraordinary action on the field.

Beginning in 1968, the calculation changed. Now Candlestick had to stand up to scrutiny in direct comparison to the Oakland Coliseum, and it wasn't a pretty picture. While the two ballparks were only about nine miles apart, directly across the bay, the complex geography of the Bay Area creates remarkably diverse mini-climates, and at the Coliseum—located at the southeast frontier of the Oakland city limits, cozily protected from much of the bay's wind and fog behind Bay Farm Island and Alameda Island—the weather was distinctly and reliably nicer than Candlestick's. Getting into and out of the Coliseum parking lot was far more efficient than the process at Candlestick, and the Coliseum, a half-decade more modern in design in a period when the architecture of sports stadiums was in a state of revolutionary advance, was just a more sleek and smooth facility.

Thus, an irreducible constant in the competitive dynamic between the Giants and Athletics in the Bay Area was the mismatch in the contest between venues. And for fans residing at more or less equal distance from both ballparks—in other words, for most fans in San Jose and the Santa Clara Valley, the region within the Bay Area now growing at a much faster rate than either San Francisco or Oakland—the decision of which game to attend could readily be influenced by the quality of the ballpark experience, and to that extent the Giants were weighted with a permanent competitive drag.[20]

But as the 1970s dawned, there was a glimmer of hope in that regard. The City of San Francisco had committed to a major renovation of Candlestick Park, for the NFL-driven purpose of converting the facility into the full-time home of the San Francisco 49ers as well as the Giants.[21] The existing V-shaped double-decked grandstand would be fully enclosed with a wraparound second deck, expanding seating capacity to greater than sixty thousand. The dramatically remodeled configuration held out the promise, or at least the possibility, of less penetration by wind and fog. (It would have little effect.) The construction would take place in two phases, one prior to and one following the 1970 baseball season. Phase 1 converted the natural grass playing field to artificial turf, marking Candlestick as the fifth National League ballpark so carpeted by 1970.[22]

Ballparks aside, the Giants did hold some meaningful advantages in the competition with the A's. Charlie Finley, for all of his enthusiasm for zany promotions—for reasons unknown, he tirelessly presented a mule named "Charlie O" as his team's mascot, and he installed a mechanical "rabbit" that rose from its lair in an underground box behind home plate to replenish the umpire's supply of fresh baseballs, thus solving a problem no one had ever diagnosed—Finley somehow never grasped the far deeper strategic importance of broad-based marketing, especially radio and television broadcasting. He did broadcast his games (indeed, twenty-five A's road games were televised each year, against seventeen for the Giants) but only on low-budget local outlets with far less reach than those of the Giants. Radio station KSFO, the Giants flagship, itself had a powerful signal and drew enormous ratings and also operated under the umbrella of Gene Autry's Golden West Broadcasting network, on whose affiliated stations the Giants' broadcasts blanketed Northern California and even reached into Nevada. Television station KTVU, which carried the Giants' games, was another Bay Area institution and ratings powerhouse. Russ Hodges and Lon Simmons were huge celebrities in the Bay Area, while the A's primary broadcaster, Monte Moore, imported by Finley from Kansas City, was unable to establish much of an image beyond Finley-loyal homer, and he worked with a different second banana each year.[23] As a result, the cultural foothold the Giants already held, having a ten-year head start on the Athletics in the Bay Area, remained deep and strong.

There's no better illustration of the authentic bond the Giants had successfully established than a fan club that formed in the late 1960s, calling itself the "Giant Boosters." The brainchild of a Bay Area insurance man named Allan Murray, the Boosters were quite something. They not only vigorously cheered for the Giants; they traveled with them—at first on tours to Arizona for spring training, then alongside the team on road trips throughout the regular season. Comprised of many women as well as men, the typical Booster was old enough to well remember the repeal of alcohol prohibition and staunchly dedicated to that event's continued celebration. Jack Kane, who managed the Giants' hospitality operations at Casa Grande, asked Stoneham: "Where'd you get this group? They're not only older than you are, but they drink more!" In fact, the Boosters became the largest and most enthusiastic organized fan club in baseball, and they adored their Giants. Said one of the Giants' enthusiastically back-slapped players, "Christ, they never sleep!"[24]

It's important to understand that the Boosters arose organically and independently from the Giants organization. They weren't a creation of the Giants' marketing department; indeed, the team's interaction with the Boosters was largely reactive. The Giants' fan base in this case did its own marketing. To be sure, the team did mount a marketing campaign: Garry Schumacher came with the organization from New York as the director of public relations, and in San Francisco they established a group sales effort headed by John Taddeucci. But it was old-fashioned, low-budget, and not sophisticated. A direct mail campaign to potential season ticket buyers, employing a full-color multipage brochure and a fresh slogan ("Baseball's Most Exciting Team"), wouldn't be undertaken until 1971.[25] In 1969 the Giants outdrew the A's, 870,000 to 780,000, but that was small comfort. The teams' combined attendance of 1.65 million was a healthy figure, but by splitting it in half, neither was going to be able to thrive.

In the December 1969 winter meetings in Bal Harbour, while his nephew was being drafted by the National League, Stoneham was busy with trade talks. He completed three deals, with the San Diego Padres, New York Mets, and Seattle Pilots (soon to become the Milwaukee Brewers), in which the Giants surrendered mid-tier pitchers Ray Sadecki, Bob Bolin, and Ron Herbel, along with some fluff for, well, mostly a bunch of fluff; the best talents acquired were pitcher Frank Reberger and infielder Bob Heise, neither of whom was much. But that wasn't the point; the point was payroll trimming while simultaneously clearing room for the organization's emerging crop of youngsters.

More payroll trimming occurred at the conclusion of 1970 spring training, when the club decisively committed to Dick Dietz as the fully regular catcher, instead of continuing to alternate him in tandem with Jack Hiatt, who was sold to Montreal. The pattern continued. In May the Giants traded twenty-nine-year-old relief ace Frank Linzy to the Cardinals for twenty-six-year-old right-hander Jerry Johnson, who was neither as accomplished a pitcher as Linzy nor as well-paid. In July thirty-one-year-old Mike McCormick was traded to the Yankees for twenty-three-year-old left-hander John Cumberland, whose salary was about one-fifth that of McCormick.

Part of the Giants' spring training schedule in 1970 involved another tour of Japan, playing exhibition games before larger paying crowds could be attracted in the Cactus League. This money-making endeavor had an unhappy chapter, however, when Juan Marichal came down with an ear infection and then suffered a severe allergic reaction to the penicillin he was prescribed. Marichal became very sick and missed the rest of spring training and the first two and a half weeks of the regular season. He then pushed himself back into action before he was fully recovered, performed badly, and exacerbated the problem.

Marichal's malady was just the beginning of the problems confounding the Giants' pitching staff in 1970. Indeed, the Giants' bland appearance in the league standings that year—they finished with an 86–76 record, in third place in the National League West—failed to reveal what a peculiar season the team had experienced. The 1970 Giants presented a tremendous offense, nearly as robust as the historically great Giants hitting teams of 1962 and 1963 and very comparable in productivity (though not in sheer power) to the 1947 Windowbreakers back in New York. Simultaneously, the team's pitching in 1970 was bad, and its fielding was worse, so in run prevention they were dreadful.

Willie McCovey and Bobby Bonds both delivered great years, and they were joined as prolific run producers by thirty-nine-year-old Willie Mays (enjoying another big rebound season, as he had in 1968), Ken Henderson (blossoming into well-rounded excellence), and Dietz (the best-hitting catcher in the majors in 1970). The Giants' pitching staff included two strong performers— Gaylord Perry, the great workhorse ace, and forty-year-old reliever Don McMahon, a 1969 stretch-run pickup who somehow avoided the salary purge—but beyond them were various degrees of pitiful. Meanwhile, three Giant defenders were the worst in the majors at their positions: catcher Dietz, second baseman Ron Hunt (whose limited range was rudely exposed by the new and fast Candlestick Park artificial turf), and third baseman Jim Ray Hart (reinstalled as the regular in the second half, in a dazzling display of hope over experience).

No single game better encapsulates the Giants' 1970 season than the one on Saturday afternoon, May 23, against the last-place San Diego Padres at Candlestick Park in front of 15,536. The

Giants jumped out to an 8–0 lead after two innings but allowed the Padres to storm right back, and by the fourth it was 8–7. The Giants took a 10–8 lead into the eighth before surrendering five more to give the Padres a 13–10 advantage. Back and forth the slugfest continued, going into extra innings tied at 14–14. In the eleventh the Padres took a 16–14 lead, only to see the Giants retie it in the bottom of the inning, before the Padres emerged victorious at last, 17–16, in fifteen innings. The ridiculous game featured not just thirty-three runs but forty-four hits—with nine home runs, twenty-two walks, and four errors—and it consumed five and a half hours.

That evening Horace Stoneham fired Clyde King. Stoneham had been considering a managerial change for at least a few weeks; indeed, it may well be the case that King had been on thin ice ever since the blowup with Mays back in 1969. But Stoneham gave his rookie manager the chance to work through that, and the Giants played well over the second half of '69. But the team was not playing well in early 1970. They entered the exceptionally wild game against the Padres with a record of 19–22 and hadn't been over .500 since mid-April. Moreover, King's stock in trade was working with pitchers, and the Giants' staff was a mess. The Giants were on pace to surrender nearly one thousand runs, more than any major league team had allowed since the 1930s. If nothing else, this was embarrassing.

To replace King, Stoneham promoted forty-eight-year-old Charlie Fox from Phoenix, where he'd replaced King in 1969. Like King, and every other managerial hire Stoneham had made except Leo Durocher, Fox was a rookie major league manager, but that was the extent of similarities between King and Fox. Apart from his service in the U.S. military in World War II, Fox was an organizational lifer with Stoneham's Giants. A New York City kid who had attended James Monroe High School in the Bronx, "Irish" Fox was signed by the Giants as a catcher in 1942 and played in his only three major league games that September. For the rest of his playing career, which lasted until 1956, Fox never rose above Class B, but beginning in 1947, at the age of twenty-five, he was always a playing manager anyway.

Fox then served the Giants as a scout from 1957 to 1963, managed the Arizona Fall League team from 1963 through 1967, was the manager at AAA Tacoma in 1964, and was a coach under Herman Franks with the major league team from 1965 through 1968. Charlie Fox wasn't just familiar with the history and culture of the Stoneham Giants' organization; he was its walking embodiment. The only curious aspect about his being promoted by Stoneham to manage the major league club in 1970 is why he hadn't been, instead of King, in 1968.

Fox was also very different in personality from the quiet, reserved King. Fox was jovial and high-spirited, the life of the party, and quite happy to drink with Stoneham. He wasn't gruff and crude like Herman Franks, but otherwise, his managerial style was in the Franks mold: Fox was a "players' manager," not a stickler for rules and fines, and just like Franks, he saw it as a top priority to cater to Willie Mays. Upon Fox's appointment, Mays was immediately returned to the assistant manager status he'd enjoyed under Franks and granted every privilege.

The Giants' performance didn't immediately turn around under Fox. But as the season went on, they did better and better, finally gaining some success at run prevention. Marichal in the second half rounded into something like his old form, and Jerry Johnson, the young pitcher acquired in the Frank Linzy trade, began to find a groove as a hard-throwing reliever. In the season's final months Fox benched Ron Hunt and replaced him with Tito Fuentes at second base, restoring defensive competence at that key position.

Stoneham had trimmed the payroll in 1970. Doing so mitigated the team's fiscal emergency but by no means resolved it, as the reduction in revenue just got worse. The Giants' poor start and subsequent lack of title contention (the Cincinnati Reds ran away with the division in 1970) drove Candlestick Park attendance down to its lowest level yet, just 740,000. The only NL teams to draw fewer were the cellar-dwelling San Diego Padres and Philadelphia Phillies.

In December 1970 Stoneham engineered another salary dump, and this one was extremely odd. Ron Hunt was traded to the Montreal Expos for a twenty-seven-year-old minor league journeyman first baseman named Dave McDonald, a marginality with zero chance of making the Giants' big-league roster in 1971. No doubt, Hunt's market value was diminished by his defensive decline, but the notion that Stoneham could attract no better offer than this suggests that he expended little effort at it. In spring training in 1971 McDonald was indeed sent packing, sold directly back to the Expos organization, meaning that all the Giants received in exchange for Ron Hunt—who would play four more years as a first-string major leaguer—was the modest cash value of Dave McDonald's contract. There can be no characterization of this episode as other than a plain blunder, a lapse in judgment on Stoneham's part. It wouldn't be the last.

The only other major alterations to the roster for 1971 were sourced from within the organization. The key move was Stoneham's decision at the end of spring training to promote twenty-year-old Chris Speier to the majors, with just one year of AA experience, and let Fox install him as the first-string shortstop. Speier's extraordinary defensive ability, especially the quick lateral capacity so important on artificial turf, bowled everyone over, and his rapid emergence at last removed Hal Lanier from the starting lineup. For Speier, born and raised in Alameda and a diehard Giants fan since he was a second grader, it was a dream come true. "We were proud when we put on the Giant uniform because the Giant organization was a solid organization," he would recall. "Mr. Stoneham was a good man and it was almost like a family atmosphere."[26]

The Giants' infield defense would be further strengthened in 1971, indirectly, by the latest setback in the flagging career of twenty-nine-year-old Jim Ray Hart. Hart's bad shoulder took another turn for the worse in the spring of '71, and he would begin the season back in AAA. Hart's chronic injury issue was genuine, but so, by now, were those of his drinking and his weight. So, Fox in 1971 committed at third base to twenty-five-year-old sophomore Alan "Dirty Al" Gallagher, with Lanier as a frequent late-inning defensive replacement. Gallagher was a modestly good singles and doubles hitter with minimal athletic tools, a gritty hustler who, Pete Rose style, sprinted to first base after a base on balls, and he was an average-at-best defensive third baseman—making him far better with the glove than Hart.

Two other rookies made the 1971 Opening Day roster and were deployed by Fox in significant roles. Right-handed pitcher Steve Stone, with just eight games of AAA experience, was inserted into the starting rotation, and George Foster, who'd jumped from A to AAA in 1970, was now the Giants fourth outfielder.

On February 23, 1971, Stoneham received a telegram that no doubt broke his heart. Seventy-eight-year-old secretary Eddie Brannick regretfully informed his boss that due to declining health, he'd decided to retire. When Stoneham made the announcement to the press, his voice quavered with emotion.[27]

Eddie Brannick wasn't just a link to the old New York days; he represented the very core and history of the franchise itself. A product of Hell's Kitchen on the West Side of Manhattan, Brannick had begun his sixty-five-year-career with the Giants as an office boy for John T. Brush, a decade and a half before C. A. Stoneham purchased the franchise. In the 1920s, when Horace Stoneham was performing his apprenticeship in the various offices of the Polo Grounds, it was Brannick serving as his particular mentor. When Horace took over as president, his first move was to promote Brannick to become club secretary. The two had worked closely together for all of Stoneham's adult life.

Brannick was a frantically energetic, singularly eccentric character, straight out of a Damon Runyon yarn. The greatest sportswriters of the mid-twentieth century never tired of marveling about Eddie. In John Drebinger's description:

> He has legions of friends, remembers the birthdays of many of them, yet once couldn't recall the date of his own. A gourmet of rare taste, he knows how and where to dine and will order a meal of excellence only to touch scarcely any of it because he is forever hopping up and down, answering phone calls and attending to the difficulties of others. Attired in the height of fashion with a blazing foulard that will knock your eye out at 40 paces, he thinks nothing

of also wearing a beard two days old, because his whiskers are very tough, he cannot shave himself and he does not find time to sit long enough in a barber's chair to have them removed. And, though he has seen thousands of ball games, he has never sat through a complete game in his life.[28]

Wrote Jimmy Cannon: "He was a dude, from his floppy Panama hat to the two-toned black and white shoes. The sports coats are a boisterous plaid, and his neckties are designed to frighten horses." And in the estimation of Red Smith: "Eddie was a priceless goodwill man for the whole game. He was naturally gregarious with a genuine liking for people. He didn't drink, but he could stay up all night buying. Wherever he went he made friends for baseball and the Giants. He was at home in the New York of Delmonico's and Rector's and in the New York of Jim Moore's, 21, and Toots Shor's. He was also at home in Chicago and St. Louis and Miami. To a lot of people in those towns, he epitomized New York."[29]

Quite unlike Horace Stoneham, Brannick's enormous circle of friends extended far beyond the realm of baseball. He was well known to just about everybody who was anybody in New York, including Broadway actors, politicians, and business big shots. Indeed, when Stoneham came to the decision to move the Giants to San Francisco, it presented a particular dilemma to Brannick, the quintessential New Yorker: how could he leave the place he loved and where he was so loved, yet how could he forsake the Giants, the only employer he'd ever known? He settled on a happy compromise: he and his wife, Kathleen (to whom he would be married for fifty-three years), moved to San Francisco and lived there during the baseball season, but they kept an apartment in Manhattan and spent the off-seasons there. Quickly, Brannick was as popular in downtown San Francisco as he would always be in New York.

In 1963 Brannick came down with pneumonia, causing him to miss spring training for the first time since 1916. He recovered and returned to work, but he cut back on his traveling schedule, and for his last several years with the Giants he handled few more serious responsibilities than merrily chatting it up with everyone over great meals. But Stoneham wouldn't dream of cutting Brannick from the payroll until he voluntarily retired. Eddie and Kathleen moved to West Palm Beach, Florida, where he would pass away in 1975.

Losing his nephew Chub Feeney from his inner circle had been hard enough for Stoneham, but losing Brannick might have been even harder. Of course, no one knew better than Horace Stoneham that nothing lasts forever, that change is inevitable, but knowing a hard truth is one thing, and living through it is another.

On the first pitch thrown to him in the 1971 season, Willie Mays blasted the 629th home run of his career.[30] He would hit four homers in the season's first four games. Twenty years after his big-league debut, Mays was off to one of his hottest starts, and the team was right with him. They won twelve of their first fourteen and finished April at 18–5, their best since 1962.

On Thursday evening, May 6, 1971, Horace Stoneham hosted a huge party in celebration of Mays's fortieth birthday. The event was held in the Grand Ballroom of the Fairmont Hotel atop Nob Hill in downtown San Francisco. Tickets were sold for twenty-four dollars per plate, in recognition of Mays's uniform number, with proceeds benefiting the Hunters Point Fund charity. The ballroom was festooned with pennants from all twenty-four major league teams. That Mays was hitting .368 contributed to the theme of the star as a timeless wonder. Some seven hundred celebrants showed up to marvel at a front table seating Mays, Hank Aaron (in town with the visiting Atlanta Braves), and Joe DiMaggio. In a rare speech the fifty-six-year-old Yankee Clipper said: "I know you're going to wind up in the Hall of Fame, but I don't know if I'll be around to see you get in. There's a rule, you know, that you have to wait five years after you retire to be elected."

Stoneham felt obligated to say a few words, though he was never comfortable as a public speaker. In brief remarks he had difficulty controlling his deep emotions and almost broke down. In his turn to speak the always-composed Chub Feeney said,

"Those of us who saw him break in 20 years ago have all grown older, but he hasn't." San Francisco supervisor Dianne Feinstein presented Mays with a plaque that read, "Mr. Mays, you are a very bright light in San Francisco." Charlie Fox, in his finest Irish tenor, sang to the tune of "Danny Boy":

Friends may forsake me
Let them all forsake me
I still have you
Willie boy.

The evening's most poignant moment occurred with a remembrance of Russ Hodges, who'd died of a heart attack three weeks earlier, at the age of sixty. Hodges had been the voice of the Giants for twenty-two years and had witnessed all but three of Mays's home runs. Mays was among the first notified of his death. "Willie broke up over the phone," a member of his family told the press. "He couldn't talk." At the birthday celebration Hodges's call of Mays's at bat in Houston in 1965, when he kept fouling off Claude Raymond fastballs until he finally hit the game-tying homer, was dramatically played to a tearful audience.[31]

The day after Mays's party, the Giants began a weekend series at Candlestick against the Braves, in which Mays delivered seven hits, including two home runs, to raise his early-season batting average to .385. Then the National League defending champion Cincinnati Reds came into town for a three-game series, and the Giants swept it. This raised their record to 25–9, the very best in major league baseball.

Predicted by no pundits to play as they were playing, the 1971 Giants were suddenly a big national story. Among those whose attention they attracted was the *New Yorker*'s Roger Angell, who made a cross-country trip to San Francisco to take in the next series against the archrival Dodgers, who along with the rest of the National League West were eating the Giants' dust. Angell reported on large crowds "accoutered in mackinaws, scarves, gloves, and watch caps, and carrying steamer rugs and Thermosed fortifiers" cheerfully trekking into Candlestick Park, normally "an excellent place to avoid—a dour, wind-whipped gray concrete tureen." He witnessed Speier hit his first big-league home run, and on the next pitch Mays hit one too, which "raised the record for most combined home runs by a still active shortstop and center fielder on the same team to 637."[32] Indeed, it was the colorful duo of Speier and Mays taking star turns together that most captivated Angell:

> Chris Speier, I suspect, is a model of baseball's infielder of the future, the AstroPlayer—wide-ranging, with extremely quick hands and the ability to get off deep, rifle-shot throws with almost no visible arm-cocking or wind-up. Old-time Giant front-office men think he may turn out to be the finest Giant shortstop since Travis Jackson, back in the early thirties. (Speier, by the way, is a local product, who still lives at home in Alameda, across the Bay. His 14-year-old brother, Bill, one may imagine, is grappling with something of a sibling problem this year. When a reporter recently asked Speier if Bill gave him much flak at the family's breakfast table, the new star shrugged and said, "Not much. I mean, what can he *say*?")
>
> Candlestick's classic pastime—and the best entertainment in baseball this year—is watching Willie Mays. Now just turned 40, and beginning his 21st year in the majors, he is hitting better than he has hit at any time in the past six or seven seasons, and playing the game with enormous visible pleasure. Veteran curators in the press box like to expound upon various Maysian specialties—the defensive gem, the basket catch, the looped throw, the hitched swing, and so forth. My favorite is his base-running. He may have lost a half-second or so in getting down to first base, but I doubt whether Willie Davis or Ralph Garr or any of the other new flashes can beat Mays from first to third, or can accelerate just as he does, with his whole body suddenly seeming to sink lower when, taking his turn at first and intently following the distant ball and outfielder, he suddenly sees his chance. Watching him this year, seeing him drift across a base and then sink into full speed, I noticed all at once how much he resembles a marvelous skier in midturn down some steep pitch of fast powder. *Nobody* like him.[33]

On Friday night, May 28, 1971, the Giants defeated the Montreal Expos at Candlestick, 3–1. Steve Stone took the win, his fourth, and Jerry Johnson the save, his fifth. The win improved their record to 33–14 and widened their National League West lead to nine and a half games. At precisely the same point in the season, the pennant-winning 1962 Giants were also 33–14.

Obviously, just about everything was going right for the 1971 Giants. The ageless Mays was performing his best in years. McCovey missed some early time with knee trouble but was still hitting a ton, as were Bonds and Dietz. On the mound Marichal and Perry were both cruising, while twenty-three-year-old southpaw Ron Bryant was blossoming in his second full big-league season.

The revamped infield was doing fine. Fuentes was providing solid second base defense, third baseman Gallagher was holding his own, and Speier was displaying startling defense and hitting solidly. The only regular not doing as well or better than expected was left fielder Ken Henderson, who'd missed some time with minor injuries. But Henderson's absences created an extra opportunity for rookie George Foster, who'd appeared in thirty-six of the Giants' forty-seven games, starting twenty-four, and was hitting .267, with five doubles and three homers in 105 at bats.

Then out of the blue, on Saturday, May 29, Stoneham traded Foster to the Cincinnati Reds. In return the Giants received Frank Duffy, a twenty-four-year-old rookie shortstop with twenty-seven major league at bats under his belt, as well as Vern Geishert, a twenty-five-year-old AAA journeyman pitcher.

It was an utterly baffling move. Duffy was a decent prospect but not remotely as good as Chris Speier. The Giants had no role for him other than infield scrub. Foster, meanwhile, had been productively filling a need, and to replace him, Stoneham called up rookie Bernie Williams, who wasn't as good. So, this deal weakened the team in the fourth outfielder role that was having a significant impact, for no purpose. Stoneham can't be faulted for failing to realize that Foster would develop into an MVP-winning superstar; no one predicted that. But everyone in 1971 regarded Foster as a high-potential young player, certainly superior to Duffy. What was Stoneham thinking?

Consider that the Foster-for-Duffy trade bore interesting similarity to another puzzling trade Stoneham had executed back in 1964, when he swapped José Cardenal for Jack Hiatt. In both cases the Giants surrendered a very young, athletic, high-ceiling outfielder in exchange for a decent prospect at a high-skill defensive position—but a position that was already amply filled on the roster, creating a new surplus. In the Cardenal case the explanation was the Giants' concern about his unruly personality, while Foster wasn't like that at all: he was painfully shy, so soft-spoken as to be almost silent.

But there's another thing these two trades had in common: in both cases the Giants traded away a player of color and received a white player in return. This uncomfortable aspect was present in many Giants trades going back more than a decade. Whatever their various talent-for-talent merits, the Black-for-white dynamic was repeated in the Willie Kirkland–for–Harvey Kuenn deal in 1960, Manny Mota–for–Joey Amalfitano in 1962, Felipe Alou–for–Bob Shaw in 1963, Matty Alou–for–Joe Gibbon in 1965, and Orlando Cepeda–for–Ray Sadecki in 1966. Meanwhile, the Giants hadn't traded *for* a significant player of color since the Bill White–for–Sam Jones deal in 1959 (which was Black-for-Black), and never had they made a white-for-Black trade. Because the Giants had been such a pioneering organization in signing and developing players of color, structurally the Giants were presented with greater opportunities for Black-for-white trades than most other teams, but still, the pattern is striking.

This isn't to suggest an overtly racist motivation on Stoneham's part; after all, it was his organization that had signed and developed all of these players of color in the first place. But it does indicate something more subtle, and likely subconscious, shaping Stoneham's perceptions and the perceptions of his inner circle of advisors. George Foster in 1971 was a reticent African American from South-Central Los Angeles, while the freckle-faced Irish American Frank Duffy had a psychology degree from Stanford. Duffy presented an image that Foster simply couldn't match. The *idea* of Frank Duffy was so much more attractive to Stoneham's Giants than that of George Foster that the actual and potential abilities of the two players, and the authentic needs of the team, were obscured.

The Giants completed a rare five-game series sweep of the Montreal Expos to close out the month of May at 37–14, ten and a half games in front. It was a pace, of course, that no team could be expected to sustain. At some point they were bound to hit a rough patch.

These being the Giants, the rough patch arrived precisely as the calendar turned to June: they swooned to eight losses in nine games and played under .500 for the month. The issue was a team-wide hitting slump. Willie McCovey had torn cartilage in his left knee at the end of spring training and opted to play through the pain rather than undergo season-ending surgery. "Every town we went to I had to have it drained because it would swell up as big as my head," McCovey recalled. "I was on medication throughout the year to try to keep the soreness and inflammation to a minimum."[34] He'd hit well in a reduced playing schedule in April and May, but in June he struggled and finally spent a couple of weeks on the disabled list.

Willie Mays played a lot of first base in McCovey's place, but he, too, ran out of steam after his sizzling start. Suddenly looking fatigued, Mays was struggling to catch up with fastballs, striking out far more frequently than ever before. Often getting deep into counts, Mays was also drawing walks at a career-high rate, and on base a lot without McCovey batting behind him, despite his mounting exhaustion, Mays stole bases more readily than he had in a decade. Meanwhile, Mays's fielding at first base was remarkably bad, as time and again his sloppy footwork led to ground balls eating him up.[35]

With Mays often playing first, new call-up Bernie Williams was thrust into the prominent outfield role recently vacated by Foster, and this rookie bombed: in seventy-three June plate appearances, he hit .180 with just two runs batted in. Williams was then sent back to the minors. (Meanwhile, in Cincinnati, Foster took over as the everyday center fielder and performed well.)

In July the good news was that the Giants bats warmed up again. The bad news was that now it was the pitching losing it way. Rookie Steve Stone was in a tailspin, and he, too, was demoted to AAA. Ron Bryant, also struggling after a hot start, would go on the disabled list with a sore elbow, his season essentially over. Top reliever Jerry Johnson, nearly unhittable in the early season, was now arm-weary. The team spent another month treading water, but the second-place Dodgers, after narrowing the Giants' once-huge lead, hit a slump of their own, and by month's end the Giants were back up to a cushion of eight and a half.

On July 30, 1971, Stoneham decided it was time to promote twenty-two-year-old first baseman–outfielder Dave Kingman from Phoenix. Towering (six foot six), broad-shouldered yet slender (210 pounds), Kingman had been drafted just thirteen months earlier off the University of Southern California campus, where he'd helped win the College World Series. Prodigiously powerful, the young Kingman also ran well and had a cannon arm (he'd pitched in high school and college) and had torched minor league pitching: in 602 at bats he'd loudly produced 85 extra-base hits, including 41 home runs—alas, also 169 strikeouts, which limited his minor league batting average to .284. Arriving in the majors, he made a big splash: in his second game Kingman delivered a grand slam and an RBI double.

In the month of August the Giants pitching staff stabilized, as helpful contributions came from young southpaw John Cumberland and rookie right-handers Don Carrithers and Jim Barr. Again, the Dodgers mounted a charge and reduced the gap, but the Giants finished August strongly and entered September with an eight-game division lead.

The Los Angeles Dodgers of 1971 were an interesting ball club. They were of a kind with the pennant-winning Dodger team of 1959, in that they weren't a finished product but, rather, a roster in the midst of a methodical multiyear rebuilding. Following the 1966 peak-career retirement of Sandy Koufax, general manager Buzzie Bavasi traded away nearly all of their veterans. The team took some lumps, dropping out of contention for a few years, but a new foundation was being prepared as the roster was repopulated with talent from the organization's farm.

In 1971 they weren't all the way back, but they were getting close. They still featured several key players from the mid-1960s champions: shortstop Maury Wills, center fielder Willie Davis, starting pitchers Don Sutton and Claude Osteen, ace reliever Jim Brewer, first baseman–outfielder Wes Parker, and infielder Jim Lefebvre. Blended with those familiar faces were shrewd trade acquisitions, including prolific slugger and problematic defender Dick Allen (still known as "Richie" in 1971), veteran starting pitcher Al Downing, veteran catchers Duane "Duke" Sims and old friend Tom Haller, and veteran outfielder–pinch hitter Manny Mota. And then there were the kids, including outfielders Willie Crawford and Bill Buckner; infielders Bobby Valentine, Bill Russell, and Steve Garvey; catcher Joe Ferguson; and pitcher Doyle Alexander. It was a remarkably deep and complicated roster, with seemingly endless lineup options, and extraordinary manager Walt Alston, in his eighteenth season at the Dodger helm, was perhaps never better at making productive use of everyone through multidimensional platooning schemes. The Dodgers in 1971 weren't great, but they were good, and in September they would play at their best.

On Monday, September 6, the Giants breezed into Dodger Stadium for a three-game series. The division lead was eight games with twenty-two left to play, and if the Dodgers were to have any realistic chance, sweeping this series was essential. Sweep it they did, and the Giants' lead was down to five.

A week later, when the Dodgers and Giants met for a two-game series at Candlestick, the lead had shrunk to an uncomfortable three games. The opener was a wild contest featuring multiple hit batsmen, a bench-clearing brawl, and two ejections, and the Dodgers prevailed 5–4. In the next evening's game the Giants rallied from behind and took a 5–3 lead into the ninth inning, but Manny Mota delivered a pinch-hit three-run double, and the Dodgers hung on to win 6–5.

It was a bone crusher for the Giants. They were still in first place, but the margin was now a single flimsy game, and it was plain to see that the Giants were toast. They'd lost nine of their last ten, and the world cringingly awaited news of the latest landing-again-in-second-place fiasco pulled off by the San Francisco Giants.

But that didn't happen. The Giants managed to stagger through the season's final two weeks, winning as many as they lost, and the Dodgers were unable to seize the opportunity to catch them. It came down to the very last day, with the Giants still clinging to a one-game lead. The Dodgers kept the pressure on with a 2–1 win over Houston, while the Giants faced the Padres in San Diego. In a scoreless game Tito Fuentes led off the fourth with a single. Willie Mays was running on fumes, hitting .194 for the month, and had struck out eight times in his past thirteen at bats. But here he clouted one off the center field wall for an RBI double, and the Giants led 1–0. One out later, Kingman blasted a two-run homer, and it was 3–0. That was more than Juan Marichal would need, as he tossed a five-hit, zero-walk, zero–earned run complete game masterpiece on just eighty-one pitches. The Giants won 5–1, nailing down the division title at long last.

From the brink of humiliating disaster in mid-September, the Giants had held off their challenger. Their celebration in the visitors' clubhouse in San Diego was understandably raucous, in joyful relief from the tension and worry of the past several weeks. They sprayed champagne, romped around, and happily denigrated the Dodgers. "They kept saying we were a dead horse," Marichal said. "Who's dead now?" Dick Dietz gleefully shouted into the KSFO microphone. "The Dodgers can go to HELL!"

Reporters clustered around Mays. When Kingman poured champagne over his head, all the plainly exhausted Mays could do was wipe it from his eyes. He spoke almost as if he were watching another team. "Let them celebrate," he said. "That's for the kids. I'm really happy for them. We're not there yet. They don't think like me. We still got the Pirates to worry about."

Mays ran his hand over his sunken face. "Man, this was a long time coming." Asked if he was tired, he could barely speak the words. "Oh, man, I've been so tired for the last month or so. Everybody on the team's known it, but I had to play. I had to be in there. These kids need me. They come to me and I go to them with advice. Some of them look on me as their father."

McCovey paid homage. "You know who I'm happiest for?" he said. "Willie. He played too much. He played when I couldn't because one of us had to be in there."[36]

The National League East Division champion Pittsburgh Pirates, whom the Giants would face in the best-three-of-five National League Championship Series (LCS), were a formidable opponent. Unlike the Giants, they hadn't led their division wire to wire, but after taking possession of first place in June, they'd never been threatened. Since May the Giants had gone 53–58 and the Pirates 68–46, and in September the Giants were 11–16, while the Pirates were 16–9. Moreover, since Pittsburgh hadn't been forced to grind it out to the last day, manager Danny Murtaugh had been able to give his regulars some rest and get his pitching rotation set up, while the Giants came in ragged.

The Pirates' two best players in 1971 were the same two future Hall of Famers from back in 1966: right fielder Roberto Clemente and left fielder Willie Stargell. But the cast around them was different now, and deeply talented, including line drive hitters Manny Sanguillen, Al Oliver, and Richie Hebner; slugger Bob Robertson; solid starting pitchers Steve Blass and Dock Ellis; and relief ace Dave Giusti. Prognosticators heavily favored Pittsburgh in this matchup.

The resilient Giants gave them a battle. In the first game, on a sunny Saturday at Candlestick Park before 40,977, Blass was dominant, with nine strikeouts in the first four innings. But in the bottom of the fifth, holding a 2–1 lead over Gaylord Perry, with two outs, Blass faced Tito Fuentes with a runner on base. Batting from the left side against the right-hander Blass—the side from which Fuentes had virtually no power and instead relied on just slapping grounders—Fuentes nonetheless lofted a soft, harmless-looking fly ball down the right field line that somehow carried *just barely* over the fence for a silly-looking two-run homer, and the Giants suddenly had a 3–2 lead. Mays then drew a walk, and up stepped McCovey. As if to say, "I'll show you a *real* home run," McCovey launched a rocket into the newly constructed movable football seats high above right field. Roger Angell described it as an "intercontinental ballistic missile," whose velocity was terrifying to behold. The Giants now led 5–2. Perry, who didn't have his best stuff, bent but never broke, going the distance as the Giants hung on to win 5–4.[37]

But the Giants were running out of options. A worn-out John Cumberland, who hadn't lasted beyond the fifth inning in either of his final two regular season starts, took the mound in game two, and this time he was knocked out in the fourth. Bob Robertson walloped three home runs, and the Pirates easily took it 9–4 to even up the series. The teams traveled to Pittsburgh, where Marichal pitched well, but surrendered solo homers to Robertson and Hebner, while the Giants were stifled by Pirates starter Bob Johnson, and the Bucs won 2–1. Much critical attention in this close game was focused on Mays, for his impromptu attempt at a sacrifice bunt with a runner on second and nobody out in the sixth inning. It was not a good look. The next day an exhausted Perry took a beating, the Pirates romped 9–5, and it was over.

So, 1971 was a semi-triumphant season. Adding to the bittersweet mood was the sense that the deep physical and mental stress borne by the wondrous Willie Mays this year had taken a hard and lasting toll. He'd received about ten cortisone shots during the year. On June 1 he was hitting .340 with twelve homers; the rest of the way he hit .230 with six, and over the closing three weeks of the regular season, Mays went six for fifty-two (.115) while striking out twenty-three times.

The night before the final game of the regular season, Giant trainer Leo "Doc" Hughes was ready to give him another injection for the bursitis in his right shoulder, which had not only inhibited his throwing but prevented him from holding his bat properly aloft. Mays refused because he would have to wait twenty-four hours to play, and he had no intention of sitting out the finale. By the end of the League Championship Series, Mays couldn't muster the energy to fly home from Pittsburgh with the team, choosing solitude. Tito Fuentes recalled: "I believe he was hurt and embarrassed. It ate him alive, and he wanted to think about it."[38]

Roger Angell, who'd written so glowingly of Mays when he'd

watched him back in the heady days of May, expressed shock and sorrow at the Mays he was now observing in the League Championship Series, who'd seemingly aged years in just a few months' time:

> A missing name in this account, it may be noticed, is that of Willie Mays. He played in all four games and did not exactly or entirely fail: two doubles, one homer, a stolen base, four hits. But these totals do not suggest the true level of his contribution, and by this, for once, I mean that he was less of a player than the statistics suggest—a much older player, who looked every year and month of his 40 years; a player gone quite gray-faced with exhaustion and pain and the pressures of leadership. Willie had seen all of his early-season triumphs worn away. . . . During the playoffs, after I had seen Mays taking called third strikes or trying to bunt his way aboard or slicing a weak little pop hit on a fastball he could no longer get around on, I began—for the first time in my life, and with enormous sadness— not to want him to come up to the plate. I dreaded it, in fact, and I was embarrassed by the feeling, and ashamed of myself. But I still feel the same way, and I think it should be said: Hang them up, Willie, please. Retire.[39]

The possibility that Horace Stoneham ever read these particular words is quite low, as Stoneham was, shall we say, not a regular reader of the *New Yorker*. But Stoneham watched exactly the same series that Angell did, and indeed, Stoneham had observed, undoubtedly with anguish, Mays's struggles while playing hurt, in 1967, in 1969, and again over so much of the intense season of 1971. Stoneham knew that Mays wasn't ready to retire, and Stoneham didn't want him to. Nonetheless, Stoneham knew that reality was beckoning. He considered what he should do.

14

I Never Thought I Would Trade Willie

Gaylord Perry was very big and very strong and, his spitball notwithstanding, still threw damn hard. At the age of thirty-two, in 1971, he'd delivered a season that would be considered terrific by any pitcher except one of his exceptional quality. He was fourth in the league in innings pitched and eighth in earned run average and overall clearly among the league's elite starting pitchers. But Perry's own standard was indeed extraordinary, and in that rarified light his 1971 performance suggested a couple of points of concern: both his complete game rate and his strikeout rate were down from previous years.

Sam McDowell was four years younger than Perry and even bigger and stronger, six foot five and 220 pounds. "Sudden Sam" was one of the very hardest throwers of the era, comparable in velocity with Sandy Koufax, Dick Radatz, and Bob Veale. Since bursting into stardom at the age of twenty-two in 1965, he'd led the American League in strikeouts five times and made six All-Star teams. His success at winning games was less consistent, though much of that could be attributed to toiling for unimpressive Cleveland Indians teams. He'd enjoyed peak form seasons in 1968, '69, and '70 but tailed off badly in '71.

McDowell's uneasy 1971 season began with a five-day holdout in spring training and a threat to retire. He was demanding a salary of $100,000. After bitter and extended negotiations with (interestingly enough) Cleveland general manager Alvin Dark—serving in an old-school dual GM–field manager role— McDowell signed a contract with a base of just $72,000 but laden with performance-based incentives. However, Dark was ignorant of the fact that such contracts were illegal under the collectively bargained contract rules of major league baseball, and on June 11 McDowell's contract was voided by Commissioner Kuhn. (Kuhn also voided similar incentive-laden contracts of fellow Cleveland players Ken Harrelson, Graig Nettles, and Vada Pinson.)

A couple of weeks after Kuhn's ruling, McDowell left the team and was placed under suspension. His contention was that since the contract had been voided, he should be declared a free agent. When he realized that wouldn't happen, he signed a new deal for a flat $75,000, and returned. But shortly thereafter, McDowell again left the club. The Indians suspended him again and filed a grievance under the contract with the Major League Baseball Players Association (MLBPA). After ten days McDowell again returned.

At another point in 1971 McDowell was fined $1,000 for "rowdyism" on the team bus going from the Los Angeles airport to Anaheim. The Indians then prohibited the consumption of alcohol on all future team flights.[1]

If Gaylord Perry's 1971 statistics subtly suggested reasons for concern going forward, McDowell's stat line was festooned with red flags. His complete game rate and his strikeout rate were both down even more significantly than Perry's, and quite unlike Perry, McDowell's walk rate, always high, soared to a completely unsustainable major league–worst level in 1971, twice what it had been as recently as 1969. Plus, there was that being suspended and rowdy drinking stuff.

Yet on November 29, 1971, the Giants traded Perry—along with none other than infielder Frank Duffy—to Cleveland in exchange for Sudden Sam McDowell. There was no payroll factor in the deal, as both Perry and McDowell were commanding $75,000 contracts. Many observers pointed to the four-year age difference as a key advantage gained by the Giants while failing to note that Perry had routinely been more durable than McDowell, especially in 1971.

In this trade Stoneham guessed terribly wrong, both that the ultra-durable Perry was nearing the end of his productive years and that the hard-throwing, hard-drinking McDowell had big seasons yet to come. Few deals in baseball history have turned out as disastrously as this one.[2] To be fair, no observers at the time predicted McDowell's imminent collapse, and no one could have foreseen just how exceptional Perry's pitching longevity would be.

This trade can be seen to have something in common with the Foster-for-Duffy acquisition: it was made less on the basis of logical analysis of the talent involved or of the team's needs than it was on the basis of the comparative images of the players involved. Perry was a dour character, short on charisma, and though he was a remarkable pitcher, he'd never become a particular favorite of Bay Area fans. (Competing for attention with Mays, McCovey, and Marichal had much to do with that.) McDowell, wild in his pitches and his behavior, was perceived by Stoneham as a much more exciting figure, a strikeout king and a headline grabber. In acquiring McDowell, Stoneham's Giants were capturing the *idea* of a flashy, young fastballing ace. The reality of McDowell's physical and mental condition was not so attractive, but Stoneham was too dazzled by the image to pay attention and perform due diligence in scouting and vetting.

In the spring of 1972 baseball encountered its first player strike of the twentieth century. The issue at stake wasn't free agency nor even anything having to do with salaries. The Major League Baseball Players Association and baseball's owners were at odds over ownership's rate of annual contributions to the union's old-age pension fund. The players' request was to increase the owners' annual contribution to the plan to keep pace with inflation. The difference between the players' proposal and the owners' counteroffer was $400,000 per year in pension fund contributions. Even in 1972 dollars, these amounts of money weren't large. In purely economic terms the disputed pension funding wasn't really a huge deal to the players, nor did it represent a significant expense to the owners. But it quickly became clear that for both sides the economic particulars weren't really the issue. What was really at stake for both sides was the principle of the matter. In the spring of 1972 relations between players and owners had reached a state in which "backing down" was for both sides an entirely unacceptable option.

The executive director of the MLBPA was Marvin Miller. Prior to his arrival in 1966, the union had been ineffectual, and while Miller hadn't yet been able to accomplish many tangible gains in his tenure, he'd brought erudite professionalism and a sense of focus and clarity to the union. Before he arrived, ownership had regarded the MLBPA in a bemused, condescending manner. Miller refused to be patronized, and his mature, persistent presence was a key factor in fostering a palpable change in the temper of the players, who became far less compliant than before. The owners resented Miller for this, and if the one thing he'd achieved by 1972 was to earn their ill will, that was an achievement that earned him the respect of many players.[3]

Most owners felt that the players had no right to behave in the manner they were, and they were angry, spoiling for a fight. If the players were actually going to be foolish enough to strike over the silly pension issue, then the owners were eager to have them do so; this would be the opportunity for the owners to humiliate and weaken Miller and the MLBPA and perhaps even break the union once and for all.[4] St. Louis Cardinals owner August "Gussie" Busch put it plainly on March 22: "We voted unanimously to take a stand. We're not going to give them another goddamn cent. If they want to strike—let 'em."[5]

All of this put Horace Stoneham in an awkward spot. He was certainly not among the snarling hard-liner faction of owners. Indeed, Stoneham had spent his career avoiding adversarial relationships with his players, and he held as a point of pride that his reputation among players had long been genuinely positive, that he was regarded as respectful in contract negotiations and generous in his provision of accommodations and amenities. The last thing he sought was an angry confrontation with the union. But neither, of course, had Stoneham ever been a rebel within the community of owners; he'd always gone along with the majority sentiment, and the majority sentiment was dead set against compromise. On top of that, with his financial distress in recent years, Stoneham was in no position of influence. He fretfully went along with his fellow owners.

What those owners failed to properly comprehend was the mood of the players. Busch's bellicose quotation, printed in the newspapers, was tacked up on clubhouse bulletin boards throughout the Grapefruit and Cactus Leagues. It was passed along by word of mouth, becoming more provocative with each retelling. The players were coming to a boil.[6] They were fully aware that the $400,000 in dispute was a trivial sum in the context of the many millions of dollars of MLB revenues. They were increasingly resentful that modest and reasonable proposals such as this invariably prompted bitter and bombastic reactions. The players were fed up with having affordable suggestions rejected as catastrophic, and they were fed up with not being treated with basic respect.

Despite Miller's recommendation to keep negotiating, on March 31 the player representatives, gathered in Dallas, unanimously voted to strike.[7] The next day the first work stoppage in modern U.S. sports history began. Opening Day of 1972 was postponed. As Miller had warned, the striking players received withering criticism from the press and public. Even former star big-league players blasted Miller and the striking players; one of them, Robin Roberts, had been instrumental in leading the early players' union.[8]

In a strange twist the Giants' player representative to the MLBPA in the spring of 1972 was none other than Willie Mays. The highly paid superstar had never been much involved in union activity, but with both the Giants' previous player rep (Gaylord Perry, traded in November) and the alternate (Hal Lanier, sold to the Yankees in February) absent, it was Mays stepping up to help his teammates and his union brothers. "I know it's hard being away from the game and our paychecks and our normal life," he said. "I love this game. It's been my whole life. But we made a decision in Dallas to stick together, and until we're satisfied, we *have* to stay together. This could be my last year in baseball, and if the strike lasts the entire season and I've played my last game, well, it will be painful. But if we don't hang together, everything we've worked for will be lost."[9]

Indeed, the players held firm.[10] It was the owners, for all their bluster about busting the union, who almost immediately began to splinter. The players were losing salaries, but the teams were losing revenue—vastly more revenue than the few hundred thousand dollars at stake in the pension dispute. Since they hadn't expected a strike, the owners had made no financial plans for it.[11] Within just a few days many owners were beginning to push for a settlement. After less than two weeks, the strike ended, with the owners essentially agreeing to the players' pension fund proposal.[12]

Instead of being humiliated and weakened, the union was vindicated and emboldened. Though the particular issue at hand hadn't been a big deal, the players' stunning success in pressing it gave them new confidence in plans to address their most central concern: the reserve clause. The 1972 strike set in motion the chain of events that would result in the establishment of free agency in 1976.

Horace Stoneham was never like a Gussie Busch, dishing out vituperative quotations about the players' union. It would, instead, be in Stoneham's nature to graciously welcome his players back after the strike and let bygones be bygones. Yet his actions regarding Dick Dietz in the spring of 1972 were truly odd and puzzling in this context.

Dietz, six foot one and two hundred pounds, was not a graceful athlete. His nickname among teammates was "Mule," in reference to his brute strength as well as his stubborn resilience. He was a powerful and excellent hitter with extraordinary strike zone discipline, a dreadfully slow runner, and one of history's worst defensive catchers. His basic problem was receiving the ball cleanly; it's simply the case that Dick Dietz was a catcher who wasn't very good at, well, catching. Thus, he racked up piles of passed balls and wild pitches and was also notoriously unreliable on tag plays at the plate.

Nevertheless, his offensive contribution was so remarkably good that, on balance, Dietz was a significant asset, a low-magnitude star. In 1971 he didn't hit as superbly as he had in 1970, but he remained highly durable and productive, and his 3.8

WAR value—which incorporates defense along with offense—was fifth best among all catchers. In September 1971, amid the searing tension of the division race, Dietz was beaned by a pitch that split the skin on his skull, requiring thirteen stitches; after sitting out three games, Dietz was bravely back in the lineup until the end. His head wrapped in a white bandage that suggested the iconic "Spirit of '76" Yankee Doodle image, in that final crucial week Dietz hit .350 with a double, a home run, and six runs batted in.

In spring training the Giants' players voted Mays as their new player rep and Dietz as the alternate. Whether that development had anything to do with it, Stoneham seriously considered trading Dietz that spring; the rumor was that Dietz would be traded to the American League's California Angels—who could really use him—in exchange for Rudy May, a solid starting pitcher. As good as Dietz was, that deal would be sensible for the Giants, given that Dietz was now thirty years old and had endured an extremely heavy workload in 1970–71; the Giants had two promising young catchers on hand in sophomore Fran Healy and rookie Dave Rader; and May was only twenty-seven, and no team can ever have enough good pitching.

However, the autumn and winter interleague trading season was over: in the spring, to execute a trade between the leagues required the players involved to clear league waivers. So, any National League team that wanted Dietz could stake a claim on him, meaning the Giants would be forced either to deal Dietz to that team or to remove him from the waiver list and keep him. Dietz described the situation from his perspective:

> In 1972 I knew they were going to do something with me. They were talking trade. . . . In spring training they were showcasing me for all the American League clubs. And 1972 was the year of the strike. We were in Yuma, Arizona and we had voted to go back to San Francisco and wait it out. The players didn't *want* to strike, but we did. We had a Players Association which we stood behind. There were some things that needed to be ironed out. The strike went on and the writers were getting different opinions from the ballplayers

and I said what everybody else said, that we stood behind the Association one hundred per cent, that the players didn't want a strike.

Guess what comes out in the *San Francisco Chronicle* the next morning? Headlines, *Dietz Supports Strike*. If you go on to read the article, I said what everybody else said, but I was pinpointed. So, as the old Mafia saying goes, that was the kiss of death. I believe the fans were behind me, they respected me for the ballplayer that I was. I did a good job, I played hard. They knew that, and I believe this article was meant to smooth things over for when I got traded.[13]

In any case what happened next was stunning. On April 14, 1972, just a few days after the strike was resolved and the day before the season was to belatedly begin, Dietz was indeed gone—but not traded to the Angels. He was released on waivers to none other than the Los Angeles Dodgers. All the Giants received in return was the waiver fee from the Dodgers, a nominal figure vastly less than Dietz's worth in the market. They had essentially given Dietz away—and to their fiercest competitor. It was unbelievable.

Apparently, the dynamic was that Dietz was indeed placed on waivers for the purpose of being traded to the American League, but the Dodgers—and only the Dodgers—placed a claim on him, not because they especially needed Dietz but for the purpose of preventing the division-rival Giants from improving themselves with the trade. The stunning part wasn't that the Dodgers did that—though teams often let players pass through waivers on a gentleman's agreement basis, they certainly don't always; the stunning part was that the Giants didn't immediately pull Dietz back off waivers to keep him and then perhaps seek to trade him to a National League team. No one was more shocked than Dietz himself:

> Well, I ended up with the Dodgers, who as a Giant I hated. It was a big adjustment. Charlie Fox called me and said, "We put you out on waivers and you've been picked up." I said, "By whom?" He said, "The Dodgers." And I almost fell out of my chair.
>
> ... [Dodgers GM Al] Campanis told me they had no idea they were going to get me. They did it for a reason, to keep the Giants from get-

ting a pitcher. The Dodgers were the last club where I had cleared the rest of them. You tell me how I cleared the rest of them to get to the Dodgers. There had to be some back-scratching going on there. The Dodgers, with the heated rivalry between the two, they said, "Well, we'll put a stop to that."[14]

As a pure baseball move, it made absolutely no sense for the Giants to do what they did. It cut payroll, as Dave Rader was making quite a bit less than Dietz, but it actively degraded the team's roster while simultaneously improving that of its direct rival. Thus, it invited speculation that the overriding intent was to humiliate Dietz, and the only cause for that would seem to be his prominence in the union. That's definitely how it was perceived by the players. John D'Acquisto, a top minor league prospect who participated in his first major league spring training camp in 1972, saw it that way:

> Dick Dietz was our labor representative at the time of the Major League Baseball players strike that spring. He was also coming off two incredible seasons, most certainly an All-Star caliber backstop. Muley made the mistake of crossing management during the labor negotiations. When the players returned to the field in April of 1972, Dietz was gone. Stoneham didn't even trade poor Muley; he placed him on waivers. The hated Dodgers didn't think twice about scooping Dietz off the waiver wire almost immediately. There was talk about some "*clerical error*" in the Giants' front office, but we all knew the truth. Dietz was let go for his attitude during the negotiations.[15]

That might be the truth. A plausible reading of the circumstances supports that conclusion. But such behavior was utterly out of character for Horace Stoneham, who'd never before demonstrated bitterness or spite in his dealings with players and never would again.

Therefore, the more likely explanation for this bizarre episode isn't a vengeful tantrum on Stoneham's part but, instead, an inattentive blunder. The "clerical error" talk was likely accurate: once the league notified the Giants that the Dodgers had placed the claim on Dietz, they had twenty-four hours to recall him from waivers before the Dodgers' claim would be awarded. Most likely, Stoneham simply failed to instruct his front office staff in time to pull Dietz. It was the day before the season was to belatedly start, there was a lot of frantic last-minute activity of all kinds going on, and Stoneham just dropped that ball.

This explanation is consistent with an owner who was sixty-nine years old, was handling an extremely full plate of executive responsibility, was enduring the overbearing stress of existential fiscal threat, and was prone to drink too much. It's also consistent with a pattern, beginning to develop, of erratic and poorly conceived player transactions, which would include the baffling Ron Hunt trade in December 1970, the Frank Duffy acquisition in May 1971, and the Sam McDowell acquisition in November 1971. The probable truth is that Horace Stoneham held no ill will toward Dick Dietz whatsoever, but he was now struggling to keep up with the basic demands of his job.

Willie Mays was not ready to retire. Part of the reason may well have been that he wasn't emotionally ready to leave behind the competition and the camaraderie he loved. But what's certain is that he wasn't financially ready. Though he'd received a raise in 1971 from $125,000 to $150,000 annually, it was only within recent years that he'd gotten out of debt and begun to save money, and he hadn't yet established long-term financial security. To that end, in 1971 Mays and his financial advisor, Herman Franks, had asked Stoneham about the possibility of a ten-year contract, to cover the remainder of his playing career and then converting to a coaching position, at $75,000 annually. Stoneham, without question, would have loved to do just that. But he turned them down because he just didn't have the financial capacity to commit to anything close to it.

In the spring of 1972 the issue remained unresolved, and for the first time in his life Mays became a holdout. Columnists in the Bay Area sports sections disparaged Mays for his "ego trip." In fact, the dealing was between two good friends—Franks and Stoneham—and it was honest and reasonable. The problem was simply that Stoneham was beginning to run out of money.

The impasse was resolved when the parties agreed to a two-year contract calling for a $165,000 annual salary. Neither Mays nor Stoneham took delight in the deal. Mays would have settled for far less in salary in exchange for the security of a long-term contract, whereas Stoneham wasn't even sure he could finance the two-year deal. He was marking time while he sought to find someone else to guarantee Mays's well-deserved financial security. That particular someone was two someones—President Joan Whitney Payson and Chairman M. Donald Grant of the New York Mets, both of whom had been shareholders and board members of the Giants before the move to San Francisco.[16] Stoneham didn't tell Mays what he was contemplating. Instead, Mays went to spring training and then waited out the eleven-day strike, unsure what the future held.

A year earlier Mays had displayed remarkable spark in his legs and thunder in his bat. But he'd sagged badly over the second half of 1971, and when the 1972 regular season finally got going in mid-April, Mays wasn't looking sharp at all. Though he'd had plenty of time to recover from the previous season's exhaustion, the almost forty-one-year-old Mays was still lost at the plate. He started in center field in each of the Giants' first nine games and went four for thirty-two (.125), without a home run. The only aspect in which he did well was drawing bases on balls, with nine, but it was jarring to see the mighty Willie Mays reduced to a parody of Eddie Stanky.

Meanwhile, in Phoenix twenty-two-year-old center fielder Garry Maddox—a special prospect, tall, slender, and very fast, who'd jumped from single-a, where he'd hit thirty homers in 1971—was off to a spectacular start, hitting .438 with nine home runs in eleven games. On April 25 Stoneham promoted Maddox to the majors. Charlie Fox started the rookie in center field that night, with Mays on the bench. For the first time since his own rookie year more than twenty years earlier, Mays now felt unconfident and insecure about his status.

Over the next two weeks Mays started just four times. He was morose, and the team was playing terribly. In the season's first home stand, the Giants lost eleven of thirteen, and they were in last place. In just four of those thirteen games did the team draw more than seven thousand. Stoneham faced the profoundly sad truth: the Giants were going broke and could no longer afford Willie Mays.

Because of the Giants' exciting division race and championship in 1971, attendance had surged—but only to 1,106,043 in the regular season, plus 83,539 in the two LCS games at Candlestick. Even when including the postseason gate, that total was just tenth among the twelve National League teams. The National Exhibition Company in 1971 eked out a profit of $460,000, a rare occurrence in recent years, but eliminated all dividends on common and preferred shares. Stoneham retained his $80,000 salary, but his loss in dividend income cost him at least $47,000. With the trajectory presented early in 1972, it was obvious that the 1971 profitability was unsustainable, and Stoneham's investors, already receiving no dividends, weren't happy.

The Mets had been wishing to acquire Mays for many years. It was said, and it was almost true, that Joan Payson had bankrolled the Mets so that Mays would play nine games a year in New York. Several times during the 1960s, she offered Stoneham princely sums to purchase the superstar center fielder, though it was a purely ceremonial dance, as Payson well knew that Stoneham wouldn't possibly consent. But time had passed, and it wasn't kind to the Giants. Stoneham wasn't just consenting now; he was initiating the call.

As late as 1971, Dick Young reported in the *New York Daily News* that Payson had bid $1 million for Mays, but Stoneham wasn't ready. In early 1972, however, the Giants were reeling, and Mays was finally expendable. But with his batting average now below .200, the market had shifted, quite a bit more significantly than Stoneham anticipated.

Stoneham wanted the Mets to assume Mays's current contract and provide him a long-term deal on top of that. He also wanted some young players in return. He traveled to New York in early May, and in four days of negotiations, he pressed for infielder Ted Martinez and one of two pitchers—Jon Matlack or Jim McAndrew. He got none of them. The Mets, led by Grant,

Payson's stockbroker, who served as the organization's chairman of the board, assessed Mays as no longer worthy of a single major league player and certainly not $1 million. The negotiations stalled.[17]

Grant, knowing that Stoneham was desperate, drove a harsh bargain. The deal that was eventually announced on May 11, 1972, was far less grand than what Stoneham had sought: it was Mays to the Mets in exchange for minor league pitcher Charlie Williams as well as an "unspecified" amount of cash. Williams was no Matlack or even a McAndrew; he was a twenty-four-year-old marginality who'd toiled ineffectively for the Mets as a rookie long reliever–spot starter in 1971 and was back in AAA with a 4.50 ERA early in '72.

The fact that Williams was such a forgettable token led the pundits to speculate that the cash portion of the deal must have been substantial; the commonly accepted estimate was $50,000, with some guessing as high as $100,000. But years later Stoneham would admit that in fact there was no cash involved at all; Stoneham and the Mets were merely pretending so, as a means of helping Mays save face, to cover the truth that his market value was now truly this meager.[18]

Stoneham's priority, obviously, wasn't in getting value to the Giants in return for Mays but, instead, was in gaining the commitment from the Mets to provide Mays with a long-term "coaching" contract after his $165,000 annual playing contract expired at the end of 1973. That they did: the agreement was that following his retirement as a player, the Mets would pay Mays $50,000 per year for ten years, the most lucrative "coach" salary in baseball history. For this the Giants owner deserves great credit: he was sincerely doing what was best for Willie Mays, ensuring that Mays would attain the long-term financial security that Stoneham was unable to provide. Moreover, the choice of the New York Mets as his destination was quite purposeful as well, as Stoneham truly wanted Mays to go to a place he loved and where there was a fan base and an ownership who already knew him and loved him. Even if, say, Atlanta or Boston or Kansas City had been willing to outbid the Mets for Mays, Stoneham surely wouldn't have taken it because he was dedicated to doing what was best for Mays. That, too, is to Stoneham's credit.

However, the manner in which Stoneham conducted the business was not to his credit. Through the entire process, from conceiving of the idea to proposing it to the Mets and negotiating the terms, Mays was left completely in the dark. Stoneham never provided Mays with the basic courtesy of a consultation, let alone a request for his permission, before orchestrating an arrangement that would relocate Mays across the continent and completely change his life for at least the next decade. Stoneham just did it.

His logic in not telling Mays was that Stoneham wasn't certain the Mets would agree to the deal, and he feared building up Mays's hope and then disappointing him. But his strategy treated Mays like a child needing to be protected, instead of a forty-one-year-old adult with independent agency. It was paternalism taken to a disturbingly disrespectful degree, particularly given the racial dynamic. Worse yet was that the press, not surprisingly, got wind of the fact that Stoneham was in New York and meeting with Mets ownership and started digging to determine what was going on. Therefore, the way Mays learned about the whole thing was by a phone call from a reporter shortly before the deal was finalized. Mays was stunned, embarrassed, confused, and most of all hurt that Stoneham had never had the decency to talk with him about it.

The official announcement took place at a press conference at the Mayfair Hotel in Midtown Manhattan. Stoneham was tearful. "I never thought I would trade Willie," he said. "But with two teams in the Bay Area, our financial situation is such that we could not afford to keep Willie and his big salary as well as the Mets. The Mets are the only club that could take care of him. Don and Mrs. Payson are as much in love with Willie as I am."

Grant conceded that the trade had little to do with improving his team. This was about helping Willie. "There was a lot of sentiment and pride" in bringing Mays back to New York, Grant said, with the overriding purpose being that "Willie would be taken care of just as Mr. Stoneham would want him to be."[19] Mays was customarily gracious in public. He participated in the press conference and made it a point to thank Stoneham, sharing none of the bitterness he felt about being kept out of the loop.

The reaction to the news back in the San Francisco Bay Area and on the Giants ball club itself was unmitigated agony and sorrow. No one had ever imagined that such a thing could come to pass. San Francisco mayor Joseph Alioto said in a statement: "There is no joy in Frisco. The mighty Stoneham has struck out." Clubhouse superintendent Mike Murphy, who'd started as a batboy in 1958, openly cried. So did Tito Fuentes and Bobby Bonds. Manager Charlie Fox, in a clubhouse meeting, explained to the players that the trade was in Willie's best interest. He asserted, "We should all get down on our knees tonight and pray to God that what has happened to Willie will happen to us when we're through." But that was no consolation to Bonds, who utterly revered Mays. "I don't think I've ever been so disappointed or hurt," he later said. "It was like they cut me down the middle and traded part of me. It was like only half of me was playing for the rest of the year."[20]

Chris Speier put it this way: "Losing Mays in '72 definitely affected the ball club. He was such a force, we put a lot of responsibility on his shoulders and when we got in a jam everyone looked to him. And when he left it was like taking part of the heart, taking part of something away and making it incomplete. And that's what we felt. We felt very uncomfortable for a while. He was such a tremendous fixture, such a tremendous individual in the Giant organization."[21]

The gut punch to the team's fans and players was a one-two combination. First was the shock of the departure of their beloved superstar in such a sudden and unceremonious way. Second was the deepening realization that the ball club truly was facing dire financial trouble. Everyone knew about the collapse in Candlestick Park attendance since the mid-1960s, of course, but until now that condition hadn't resulted in serious consequences. Winning the division and drawing (just) over a million fans in 1971 had been wishfully interpreted as signs that things were getting better, but Stoneham's cutting Mays loose was a splash of cold water. Everyone knew how much Stoneham loved Mays, and it was obvious how torturous this was for him, so the fact that he'd had to do it meant that things were really, really bad, and if they were that bad, they were probably going to get worse.

Mays, as only he could, added his own sly twist to the story. As fate would have it, his first appearance with the Mets was against the Giants, on Sunday afternoon, May 14, at Shea Stadium. With the game tied at 4–4 in the fifth inning, he untied it by launching his first home run of the year, and the Mets won 5–4. On Friday evening, July 21, Mays made his first visit to Candlestick Park with the Mets. The crowd of 18,117 was a large one by 1972 Candlestick standards, and Mays was showered with standing ovations at every turn. In the fifth inning he connected for another homer, resulting in perhaps the most tumultuous applause for a visitor's home run in the history of baseball. The Mets won, 3–1. Take that, Mr. Stoneham.

At age thirty-three in 1971, Juan Marichal had enjoyed an outstanding season, a strong rebound from his struggles of 1970. He was no longer the superstar of his peak years but still a legitimate ace. It was Stoneham's vision that Marichal would team with Sam McDowell in 1972 to create a colorful duo at the top of the rotation: the righty Marichal, the control artist master of every conceivable pitch; and the southpaw McDowell, the straight-ahead flamethrower.

Marichal opened the 1972 season with eight shutout innings in Houston as the Giants won, 5–0. For the next month he continued to pitch well. But he then developed back trouble, and both his fastball velocity and his usual microdot control were degraded. He sat out three weeks in late June as well as most of September and staggered at age thirty-four to the worst season he'd ever encountered, finishing at 6–16.

As for McDowell, consider the observations John D'Acquisto presented in his memoir. In the spring of 1972 D'Acquisto was an impressionable twenty-year-old, a minor leaguer with special promise, invited to the Giants' major league spring training camp at Casa Grande for the first time. After the first day's

workouts and showers, the team gathered to relax and social-
ize before dinner. D'Acquisto describes the stereo pounding out
Sly and the Family Stone while players enjoyed card games and
friendly, funny banter. Bobby Bonds asked D'Acquisto to grab
him a beer from the cooler, and the deferential rookie complied.
Then McDowell handed D'Acqusito his room key and requested
that he go upstairs and fetch a bottle of vodka from McDowell's
room. Again, the rookie was eager to be of assistance.

But then: "As I entered Sam's room moments later, I saw worn
suits folded on the bed, uniform pants and jerseys dangling off
a desk chair, [a] couple emptied suitcases and travel bags. . . .
*And 25 bottles of Smirnoff lined up in boxes and all along the wall
ledge.* . . . One on top of the other, like a warehouse for a small
local distributor, more alcohol than a single human being could
ever drink in a lifetime, let alone six weeks in Phoenix. From one
end of the wall to the other—double stacked."[22]

D'Acquisto brought one of the bottles downstairs to McDowell,
expecting him to pour a cocktail. Instead, McDowell twisted the
cap off the bottle, leaned his head back, and chugged it, terribly
deeply—"the chug seemed to last five minutes"—before putting
it down and saying, nonchalantly, "Deal the cards." This was the
ace pitcher for whom Stoneham had expended Gaylord Perry.

McDowell actually started well in 1972: in his first six starts he
was 5–0, with three complete games and a 2.57 ERA. Then things
went south in a hurry: from that point until mid-July, he went 3–7,
with an earned run average of 5.55. Complaining of a sore shoulder, McDowell then spent six weeks on the disabled list. His 1972
strikeout rate was far below his career norm and his hits allowed
rate far above it. Meanwhile, in Cleveland, Perry was winning
twenty-four games and the American League Cy Young Award.

Willie McCovey, immediately following the 1971 season, underwent
his long-needed knee surgery. This allowed the full off-season for
rehabilitation. By spring training of 1972 he was looking good—or
at least as good someone with Willie McCovey's thirty-four-year-old
surgery-repaired knees could look. With McCovey back to a more
or less full-time presence at first base, the question for Charlie Fox

turned to what to do with Dave Kingman. The young slugger was way too good to be limited to a strict backing-up-McCovey role. But where to play him? He wasn't going to supplant the strong-all-around Ken Henderson in left field and certainly not the brilliant Bobby Bonds in right. And in the spring of 1972 Mays was still in center field, with Garry Maddox on his heels.

So, Fox took a look across the diamond, to third base. Alan Gallagher was a competent player who'd delivered a satisfactory performance as the Giants' primary third baseman in 1971. But he had no star potential; Gallagher was a placeholder, adequate until the team could come up with someone better. Charlie Fox thought he might do just that.

Twenty-three-year-old Dave Kingman had never played third base. Always the tallest kid on his team, the six-foot-six-inch Kingman had pitched and played first base and the outfield. In the history of major league baseball, only one player as tall as Kingman had ever played third base and then in just five games: Dick Hall, a twenty-one-year-old rookie with the woebegone 1952 Pittsburgh Pirates.[23] The tallest third baseman to see a significant amount of action was six-foot-four-inch Don Demeter, who battled the position through 148 games in 1962–63; the tallest third baseman to succeed as a career regular had been solid-fielding six-foot-three Ken McMullen, the onetime Dodger hopeful who'd been a steady first-stringer with the Senators and Angels since 1965.

But Kingman had more than enough arm strength for third base, and in his early twenties he was slender, reasonably agile, and quick on his feet; he would steal sixteen bases in twenty-two attempts in 1972. As had been the case with Orlando Cepeda, Bobby Thomson, Sid Gordon, and Mel Ott before him, Kingman wouldn't need to become a top-notch fielder at third base for the move to pay off positively for the Giants. If he could perform just adequately with the glove, making the routine plays, the placement of his powerful bat in the everyday lineup right behind McCovey's was a rousing concept. In spring training Fox proclaimed that Dave Kingman would be his third baseman in 1972 and played him there extensively in the Cactus League.

Perhaps Kingman, provided with the opportunity of sustained experience at the position, might have developed into a reliable fielder at third base. But Fox, mysteriously, would never give it. Kingman started at third for the first four games of the 1972 season and handled twelve chances without an error. But in that fourth game of the year, Willie McCovey fractured his forearm in a collision at first base and would miss a month and a half. Rather than persist with Kingman at third, Fox moved him back to first base for most of McCovey's absence. And even when McCovey returned, Kingman was never reestablished as the third baseman. Fox would play him there for a while and then shift him to left field for a spell and also have him fill in for McCovey at first. Altogether Kingman appeared in fifty-nine games at third base in 1972 but never on a prolonged basis. It was a particularly difficult way for a player to meet the challenge of learning a new position, yet through it all Kingman's defensive statistics at third base in '72 weren't bad: while quite error prone, he demonstrated better-than-average range.

Following the 1971 season, the Giants' pitching coach, Larry Jansen, was hired away by his old manager Leo Durocher to coach for the Chicago Cubs, likely because the Cubs could afford a better salary than Stoneham's Giants. So Stoneham endeavored to fill the opening in the most fiscally conservative way. He reasoned that forty-two-year-old Don McMahon, who'd been modestly effective in 1971 as the second-in-line reliever behind new ace Jerry Johnson, had ample experience and pitching smarts to serve as pitching coach while also holding down a bullpen spot. McMahon wasn't enthusiastic about it, but he accepted the assignment and gave it his best, later recalling: "It was tough being both a pitcher and a coach because you had to worry about the feelings of the other guys. I tried to put the two things out of my mind most of the time, but I think it hurt me more than it helped pitching-wise. . . . It was a difficult situation, but the guys were good. I got along with the guys well, and they knew I wasn't trying to build up my own thing. I was just trying to win. That's all we wanted to do, put the best guy in at the best time. But I think it might have stopped me from working more on myself. Where I worked with other guys, I could be throwing myself."[24]

While juggling the dual role, McMahon would once again perform positively as a reliever in 1972. However, the Giants' team struggles in the early months of that season were extreme. The defending division champions were 6–10 in April and then 9–21 in May, for the team's worst month since 1957. Never in San Francisco had they been remotely this bad. They hit bottom on June 20, at 21–44. No Giants team had been that many games under .500 since 1956, and no Giants team had a comparable record at that point in a season since 1902—that is to say, since before the arrival of John McGraw.

The Giants' problem in early 1972 wasn't offense; it was, as in 1970, run prevention. This weakness was again a team effort between the fielding and the pitching—normally sure-handed second baseman Tito Fuentes coughed up a twenty-nine-error season in 1972—but most of the fault in early '72 was poor pitching. As in 1970, the Giants in 1972 were able to turn it around midyear; following the low point in June, they went 48–42 the rest of the way. Distinctly improved second-half pitching was led by Ron Bryant, sophomore Jim Barr, and rookie right-hander Jim Willoughby.

The Giants' best player in 1972 was Chris Speier, better even than Bobby Bonds. Speier, at just twenty-two, added an excellent bat on top of his already superb defensive game, and it seemed that the Giants had come up with yet another extraordinary star. Dave Kingman, deployed as a defensive nomad, delivered mixed results: he struck out in more than a quarter of his plate appearances, and his batting average was a lowly .225, but his thunderous power production at age twenty-three suggested that he could develop into an elite slugger if the Giants could just figure out a way to play him every day. Rookie center fielder Garry Maddox was raw, lacking in strike zone discipline, but he impressed with his power, speed, and dazzling outfield range. Another rookie, catcher Dave Rader, won the regular job over Fran Healy and delivered a fundamentally sound, steady performance.

Along with Marichal and McDowell, the third high-salaried veteran star remaining on the roster was Willie McCovey, and just like the other two, McCovey endured a dreadful year in 1972.

When he returned in early June from his six-week recovery from the broken arm, it was essentially spring training all over again for him, and he never found his batting stroke. In eighty-one games he finished at .213, with fourteen home runs, and at the age of thirty-four his future was deeply in question. It was the failure of all three big-name veterans to capably fill their assignments that doomed the 1972 Giants to fall from contender to also-ran.

But the dimming of those stars helped turn attention to the remarkable abundance of impressive young talent that continued to emerge from the organization's amazing farm system. Despite his financial crisis, Stoneham had refused to cut the payroll of his extensive and far-flung scouting department, and the team continued to reap its benefits. The very long list of scouts who would work fifteen or more years for Stoneham and Hubbell included Frank Burke, Walker Cress, Frank "Chick" Genovese, Herm Hannah, John Hudson, Tom Hull, Carl Kentling, Hans Lobert, Ray Lucas, Sal Margoglione, Dickey Martin, Horacio "Rabbit" Marttínez, J. R. McLean, Eddie Montague, Hugh Poland, Evo Pusich, Tony Ravish, Walter "Dutch" Ruether, Frank Shellenback, Nick Shinkoff, Gene Thompson, and Pedro Zorrilla. Following the attendance dive of 1968, Stoneham had only minimally reduced the size of his minor league chain, cutting it from six affiliates to five in 1969 by eliminating one Class A team.

Thus, even with McCovey, Marichal, and McMahon on the roster, the 1972 Giants were one of the very youngest teams in baseball and impressively athletic: despite their losing record, the Giants led all major league teams in home runs (150) while stealing the third-most bases (123) with the very best stolen base percentage (73 percent). Though this suggested the likelihood of a return to contending status in the future, within the present of 1972 the Giants were in a very bad way indeed.

The team's terrible 1972 start killed any hope of title contention, and as a result, attendance at Candlestick Park sunk to its lowest point yet, at 647,000. Giants' attendance was now down to what it had been during the bleak final Polo Grounds seasons of 1956 and '57. In the final two games of the 1972 season, a Tuesday night and a Wednesday afternoon at Candlestick against the last-place San Diego Padres, the Giants set new records for their least-attended games since arriving in San Francisco, with "crowds" of 1,755 and 1,578, respectively.

The year brought two more retirements of long-tenured front office executives. Garry Schumacher, a former sportswriter, had joined the Giants in 1947 to perform the newly created job of publicity manager. In 1952 his role was modified to promotions director, and with the move to San Francisco, he became the organization's first public relations director, the position he fulfilled until his retirement. Edgar Feeley, who'd served as the club's treasurer since 1945, when he took over for Leo Bondy, retired in 1972 as well. Two more candles burning the institutional flame from the Polo Grounds were extinguished. The only members of Stoneham's old guard remaining were Carl Hubbell and Jack Schwartz.

With Feeley's departure, Chuck Rupert assumed primary responsibility for operating the business, his title now executive vice president and secretary-treasurer. He and Jerry Donovan, who'd been promoted from business manager to assistant to the president when Eddie Brannick retired, alongside Hubbell, Schwarz, and Hank Sauer—who'd been promoted in 1970 from organizational hitting instructor to help oversee the farm system—were now Stoneham's inner circle, his brain trust. This would be the final crew.

Perhaps it was because the executive retirements had provided some payroll relief for Stoneham, but the player transactions the Giants undertook in the 1972–73 off-season included no further salary dumps. Juan Marichal took a pay cut from $140,000 to $135,000, but Willie McCovey's contract remained at $125,000 and Sam McDowell's at $75,000, and all would return for 1973— at least to start the season. Meanwhile, Chris Speier got a big raise, from $30,000 to $45,000, while Bobby Bonds remained in the $80,000 range.

Stoneham executed just one significant trade. On November 29, 1972, he sent outfielder Ken Henderson along with sophomore starter-reliever Steve Stone to the Chicago White Sox and received right-handed starting pitcher Tom Bradley. The multitalented twenty-six-year-old Henderson had delivered an inconsistent performance with the bat in 1972, and he was expendable because of the arrival in September of twenty-one-year-old Gary Matthews, yet another terrific power-and-speed whiz kid outfielder served up by the amazing Giants' system. The twenty-five-year-old Stone had established himself as a solid major leaguer but didn't project star potential. Bradley, who would turn twenty-six in March 1973, had already achieved stardom, or something close to it. He'd been remarkably durable for the White Sox in 1971 and '72, and while his win-loss record over those two seasons was just 30–29, he'd posted strong earned run averages and terrific strikeout-to-walk ratios. He was an outstanding young pitcher, and this was a smart trade by Stoneham.

It was in the spring of 1973 that Stoneham tended to some payroll shaving. He let Jerry Johnson go on waivers, traded Fran Healy and Alan Gallagher for minor leaguers, and sold Jim Ray Hart—undoubtedly a sad day for Stoneham, who'd always loved Jimmy Ray—and those roster spots were filled by low-salaried rookies.

At Don McMahon's urging, Charlie Fox attempted to convert Sam McDowell into a relief pitcher. McMahon's reasoning was twofold: first, at age thirty and following back-to-back poor years, it seemed evident that McDowell's capacity to succeed as a flame-throwing starting pitcher was gone, and working in short stints out of the bullpen would be easier on his arm and would help mitigate his problems of reduced velocity and endurance; and second, with fewer nights per week in which McDowell knew he wouldn't be pitching the next day, he might stand a better chance of getting a handle on his egregious drinking.[25] It was a sensible idea, but at least in the short window of opportunity Fox provided, McDowell succeeded neither in pitching effectively nor in curbing his copious Smirnoff consumption. On June 7, 1973, Stoneham pulled the plug on Sudden Sam, selling him to the New York Yankees, closing the sad book on the very worst transaction Stoneham executed in his four decades at the Giants' helm.

The Giants' marketing campaign for 1973, spearheaded by Rupert, Donovan, and John Taddeucci, focused on the team's young talent core, touting them as "the Young Giants." Altogether, seventeen of the team's twenty-five regular-season roster spots were held by either rookies, sophomores, or third-year players. The organizational resilience in the face of peril was remarkable.

On Tuesday evening, May 1, 1973, the Giants played the East Division defending champion Pittsburgh Pirates at Candlestick Park, before a "crowd" of 7,972. In the bottom of the ninth inning, with two outs and a runner on first, the Pirates held a commanding 7–1 lead. But then the Giants mounted a stunning rally, climaxed by a Bobby Bonds three-run double, to win the game 8–7. This amazing comeback was extraordinary, of course, but it was emblematic of the inspired play of the Young Giants in the opening weeks of 1973. That win put their record at 19–6, and they held a four-game lead in the National League West Division. The Giants would play near-precisely .500 ball for the rest of the season, surrendering first place in mid-June, and they finished in third, at 88–74, eleven games behind the division-winning Cincinnati Reds. Still, 1973 was a highly positive season on the field for Stoneham's Giants, as they emphatically bounced back from the flop of 1972, delivering competitive, colorful baseball.

The team's key strength was a tremendous outfield. Right fielder Bobby Bonds delivered the best season of his career and was named *The Sporting News* National League Player of the Year; he won a Gold Glove, stole forty-three bases, and hit a personal-best thirty-nine home runs, very nearly becoming the first player in major league history to achieve "40–40." Sophomore center fielder Garry Maddox resolved to reduce his strikeouts and improve his batting average, and by adopting an extra-wide stance and a short, bat-controlling stride, he sacrificed some home run production but still produced extra-base power, while his average soared to third highest in the league. In left field Matthews was the National League Rookie of the Year, doing everything well. All three were speedy defensive standouts. Maddox recalled, "We had on the Giants what was considered the fastest outfield. . . . We took pride in not letting the ball get to the wall."[26] Bonds echoed, "I believe that Gary Matthews and Garry Maddox and I were the fastest outfield that's ever been put on a baseball field. . . . I honestly cannot remember five balls that hit the right-center field wall. We cut off everything. It was something we took pride in."[27]

Southpaw Ron Bryant's fastball wasn't outstanding, but his curve was, an old-fashioned roundhouse knee buckler. He could struggle to get the big breaker into the strike zone, but when he was getting Uncle Charlie over, it set up his sinking, tailing fastball beautifully, and Bryant could be tough to hit. At age twenty-five in 1973, he enjoyed the year of his life, with a major league–leading twenty-four wins. Bryant's gaudy win total was the result of extravagant run support, as no pitcher in major league baseball had won so many games with such a high earned run average (3.53) since 1933. Still, Bryant was very good, providing the Giants the durable rotation anchor they'd lacked in 1972. Another Giant who was at his best in a key role in 1973 was Tito Fuentes, who rebounded from a dismal season with the glove in 1972 to a great fielding season in '73, achieving a major league record for fewest second base errors, with just six.

On the heels of his 1972 breakout performance, in April 1973 twenty-three-year-old shortstop Chris Speier was featured on the covers of both *The Sporting News* (caption: "BUDDING STAR") and *Sports Illustrated* ("GIANT AMONG GIANTS"). Through the season's first half he lived up to the billing, continuing to hit well and starting in the All-Star Game. But then he encountered an unspecified midseason injury; he didn't go on the disabled list but missed some playing time, hit weakly over the second half, and saw his season's error total balloon from twenty to thirty-three. Another whose season failed to meet expectations was newcomer Tom Bradley. He missed nearly a month with an ankle injury and had some good stretches but was plagued with inconsistency. He wasn't bad, but he was not nearly as good as he'd been with the White Sox.

Willie McCovey was healthy in 1973—or as healthy as he was going to be at this point—and he enjoyed a strong comeback season, hitting his best since 1970. Thus, with first base being even less an option for Dave Kingman than in it had been in '72, third base would truly seem to be Kingman's position now. But Charlie Fox's commitment to developing the twenty-four-year-old Kingman into a third baseman was even less resolute this time around, as the manager came to the baffling decision to give the starting hot corner job not to Kingman but to Ed Goodson, a twenty-five-year-old sophomore. Goodson was a lefty-swinging line drive hitter with medium power but a slow runner and poor fielder, with nothing approaching Kingman's athleticism. Yet for most of 1973 Kingman was relegated to backing up McCovey and Goodson. In the utility role Kingman was unable to get his all-or-nothing swing into rhythm, and he hit miserably. Only when Goodson suffered a finger injury in August and was shelved for the season did Kingman finally get a shot at everyday play, and he made the most of it, blasting thirteen home runs and drawing twenty-eight walks in thirty-five games, good for an amazing OPS+ of 174 down the stretch.

Yet however foolish it was to play Goodson ahead of Kingman, such quibbles were the least of the franchise's worries. Even with the improved play of 1973, attendance at Candlestick Park was just 834,000, ranking twentieth among the twenty-four major league teams. Across the bay the Oakland A's, winning their second straight pennant and World Series title, reached the one million threshold for the first time. The Giants' good play in 1973 staved off disaster, but the business remained severely unhealthy.

Horace Stoneham's problems compounded. The owner's vision was that his earnings from the Giants would be augmented by earnings from his Casa Grande resort in Arizona, in a manner comparable to the way in which, decades earlier, the pure baseball revenue in New York had been augmented by renting out the Polo Grounds as a multisport entertainment venue. By this point in the early 1970s—fifteen years following the Casa Grande groundbreaking—the master plan had called for the Arizona property to be generating not just seasonal revenue as a vacation hotel but also attracting buyers of vacation homes to be developed on Stoneham's real estate lots surrounding the resort and golf course. But it wasn't happening.

The issue stemmed from the choice of Casa Grande as the location, instead of somewhere closer to either Phoenix or Tucson. As had been forecasted decades earlier, the state of Arizona was indeed rapidly growing in the 1960s and '70s as a vacation and retirement destination. But that economic development turned out to be focused in and around Phoenix and to a lesser extent in Tucson, and it just wasn't taking place in Casa Grande, forlornly sitting out there in the dusty desert far from the two poles of growth. The Giant Boosters were coming out there to heartily enjoy spring training vacations, but that was about it. The anticipated attractiveness of Casa Grande as a more broadly based golf resort hadn't materialized, so the hulking Francisco Grande Hotel was standing empty for most of the year, and the sale of residential lots wasn't going on at all. As Giants front office executive John Taddeucci would put it, the Casa Grande venture was now "soaking up money as quickly as the desert soaks up the rain."[28] If anyone couldn't afford that, it was Horace Stoneham.

Thus, the watchword, as Stoneham considered roster changes for 1974, was, once again, *payroll reduction*. The first contract to go would be Willie McCovey's $125,000. After Willie Mays had been pensioned off to the Mets, it was McCovey who naturally assumed the role of clubhouse leader. McCovey's personality was different from Mays's; he was calmer and funnier, and his steadfast tolerance of chronic pain and tireless commitment to the welfare of the team earned McCovey genuine moral authority. His teammates didn't just respect Willie McCovey; they loved him. He was the emotional center of gravity.[29]

Stoneham certainly understood this and well knew that in sending McCovey away he would be costing his ball club much more than a still-huge bat in the middle of the order. But the hard math of $125,000 was pitiless, and moreover, Stoneham wanted, just as he had with Mays, to do what was best for McCovey's financial future. Some additional hard truths were that McCovey would be thirty-six in 1974, and he was really hobbling now, his top speed a painful-looking trot, thus a distinct liability on the bases and in the field. Moreover, the Giants had multiple young and promising first base alternatives. So, though Stoneham surely didn't like it, McCovey had to go.

Nor was McCovey surprised by it. Perhaps Stoneham now recognized that the secretive way he'd handled it with Mays was the wrong approach, so the owner was candid with McCovey in late

1973. He admitted the sad economic facts of the situation and asked McCovey where he would prefer to go. McCovey gratefully appreciated the consideration and responded that he'd like to stay on the West Coast and that a warmer climate than the Bay Area would be best for his aching knees. Fortunately for McCovey, Stoneham was able to find a trading partner who checked both of those boxes.[30]

The San Diego Padres' roster had been constructed from the ground up by Buzzie Bavasi, formerly of the Dodgers, beginning with the 1968 expansion draft. Bavasi was committed to building with youth, eschewing any short-term competitiveness that might be gained by deploying veterans. He succeeded in crafting a very young team, but the eventual improvement in performance he'd anticipated, as the kids would develop, didn't pan out: the 1973 season was the Padres' fifth and also the fifth in which they finished dead last, averaging 101 losses per year. The utterly noncompetitive young Padres had achieved no success in building a fan base; attendance at cavernous San Diego Stadium was also dead last in the National League every seasons as well. They were in even worse financial straits than the Giants.

By late 1973 the Padres were for sale.[31] A deal was worked out with a group from Washington DC to relocate the team there. But when that prospect was challenged with lawsuits, the team was instead sold to Ray Kroc, the flamboyant former McDonald's entrepreneur, who committed to keeping the Padres in San Diego. Moreover, Kroc immediately sent word to Bavasi that the days of patiently waiting for youngsters to develop were over; the Padres were hereby going to import whatever veteran talent they could find, cost be damned, and become competitive right away.

So it was that the interests of the Giants, the Padres, and Willie McCovey were suddenly in alignment, and on October 25, 1973, the Giants traded McCovey to San Diego along with outfielder Bernie Williams (who hadn't developed) in exchange for left-handed pitcher Mike Caldwell. Quite unlike Charlie Williams, Caldwell was no marginal token; though not yet twenty-five years old, he was an established major leaguer who'd performed encouragingly for the Padres in a starter-reliever swingman role in both

1972 and '73. Stoneham didn't simply dump McCovey's salary; he got back fair value for him.

Still, it was profoundly hard to send Stretch away. McCovey would always acknowledge his (well-earned) personal wealth of friendships throughout the Giants organization, or—without irony, as Stoneham dearly perceived it, within the Giants *family*: "When I left the Giants I never felt the same, with the Padres or the A's, as I did when I was with the Giants. They signed me when I was just a kid, 17 years old, and I've been very close to everybody in the organization. They've always treated me like their son. Every manager I've played for, everybody in the front office from Horace Stoneham on down, there was always that feeling of closeness and family."[32]

Next on Stoneham's shopping-around list was Juan Marichal. At age thirty-five in 1973, the former elite ace hadn't struggled as badly as he had in '72, but his performance was just mediocre. John D'Acquisto, the raw kid from spring training in 1972, had been called up to the Giants' major league roster in September 1973, and he spent that month as Marichal's teammate. D'Acquisto would observe: "Juan had pitched for the Giants since 1960, was beloved in the community, the ballpark, and the clubhouse, especially the clubhouse, a nine-time All-Star on a team once full of them. This was the September of his career, [he] had lost 4–5 MPH off his fastball, plus with the financial issues of the organization, everyone knew this would most likely be his final month in San Francisco."[33]

Whether Marichal provided input to Stoneham as to where he might prefer to be sent is unrecorded. What's clear is that Stoneham was unsuccessful in attracting any trade offers for Marichal, who was carrying a salary of $135,000, and so settled for just selling him to the Boston Red Sox on December 7, 1973. The sale price was reported as "an undisclosed amount," which is code for "not very much." This was just a salary dump. The last of Stoneham's prodigious core of homegrown Hall of Fame–bound superstars, who'd led the Giants to the 1962 pennant and so many close contentions in the 1960s, was gone.

15

You Can't Get Discouraged

s Stoneham's San Francisco Giants entered the 1974 season, they weren't quite in a state of crisis, though that was visibly looming. The odds against it were long, but the franchise could still pull through. The scenario for success was ambitious: it required the team on the field to be not merely competitive but to *win* and regain strong attendance at Candlestick Park. No doubt, that scenario would be best served by the Oakland Athletics not achieving championships of their own year after year, but that part was beyond the Giants' control.

Certainly, the Giants' predicament was dire: they were, one might say, trailing by several runs in the bottom of the ninth inning and needing a last-chance big rally. But such a rally wasn't a ridiculous notion, because the roster Stoneham had fashioned was truly impressive, and the potential for this team to emerge as a great one was genuine.

In Bobby Bonds the team featured a superstar in the prime of his career. Bonds was joined in the lineup by outstanding all-around young stars Chris Speier, Garry Maddox, and Gary Matthews. It was a lineup with no holes; while second baseman Tito Fuentes and catcher Dave Rader weren't stars, they were sound and solid regulars.

The team's question marks were at first base and third base. However, at both positions there were multiple good options at hand for manager Charlie Fox, and there was indeed a significant possibility that one or the other corner infield spot would be filled by another young star: twenty-five-year-old Dave King-man. To be sure, Kingman hadn't yet attained stardom, but he plainly had the potential to do so. The robust production King-man displayed in the closing weeks of 1973 suggested that he was ready, over a full season, to deliver a forty-homer, 100-RBI performance. No doubt Kingman would also challenge Bonds's major league strikeout record, but Bonds himself had vividly demonstrated that a record-breaking strikeout rate was hardly incompatible with high-grade offensive production. The 1974 season was Kingman's golden opportunity to break through.

With McCovey departed, one obvious choice for Fox was to just forget about the Kingman-at-third-base experiment and play him full-time at first base. Yet they could still deploy Kingman at third; though he hadn't been a good-fielding third baseman in 1972 or '73, he hadn't been terrible; Kingman wasn't as bad defensively as Ed Goodson. Another third base option was rookie Steve Ontiveros, not a good fielder at third either, but capable of handling it, and a line drive–hitting switch hitter with excellent strike zone discipline. Yet another good young player in the mix was twenty-two-year-old left-handed sophomore Gary Thom-asson, powerful enough to be a serious candidate at first base while speedy enough to handle center field.

The Giants' pitching staff lacked a first-rate ace—someone like, say, Gaylord Perry—but in Ron Bryant, Tom Bradley, and Jim Barr they had three good starters, and Mike Caldwell appeared ready to step forward as a fourth. And in twenty-two-year-old fireballing right-hander John D'Acquisto, ready to begin his first full big-league season in 1974, they clearly had a potential star: in three and a half minor league seasons, he'd racked up more than 750 strikeouts, and he was being compared, legitimately, to Nolan Ryan. In the bullpen the Giants featured two good young right-handers in Elias Sosa and Randy Moffitt.[1] The one compo-nent the Giants' pen was lacking was a reliable left-hander—if only Sam McDowell could have pulled off that assignment.

Altogether the team the Giants were presenting in 1974 looked to be excellent, with ample capability to strongly contend. And while the 1973 edition had been touted as "The Young Giants," this time around, with McCovey and Marichal removed, they were even younger. The virtue of a young team—in addition to its being low salaried—is that it's likely to improve. These Giants were already good and poised to continue delivering strong results for the foreseeable future. Stoneham needed everything to go just right—no doubt about that—but it was the case that the team he'd put together was capable of delivering the come-from-behind rally.

The first sign that things wouldn't go as hoped came from Ron Bryant. He was a pudgy, easygoing sort who carried the nickname of "Teddy Bear," as a play on the famous University of Alabama football coach Paul "Bear" Bryant, whose gruff, tough persona was the antithesis of Ron Bryant's. Someone (probably a Giants booster) presented Bryant with a huge actual teddy bear, and he was merrily photographed alongside it, in the clubhouse and in the dugout. All indications are that Bryant never met a party he didn't like, and the young pitcher heartily enjoyed the celebrity he was afforded with his big year of 1973.

On March 15, 1974, the Giants were in Palm Springs, California, to play the Angels in a spring training game. That evening at their hotel, Bryant suffered a major injury, a deep gash in his side, a wound requiring twenty-five stitches to bind. The explanation for this accident, reported in the papers, was that Bryant "tumbled off a pool slide . . . and hit the side of a hotel swimming pool before going into the water."[2]

How, exactly, could one manage to do that? It seemed to be the sort of thing that one would have to expend some effort to bring off. Don McMahon explained that it was exactly that: "Ronny tries to slide down like he's Pete Rose, next thing you know, the dumb shit slips off the slide, scrapes his body against the coping of the pool and splits his side open. All cut up. Screaming in pain. Ambulance came and everything. It was a big, bloody, fuckin' mess."[3] It was a remarkably unintelligent thing for Bryant to do, but he'd done it. Precisely how inebriated he was at the time was open to speculation. He would open the season on the disabled list.

Additional injuries emerged. On Opening Day, Tito Fuentes's back seized up, and he would be sidelined for nearly a month. Ed Goodson was nagged by a slow-to-heal hamstring pull and was mostly on the DL until mid-May.

Despite the injury problems, the 1974 Giants jumped out of the gate nicely. In the season opener at Candlestick Park—which attracted just 17,527—Maddox hit a three-run homer, Bradley took a shutout into the ninth, and the Giants handily defeated the Houston Astros, 5–1. The next day Ontiveros homered, and Caldwell got the 3–2 win in his San Francisco debut, and then the Giants made it a sweep in a romp, 8–4, with Kingman detonating a three-run bomb. Following that, the Giants took two out of three from the defending division champion Cincinnati Reds—John D'Acquisto picked up his first win of the year in that series—and a week into the season they were at 5–1, tied for first place with the Dodgers.

But over the next month and a half, the Giants played mediocre baseball. At the end of May they were 27–25—not a bad record but not good, and while they'd been plodding along, the Dodgers were sprinting away to their best start since 1962. The Giants were already ten games behind, languishing in fifth place. The strongly contending season the franchise so desperately needed was looming out of reach before summer had even begun.

Without a pennant race to stimulate interest, the fan base was paying less and less attention. In the months of April and May the Giants attracted an average of 8,770 per game, which would give them attendance of just over 700,000 for the season. That would be significantly below even the modest attendance achieved in 1973, and the growth in ticket and concessions revenue the franchise so desperately needed was simply not materializing.

Everyone understood this meant disaster. Stoneham and the front office were agitated, and Fox was feeling intense pressure. The Giants' clubhouse was gloomy. As the bitter mood pervaded, it was evident that more than the power of his bat, the Giants as a fraternity missed the presence and leadership of Willie McCovey.

After McCovey was traded, twenty-eight-year-old Bobby Bonds took it upon himself to become the new clubhouse leader. He felt he deserved it, as the reigning star, that it was his time and his responsibility. That much was fine. However, Bonds exhibited personality traits that, shall we say, weren't recommended in leadership manuals. He was smart and gregarious but also high-strung, somehow not quite comfortable in his own skin. He chain-smoked and drank heedlessly, or perhaps compulsively. Charlie Fox wasn't persuaded that it should be Bonds taking the mantel of team leader, as in Fox's estimation Bonds didn't set the best example for the team's many young players to emulate. The relationship between Fox and Bonds had been positive in previous years, but in 1974, as the scrutiny mounted on both and each warily eyed the other as a rival for the team's allegiance, that relationship deteriorated.

Through the end of May, Bonds had been performing well but not keeping pace with the great standard he'd set in 1973. As the team failed to catch a hot streak, Bonds grew ever more tense. Then the calendar turned to June, and right on cue, the swoon began. By Tuesday, June 11, before a Candlestick Park throng of 3,311—no, not the smallest home crowd of the year so far, not by a long shot—when the Giants lost to the Cubs, 7–4, they dropped to 30–31. Still mired in fifth place, they were now below .500. Fox was worried about his job, he was concerned that Bonds was drinking more heavily, and a confrontation brewed.

Two days later, after a Thursday afternoon game (attendance 2,342), the Giants went to San Francisco Airport to board a cross-country flight. D'Acquisto recounted the scene:

> We were at the airport waiting for our flight to Pittsburgh when Bobby approached me in the executive club for charter passengers. He was carrying a paper bag.
>
> "Hey, Rook," he said quietly. "Bring this on for me, will ya?" I looked in the bag, sorted through about a half-dozen airplane bottles of Johnny Walker and Jack Daniels. I was a rookie. I didn't ask any questions. I always did what I was told.
>
> "Sure, no problem, BB," I replied, grabbing the bag as the stewardess announced it was time to board the plane. I passed Charlie, who was sitting up front. He smiled at me for a moment, then glanced

at the bag. He knew the moment his eyes caught mine. He excused himself from Joey Amalfitano, one of our coaches sitting beside him, and called me over to the flight attendant's food prep station.

"Whose is that?" Charlie asked pointedly.

"Just some stuff for the flight."

Charlie said *"lemme see"* with his fingers, and sifted through the small bag. "There's no tequila in here," Charlie said, finding nothing but whiskey and vodka. [Fox knew that the young D'Acquisto's only familiar liquor was tequila.]

"Whose is this?" he asked again.

"Just thought I'd try some . . ." I fumbled my words as Charlie gently took the bag from my hands.

"You're a good teammate, Johnny," Charlie fumed as he folded up the bag. "Go sit down."

As I stepped toward the back of the plane, I grabbed my seat. . . . I looked over at the front and watched as Bobby was the last player to enter the cabin. Charlie stopped him and they walked to the stewardess's station. Judging from Bobby's contained grimace, it wasn't a pleasant conversation. Bobby eventually came by me. I felt awful putting Bobby in that situation.

"Hey, man, I'm sorry," I pleaded, but Bobby just tapped me on the shoulder reassuringly.

"It's okay, Rook, we're cool, we're cool," with the forced smile of an older brother trying to calm his younger sibling as he took his seat a few rows behind me.

The post-game chats in Charlie's office with Bobby continued for the next couple of weeks, only they weren't friendly, open visits between manager and team leader, but rather closed-door shouting matches.[4]

The Giants lost four out of six in Pittsburgh and St. Louis, then flew to Los Angeles for three games against the first-place Dodgers. The Giants were 33–36 and twelve games behind, and if they were to have any chance of turning it around, this opportunity was crucial.

The Giants lost all three, each by one run, with three straight late-inning blown leads and three straight walk-off hits for the

Dodgers. The Giants were now 33–39 and fifteen games behind. It couldn't possibly have been a more depressing weekend. Horace Stoneham's Giants were now, as never before, finished, in multiple ways.

A few days later Charlie Fox "resigned in the best interest of the club."[5] It's unknown just how voluntary Fox's decision was—probably not very. Stoneham kept Fox in the organization, reassigning him to be the club's chief major league scout; he swapped jobs with Wes Westrum.

Westrum wasn't quite one of Stoneham's organizational lifers, but he was close. He was first acquired as an eighteen-year-old minor league catcher in 1941, played in the majors with the Giants from 1947 to 1957, and coached with them from 1958 through 1963. He went to the New York Mets to coach under Casey Stengel and then, in 1965, replaced the retiring Stengel as manager of the Mets. Westrum held that job until late 1967, then returned to Stoneham's organization to coach from 1968 through 1971. He'd been the Giants' major league and special assignment scout since 1972.

Westrum was well qualified to take over as manager, and Stoneham used no "interim" language in making the announcement. Westrum was an even-tempered, no-drama personality, less intense and emotional than Fox. The team he took over was in free fall. The Giants ended June 1974 with a month's record of 7–20, the worst full month of play by any Giants team since July 1901. Under Westrum the Giants slogged in to finish at 72–90, in fifth place, thirty games behind the division-winning Dodgers.

The dreary death march of the second half was brightened by just one refreshing positive: on September 3, against the Dodgers in Los Angeles, a talkative rookie pitcher named John Montefusco enjoyed a major league debut for the ages. Inserted into the game in emergency first-inning relief, Montefusco pitched out of a bases-loaded, one-out jam. Batting for himself in the second inning, Montefusco drew a walk and came around to score a run. And in the third Montefusco launched a two-run homer as his first major league hit. On the mound he went the distance, logging a full nine innings in relief while allowing just six hits and a run, striking out seven, as the Giants won 9–5. In that final month of the season, Montefusco would win two more games—one of them a complete game shutout of the heavy-hitting Reds, a game in which he also hit another home run—while charming the print and broadcast media as one of the most brazenly quotable characters in all of baseball. A new star had suddenly and flamboyantly arrived.

But Montefusco couldn't salvage the season. Their ninety losses were the most by a Giants team since 1946. What happened to this ball club that had been so good the year before and whose young roster was so promising?

Not everything went badly. John D'Acquisto delivered a solid first full season, finishing tenth in the league in strikeouts and being voted National League Rookie Pitcher of the Year by *The Sporting News*. Sophomore left fielder Gary Matthews essentially replicated the all-around production that had earned him Rookie of the Year honors in 1973. Starting pitchers Jim Barr and Mike Caldwell both had fine years, and catcher Dave Rader delivered a career-best batting average.

But that was it for the good news. Bobby Bonds suffered a big drop-off in power production and delivered the lowest WAR rate of his seven-year major league career. Garry Maddox was doing great into June but then encountered injuries and hit poorly the rest of the way. Chris Speier was blandly so-so, unable to regain the sparkling form that had earlier propelled him to national stardom, and would grace no more magazine covers. Speier's double play partner, Tito Fuentes, plagued by the back trouble that had afflicted him on Opening Day, appeared in just 108 games. and neither hit nor fielded well.

Fox opened the 1974 season with Dave Kingman as his third baseman, but his commitment to that decision lasted just two weeks, as Fox moved him back to first base and went with Steve Ontiveros at third. In late May, Kingman was among the league leaders in home runs, but he then suffered a groin pull and played sporadically for the next couple of months. Through that period, making just nineteen starts, he hit a ghastly .145. Over the season's final weeks Kingman regained his regular status and hit pretty well, but the dreadful midseason struggle had wrecked his year. The abundantly potential star's development remained stalled.

Tom Bradley began the season strongly, but that would be the final stretch of effective pitching in the twenty-seven-year-old's career. In mid-May, in a game in which the Giants' bullpen had been depleted, Fox asked Bradley to take an inning of mop-up relief. In that outing Bradley "felt something pop" in his shoulder.[6] In accordance with the norms of the time, he didn't tell management (or if he did, they didn't listen), but instead, Bradley attempted to pitch through the increasing pain. The results were disastrous, and Fox eventually yanked him from the rotation. Under Westrum, in the second half Bradley got just five starts and eight relief appearances, in which his earned run average was 7.20.

But of all the Giants who encountered disappointing seasons in 1974, none would compare with the catastrophic showing of Ron Bryant. Embarrassed by his swimming pool slide fiasco, Bryant rushed himself back into action, almost as soon as his stitches were pulled, without having benefit of a real spring training. He'd never been a stickler for conditioning anyway, but now he was clearly not in game shape. Bryant's form in 1974 was a mess, and his results were worse: he didn't manage to get his ERA below 8.00 until mid-June and wound up with a mark of 5.61 and a win-loss record of 3–15. Never before in major league history had a twenty-game winner fallen to such immediate ruin.

So, the collapse of the 1974 Giants was a rich combination of injuries, slumps, and underperformance of both mundane and spectacular varieties. It's unusual for a ball club with such a breadth of outstanding young talent to fall apart like that, but such things do occasionally happen. However, for Horace Stoneham's Giants in 1974, whose slim hope of economic survival required fielding a winner to revive fan interest, it was a mortal blow.

Candlestick Park attendance had been a dismal 8,770 per game through May, on average, and once the team was a proven dud, it went steadily downhill from there: over June and July they drew an average of just 5,970, and for the season's final two months they attracted 4,884 per game. In a Monday afternoon game on September 16 against the Atlanta Braves, attendance at Candlestick was an appalling 748—not just the smallest in the Giants' San Francisco history but the smallest in all of Horace Stoneham's thirty-nine-year tenure as owner of the franchise. The season's attendance of 519,987 was last in the major leagues in 1974 and the lowest figure for a Giants' team since the wartime year of 1943. At the close of the year it was Stoneham's awful duty to announce to his shareholders that the National Exhibition Company had posted an annual loss of $1.7 million.[7] There was no more means of forestalling the worst: the San Francisco Giants were now facing insolvency.

Horace Stoneham's state of mind in the autumn of 1974 can only be imagined because, of course, being Horace Stoneham, he issued no public statements. But the imagining is easy: it couldn't be anything but the worst autumn of his life. The Giants weren't just the Stoneham family business—it was more than that. The Giants were the grand gift that had been so enthusiastically presented to Horace by his father, way back in 1919. The Giants were the one asset, the single possession that his father had refused to relinquish as his once-vast personal fortune was picked to the bone by Great Depression creditors. The Giants were the essential crown jewel, the core element that old Pop had made sure he could provide to his son.

In the 1950s, when Horace Stoneham came to the agonizing decision to relocate the team away from the Polo Grounds—and away even from New York, as wrenching as that had been—the guiding and clarifying principle was that he was acting in the best interest of the franchise. The *Giants* were the thing, the key thing. Everything else was secondary.

How terrible it was, then, in the aftermath of the disastrous 1974 season, that Horace Stoneham now faced the desolate truth that he was going to lose that very thing. He simply couldn't afford another season like 1974 without going broke. The irreducible reality was that he'd reached the point at which the only viable option was to sell. The only questions left were to whom and for how much. For Stoneham nothing could possibly be sadder.

As he comprehended these bleak facts and pondered the conditions of sale of his beloved Giants, somehow Horace Stoneham in the autumn of 1974 tore into the annual trading season with zeal. Facing existential oblivion, Stoneham nonetheless behaved like an owner with a long-term vision for enterprise success. He executed three significant trades.

On October 14, 1974, Stoneham sent reliever Elias Sosa along with backup catcher Ken Rudolph to the St. Louis Cardinals for twenty-two-year-old minor league catcher Marc Hill, a highly regarded defensive prospect who'd hit well in AAA in 1974. Sosa—who'd been excellent in 1973 but just so-so in '74—was a fair price to pay. Hill didn't project to immediately challenge incumbent Dave Rader, but he would likely fit in as at least a platoon partner for now, and the team's long-term strength at the vital position was plainly improved.

On December 6, 1974, Stoneham dealt Tito Fuentes along with minor league pitcher Clarence "Butch" Metzger to San Diego in exchange for twenty-four-year-old Derrel Thomas, a versatile fielder who could handle second base or center field and shortstop in a pinch while being quick on the bases and swinging a decent switch-hitting bat. This deal was an example of Ray Kroc's Padres overpaying to acquire a familiar veteran name, and it was a clearly good move on Stoneham's part.

These trades shared a common two-for-one structure of upgrading the talent while getting younger at the same time. And in between those deals, on October 22, 1974, Stoneham executed a very different kind of trade, one of the most significant transactions of his entire tenure.

Bobby Bonds and Bobby Murcer had more in common than a first name. Each was born in 1946. Each arrived in the major leagues as an extraordinarily talented young prospect. Each was forced to deal with the unenviable pressure of constant comparison with his team's aging superstar: the African American Bonds, with his spectacular combination of speed and power, was inevitably characterized as "the next Willie Mays," and the fair-haired Murcer with the Yankees, a shortstop–turned–center fielder with an Oklahoma drawl and a home run bat, was "the next Mickey Mantle."

Both players handled the patently unfair expectations with commendable poise. By the early 1970s it was obvious that neither was going to be the player to whom he had been compared, but each had proven to be a terrific performer in his own right. When Mays departed the Giants and Mantle the Yankees, Bonds and Murcer each became his team's primary star.

But it would be incorrect to consider Bonds and Murcer as equal talents. Bonds had one weakness that Murcer didn't, in that Bonds was highly strikeout prone. This flaw prevented Bonds from sustaining a high batting average, and Murcer consistently hit for a better average. But this was the only way in which Bonds wasn't clearly superior: Bonds hit more home runs than Murcer and stole far more bases; he earned more WAR per season, won more Gold Gloves, and attracted more MVP votes. The objective statistical record along with the contemporary assessment of award voters are in firm agreement that Murcer was an excellent player, but Bonds was significantly better.

Yet Horace Stoneham traded Bonds for Murcer, one for one, in October 1974. Stoneham bet that Murcer's future would be better than Bonds's, despite the fact that Bonds had enjoyed a demonstrably better past. Yankees GM Tal Smith was quick to take him up on the offer.

The explanation could only be that Stoneham had simply lost confidence in Bonds. The deal didn't make the roster any younger or any cheaper (indeed, Bonds was making $100,000 in 1974, but Murcer was making $110,000). And Stoneham, unlike Charlie Fox, had continued to get along well with Bonds—in his memoir D'Acquisto recounts an anecdote of Stoneham and Bonds happily laughing and drinking together in Stoneham's office while the ax was about to fall on Fox; in D'Acquisto's perception Stoneham's firing of Fox was his way of choosing to side with his star player over his manager.[8] But here Stoneham, the owner who treated his players like family and who hated to trade anyone away, swiftly and decisively cut Bonds loose. Certainly, the compelling issue might have been Bonds's drinking, particularly given what the team had just been through with Sam McDowell, but that issue, shall we say, had rarely been something Horace

Stoneham appeared to worry about. Whatever motivated this decision, it was the most dramatic of the ways in which Stoneham's actions in late 1974 didn't seem like those of a short-timer who was ready to throw in the towel. The wisdom of this trade can be questioned, but the passion it revealed was as intense as ever.

As the calendar turned from 1974 to 1975, the United States economy was in recession and struggling with high unemployment and soaring gasoline and energy prices. In the spring of 1975 the South Vietnamese capital of Saigon fell to the North Vietnamese army, ending the twenty-year-long Vietnam War in the first military defeat in United States history. Desperate and chaotic mass evacuations of U.S. military troops and South Vietnamese civilians ensued.

In San Francisco, in September 1975, twenty-one-year-old newspaper heiress Patricia Hearst was arrested on several felony warrants. She had been kidnapped by Symbionese Liberation Army terrorists in 1974 but subsequently seemed to have joined the gang, which committed multiple robberies and murders in California between 1973 and 1975. Also in San Francisco in September 1975, forty-five-year-old Sara Jane Moore, who'd become obsessed with the Hearst case, attempted to shoot President Gerald Ford, narrowly missing due to a faulty sight on her .38 caliber revolver. It was the second assassination attempt on Ford within a span of three weeks. Horace Stoneham's final months of ownership of the Giants took place within a weirdly dispiriting period in which the United States was weak and demoralized like no time since the Great Depression.

If the player transactions Horace Stoneham executed in the fall of 1974 didn't seem to have any relation to the financial crisis overwhelming the franchise, the big deal he made in early 1975 was a stark reminder of his distress. On February 28, 1975, at the outset of spring training, Stoneham's Giants sold Dave Kingman to the New York Mets for a straight $150,000 in cash. This wasn't a trade, a strategic gamble that giving up this will gain that. Nor was it a salary dump, along the lines of the dismissals of the great veterans Mays, McCovey, and Marichal. This was a plain desperation move, a public confession of hopelessness.

Certainly, Kingman had been an enigma with the Giants, a frustrating case of unfulfilled potential. But he was still just twenty-six, and the team was nothing close to a point at which it would make sense for them to just give up on him, to conclude that he'd never get it together. It was still entirely plausible for Kingman to grandly turn the corner and bust out as a slugging star. He was one of the team's most precious assets.

Stoneham had issued no public statements regarding the team's financial predicament. There was speculation and rumor aplenty in the press, of course, but no substantive story had yet developed about just where the Giants were as a business and what was going to happen. But Stoneham's abrupt late-winter move to liquidate Kingman's value served as a public admission, without uttering a word, that the condition of the franchise was dire. Selling off significant still-young major league talent was a last-ditch survival tactic not exhibited in major league baseball since the final desperate years of the St. Louis Browns in the late 1940s. This was burning the furniture to heat the house.

The $150,000 that Kingman fetched was desperately needed to help cover ongoing expenses such as payroll and stadium rental. Stoneham didn't need to say anything. The death spiral was obviously underway, and with that, serious conversations now took place between seriously concerned parties, not all of them within the Giants organization. Other front offices as well as the National League and Major League offices had been worriedly eyeing the Giants for several years, and now phones began ringing, including Stoneham's.

The president of the National League was, lest we forget, Horace Stoneham's nephew. Chub Feeney was now quietly, respectfully, but firmly at his uncle's side to attend to what needed to be done. Feeney had the full commitment of the league's ownerships behind him, none more fully than Walter O'Malley's Dodgers, to help out. Feeney saw to it that Stoneham was now provided with access to substantial lines of credit from the league. Thus, Stoneham was going to be spared much of the day-to-day indignity of struggling with a bankruptcy in progress, as the league would cover any shortages in his expenditures while he conducted the sale of the franchise. Make no mistake: the loans were to be taken against Stoneham's eventual big payday, and it was further understood that the league was planning to hold the vote to approve the Giants' sale in the fall, as soon as the World Series was over. (This last bit would prove overly optimistic.)

So, it was all but official now, and in early May 1975 it was official. Horace Stoneham announced to the board of the National Exhibition Company, and then to the press, that the San Francisco Giants, the National League franchise proudly owned by Stonehams since 1919, was for sale.

Among the many calls Stoneham took in the wake of this bombshell was one from the *New Yorker*'s Roger Angell. Upon reading the news that the legendary franchise was on the market for the first time in nearly sixty years, Angell jumped at the chance to grab an angle on this piece of living baseball history. Angell had grown up a diehard New York Giants fan. He'd never met Stoneham, so his request for an interview was relayed through friends of friends. The message Angell delivered was that he had no desire to inquire about "attendance figures or sales prices" but "just wanted to talk baseball" with Stoneham. Stoneham called Angell immediately. "'Come on out,' he said in a cheerful, gravelly, Polo Grounds sort of voice. 'Come out, and we'll go to the game together.'"[9]

The date that Angell and Stoneham settled upon was Wednesday afternoon, June 18, 1975, against the San Diego Padres at Candlestick. Angell caught the early-morning direct flight from JFK to SFO, rented a car at the airport, and drove straight to the ballpark to meet Stoneham in his office. Angell had been to the Bay Area a few times (we remember his dispatches from 1962 and 1971) but wasn't experienced enough to think through his clothing for a summer afternoon at Candlestick Park. Angell reported: "I had dressed all wrong for it, of course. . . . He shook my hand and examined my airy East Coast midsummer getup and said, 'Oh, no, this won't do.' He went to a closet and produced a voluminous, ancient camel's-hair polo coat and helped me into it. He is a round, pink-faced man with close-cropped white hair, round horn-rimmed spectacles, and a hospitable Irish smile, and he looked much younger than I had expected. (He is 72.) He was wearing tweeds, with an expensive-looking silk tie—a gambler's tie—but he, too, put on a topcoat and buttoned it up before we went out in the sunshine."[10]

Angell didn't so much interview Stoneham that afternoon as just let him talk. Angell recorded the discussion on a portable cassette device, rather than attempt to take notes, which would have been futile. Stoneham rambled widely and freely—his voice on the tape is deep and strong, his New York brogue salty as a pickled egg, and his mood pleasant, easy, clearly cognizant of wanting to help Angell by providing good stories but not forcing it, just letting the afternoon's conversation flow naturally. It was a remarkable capturing by Angell of a personage who'd seen just about everything that he could have seen with regard to baseball over the preceding half-century, who'd plainly loved it and, seemingly genuinely, had no regrets. In Angell's description: "Stoneham talked in an energetic, good-humored way. He reminded me of a good standup, middle-of-the-night bar conversationalist."[11]

Angell noted a fourth-inning interlude in which Stoneham excused himself to take a phone call dealing with the sad news that 1940s and '50s Giants' player Sid Gordon had died of a heart attack at the age of fifty-seven. Stoneham—of course—loved Sid Gordon. He'd sent flowers and written a personal note to Gordon's widow.

In mid-game Stoneham and Angell were joined in the owner's box by Garry Schumacher, now retired but still a regular favorite chum of Stoneham. Schumacher suggested, as subjects for conversation, Sal Maglie and Roy Campanella, then Juan Marichal and Warren Spahn, and Stoneham was off to the races. Angell observed that "Schumacher and his other friends had probably talked together hundreds of times about each of these famous games and vanished companions. Old afternoons were fresh and past players stayed young, and it was the talking that kept them that way."[12]

Later the subject of the upcoming 1975 All-Star Game arose, and Stoneham volunteered that he'd decided to skip it: "They're having business meetings all day, before the game. Who wants *that*? That used to be a holiday. You'd go to the game and then you'd see your friends in the evening. It's the same way at our board meetings. When I first came on our board, all the conversation was about baseball. We'd sit and talk about the game. Now the lawyers outnumber the baseball people. In the old days, it was nothing but baseball with people on the ball clubs—it was a personal thing. Even somebody like Mr. Wrigley, it was him that owned the team, not the company."[13]

This day's game at Candlestick Park was a happy one, the Giants romping to an 8–1 victory behind none other than John Montefusco. At its conclusion Angell and Stoneham retreated from the outdoor balcony seats to the owner's interior office, where Stoneham helped his guest out of the polo coat and hung it back in the closet. Angell was struck with the notion of how many games and how many guests that big helpful garment had known. Angell waited as Stoneham attended to some business at his desk, and finally the Giants' owner buzzed his secretary on the office intercom: "I'm getting a haircut in the morning, so I'll be a little late getting in. Good night, Florence."

Angell described his parting with Horace Stoneham: "We went outside and walked down a ramp in the sunshine. The wind had dropped, and the low hills around the Bay were all alight. It was one of those afternoons when you felt that summer might never end. I started to say something to Stoneham about his parting with the Giants and how I felt about it, but he smiled and cut me off. . . . 'You can't get discouraged over a few bad breaks,' he said. 'In this game, you're always losing sometimes. You can't let yourself complain or feel sorry for yourself.' He walked me to my car in the parking lot, and we shook hands and said goodbye."[14]

The San Francisco Giants' 1975 performance—the actual playing of baseball—was plainly an irrelevance, as attention was focused on the upcoming sale and its many implications. Yet through it all, Stoneham himself, as though unable to help himself, remained attentive to the ball club itself on the field, attempting to improve it—though for the first time, perhaps, the short-timer may have betrayed some immediate-term gratification at the expense of long-term sensibility.

In January, Stoneham executed what seemed to be a marginal transaction, claiming twenty-seven-year-old backup outfielder Von Joshua off waivers from the Dodgers. Other than being the rare instance of a deal between the archrivals, nothing else about this was significant: Joshua had been a scrub for the Dodgers and would likely be one for the Giants, if he would even make the team. But Joshua hit well in spring training and made the team. When the regular season began, Garry Maddox, the exciting young center fielder who'd starred through 1973 and early 1974, found himself in a hitting slump. Manager Wes Westrum gave some center field starts to Joshua, who squared up line drives, and that got him some more starts.

At first base, with Kingman gone, Westrum had turned to Ed Goodson and Gary Thomasson. Presented with a grand opportunity to win the starting job, neither seized it. Meanwhile, Maddox was grumbling to Westrum about his playing time, and Stoneham assessed the situation: the team was doing so-so (11–11), while Maddox was hitting .135, Joshua was hitting .348, and Goodson and Thomasson at first base had combined for .167. Stoneham reasoned that with the emergence of Joshua, the unhappy Maddox was expendable, and the team had a hole at first base. So, on May 4, 1975, Stoneham accepted an offer from the Philadelphia Phillies and traded Maddox straight up for first baseman Willie Montanez.

Montanez was a good player, and he shared with Maddox an interesting attribute: each had carefully reconstructed his swing at the major league level, transforming from a pull-hitting slugger with strikeout issues to a contact-oriented line drive sprayer. While Maddox had started 1975 badly, Montanez was hitting just fine. Certainly, Montanez presented an immediate upgrade for the Giants at first base, but he was a year and a half older than Maddox and not nearly as well-rounded an athlete, less likely to age well. Joshua would take remarkable advantage of his chance, enjoying an out-of-nowhere dream season at .318 with forty-two extra-base hits. Montanez settled in to deliver a solid year at first base, and regardless of the long run, Stoneham had succeeded at providing the team with positive production at both positions over the balance of 1975.

Bobby Murcer was devastated at being traded away by the Yankees and never pretended to want to be playing for the Giants, especially at Candlestick Park. Still, he conducted himself as a professional, and while he didn't provide the power or speed of Bobby Bonds, Murcer performed well.

The big story of the 1975 Giants was John Montefusco. In his first full big-league season, his combination of on-field success and brash personality quickly brought him notoriety. He eagerly presented himself as a cheerfully inoffensive braggart, a rare trick pulled off only by the likes of Dizzy Dean or Muhammad Ali. Montefusco made hilariously bold predictions, not just that he would win his next game but that he'd do it while pitching a shutout and/or striking out the opponent's most feared slugger. Sometimes he would succeed—which was amazing—and sometimes he'd fail, but when he failed, he did so with good humor, which endeared him all the more to the media and to the Giants' fan base.

Giants' broadcaster Al Michaels—who'd replaced the temporarily retired Lon Simmons in 1974 and would stay with the team through 1976, before embarking on his long national network career—coined the nickname "The Count" for Montefusco, as a play on the title character of the nineteenth-century adventure classic *The Count of Monte Cristo*.[15] More than just a zany personality, Montefusco was a terrific pitcher. He threw hard but didn't rely on pure velocity; despite his lack of experience, this rookie expertly changed speeds and spotted locations. He finished the 1975 season second in the league in strikeouts and seventh in ERA, was fourth in the league's Cy Young Award balloting, and beat out Gary Carter to win Rookie of the Year.

Altogether, the Giants in 1975 were a steadfastly middling ball club, strengths neatly matched by weaknesses, and they spent all season hovering around .500 and finished at 80–81, in third place. They were an improvement over the disaster of 1974 but not as good as the contender of 1973. Horace Stoneham thus bowed out with a mediocre finale. In any case, the only folks paying attention to the Giants anymore were the diehards. The team remained last in the major leagues in attendance, at 522,919. There was no hint of last-minute financial hope.

Robert Alfred "Bob" Lurie was born in San Francisco in 1929, the son of Louis Lurie, one of the most successful and prominent commercial real estate developers in the city. The list of Lurie-owned properties was a tour of top-end downtown landmarks, including the Mark Hopkins Hotel, the Curran Theatre, and the Bank of America headquarters building at 555 California Street. Louis Lurie enjoyed a position of power and influence in high places in and around San Francisco. His regular lunch table at Jack's Restaurant on Sacramento Street featured celebrities from the entertainment and sports worlds as well as politicians and fellow business big shots. As *San Francisco Chronicle* columnist Wells Twombly put it, if in Boston there are the Cabots and the Lodges, in San Francisco there are the Luries.[16]

Young Bob Lurie prepped at elite Menlo School on the San Francisco peninsula, then went to Chicago to obtain a business degree at Northwestern University. In the early 1950s he began working for his father, learning the real estate and property management business and, rather in the manner that Horace Stoneham had once done with the Giants, gradually taking on greater responsibility within the family enterprise. Like his own father, Bob Lurie became well-known, well-liked, and well-respected. An avid golfer, young Bob was regularly seen at the area's most prestigious courses and became an annual participant in Bing Crosby's Pro-Am tournament at Pebble Beach in Monterey.

When the Giants arrived in San Francisco in 1958, the up-and-coming Bob Lurie was invited to take a seat on the board of the National Exhibition Company. He was a natural fit, providing Stoneham and the rest of the New Yorkers on the board with a fresh young San Francisco perspective and connections to the Bay Area's social, corporate, and political power centers. In this role Lurie developed close friendships with Stoneham and with Chub Feeney. When the Giants began to encounter financial problems in the early 1970s, there was speculation in the local press that if Stoneham were ever inclined to sell the franchise, Bob Lurie would be a logical candidate to buy it.[17]

In 1974, before Stoneham had come to the decision to sell, Lurie privately approached him and acknowledged that in that event he'd be interested. So, it was a natural development that in early May 1975, prior to his formal announcement that the team was being put up for sale, Stoneham took Lurie aside and let him know that the inside track was his to pursue.[18] Lurie thanked him but told Stoneham that while he would seriously undertake the consideration, he needed time to recruit an investment partner or partners, and he wasn't ready to make an immediate offer.[19]

That was reasonable, and Stoneham understood it, but it was also the case he was in no position to patiently wait for Lurie to decide. In Stoneham's public statements he stressed that he preferred a local buyer who would keep the team in San Francisco, but he was open to considering serious proposals from anyone, anywhere.[20]

Among the first people Lurie talked with about the possibility of buying the Giants was Chub Feeney. Whether or not their conversations went very far in the direction of Feeney himself buying in as a partner with Lurie, speculation to that effect immediately appeared in the local papers. The idea of it made obvious sense: Lurie would be the local connection and the financial anchor, while Feeney would be a natural to run the baseball operation, as no one except Stoneham himself was more steeped than Chub Feeney in the organization's history and culture.[21] However, Feeney was now happily engaged in the role of National League president, and, significantly, the league's key owners, including Walter O'Malley, were happy with Feeney there and weren't comfortable with the idea of solving one problem (ownership of the Giants) by creating another (needing to find a new president). Feeney, likely prodded to do so, put the speculation to rest with a formal statement in mid-May: "It is common knowledge that I am a friend of Bob Lurie, a member of the Giants' board of directors, who reportedly may make an offer to purchase the club from Horace Stoneham. At this time, I wish to clear the air and state that I am not now involved with Lurie or any group in the possible purchase of the club. As president of the National League, a position I enjoy, it is my hope to continue in this position for as long as my presence in this office is desired by the owners of the 12 National League clubs."[22]

With Feeney out as a partner, Lurie's enthusiasm for the concept of purchasing the Giants seemed to cool. As a board member, he well understood the financial distress facing the franchise and the two implacable problems causing it: the direct competition from the Oakland Athletics for the Bay Area's fan population, and the rank unattractiveness of Candlestick Park as the venue presenting the games. The problem with committing to keeping the Giants in San Francisco was that the new owner was committing to taking on the very issues that had driven Stoneham to insolvency. While as a proud San Franciscan and a loyal Giants' fan Lurie wanted to do the right thing, as a prudent businessman he couldn't figure out a way to make the math work. He didn't withdraw his name as a potential buyer, but neither, over the summer of 1975, did he move toward formulating an offer.

With this, Stoneham's, and the National League's, hopes of promptly wrapping up the sale were dashed. This process was going to be long, and the possibility that the team would be relocated grew very real. Lurie's presence in the considerations remained, but he stayed in the background while a variety of other potential buyers emerged. In May, Robert Post, the owner of a Beverly Hills–based mortgage company called American Funding, announced that he was interested but, after he was given a look at the team's books, decided to withdraw. This would be a repeated pattern. In July a group from Japan indicated interest not just in the ball club but also in the Casa Grande real estate holdings in Arizona, but they soon reconsidered. Stoneham's good friend Herman Franks said it was something he was looking into, but he was thinking only of the ball club and didn't want a bundled real estate deal. These and other rumors consumed many news cycles as summer faded into autumn, but actual progress toward finalizing an actual deal was absent.[23]

In late September the National League authorized another $500,000 to cover the Giants' expenses through the end of the year, and patience was beginning to fray.[24] By November—the point at which the league had anticipated holding a vote to approve the sale—with no offers on the table, the league looked for ways to force the issue. Stoneham was persuaded to issue uncondi- tional releases to manager Wes Westrum and his entire coaching staff, as a means of presenting a clean slate for the new owner. The league hired fifty-three-year-old Harold "Spec" Richardson, who'd been the general manager of the Houston Astros from 1967 until being fired in July 1975, to act as the interim GM of the Giants, represent them at the upcoming winter meetings, and undertake player transactions. Though he still owned the fran- chise, Stoneham was now completely out as its operator, as the Giants were a ward of the National League.[25]

At the winter meetings, held in Hollywood, Florida, in early December, Richardson executed one trade, sending young starting pitcher Pete Falcone—who'd won twelve games for the Giants as a rookie in 1975—to the St. Louis Cardinals for light-hitting Gold Glove third baseman Ken Reitz. Also at that meeting, the National League appointed a "San Francisco Committee," chaired by O'Malley and also including Pirates' owner John Galbreath and Expos' owner Charles Bronfman, to drive the Giants' situation to resolution.[26]

New potential offers emerged. Entertainer Danny Kaye, Leo Durocher's old Stoneham-trashing buddy, came forward repre- senting a group interested in buying the franchise and moving it to Seattle but never made a formal offer.[27] Former Giants' pitcher Mike McCormick headed a Bay Area group, as did Allan Mur- ray, the Giant Boosters organizer; both groups did submit bids, but neither met the National Exhibition Company's ask price.[28] Two additional offers were mustered, one from Bob Short, the former owner of the American League's Texas Rangers, who'd relocated that franchise from Washington DC in 1972, and the other from an investment group in Toronto, Canada. Both of these bids also fell through.[29]

The increasing possibility of the franchise's relocation stim- ulated vocal action from concerned fans, who organized "Save

Our Giants" campaigns and even articulated the concept of creating a publicly held cooperative to purchase and own the team, along the lines of the NFL's Green Bay Packers. For his part Walter O'Malley expressed a strong desire to keep the Giants from moving. Through his committee he warned his fellow owners that it would be a strategic blunder to cede the entire Bay Area market to the American League. Of course, O'Malley had a selfish interest as well; even when the Giants were drawing poorly in San Francisco, their three yearly visits to Dodger Stadium always stimulated near-sellouts. O'Malley justifiably didn't want to lose that.[30]

Yet no local buyer had been found who was ready to meet Stoneham's price. Thus, it was a highly significant turn of event when in early January the first offer came through that Stoneham was willing to accept, and it wasn't local. Another group from Toronto, this one headed by the Labatt Brewing Company, offered $8 million cash for the ball club, plus an additional $5.25 million to be posted in escrow to cover legal expenses—which meant, practically, covering the franchise's penalties to the City and County of San Francisco for breaking the lease on Candlestick Park. On January 9, 1976, Stoneham announced to his board that he'd agreed to the offer in principle, and the next day the headline in the San Francisco Examiner read, "GIANTS MOVING TO TORONTO."[31]

The same week that bombshell dropped, forty-six-year-old George Moscone was sworn in as the incoming mayor of San Francisco.[32] A native of the city—indeed, a former all-city basketball star at St. Ignatius Prep near Golden Gate Park—Moscone viewed with horror the idea of San Francisco losing the Giants, especially as the very opening event of his term in office. Moscone immediately proclaimed a "not on my watch" campaign in which he pledged to do everything he possibly could to prevent the team from leaving.[33] His first task was to file suit against the Giants (which Stoneham was plainly anticipating) for breaking their Candlestick Park lease, which was in effect through 1994. That filing then quickly triggered a temporary restraining order that prevented Stoneham from finalizing the sale and prevented the National League from approving it.

This move bought Moscone time, and he didn't waste any. On January 14 the mayor flew to Phoenix, where National League owners were meeting to discuss the situation. Moscone forcefully and persuasively presented San Francisco's case. He gained the owners' trust that he'd be able to do what he was vowing to do, which was return to the league within a short time with a serious and credible buyer willing and able to meet Stoneham's price while keeping the team at Candlestick. They agreed to not do anything for the time being, but the clock was loudly ticking.

Moscone had several potential investors in mind, and after vetting it out, the partnership he decided to support would be between Bob Lurie and Bob Short. The Lurie-Short pairing—sensible in that Lurie provided local connections, while Short brought experience as a major league franchise owner—committed to match the Labatt offer. This maneuver succeeded in persuading Judge John Benson, in a hearing on February 11, 1976, to order an injunction that forced the National League to vote up or down on this new Moscone-brokered offer.

However, that didn't pan out either, as NL owners, wary of Short's highly controversial tenure as Senators-Rangers owner just a few years earlier, voted in a special meeting on February 24 to approve the sale only if Lurie would be designated as the controlling partner, with Short restricted to minority owner status. Short wouldn't hear of this arrangement and backed out.

Thus, it seemed as though nothing could now prevent the sale to the Toronto group, which meant the end of the Giants in San Francisco. But on the morning of March 2, 1976, with literally just hours left on the league's deadline to resolve the question, Mayor Moscone's office received a telephone call from someone named Adolph "Bud" Herseth, a cattleman in Phoenix, Arizona. Herseth claimed to be willing to put up the necessary $4 million to partner with Lurie and purchase the Giants.

No one in San Francisco, or in baseball generally, had ever heard of Herseth, and frantic efforts were undertaken to verify and vet him. He checked out, and with the minutes ticking, Herseth was placed on a phone call with Lurie. The prospective partners met, by voice, and hastily agreed on their arrangement:

Lurie would be the managing partner and Herseth a silent investor, even though he was forking over half of the cash.[34]

It was amazing, but true, and all resolved within that very afternoon. That evening, March 2, 1976, via telephone conference call, the National League approved the sale of the San Francisco Giants franchise from Horace Stoneham's National Exhibition Company to the partnership of Bob Lurie and Bud Herseth. For the first time since 1918, Horace Stoneham and his family were out of the baseball business.

Epilogue

orace Stoneham entered the business of professional baseball in the early 1920s, a point when games had rarely been
broadcast via radio. He'd owned and operated the Giants
since the mid-1930s, a point when the concept of night games was
just being introduced. By the 1960s and '70s not only had every
game been broadcast on radio for decades, but games were often
nationally televised, with the communication signal relayed by
a satellite in geosynchronous orbit. Most games were played at
night, and moreover, artificial turf was widely employed in baseball parks—including one that was entirely indoors. The sweep
of changes Stoneham grappled with, in the business of baseball
and in the world at large, was stunning.

Stoneham was that vanishingly rare individual fortunate
enough to pursue his one and abiding passion as his vocation
for his entire working life. Not every exorbitantly rich kid under-
stands just how stupidly lucky he or she is, but Stoneham—at
least after his Copperopolis sojourn—really seemed to get that.
He'd been handed his favorite thing in the world on a platter, and
he took his responsibility seriously, to attend to its success to the
best of his ability. He wasn't brilliant: he knew it and didn't pretend to be. But Stoneham was smart, hardworking, and effective. He was a good manager, whose employees respected him
and rewarded him with endless loyalty. His strong inclination
was to avoid attention, and thus his trailblazing strides in successfully effecting the racial, cultural, and international integration of the sport have rarely been understood and acknowledged.

He had his share of faults and made his share of mistakes. He was mostly successful but rarely a champion in his competition. He boldly sidestepped a potentially devastating threat to his business in midcareer but a couple of decades later was unable to avoid the killing impact of another. His life's great pain was to behold the failure of his only son to succeed at assuming the role and responsibility of heir, as Horace himself had so diligently done for his own father. Horace Stoneham's experience with, and imprint upon, the sport and the business of professional baseball was intricate.

Stoneham's Giants weren't the last of the family-owned-and-run operations in major league baseball, but they were among a dwindling few. The Stoneham family's circumstances in the business was most similar to that of the Griffiths. Clark Griffith, a onetime star major league pitcher and then a manager, purchased the Washington Senators in 1920; when he died, in 1955, his son Calvin inherited ownership. In 1961 Calvin relocated the franchise to Minneapolis–St. Paul (thus claiming the new market Stoneham had nearly chosen), where they became the Twins. He was still operating there when Stoneham sold the Giants, and Griffith would hang on until finally forced to sell in 1984 to billionaire Carl Pohlad. The Griffith family's situation was comparable to that of Horace Stoneham with the Giants, in that they were in no business other than baseball: it wasn't just a family business; it was *the* family business.

Phil Wrigley was similar to Stoneham and Griffith in that he inherited the Chicago Cubs when his father, William, died in 1932. The key difference, of course, is that in addition to the Cubs, Wrigley had inherited the massively successful chewing gum company that bore the family's name, and the baseball team would never be close to Phil Wrigley's primary source of income. Wrigley was still the owner of the Cubs in the mid-1970s, but he was in declining health and would die in 1977. The Wrigley family would sell the Cubs to the Tribune Company in 1981.

Though it may not have seemed comparable at the time, in fact the Los Angeles Dodgers of Walter O'Malley—a much more prosperous enterprise than the Giants or just about any other

baseball franchise for that matter—were O'Malley's principal business, and when he passed away in 1979, his son, Peter,
inherited ownership, and the family would retain ownership
and operation of the Dodgers until selling to none other than
Rupert Murdoch in 1998.

The sale price for the San Francisco Giants franchise in 1976
was $8 million, but of course Horace Stoneham didn't yield that
total personally. He was the principal owner but didn't own 100
percent of the shares, and moreover, there were the substantial
loans advanced by the National League to be paid off. Nevertheless,
he was far from destitute. Particularly with the sale of their Telegraph Hill house in San Francisco, Horace and Valleda had more
than enough in the bank to retire very comfortably in Scottsdale.

In the first several years of his retirement, Stoneham (and
often Valleda as well) would frequently go to watch the Giants at
spring training workouts and games. But as the seasons passed
and he had less familiarity with the players and the organizational staff, he appeared more rarely. With the sale of his Giants,
Horace Stoneham had closed the book on his life as a public figure. He attended no official major league baseball functions and
undertook no interviews with the media.[1]

It was a placid retirement. In particular, Horace and Valleda
enjoyed hosting visits with their grandchildren, now grown or
growing up. Also, friends would come to visit, and Stoneham
never tired of drinking and reminiscing with his many baseball buddies.

The family was visited with sadness in the mid-1980s. Chuck
Rupert, their beloved son-in-law and father to the grandchildren, developed lung cancer and died, at age sixty-five, in 1985.

Stoneham enjoyed good health past his eightieth birthday. But
a few years later he began to exhibit dementia. Among the symptoms that indicated something was amiss was that the always
impeccably groomed and dressed Horace Stoneham began to
let his hair grow long and unkempt and allow his face to go
unshaven. He died in Scottsdale on January 7, 1990, at the age
of eighty-six. Per his wishes, there was no large public funeral
service, just a low-key family event.

Following Horace's death, Valleda kept the Scottsdale house as her primary residence but spent much of her time visiting daughter Mary ("Wootchie") at her home in Atherton, California. Valleda passed away in 1994, a couple of weeks shy of her ninety-first birthday. Horace and Valleda's son, Pete, mostly lived in Hawaii through these years, but he died in San Francisco in 1996, at the age of sixty-eight. Wootchie remained in Atherton and passed away at age seventy-six in 2001.

As for the San Francisco Giants, the shotgun wedding between Bob Lurie and Bud Herseth served its purpose of saving the franchise from departing the Bay Area. But it wasn't a relationship built to last, as their personalities proved to be thoroughly incompatible. Within a few years Lurie raised the necessary cash to buy out Herseth's share and became sole owner.

Lurie's ownership tenure would last until the early 1990s. By and large his Giants teams endured frustration: in his seventeen seasons, they finished with a losing record ten times. Still, he enjoyed some high moments. During spring training of 1978, Lurie pulled the trigger on a massive trade with the Oakland Athletics that sent seven young players and $300,000 cash across the bay in exchange for ace pitcher Vida Blue. The 1978 Giants, led by the star performances of Blue and blossoming young slugger Jack Clark (a sweet parting gift from Horace Stoneham's amazing farm system), spent most of the season in first place, before finishing a strong third.

Blue was available because Charlie Finley's championship A's team had been wiped out in 1976–77 with the introduction of free agency to major league baseball, as nobody wanted to play for Finley. The sudden collapse of the Athletics cratered their attendance and presented an opportunity for the Giants to reclaim their status as the top attraction in Bay Area baseball. In the excitement of 1978 Bob Lurie's team drew 1.74 million—very nearly matching the franchise record of 1.79 million, set in Candlestick Park's inaugural season 1960—while the A's were now attendance starved. But the Giants fell apart in 1979, and by 1980 their attendance had fallen back to the bottom of the league.

In 1981 Lurie hired Frank Robinson to become the first Black manager in National League history. Under Robinson's forceful leadership, in 1982 the Giants again emerged as a surprise contender, streaking out of nowhere with a 20–7 September to very nearly capture the division. Though again they finished third, the franchise gained some measure of satisfaction that year by preventing the archrival Dodgers from winning the flag, knocking them out with a dramatic win at Candlestick Park on the season's final day. Alas, in subsequent seasons that Giants team quickly declined as well.

Following that stretch, Lurie hired Al Rosen as general manager and Roger Craig as field manager, and in the latter part of the 1980s the Giants finally sustained on-field success. They were Western Division champions in 1987 (though they lost a tough seven-game League Championship Series to the St. Louis Cardinals), and National League pennant winners in 1989 (though they lost the World Series in a four-straight blowout to the resurgent Athletics—now owned by Walter Haas—a result overshadowed by the deadly Loma Prieta earthquake that interrupted the competition).

In the 1980s Lurie was able to work with the city of San Francisco to enact some improvements in the fan amenities at Candlestick Park. Nevertheless, the windswept stadium remained as bad a venue as there was in major league baseball, and just like Stoneham before him, Lurie was finally unable to escape financial distress. Beginning in the late 1980s, Lurie devoted his strategic energy to raising public support for the construction of a new taxpayer-funded ballpark, first in San Francisco, and when that failed, down in Silicon Valley, in Santa Clara or San Jose. But the voters weren't sympathetic, and in 1992 Lurie put the franchise up for sale. In a turn of events eerily similar to those of 1975–76, it appeared that the only viable offer for the Giants was from a group wishing to relocate the ball club, this time to Tampa–St. Petersburg, Florida. But at the last minute, in late 1992, a bid from a group headed by Peter Magowan saved the day and kept the Giants in San Francisco yet again.

The National League franchise that C. A. Stoneham bought in 1918 had a market value of nearly $1.9 million; when Horace

Stoneham sold it in 1976 for $8 million, the escalation was almost exactly equal to the rate of U.S. inflation over that six-decade period. When Lurie sold the franchise in 1992, it went for a cool $100 million, a price appreciation five times greater than the 1976–92 inflation rate—a vivid demonstration of the degree to which the business of major league baseball, by the 1990s, was exploding into an economic magnitude the Stonehams could barely have imagined.

Acknowledgments

The idea to write this book was suggested to me by my friend and fellow lifelong Giants fan Rob Garratt. When he offered this suggestion, Rob was well underway in the process of researching his own book on the related topic of the history of the Giants franchise in San Francisco. He generously provided me with access to all of the relevant research material he'd gathered and also delivered candid feedback on several of the early drafts that would eventually become this book.

My own research could not have been completed without the thorough and professional assistance of Gabriel Schechter, combing through the Hall of Fame archives in Cooperstown, New York.

Others who provided extremely helpful input by reading and reacting to draft sections of the manuscript were Andy McCue, Steve Gietschier, and especially, Dan Levitt.

My editor at the University of Nebraska Press, Rob Taylor, has been a patient and effective coach and guide.

I am sincerely appreciative of the time and attention granted to me by Horace Stoneham's granddaughters, Kim, Jaime, and Sonja Rupert, and their generous sharing with me of a treasure trove of family photographs and heirlooms.

By far my greatest debt of gratitude goes to my wife, Pam, whose steadfast support and tolerance at every turn is of a depth beyond the capacity of words.

Notes

1. Horrie, I Bought You a Ball Club

1. It's unknown whether this is exactly true, but it seems true enough.

2. All of those stars would be elected to the Baseball Hall of Fame: Ewing in 1939, O'Rourke in 1945, Keefe in 1964, Welch in 1973, and Connor in 1976.

3. Henry D. Fetter, *Taking On the Yankees: Winning and Losing in the Business of Baseball, 1903–2003* (New York: W. W. Norton, 2003), 63–64.

4. *New York Times*, May 7, 1905, 2.

5. And though the first World Series between the National and American League champions had been successfully held in 1903, none was played in 1904 because the Giants refused to take part. Both McGraw and John T. Brush, who now owned the Giants, remained implacable enemies of Ban Johnson. In 1905, when the Giants repeated as NL pennant winners, they would finally be persuaded to engage in the World Series (probably by the free money they were leaving on the table by not playing).

6. Robert E. Murphy, *After Many a Summer: The Passing of the Giants and Dodgers and a Golden Age in New York Baseball* (New York: Union Square Press, 2009), 11.

7. *New York Times*, January 16, 1908, 2.

8. Murphy, *After Many a Summer*, 28.

9. Frank Graham, *McGraw of the Giants: An Informal Biography* (New York: G. P. Putnam's Sons, 1944), 113–14.

10. Interview with Horace Stoneham's granddaughters Kim and Jaime Rupert, June 20, 2015.

11. Leo Katcher, *The Big Bankroll: The Life and Times of Arnold Rothstein* (New York: Da Capo Press, 1959), 8.

12. Nat Ferber, *I Found Out: A Confidential Chronicle of the Twenties* (New York: Dial Press, 1939), 195.

13. Murphy, *After Many a Summer*, 30.

14. The surrender was not unconditional. In the settlement Federal League ownership groups were arranged to purchase the American League's St. Louis Browns and the National's Chicago Cubs, a deal that included Wrigley Field as a ballpark to be named later.

15. The New York Giants community was hit hard by the combat death in France on October 5, 1918, of Captain Edward Leslie "Harvard Eddie" Grant, an infielder who'd played for the Giants as recently as 1915. In 1921 a monument to Grant was erected in deepest center field of the Polo Grounds.

16. Roger Angell, "The Companions of the Game," *Five Seasons: A Baseball Companion* (New York: Simon & Schuster, 1977), 267.

17. Noel Hynd, *The Giants of the Polo Grounds: The Glorious Times of Baseball's New York Giants* (Dallas: Taylor, 1988), 210–11.

18. David Pietrusza, *Rothstein: The Life, Times, and Murder of the Criminal Genius Who Fixed the 1919 World Series* (New York: Basic Books, 2003), 129.

19. Pietrusza, *Rothstein*, 129.

20. Lee Allen, *The Giants and the Dodgers: The Fabulous Story of Baseball's Fiercest Feud* (New York: G. P. Putnam's Sons, 1964), 106–7.

21. "At the time of the sale, [Arnold] Rothstein had bribed Judge McQuade in a case involving a fatal shooting at one of his illegal casinos, a joint known as The Partridge Club." Hynd, *Giants of the Polo Grounds*, 211.

22. Allen, *Giants and the Dodgers*, 108. The sale price was the highest yet commanded by a baseball franchise. Stoneham's holding was thirteen hundred shares, and McQuade and McGraw each purchased seventy shares.

23. See Robert Shaplen, "The Lonely, Loyal Mr. Stoneham," *Sports Illustrated*, May 5, 1958, 74; and Frank Graham, "The Shy Boss of the Giants," *Sport* 21, no. 35 (May 1956): 49.

2. Roaring into the Twenties

1. Bruce Kuklick, *To Every Thing a Season: Shibe Park and Urban Philadelphia, 1909–1976* (Princeton NJ: Princeton University Press, 1993).

2. Bruce Allardice, "Out of the Shadows: Joseph 'Sport' Sullivan," *SABR Black Sox Research Committee Newsletter* 6, no. 1 (June 2014): 9. https://famous-trials.com/blacksox.

3. Douglas Linder, "The Black Sox Trial: An Account," University of Missouri–Kansas City School of Law, https://famous-trials.com/blacksox.

4. Joe King, *The San Francisco Giants* (Englewood Cliffs NJ: Prentice-Hall, 1958), 126.

5. *New York Tribune*, January 15, 1919.

6. King, *San Francisco Giants*, 159.

7. Allen, *Giants and the Dodgers*, 116.

8. Daniel R. Levitt, *Ed Barrow: The Bulldog Who Built the Yankees' First Dynasty* (Lincoln: University of Nebraska Press, 2008), 197.

9. Jacob L. Ruppert, as told to Dan Daniel, "Behind the Scenes of the Yankees . . . Ruppert Almost Broke Up AL," *New York World Telegram*, February 16, 1938.

10. Neil J. Sullivan, *The Diamond in the Bronx: Yankee Stadium and the Politics of New York* (New York: Oxford University Press, 2001), 28–29.

11. Lyle Spatz and Steve Steinberg, *1921: The Yankees, the Giants, and the Battle for Baseball Supremacy in New York* (Lincoln: University of Nebraska Press, 2010), 80.

12. Don Jensen, "John McGraw," SABR BioProject essay, Society for American Baseball Research, http://sabr.org/bioproj/person/fef5035f.

13. King, *San Francisco Giants*, 126.

14. James Damschroder, "Former Giants Owner Got an Education in Copperopolis," *Sonora Union Democrat*, March 31, 2008.

15. Damschroder, "Former Giants Owner."

3. Hard Truths

1. Fetter, *Taking On the Yankees*, 89–92.

2. Fetter, *Taking On the Yankees*, 89.

3. Fetter, *Taking On the Yankees*, 89.

4. Spatz and Steinberg, *1921*, 20.

5. Angell, "Companions of the Game," 269.

6. Interview with Kim and Jaime Rupert, June 20, 2015.

7. Angell, "Companions of the Game," 269–70.

8. Angell, "Companions of the Game," 269.

9. Fred Stein, "Frankie Frisch," in *The 1934 St. Louis Cardinals: The World Champion Gas House Gang*, ed. Charles H. Faber (Phoenix AZ: Society for American Baseball Research Digital Library, 2014), 20:109.

10. Dick Bartell and Norman L. Macht, *Rowdy Richard: A First-Hand Account of the National League Baseball Wars of the 1930s and the Men Who Fought Them* (Berkeley CA: North Atlantic Books, 1993), 223.

11. McGraw, with Stoneham's enthusiastic support, had long sought to find a way to persuade general manager Branch Rickey of the Cardinals to part with Hornsby in some manner of sale or trade. Lee Lowenfish, *Branch Rickey: Baseball's Ferocious Gentleman* (Lincoln: University of Nebraska Press, 2007), 115–16.

While the Frisch-for-Hornsby core concept of the deal was forged between McGraw and Rickey, the final negotiation was handled strictly between Stoneham and Cardinals' owner Sam Breadon. Lowenfish, *Branch Rickey*, 173.

12. The stunning deal included still another complicated piece: "Hornsby . . . owned stock in the St. Louis Cardinals and demanded $116 a share for it from Sam Breadon, Cards owner. Breadon pointed out that the stock had cost Hornsby $45 a share. Stoneham fought the league when members suggested the Giants make up the difference. When the league ruled that Hornsby could not play

with the Giants while owning St. Louis stock, Stoneham instructed his lawyer, Leo J. Bondy, to apply for an injunction against John Heydler, league president. The league surrendered and made up the difference between Hornsby's asking price and Breadon's offer." King, *San Francisco Giants*, 128.

13. Graham, *McGraw of the Giants*, 215.

14. McGraw's primary complaint was severe sinusitis, which caused headaches and blurred vision, but he also suffered from chronic digestive problems exacerbated by years of heavy drinking. Hornsby handled the managerial role in thirty-two Giants' games in 1927. In 1924 and 1925 McGraw had missed a total of seventy-six games, and at that time his substitute was coach Hughie Jennings, McGraw's friend and teammate from his Baltimore days.

15. OPS+ is the calculation of on-base percentage plus slugging percentage, normalized for ballpark and league context, such that 100 is defined as league-average performance. Hornsby's OPS+ in 1927 was 175, the highest mark achieved by any Giants' batter since Roger Connor's 176 in 1888.

16. Hynd, *Giants of the Polo Grounds*, 270–71.

17. McQuade would sue for breach of contract. In 1931 he would win an award for back salary, but that judgement would be overturned on appeal. Allen, *Giants and the Dodgers*, 145.

18. King, *San Francisco Giants*, 128–29.

19. Roger Kahn, *The Era: 1947–1957, When the Yankees, the Dodgers, and the Giants Ruled the Baseball World* (New York: Ticknor & Fields, 1993), 20.

20. Peter Williams, *When the Giants Were Giants: Bill Terry and the Golden Age of New York Baseball* (Chapel Hill NC: Algonquin Books, 1994), 12.

21. Williams, *When the Giants Were Giants*, 13.

22. Williams, *When the Giants Were Giants*, 43–45.

23. William Manchester, *The Glory and the Dream: A Narrative History of America, 1932–1972* (New York: Bantam Books, 1974), 31–36.

24. Allen, *Giants and the Dodgers*, 150.

25. Mathewson had died in 1925 from tuberculosis at the age of forty-five and Youngs in 1927 from kidney failure at the age of thirty. Both tragedies hit McGraw very hard.

26. Williams, *When the Giants Were Giants*, 121–22.

27. Allen, *Giants and the Dodgers*, 150.

28. Hynd, *Giants of the Polo Grounds*, 274.

29. Frank Graham, "The San Francisco Giants," in *The National League*, ed. Ed Fitzgerald (New York: Grosset & Dunlap, 1966), 270.

30. Williams, *When the Giants Were Giants*, 123–24.

31. Levitt, *Ed Barrow*, 3–4.

32. Lee Allen, *The National League Story: The Official History* (New York: Hill & Wang, 1961), 183.

33. Lowenfish, *Branch Rickey*, 125.

34. Levitt, *Ed Barrow*, 261–77.

35. The dire economic circumstances of the time impacted everything, of course. Many, if not most, minor league teams were in desperate straits in the early 1930s and thus suddenly eager to accept controls imposed by "parent" major teams that they'd resisted for years, so long as those controls came with dependable revenue.

36. Williams, *When the Giants Were Giants*, 127–29. Lindstrom's expectation that it would be him rather than Terry to be promoted to manager upon McGraw's retirement wasn't very realistic, as Lindstrom was still only twenty-six years old in 1932 (Terry was thirty-three), and even in that era of frequent player-managers, very few were nearly that young.

37. Allen, *Giants and the Dodgers*, 153.

38. On July 2, 1933, at the Polo Grounds, Hubbell pitched one of history's all-time greatest games, an eighteen-inning complete game 1–0 shutout of the St. Louis Cardinals in which he surrendered just six hits while walking none and striking out twelve. That remarkable feat took place in the first game of a doubleheader between the first-place Giants and second-place Cardinals, and in the second game Giants' right-hander Roy Parmelee outdueled none other than Dizzy Dean, winning again by just 1–0 while striking out thirteen (and again, amazingly, with zero walks) in nine innings.

39. Williams, *When the Giants Were Giants*, 156.

40. Graham, *McGraw of the Giants*, 264.

41. Graham, *McGraw of the Giants*, 264.

42. Hynd, *Giants of the Polo Grounds*, 291.

43. Allen, *Giants and the Dodgers*, 156.

44. Hynd, *Giants of the Polo Grounds*, 292.

45. George Genovese with Dan Taylor, *A Scout's Report: My 70 Years in Baseball*, (Jefferson NC: McFarland & Company, 2015), 107.

46. Allen, *Giants and the Dodgers*, 162.

47. Williams, *When the Giants Were Giants*, 193.

48. Williams, *When the Giants Were Giants*, 193.

49. Williams, *When the Giants Were Giants*, 194.

50. Murphy, *After Many a Summer*, 32–33.

51. "Stoneham's Son Is Likely to Direct Giants," *Brooklyn Daily Eagle*, January 7, 1936, 18–19.

4. Brooklyn Is Still in the League

1. Allen, *Giants and the Dodgers*, 162.

2. King, *San Francisco Giants*, 130.

3. Arthur E. Patterson, "Polo Grounds Pageant Celebrates League's Birth Today," *New York Herald Tribune*, August 13, 1936, 18.

4. Hynd, *Giants of the Polo Grounds*, 301.

5. Paul Mickelson, "Giants' Stoneham Oozes Optimism," *Rochester Democrat and Chronicle*, September 1, 1936, 18.

6. Fred Stein, *Mel Ott: The Little Giant of Baseball* (Jefferson NC: McFarland & Company, 1999), 81.

7. Stein, *Mel Ott*, 88.

8. Fred Stein, *Under Coogan's Bluff: A Fan's Recollections of the Giants under Terry and Ott* (Alexandria VA: self-published, 1978), 59.

9. Allen, *Giants and the Dodgers*, 166.

10. Tim Wendel, "Horace Stoneham," National Pastime Museum, December 28, 2014, https://web.archive.org/web/20161117142055/http:/www.thenationalpastimemuseum.com/article/horace-stoneham.

11. Murphy, *After Many a Summer*, 37.

12. Murphy, *After Many a Summer*, 178.

13. Kahn, *Era*, 74.

14. Kahn, *Era*, 21–22.

15. Interview with Stoneham granddaughters Sonja and Kim Rupert, August 2016.

16. Allen, *Giants and the Dodgers*, 166.

17. Allen, *Giants and the Dodgers*, 168.

18. Allen, *Giants and the Dodgers*, 181.

19. Allen, *Giants and the Dodgers*, 173–74.

20. Gelernter, *1939*, 1–2.

21. *Challenge trade* is a term coined by Bill James to describe a trade that, instead of expending surplus talent from one position in exchange for needed talent at a different position, exchanges players directly at the same position. In this sense it is a stark "challenge," a wager by both sides that the player being received will perform better at this position than the player expended.

22. *Indianapolis Star*, December 12, 1938, 17.

23. Stein, *Under Coogan's Bluff*, 69.

24. Stein, *Mel Ott*, 110.

25. Stein, *Under Coogan's Bluff*, 75

26. Joshua Prager, *The Echoing Green: The Untold Story of Bobby Thomson, Ralph Branca, and the Shot Heard Round the World* (New York: Pantheon, 2006), 42.

27. Ben Gold, "Young Makes Giants Forget All about Zeke," *Brooklyn Daily Eagle*, April 27, 1940, 11.

28. Williams, *When the Giants Were Giants*, 272.

29. King, *San Francisco Giants*, 131.

30. Stein, *Mel Ott*, 110–11.

31. Williams, *When the Giants Were Giants*, 277.

32. Stein, *Mel Ott*, 113.

33. Stein, *Mel Ott*, 114.

34. Williams, *When the Giants Were Giants*, 275–76.

35. Judson Bailey, "2-Year Contracts Granted Both by Stoneham," *Rochester Democrat and Chronicle*, December 3, 1941, 26.

5. War, Peace, and Nice Guys

1. George Q. Flynn, *The Draft: 1940–1973* (Lawrence: University Press of Kansas, 1993), 46.

2. Erasmo Gamboa, "On the Nation's Periphery: Mexican Braceros and the Pacific Northwest Railroad Industry, 1943–1946," in *Mexican-Americans and World War II*, ed. Maggie Rivas-Rodriguez (Austin: University of Texas Press, 2005), 269.

3. Duane Ernest Miller, "Barbed-Wire Farm Laborers: Michigan's Prisoners of War Experience during World War II," *Michigan History* 73, no. 5 (September 1989): 12–17.

4. Paul A. C. Koistinen, *Arsenal of World War II: The Political Economy of American Warfare, 1940–1945* (Lawrence: University Press of Kansas, 2004), 410.

5. Harold G. Vatter, *The U.S. Economy in World War II* (New York: Columbia University Press, 1985), 27–31.

6. Daniel Kryder, *Divided Arsenal: Race and the American State during World War II* (Cambridge: Cambridge University Press, 2000), 113–29.

7. Two former major leaguers sacrificed their lives in battle: Elmer Gedeon, an outfielder who'd sipped a cup of coffee with the Senators in 1939, was a bomber pilot whose B-26 was shot down in France in April 1944, and Harry O'Neill, who'd appeared as a catcher in a single inning for the Athletics in '39, was a U.S. Marine Corps lieutenant killed by a sniper on Iwo Jima in March 1945. At least 137 additional players with strictly minor league experience gave their full last measure of devotion. See William B. Mead, *Even the Browns* (Chicago: Contemporary Books, 1978), 189–201.

8. Allen, *Giants and the Dodgers*, 180.

9. "Giants on Rebound, Loom as Flag Threat," *Rochester Democrat and Chronicle*, December 13, 1941, 17.

10. Ott led the National League in OPS+ in 1932, 1934, 1936, and 1938. Mize led in 1937, 1939, and 1940.

11. Hynd, *Giants of the Polo Grounds*, 321.

12. Ott removed Young for a defensive replacement in twenty-three of his fifty-four center field starts in 1942.

13. "Reds Get Babe Young," *Cincinnati Enquirer*, June 8, 1947, 26.

14. Ott led the 1942 National League in OPS+ with 165, and Mize was third at 161.

15. Hynd, *Giants of the Polo Grounds*, 323–24.

16. Allen, *Giants and the Dodgers*, 186.

17. Allen, *Giants and the Dodgers*, 181.

18. Andy McCue, "Branch Rickey," in *The Team That Changed Baseball and America Forever*, ed. Lyle Spatz (Lincoln: University of Nebraska Press, 2012).

19. Allen, *Giants and the Dodgers*, 182.

20. Allen, *Giants and the Dodgers*, 186.

21. Williams, *When the Giants Were Giants*, 283–87.

22. Damschroder, "Former Giants Owner."

23. Allen, *Giants and the Dodgers*, 184.

24. King, *San Francisco Giants*, 109–10.

25. Adrian Burgos Jr., *Cuban Star: How One Negro-League Owner Changed the Face of Baseball* (New York: Hill & Wang, 2011), 158.

26. Allen, *Giants and the Dodgers*, 187–88.

27. Jules Tygiel, *Baseball's Great Experiment: Jackie Robinson and His Legacy* (New York: Oxford University Press, 1997), 69.

28. Tygiel, *Baseball's Great Experiment*, 80.

29. Adams had blossomed under Mel Ott in a very modern high-usage mode, with an unprecedented run of four consecutive seasons of over 60 appearances in 1942–45, including a twentieth-century-record 70 games in 1943. Adams's four-year total of 261 pitching appearances—all but 7 of them in relief—wouldn't be exceeded until 1962–65, when both Ron Perranoski and Dick Radatz made 270.

30. "Cardinals Sell Cooper to NY for $175,000," *Syracuse Post-Standard*, January 6, 1946, 47.

31. *San Francisco Examiner*, January 10, 1946.

32. Gerald Eskenazi, *The Lip: A Biography of Leo Durocher* (New York: William Morrow, 1993), 229.

33. *New York Journal-American*, July 7, 1946.

34. *The Sporting News*, July 17, 1946.

35. Murphy, *After Many a Summer*, 38–39.

36. Stein, *Mel Ott*, 162–63.

6. We Knew Segregation Was Wrong

1. Meanwhile, the park's enormous expanse of foul territory had a depressive effect on batting averages, and on balance it played as a neutral to slightly above-average scoring environment.

2. Eskenazi, *Lip*, 205–6.

3. Red Barber, *1947: When All Hell Broke Loose in Baseball* (New York: Doubleday, 1982), 213.

4. Lowenfish, *Branch Rickey*, 446–47.

5. Lowenfish, *Branch Rickey*, 447–48.

6. Lowenfish, *Branch Rickey*, 458–59.

7. Lowenfish, *Branch Rickey*, 459.

8. By 1950 the *New York Daily News*, under sports editor Jimmy Cannon and featuring brash young columnist Dick Young, openly feuding with Rickey, adopted a policy of refusing to mention Burt Shotton by name, instead using the acronym KOBS (for Kindly Old Burt Shotton). See Roger Kahn, *The Boys of Summer* (New York: Signet, 1973), 105.

9. Stein, *Mel Ott*, 177–78.

10. Eskenazi, *Lip*, 227–28.

11. Murphy, *After Many a Summer*, 39.

12. Kahn, *Era*, 153.

13. *New York Herald Tribune*, July 17, 1948.

14. Arnold Hano, *Greatest Giants of Them All* (New York: G. P. Putnam, 1967), 59.

15. Stein, *Mel Ott*, 180–81.

16. Hynd, *Giants of the Polo Grounds*, 354–55.

17. "MARY V. STONEHAM BRIDE OF OFFICER," *New York Times*, June 5, 1949.

18. Barber, *1947*, 248–49.

19. Tygiel, *Baseball's Great Experiment*, 212–14.

20. Tygiel, *Baseball's Great Experiment*, 221–22.

21. Tygiel, *Baseball's Great Experiment*, 224.

22. Tygiel, *Baseball's Great Experiment*, 224.

23. Tygiel, *Baseball's Great Experiment*, 243.

24. Kahn, *Era*, 188.

25. Burgos, *Cuban Star*, 182–83.

26. Stew Thornley, "Voice of the Giants: Russ Hodges," in *The Polo Grounds: Essays and Memories of New York City's Historic Ballpark, 1880–1963*, ed. Stew Thornley (Jefferson City NC: McFarland, 2019), 163.

27. Allen, *Giants and the Dodgers*, 202–3.

28. Larry Moffi and Jonathan Kronstadt, *Crossing the Line: Black Major Leaguers, 1947–1959* (Iowa City: University of Iowa Press, 1994), 40.

29. Ralph Roden, "Yanks Purchase Mize in Surprise Transaction," *Syracuse Post-Standard*, August 23, 1949, 12.

30. "Braves Trade Dark, Stanky for Giants' Kerr, Gordon, Marshall, Hurler Sam Webb," *Rochester Democrat and Chronicle*, December 15, 1949, 40.

31. "Braves Trade Dark, Stanky," 40.

32. Lowenfish, *Branch Rickey*, 398.

33. Angell, "Companions of the Game," 271.

34. Murphy, *After Many a Summer*, 41.

35. Harshman delivered prodigious minor league home run totals but also lots of strikeouts and low batting averages. In 1952 he would be converted from a first baseman to a pitcher, and in that role he would thrive. The Giants sold him to the Chicago White Sox, and in the American League from 1954 through 1960, Harshman would win sixty-nine games.

36. Clint Hartung, "the Hondo Hurricane," had been a sensation in the New York papers in early 1947. A green twenty-four-year-old rookie straight out of four years of service in the army air corps, Hartung enjoyed a terrific spring training. Ott and Stoneham, unwisely, placed him directly onto the Giants' 1947 major league roster as an old-fashioned two-way pitcher-outfielder. Big and strong (six foot five, 210 pounds), Hartung captured wide attention that year with some big moments both on the mound and at the

plate. But his talent, while prodigious, was entirely raw: as a pitcher, his fast-ball was hard but straight, and he was unable to command breaking stuff to support it, while as a hitter, he showed fine power but little capacity to master the strike zone.

37. James and Neyer, *Neyer/James Guide to Pitchers*, 238.

38. Jim Hearn's combined earned run average in 1950 with the Cardinals and the Giants was 2.49 in 134 innings of work. Under the rules in effect at the time, ten complete games was the qualifying minimum for the league's ERA title, so Hearn was honored as the league's ERA champion. The very next year the major league standard would be changed, and pitchers would need to work at least one inning per scheduled game (154 in those days, 162 beginning in the 1960s) to qualify. Had that standard applied in 1950, the National League ERA leader would have been Sal Maglie, at 2.71. See Macmillan, *The Baseball Encyclopedia: The Complete and Official Record of Major League Baseball* (New York: Information Concepts Incorporated, 1969), 2335.

39. James S. Hirsch, *Willie Mays: The Life, the Legend* (New York: Scribner, 2010), 79.

40. Hirsch, *Willie Mays*, 79–80.

41. Allen, *Giants and the Dodgers*, 205.

7. Stoneham Has Finally Got a Winner

1. Eskenazi, *Lip*, 247.

2. Monte Irvin with James A. Riley, *Monte Irvin: Nice Guys Finish First* (New York: Carroll & Graf, 1996), 152.

3. Arnold Hano, *Willie Mays* (New York: Grosset & Dunlap, 1966), 74.

4. Hano, *Willie Mays*, 55.

5. *Brooklyn Daily Eagle*, May 25, 1951, 16.

6. Hano, *Willie Mays*, 57.

7. J. G. Taylor Spink, ed., *Baseball Guide and Record Book, 1951* (St. Louis: Charles C. Spink & Son, 1951), 49.

8. Hirsch, *Willie Mays*, 117–18.

9. Hirsch, *Willie Mays*, 118–19.

10. Eskenazi, *Lip*, 249.

11. Hano, *Willie Mays*, 58–59.

12. Hirsch, *Willie Mays*, 121.

13. John Drebinger, *New York Times*, May 26, 1951.

14. Hirsch, *Willie Mays*, 122–23.

15. Hano, *Willie Mays*, 64.

16. Allen, *Giants and the Dodgers*, 212.

17. Hano, *Willie Mays*, 69–70.

18. Mike Mandel, *SF Giants: An Oral History* (Santa Cruz CA: self-published, 1979), 30.

19. Rosenbaum and Stevens, *Giants of San Francisco*, 130–32.

20. Andy McCue, *Mover and Shaker: Walter O'Malley, the Dodgers, and Baseball's Westward Expansion* (Lincoln: University of Nebraska Press, 2014), 90.

21. Allen, *Giants and the Dodgers*, 214.

22. Prager, *Echoing Green*, 64.

23. Hirsch, *Willie Mays*, 152–53.

24. Hano, *Willie Mays*, 68.

25. Hano, *Willie Mays*, 73–74.

26. And of course, the Giants' sign stealing at the Polo Grounds had no bearing on their run prevention.

27. Eskenazi, *Lip*, 256.

28. Irvin with Riley, *Monte Irvin*, 158.

29. The Hodges call became available to the world, preserved as an object of recorded sound, only because an amateur hobbyist taped it off his home radio speaker. Magnetic tape recording itself was still a new and rare technology in 1951, and the broadcast communications business had not yet established the practice of recording and archiving productions.

30. Don DeLillo, *Underworld* (New York: Simon & Schuster, 1997), 40–44. The novel's opening chapter was adapted from DeLillo's 1992 novella *Pafko at the Wall*. In both versions the narrative of the game and the climactic home run is interspersed with darkly hilarious interactions among a particular party of four in the box seats: J. Edgar Hoover, Jackie Gleason, Frank Sinatra, and Toots Shor.

31. Steve Bitker, *The Original San Francisco Giants: The Giants of '58* (Champaign IL: Sports Publishing, 1998), 61.

32. "STANKY MAKES IT OFFICIAL," *Brooklyn Daily Eagle*, December 12, 1951, 23. Stoneham asked for Enos Slaughter in return, but the Cards said no.

33. Dick Schaap, "Hoyt Wilhelm: Nothing but Knucklers," in *Baseball Stars of 1960*, ed. Ray Robinson (New York: Pyramid, 1960), 57.

34. Had the ten complete games qualifying standard still been in place in 1952, as it had for Jim Hearn in 1950, then Wilhelm would not have qualified for the league's ERA title, and the champion would have instead been the Chicago Cubs' Warren Hacker, at 2.58.

35. Allen, *Giants and the Dodgers*, 212.

36. Eskenazi, *Lip*, 265.

37. James R. Walker and Robert V. Bellamy, *Center Field Shot: A History of Baseball on Television* (Lincoln: University of Nebraska Press, 2008), 182.

38. Walker and Bellamy, *Center Field Shot*, 188.

39. Walker and Bellamy, *Center Field Shot*, 191.

40. King, *San Francisco Giants*, 103.

41. "Baseball Box Office Hit by Video," *New York Times*, November 15, 1948.

42. While packing up the crew and equipment and televising from the road was technically feasible in this era, the cost of renting access to AT&T's coaxial cable lines to relay the signal home was still prohibitively expensive.

43. Harada was wounded three separate times during his military intelligence service.

44. Robert K. Fitts, *Mashi: The Unfulfilled Baseball Dreams of Masanori Murakami, the First Japanese Major Leaguer* (Lincoln: University of Nebraska Press, 2014), 38.

45. "STONEHAM, II, LEARNING ROPES," *New York Times*, May 9, 1946.

46. "Young Stoneham Has Trenton Giants Job," *New York Times*, April 30, 1950.

47. Bill Corum, "Pete Stoneham Looms Giants' Future Prexy," *New York Journal-American*, December 28, 1951, 18.

48. Moffi and Kronstadt, *Crossing the Line*, 93.

49. Hirsch, *Willie Mays*, 194–96.

50. John Drebinger, "Giants Trade Thomson to Braves; '51 Pennant Hero in 6-Player Deal to Milwaukee," *New York Times*, February 2, 1954, 1.

51. The term *bonus baby* was applied in this period to players signed as amateurs to contracts with bonus payment amounts large enough to trigger a rule, then in effect, requiring the signing team to immediately place the rookie on the active major league roster, prohibited from being farmed to the minors without going through waivers. See Steve Treder, "Cash in the Cradle: The Bonus Babies," *Hardball Times*, November 1, 2004, www.fangraphs.com /tht/cash-in-the-cradle-the-bonus-babies/.

52. Red Smith, "Views of Sports," *New York Herald Tribune*, February 2, 1954.

53. Mays's OPS+ of 175 was exactly equal to that of Hornsby in 1927, his one season with the Giants.

54. Hano, *Willie Mays*, 99–100.

55. Hano, *Willie Mays*, 95–96.

56. Hano, *Willie Mays*, 105–6.

57. Estimated runs saved above average is calculated by comparing every opposing batter's career rates of outs by position (for example, if 30 percent of a batter's outs are hit to the shortstop, then every time that batter gets a hit, the shortstop is charged 0.3 hits) against his actual rate of outs against a specific fielder in an individual season. This is calculated for every position and performed separately when batting against right-handed and left-handed pitching separately, as switch hitters will have very different ball in play distributions depending on which side of the plate they hit from. The fractional hits are summed for every fielder, combined with plays made and errors, to produce a "totalzone" score, which is then adjusted by ballpark and converted to runs. See Sean Smith, BaseballProjection.com, http://apps.baseballprojection.com/blog/.

58. Angell, "Companions of the Game," 273.

59. ERA+ converts raw earned run average into a figure normalized for ballpark and league context, such that 100 is defined as league-average performance.

60. Will Grimsley, "Introducing Mr. Dusty Rhodes, Pinup Boy of New York Giants," *Florence Morning News*, October 1, 1954, 15.

61. Arnold Hano, *A Day in the Bleachers* (New York: Cromwell, 1955), 116–24.

62. Roscoe McGowen, "Champions Quietly Happy after Humbling Cleveland," *New York Times*, October 3, 1954.

63. King, *San Francisco Giants*, 112–13.

64. Eskenazi, *Lip*, 280.

8. We Have No Chance to Survive Here

1. Eskenazi, *Lip*, 271–72.

2. Kahn, *Era*, 326–27.

3. Eskenazi, *Lip*, 281.

4. Bill Veeck, with Ed Linn, *The Hustler's Handbook* (New York: Putnam, 1965), 89.

5. Williams's issues with his back were undoubtedly not helped when he was bowled over by the Dodgers' Jackie Robinson in a violent and controversial collision as Williams was covering first base on a bunt on April 23, 1955. However, that play in itself did not ruin Williams's career, as some accounts insist. His back condition was a problem already—he'd missed much of the 1953 season because of it—and he remained in the game following the Robinson incident and did not go on the disabled list at that point. But it continued to worsen. In August he was sent to the Mayo Clinic and diagnosed with an incurable arthritic spinal condition and advised to quit playing baseball. Williams was disappointed with Robinson regarding that play but bore no lasting ill will toward him and indeed admired him. C. Paul Rodgers III, "Davey Williams," SABR BioProject essay, Society for American Baseball Research, https://sabr.org/bioproj/person/00b5ef8b.

6. Kahn, *Era*, 323.

7. Allen, *Giants and the Dodgers*, 219.

8. Allen, *Giants and the Dodgers*, 219–20.

9. Williams, *When the Giants Were Giants*, 295–96.

10. McCue, *Mover and Shaker*, 145.

11. Allen, *Giants and the Dodgers*, 222–23.

12. Allen, *Giants and the Dodgers*, 224.

13. King, *San Francisco Giants*, 133–34.

14. McCue, *Mover and Shaker*, 146.

15. There had been much discussion regarding the possibility of placing a major league team or teams in California for many years before 1957, of course. The St. Louis Browns were supposedly poised to propose a relocation to Los Angeles as early as 1941, before that idea was scuttled by World War II. But as a practical matter, it wasn't until the mid-1950s, when the introduction of jet engine passenger airplanes significantly reduced travel time, that scheduling would be economically feasible. And even with jet aircraft available, the logistical inefficiency of placing just one team on the West Coast remained an issue. It made far more sense for a league to put two (or more) teams there rather than just one.

16. Art Rosenbaum and Bob Stevens, *The Giants of San Francisco* (New York: Coward-McCann, 1963), 64–66.

17. Allen, *Giants and the Dodgers*, 225.

18. McCue, *Mover and Shaker*, 149.

19. Allen, *Giants and the Dodgers*, 226.

20. The lone board member who voted against the relocation was M. Donald Grant, who would become a founding minority owner of the New York Mets.

21. McCue, *Mover and Shaker*, 357.

22. Harvey Frommer, *New York City Baseball: The Golden Age, 1947–1957* (Lanham MD: Taylor Trade Publishing, 1980), 8.

23. Frommer, *New York City Baseball*, 10.

24. Robert F. Garratt, *Home Team: The Turbulent History of the San Francisco Giants* (Lincoln: University of Nebraska Press, 2017), 23.

25. Garratt, *Home Team*, 24.

26. Murphy, *After Many a Summer*, 40.

27. Shaplen, "Lonely Loyal Mr. Stoneham."

28. Robert Creamer, *Sports Illustrated*, May 20, 1957.

29. Veeck, *Hustler's Handbook*, 78–82.

30. Murphy, *After Many a Summer*, 41–42.

31. Garratt, *Home Team*, 19.

32. Murphy, *After Many a Summer*, 41.

33. Murphy, *After Many a Summer*, 316–17.

34. Walker and Bellamy, *Center Field Shot*, 57–58.

35. Garratt, *Home Team*, 24–25.

36. Rosenbaum and Stevens, *Giants of San Francisco*, 62.

37. Garratt, *Home Team*, 25–26.

38. Walker and Bellamy, *Center Field Shot*, 59.

39. Garratt, *Home Team*, 27–28.

40. Garratt, *Home Team*, 36–37.

41. "STONEHAM SON ACCUSED, Coroner's Jury Rules Him Negligent in Fatal Crash," *New York Times*, February 8, 1958, 22.

9. Open Your Golden Gate

1. Garratt, *Home Team*, 20.

2. Bitker, *Original San Francisco Giants*, 11–12.

3. "Charles Horace (Pete) Stoneham, 30 years old, son of the president of the San Francisco Giants baseball club, was sued for $250,000 today in the death of a Canadian woman and the injury of her husband in an automobile accident. Also named as defendants in the United States District Court suit filed by William B. Leach of Victoria, B.C., were young Stoneham's father, Horace, and the San Francisco Giants." "STONEHAM'S SON SUED, Giants' Owner Also Is Named in Fatal Car Crash Case," Associated Press, March 19, 1958.

4. Shaplen, "Lonely Loyal Mr. Stoneham."

5. Rosenbaum and Stevens, *Giants of San Francisco*, 70–71.

6. Rosenbaum and Stevens, *Giants of San Francisco*, 72.

7. Bitker, *Original San Francisco Giants*, 14.

8. Bitker, *Original San Francisco Giants*, 15.

9. Walker and Bellamy, *Center Field Shot*, 324–25, 330–31.

10. Rosenbaum and Stevens, *Giants of San Francisco*, 73.

11. Stein, *Mel Ott*, 190.

12. "Mel Ott and Wife Are Critically Hurt in Auto Accident That Kills a Man," *New York Times*, November 15, 1958. Some historians have wondered about the legitimacy of the no-fault coroner's jury verdict, given that Leslie Curry, the driver, who was instantly killed and thus unable to offer testimony, was African American; that Mel Ott wasn't just white but was a local hero of immense magnitude; and that this was rural Mississippi in 1958. It's possible that Ott, having just consumed dinner, was under the influence of alcohol; while never known as a heavy drinker, Ott was no teetotaler. But there is no evidence to resolve the question. The official conclusion was that it was a blameless accident, and more than that is unknowable.

13. "Mel Ott, 49, Dies of Crash Injuries," *New York Times*, November 22, 1958.

14. "MEL OTT DIES OF INJURIES SUFFERED IN AUTO ACCIDENT," Associated Press, November 22, 1958.

15. Stein, *Mel Ott*, 191.

16. The sophisticated modern statistic of wins above replacement (WAR) for pitchers assesses Sam Jones as tied with Robin Roberts as the best pitcher in the National League in 1958.

17. The African American Bill White had requested that the Giants trade him, and he was accommodated. "I asked to be traded. I don't think Stoneham wanted to keep me anyway. I was uppity [laughs]. I think Stoneham and the people who ran the Giants felt that way because I would hold out. I would say, 'I don't have to play baseball,' and I'd go back to school. I'd hold out by staying in school. I think I left the Danville team in the playoffs, so I could get back in school. Baseball was not everything. It was there, and I played it. But I wanted to get an education. So I'd leave whenever I had to get back in school. Plus, I didn't take shit." Bitker, *Original San Francisco Giants*, 211.

18. Rosenbaum and Stevens, *Giants of San Francisco*, 79–80.

19. Wolfe, "Candlestick Swindle," https://www.foundsf.org/index.php?title=Candlestick_Swindle.

20. Garratt, *Home Team*, 53.

21. Rosenbaum and Stevens, *Giants of San Francisco*, 77.

22. Garratt, *Home Team*, 55.

23. Wolfe, "Candlestick Swindle."

24. Garratt, *Home Team*, 57–58.

25. Garratt, *Home Team*, 55–56.

26. Rosenbaum and Stevens, *Giants of San Francisco*, 75–76.

27. Rory Costello and Lyle Wilson, "André Rodgers," SABR BioProject essay, Society for American Baseball Research, https://sabr.org/bioproj/person /c638d820.

28. Joe Reichler, "Tony Kubek, André Rodgers Choice for Rookie-of-Year," Associated Press, March 22, 1957. Reichler would be proved correct in his prediction for Kubek.

29. Rosenbaum and Stevens, *Giants of San Francisco*, 86.

30. The Braves had solved a second base problem in mid-1957 by acquiring Red Schoendienst from the Giants, and he performed marvelously for them that year. But over the course of the 1958 season, he fell ill and was eventually diagnosed with tuberculosis, causing him to sit out virtually all of 1959.

31. Rosenbaum and Stevens, *Giants of San Francisco*, 145.

32. Rosenbaum and Stevens, *Giants of San Francisco*, 145.

33. Rosenbaum and Stevens, *Giants of San Francisco*, 145–46.

34. Rosenbaum and Stevens, *Giants of San Francisco*, 92.

35. Jones was brilliant for the Giants in 1959, leading the league in wins and ERA. He finished second to Early Wynn of the Chicago White Sox in Cy Young Award balloting, which was in those days major league–wide. Had there been a National League Cy Young Award in 1959, Jones would have won it, deservedly.

36. Rosenbaum and Stevens, *Giants of San Francisco*, 93–94.

37. Roy Terrell, *Sports Illustrated*, October 5, 1959.

38. *San Francisco Examiner*, September 19, 1959.

10. It's Bye-Bye Baby

1. Prescott Sullivan, *San Francisco Examiner*, October 21, 1959.

2. Charles Einstein, *San Francisco Examiner*, October 28, 1959.

3. Horace Stoneham, *San Francisco Examiner*, November 10, 1959.

4. *San Francisco Examiner*, November 20, 1959.

5. Rosenbaum and Stevens, *Giants of San Francisco*, 113–14.

6. Angell, "Companions of the Game," 269.

7. Rosenbaum and Stevens, *Giants of San Francisco*, 95–96.

8. Rosenbaum and Stevens, *Giants of San Francisco*, 97–98.

9. Roger Angell, "A Tale of Three Cities," *The Summer Game* (New York: Viking Press, 1972), 81–82.

10. Rosenbaum and Stevens, *Giants of San Francisco*, 10.

11. Hano, *Willie Mays*, 153.

12. Mandel, *SF Giants*, 7.

13. Hano, *Willie Mays*, 152.

14. Rosenbaum and Stevens, *Giants of San Francisco*, 98–99.

15. Bitker, *Original San Francisco Giants*, 53.

16. Mandel, *SF Giants*, 7.

17. Allen, *Giants and the Dodgers*, 239.

18. Rosenbaum and Stevens, *Giants of San Francisco*, 99.

19. Allen, *Giants and the Dodgers*, 239–40.

20. Hano, *Willie Mays*, 153.

21. Bitker, *Original San Francisco Giants*, 153.

22. Rosenbaum and Stevens, *Giants of San Francisco*, 100.

23. Allen, *Giants and the Dodgers*, 241–42.

24. Hano, *Day in the Bleachers*, 95–96.

25. Jim Bouton, edited by Leonard Shecter, *Ball Four: My Life and Times Throwing the Knuckleball in the Big Leagues* (New York: World, 1970), 119–20.

26. Rosenbaum and Stevens, *Giants of San Francisco*, 135–36.

27. Alvin Dark and John Underwood, *When in Doubt, Fire the Manager: My Life and Times in Baseball* (New York: E. P. Dutton, 1980), 71–72, 96.

28. Hirsch, *Willie Mays*, 418.

29. Mandel, *SF Giants*, 46–47.

30. Rosenbaum and Stevens, *Giants of San Francisco*, 96.

31. Rosenbaum and Stevens, *Giants of San Francisco*, 101.

32. Clifford S. Kachline, "Engineer Throws Home Run Light on Candlestick, Predicts 50 Limit," *The Sporting News*, April 27, 1960, 31.

33. Rosenbaum and Stevens, *Giants of San Francisco*, 101.

34. The Giants also sent a player to be named later to the Reds—pitcher Sherman Jones, delivered on May 13.

35. It was actually the first of two major league All-Star games that year, which were presented in a two-games-per-year format from 1959 through 1962.

36. Rosenbaum and Stevens, *Giants of San Francisco*, 103–4.

37. Rosenbaum and Stevens, *Giants of San Francisco*, 108.

38. Rosenbaum and Stevens, *Giants of San Francisco*, 108–9.

39. Rosenbaum and Stevens, *Giants of San Francisco*, 109–10.

40. Rosenbaum and Stevens, *Giants of San Francisco*, 148.

41. Ron Fimrite, "The Heart of a Giant," *Sports Illustrated*, October 16, 1991.

42. Fimrite, "Heart of a Giant."

43. Rosenbaum and Stevens, *Giants of San Francisco*, 148.

44. Bill James, *The Bill James Historical Baseball Abstract* (New York: Villard Books, 1986), 336.

45. Rosenbaum and Stevens, *Giants of San Francisco*, 144.

46. KSFO was owned by San Jose native Franklin Mieuli. The station also broadcast San Francisco 49ers football games, and in 1962 Mieuli purchased the Philadelphia Warriors of the National Basketball League and relocated them to San Francisco, and KSFO carried those games as well. Mieuli wasn't just the owner of the radio station; he actively produced the sports broadcasts. He hired Russ Hodges to move out from New York with the Giants and paired him with younger, local voices Lon Simmons and Bill King, both of whom would forge legendary Bay Area multisport broadcasting careers and both of whom would join Hodges as recipients of the Ford C. Frick Award from the Baseball Hall of Fame.

47. Mandel, *SF Giants*, 99.

48. Russ Hodges, KSFO, Candlestick Park, San Francisco, April 10, 1962, radio broadcast.

49. In the seventh inning of this game, Orlando Cepeda stole home while the Giants were leading 17–3.

50. This was the first regular season return to New York. On July 24, 1961, the Giants had visited Yankee Stadium to play an exhibition game against the Yankees. The Giants' players, mostly unfamiliar to New York fans, received a tepid greeting, until the public address announcer presented the name of Willie Mays. Charles Einstein described the cheers: "An unbroken, throat-swelling peal of adulation sprang from the hearts of Giant-starved New Yorkers. It rolled and volleyed off the great tiering of this triple-decked palace and against the vague outline of the Bronx County courthouse, looming in the gray black mist out beyond the huge scoreboard in right center field. They rocked and tottered and shouted and stamped and sang. It was joy and love and welcome, and you never heard a cascade of sound quite like it." Charles Einstein, *A Flag for San Francisco: The Stormy Honeymoon of a Proud City and Divorced Baseball Team* (New York: Simon & Schuster, 1962), 225.

51. Roger Angell, "The 'Go' Shouters," *The Summer Game* (New York: Viking Press, 1972), 44–46.

52. Allen, *Giants and the Dodgers*, 250.

53. Rosenbaum and Stevens, *Giants of San Francisco*, 164.

54. Hodges, KSFO, Candlestick Park, San Francisco, August 11, 1962, radio broadcast.

55. Charles Einstein, "Hey, Lay Off McCovey," *Sport*, July 1963, 34.

56. Bill King, KSFO, Candlestick Park, San Francisco, September 29, 1962, radio broadcast. King was working this game because Simmons was working the 49ers game at Kezar Stadium.

57. Hodges, KSFO, Candlestick Park, San Francisco, September 29, 1962, radio broadcast.

58. Rosenbaum and Stevens, *Giants of San Francisco*, 169.

59. Hodges, KSFO, Candlestick Park, September 29, 1962, radio broadcast. The St. Louis second baseman was Julian Javier.

60. Angell, "Tale of Three Cities," 76.

61. This unfortunate mark wouldn't be surpassed until a Yankees–Red Sox glacier in 2006.

62. Hano, *Willie Mays*, 168.

63. Rosenbaum and Stevens, *Giants of San Francisco*, 178–80.

64. Angell, "Tale of Three Cities," 79–80.

65. Angell, "Tale of Three Cities," 80.

66. Angell, "Tale of Three Cities," 83.

67. Hano, *Willie Mays*, 171–72.

68. Rosenbaum and Stevens, *Giants of San Francisco*, 191.

11. No Cigar

1. Bill James, *The New Bill James Historical Baseball Abstract* (New York: Free Press, 2001), 854.

2. Mays's OPS+ was 175, Cepeda's was 165, and McCovey's was 161, good for second, third, and fourth in the league behind Hank Aaron, at 179. The only other team in major league history with three everyday regulars with an OPS+ over 160 was the 1895 Philadelphia Phillies, with Ed Delahanty (187), Sam Thompson (177), and Jack Clements (171), and that was on a 132-game schedule.

3. Dark and Underwood, *When in Doubt, Fire the Manager*, 106–7.

4. Quoted in Charles Einstein, *Willie's Time* (New York: J. B. Lippincott, 1979), 201–2.

5. Hirsch, *Willie Mays*, 492–93.

6. Alex Kupfer, "Lew Burdette," SABR BioProject essay, Society for American Baseball Research, https://sabr.org/bioproj/person/bc3fde89.

7. Mark Armour, "Gaylord Perry," SABR BioProject essay, Society for American Baseball Research, https://sabr.org/bioproj/person/f7cb0d3e.

8. Armour, "Gaylord Perry."

9. Bryan Curtis, "No Chattering in the Press Box: The Lost Tribe of Sportswriters Known as the Chipmunks," *Grantland*, May 3, 2012, http://grantland.com/features/larry-merchant-leonard-shecter-chipmunks-sportswriting-clan/.

10. Hirsch, *Willie Mays*, 498.

11. Einstein, *Willie's Time*, 209.

12. Hirsch, *Willie Mays*, 499.

13. Hirsch, *Willie Mays*, 499–500.

14. Einstein, *Willie's Time*, 212–14.

15. Mark Armour, "Willie McCovey," SABR BioProject essay, Society for American Baseball Research, https://sabr.org/bioproj/person/2a692514.

16. Fitts, *Mashi*, 39.

17. In the early 1950s Harada had been instrumental in bringing fellow Japanese American Wally Yonamine, who had played running back for the San Francisco 49ers of the NFL, to Japan to play for the Yomiuri Giants, forging a career that would propel him into the Japanese Baseball Hall of Fame. Fitts, *Mashi*, 38.

18. Fitts, *Mashi*, 39–41.

19. Fitts, *Mashi*, 48–49, 55.

20. Burgos, *Cuban Star*, 230, 234.

21. Mandel, *SF Giants*, 47.

22. Jack Zanger, *Major League Baseball 1967* (New York: Pocket Books, 1967), 98–99.

23. Hirsch, *Willie Mays*, 509.

24. *Seattle Daily Times*, February 4, 1965.

25. Mandel, *SF Giants*, 98.

26. John Rosengren, *The Fight of Their Lives* (Guilford CT: Lyons Press, 2014), 91–92.

27. Fitts, *Mashi*, 126–34.

28. Armour, "Willie McCovey."

29. Spahn would do well for the Giants in 1965, delivering eleven starts, five relief appearances, and seventy-one much-needed innings of solid work in the closing act of his magnificent major league career.

30. Hano, *Willie Mays*, 184.

31. Rosengren, *Fight of Their Lives*, 100–101.

32. Rosengren, *Fight of Their Lives*, 102.

33. Rosengren, *Fight of Their Lives*, 82.

34. Hano, *Willie Mays*, 9–10.

35. Hirsch, *Willie Mays*, 518.

36. Rosengren, *Fight of Their Lives*, 111–12.

37. Hirsch, *Willie Mays*, 519.

38. Rosengren, *Fight of Their Lives*, 113–14.

39. Hirsch, *Willie Mays*, 521–22.

40. Hano, *Willie Mays*, 10.

41. Hirsch, *Willie Mays*, 522–23.

42. Rosengren, *Fight of Their Lives*, 118.

43. Hirsch, *Willie Mays*, 523.

44. Hirsch, *Willie Mays*, 523.

45. Hirsch, *Willie Mays*, 527–29.

46. Roger Connor had an OPS+ of 200 for the New York Giants in 1885, when the game was very different. That's the only one higher than Mays's 185 through 1965. Rogers Hornsby achieved marks higher than 185 six times in his career, but in his lone season with the Giants, in 1927, his OPS+ was 175— high enough to lead the league by plenty.

12. Certainly the Move Will Hurt Us

1. Matty Alou would famously blossom with the Pittsburgh Pirates as a batting average champion. Pirates manager Harry Walker, also serving as the team's hitting coach, replaced the light bat Alou had been using with the Giants and instead handed him a thirty-eight-ounce war club and instructed him to choke far up and focus on chopping grounders up the middle and to the opposite field. To his credit, Alou took the coaching to heart and succeeded brilliantly with the new approach.

2. Under manager Leo Durocher in Chicago, Hundley and Hands would both surpass expectations and emerge as stars, but it's also the case that neither was going to get the same opportunity to play with the Giants that they got with the rebuilding Cubs.

3. Moreover, the Giants and Dodgers almost never engaged in transactions.

4. Einstein, *Willie's Time*, 209.

5. Hirsch, *Willie Mays*, 550.

6. Einstein, *Willie's Time*, 250–51.

7. Hirsch, *Willie Mays*, 551.

8. Einstein, *Willie's Time*, 252–53.

9. Hirsch, *Willie Mays*, 551–52.

10. The Castro neighborhood would, in subsequent decades, become the center and symbol of lesbian, gay, bisexual, and transgender pride and activism in San Francisco.

11. Warren Corbett, "Mike McCormick," SABR BioProject essay, Society for American Baseball Research, https://sabr.org/bioproj/person/a0de4b6f.

12. Mark Armour, "Jesus Alou," SABR BioProject essay, Society for American Baseball Research, https://sabr.org/bioproj/person/e8c21d8d.

13. Hirsch, *Willie Mays*, 554.

14. Hirsch, *Willie Mays*, 554.

15. Furman Bisher, *Atlanta Constitution*, August 15, 1967.

16. Rosengren, *Fight of Their Lives*, 154–55.

17. Jack Zanger, *Major League Baseball 1968* (New York: Pocket Books, 1968), 96.

18. The writer Gertrude Stein spent most of her childhood in Oakland, beginning in the late 1870s. In her 1937 autobiography Stein famously wrote, "There is no there, there." What she was specifically addressing with that clever phrase was the degree to which the industrialized Oakland of the 1930s bore no resemblance to her quaint town of a half-century earlier. But the saying has often been more broadly interpreted as a comment on modern Oakland's image (however accurate) of bland forgettability.

19. Now part of the interstate system and designated as I-880, in the 1960s the freeway was California Route 17. Also, though it wouldn't begin passenger service until 1972, the Bay Area Rapid Transit (BART) electric railway system has an adjacent line and a station serving the Coliseum.

20. The Raiders would play their 1960 home games at Kezar Stadium in San Francisco, home of the 49ers, and in 1961 at Candlestick Park. In 1962 Frank Youell Field was completed for them in Oakland as a temporary facility until the Coliseum was opened.

21. In 1969 both leagues would add a third team on the West Coast, with the American League expanding to Seattle and the National to San Diego.

22. Mark Armour, *Joe Cronin: A Life in Baseball* (Lincoln: University of Nebraska Press, 2010), 280–82, 297–99.

23. *The Sporting News*, November 4, 1967.

24. Manchester, *Glory and the Dream*, 1122–23, 1134–35.

25. Thom Loverro, "Sports, Politics Conflicted 50 Years Ago with Mourning of RFK's Death," *Washington Times*, June 7, 2018. The postponed Giants Opening Day game against the New York Mets was played as part of a doubleheader at Candlestick Park on Saturday, August 10, 1968, and the postponed June game was played as part of a doubleheader the next day, Sunday, August 11.

26. Roger Angell, "A Little Noise at Twilight," *The Summer Game* (New York: Viking Press, 1972), 182–83.

27. The last time a Giants-Dodgers transaction had occurred was the unsuccessful attempt to trade Jackie Robinson in December 1956; the last time a transaction had been fully consummated was the sale of utility player John "Spider" Jorgensen by the Dodgers to the Giants in May 1950; and the last significant transaction between the clubs was Bill Terry's trade of Freddie Fitzsimmons to Brooklyn in June 1937, barely a year and a half into Horace Stoneham's ownership tenure.

28. Despite appearing in only ninety total games and seventy-two complete games behind the plate, Dietz led the league in catcher errors and stolen bases allowed, was second in passed balls, and was sixth in wild pitches allowed.

13. Resilience

1. Franks would return to baseball twice, first as an interim midseason pitching coach for his old mentor Leo Durocher with the Chicago Cubs in 1970 and then as manager of the Cubs in 1977–79.

2. Hirsch, *Willie Mays*, 574.

3. Einstein, *Willie's Time*, 316.

4. Hirsch, *Willie Mays*, 573.

5. Hirsch, *Willie Mays*, 575.

6. Einstein, *Willie's Time*, 315–16.

7. Hirsch, *Willie Mays*, 576–77.

8. Topping even Roger Connor's 200 from 1885.

9. It should be noted that the statistic of intentional bases on balls had only been officially recorded since 1955; it's possible that in his peak years Babe Ruth received a very large number of intentional passes, but they weren't recorded, so it's unknown. To this day the only player known to have surpassed McCovey's 1969 total of forty-five was Barry Bonds, in 2002, 2003, and 2004.

10. Hirsch, *Willie Mays*, 578.

11. Ron Fimrite, "The Heart of a Giant," *San Francisco Chronicle*, September 23, 1969.

12. Hirsch, *Willie Mays*, 578–79.

13. John Helyar, *Lords of the Realm: The Real History of Baseball* (New York: Ballantine Books, 1994), 80–81.

14. Helyar, *Lords of the Realm*, 81.

15. Helyar, *Lords of the Realm*, 81–82.

16. Edwin Shrake, "A Man and a Mule in Missouri," *Sports Illustrated*, July 27, 1965, 43.

17. Helyar, *Lords of the Realm*, 80, 82.

18. Helyar, *Lords of the Realm*, 97–98.

19. As a condition of accepting the job, Feeney established the National League headquarters office in San Francisco rather than move to New York, as Com-

missioner Kuhn preferred, but after a few years Feeney would relent on that point and relocate back across the country to his old hometown.

20. The moniker *Silicon Valley* would be coined in 1971 and enter general use in the 1980s, but the economic and social impact of the exploding high technology industry in Santa Clara County had begun in the 1940s and '50s and was fully underway by the 1960s.

21. Ever since their inaugural season of 1946, the 49ers had played at Kezar Stadium, a modest small college–sized facility dating from the 1920s, located in Golden Gate Park, completely outmoded in every respect by the rapidly elevating standards of the NFL in the 1960s and '70s.

22. The others were the Astrodome in Houston, Busch Stadium in St. Louis, Three Rivers Stadium in Pittsburgh, and Riverfront Stadium in Cincinnati. In 1971 Veterans Stadium in Philadelphia would open with the sixth artificial surface in the twelve-team league.

23. In 1970 the second broadcaster was none other than Harry Caray, hired by Finley after the St. Louis Cardinals let him go following a twenty-five-year run there. But Caray and Finley got along poorly, and after just one year, Caray went to the Chicago White Sox. Another, in 1974, was twenty-two-year-old Jon Miller, in his first professional play-by-play job.

24. Einstein, *Willie's Time*, 317.

25. The "Baseball's Most Exciting Team" idea was based on the logic that run scoring was exciting, and in 1970 the Giants had led the major leagues in runs scored and also in runs allowed.

26. Mandel, *SF Giants*, 193.

27. R. J. Lesch, "Eddie Brannick," SABR BioProject essay, Society for American Baseball Research, https://sabr.org/bioproj/person/f0d59a5f.

28. Lesch, "Eddie Brannick."

29. Lesch, "Eddie Brannick."

30. Ray Robinson, "Willie Mays: Twilight Time," in *Baseball Stars of 1972*, ed. Ray Robinson (New York: Pyramid, , 1972), 61.

31. Hirsch, *Willie Mays*, 588–89.

32. Roger Angell, "Part of a Season: Bay and Back Bay," *The Summer Game* (New York: Viking Press, 1972), 256–57.

33. Angell, "Part of a Season," 258.

34. Mandel, *SF Giants*, 91.

35. Mays had forty-two ground ball chances at first base in 1971 and booted seven of them, a terrible rate.

36. Hirsch, *Willie Mays*, 594–95.

37. Roger Angell, "Some Pirates and Lesser Men," *The Summer Game* (New York: Viking Press, 1972), 274.

38. Hirsch, *Willie Mays*, 594.

39. Angell, "Some Pirates and Lesser Men," 275.

14. I Never Thought I Would Trade Willie

1. Joseph Wancho, "Sam McDowell," SABR BioProject essay, Society for American Baseball Research, https://sabr.org/bioproj/person/0c9cecef.

2. With the two Frank Duffy transactions coming in such rapid succession, the Giants' exchange effectively netted out as Foster and Perry for McDowell and Vern Geishert. Doing the math on this parlay: Foster, post-1971, played fifteen seasons and hit 334 home runs, while Perry, post-1971, played twelve seasons and won 180 games. McDowell, post-1971, played four seasons and won nineteen games, while Geishert was injured and never pitched a professional inning after being acquired by the Giants.

3. "Miller would elicit [strong negative] reactions [from management]. Everywhere the owners turned now, he seemed to be on the attack: in court, in arbitration, in bargaining. He was cool and calculating and contemptuous of their great institution. The Lords were beginning to take this personally.

"They often referred to him not by name but as 'that gimpy-armed Jew bastard.' [Phillies' owner] Bob Carpenter, who had more breeding, preferred 'that plebian socialist.' Leo Durocher, an old-schooler of the first rank, disrupted one of Miller's spring training meetings by fungoing fly balls into the outfield, where he was clustered with the Astros players.

"'It was vitriolic,' recalled Tim McCarver. 'You talk about thick skin—this guy was a rhinoceros.'" Helyar, *Lords of the Realm*, 115–16.

4. "It is clear that some of the more dedicated Cro-Magnons among the owners (including the Cardinals' Gussie Busch, the Reds' Frank Dale, the Mets' Donald Grant, and the Royals' Ewing Kauffman) saw the strike as a precious opportunity to strain, and perhaps crack, the labor union of their upstart, ungrateful young employees and, above all, to discredit its executive director, Marvin Miller. Most of the owners, to be sure, would deny such an intention, but the unchanging and apparently unchangeable characteristic of their fraternity is its total distaste for self-discipline—a flaw that characterizes the entire body and repeatedly renders it victim to its loudest and least responsible minority." Roger Angell, "Starting to Belong," *Five Seasons: A Baseball Companion* (New York: Simon & Schuster, 1977), 27.

5. Helyar, *Lords of the Realm*, 119.

6. Helyar, *Lords of the Realm*, 119.

7. Technically, the vote was all in favor, with one abstention. Only one of the forty-eight player representatives (two from each of the twenty-four teams) at the meeting was in agreement with Miller's recommendation: Wes Parker of the Dodgers, who explained that he had just bought a new house and couldn't afford to strike. He was hooted down and then chose to abstain. See Helyar, *Lords of the Realm*, 121–22.

8. Roberts had in fact been the player representative who had initially contacted Miller and championed his hiring in 1966. But Roberts was appalled that

things had gotten so far out of hand to lead to a strike, seeing this as a failure of effective negotiation on Miller's part. Jackie Jensen, an MVP winner in the 1950s, was another high-profile critic: "I think playing baseball is a privilege. I enjoyed it and it was a game to me. It doesn't look like it is anymore. And if it isn't, it isn't going to be much fun from here on in—either to the fans or the players. And I think that's a tragedy." See Helyar, *Lords of the Realm*, 126–27.

9. Helyar, *Lords of the Realm*, 125.

10. "Players across baseball hung together. The Twins' Jim Perry lined up housing for strapped younger players with better-fixed veterans. He arranged for a place for the team to work out and a bus to transport players there. The Braves practiced on a high school field until they ran out of balls. Hank Aaron had hit them all into a grove of trees. Chris Cannizzaro of the Dodgers worked out with the Padres in San Diego, where he lived. Vada Pinson of the Angels worked out with the Athletics in Oakland, where he lived. Miller hustled around keeping up players' spirits between negotiating sessions." Helyar, *Lords of the Realm*, 125.

11. Ownership's lack of planning for the eventuality of a strike—indeed, the glaring absence of coordinated activity of pretty much any kind on their part—was remarkable. To understand why is to recognize the degree to which the owners were generally fiercely independent old-school tycoons, not taken to such activities as cooperating or, really, listening. As Angell put it: "Commissioner Bowie Kuhn, who has been criticized for not playing a stronger hand in settling the strike, does not in fact have any power over the owners in such a crucial situation; these businessmen, in contrast to the players, chose to remain undirected and largely unadvised throughout the crisis." Angell, "Starting to Belong," 27.

12. The owners agreed to increase the pension fund by $490,000 annually, resulting in a 14 percent cost of living increase in fixed retirement benefits and a total increase of $4.9 million over a ten-year period. It was estimated that the players lost a total of about $960,000 in salaries during the strike. The clubs lost an estimated $175,000 to $200,000 each in revenues during the strike, for a total of between $4 million and $5 million. See Holtzman in *Official Baseball Guide for 1973*, ed. Joe Marcin, Chis Roewe, Larry Wigge, and Larry Vickrey (St. Louis: The Sporting News, 1973), 279.

13. Mandel, *SF Giants*, 160.

14. Mandel, *SF Giants*, 161–62.

15. John D'Acquisto and Dave Jordan, *Fastball John* (New York: Instream Books, 2015), 72.

16. Einstein, *Willie's Time*, 328–29.

17. Hirsch, *Willie Mays*, 602–3.

18. Einstein, *Willie's Time*, 331.

19. Hirsch, *Willie Mays*, 604.

20. Hirsch, *Willie Mays*, 605.

21. Mandel, *SF Giants*, 195.

22. D'Acquisto and Jordan, *Fastball John*, 69–71.

23. Odder still, Hall played in seven games at second base for the Pirates in 1953—still the tallest second baseman in major league history. Hall would gain far more notice as a first-rate relief pitcher in the 1960s.

24. Mandel, *SF Giants*, 175.

25. Mandel, *SF Giants*, 177.

26. Mandel, *SF Giants*, 198.

27. Mandel, *SF Giants*, 170.

28. Garratt, *Home Team*, 87.

29. Following McCovey's retirement as a player in 1980, the Giants created the Willie Mac Award. At the end of each season the players, coaches, and clubhouse staff vote to honor that year's Giants player who best embodies McCovey's spirit of competitive dedication and team commitment.

30. Armour, "Willie McCovey."

31. Along with their considerable financial distress, the Padres were for sale because their primary owner, San Diego business tycoon C. Arnholt Smith (a crony of Richard Nixon), also owned the United States National Bank of San Diego, which was in the process of failing in the autumn of 1973—at the time the largest bank failure in history—and on top of that Smith was being sued by the Internal Revenue Service for twenty-three million dollars in unpaid back taxes.

32. Mandel, *SF Giants*, 91.

33. D'Acquisto and Jordan, *Fastball John*, 110.

15. You Can't Get Discouraged

1. Moffitt was the brother of tennis legend Billie Jean King, who transcended great athletic achievement to become a significant leader in the work for gender equality.

2. *New York Times*, March 16, 1974.

3. D'Acquisto and Jordan, *Fastball John*, 132.

4. D'Acquisto and Jordan, *Fastball John*, 137–38.

5. "Skipper Fox Resigns—Westrum Takes Helm," *The Sporting News*, July 13, 1974, 16.

6. John Gabcik, "Tom Bradley," SABR BioProject essay, Society for American Baseball Research, https://sabr.org/bioproj/person/334c0314.

7. *San Francisco Examiner*, April 29, 1975.

8. D'Acquisto and Jordan, *Fastball John*, 139.

9. Angell, "Companions of the Game," 265.

10. Angell, "Companions of the Game," 265.

11. Angell, "Companions of the Game," 266.

12. Angell, "Companions of the Game," 272–73.

13. Angell, "Companions of the Game," 275–76.

14. Angell, "Companions of the Game," 276–77.

15. Bob Hurte, "John Montefusco," SABR BioProject essay, Society for American Baseball Research, https://sabr.org/bioproj/person/5e3343be.

16. Wells Twombly, "A Look at the Giants' Odd Couple," *San Francisco Chronicle*, February 15, 1976.

17. Art Rosenbaum, "Lots of Buyers for Giants," *San Francisco Chronicle*, August 18, 1972.

18. Wells Twombly, "Stoneham Makes a Noble Gesture," *San Francisco Chronicle*, May 8, 1975.

19. Garratt, *Home Team*, 93.

20. *The Sporting News*, May 24, 1975.

21. *San Francisco Chronicle*, May 7, 1975; *San Francisco Examiner*, May 8, 1975.

22. *San Francisco Examiner*, May 14, 1975.

23. Garratt, *Home Team*, 95–96.

24. Minutes from Special Meeting of the National League, September 24, 1975, Major League Baseball archives.

25. Jerome Holtzman, "Review of 1975," in *Official Baseball Guide for 1976*, ed. Joe Marcin, Chris Roewe, Larry Vickrey, and Larry Wigge (St. Louis: The Sporting News, 1976), 284.

26. Minutes from Meeting of the National League, December 10, 1975, Major League Baseball archives.

27. *The Sporting News*, January 10, 1976.

28. *The Sporting News*, December 27, 1975.

29. Garratt, *Home Team*, 97.

30. *San Francisco Chronicle*, January 13, 1976.

31. *San Francisco Chronicle*, January 10, 1976; *San Francisco Examiner*, January 10, 1976.

32. On November 27, 1978, Moscone would be assassinated, along with San Francisco city supervisor Harvey Milk, by former supervisor Dan White.

33. *San Francisco Examiner*, January 11, 1976.

34. Garratt, *Home Team*, 101–5.

Epilogue

1. With one exception: in 1978 Stoneham consented to several telephone calls with writer Charles Einstein for his book *Willie's Time*. It was in one of these conversations that Stoneham admitted, for the first and only time, that there had been no cash included in the deal that sent Willie Mays to the New York Mets in 1972.

Bibliography

Allardice, Bruce. "Out of the Shadows: Joseph 'Sport' Sullivan." SABR *Black Sox Research Committee Newsletter* 6, no. 1 (June 2014).

Allen, Lee. *The Giants and the Dodgers: The Fabulous Story of Baseball's Fiercest Feud.* New York: G. P. Putnam's Sons, 1964.

———. *The National League Story: The Official History.* New York: Hill & Wang, 1961

Angell, Roger. *Five Seasons: A Baseball Companion.* New York: Simon & Schuster, 1977.

———. *The Summer Game.* New York: Viking Press, 1972.

Ardell, Jean Hastings, and Andy McCue, eds. *Endless Seasons: Baseball in Southern California, The National Pastime.* No. 41. Phoenix: Society for American Baseball Research, 2011.

Armour, Mark. "Gaylord Perry." SABR BioProject essay. Society for American Baseball Research. https://sabr.org/bioproj/person/f7cb0d3e.

———. "Jesus Alou," Society for American Baseball Research, https://sabr.org/bioproj/person/e8c21d8d.

———. *Joe Cronin: A Life in Baseball.* Lincoln: University of Nebraska Press, 2010.

———. "Willie McCovey." SABR BioProject essay. Society for American Baseball Research. https://sabr.org/bioproj/person/2a692514.

Barber, Red. *1947: When All Hell Broke Loose in Baseball.* New York: Doubleday, 1982.

Bartell, Dick, and Norman L. Macht. *Rowdy Richard: A First-Hand Account of the National League Baseball Wars of the 1930s and the Men Who Fought Them.* Berkeley CA: North Atlantic Books, 1993.

Bitker, Steve. *The Original San Francisco Giants: The Giants of '58.* Champaign IL: Sports Publishing, 1998.

Bouton, Jim, edited by Leonard Schecter. *Ball Four: My Life and Times Throwing the Knuckleball in the Big Leagues.* New York: World, 1970.

Burgos, Adrian, Jr. *Cuban Star: How One Negro-League Owner Changed the Face of Baseball.* New York: Hill & Wang, 2011.

Corbett, Warren. "Mike McCormick." SABR BioProject essay. Society for American Baseball Research. https://sabr.org/bioproj/person/a0de4b6f.

Corbett, Warren. *The Wizard of Waxahachie: Paul Richards and the End of Baseball as We Knew It.* Dallas: Southern Methodist University Press, 2009.

Costello, Rory, and Lyle Wilson. "André Rodgers." SABR BioProject essay. Society for American Baseball Research. https://sabr.org/bioproj/person/c638d820.

Curtis, Bryan. "No Chattering in the Press Box: The Lost Tribe of Sportswriters Known as the Chipmunks." *Grantland,* May 3, 2012. http://grantland.com/features/larry-merchant-leonard-shecter-chipmunks-sportswriting-clan/.

D'Acquisto, John, and Dave Jordan. *Fastball John.* New York: Instream Books, 2015.

Dark, Alvin, and John Underwood. *When in Doubt, Fire the Manager: My Life and Times in Baseball.* New York: E. P. Dutton, 1980.

DeLillo, Don. *Underworld.* New York: Simon & Schuster, 1997.

Einstein, Charles. *A Flag for San Francisco: The Stormy Honeymoon of a Proud City and Divorced Baseball Team.* New York: Simon & Schuster, 1962.

———. *Willie's Time.* New York: J. B. Lippincott, 1979.

Eskenazi, Gerald. *The Lip: A Biography of Leo Durocher.* New York: William Morrow, 1993.

Faber Charles H., ed. *The 1934 St. Louis Cardinals: The World Champion Gas House Gang.* SABR Digital Library, vol. 20. Phoenix: Society for American Baseball Research, 2014.

Ferber, Nat. *I Found Out: A Confidential Chronicle of the Twenties.* New York: Dial Press, 1939.

Fetter, Henry D. *Taking On the Yankees: Winning and Losing in the Business of Baseball, 1903–2003.* New York: W. W. Norton, 2003.

Fitts, Robert K. *Mashi: The Unfulfilled Baseball Dreams of Masanori Murakami, the First Japanese Major Leaguer.* Lincoln: University of Nebraska Press, 2014.

Fitzgerald, Ed, ed. *The National League.* New York: Grosset & Dunlap, 1966.

Flynn, George Q. *The Draft: 1940–1973.* Lawrence: University Press of Kansas, 1993.

Frommer, Harvey. *New York City Baseball: The Golden Age, 1947–1957.* Lanham MD: Taylor Trade Publishing, 1980.

Gabcik, John. "Tom Bradley." SABR BioProject essay. Society for American Baseball Research. https://sabr.org/bioproj/person/334c0314.

Garratt, Robert F. *Home Team: The Turbulent History of the San Francisco Giants.* Lincoln: University of Nebraska Press, 2017.

Genovese, George, with Dan Taylor. *A Scout's Report: My 70 Years in Baseball.* Jefferson NC: McFarland, 2015.

Gelernter, David. *1939: The Lost World of the Fair.* New York: Avon Books, 1995.

Graham, Frank. *McGraw of the Giants: An Informal Biography.* New York: G. P. Putnam's Sons, 1944.

Hano, Arnold. *A Day in the Bleachers.* New York: Cromwell, 1955.

———. *Greatest Giants of Them All.* New York: G. P. Putnam, 1967.

———. *Willie Mays.* New York: Grosset & Dunlap, 1966.

Helyar, John. *Lords of the Realm: The Real History of Baseball.* New York: Ballantine Books, 1994.

Hirsch, James S. *Willie Mays: The Life, the Legend.* New York: Scribner, 2010.

Hurte, Bob. "John Montefusco." SABR BioProject essay. Society for American Baseball Research. https://sabr.org/bioproj/person/5e3343be.

Hynd, Noel. *The Giants of the Polo Grounds: The Glorious Times of Baseball's New York Giants.* Dallas: Taylor, 1988.

Irvin, Monte, with James A. Riley. *Monte Irvin: Nice Guys Finish First.* New York: Carroll & Graf, 1996.

James, Bill, *The Bill James Historical Baseball Abstract.* New York: Villard Books, 1986.

———. *The New Bill James Historical Baseball Abstract.* New York: Free Press, 2001.

James, Bill, and Rob Neyer. *The Neyer/James Guide to Pitchers: An Historical Compendium of Pitching, Pitchers, and Pitches.* New York: Simon & Schuster, 2004.

Jensen, Don. "John McGraw." SABR BioProject essay. Society for American Baseball Research. http://sabr.org/bioproj/person/fef5035f.

Kahn, Roger. *The Boys of Summer.* New York: Signet, 1973.

———. *The Era: 1947–1957, When the Yankees, the Dodgers, and the Giants Ruled the Baseball World.* New York: Ticknor & Fields, 1993.

Katcher, Leo. *The Big Bankroll: The Life and Times of Arnold Rothstein.* New York: Da Capo Press, 1959.

King, Joe. *The San Francisco Giants.* Englewood Cliffs NJ: Prentice-Hall, 1958.

Koistinen, Paul A. C. *Arsenal of World War II: The Political Economy of American Warfare, 1940–1945.* Lawrence: University Press of Kansas, 2004.

Kryder, Daniel. *Divided Arsenal: Race and the American State during World War II.* Cambridge: Cambridge University Press, 2000.

Kuklick, Bruce. *To Every Thing a Season: Shibe Park and Urban Philadelphia, 1909–1976.* Princeton NJ: Princeton University Press, 1993.

Lesch, R. J. "Eddie Brannick." SABR BioProject essay. Society for American Baseball Research. https://sabr.org/bioproj/person/f0d59a5f.

Levitt, Daniel R. *Ed Barrow: The Bulldog Who Built the Yankees' First Dynasty.* Lincoln: University of Nebraska Press, 2008.

Linder, Douglas O. "The Black Sox Trial: An Account." Famous Trials website, 2010. University of Missouri–Kansas City School of Law. http://law2.umkc.edu/faculty/projects/ftrials/blacksox/blacksoxaccount.html.

Lowenfish, Lee. *Branch Rickey: Baseball's Ferocious Gentleman*. Lincoln: University of Nebraska Press, 2007.

MacFarlane, Paul, Chris Roewe, Larry Vickrey, and Larry Wigge, eds. *Official Baseball Guide for 1970*. St. Louis: The Sporting News, 1970.

Macmillan. *The Baseball Encyclopedia: The Complete and Official Record of Major League Baseball*. New York: Macmillan, Information Concepts, 1969.

Manchester, William. *The Glory and the Dream: A Narrative History of America, 1932–1972*. New York: Bantam Books, 1974.

Mandel, Mike. *SF Giants: An Oral History*. Santa Cruz CA: by the author, 1979.

Marcin, Joe, Chris Roewe, Larry Vickrey, and Larry Wigge, eds. *Official Baseball Guide for 1973*. St. Louis: The Sporting News, 1973.

———, eds. *Official Baseball Guide for 1976*. St. Louis: The Sporting News, 1976.

Martel, Gordon. *The Month That Changed the World: July 1914 and WWI*. Oxford: Oxford University Press, 2014.

McCue, Andy. *Mover and Shaker: Walter O'Malley, the Dodgers, and Baseball's Westward Expansion*. Lincoln: University of Nebraska Press, 2014.

Mead, William B. *Even the Browns*. Chicago: Contemporary Books, 1978.

Miller, Duane Ernest. "Barbed-Wire Farm Laborers: Michigan's Prisoners of War Experience during World War II." *Michigan History* 73, no. 5 (September 1989).

Moffi, Larry, and Jonathan Kronstadt. *Crossing the Line: Black Major Leaguers, 1947–1959*. Iowa City: University of Iowa Press, 1994.

Murphy, Robert E. *After Many a Summer: The Passing of the Giants and Dodgers and a Golden Age in New York Baseball*. New York: Union Square Press, 2009.

Pietrusza, David. *Rothstein: The Life, Times, and Murder of the Criminal Genius Who Fixed the 1919 World Series*. New York: Basic Books, 2003.

Prager, Joshua. *The Echoing Green: The Untold Story of Bobby Thomson, Ralph Branca, and the Shot Heard Round the World*. New York: Pantheon, 2006.

Rivas-Rodriguez, Maggie, ed. *Mexican-Americans and World War II*. Austin: University of Texas Press, 2005.

Robinson, Ray, ed. *Baseball Stars of 1960*. New York: Pyramid, 1960.

———, ed. *Baseball Stars of 1972*. New York: Pyramid, 1972.

Rodgers, C. Paul, III. "Davey Williams." SABR BioProject essay. Society for American Baseball Research. https://sabr.org/bioproj/person/00b5ef8b.

Rosenbaum, Art, and Bob Stevens. *The Giants of San Francisco*. New York: Coward-McCann, 1963.

Rosengren, John. *The Fight of Their Lives*. Guilford CT: Lyons Press, 2014.

Spatz, Lyle, ed. *The Team That Changed Baseball and America Forever*. Lincoln: University of Nebraska Press, 2012.

Spatz, Lyle, and Steve Steinberg. *1921: The Yankees, the Giants, and the Battle for Baseball Supremacy in New York*. Lincoln: University of Nebraska Press, 2010.

Spink, J. G. Taylor, ed. *Baseball Guide and Record Book 1951*. St. Louis: Charles C. Spink & Son, 1951.

Stein, Fred. *Under Coogan's Bluff: A Fan's Recollections of the Giants under Terry and Ott*. Alexandria VA: by the author, 1978.

———. *Mel Ott: The Little Giant of Baseball*. Jefferson NC: McFarland, 1999.

Sullivan, Neil J. *The Diamond in the Bronx: Yankee Stadium and the Politics of New York*. New York: Oxford University Press, 2001.

Thorn, John, Pete Palmer, and David Reuther, eds. *Total Baseball*. New York: Warner Books, 1989.

Thornley, Stew, ed. *The Polo Grounds: Essays and Memories of New York City's Historic Ballpark, 1880–1963*. Jefferson City NC: McFarland, 2019.

Treder, Steve. "Cash in the Cradle: The Bonus Babies." *Hardball Times*, November 1, 2004. www.fangraphs.com/tht/cash-in-the-cradle-the-bonus-babies/.

Tygiel, Jules. *Baseball's Great Experiment: Jackie Robinson and His Legacy*. New York: Oxford University Press, 1997.

Vatter, Harold G. *The U.S. Economy in World War II*. New York: Columbia University Press, 1985.

Veeck, Bill, with Ed Linn. *The Hustler's Handbook*. New York: Putnam, 1965.

Walker, James R. *Crack of the Bat: A History of Baseball on the Radio*. Lincoln: University of Nebraska Press, 2015.

Walker, James R., and Robert V. Bellamy. *Center Field Shot: A History of Baseball on Television*. Lincoln: University of Nebraska Press, 2008.

Wancho, Joseph. "Sam McDowell." SABR BioProject essay. Society for American Baseball Research. https://sabr.org/bioproj/person/0c9cecef.

Wendel, Tim. "Horace Stoneham." National Pastime Museum, December 28, 2014. https://web.archive.org/web/20161117142055/http:/www.thenationalpastimemuseum.com/article/horace-stoneham.

Williams, Peter. *When the Giants Were Giants: Bill Terry and the Golden Age of New York Baseball*. Chapel Hill: Algonquin Books, 1994.

Wise, Bill, ed. *1964 Official Baseball Almanac*. Greenwich CT: Fawcett, 1964.

Wolfe, Burton H. "Candlestick Swindle: Historical Essay." *FoundSF* (1972).

Zanger, Jack. *Major League Baseball 1967*. New York: Pocket Books, 1967.

———. *Major League Baseball 1968*. New York: Pocket Books, 1968.

Index

Aaron, Hank, 223, 339, 356

Adams, Ace, 110

Alcohol prohibition, 21, 33–34, 59, 348

Alexander, Doyle, 363

Alioto, Joseph, 382

Allen, Dick "Richie," 225, 363

Allen, Mel, 83

Alley, Gene, 309

All-Star Game: of 1933, 60; of 1934, 61–62; of 1961, 243–44; of 1967, 318; of 1973, 392; of 1975, 412–13

Alou, Felipe, 210, 213, 236, 242, 250, 253, 257, 259, 266, 268, 270–71, 273, 289, 360

Alou, Jesús, 269, 271, 282, 289, 309, 315–17, 319, 329, 331, 335, 338

Alou, Mateo "Matty," 259, 266, 271, 293, 300, 305–6, 360

Alston, Walter "Walt," 257, 260, 311, 363

Amalfitano, Joseph "Joe," "Joey" 233, 242, 246, 269, 271, 360, 402

American Association (major league), 3–4, 9

American Association (minor league), 49, 105, 145, 185

American League, 9, 15–16, 22, 25–29, 30–31, 62, 73, 79, 84, 108, 132, 170, 174, 190, 243, 263, 308, 322–23, 345, 368, 374–75, 384, 419–20

Angell, Roger, 232, 251, 258, 261, 264, 327, 357–58, 366–67, 411–13

Anson, Adrian "Cap," 5

Antonelli, John, 170–71, 174, 213, 221, 241

Atlanta Braves, 312, 339, 341, 356, 406

Autry, Gene, 348

Avila, Roberto "Bobby," 174, 176

Bailey, Ed, 242, 250, 254–55, 257, 260, 267, 268, 270, 273, 288, 293

Baltimore Orioles (American League), 9–10, 25, 183, 269, 316

Baltimore Orioles (National League), 9

Bamberger, J. J. 8

Bancroft, Dave, 30

Bando, Sal, 332

Bankhead, Dan, 132

Banks, Ernie, 318

Barber, Walter "Red," 82–83, 112–13, 131, 135, 157

Barna, Herbert "Babe," 89

Barnes, Virgil, 30

Barnhill, Dave, 134

Barr, Jim, 362, 387, 398, 404

Barrow, Ed, viii, 38, 55, 57, 81, 83

Bartell, Dick, 63, 70, 84, 86, 89

Barton, Bob, 288, 329

Bavasi, Emil "Buzzie," 142, 151, 291, 362, 395

Beane, Billy, viii

Beaumont, Clarence "Ginger," 7

Bell, Bert, 139

Belli, Melvin, 244–46

Benson, John, 421

Bentley, Jack, 30

Berger, Wally, 72

Berra, Larry "Yogi," 158, 264

Bertell, Dick, 293

Birmingham Black Barons, 14142, 145

Bisher, Furman, 318

Black, Joe, 160

Black, Shirley Temple, 210

Blasingame, Don, 229–30, 234, 242, 246

Blass, Steve, 365

Blue, Vida, 426

Bolin, Bob, 250, 258, 268, 306, 316, 331, 338, 349

Bolles, John, 220–21

Bolton, Joe, 83

Bonds, Barry, 248, 330

Bonds, Bobby, 329–30, 336, 338, 350, 382, 384–85, 387, 389, 391–92, 397, 400–402, 404, 407–8, 415

Bondy, Leo, 67–68, 70, 86–88, 389

Bonilla, Bobby, 225

Bonura, Henry "Zeke," 84–86

Boston Americans, 7

Boston Bees, 72

Boston Braves, 15, 21, 23, 43, 58, 121, 133, 137–39, 141, 147, 160, 166

Boston Red Sox, 26–27, 108, 190, 201, 212, 396

Boudreau, Lou, 131

Bouton, Jim, 238

Bowman, "Doc," 201

Boyer, Clete, 263

Bradley, Alva, 73, 108–9

Bradley, Tom, 389–90, 392, 398, 405

Branca, Ralph, 151, 153, 155–56

Brandt, Jackie, 185, 210, 213, 221, 229

Brannick, Eddie, 24, 56, 70, 117, 154, 201, 209, 354–56, 389

Breadon, Sam, 42, 55, 81–82, 102, 113

Bresnahan, Roger, 10

Bressoud, Eddie, 185, 222, 226, 234, 236, 242, 246

Brewer, Jim, 363

Bronfman, Charles, 419

Brooklyn Dodgers: from 1943–51, 101–8, 112–14, 116, 118–19, 121–24, 130–34, 136–38, 142–43, 151–57; from 1952–57, 161, 165, 169, 173, 180, 183, 185–92, 195, 223, 274, 281; known as the Superbas, 26; nicknamed the Robins, 77; through 1942, 29, 60, 62–63, 70, 73–74, 77–80, 82–83, 85–87

Brown, Edmund G. "Pat," 296

Brown, Ollie "Downtown," 309, 316–17, 319, 329, 335

Brown, Willard, 131–32

Brush, John T., 10–11, 16, 18, 23, 56, 88, 354

Bryant, Ron, 359, 362, 387, 392, 398–99, 405

Buckner, Bill, 363

Buhl, Bob, 224

Buhler, Bill, 300–301

Burdette, Lew, 224, 277

Burke, Frank, 388

Burke, Mike, 345

Burns, George, 195

Burright, Larry, 260

Busch, August "Gussie," 371–73

Cabrera, Miguel, 225

Cactus League, 199, 210, 350, 372, 385

Caen, Herb, 202, 232

Cahill, Tom, 312

Caldwell, Mike, 395–96, 398, 400, 404

California Angels, 374, 399

California League, 204–5, 284–85

Camilli, Dolph, 79, 87, 205

Campanella, Roy, 133, 137, 145, 412

Campanis, Al, 375

Candlestick Park, San Francisco, xvi; conception–1965, 220–21, 229–34, 237, 240–46, 249–50, 252–58, 264–67, 278, 291, 297–302; from 1966–71, 311, 314–15, 318–20, 330, 332–33, 339, 341, 346–47, 350, 352, 357–58, 363, 365–66, 379; post-1971, 382–83, 388–89, 391, 393, 397, 400–401, 405–6, 411–13, 415, 418, 420–21, 426–27

Cannon, Jimmy, 278, 355

Cardenal, José, 269, 287–88, 360

Carpenter, Bob (ballplayer), 101

Carpenter, Bob (owner), 163

Carr, Rex, 329

Carrithers, Don, 362

Carter, Gary, 415

Cartwright, Alexander, 204

Casa Grande AZ, 200, 249, 284, 348, 383, 393–94, 418

Casey, Hugh, 80

Castleman, Foster, 185, 209

Celler, Emanuel, 195

Cepeda, Orlando, 209–12, 223–26, 236, 240, 242–43, 247–48, 250–51, 257, 260, 266–68, 270, 279–81, 286, 292, 294, 385; trade to St. Louis Cardinals, 306–9, 316–17, 360

Chandler, Albert "Happy," 108, 110, 119, 343

Chester, Hilda, 80

Chicago Cubs, 16, 57, 66, 71, 73, 78, 81, 84, 86–87, 116, 130, 151, 163, 179, 227, 293, 305, 386, 401, 424

Chicago White Sox, 21–22, 81, 246–47, 389–90, 392

Chicago White Stockings, 5

Chiozza, Lou, 72–73

Choate, Don, 215

Christopher, George, 189–91, 210, 216–21

Cincinnati Reds, 10, 21–22, 78–79, 82, 135, 190, 242, 332, 339, 352, 357, 359, 361, 391, 400

Clapp, John, 3

Clark, Jack, 426

Clemente, Roberto, 309, 365

Cleveland Indians, 57, 73, 108, 130–33, 136, 174–76, 180, 190, 198–99, 241, 368–69

Cline, Ty, 318, 335

Cobb, Ty, 100, 206, 211

Coffman, Dick, 70–71

Cohan, George M., 18, 21

Coker, Jimmie, 269–70

Collins, Eddie, 108

Collins, Jack, 155

Connor, Roger, 5

Considine, Bob, 90

Continental League, 228–29

Cook, Jack, 85

Cooper, Walker, 111–12, 114, 117, 135–36

Copperopolis CA, 34–36, 198, 423

Corkins, Mike, 340

Corum, Bill, 123

Cox, Billy, 121, 153–54

Craig, Roger, 223, 427

Crandall, Del, 273, 288

Crawford, Henry "Shag," 298

Crawford, Willie, 296, 363

Creamer, Robert, 194

Cress, Walker, 388

Cronin, Joe, 62, 205, 323

Cuellar, Miguel "Mike," 308

Cumberland, John, 349, 362, 366

Curran Theatre, San Francisco, 260, 416

Curry, Leslie, 214

D'Acquisto, John, 376, 383–84, 396, 398, 400–402, 404

Daley, Arthur, 243

Dandridge, Ray, 134

Daniel, Dan, 90, 183

Danning, Harry, 64, 87, 101

Dark, Alvin: as manager, 237–40, 242, 246–48, 250, 253, 258, 260, 265, 267, 270–83, 286–87, 292, 294, 368–69; as player, 137–38, 140, 156, 178, 180, 185

Dartmouth College, 130

Davenport, Jim, 209, 225, 233, 250, 257, 260, 268, 271, 273–74, 329, 331, 338

Davis, Ben, 107

Davis, George "Kiddo," 58

Davis, Tommy, 259, 292

Davis, Willie, 251, 358, 363

Day, John B., 2–3, 5, 9

DeBerry, Hank, 105

Demaree, Frank, 84

Demeter, Don, 385

Desmond, Connie, 83

Detroit Tigers, 57, 214

DeWitt, Bill, 131, 133

Diering, Chuck, 159

Dietz, Dick, 288, 329, 331, 336, 349–50, 359, 364, 373–77

DiMaggio, Joe, 64, 72, 75, 110, 158, 205, 356

Doby, Larry, 131–33, 174–75

Dodger Stadium, 219, 254–55, 257–59, 295–96, 310, 363, 420

Dominican Civil War, 289–91

Donovan, Jerry, 201, 389

Douglas, Jane, 173

Downing, Al, 363

Doyle, Larry, 195

Drebinger, John, 147, 164, 219, 354

Dressen, Charles "Chuck," 142, 152, 154, 156

Drysdale, Don, 223, 226, 253, 258, 270, 277, 297

Duffy, Frank, 359–60, 369–70, 377

Durocher, Leo: with Brooklyn Dodgers, 73–75, 78, 80, 85–87, 112–13, 118–19, 121–23, 281; with Chicago Cubs, 386; with New York Giants, 124–27, 135–41, 143–44, 146–48, 150, 160–61, 169, 174–81, 185, 188, 196, 235, 239, 272, 287, 351, 419

Ebbets Field, Brooklyn, 77, 79–80, 112, 121, 123, 131, 137, 154–55, 183, 187

Eckert, William "Spike," 325–26, 342, 344

Einstein, Charles, 228, 279, 335

Elberfeld, Norman "Kid," 47, 56

Elliott, Bob, 160, 225

Ellis, Dock, 365

Epstein, Theo, viii

Ewing, William "Buck," 5

Face, Elroy, 224

Fairly, Ron, 251, 298

Falcone, Pete, 419

Farrell, Dick "Turk," 254–55

Federal League, 14–16, 18

Feeley, Edgar, 201, 314, 389

Feeney, Charles "Chub": with Giants, 67, 129–30, 134, 168, 186, 201, 209, 230, 237–39, 261, 280, 285, 309, 323, 326, 337, 341–42; as National League president, 356–57, 410, 417–18; transition from Giants, 344–46

Feinstein, Dianne, 357

Feller, Bob, 110

Fenway Park, Boston, 27

Ferguson, Allyn, 249

Ferguson, Joe, 363

Fimrite, Ron, 340

Finley, Charles O. "Charlie," ix, 322–23, 332, 344, 347–48, 426

Fisher, Jack, 269–71

Fitzsimmons, Fred "Fat Freddie," 46, 60, 141

Foley, Thomas "Big Tom," 13, 37

Forbes, Frank, 148–49

Forbes Field, Pittsburgh, 71, 271

Ford, Ed "Whitey," 263–65, 276–77

Fordham University, 33, 130

Foster, George, 340, 354, 359–61, 370

Fox, Charlie, 351–54, 357, 375, 378, 382, 384–86, 390, 392–93, 397–98, 401–3, 408

Fox, Matthew "Matty," 197–98

Foxx, Jimmie, 62, 339

Franks, Herman, 150, 280, 282, 286–87, 293, 303, 306–7, 309–10, 318–19, 329, 331, 333–34, 352, 377, 418

Frazee, Harry, 27

Freedman, Andrew, 9–10

Fresno Giants, 284

Frick, Ford C., 77, 108, 124, 182, 191, 265, 281, 290, 343–44

Frisch, Frankie, 30, 41–44, 49

Frommer, Harvey, 193

Fuentes, Rigoberto "Tito," 294, 306, 315, 319, 329, 338, 352, 359, 364–66, 382, 387, 392, 397, 400, 404, 407

Furillo, Carl, 153–54

Gabrielson, Len, 293, 309, 316–17

Galbreath, John, 419

Gallagher, Alan "Dirty Al," 353–54, 359, 385, 390

Gandil, Arnold "Chick," 21

Garcia, Mike, 174, 176

Gardella, Danny, 110

Garratt, Robert, 193

Garvey, Steve, 363

Gee, Sammy, 133

Gehrig, Lou, 62, 72, 116

Gehringer, Charlie, 62

Geishert, Vern, 359

Genovese, Frank "Chick," 236, 388

Gibbon, Joe, 305–6, 316, 360

Gibson, Bob, 271

Gilbert, Harold "Tookie," 140

Giles, Warren, 192, 302, 326, 346

Gilliam, Jim "Junior," 222, 257

Gillick, Pat, viii

Giusti, Dave, 365

Glossop, Al, 86

Gomez, Ruben, 169, 174, 211, 215
Gomez, Vernon "Lefty," 205
Gooding, Gladys, 80
Goodson, Ed, 393, 398, 400, 414
Goosby, Ann, 173
Gordon, Sid, 121, 137–39, 195, 225, 385, 412
Graham, Charley, 190
Grant, M. Donald, 378–81
Gray, Olivia, 8, 13
Great Depression, 44–45, 50–51, 59, 406
Green Bay Packers, 84, 420
Grieve, Curley, 202, 217, 219
Griffith, Calvin, 424
Griffith, Clark, 84, 424
Grimes, Burleigh, 73, 277
Grissom, Marv, 174
Guerrero, Pedro, 225

Haddix, Harvey, 224
Hall, Dick, 385
Haller, Tom, 250, 268, 270, 273, 277, 294, 315, 318, 328–29, 363
Hands, Bill, 305–6
Hannah, Herm, 388
Hano, Arnold, 175, 237, 294, 297
Harada, Tsuneo "Cappy," 167, 283, 290
Harmon, Chuck, 133
Harney, Charles, 216, 218–21
Harridge, Will, 108
Harris, Bill, 142
Harris, Gail, 209
Harris, Stanley "Bucky," 84
Harshman, Jack, 140
Hart, Jim Ray, 269, 271, 273, 282, 307, 315, 319, 329, 331, 336–38, 350, 353–54, 390
Hartnett, Charles "Gabby," 89
Hartung, Clint, 141, 156
Hausmann, George, 110
Healy, Fran, 374, 387
Hearn, Jim, 141, 155
Hearst, William Randolph, 37
Heath, Tommy, 144
Hebner, Richie, 365
Heilmann, Harry, 205
Heise, Bob, 349
Heller, Hugh, 249
Hempstead, Harry, 16, 18

Henderson, Ken, 338, 350, 359, 385, 389–90
Hendley, Bob, 273, 293
Herbel, Ron, 276, 302, 306, 349
Herrmann, Garry, 22
Herseth, Adolph "Bud," 421–22, 426
Hiatt, Jack, 287–88, 329, 336, 349, 360
Higbe, Kirby, 87
Hill, Marc, 407
Hiller, Chuck, 242, 246, 250, 257, 259, 264, 266, 268–69, 271, 273–74, 288
Hilltop Park, New York, 26
Hodges, Gil, 156, 211
Hodges, Russ, 134–35, 147–48, 153–54, 157, 196, 222, 249–50, 253–57, 312, 348, 357
Hoeft, Billy, 269–71, 273
Hogan, Frank "Shanty," 43, 56, 58
Hoover, Herbert, 51, 58
Hopper, Clay, 118
Hornsby, Rogers "Rajah," 42–43, 49, 56, 172
Hotel Lexington, New York, 191
Houk, Ralph, 264–65, 267
Houston Astros, 269, 303, 308, 325, 337, 339, 341, 364, 383, 400, 419
Houston Colt .45s, 246, 254–55
Howard, Elston, 263, 267
Howard, Frank, 251
Hubbell, Carl, as player, 46, 59–60, 62, 71–72, 78, 85, 88; as farm director, 105–6, 111, 114, 125, 134, 142, 144, 164, 195, 201, 209, 388–89
Hudson, John, 388
Hughes, Leo "Doc," 366
Hull, Tom, 388
Hundley, Randy, 288, 305–6
Hunt, Ron, 328–30, 340, 350, 352–53, 377
Hunter, Bob, 253
Hunter, Jim "Catfish," 332
Hunters Point riots, 311–13
Huntington Grounds, Boston, 7
Huston, Tillinghast L'Hommedieu "Cap," 26

International League, 54, 58, 72, 105, 118, 140
Inter-State League, 142, 168
Irvin, Monte, 133, 136–37, 139–40, 143, 146, 150, 155–56, 159–60, 171, 174, 180
Isaacs, Stan, 278–79

Jablonski, Ray, 215–16
Jack, Hulan, 186
Jackson, Al, 308
Jackson, Reggie, 332
Jackson, Travis, 30, 63, 358
James, Bill, 248, 268
James, Charlie, 256
Jansen, Larry, 115, 118, 141, 166, 277, 337, 386
Japanese professional baseball, 167, 283–86, 289–91
Jaster, Larry, 308
Javier, Julian, 257
Jersey City Giants, 79
Johnson, Arnold, 322
Johnson, Bob, 366
Johnson, Byron Bancroft "Ban," 9–10, 27–29
Johnson, Frank, 310
Johnson, Jerry, 349, 352, 359, 362, 386, 390
Johnson, Lou, 292, 310
Johnson, Lyndon B., 274, 325
Johnson, Walter, 31
Jones, Sam "Toothpick Sam," 215–16, 221–22, 226, 233, 246, 360
Jones, Sheldon, 127, 141, 160
Jonnard, Clarence "Bubber," 111
Joshua, Von, 414
Jurges, Billy, 84–85, 89

Kansas City Athletics, 182–83, 188, 212, 322–23
Kansas City Municipal Stadium, 323
Kaye, Danny, 179, 419
Keefe, Tim, 5
Kelley, Joe, 10
Kelly, George, 30
Kennedy, John, 291–92
Kennedy, Monte, 115, 141, 171
Kennedy, Robert F., 325–26
Kentling, Carl, 388
Kerr, John "Buddy," 137–38
Killebrew, Harmon, 225
King, Bill, 254–55
King, Clyde, 334–38, 340, 351–52
King, Martin Luther, Jr., 274, 325
Kingman, Dave, 362, 364, 385–87, 392–93, 398, 400, 404–5, 409–10
Kingsley, Robert, 241–42

Kirkland, Willie, 210, 213, 226, 241, 360
Kleiner, Dick, 173
Klem, Bill, 56
Knickerbocker Base Ball Club, 204
Knowles, "Doc," 52
Koslo, Dave, 101, 115, 141, 171
Koufax, Sandy, 252, 257, 270, 291, 297–99, 301–2, 304, 311, 346, 362, 368
Kratter, Marvin, 187
Kroc, Ray, 395, 407
KSFO, 249–50, 254, 348, 364
KTVU, 243, 312, 348
Kubek, Tony, 263, 265
Kuenn, Harvey, 241–42, 250–51, 257, 259, 266, 268, 270, 293, 360
Kuhn, Bowie, 345, 369

Labine, Clem, 155–56
Lafata, Joe, 137
LaGuardia, Fiorello, 108
Landis, Kenesaw Mountain, 22–23, 56–57, 95–96, 102, 342–43
Landrith, Hobie, 246
Lane, Frank, 230
Laney, Al, 125
Lanier, Hal, 274, 282, 294, 315, 319, 331, 338, 353, 372
Lanier, Max, 159, 171
Larsen, Don, 247, 250, 258, 268
Laurice, Shorty, 80
Lazzeri, Tony, 205
Leach, Mrs. William, 203
Leach, William, 203
Lefebvre, Jim, 292, 310, 363
Lehner, Paul, 132
Leiber, Hank, 64, 84, 86
LeMay, Dick, 269
Lemon, Bob, 69, 174–76
Leslie, Sam, 60, 70, 72
Liddle, Don, 170–71, 175
Lindstrom, Fred, 58
Linzy, Frank, 306, 311, 316, 349, 352
Lobert, Hans, 388
Lockman, Carroll "Whitey," 121, 140, 143–44, 150, 153, 156, 171, 185, 188, 196, 254–55
Loesser, Frank, 14

Loft, George, 18

Logan, Eddie, 125, 201

Logan, Mel, 105

Lohrke, Jack "Lucky," 117

Lohrman, Bill, 98

Lombardi, Ernie, 205

Lopat, Eddie, 158

Los Angeles Angels, 287, 294

Los Angeles Dodgers: from 1958–65, 222–23, 226–28, 234, 251–60, 262, 270, 291–93, 295–305; from 1966–71, 308–11, 315, 325, 328, 330, 339, 346, 357, 362–64; post-1971, 375–77, 400, 402–3, 410, 414, 420, 424–25

Lucas, Ray, 388

Lurie, Bob, 416–18, 421–22, 426–28

Lurie, Louis, 416

Mack, Connie, 21, 108, 119

Mack, George, 105

MacPhail, Lee, 344

MacPhail, Leland "Larry," ix, 77–80, 82, 86–87, 100–102, 106, 230

Maddox, Garry, 378, 385, 387, 391, 397, 400, 404, 414

Maglie, Sal, 110, 141, 156, 158, 174–75, 180, 195, 412

Magowan, Peter, 427

Maguire, Gordon, 105

Mahan, John, 10

Major League Baseball Players Association (MLBA), 344, 370–73

Manchester, William, 50, 324

Mancuso, Gus, 57–58, 60, 64, 84

Mantle, Mickey, 158, 263–64, 266, 284, 318, 407–8

Manush, Henry "Heinie," 62

Margoglione, Sal, 388

Marichal, Juan, from 1960–67, 237, 250, 259, 265, 268, 270–71, 277, 280, 289, 297–302, 306, 315–16, 319–20; 1968–73, 330, 338, 350, 352, 359, 364, 366, 370, 383, 387–89, 396, 399, 409, 412

Maris, Roger, 263, 266–67

Marks, Garnett, 83

Marquard, Richard "Rube," 195

Marshall, Willard, 101, 115, 117, 137–39

Martin, Dickey, 388

Martínez, Horacio "Rabbit," 149, 236, 388

Martínez, Ted, 379

Mathews, Eddie, 170, 223

Mathewson, Christy, 11, 16, 30, 32, 48, 52–53, 192, 196

Matlack, Jon, 379–80

Matthews, Gary, 390–91, 397, 404

Maughn, Bill, 141

May, Rudy, 374

Mays, Willie, 169–70, 407–8; fortieth birthday celebration, 356–57; as player from 1950–52, 141–42, 144–50, 153–54, 161; as player from 1954–57, 171–73, 175–77, 180, 185, 196, 202; as player from 1958–62, 210–12, 223, 226, 236, 243, 250, 252–53, 255, 257, 259, 266, 268; as player from 1963–66, 270, 284, 293–95, 298, 301–4, 307, 310, 312–13, 315; as player from 1967–70, 317–20, 329–30, 333–37, 339–41, 350, 352; as player from 1971–72, 356–59, 361, 364–67, 372, 374, 377–78, 383, 385; as team captain, 274–76, 278–82, 287, 300–301, 364–65, 382; trade to New York Mets, 379–83, 394, 409

Mazeroski, Bill, 309

McAndrew, Jim, 379–80

McCall, John "Windy," 171

McCarthy, Johnny, 72, 98

McCarty, Francis, 190

McCormick, Mike, 221, 250, 269–70, 316–17, 319, 331, 349, 419

McCovey, Willie: from 1959–64, 223–26, 229, 236, 242, 247–49, 253, 255, 259, 264, 266–70, 276, 281–83; from 1965–73, 292–93, 297, 303, 306–7, 309, 315, 319–20, 330, 336–39, 350, 359, 361, 365–66, 370, 384–89, 392–93; trade to San Diego Padres, 394–96, 398–400, 409

McDaniel, Lindy, 305–6, 316

McDonald, Arch, 83

McDonald, Dave, 353

McDowell, Sam, 368–70, 377, 383–84, 387, 389–90, 398, 408

McGann, Dan, 10

McGinnity, Joe, 10

McGowen, Roscoe, 62, 152

McGraw, Blanche, 53, 60, 195, 210

McGraw, John, 9–12, 15, 17–18, 23–24, 28–32, 40–54, 56–57, 59–61, 65, 67, 77, 88, 103, 176, 190, 192, 213, 387

McHale, John, 237

McKeever, Steve, 82

McLean, J. R., 388

McMahon, Clarissa, 244

McMahon, Don, 350, 386–88, 390, 399

McMullen, Ken, 256, 385

McQuade, Francis, 18, 24, 37–38, 44, 65

McQuillan, Hugh, 30

Medwick, Joe "Ducky," 87

Melton, Cliff, 72

Metzger, Clarence "Butch," 407

Meusel, Emil "Irish," 30

Mexican League, 109–10, 141

Meyers, John "Chief," 16

Michaels, Al, 415

Miller, Marvin, 344, 371–72

Miller, Stu, 213, 221, 236, 243–44, 250, 255, 268, 269–71

Milwaukee Braves, 166, 170–71, 182, 186, 189, 211–12, 216, 223, 226–27, 234, 237, 250, 273, 277

Milwaukee Brewers, 349

Milwaukee County Stadium, 186

Minneapolis Millers, 144–45, 169, 185, 201

Minnesota Twins, 424

Mize, Johnny, 98–101, 110, 112, 114, 117, 137, 140, 225, 304

Moeller, Joe, 310

Moffitt, Randy, 398

Montague, Eddie, 141–42, 388

Montanez, Willie, 414

Montefusco, John, xviii, 403–4, 413, 415

Montreal Expos, 335, 349, 352–53, 358, 361

Montreal Royals, 105, 118, 133, 142

Moore, Joe "Jo-Jo," 54, 58, 60

Moore, Monte, 348

Moscone, George, 420–21

Mota, Manny, 269, 360, 363

Muckerman, Richard, 131

Mueller, Don, 139–40, 150, 154, 156, 171, 196, 209

Mueller, Ray, 135

Murakami, Masanori "Mashi," 283–85, 289–91, 302, 305

Murcer, Bobby, 407–8, 415

Murphy, Mike, 382

Murray, Allan, 348, 419

Murtaugh, Danny, 365

Musial, Stan, 110

Mutrie, Jim, 2–5, 9, 24–25, 32, 192

Mutual Baseball Club of New York, 1

Mylod, Charles J., 187

Nankai Hawks, 283–86, 289–91

National Association, 7, 14

National Association of Professional Base Ball Players, 1–2

National Commission, 22

National Exhibition Company, 19, 39, 130, 192, 379, 406, 411, 416

National Football League, 139, 186, 344, 347, 420

National League Championship Series, of 1971, 365–67; of 1987, 427

National League playoff: of 1946, 112, 155; of 1951, 155–58; of 1962, 257–60

Negro Leagues, 119–20, 131–34, 136, 141–42, 146, 149

Nehf, Art, 23, 30

Newcombe, Don, 133, 137, 145, 156

New York Cubans, 106, 134, 149

New York Giants (football), 32, 84, 139, 186

New York Gothams, 3

New York Highlanders, 26

New York Metropolitans, 2–4

New York Mets, 201, 246, 251, 276–77, 282, 285, 288, 294–95, 320, 326, 349, 379–81, 383, 394, 403, 409

New York Yankees: from 1903–41, 26–31, 37–38, 42, 44, 55, 57, 63, 72–73, 79–83, 87, 116; from 1949–55, 134–35, 137, 158–59, 165, 169, 172, 174, 177, 180, 184, 199; from 1962–75, 262–68, 291, 343, 345, 349, 372, 390, 407–8, 415

Niekro, Phil, 339, 341

Noble, Rafael "Ray," 134

Nomo, Hideo, 291

North, Henry, 219–20

Oakland-Alameda County Arena, 321

Oakland-Alameda County Coliseum, 321, 346–47

Oakland Athletics, 323–24, 332, 346–49, 393, 396–97, 418, 426–27

Oakland Oaks, 205, 214, 321

O'Connell, Danny, 221

O'Dea, Hank, 84, 98

O'Dell, Billy, 229, 249–50, 253–55, 258, 266, 268, 288

O'Doul, Frank "Lefty," 60, 114, 166–67, 228, 284

Oliver, Al, 365

Oliver, Gene, 256

Oliver, Nate "Pee Wee," 328

O'Malley, Peter, 425

O'Malley, Walter, ix–x, 102, 106–7, 122, 142, 157–58, 183–84, 186–95, 197–98, 219, 297, 328, 344–45, 410, 417, 419–20, 424–25

Ontiveros, Steve, 398, 400

Oriental Park Racetrack, Havana, Cuba, 17

O'Rourke, Jim, 5

Orsino, John, 269–71

Osteen, Claude, 291, 363

Ott, Mel, 129, 167, 172, 192, 196, 225, 239, 304, 339, 385; death, 213–15; as player, 46, 60, 70–73, 78, 85; as player-manager, 88–91, 98–100, 110–16, 121, 123–27

Ott, Mildred "Mickey," 89, 125, 214

Owens, Reuben, 231

Pacific Coast League, 105, 115, 166, 190, 201, 205–6, 214, 321

Pafko, Andy, 151, 154

Pagán, José, 240, 242, 250, 257, 260, 268, 271, 274, 292–93

Paige, Leroy "Satchel," 133

Park, Charlie, 222

Parker, Wes, 291, 363

Parker, William H., 295

Parrott, Harold, 123

Pasquel, Jorge, 109–10

Patrick, Van, 214

Patterson, Arthur "Red," 187

Payson, Joan Whitney, 378–81

Pegler, Westbrook, 53–54

Perez, Tony, 225

Perini, Lou, 133

Perranoski, Ron, 260

Perry, Alonzo, 141–42

Perry, Gaylord, 269, 276–77, 294, 306, 315–16, 319, 330, 337–38, 350, 359, 365–66, 368–70, 372, 384, 398

Peterson, Charles "Cap," 269, 316–17

Phelps, Ernest "Babe," 86

Philadelphia Athletics, 21, 97, 108, 182–83, 190, 322

Philadelphia Phillies, 51, 57–58, 63, 79, 87, 140, 146–47, 151–52, 163, 215, 223, 237, 282, 325, 352, 414

Phoenix Giants, 201, 223, 329, 334, 351, 362, 378

Pierce, Billy, 247, 250, 253, 257–58, 260, 265, 268

Pierre, Bill, 105

Pinson, Vada, 369

Pittsburgh Pirates, 7, 30, 43, 57–58, 71, 116, 121, 142, 195, 234, 288, 292, 305, 309, 311, 325, 334, 364–66, 385, 391

Podres, Johnny, 255–56

Pohlad, Carl, 424

Poland, Hugh, 388

Polo Grounds, New York, 334, 354, 388–89, 393, 406, 411; from 1883–1945, 3, 14–16, 19, 24–33, 40, 44, 48–49, 51, 53–54, 63, 69–70, 76–77, 86–87, 98–99, 103, 106; from 1946–54, 112, 115, 117, 125, 134, 137, 139, 145, 147, 150, 152–53, 155–59, 164, 172, 175–76; from 1955–57, 181, 184–86, 188–89, 194–96, 201; in 1962, 251–52

Pompez, Alejandro "Alex," 106, 134, 149–50, 169, 209, 237, 286

Pope, Dave, 176

Post, Robert, 418

Post, Wally, 224

Poulson, Norris, 189, 191

Priddy, Bob, 316

Pujols, Albert, 225

Purtell, Marty, 105

Pusich, Evo, 388

Quinn, John, 137–38, 171

Radatz, Dick, 368

Rader, Dave, 374, 376, 387, 397, 404, 407

Raschi, Vic, 159

Ravish, Tony, 388
Raymond, Claude, 303, 357
Reberger, Frank, 349
Reese, Harold "Pee Wee," 211
Reiser, Pete, 87
Reitz, Ken, 419
Reyes, Nap, 110
Reynolds, Allie, 159
Rhodes, Jim "Dusty," 174, 176–77
Rice, George Graham, 13
Richards, Paul, 243
Richardson, Bobby, 263, 267
Richardson, Harold "Spec," 419
Rickey, Branch, viii–ix, 42, 55–57, 98–
    100, 102, 104–9, 112–13, 118–19, 121–
    24, 130–33, 136, 138, 142, 193–94
Rickey, Frank, 105
Rigney, Bill, 158, 185, 195–96, 202, 210, 213,
    221–23, 226, 228, 232–36, 238–39, 247
Ring, Jimmy, 42
Ripple, Jimmy, 73
Roberts, Robin, 223–24, 372
Robertson, Bob, 365–66
Robinson, Elmer, 216
Robinson, Frank, 427
Robinson, Jackie, 69, 108, 118–22, 130–
    32, 136–37, 144–45, 154, 188–89, 199,
    274, 279, 281
Robinson, Wilbert, 10, 29, 61, 77
Rockwood, Jackie, 272
Rodgers, André, 221–22, 233, 237
Roe, Elwin "Preacher," 121
Roebuck, Ed, 259
Roosevelt, Franklin D., 58, 95–96
Roosevelt Hotel, in New York, 62, 285
Rose, Pete, 354, 399
Roseboro, John, 296–302, 310
Rosen, Al, 174–75, 427
Rothstein, Arnold, 14, 17, 22–23
Rucker, Johnny, 88
Rudolph, Ken, 407
Ruel, Harold "Muddy," 131–32
Ruether, Walter "Dutch," 388
Rupert, Charles "Chuck," 128–29, 314–15,
    342, 389–90, 425
Rupert, Jaime, 314–15
Rupert, Kim, 314–15

Rupert, Peter, 314–15
Rupert, Sonja, 314–15
Rupert, Valleda Mary Stoneham "Woo-
    tchie," 40, 76, 125, 128–29, 314, 426
Ruppert, Jacob, 26–29, 38, 55, 57, 82
Russell, Bill, 363
Ruth, George "Babe," 26–28, 30–31, 42,
    44, 62, 64, 79, 172, 339–40
Ryan, John "Blondy," 58, 60
Ryan, Nolan, 398
Ryan, Wilfred "Rosy," 30, 195

Sadecki, Ray, 307–9, 316, 319, 330–31,
    338, 349, 360
Saigh, Fred, 343
San Diego Municipal Stadium, 339–40, 395
San Diego Padres, 335, 339, 341, 349,
    350–52, 364, 389, 395–96, 407, 411
Sanford, Jack, 215, 221, 234, 236, 250,
    258, 264–66, 268, 294
San Francisco 49ers, 139, 347
San Francisco International Airport,
    260–61, 411
San Francisco Seals, 105, 114, 166, 171,
    190, 201, 205, 284
Sanguillen, Manny, 365
Sauer, Henry "Hank," 188, 210, 213, 389
Schmidt, Bob, 210, 242
Schmitz, Andrew, 106
Schoendienst, Albert "Red," 185, 189
Schofield, Dick "Ducky," 292–94, 306
Schuerholz, John, viii
Schumacher, Garry, 201, 231, 349, 389, 412
Schumacher, Hal, 60, 101, 195
Schwab, Matty, 201, 220, 253
Schwarz, John "Jack," 64, 88, 103, 111,
    142, 149, 165, 201, 209, 284, 389
Seals Stadium, San Francisco, 190, 206–
    7, 210–11, 221, 223, 226
Seattle Pilots, 349
Seymour, James "Cy," 10
Shaplen, Robert, 194, 208
Shaw, Bob, 273, 277, 306, 360
Shea Stadium, New York, 276–77, 281,
    285, 383
Sheehan, Tom "Clancy," 201, 235–36,
    239, 309

Shellenback, Frank, 141, 201, 388

Shelley, Jack, 312

Sherry, Larry, 223

Shinkoff, Nick, 388

Shor, Bernard "Toots," 75–76, 90, 126, 202, 215, 355

Short, Bob, 419, 421

Shotton, Burt, 119, 122–24, 137, 142

Simmons, Al, 62

Simmons, Curt, 255–57, 271, 308

Simmons, Lon, 104, 254, 312, 348, 415

Sims, Duane "Duke," 363

Sinclair, Harry, 18

Skowron, Bill, 263

Smith, Al, 13

Smith, John, 107

Smith, John Ford "Speedball," 133

Smith, Tal, 408

Smith, Walter "Red," 171, 355

Snider, Ed "Duke," 211

Snyder, Frank, 30

Sosa, Elias, 398, 407

Spahn, Warren, 147–48, 170, 223–24, 250, 271, 294, 412

Speaker, Tris, 100

Speier, Chris, 353, 358–59, 382, 387, 392, 397, 404

Spencer, Daryl, 169, 171, 185, 211, 221, 226, 229–30

Sportsman's Park, St. Louis, 82, 132

Stanky, Eddie, 121–22, 137–38, 140, 150, 159, 237, 329, 378

Stargell, Willie, 309, 365

Steinbrenner, George, viii

Stengel, Charles "Casey," 12, 30, 159, 403

St. Louis Browns, 57, 70, 82, 97, 131–33, 170, 182–83, 190, 410

St. Louis Cardinals, from 1926–60, 42–44, 55–57, 63, 66, 73, 81–82, 87, 98–102, 111–13, 122, 141, 159, 185, 215, 229, 233; from 1962–87, 254, 256, 271, 282, 307–9, 317, 329–30, 343, 349, 371, 407, 419, 427

Stone, Steve, 354, 358, 362, 389–90

Stoneham, Bartholomew, 4

Stoneham, Charles Abraham "Charley," "C. A.," 61, 126, 158, 177, 179–80, 188, 192, 213, 406; bigamy, 6, 67–68; birth and child-hood, 4–5; death, 65–67; drinking alcohol, 18, 33, 44, 66; financial scandal, 13, 37–38; gambling, 5, 14, 17, 23; marital scandal, 8–9; owner of New York Giants, 21–25, 30, 38, 43–46, 51–52, 56–57, 59, 64–65; personality, xi, 24, 32–34, 40, 65; purchase of New York Giants, 17–19; relationship with Horace, xii, 16–17, 19, 32–35, 33–37, 39, 65, 67; securities trading, 5, 13, 17, 32, 45

Stoneham, Charles Horace "Pete," xiii, 40, 76, 128–30, 168–69, 202–3, 207–9, 314, 342, 426

Stoneham, Hannah Monahan, 6, 8–9, 14, 67

Stoneham, Horace Abraham, 67

Stoneham, Horace Charles, viii, xv–xviii, 19, 32–36, 39–40, 45–46, 65–77, 84–91, 103–6, 110–11, 113–15, 117, 121, 123–30, 137–39, 143–49, 157–61, 164–71, 173, 176–81, 183–86, 188–203, 206–19, 221, 223, 225, 227–30, 232–41, 245–49, 262, 265, 268–74, 280, 282–83, 285–88, 292–94, 297, 305–9, 312, 314–18, 322–24, 326, 328–29, 331, 334–35, 337, 341–42, 344–46, 348–49, 351–56, 359–60, 362, 367, 369–74, 376–83, 388–90, 393–97, 399–400, 403, 405–27; birth and childhood, 6, 14, 16–17; death, 425; drinking alcohol, xi, xv, 33–34, 36, 74, 90, 104, 126, 169, 179, 181, 194, 208–9, 234, 236, 272, 286, 348, 377; education, 17, 32–33; financial problems, 185–86, 188, 192, 323–24, 335, 341, 344, 349, 352, 371, 377, 379, 382, 386, 388–90, 393–94, 405–6, 409–10; Japanese baseball, 167, 237, 283, 290; marriage, xvi, 39–40, 74, 76, 128–29, 201–2, 315, 425; personality, ix–xii, xvii, 33, 39–40, 74, 103–4, 113–14, 193–94, 208–9; racial integration of baseball, xiii, 108–9, 133–34, 149, 271–72, 286, 360; radio and television broadcasting of baseball, 83, 165, 196–98, 212, 243; relationships with employees and players, 90–91, 114, 125, 138–39, 148–49, 161, 178–80, 184, 201, 213–15, 228, 230, 233–34, 238–39, 249, 272, 288, 309, 318, 356, 371, 373, 380–81, 383; sale of Giants, 411, 417–22

Stoneham, Margaret Leonard, 67

Stoneham, Mary Alice, 6, 67

Stoneham, Mary Holwell, 4

Stoneham, Valleda Pyke, xvi, 39–40, 74,
76, 128–29, 201–2, 315, 425–26

Sullivan, Joseph "Sport," 21

Sullivan, Prescott, 202, 228, 337

Summer of Love, 313–14

Sutton, Don, 363

Symington, Stuart, 323

Taddeucci, John, 349, 390, 394

Takahashi, Hiroshi, 283–84

Tammany Hall, 8, 13, 18, 37

Tanaka, Tatsuhiko, 283–84

Telegraph Hill, San Francisco, 202, 425

Tendler, Lew, 31–32

Terry, Bill, ix, 46–55, 57–68, 70–73, 78,
84–91, 98, 102–4, 183–84, 192

Terry, Ralph, 264–67

Texas Rangers, 419, 421

Thomas, Derrel, 407

Thomas, Frank, 225

Thomasson, Gary, 398, 414

Thompson, Gene, 388

Thompson, Hank, 131–33, 136, 139–40,
150, 169, 171, 180

Thomson, Bobby, 115–17, 140, 150–51, 154–
58, 169–71, 189, 196, 209, 225, 249, 385

Tiernan, Mike, 5, 9, 32

Tierney, Jim, 44, 52, 56, 70

Topping, Dan, 343

Torre, Frank, 340–41

Tracy, Spencer, 181

the Treniers, 173

Tresh, Tom, 263, 266

Turkel, Henry, 231

Twombly, Wells, 416

Uchimura, Yushi, 290

Valentine, Bobby, 363

Vasquez, Pedro, 149

Veale, Bob, 368

Veeck, Bill, Jr., viii–ix, 130–31, 133, 170,
179–80, 194, 198–99

Veeck, Bill, Sr., 81, 94, 179

Venzon, Tony, 310

Vergez, Johnny, 63, 105

Vietnam War, 324–25, 409

Virgil, Ozzie, 209

Wagner, Leon, 210, 213, 221, 229

Wagner, Robert F., 183

Walker, Bill, 57

Walker, Fred "Dixie," 118, 121

Waner, Paul, 43

Washington Senators (expansion), 316–
17, 419, 421

Washington Senators (original), 31, 59,
84, 86, 135, 190, 424

Watts riots, 295–97, 300

Webb, Del, 199, 343

Weiss, George, viii, 57

Welch, Mickey, 5

Welsh, Jimmy, 43

Werle, Bill, 284

Wertz, Vic, 174–75

Westrum, Wes, 135, 140, 150, 153–54, 171,
180, 196, 209, 255, 403, 405, 419

White, Bill, 185, 210, 213, 215–16,
308, 360

Whitehead, Burgess, 66, 70–71, 86

Wilhelm, Hoyt, 159–60, 174, 243

Williams, Bernie, 359, 361, 395

Williams, Charlie, 380, 395

Williams, Davey, 159, 171, 180

Williams, Stan, 260

Williams, Ted, 69, 110, 339

Willoughby, Jim, 387

Wills, Maury, 251–53, 256, 258–59,
298, 363

Wilson, Lewis "Hack," 40, 116

Witek, Mickey, 86

World Series: of 1888 and 1889, 9; of
1903, 7; of 1914, 21; of 1918, 16; of 1919,
21; of 1921 and 1922, 30–31; of 1923 and
1924, 31; of 1926, 42; of 1933 59; of 1936,
72; of 1937, 73–74; of 1948, 133; of 1951,
158–59; of 1954, 174–77; of 1962, 262–
67; of 1989, 427

World War I (the Great War), 15–16, 20–
21, 92, 95

World War II, 91–98, 100–102, 104–5, 107

Worthington, Al, 221

Wrigley, Phil, 163, 413, 424
Wrigley, William, 424
Wyatt, Whitlow, 87
Wynn, Early, 174, 176

Yankee Stadium, New York, 29, 31, 44, 139, 159, 184, 186, 191, 263–64
Yomiuri Giants, 167

Young, Denton "Cy," 7
Young, Dick, 211, 235, 379
Young, Norman "Babe," 99–100, 112
Youngs, Ross, 30, 40, 49, 52–53
Yvars, Sal, 151

Zabala, Adrian, 110
Zorrilla, Pedro, 149, 388